BASIC MACROECONOMICS

BASIC MACROECONOMICS

SECOND EDITION

EDWIN G. DOLAN

GEORGE MASON UNIVERSITY

IN COLLABORATION WITH **DAVID E. LINDSEY**

CHIEF, BANKING SECTION · DIVISION OF RESEARCH AND STATISTICS · BOARD OF GOVERNORS OF THE FEDERAL RESERVE SYSTEM

THE DRYDEN PRESS · HINSDALE, ILLINOIS

Text and cover design by Stephen Rapley
Copy editing and indexing by Jo-Anne Naples
Photo research by Mili Ve McNiece

A division of Holt, Rinehart and Winston, Publishers

Library of Congress Catalog Card Number: 79-51108
ISBN: 0-03-051276-X
Printed in the United States of America
012 032 987654321

Credits and Acknowledgments
Print of Adam Smith, page 11, reproduced from the collection of the Library of Congress. Photo of Friedrich August von Hayek, page 30, courtesy of Wide World Photos. Photo of Alfred Marshall, page 38, courtesy of Historical Pictures Service, Inc., Chicago. Print of John Stuart Mill, page 122, reproduced from the collection of the Library of Congress. Photo of John Maynard Keynes, page 128, courtesy of the Bettmann Archive. Photo of Paul Anthony Samuelson, page 156, courtesy of Professor Samuelson. Photo of Milton Friedman, page 239, by C. G. Bloom, courtesy of the University of Chicago Office of Public Information. Photo of Arthur Okun, page 268, courtesy of Mr. Okun. Photo of Robert Lucas, page 311, by Patricia Evans, courtesy of the University of Chicago Office of Public Information. Print of Thomas Robert Malthus, page 367, courtesy of the Bettmann Archive. Photo of William Arthur Lewis, page 376, courtesy of Princeton University. Photo of Theodore W. Schultz, page 376, © Patricia Evans, 1978, courtesy of the University of Chicago. Print of David Ricardo, page 385, courtesy of Culver Pictures, Inc.

PREFACE

Teaching economics in the 1980s is more of a challenge than ever before. A recent poll taken by *Fortune* magazine found that two out of three economics professors feel there is a sense of lost moorings in economics. Three out of four feel increasing doubt about the accuracy of macroeconomic models. Seven out of eight have less confidence than they used to in government programs as solutions to economic problems. The result is that 98 percent of all professors polled said they were teaching economics differently than they did five years ago.[1]

Despite this sense of lost moorings, most economists realize that the last decade has been a very productive one in terms of economic knowledge. In macroeconomics, great strides have been made in understanding the dynamics of inflation and unemployment, the role of monetary policy in the economy, the operation of the labor market, and the importance of expectations as a determinant of economic behavior. In microeconomics, such established fields of study as industrial organization and regulation have taken on a new life, while the fields of energy and the environment have under the pressure of events, blossomed from obscure specialties into major branches of the discipline.

All this means that teaching economics in the 1980s requires a new kind of textbook—one that brings into the classroom the new learning and new controversies of today's economic science. Students have an uncanny ability, from the first day of class, to pose exactly those questions that are being debated in the latest professional journals. They deserve the best answers that can be given; and in cases where there is no universally acceptable right answer, they deserve honest explanations of why disagreement persists.

Here, in brief, is the strategy used in *Basic Macroeconomics*, second edition, to meet the challenge.

MACROECONOMICS

The effects of monetary and fiscal policy have always been a central theme in teaching macroeconomics at the principles level, and this emphasis is continued in *Basic Macroeconomics*. However, the book reflects a major shift that has taken place in how fiscal and monetary policies are perceived by economists to operate. As Arthur Okun has put it: "The evidence of recent years suggests that through its fiscal and monetary policies the federal government can control—within a reasonable margin—the total growth of GNP measured in dol-

[1] Walter Guzzardi, Jr., "The New Down-to-Earth Economics," *Fortune*, December 31, 1978, p. 77.

lars. But it cannot control the division of that growth between increases in output and increases in the price level."[2]

In accordance with this view of how the economy works, *Basic Macroeconomics* introduces the crucial distinction between nominal quantities, measured in current dollars, and real quantities, adjusted for changes in the price level, early in the book (Chapters 6 and 7). It then portrays the multiplier effects of fiscal policy and the effects of monetary policy as having their primary impact on nominal GNP; it also offers the continual reminder that changes in nominal GNP may represent changes in either real output, the price level, or both (Chapters 8 to 14). To answer the crucial question of how changes in nominal GNP are split up between inflation and changes in real output, the book turns to the supply side of the economy. Chapter 15 introduces the Phillips curve and draws initial distinctions between demand-pull and cost-push inflation. Chapter 16 deals with the labor market and the determination of the unemployment rate in terms of job search theory. Chapter 17 discusses the short-run dynamics of inflation, with special emphasis on the role of inflationary expectations and the phenomenon of inflationary recession. Chapter 18 explains the major policy alternatives to traditional fiscal and monetary fine-tuning. The result is a thorough integration of the traditional theory of income determination with modern theories of inflation and unemployment.

APPLICATIONS

Basic Macroeconomics contains a number of chapters that put the students' newly acquired theoretical tools to work on problems of contemporary policy significance. Chapter 19, on environmental economics, applies marginal analysis to the issue of command-and-control regulation versus economic incentives. Chapter 20, entirely devoted to the economics of energy, is divided into two parts. The first introduces the elements of the theory of the mine and applies this theory to oil and gas policy. The second discusses coal, nuclear power, and solar power as major energy alternatives to oil and gas, emphasizing the economic strengths and weaknesses of each alternative. Chapter 21 discusses the economics of population and development. International economics—especially problems of the balance of payments and exchange rate determination—is a final area of application emphasizing the latest empirical and theoretical research.

TEACHING AND LEARNING AIDS

The substantive content of a textbook is only part of what makes it usable in the classroom; for the book to be effective, its content must be taught by instructors and learned by students. To facilitate the process as much as possible, this book pays particular attention to teaching and learning aids.

The Cases According to a time-honored principle, each generalization should receive a specific illustration, and each illustration should lead to a generaliza-

[2]Arthur Okun, "An Efficient Strategy to Combat Inflation," *Brookings Bulletin* 15 (Spring 1979): 4.

tion. Following this principle, numerous short case studies are included in the book. Some of them illustrate general statements about economic policy with specific episodes—for example, Nixon's wage and price controls and the regulation of pollution from steel mills. Other cases introduce empirical material supporting the discussion in the text—for example, inflation-unemployment trends or data on economies of scale. All cases are short and to the point; and they are placed directly in the text, just where they will do the most good—not at the end of the chapters. Thus they serve as an integral part of the learning process, not just as entertainment or digression.

Readability In *Basic Macroeconomics,* readability means three things. First, it means a lively writing style that draws students into the subject matter. Second, it means complete control of the level of difficulty, as measured by standard readability formulas; in this respect, the book corresponds to the actual reading abilities of today's undergraduate students. Third, it means elimination of the "alphabet soup" style of textbook writing. When terms such as average propensity to consume and marginal propensity to consume occur, the text uses the actual words, not a thicket of APCs and MPCs that quickly bewilder the students.

Vocabulary For many students, vocabulary is one of the big stumbling blocks to learning economics. This book uses a unique three-level reinforcement technique to handle the problem. First, each new term is printed in boldface at the point it is first used and defined. Next, the term and its definition are repeated on the same page in a marginal vocabulary box. Finally, a complete alphabetical glossary of terms appears at the end of the book.

Graphs For the benefit of students who may not be used to working with graphs, an appendix on the subject has been added to Chapter 1. This appendix does more than just explain techniques. It also addresses the most common problems students have in working with graphs. One of these problems is the tendency to memorize graphs as meaningless patterns of lines, without understanding their meaning. Another is the inability to draw original graphs when they are needed in note-taking or on examinations. The Chapter 1 appendix warns of these pitfalls and carefully explains how they can be avoided. As an added bonus throughout the book, the large page size and single-column format make it especially easy to put graphs exactly where they are needed in relation to the written text.

Appendixes In addition to the Chapter 1 appendix on working with graphs, appendixes are used at other points in the book to cover topics that some instructors like to include and others do not. One example is the Appendix to Chapter 8, which discusses investment decision making. Some appendixes serve the special function of providing a brief algebraic statement of the argument in the corresponding chapter. The text itself uses no algebra at all, an approach that best serves the requirements of most students and instructors. Nonetheless, every class contains some students who are very good at mathematics and who can actually catch on faster to a set of equations than to a whole chapter of verbal exposition. In some classes, there will be enough such students that the instructor will want to teach the appendix material as an integrated part of the course. In addition, instructors will find the algebraic statement of the model underlying the text useful in constructing classroom examples.

Chapter Front and Back Matter To further facilitate the learning process, each chapter is preceded by a brief statement of learning objectives and a list of terms for review. Each chapter is followed by a concise summary and a set of review questions, and most have an annotated list of suggestions for further reading.

Student Guide A comprehensive student guide, published separately, completes the package of learning aids. This guide was developed and written by the author of the text, which makes for unusually close coordination between the text and this important supplement. Each chapter in the student guide consists of four elements: a list of learning objectives (somewhat more detailed than those given in the chapter openings in the text), a narrative synopsis of the chapter, a programmed review requiring active student involvement and problem solving for immediate reinforcement, and a self-test. (The self-test items are carefully coordinated with the test bank in terms of format, coverage, and level of difficulty. Answers to self-test items, with explanations where necessary, are at the back of the study guide.)

Teaching Aids The text is also accompanied by a complete package of teaching aids. Foremost among them is an instructor's manual, by the author of the text. This manual contains instructional objectives, lecture notes, and answers to the text's end-of-chapter questions. It also contains a special section entitled "What's Different Here, and Why." This section compares the terminology, topic sequence, and underlying models of *Basic Macroeconomics* with those of other leading textbooks to help instructors who have used other books in the past convert their courses and lecture notes. For the benefit of users of the first edition of *Basic Macroeconomics,* this section of the instructor's manual also summarizes changes that appear in the second edition and explains why they were made.

Test Bank The test bank, provided on request to users of the textbook, has a number of features that make it a particularly powerful instructional tool. It is divided into two sections, A and B, each containing ten true-and-false and fifteen multiple choice questions for each chapter (two thousand test items in all). The two sections closely parallel one another in terms of coverage and level of difficulty, so that they can be used in alternate semesters or in different sections of the same course and still allow comparability for grading. The test items are distributed as evenly as possible among three levels of difficulty: recognition and understanding, simple application, and complex application. Individual items are coded in terms of level of difficulty and topic covered. The test items were developed by the author of the text and Elizabeth Craig of the University of Delaware. Before publication, they were reviewed by a panel of experienced instructors to eliminate any weak or ambiguous items.

Paperback Micro Edition and Hardbound Edition For maximum flexibility in suiting the varied requirements of instructors, a companion volume, *Basic Microeconomics,* is also published. That book begins with the same introductory chapters as *Basic Macroeconomics* so the two paperback volumes can be used in any order. In addition, there is an integrated hardbound volume, *Basic Economics,* that includes all the material in both *Basic Macroeconomics* and *Basic Microeconomics.* All ancillary items can be used with any of the three books.

Transparencies and Masters As a further teaching aid, fifty transparency acetates of the most important diagrams from the text are provided to instructors on request. In addition, transparency masters are available for the remaining diagrams. The instructor's manual contains suggestions for the use of these transparencies and transparency masters.

The Newsletter The teaching aid package is rounded out by a twice-yearly newsletter available to all instructors adopting the textbook. This newsletter serves three purposes. First, it contains fresh case studies to supplement those included in the text. Second, it updates the suggestions for further reading with brief reviews of new books suitable for use in the principles course. Finally, it updates statistical series and key diagrams of the text as new data become available.

CHANGES IN THE SECOND EDITION

The second edition of *Basic Macroeconomics* is the fruit of two years of planning and effort by the author, the publisher, and dozens of reviewers and users of the first edition. Several entirely new chapters, appendixes, and case studies have been added; others have been thoroughly rewritten to reflect the latest developments in theory and policy. No paragraph has escaped refining and polishing, even where content is substantially unchanged. In order to maintain the relatively short overall length that was an attractive feature of the first edition, redundant material has been deleted as appropriate. Only the highlights of the revision can be mentioned here; a chapter-by-chapter discussion of revisions appears in the instructor's manual.

Monetary Policy and Institutions As many contributions of the monetarist school become integrated into the common body of theory accepted by all economists, and as monetary institutions continue to change at a rapid pace, monetary economics requires increasing emphasis in the principles course. To satisfy this need, the section on monetary policy and institutions has been expanded from three chapters in the first edition to four in the second. Chapter 11, which is entirely new, discusses the commercial banking system and other financial intermediaries, including thrift institutions, insurance companies, and security markets. Chapter 12 is now entirely devoted to the money supply. It opens with a new section devoted to the problem of defining money, which includes a description of proposed new definitions of monetary aggregates. Next it discusses the process of money creation by the commercial banking system, using a complete T-account approach rather than the abbreviated exposition of the first edition. The remainder of Chapter 12 is devoted to Federal Reserve policy, including an expanded discussion of monetary policy targets and of the reasons the Fed sometimes has difficulty meeting them. Chapter 13, on money demand, covers the same ground as the corresponding chapter in the first edition. Chapter 14 is reorganized to include the material on real versus nominal interest rates that was previously relegated to an appendix.

Inflation and Unemployment Two significant changes have been made in the treatment of inflation and unemployment. First, an entirely new Chapter 7 has been added; it deals with the macroeconomic goals of full employment, price stability, and economic growth in the context of the Humphrey-Hawkins Act of 1978. Each of the three goals is discussed in terms of measurement problems, distributional impacts, and the actual performance of the economy. The second major change comes in Chapter 17, which discusses the dynamics of inflation and unemployment. The main body of this chapter now incorporates a greatly streamlined diagrammatic exposition of the accelerationist argument while covering the same content as before. The more complex diagrams of the first edition are now included in an appendix, where they are supplemented by a fully determinate, although simplified, algebraic model. Minor revisions include a new section on balanced budgets and the national debt, increased attention to the contributions of the rational expectations school, a discussion of tax-based incomes policy (TIP), and several new cases.

Applied Topics Several of the applied chapters are new or thoroughly revised. The chapter on poverty has been extensively updated. An entirely new chapter on the economics of energy has been added. The material on population and development has been reorganized to fit into one tighter chapter. The chapter on international monetary issues has been rewritten from start to finish to keep up with the latest developments.

A WORD OR TWO OF THANKS

I have been extremely fortunate in getting help of many kinds from many quarters while writing this book. It is a pleasure to acknowledge that help here.

I owe the greatest thanks to my collaborating author, David E. Lindsey. David, my longtime friend and professional colleague, provided the theoretical inspiration and many of the technical details for the underlying macroeconomic model of this book. The approach is one he developed over many years of teaching at Ohio State University and Macalester College. Although the heavy commitments he now has as chief of the banking section of the division of research and statistics of the Federal Reserve Board of Governors prevented him from participating actively in the actual writing of the book, he worked through the macro section page by page and suggested many substantive additions on the basis of his own recent experience. Of course, the contributions are his personally and do not necessarily represent the views of the Board of Governors or other staff members of the Federal Reserve System. Any errors or shortcomings in the book are, just as much as elsewhere, my responsibility, not his.

Next, I must thank the many reviewers who commented on various drafts of the manuscript and suggested countless improvements:

Richard K. Anderson
Texas A&M University

Robert Y. Awh
Mississippi State University

A. H. Barnett
University of South Carolina

Thomas Bible
Oregon State University

David Denslow, Jr.
University of Florida, Gainesville

Marc P. Freiman
Wayne State University

Richard M. Friedman
California State University, Northridge

Joseph C. Gallo
University of Cincinnati

John C. Gilliam
Texas Tech University

Fred Gottheil
University of Illinois

Thomas J. Grennes
North Carolina State University

Raouf S. Hanna
Eastern Michigan University

Ziad Keilany
University of Tennessee, Chattanooga

Calvin A. Kent
Baylor University

Robert L. Lawson
Ball State University

Lucinda M. Lewis
University of Pennsylvania

Lawrence W. Lovik
Macon Junior College

Bernard J. McCarney
Illinois State University

Roger W. Mack
DeAnza College

Allan Mandelstamm
Virginia Polytechnic Institute and State University

Geoffrey Nunn
San Jose State University

Kent W. Olson
Oklahoma State University

Michael J. Piette
University of Hartford

John Pisciotta
Southern Colorado State College

Robert Pollard
University of Texas, Austin

Anthony A. Romeo
University of Connecticut

Francis W. Rushing
Georgia State University

Don Tailby
University of New Mexico

Edward Vento
Missouri Southern State College

Percy O. Vera
Sinclair Community College

Allen J. Wilkins
University of Wisconsin, Madison

Travis Wilson
DeKalb Community College

William J. Zeis
Bucks County Community College

In addition, I am indebted to those reviewers who made helpful comments on the first edition, the Test Bank, and the Study Guide:

Richard K. Anderson
Texas A&M University

Dwight M. Blood
Colorado State University

John A. Coupe
University of Maine, Orono

Edward J. Deak
Fairfield University

Keith D. Evans
California State University, Northridge

Jeff D. Gibbs
Macon Junior College

Kathie S. Gilbert
Mississippi State University

Richard F. Gleisner
St. Cloud State University

Douglas A. Greenley
Moorhead State University

James Halteman
Wheaton College

Jan Hansen
Capital University

W. H. Heiman
Central Connecticut State College

Willard D. Machen
Amarillo College

Bruce McCrea
Lansing Community College

H. L. Minton
DeKalb Community College

Dennis Olson
Central Michigan University

Benjamin A. Rogge
Wabash College

Milton Shapiro
California State Polytechnic University, Pomona

Frank Slesnick
Bellarmine College

Gerald A. Smith
Louisiana State University

Sheldon Stein
Cleveland State University

Dave Streifford
St. Louis Community College, Forest Park

Norman Van Cott
Ball State University

Gregory H. Wassall
University of Hartford

Darwin Wassink
University of Wisconsin, Eau Claire

Last, but not least, I would like to thank Gail Cooper and Wanda Farmer of Arlington, Virginia, who typed literally thousands of pages of manuscript, working much of the time under the pressure of overly tight deadlines.

Dozens of other people who go unnamed here—publishers, editors, designers, and staff—have worked hard to make this book what it is. They will recognize their own individual contributions that have gone to make this a better book.

C O N T E N T S

PART ONE / AN OVERVIEW OF THE MARKET ECONOMY

PART THREE / THE THEORY OF PRICES AND MARKETS

CHAPTER 19 / THE ECONOMICS OF POLLUTION

CHAPTER 20 / THE ECONOMICS OF ENERGY

CHAPTER 21 / THE ECONOMICS OF POPULATION AND DEVELOPMENT

PART FOUR / THE WORLD ECONOMY

CHAPTER 22 / INTERNATIONAL TRADE AND COMPARATIVE ADVANTAGE

CHAPTER 23 / THE BALANCE OF PAYMENTS AND THE INTERNATIONAL MONETARY SYSTEM

PART ONE

AN OVERVIEW OF THE MARKET ECONOMY

CHAPTER 1
WHAT ECONOMICS IS ALL ABOUT

WHAT YOU WILL LEARN IN THIS CHAPTER

As economists struggle to understand the dramatic economic events of recent years, they are placing increased emphasis on the basics: how individual markets work and how individual people react to changing economic conditions and policies. This chapter will begin explaining these basics with a discussion of the concepts of economic scarcity and choice. It will also distinguish between economics as a science and as policy. The Appendix to Chapter 1 will introduce the use of graphs in economics.

The 1970s were years of dramatic change for the U.S. economy. Unemployment and inflation struck in combinations that not so long ago would have been thought flatly impossible. Energy and environmental quality, long ignored or taken for granted, became subjects of national debate and targets of sweeping programs of federal regulation. The international monetary system was revolutionized, and the U.S. dollar lost, perhaps forever, its status as the strongest and most stable of currencies.

Not surprisingly, all this change and turmoil pushed public interest in economics to new heights. Enrollments in economics have never been higher. Newspapers and television have greatly increased their coverage of economic affairs. The specialized business press has prospered. People want to understand the economic events they are witnessing, and they expect economists to explain them.

Economists are trying hard to do so, and this book is part of the effort. Together with the course of which it is a part, it will help readers become more perceptive of economic news and more constructive participants in discussions of economic issues.

Economics has been undergoing a revolution, part of which has been an increase in modesty among economists. Economists are beginning to understand why the theories and forecasting methods of which they were once so proud came to grief in the 1970s, but they are not fully agreed on what to replace them with. They are beginning to understand why economic policies of the past have not always had the intended effects, but they are not fully agreed on how to design policies that will do better.

There is, however, one thing that economists today seem to agree on: More emphasis on the basics is needed. That means paying more attention to how individual markets operate and how individual people react to changing economic conditions and policies. This emphasis will be very much in evidence throughout the book. The discussion will begin with two of the most basic economic concepts of all: scarcity and choice.

SCARCITY AND CHOICE IN ECONOMICS

Learning economics means learning to look in a special way at what people do, singling out some features for close attention and placing others in the background. In this respect, economics is much like other social sciences, each of which has its particular way of looking at the world. Psychology emphasizes how people's motivations and personalities shape their behavior toward one another. Political science takes special note of how people's actions are shaped by power relationships within formal and informal political institutions. Economics emphasizes how human actions are influenced by the fact of scarcity and the necessity of choice.

Scarcity

In economics, *scarcity* means that people do not have as much of everything as they want. Economic scarcity is a subjective concept; it is not measurable by any objective, physical standard. A geologist might say that tin ore is scarce but that iron ore is abundant, meaning that the earth's crust contains much more iron than tin. But an economist would say that both are scarce because people do not have as much of either as they want. An environmentalist might say that sperm whales have become scarce, meaning that there are now barely enough of them to maintain a breeding population. But an economist would say that sperm whales are less scarce than they once were. A century and a half ago, before the discovery of kerosene, whale oil was much in demand as a lamp fuel; today, there are relatively abundant substitutes.

Scarcity as an imbalance between what people have and what they want is sometimes said to be artificial. If people could only learn to limit their wants, then they would solve the problem once and for all. But scarcity is inescapable. Suppose, for example, that you limited your material desires to a single bowl of rice a day and went out into the wilderness to meditate. As soon as you began looking for twigs to build a fire to cook your rice, you would discover that twigs are scarce. You would have to take time off from meditation to look for them. You would build your fire carefully, in such a way as to boil the water without wasting fuel. And in so doing, you would be drawn to meditate that your behavior in the wilderness was shaped by scarcity, much as it was in the world you had left.

Choice

Economics accepts scarcity as a fact of life; but what makes life interesting, economically speaking, is not scarcity itself so much as the necessity of choosing among ways of coping with it. Earthworms must live with a scarcity of good soil in which to dig their burrows, but they have no choice but to dig. As a result, economists find earthworms nowhere nearly as interesting as people, who can earn their sustenance by burrowing in the soil, by fishing in the sea, or by lecturing on economics to the burrowers and fishers.

As soon as the element of choice is added to that of scarcity, a whole world of economics opens up. How does each person decide how much time to spend fishing and how much to spend burrowing for edible roots? Is it better to fish with a pole or a net, to dig with a flat rock or a pointed stick? Why do some people specialize in fishing and others in lecturing on economics? Why is one fish traded for three roots when fishers and diggers meet at the Saturday market? These are questions about how human actions and interactions are shaped by the choices people make among alternatives for coping with scarcity.

Objectives, Alternative Activities, and Constraints

People make a number of different kinds of economic choices every day. Despite the great diversity, however, most of the situations calling for economic choice can be described in terms of three features: objectives, alternatives, and constraints.

Economic *objectives* can usually be described in terms of maximizing or minimizing something. Business firms, for example, are conventionally held to make decisions with the objective of maximizing profits. Consumers seek maximum satisfaction—or maximum "utility," as economists quaintly put it. More specialized kinds of economic decisions may aim at such objectives as minimizing the cost of transporting a given quantity of freight from a set of origins to a set of destinations. The variety of objectives pursued is endless.

In addition to having an objective, every situation calling for an economic decision must be characterized by two or more *alternative activities* by means of which the objective can be pursued. For a farmer, the activities might be growing different crops or using different techniques for growing a given crop. For a shopper in a supermarket, the different activities might be purchasing different kinds of foods. For the railroad traffic manager, the different activities might be different possible routings for trains. Whatever the particulars, the job of the decision maker is to choose that pattern of activities best serving the relevant objective.

Finally, in addition to objectives and alternative activities, economic decisions involve *constraints*. In one way or another, these constraints limit people's ability to achieve their objectives. A farmer might be constrained by the acreage available and a manufacturing firm by the size of its plant. Consumers are constrained by limited budgets. The railroad traffic manager is constrained in minimizing costs by the fact that a certain quantity of freight must somehow be moved to certain points. Constraints, in short, represent the element of scarcity always present in economic life.

Pure Economizing and Entrepreneurship

Objectives, alternative activities, and constraints are present in all situations calling for economic decisions, but they are not always equally well-defined or inflexible. In the simplest case, the objectives, alternative activities, and constraints are all clearly defined and known with certainty by the person making the decision. Economic decision making then becomes a matter of solving a problem with mathematical precision—of identifying from among the available alternatives the pattern of activities that best serves the objectives, given the prevailing constraints. There is one best solution, and an independent check can be made to determine whether a particular solution is the right one. This kind of economic decision making, which consists of finding the

Pure economizing The aspect of economic decision making that consists of choosing a pattern of activities from among a given set of alternative activities that will best serve a well-defined objective, subject to known constraints.

right answer when objectives, alternative activities, and constraints are given, can be called **pure economizing.**

In practice, economic decisions are rarely so clear-cut. People do not always know what all of their alternatives are; they have to explore the world around them, be alert to new possibilities, even actively invent new possibilities. They do not always know exactly what constraints they face or whether today's constraints will change tomorrow, so they have to take risks and rely on guesswork. People do not always even know what their own objectives are; they may question the goals they have set for themselves and may experiment with new ones. These activities—exploration, experimentation, alertness to changing circumstances, guesswork, and risk-taking—are all important parts of economic decision making, but they do not fit within the narrow framework of pure economizing. Lumped together, they can be referred to as **entrepreneurship.**

Entrepreneurship The aspect of economic decision making that consists of exploring for new alternatives, inventing new ways of doing things, being alert to new opportunities, taking risks, overcoming constraints, and experimenting with new objectives.

Traditionally, entrepreneurship is associated with founding new business firms and pure economizing with the management of existing ones. It is easy to understand why. A Henry Ford starting off to produce a new product for a new market using new technology clearly must do a lot of exploration and experimentation and must take a lot of risks. The current manager of a Ford Motor Company assembly plant, by comparison, has a much more clear-cut problem—meeting a specified schedule of deliveries at minimum cost, using known production techniques and working within known constraints. In practice, of course, entrepreneurship and pure economizing are never completely separated. Even in the most standardized situation, something unexpected can occur. Then the manager must become an entrepreneur and discover a way of coping with changed circumstances. Similarly, even the most innovative entrepreneur must begin to manage the new enterprise on a day-to-day basis—or hire someone to manage it—as soon as it is set up.

Despite the fact that pure economizing and entrepreneurship always get mixed together in the real world, it can be useful for purposes of discussion to separate the two. This book will often pose the question of what consumers, managers, or investors would do if they were faced by a given, well-defined set of objectives, alternative activities, and constraints. Answering that sort of question frequently provides a solid basis for understanding the more complicated entrepreneurial aspects of economic activities as well.

Opportunity Cost

The concept of *cost* is central to all economic decision making, including entrepreneurial decision making and pure economizing. The key to understanding how cost enters into economic decisions is the concept of **opportunity cost.**

Opportunity cost The cost of doing something measured in terms of the loss of the opportunity to pursue the best alternative activity with the same time or resources.

To economists, the opportunity cost of doing something means the loss of opportunity to pursue the best alternative activity with the same time or resources. In many cases, the opportunity cost of doing something is properly measured in terms of money out of pocket. For example, the opportunity cost of spending a dollar for a hamburger is the loss of the opportunity to spend the same dollar on something else. In other cases, activities that have no money cost have an important opportunity cost in terms of time. For example, an hour spent studying economics is an hour unavailable for studying biology or French. The following case study uses a familiar situation to illustrate the concept of opportunity cost.

Case 1.1
The Opportunity Cost of a College Education

How much does it cost you to go to college? If you are a resident student at an average four-year private college in the United States, you will probably answer this question by drawing up a budget like the one shown in Exhibit 1.1a. This budget bears the heading "out-of-pocket costs" because it includes all the items, and only those items, for which you or your parents will actually have to pay during the year.

Your own out-of-pocket costs may be considerably higher or lower than these average figures, but chances are that the items in this budget are the ones that will come to your mind if you are asked about the matter. As you begin to think in economic terms, however, you may want to revise your budget in accordance with the concept of opportunity costs. Which of the items in Exhibit 1.1a represent opportunities foregone in order to go to college? Are there any foregone opportunities that are missing from the table? To see the answers, compare this out-of-pocket budget with the opportunity cost budget shown in Exhibit 1.1b. The first three items in the out-of-pocket budget show up again in the opportunity cost budget. In order to spend $3,017 on tuition and fees and $246 on books and supplies, you have to give up the opportunity to buy other goods and services, say a car or a house. In order to spend $271 getting to and from college, you have to pass up the opportunity to travel somewhere else or to spend the money on something other than travel. But the last two items in the out-of-pocket budget are not opportunity costs of college. By spending $2,228 on room, board, and personal expenses during the year, you are not really giving up an opportunity to do something that you could have done if you had not gone to college. Whether you went to college or not, you would have to eat, to live somewhere, to buy clothing. Because these are expenses you would have to meet in any case, they are not specific opportunity costs of going to college.

Thinking about what you would have done if you had not gone to college suggests one major item that must be added to your opportunity cost budget and that does not show up at all in the out-of-pocket budget. If you had not gone to college, you probably would have taken a job and started earning money soon after leaving high school. The level of average weekly earnings for sixteen to twenty-four year olds is about $175. Multiplying this by thirty-two weeks (assum-

Exhibit 1.1
Budget for one year at college

a. Budget of Out-of-Pocket Costs[a]	
Tuition and fees	$3,017
Books and supplies	246
Transportation to and from home	271
Room and board	1,704
Personal expenses	524
Total out-of-pocket costs	$5,762
b. Budget of Opportunity Costs	
Tuition and fees	$3,017
Books and supplies	246
Transportation to and from home	271
Foregone income	5,600
Total opportunity costs	$9,134

[a] Based on average costs for private four-year colleges, as reported in *Student Expenses at Postsecondary Institutions, 1978–79* (New York: College Entrance Examination Board, 1978), Tables 1–5, projected to 1980–81 using factors given in Tables 11 and 13.

ing you work during vacation if you go to college) comes to $5,600 per year of college. These potential earnings are something you have to forego to go to college, so the item appears in the opportunity cost budget.

Which budget you use, of course, depends on what kind of decision you are making. If you are already committed to college and are simply doing your financial planning for the year, then you will use the out-of-pocket cost budget to make sure you have enough in savings, scholarships, loans, and parents' contributions to make ends meet. But suppose you are making the more basic economic decision of whether to go to college or to pursue some alternative career pattern that does not require college. Then it is the opportunity cost of college that you should take into account, weighing this cost against the benefit of greater earnings or greater personal satisfaction that you expect to get from a college degree.

Trade-offs The discussion of opportunity cost offers a good chance to show how economists use diagrams to put their ideas across vividly.[1] Case 1.1 shows that a college education involves certain opportunity costs, which suggests that for the economy as a whole, there is a trade-off between producing education and producing other desired goods. The simple diagram in Exhibit 1.2 can give a visual image of what that trade-off is like. The horizontal axis of the figure measures the quantity of education produced in terms of the number of college graduates produced per year. The vertical axis measures the production of all other goods in billions of dollars per year. Any combination of education and other goods that is produced in the economy in some year can be shown as a point in the space between the two axes. For example, the production of 10 million college graduates and $500 billion worth of other goods is represented by Point E.

[1]For a quick brush-up on how to work with graphs, see the Appendix to Chapter 1.

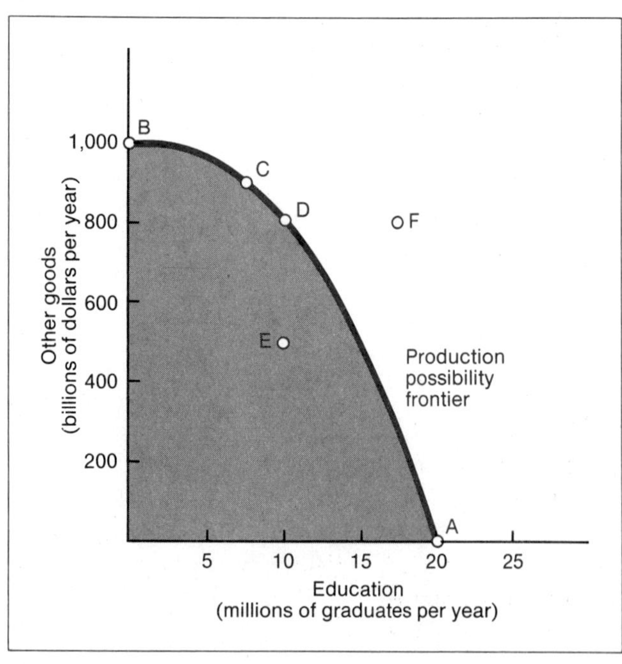

Exhibit 1.2
A production possibility frontier for education and other goods
This diagram shows a production possibility frontier for education and other goods. Point A represents the maximum production of education if no other goods are produced, and Point B represents the maximum production of other goods if no education is produced. A, B, C, D, and all other points along the frontier, as well as points such as E in the shaded area under it, are possible. Points such as F, outside the frontier, are not possible given the quantity and quality of resources available.

The Production Possibility Frontier Even if all people devoted all their time and resources to education, there would be a limit to the quantity of education that could be produced each year. For the sake of illustration, suppose that the limit is 20 million graduates per year. The extreme possibility of producing 20 million graduates and nothing else is shown by Point A in Exhibit 1.2. The maximum rate of output of other goods if no resources at all are put into education is $1,000 billion, shown by Point B. Between these two extremes is a whole range of possibilities for producing education and other goods in combination. These intermediate possibilities are represented by points such as C and D, which fall along the curve in the diagram. This curve is called a **production possibility frontier.**

Production possibility frontier A curve showing the possible combinations of goods that can be produced by an economy, given the quantity and quality of factors of production available.

It is a *frontier* because it is a boundary between the combinations of education and other goods that can be produced and the combinations that cannot possibly be produced. Points A, B, C, and D, which lie right on the curve, represent combinations of education and other goods that can be produced. A combination such as that represented by Point E in the shaded area under the production possibility frontier can be produced even if some resources remain unemployed or are used wastefully. In contrast, a combination of education and other goods such as that represented by Point F cannot possibly be produced in one year. All the points outside the shaded area are impossible.

At any point along the production possibility frontier, there is a trade-off between education and other goods. More of one cannot be produced without giving up some of the other. For example, suppose we began at Point C, where 8 million students were graduating from college each year and $900 billion of other goods were being produced. If we wanted to increase the output of graduates by 10 million per year, we would have to give up some other goods and use those resources to build classrooms, print books, and staff lecture halls. What is more, we would lose the output those students could have produced if they had taken jobs rather than going to class nine months out of the year. That would move us to Point D, which represents 10 million graduates and only $800 billion of other goods.

Now we can see how the production possibility curve allows us to visualize the concept of opportunity cost. In moving from C to D on the production possibility frontier, 2 million extra graduates can be obtained at the opportunity cost of $100 billion in other goods. Putting this on a per student basis, the opportunity cost of college education (in the range between C and D) is approximately $50,000 per additional graduate. Geometrically, the opportunity cost of education in terms of other goods is given by the slope of the production possibility frontier.

Why Is the Frontier Curved? Why is the production possibility frontier a curve rather than a straight line? If it were a straight line, that would mean that the opportunity cost of educating an additional college graduate, measured in terms of other goods, would be the same no matter how people chose to divide their efforts and resources between education and other activities. Why is this not the case?

The answer is that not all resources are **homogeneous.** That is, individual units of any resource are not all alike. Most importantly, people are not all alike. Some are suited to specializing in the production of one thing; others are

Homogeneous Having the property that every unit is just like every other unit.

suited to something else. It is easy to see why this puts a curve in the production possibility frontier.

Imagine that starting today we wanted to increase the output of college graduates. The first thing we would need would be more teachers. The opportunity cost of getting the first few teachers would be low. We could call on professors who had just retired, on their spouses who were qualified but not currently working, or on graduate students who could combine teaching with learning. Few other goods would be lost by engaging these people. Next we might turn to industry and hire chemists, engineers, or economists working there to staff additional classrooms. These people might make equally good teachers, but they would be sorely missed by the firms that had employed them, and there would be a noticeable drop in the output of other goods. The opportunity cost of education would rise, and the production possibility curve would begin to bend as we moved along it.

Pretty soon we would have to start calling in people who were not even well-qualified to be teachers, even though they might be doing a good job at something else. These people would not add much to the output of education, but a lot would be lost elsewhere. The production possibility frontier would bend still more sharply. In short, differences of ability and specialization among people (and differences among units of other factors) can be counted on to give the production possibility frontier its typical bowed-out shape.

The Division of Labor Because people are not interchangeable parts, we must pay careful attention to the division of labor—who gets which job—if we are to do well in our struggle against scarcity. Once again we can use the production possibility frontier to show why. Suppose that for some reason or other we chose to devote half the nation's labor power to producing education and half to producing other goods, but that we used the wrong half in each place. Skilled

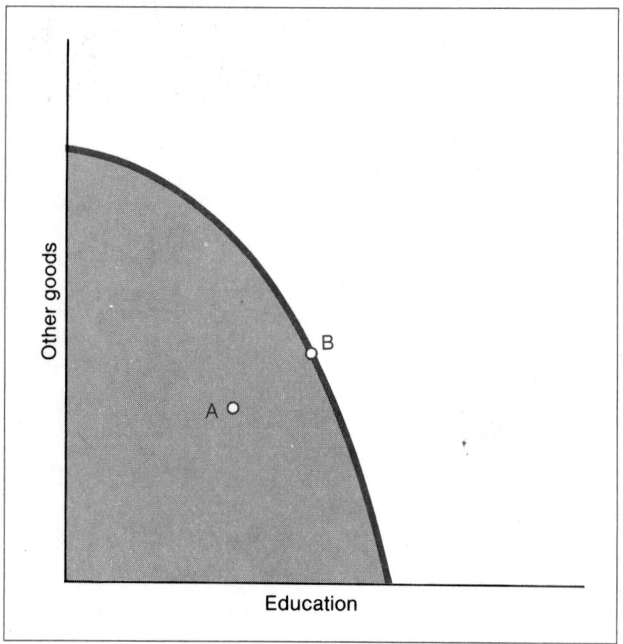

Exhibit 1.3
Effects of a poorly organized division of labor
Poor organization of the division of labor can cause the economy to drop off the production possibility frontier and end up at an interior point such as A in this diagram. This could happen even if all resources were fully employed, just because the right people were not doing the right jobs. With an improved organization of the division of labor, the economy could end up at Point B.

production workers would awkwardly mumble their way through lecture notes on Greek history, while professors got their thumbs jammed in delicate factory machinery. We would not produce as much as possible of either education or other goods. The economy would drop right off the production possibility frontier and end up at some interior point, such as Point A in Exhibit 1.3. Just by using the proper division of labor, we could produce the output combination indicated by Point B and have more of both goods.

More than two hundred years ago, Adam Smith began the most famous economics book of all time with an example emphasizing the importance of the division of labor. Smith had visited a pin factory and had seen that when one worker specialized in putting heads on the pins, another in sharpening the points, another in placing them on cards, and so on, they all could produce a hundred times more than could the same number of people working separately. Smith went on to show how free markets and private enterprise solve the problem of the division of labor simply by attracting people into the occupations where their potential earnings are greatest. Beginning with Chapter 2, this book will spend many chapters doing the same thing and will have time left over for a look at how governments sometimes try to improve on the market by substituting their own judgments concerning the division of labor.

Adam Smith (1723–1790)

Adam Smith was born in Kirkaldy, on the east coast of Scotland. He studied first at Glasgow University and then at Oxford. In those days, the universities of Scotland were greater centers of learning than those of England, so Smith returned to the north after finishing his studies at Oxford and obtained a chair at Glasgow. It was not, of course, a chair in economics. Economics had not yet been invented as a distinct discipline, and besides, it was not yet Smith's major interest. His specialty was moral philosophy.

During his long career, Smith wrote just two books. It was his good fortune, however, to have both bring him immediate fame. His first book was *The Theory of Moral Sentiments*, published in 1759. His second, *The Wealth of Nations*, appeared seventeen years later, in 1776. David Hume, a friend of Smith's, commented that "the reading of it necessarily requires so much attention, and the public is disposed to give so little, that I shall still doubt for some time of its being at first very popular." Hume, however, was wrong. The book sold well from the start.

The task Smith set himself first of all was to explain the workings of the economic system—that is, the sources of the "wealth of nations." The greatest source, he discovered, was the division of labor. Chapter 1 opened with the observation that "the greatest improvement in the productive powers of labor, and the greater part of the skill, dexterity, and judgment with which it is anywhere directed, or applied, seem to have been the effects of the division of labor." He then went on to give his famous pin factory example.

It was not enough for Smith to just describe the division of labor, however. He wanted to explain how it came about. His explanation was highly characteristic:

> This division of labor, from which so many advantages are derived, is not originally the effect of any human wisdom, which foresees and intends that general opulence to which it gives occasion. It is the necessary, though very slow and gradual consequence of a certain propensity in human nature which has in view no such extensive utility; the propensity to truck, barter, and exchange one thing for another.

Here, for the first time in the book, Smith emphasized the importance of the unintended consequences of human action: Each person acting in the marketplace has only narrow ends in mind, but the joint result of the actions of everyone is a general benefit that none intended.

As *The Wealth of Nations* progressed, Smith added another theme, that of the benefits of economic liberty. The free, spontaneous interaction of people in the marketplace is not just one way to bring about the general benefit of mankind; it is the best way. Government attempts to guide or regulate the market end up doing more harm than good. Smith especially attacked the privileges of legally protected monopolies, the Poor Laws (which he saw as inhibiting the mobility of labor), and the apprenticeship system (which worked against free entry into occupations). All such restraints on the market tended to force trade into "unnatural" and less beneficial channels.

Smith's book has meant various things to various people. To some it has been a handbook of laissez-faire liberalism. To others, it has been the fountainhead of economic science. Still others have found it, not without reason, to be unoriginal and crammed with errors. Whatever its faults, it is a book that continues to be read and debated. In 1976, its bicentennial brought leading economists from all over the world to Glasgow to pay tribute to the absentminded professor of moral philosophy who had lectured there so long before.

The Margin

Margin, marginal Terms referring to the effects of making a small increase in any economic activity. See glossary entries *Marginal cost, Marginal product,* and so on.

We have not yet mentioned one concept that has wide applicability to economic decision making: the idea of the **margin.** Whenever economists talk about the margin or use the adjective *marginal,* they are referring to the effects of making a small increase or decrease in some economic activity. *Margin* is an idea that is hard to define abstractly but easy to illustrate. When we talk about the "marginal cost" of producing cars at General Motors, we are referring to the added cost of producing one more car beyond the limit of the number currently being produced. When we speak of the "marginal benefit" of sewage treatment in a certain river basin, we mean the extra benefit of making a small increase in the effort put into sewage treatment in the area. These terms and quite a few others will be defined more precisely in later chapters. For now, though, one example will give a general idea of why thinking in terms of the margin is important.

Case 1.2
Marginal Cost Pricing of Domestic Oil

In the winter of 1978–79, political turmoil in Iran threatened the United States with a new energy crisis. This caused people to become more concerned than ever about the price of oil and the cost of obtaining it. But what was the cost of oil? The matter was obscured by a complex system of oil price controls that had been in force since the early 1970s.

Under the system of price controls, so-called old oil—that produced from wells drilled before 1972—could be sold to refiners for no more than about $5.80 per barrel. New oil from more recently drilled wells could be sold for as much as $12.85 per barrel. Because there was not enough of either old or new oil to supply the energy needs of the U.S. economy, huge quantities of oil were being imported at the world market price, which stood at about $16.25 per barrel in the spring of 1979. The regulations required that the price paid by the public for products refined from this oil be based on the *average* cost to the refiners of oil from all the various sources. That average worked out to about $10 per barrel.

As the world oil price rose higher, this system of average cost pricing for petroleum products came under increasingly strong attack from economists. Instead of being priced at the average cost from all sources, they said, prices should reflect the *marginal* cost of oil to the U.S. economy—that is, the cost of getting the extra barrel of oil needed to replace each barrel consumed. For all practical purposes, an extra barrel of oil consumed could be replaced only with imported oil. That meant the marginal cost of oil to the economy was the world market price of $16.25 per barrel. (A small amount of additional oil could be produced domestically using exotic secondary recovery technology, but this too was very expensive.)

By keeping the price of petroleum products below the marginal cost of replacing what was consumed, the critics argued, price controls were causing oil to be used wastefully. Some plants that would have switched to coal if they had had to pay $16.25 a barrel for oil were content to continue burning oil at $10 per barrel. With heating oil selling for a price below its marginal cost, homeowners and builders did not find it worthwhile to insulate homes as well as they would have if fuel prices had been higher. And with gasoline prices based on an artificially low cost for crude oil, motorists had little incentive to change their driving habits or buy small cars.

After listening to these arguments, the Carter administration decided in April that average cost pricing would have to go. Because raising domestic oil prices to the world level would add to inflationary pressures, at least in the short run, the decision was a sensitive one. But inflation seemed less of an evil than was the ever-increasing reliance on imported oil. So the administration began a delicate process of political negotiation and compromise that, it was hoped, would lead to a timetable for gradually introducing marginal cost pricing of oil to the U.S. economy.

ECONOMIC SCIENCE AND ECONOMIC POLICY

A great part of what one reads about economics in the newspapers or hears about it on television is focused on specific problems of economic policy. Should the federal government spend more money and run a larger budget deficit? Should price controls on oil be lifted in the hope of increasing production and decreasing consumption? Should the government encourage or discourage exports of U.S. agricultural products? If we are to learn the economic way of thinking, we must learn how economists think about policy issues as well as how they think about pure theory.

The mention of economic policies such as price controls or budget deficits tends to set little lights labeled "hurrah" or "ugh" flashing in our minds. Sometimes our mental circuits work so fast that we do not notice that, between the mention of the policy and the flashing of the lights, a chain of thinking somewhat like the following must occur:

1. If Policy X is followed, Outcome Y will result.
2. Outcome Y is a good (or bad) thing.
3. Therefore, hurrah (or ugh) for Policy X.

In order to understand the contents of this book and how to put them to work, it is important to understand the logic of the three-step chain of thinking. To that end, we will go through it one step at a time.

Positive Economics

Economic science cannot foretell the future, but it can offer predictions of the "if, then" form: "If A occurs, then B will occur, other things being equal." An economist might, then, make the assertion: "If government spending were increased, then unemployment would decline, as long as no other changes in economic conditions occurred in the meantime." Such a statement is sometimes called a **scientific prediction.** It is a statement of cause and effect but one that is valid only under specified conditions. In making scientific predictions of this form, economists rarely attempt to foretell whether A will actually occur or whether other things will actually remain constant.

Scientific prediction A conditional prediction having the form "if A, then B, other things being equal."

Positive economics The part of economics limited to making scientific predictions and purely descriptive statements.

When economists limit their attention to statements that are pure scientific predictions, they are said to be practicing **positive economics.** All sound analysis of economic policy must begin with positive economics as step 1.

Resolving Disagreements Of course, economists sometimes disagree about whether a certain scientific prediction is valid. In fact, a great deal of the day-to-day work in which economists engage is directed toward resolving disagreements on matters of positive economics. Some scientific disagreements concern matters of pure theory and are much like the disagreements among mathematicians concerning whether some unproved theorem is true or false. These disputes can, in time, be resolved by a process in which each party tries to state the reasoning as carefully as possible or to detect logical errors.

Empirical A term referring to data or methods based on observation of actual past experience or on controlled experiments.

Econometrician A specialist in the statistical analysis of economic data.

Frequently, economists try to resolve disputes over matters of positive economics by using **empirical** methods. That means looking at evidence—statistical or otherwise—based on observation of past experience. Much of this work is done by specialists in the statistical analysis of economic data who are called **econometricians.** Suppose that the scientific prediction in dispute said: "If government spending were to increase, then unemployment would decline, other things being equal." An econometrician might enter the debate with the announcement that, according to a study of postwar data on the U.S. economy, an increase in government expenditure has, in fact, been consistently associated with a decline in unemployment, taking into account the probable influence of other factors. Or the econometrician might assert that the data reveal no systematic association at all between government spending and unemployment when advanced statistical techniques are used to eliminate the influence of other changes in economic conditions. Questions of this sort are not usually resolved by a single empirical study, but repeated studies and the gradual accumulation of evidence serve to narrow areas of disagreement and contribute to scientific progress in economics.

Normative Economics

A positive economic statement of the type "if Policy X, then Outcome Y" cannot by itself resolve the issue of whether Policy X is desirable. To come to a conclusion on the desirability of the policy, one must decide whether Outcome Y is good or bad. When economists make statements of the type "Outcome Y is good," they are engaging in **normative economics.**

Normative economics The part of economics devoted to making value judgments about what economic policies or conditions are good or bad.

Most economists do not consider themselves experts in ethical theory, and few would be prepared to defend their normative statements with the same rigor and clarity they would use to defend their positive economic analysis. Nonetheless, economists who wish to speak persuasively on the subject of economic policy should be able at least to point to some general ethical principles on which their normative conclusions might plausibly be based. Economists who base their like or dislike of a particular policy on arbitrary whims are less likely to be listened to than are those who speak in terms of consistent and well thought out values. With this in mind, we will look at a few basic ideas that frequently arise in discussions of normative economics.

Efficiency The property of producing or acting with a minimum of expense, waste, and effort.

The Efficiency Standard The standard of **efficiency** occupies a prominent place among those standards by which economists judge the performance of the systems they observe. In its most general sense, the word *efficiency* means the property of producing or acting with a minimum of expense, waste, and effort. A good economic example of the difference between efficiency and inefficiency appeared in Exhibit 1.3. That diagram showed how a badly organized division of labor could cause the economy to drop off the production possibility frontier and end up at an *inefficient* interior point. A better division of labor would have permitted the production of more output with the same quantity of inputs and thus would have been more efficient.

Efficiency and Equity Most economists think that efficiency itself is a good thing. This does not mean, however, that any policy promoting efficiency is automatically a good policy. Other norms and values must be introduced into policy analysis to supplement the efficiency standard. Among the most important of the supplementary standards are those referred to in everyday speech as equity, merit, and justice.

The standard of equity has two roles to play in relation to the standard of efficiency. First, it may be used to supplement the efficiency standard in cases where the choice is between policies that are equally efficient. Efficiency alone defines not a single, unique pattern of economic life but only a range of possible patterns. Different but equally efficient patterns often involve different distributions of welfare among specific individuals. In one efficient state of the world, Jones may be rich and Smith poor; in another, Smith may be rich and Jones poor; in a third, Jones and Smith may be equally well-off. When such alternatives confront us, we may be led to reason like this:

1. Policies X and Y produce equally efficient outcomes but imply different distributions of individual welfare.
2. The distributional outcome of Policy X is more equitable.
3. Therefore, let us undertake Policy X.

A second possible use for the criterion of equity is to override the criterion of efficiency. For many people, efficiency is a goal that should not be pursued at the expense of equity but that should, if needed, be sacrificed to the pursuit of equity. In such cases, the logic might run as follows:

1. Policy X would be bad for efficiency but would help achieve greater equity.
2. The loss of efficiency is unfortunate, but the gain in equity outweighs it.
3. Therefore, in the absence of a policy that will serve both goals at once, go ahead with Policy X.

A Difficulty Whichever way it is used, the concept of equity plays an important role in policy analysis. Using it, however, involves a difficulty that did not occur in the case of efficiency. The difficulty is that equity has no universally agreed-upon meaning. It means different things to different people, depending on the values they hold and the ideologies they profess. Few things are more harmful to intelligent debate on questions of economic policy than for the parties to a discussion to use the same word to mean different things. The word *equity* and the associated words *merit* and *justice* may be the cause of more misunderstandings than any other terms in economics.

In the interest of avoiding such misunderstandings, we might wish to establish beyond doubt that a particular meaning of *equity* is the right one. But to attempt it would take us deep into details of philosophy and far from the main subject of this book. Instead we will simply suggest two meanings of the equity concept (or two classes of meanings within which are many minor variations) without choosing between them.

Distributive justice The principle of distribution according to innate merit. Roughly, the principle of "from each according to abilities, to each according to needs."

Equity as Distributive Justice The first meaning of *equity* equates it to **distributive justice.** The phrase "from each according to abilities, to each according to needs" gives a rough idea of what the principle of distributive justice means. The concept is based on the idea of innate merit; that is, all people are presumed—solely by virtue of their birth, their existence, and their common humanity—to merit some share of the total stream of goods and services turned out by the economic system. An improvement on the phrase is "to each according to innate merits."

Just what each person's innate merits are is a point that gives rise to many variations on the idea of distributive justice. For example, some people believe that all economic goods should be distributed equally among all members of society. Others think that a person's innate claims on economic goods ought to be limited to some minimum standard of living and are willing to see any surplus above this minimum distributed according to other principles. Still others conceive of innate merits as being limited to certain specific types of goods. Each person might have, for example, an innate claim to a share of food, shelter, medical care, and education, but no such claim to even a minimum share of tobacco, imported wine, or manufacturing services.

Market justice The principle of distribution according to acquired merit. The observance of property rights and the honoring of contracts. Roughly, the principle of "value for value."

Equity as Market Justice The second meaning of *equity* makes it equivalent to what can be called commutative justice, or, more simply, **market justice.** The justice of the marketplace is *value for value;* market justice is based on the idea of acquired merit. Individuals have no innate claim to a share in the total economic output but merit only whatever share they acquire through production, exchange, or voluntary donation.

The idea of market justice gives a special significance to the concepts of property and contract. Suppose that the entire mass of economic goods is divided up as the properties of specific individuals (or voluntary associations of individuals), so that for every loaf of bread, some person stands ready to say, "This bread is mine—my property to use and to exclude others from using." Then the central meaning of *market justice* becomes the movement of property from hand to hand only by fair contract (except for voluntary gifts). *Fair contract* means that each party must be satisfied that the value to him or her of the property received is at least as great as the value of the property given up. So market justice can be summed up as the observance of property rights and the honoring of contracts.

Economic Ideology

Economic ideology A set of judgments and beliefs concerning efficiency, market justice, and distributive justice as goals of economic policy, together with a set of prejudices or beliefs concerning matters of positive economics.

Each person carries out the job of policy analysis, whether in a systematic or a casual way, within a personal framework of thought that can be called an **economic ideology.** An economic ideology includes a person's judgments concerning the relative priority (and exact interpretation) of distributive justice and market justice and attitudes toward the relative importance of equity and efficiency as goals of economic policy. Often, it also includes a set of prejudices and more or less rationally founded beliefs concerning matters of positive economics. Liberalism, Marxism, libertarianism, conservatism—these and many other "isms" are the labels we use to refer to economic ideologies.

To deal with every policy issue from all possible ideological points of view would be too much to attempt in this book. Instead, we will content ourselves for the most part with pointing out the implications of various policies in terms of the standards of efficiency and equity just discussed. People will have to reach their own conclusions on the ideological level.

Why Distinguish between Positive and Normative Economics?

When policy analysis is broken down into a three-step process in which positive and normative elements are clearly separated, orderly debate on important economic issues is made easier in several ways. First, the breakdown of policy analysis into positive and normative components makes it clear that disagreements on policy questions can arise from two different sources. If you and I disagree as to whether Policy X is good or bad, it may be either because we disagree on the positive issue of whether Policy X will, in fact, result in Outcome Y or because we disagree on the normative issue of whether Outcome Y is good or bad. Our analysis also indicates that a particular sort of spurious agreement could arise between us: You might think that Policy X will cause Outcome Y and that Y is good, whereas I might think Y is bad but that X will not cause it! This sort of thing occurs surprisingly often. In any event, it is clear that intelligent policy analysis requires careful thinking.

Second, if a positive statement is associated with an unpopular normative position, it is less likely to gain acceptance. Critics must be persuaded that both are valid. People are less likely to pay serious attention to the claim that fluoridation of water harms their bodies when its opponents also claim that fluoridation is an evil communist plot. A positive statement divorced from any normative view is not disadvantaged in this way.

Third, when a positive statement is associated with a popular normative position, it may be accepted too uncritically. Why? Because reactions to value judgments are much more pronounced than are reactions to positive statements, so that value judgments surreptitiously tend to dominate thought. People are all too likely to accept a "what is" statement from someone who agrees with them about "what ought to be." This natural reaction helps explain the inability of economists to persuade politicians that increases in the legal minimum wage have worsened the employment opportunities of poor people.[2] Politicians say they want to help the poor and resent being informed that a method they support has not worked. Perhaps they even suspect that economists critical of minimum wages do not share their values. They apparently believe that minimum wage laws help the poor simply because they believe that the poor ought to be helped.

CONCLUSIONS

In a once-over fashion, this chapter has tried to give some idea of the kinds of things to which economists are sensitive when they look at the world around them. It has shown that economists think in terms of scarcity, choice, and trade-offs. It has offered some simple examples of how economists use diagrams to make it easier to visualize abstract concepts in a concrete form. It has explained how to distinguish between positive and normative economics and why that distinction is important. What can be said now to sum it all up?

---

[2] Minimum wage laws are discussed in Chapter 15.

If there is one single feature of overriding importance about the economic way of thinking, it is this: *Economics is about people.* Individual people are the units of analysis in all economic theory. Every economic principle developed in this book must be a statement about the way individuals make choices, struggle with the problem of scarcity, and respond to changes in their environment. And all economic policies must be judged in terms of their impact on the welfare of individual people.

This does not mean that economists are all rugged individualists, in the sense that they are indifferent to social issues, or that they are political know-nothings who do not care about the national interest. What it does mean is that economic science (and all valid social science, for that matter) is based on the recognition that society and the nation have no existence and no importance apart from the individual people of which they are composed. Society is not a super-being, and the nation is not a sentient creature capable of feeling pain when a pin is stuck in the national thumb. They are only the names of groups of which all people are equal members. *We* are what economics is all about.

SUMMARY

1. Learning economics means learning to look at human actions and interactions in a special way, singling out some features for close examination and placing others in the background. The economic way of thinking places particular emphasis on how people's actions are influenced by the fact of scarcity and the necessity of choice.
2. All economic decisions can be described in terms of objectives, alternatives, and constraints. The terms are not equally well-defined in all decision making situations, however. Economic decision making in which objectives, alternatives, and constraints are all well-defined and known to the decision maker is called pure economizing. Economic decision making in which they are less well-defined may require the decision maker to explore the situation, be alert to new possibilities, develop new ways of overcoming constraints, take chances, and so on. These activities are referred to as entrepreneurship.
3. The production possibility frontier shows which combinations of goods can be produced and which cannot. Its slope shows the opportunity cost of the good measured on the horizontal axis in terms of the good measured on the vertical axis. The position of the production possibility frontier depends on the quantity and quality of resources available to an economy. Over time, the frontier may expand, and the economy may grow. If the division of labor is not organized efficiently, the economy may drop off the production possibility frontier and end up at an interior point.
4. Positive economics cannot foretell the future, but it can offer scientific predictions in the form "if A occurs, then B will occur, other things being equal." Disputes in positive economics can, in principle, be resolved by reasoned discussion or by the examination of statistical data.
5. Normative economics is concerned with statements about what ought to be. Most economists think that efficiency is, in itself, a worthy goal of economic policy. The efficiency standard must, however, be supplemented by considerations of equity when policy decisions are to be made. There is no

universal agreement on what equity means. Some economists maintain that equity is primarily a matter of distributive justice; others emphasize market justice. Partly because of such disagreements on the meaning of *equity,* economists try to distinguish carefully between their positive statements and their normative statements.

6. Economics is about people. All economic principles must be framed in terms of the way individuals make choices and respond to changes in their environment, and all economic policies must be judged in terms of their impact on the welfare of individual people.

DISCUSSION QUESTIONS

1. Suppose you want to get as high a grade-point average as you can this term; yet your time and abilities are limited. Would it be possible to look at the way you spend your time as an economic problem? What constraints and alternative activities do you face? What is the opportunity cost of getting higher grades?
2. Suppose you won a lottery prize of $20 million. Would this solve all your personal economic problems of scarcity? Explain.
3. Can you give some real-world examples of how the economy, a firm, or even an individual might be operating inside the production possibility curve?
4. Can it be said that economics is about money or about goods and services rather than about people? Explain.
5. Do the animals in a forest face an economic problem? What are their objectives, constraints, and alternatives? What has happened to their economic problems as people have impinged on their habitat? Is economics about nonpeople too?
6. Should we all be entitled to our fair share of the earth's produce? Would this question be better stated if we replace "the earth's produce" with "the goods and services that Smith and Jones and Jansen and M'Boye and Li Ha Ching and . . . [listing all the earth's 4 billion people by name] produce"? To make it still easier, suppose that Smith and Jones are the only two people on earth. Is Smith entitled to a fair share of what Jones produces and vice versa?
7. Review Case 1.2. Looking at the oil situation from an economy-wide point of view, what is the opportunity cost of consuming a barrel of oil? Under price controls, is the opportunity cost of oil to the individual consumer the same as the opportunity cost of oil as seen from an economy-wide viewpoint?
8. Refer again to Case 1.2. Try to cast the argument of price control critics in terms of the three-step chain of reasoning given later in the chapter. Some people opposed marginal cost pricing of oil on the ground that higher prices would be particularly burdensome to low-income consumers. State this argument in terms of the three-step chain of reasoning.

APPENDIX TO CHAPTER 1
WORKING WITH GRAPHS

HOW ECONOMISTS USE GRAPHS

At one of our country's well-known colleges, the students have their own names for all the courses. They call the astronomy course "stars," the geology course "rocks," and the biology course "frogs." Their name for the economics course is "graphs and laughs." This choice of names indicates two things. First, it shows that the students think the professor has a sense of humor. Second, it shows that in the minds of students, economics is a matter of learning about graphs in the same sense that astronomy is a matter of learning about stars or geology a matter of learning about rocks.

To begin, then, we can say that economics is not about graphs; it is about people. It is about the way people make choices, use resources, and cooperate with one another in an effort to overcome the universal problem of scarcity. Economics is a social science, not an offshoot of analytic geometry.

The skeptical reader may reply, "If economics is not about graphs, why are there so many of them in this book?" The answer is that economists use graphs to illustrate the theories they develop about people's economic behavior in order to make them vivid, eye-catching, and easy to remember. Everything that can be said in the form of a graph can also be said in words, but saying something two different ways is a proven aid to learning. The purpose of this appendix is to show how to make maximum use of an important learning aid by explaining how to work with graphs.

PAIRS OF NUMBERS AND POINTS

The first thing to learn is how to use points on a graph to represent pairs of numbers. Consider Exhibit 1A.1. The small table in that exhibit presents six pairs of numbers. The two columns are labeled x and *y*. The first number in each pair is called the x *value,* and the second is called the *y value.* Each pair of numbers is labeled with a capital letter A through E. Pair A has an x value of 2 and a *y* value of 3; Pair B has an x value of 4 and a *y* value of 4, and so on.

Next to the table is a diagram. The lines placed at right angles to one another along the bottom and the left-hand side of the diagram are called *coordinate axes.* The horizontal axis is marked off into units and is used for measuring the x value, while the vertical axis is marked off into units for measuring the *y* value. In the space between these axes, each lettered pair of numbers from the table can be represented as a lettered point. For example, to put Point A in place, go two units to the right along the horizontal axis to represent the x value of 2 and then three units straight up, parallel to the vertical axis, to represent the *y* value of 3. The other points are placed the same way.

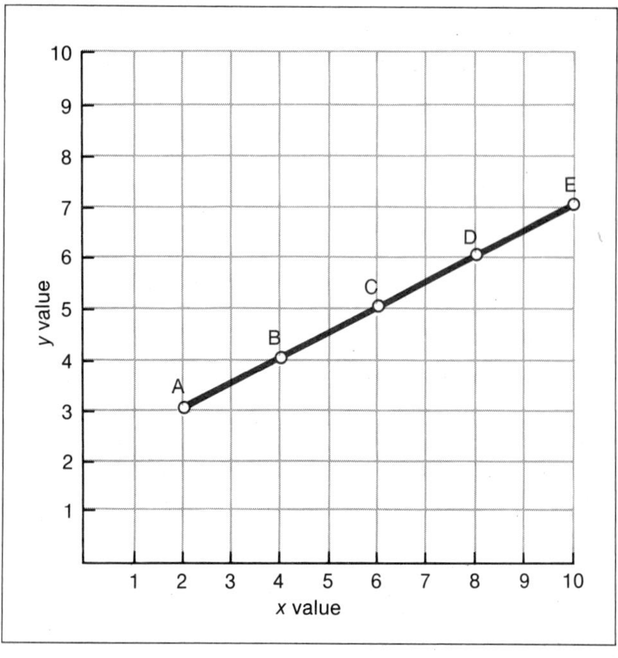

Exhibit 1A.1
Pairs of numbers and points
Each lettered pair of numbers in the table corresponds to a lettered point on the graph. The *x* value of each point corresponds to the horizontal distance of the point from the vertical axis, and the *y* value corresponds to the vertical distance from the horizontal axis.

	x	*y*
A	2	3
B	4	4
C	6	5
D	8	6
E	10	7

Usually, the visual effect of a graph is improved by connecting the points with a smooth line or curve. When this is done (as shown in the diagram), it can be seen at a glance that as the x value increases, the y value also tends to increase.

COMMON ECONOMIC GRAPHS

Economics is interested not in abstract relationships between x's and y's but in relationships concerning people and the things they do under various conditions. This means that graphs in economics are labeled in terms of the ideas used in putting together economic theories. Exhibit 1A.2 shows three common ways of labeling coordinate axes. Each of these will be encountered many times in this book.

Exhibit 1A.2a represents the relationship between the price of subway tokens in some city and the number of people who choose to ride the subway each day at any given price. The table shows that as the price of tokens goes up, fewer people choose to ride the subway. The graph shows the same thing. As a matter of tradition in economics, whenever a graph involves both money values and quantity units, the vertical axis is used to measure the money value (in this case, the price of subway tokens) and the horizontal axis to measure the quantity units (in this case, the number of riders per day).

Exhibit 1A.2b uses quantity units on both axes. Here, the problem is to represent the various combinations of milkshakes and hamburgers that can be bought at the local carry-out when milkshakes cost $.50 each, hamburgers cost $.50 each, and the buyer has exactly $2.50 to spend on lunch. The table shows that the possibilities are five burgers and no shakes, four burgers and one shake, three burgers and two shakes, and so on.

The graph offers a visual picture of the "menu" to choose from, given limited money to spend. The points from the table are drawn in and labeled, and any can be chosen. A diagonal line has been sketched in to connect these points, and if the purchase of parts of hamburgers and milkshakes is allowed, the buyer can choose from among all the points along this line (for example, 2.5 burgers and 2.5 shakes). The buyer who wanted to have some money left over could purchase a lunch represented by a point within the shaded area, such as Point G (which stands for two burgers and one shake and costs just $1.50). But unless the buyer gets more money, points outside the shaded area cannot be chosen.

Exhibit 1A.2c illustrates still another kind of graph frequently used in economics—one showing how some magnitude varies over time. This graph indicates what happened to the unemployment rate of nonwhite teenage males over the years 1969–78. The horizontal axis is used to represent the passage of time and the vertical axis to measure the percentage of nonwhite teenage males officially classified as unemployed. Graphs like this are good for getting a quick idea of trends over time. Although teenage unemployment has had its ups and downs in recent years, the trend during the 1970s was clearly upward.

SLOPES

When talking about graphs, it is frequently convenient to describe lines or curves in terms of their *slopes.* The slope of a straight line drawn between two points is defined as the ratio of the change in the y value to the change in the x value between two points. In Exhibit 1A.3, for example, the slope of the line drawn between Points A and B is 2. The y value changes by six units between these two points, while the x value changes by only three units. The slope is the ratio $6/3 = 2$.

When a line slants downward like the line between Points C and D in Exhibit 1A.3, the x value and the y value change in opposite directions. Going from Point C to Point D, the y value changes by -2 (that is, it decreases by two units), while the x value changes by $+4$ (that is, it increases by four units). The slope of this line is the ratio $-2/4 = -1/2$. A downward-sloping line such as this is said to have a negative slope.

The slope of a curved line, unlike that of a straight line, varies from point to point. The slope of a curve at any given point is defined as the slope of a straight line drawn tangent to the curve at that point. (A tangent line is one just touching the curve

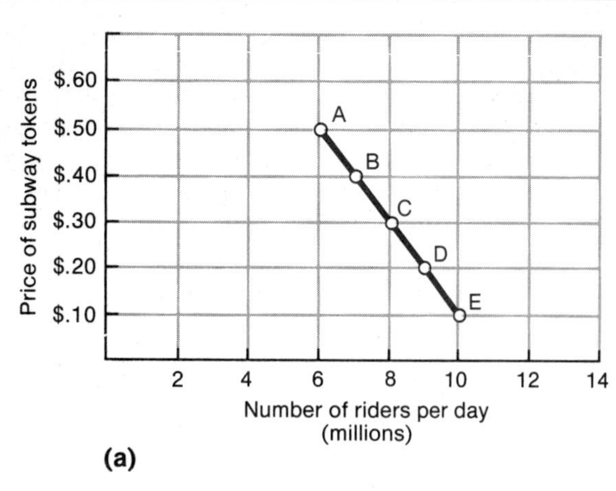

	Price of Subway Tokens	Number of Riders per Day (Millions)
A	$.50	6
B	$.40	7
C	$.30	8
D	$.20	9
E	$.10	10

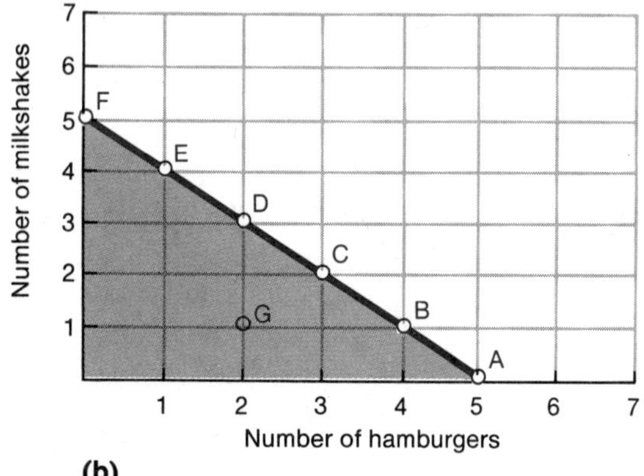

	Number of Hamburgers	Number of Milkshakes
A	5	0
B	4	1
C	3	2
D	2	3
E	1	4
F	0	5

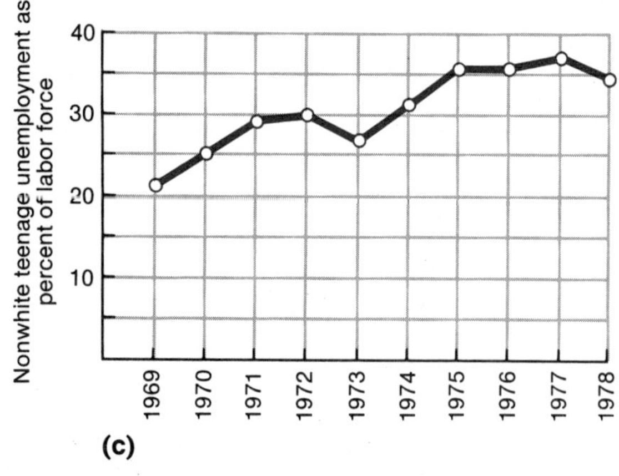

Year	Unemployment Rate (Nonwhite Males, 16–19 Years Old)
1969	21.4 %
1970	25.0
1971	28.9
1972	29.7
1973	26.9
1974	31.6
1975	35.4
1976	35.4
1977	37.0
1978	34.4

Exhibit 1A.2
Three typical economic graphs
This exhibit shows three graphs typical of those used in economics. Part a shows the relationship between the price of tokens and the number of riders per day on a certain city subway system. When a graph shows the relationship between a price and a quantity, it is conventional to put the price on the vertical axis. Part b shows the possible choices open to a person who has $2.50 to spend on lunch and can buy hamburgers at $.50 each or milkshakes at $.50 each. Part c shows how a graph can be used to represent change over time.

Source: Part c is from President's Council of Economic Advisers, *Economic Report of the President* (Washington, D.C.: Government Printing Office, 1979). Table B-30.

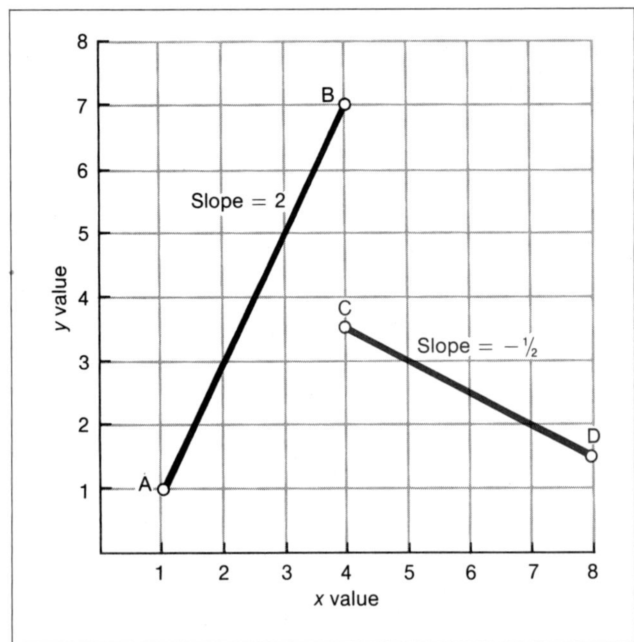

Exhibit 1A.3
Slopes of lines
The slope of a straight line drawn between two points is defined as the ratio of the change in the *y* value to the change in the *x* value between the two points. For example, the line drawn between Points A and B in this exhibit has a slope of +2, whereas the line drawn between Points C and D has a slope of −1/2.

without crossing it.) Consider the curve in Exhibit 1A.4. Applying the definition, the slope of this line at Point A is 1, and the slope at Point B is −2.

ABSTRACT GRAPHS

In all the examples so far, we have had specific numbers to work with for the x and y values. Sometimes, though, we know only the general nature of the relationship between two economic magnitudes rather than specific numbers. For example, we

Exhibit 1A.4
Slopes of curves
The slope of a curve at any given point is defined as the slope of a straight line drawn tangent to the curve at that point. A tangent line is one that just touches the curve without crossing it. In this exhibit, the slope of the curve at Point A is 1, and the slope of the curve at Point B is −2.

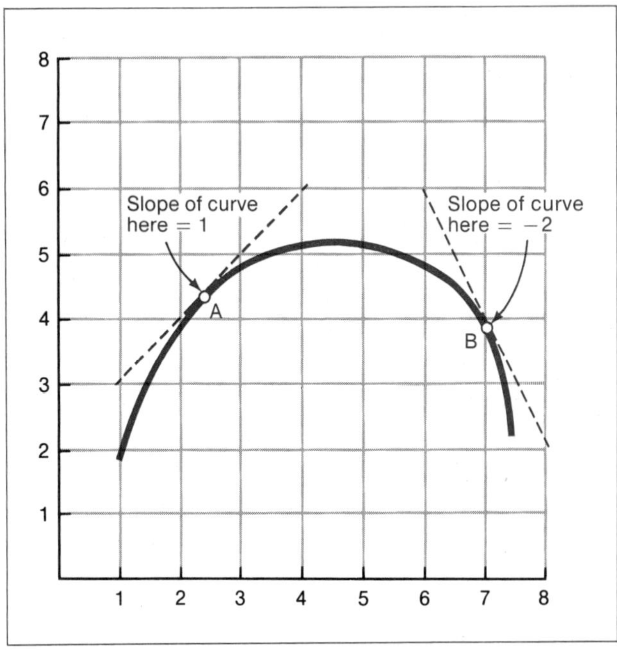

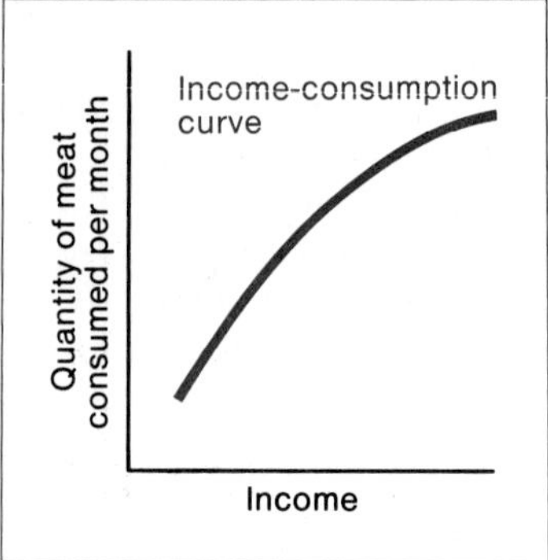

Exhibit 1A.5
An abstract graph
When we know the general form of an economic relationship but do not know the exact numbers involved, we can draw an abstract graph. Here, we know that as people's incomes rise, their consumption of meat increases rapidly at first, then levels off. Because we do not know the exact numbers for meat consumption or income, we have not marked any units on the axes.

might know that when people's incomes rise, they tend to increase their consumption of meat rapidly at first. But then, as they reach very high incomes, their meat consumption levels off. If we want to represent a relationship like this without caring about the numbers involved, we draw a graph like that shown in Exhibit 1A.5. The vertical axis is labeled "quantity of meat consumed per month," without any specific units. The horizontal axis is labeled "income," again without specific units. The curve, which rises rapidly at first and then levels off, tells us the general nature of the relationship between income and meat consumption: When income goes up, meat consumption rises, but not in proportion to the change in income. We will use abstract graphs like this one very frequently in this book. Abstract graphs express general principles, whereas graphs with numbers on the axes summarize specific known information.

STUDY HINTS FOR GRAPHS

When you come to a chapter in the book that is full of graphs, how should you study it? The first and most important rule is not to worry about memorizing graphs. I have never taught economics without having at least one student come to me after failing an exam and say: "But I learned every one of those graphs! What happened?" I always tell the students that they should have learned economics instead of learning the graphs.

Here are some specific study hints for working with graphs: After reading carefully through a chapter that uses graphs frequently, go back through the graphs one at a time. Place your hand over the explanatory note that appears beside each graph and try putting what the graph says into words. If you cannot say at least as much about the graph as the explanatory note does, read the text over again.

If you do all right going from graphs to words, half the battle is won. Next, try covering up the graph, and, using the explanatory note as a guide, sketch the graph on a piece of scratch paper. If you understand what the words mean and can comfortably go back and forth between the words and the graphs, you will find out that the two together are much easier to remember and apply than either would be separately. If you "learn the graphs" as meaningless patterns of lines, you are lost.

CONSTRUCTING YOUR OWN GRAPHS

For some students, the hardest kind of question to answer on an exam is the kind that requires construction of an original graph as part of an essay answer. Here are some hints for constructing your own graphs:

1. Put down the answer to the question in words. If you cannot do that, you might as well skip to the next question without wasting time on the graph. Try underlining the most important quantities in what you have written. The result might be

Exhibit 1A.6
Constructing a graph
To construct a graph, first put down in words what you want to say: "The larger the *number of students* at a university, the lower the *cost per student* of providing them with an education." Next, label the coordinate axes. Then, if you have exact numbers to work with, construct a table. Here we have no exact numbers, so we draw an abstract graph that slopes downward to show that cost goes down as numbers go up. For graphs with more than one curve, repeat these steps.

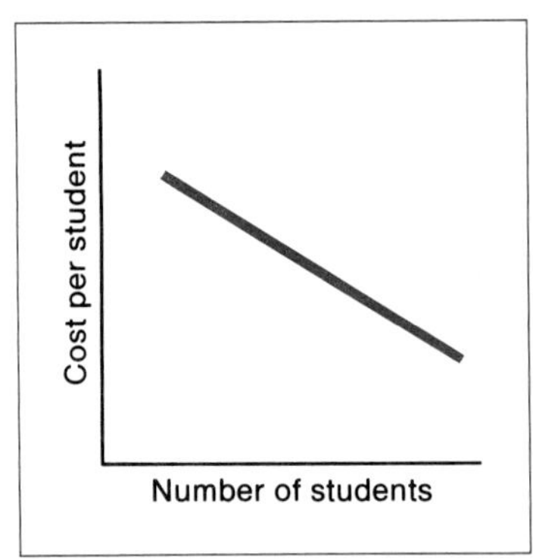

something like: "The larger the *number of students* who attend a university, the lower the *cost per student* of providing them with an education."

2. Decide how you are going to label the coordinate axes of your graph. In our example, because it is conventional to put money values on the vertical axis, we label the vertical axis "cost per student" and the horizontal axis "number of students."
3. Do you have exact numbers to work with? If you do, your next step should be to make a table showing what you know and then to use that to sketch your graph. If you do not have numbers, you will be drawing an abstract graph. In this case, all you know is that the cost per student goes down when the number of students goes up. Sketch in any convenient downward-sloping line (as in Exhibit 1A.6), and you will have done as well as can be done.
4. If your graph involves more than one relationship between pairs of economic quantities, repeat steps 1 to 3 for each relationship that you want to represent by a line or curve. When sketching graphs with more than one curve, pay particular attention to points where you think two curves ought to intersect (which will happen whenever both the x and y values of the two relationships are equal) and where you think they ought to be tangent (which will happen whenever the slopes of two curves are equal).
5. After your graph is completed, try translating it back into words. Does it really say what you wanted it to say?

A REMINDER

As you work through this book and are introduced to various specific kinds of graphs, turn back to this appendix now and then. Do not commit the fatal error of memorizing graphs as meaningless pictures. Remember that if you can go back and forth between graphs and words, the underlying theory that both are trying to express will stay with you more vividly than if you rely on either graphs or words alone. Remember that economics is about *people,* not graphs.

SUGGESTIONS FOR FURTHER READING

Bowen, William G. "Econometrics." In *Perspectives in Economics,* edited by Alan A. Brown, Egon Neuberger, and Malcolm Palmatier. New York: McGraw-Hill, 1971.
An introductory description of the important role of econometrics in modern economics. The essay on "Scope and Method of Economic Analysis" by Alan Brown and Egon Neuberger in the same volume is also useful.

Fusfeld, Daniel R. *The Age of the Economist.* Glenview, Ill.: Scott, Foresman, 1977, chap. 3.
More on Adam Smith.

Goodman, John C., and Dolan, Edwin G. *Economics of Public Policy.* St. Paul: West Publishing, 1979, chaps. 1 and 2.
Chapter 1 provides additional perspective on the relationship between positive and normative economics. Chapter 2 uses the military draft in an extended case study of the production possibility frontier.

Kirzner, Israel M. *The Economic Point of View.* Princeton, N.J.: Van Nostrand, 1960.
A commentary on the nature and history of economics by a leading representative of the "Austrian" school.

Koopmans, Tjalling C. "Economics among the Sciences." *American Economic Review* 69 (March 1979): 1–13.
A thought-provoking presidential address to the American Economics Association, organized around several fascinating case studies.

Robbins, Lionel C. *An Essay on the Nature and Significance of Economic Science,* 2d ed., rev. London: Macmillan, 1935.
The classic treatment of the topic.

CHAPTER 2

THE PRICE SYSTEM AND THE MARKET ECONOMY

WHAT YOU WILL LEARN IN THIS CHAPTER

This chapter will introduce the role played by markets in determining what is produced, how it is produced, and for whom it is produced. The chapter will explain each of three functions of markets: transmitting knowledge, providing incentives, and distributing income. It will show how the price system broadcasts information on opportunity costs and relative scarcities to buyers, how prices at the same time provide incentives to resource owners and entrepreneurs to put resources to best use, and how the incentive system operates to determine individuals' incomes. It will also introduce the questions of whether the market distributes income fairly and why it does not always operate perfectly. These questions will recur frequently as the discussion of economics progresses.

FOR REVIEW

Here are some important terms and concepts that will be put to use in this chapter. If you do not understand them, review them before proceeding.

- *Pure economizing and entrepreneurship (Chapter 1)*
- *Opportunity cost (Chapter 1)*
- *Positive and normative economics (Chapter 1)*
- *Market justice and distributive justice (Chapter 1)*

Modern economies are based on a vast division of labor, and each person within them makes a contribution to the whole system. One person installs hubcaps on Ford station wagons. Another keeps accounts in a New England branch of Woolworth's. Still another serves coffee, tea, or milk on Eastern Airlines. All these jobs have to be coordinated with others. When a team of auditors visit the branch of Woolworth's, someone must make sure that they will not run out of coffee on the airplane, that their rented Ford will not be missing a hubcap, and that the books they want to see will be balanced and ready when they arrive.

In the U.S. economy, markets play a central role in providing the necessary coordination. **Markets** are the various arrangements people have for trading with one another. They may be elaborately organized, like the New York Stock Exchange with its computers and ticker tape machines, or informal, like the word-of-mouth network that puts teenage babysitters in touch with the people who need their services. But however markets are organized, they perform

Markets All the various arrangements people have for trading with one another.

certain common functions: transmitting information, providing incentives, and distributing income.

THE FUNCTIONS OF MARKETS

Information and Its Value

Information is the most precious good in any economy. Economic prosperity depends on putting resources to their best uses, and to do this, the people who make decisions on how resources are to be used must know which uses are best. Like water, economic information is taken for granted when it is cheap and abundant. Its importance becomes apparent only when it is scarce, as the following case study illustrates.

Case 2.1
The Role of Information in the Bazaar Economy

At the foot of the Atlas Mountains in Morocco sits the ancient walled town of Sefrou. Once an important stop on the caravan route from Fez to the Sahara, it has been, for about a century now, an important *bazaar,* or market center, for some 15,000 to 30,000 people. Since the mid 1960s, anthropologist Clifford Geertz of the Institute for Advanced Study has been observing the bazaar at Sefrou. What he has discovered is instructive.

According to Geertz, information in the bazaar is poor, scarce, maldistributed, inefficiently communicated, and intensely valued. The level of ignorance about everything from product quality and going prices to market possibilities and production costs is very high. The name of the game in the bazaar is the search for information a person lacks and the protection of information a person has. As in any other economy, capital, skill, luck, privilege, and hard work contribute to individual success; but in the bazaar they do it not so much by increasing the efficiency of production as by enabling a person to secure a strategic location in the market's communications network. The primary problem facing participants in the bazaar is not to balance options but to find out what they are.

Geertz interprets the central features that distinguish the bazaar from a modern, industrialized market economy as responses to the scarcity of information. One of these features is bargaining. In a system where virtually nothing is packaged, standardized, or regulated, every transaction must be preceded by elaborate bargaining over price, quantity, quality, and credit terms. During the bargaining, buyers and sellers naturally try to conceal their minimum acceptable terms from one another, but at the same time they must manage to reveal enough information to form a basis for a mutually advantageous trade.

At this point, the efficiency of the bazaar is apparently improved by a second characteristic feature, which Geertz calls "clientalization." By this he means a tendency of buyers to return repeatedly to the same seller to engage in intensive bargaining rather than to search quickly but extensively among many sellers for the best price. Evidently, repeated bargaining within a stable client-seller relationship improves information exchange by enough to offset any loss of information resulting from frequent examination of alternative sources of supply.

In Geertz's view, the whole structure of the bazaar can be viewed as a set of communications channels designed to serve the needs of people whose interests are opposed in the act of bargaining but joined by the need to coordinate their economic activities. The same is true of any economic system; but since information is relatively scarce in the bazaar, its value is more prominently displayed.

Source: Based on Clifford Geertz, "The Bazaar Economy: Information and Search in Peasant Marketing," *American Economic Review* 68 (May 1978): 28–32. Used by permission.

The Price System

In the U.S. economy of today, bargaining and client-seller relationships are by no means unknown. Their importance as channels for the transmission of information, however, is completely overshadowed by another mechanism that exists only in rudimentary form in the bazaar economy. This mechanism is the *price system*. In the modern economy, prices typically are not subject to bargaining on a one-to-one basis between buyer and seller every time a transaction is made. Instead, they are widely advertised and published as an invitation to any buyer to enter the market on equal terms with other buyers. The price system is essentially a system for broadcasting information on opportunity costs and on the relative scarcity of various goods and services. A rise in the price of any good relative to the price of other goods signals increasing scarcity of that good. A fall in the price of any good (or, in times of inflation, a failure of its price to rise as fast as the prices of other goods) signals increasing abundance. Buyers can adjust their behavior accordingly.

The following case, supplied by Nobel prize–winning economist F. A. Hayek, brings out the contrast between the price system and the bazaar system. In Hayek's example, prices are the cheap and easily available source of information used by buyers to adjust to complex events occurring far away.

Case 2.2
Information and the Price System

Assume that somewhere in the world a new opportunity for the use of some raw material, say tin, has arisen, or that one of the sources of supply of tin has been eliminated. It does not matter for our purpose—and it is very significant that it does not matter—which of these two causes has made tin more scarce. All that the users of tin need to know is that some of the tin they used to consume is now more profitably employed elsewhere, and that in consequence they must economize tin. There is no need for the great majority of them even to know where the more urgent need has arisen, or in favor of what other needs they ought to husband the supply. If only some of them know directly of the new demand, and switch resources over to it, and if the people who are aware of the new gap thus created in turn fill it from still other sources, the effect will rapidly spread throughout the whole economic system and influence not only the uses of tin, but also those of its substitutes and the substitutes of these substitutes, the supply of the things made of tin, and their substitutes, and so on, and all this without the great majority of those instrumental in bringing about these substitutions knowing anything at all about the original cause of these changes. The whole acts as one market, not because any of its members survey the whole field, but because their limited individual fields of vision sufficiently overlap so that through many intermediaries the relevant information is communicated to all.

Source: Reprinted by permission from F. A. Hayek, "The Use of Knowledge in Society," *American Economic Review* 35 (September 1945): 519–530.

By informing people of the value and scarcity of tin, wheat, forklift trucks, and hundreds of thousands of other commodities, the price system reduces countless decisions to the level of pure economizing. Producers and consumers can observe market prices, combine them with their own knowledge of local circumstances, and arrive at valid judgments about the advantages and disadvantages of various production and consumption activities. To be sure, there is more to economic decision making than pure economizing, and the price system does not supply the answers to all economic questions. But entrepreneurial talents and energies, which in a bazaar economy are used up merely in finding out how much things cost, are now liberated to deal with the problem of finding new and better ways of doing things.

Incentives in the Market Economy

Knowledge of the best use of resources is a necessary condition for efficient coordination of economic activity, but it is not by itself sufficient. In addition to knowing the uses to which resources should be put, the people controlling them must have incentives to devote them to the known best use. Providing those incentives is the second major function of markets. As Adam Smith wrote more than two hundred years ago:

> It is not from the benevolence of the butcher, the brewer, or the baker that we expect our dinner, but from their regard to their own interest. . . . Every individual is continually exerting himself to find out the most advantageous employment for whatever capital he can command. . . . By directing that industry in such a manner as its produce may be of the greater value, he intends only his own gain, and he is in this,

---

Friedrich August von Hayek (1899-)

In 1944, a slim volume entitled *The Road to Serfdom* burst onto the world's best seller list. This book warned that an enthusiasm for economic planning and strong central government was leading Western democracies down a path that, if not checked, could end in Soviet- or Nazi-style totalitarianism. The author of the book was as surprised as anyone to find it a best seller. He was Friedrich von Hayek, then a professor at the London School of Economics.

Hayek, born and educated in Vienna, by 1944 already had a first-class international reputation as an economic theorist. He had written widely on monetary theory and on the subject now known as macroeconomics. In contrast to many of his contemporaries, he did not believe that the Great Depression of the 1930s signaled the final failure of the market economy. The market would and could work, he held, if it were freed of the distortions introduced by ill-advised government policies. Most of all, what the economies of the world did not need as a cure for their troubles was comprehensive economic planning. Planning could never replace the market as a method for utilizing knowledge and guiding the division of labor. The attempt to make it do so would lead only to a loss of political freedom, not greater economic prosperity.

In 1950, Hayek left London for the University of Chicago, where he taught for twelve years as professor of social and moral science. Much of his time he now spent writing on broad issues of law and social philosophy. His major work of the University of Chicago period was *The Constitution of Liberty.* In this book, he defended the classical liberal ideal of the limited state based on a free market economy and a written constitution.

In 1962, Hayek saw that the University of Chicago's mandatory retirement age was fast approaching. Retirement seemed such an impossible idea to him that he returned to Europe, where professors could serve for a lifetime. He is now visiting professor at the University of Salzburg in Austria and professor emeritus of the University of Freiburg in Germany. In 1974, the name Friedrich von Hayek was back in the international headlines once again. The Swedish Academy of Science had awarded him the Nobel Memorial Prize in Economics—the highest professional distinction there is. A fitting time to retire from a distinguished career? Not for Hayek. The first volume of his new work, *Law, Legislation, and Liberty,* had just appeared the year before, and there were two more volumes to complete. Asked what he would do when the job had been finished, Hayek indicated that he would then, after a detour of many years, be ready to get back to some unfinished problems of economic theory.

as in many other cases, led by an invisible hand to promote an end which was no part of his intention.

The market offers different kinds of incentives to different people. Consumers who keep themselves well informed and spend their money judiciously are rewarded by the satisfaction of more needs with their limited budgets. Workers earn higher incomes if they stay alert to job market opportunities and work where their productivity is highest. Real estate brokers earn higher commissions the more efficiently they match suitable buyers and sellers. In every case, people who acquire economic information have an incentive to act on that information and not just file it away.

No doubt the most famous of incentives in the market economy is the profit motive. Profits make up a relatively small part of all income received by individuals. As officially measured by government statisticians, wages and salaries outweigh corporate profits by more than ten to one. But profits have an importance entirely out of proportion to their magnitude because they are the reward earned by entrepreneurs for properly coordinating the contributions of workers and other resource owners. A business firm earns a profit by buying inputs at their market prices and using them to produce a product that can be sold for more than the cost of all the inputs. And just as the market rewards firms that use resources productively, it penalizes those who use them wastefully. If the value of the inputs a firm buys exceeds the value of the product it makes out of those inputs, that firm will suffer a loss and will eventually disappear from the market.

Distributing Income

As a by-product of providing incentives, markets distribute income and wealth. People who possess skills and talents or who own resources that are scarce and highly valued get richly rewarded for putting them to their best use. People whose talents or resources are less scarce or of poor quality get less well rewarded even if they use what they have as wisely as possible. Entrepreneurs who take risks and guess right make large profits; entrepreneurs who take risks that looked just as prudent at the outset but who have guessed wrong suffer losses. In short, the market tends to distribute income in proportion to the contribution each person makes to the process of production.

The distributional function of the market is a source of great controversy, much of it over the normative question of whether the distribution of income in a market economy is *fair*. Not surprisingly, the answer depends largely on what is meant by *fairness*. To those for whom fairness is the observation of market justice, the distribution of income in a market economy does appear equitable. People receive what they earn from their own labor and from the voluntary exchange of property with others. All that is required for fairness, in this view, is that the contracts and exchanges be voluntary so they will work out to the mutual benefit of buyers and sellers.

To those who view fairness in terms of distributive justice, the distribution of income in the market economy is not inherently fair. Because skills, talents, and resource ownership are not distributed equally among people, the market does not distribute income equally either.

Is Distribution Separable? The controversy over the distributive function of markets also raises an important question of positive economics: Can the function of distributing income be separated from the functions of transmitting information and providing incentives? Answers differ to this question as well.

One answer is a flat no—the distributional function cannot be separated from the others. The reasoning behind this answer begins with the observation that there are only two ways to alter the distribution of income produced by the market—either to take from some people part of what they earn in order to give it to others or to manipulate prices so that some people earn more and some earn less than they otherwise would have earned. The first alternative interferes with incentives; if people know that part of what they earn will not be theirs to keep, their incentive to put their resources to best use will be correspondingly diminished. The second alternative interferes with the transmission of information through the price system; if prices are manipulated for the purpose of affecting income distribution, they cannot at the same time carry accurate signals regarding the relative scarcity of resources.

Despite the apparent reasonableness of this argument, not everyone accepts it on a practical level. It may be true, critics say, that attempts to redistribute income always carry the danger of distorting incentives or sending false signals regarding scarcity; but in practice, the distortions can be held to an insignificant level. Many think, for example, that people will not work much less or invest their capital much differently if they are subject to income taxes than if they are not. To take another kind of example, if rents on urban housing are held down to make housing more accessible to the poor, the distortion of the incentive to build such housing can be offset with other regulations or subsidies.

IMPERFECTIONS IN THE MARKET SYSTEM

Are markets perfect? Economists from Adam Smith to Milton Friedman sometimes get so enthusiastic about the principles according to which markets operate that they forget to point out that in the real world these principles operate only as tendencies. Imperfections in the market economy stem from a number of sources. By far the most important is the fact that although the price system *cheapens* the process of transmitting information to a large degree, it does not make information *free.*

Even after the price system has done its best, there is an irreducible minimum of ignorance in the world. Producers and consumers remain at least partly ignorant of what is happening in other places and substantially ignorant of what is likely to happen in the future. They may conceal their preferences for strategic reasons when dealing with others and at the same time remain ignorant of the preferences of others. A modern industrial market economy is worlds ahead of the bazaar at Sefrou in terms of the quality of information available; but as long as information is less than perfect, mistakes will be made.

Transactions Costs

Transactions costs All costs of finding buyers or sellers to transact business with and of negotiating terms of exchanges, drawing up contracts, guarding against involuntary default or foul play, and so on.

The cost of obtaining information is only one of a number of transactions costs that prevent markets from operating perfectly in the real world. By **transactions costs,** economists mean any of the costs of finding people to do business with, negotiating terms, drawing up contracts, guarding against involuntary default or foul play, and so on. Examples of market imperfections resulting from transactions costs are easy to find.

Have you ever had the experience of trying to get tickets to a play or ball game and being turned away because all the tickets were sold? Have you ever stayed away from such an event because the ticket price was too high, even though some seats remained unsold? If you have had either of these experiences, you have witnessed a market imperfection. If ticket prices accurately reflected the scarcity of seats relative to demand for them, there would be no unsold seats and no one turned away. But the transactions costs of trying to adjust ticket prices for every performance to exactly match supply and demand are evidently prohibitive. Predicting the correct price, informing the public of it each night, settling disputes, printing tickets, and a hundred other things would become so complex and costly that trying to fine tune market performance in this way just would not pay.

A second example: Have you ever been annoyed by smokers or annoyed that you were not permitted to smoke at some particular time or place? The perpetual battle between smokers and nonsmokers could, in principle, be efficiently resolved if there were a market in smoking rights. Every time two or more people got together in a room, they could hold an auction for the right to smoke. Nonsmokers could sell smokers a permit to light up or could pay them not to light up; the rules could be set either way. Whatever the rules, with such a market in operation, smoking would take place when, and only when, the benefit to smokers at least equaled the annoyance to nonsmokers. Of course, the transactions costs of holding auctions every time people walked from room to room would far outweigh the modest gains. Cruder methods, such as designating smoking and nonsmoking areas, only approximately adjust the conflicting interests of the opposing camps, but they are enormously cheaper to administer.

Property Rights

Just how seriously transactions costs interfere with the efficient use of resources often depends on the structure of the property rights that underlie the market system. Consider, for example, the problem of efficiently exploiting a common property fishing ground, say one in international ocean waters, that is open to all comers without restriction. Overharvesting is likely to be a serious problem in such a fishing ground. Overall yield can be maximized by limiting the yearly catch or the size of fish taken or by using other conservation practices, but no individual operator will have the incentive to employ conservation practices unless all others agree to do likewise. And any attempt to negotiate privately a unanimous, binding conservation agreement among all fishers would run up against insurmountable transactions costs.

In comparison, overharvesting need never be a problem in privately owned fishing grounds, such as those maintained for sports fishing by many clubs and commercial operators. Without elaborate negotiations, club directors or commercial owners simply establish the proper conservation rules, and those not inclined to observe them are not admitted. In this case, private property appears to decrease transactions costs greatly compared with common property, thereby improving the efficiency of resource use.

In other cases, private ownership of property may be a barrier to efficient use of resources. Consider, for example, the problem of obtaining a right-of-way for a new road or power line through a stretch of countryside owned by many individual farmers. Private negotiations with each landowner could very likely involve prohibitive transactions costs. Especially troublesome would be the fact that each landowner would have the incentive to hold out in the expectation that the last owner to settle could extort the best deal from the highway department or utility in question.

To cut transactions costs in cases like this, federal, state, and local governments are frequently given the power to condemn private land for public use. The private owner is forced to sell in return for what some independent agency or arbitrator judges to be a fair price. This power to condemn private land for public purposes is, of course, open to abuse and may, on occasion, itself lead to inefficient patterns of land use. But many economists believe that the savings in transactions costs more than outweigh the occasional abuses.

The proper mix of private and public property rights, then, can often reduce transactions costs to manageable levels and improve the efficiency of markets. In no case, however, can transactions costs be entirely eliminated.

CONCLUSIONS

This chapter has given just a few examples of how markets perform their functions of transmitting information, providing incentives, and distributing income. It has also offered a few examples of market imperfections and the sources from which they arise. The chapters that follow will give many more examples. In fact, the entire book can be read as an amplification of the themes set forth in this chapter: how markets operate to determine what is produced, who produces it, and for whom it is produced; why markets do not always perform perfectly; and what can be done to improve market performance.

SUMMARY

1. Markets play a crucial role in coordinating the division of labor in the market economy. This role includes performance of three basic functions: transmitting information, providing incentives, and distributing income.
2. In an advanced industrial market economy, the price system functions as a mechanism for broadcasting information about opportunity costs and the relative scarcity of resources. Rising relative prices signal increasing scarcity; falling relative prices signal increasing abundance.
3. Knowledge of the best use of resources is a necessary but not sufficient condition for efficient coordination of economic activity. In addition to knowing the uses to which resources should be put, the people controlling those resources must have incentives to devote them to their known best use. Consumers, resource owners, and entrepreneurs all have incentives to heed the information that comes to them through the price system, because doing so increases their satisfaction, income, and profit.
4. As a by-product of their function in providing incentives, markets perform the further function of distributing income and wealth. People who possess skills and talents or who own resources that are scarce and highly valued get richly rewarded for putting the resources to their best use. People whose talents or resources are less scarce or of poor quality get less well rewarded even if they use what they have wisely.
5. Despite their acknowledged effectiveness in coordinating the division of labor, markets are neither necessarily fair nor always perfectly efficient. Whether markets are considered fair is largely a question of normative economics that is answered differently by different individuals. Whether

markets function efficiently often depends on how seriously transactions costs impede the transmission of information, the execution of contracts, and so on.

DISCUSSION QUESTIONS

1. In your opinion, do the wages or salaries of various occupations have much influence on people's decisions about whether to go to college and what to major in? Justify your answer by explaining what it has to do with the functions of markets in transmitting information, providing incentives, and distributing income.
2. If you were the manager of a division of a major automobile manufacturer and you noticed that the price of steel had been going up relative to the prices of other materials used in the manufacturing of automobiles, how would you react? What would you do and have others do to make adjustments? How would you expect your competitors to react? Explain.
3. Even in an advanced industrial economy such as that of the United States, not all transactions take place in accordance with uniform, published prices. What sorts of transactions do you know of that are still subject to bargaining between buyer and seller? Why do you think they are carried out by means of bargaining rather than by fixed prices?
4. Review Case 1.2, in which it is explained that certain U.S. energy policies have the effect of holding the market price of oil below its marginal cost. What you have learned in this chapter should give you additional insights into the effects of that policy. How does it affect the ability of the price system to transmit accurate information about opportunity costs and relative scarcities? How does it affect the distribution of income?
5. Suppose you think that you and your neighbors are being overcharged by your local supermarket, which happens to be the only one in town. You decide that you will organize a consumer owned food cooperative to provide competition and low prices. What transactions costs might you have to overcome in setting up and operating the cooperative?
6. Presuming that continually repeated auctions of smoking rights are impractical, the following approach to resolving the conflict between smokers and nonsmokers is proposed: In public places, the government should set rules permitting smoking only in designated areas and guaranteeing nonsmokers a right to clean air. In private places, rules should be established and enforced by the owners of the private property. Do you find this a reasonable approach to the problem? How would you distinguish between public and private places? Would you do it strictly on the basis of legal ownership? Or would you consider such places as restaurants, theaters, and airplanes to be "public" enough, despite private ownership, to justify government imposed rules?

SUGGESTIONS FOR FURTHER READING

Coase, R. H. "The Problem of Social Cost." *Journal of Law and Economics* 3 (October 1960): 1–44.
The classic treatment of property rights and transactions costs in economics.

Hayek, F. A. "The Use of Knowledge in Society." *American Economic Review* 35 (September 1945): 519–530.
The source of Case 2.2, worth reading in its entirety.

Manne, Henry G., ed. *The Economics of Legal Relationships.* St. Paul: West Publishing, 1975.
A collection of papers on property rights and transactions costs in economics, many accessible to beginning students. Chapter 9 reproduces Coase's article on social cost, listed above. Chapter 24 is a detailed analysis of the problem of the fishery.

CHAPTER 3

SUPPLY AND DEMAND —THE BASICS

WHAT YOU WILL LEARN IN THIS CHAPTER

Everyday experience teaches that, other things being equal, the quantity of a good that buyers are willing to purchase tends to increase as the price of the good decreases. Similarly, it teaches that the quantity of a good suppliers are willing to sell tends to increase as the price increases. This chapter will show how these commonsense ideas form the basis for supply and demand analysis—one of the most useful analytical tools in all of economics. It will show how terms such as shortage *and* surplus *can be given a precise meaning and will introduce the concept of market equilibrium. These new concepts will then be applied to practical economic problems.*

FOR REVIEW

Here are some important terms and concepts that will be put to use in this chapter. If you do not understand them, review them before proceeding.

- *Opportunity cost (Chapter 1)*
- *Working with graphs (Appendix to Chapter 1)*

The number of markets in the U.S. economy is as large as the number of different kinds of goods and services produced—and that is very large. Despite the great diversity of markets, though, there are some economic principles so powerful that they are useful in understanding all of them. The principles of supply and demand fit into this category.

The fundamental ideas of supply and demand have long been known to practical merchants and traders. For as long as there have been markets, sellers have realized that one way to encourage people to buy more of their product is to offer it at a lower price, and buyers have known that one way to get more of the goods they want is to offer to pay more for them. Only in the last hundred years, though, have economists made systematic use of the principles of supply and demand as the central basis of their science. In the English-speaking world, Alfred Marshall deserves much of the credit for showing how useful the ideas of supply and demand can be. This chapter—and the corresponding chapters in all modern textbooks—is little more than a rewrite of the principles he taught in his own famous *Principles of Economics.*

Alfred Marshall (1842–1924)

Alfred Marshall was born in London in 1842, the son of a Bank of England cashier. His father hoped that he would enter the ministry, but young Marshall had other ideas. He turned down a theological scholarship at Oxford to study mathematics instead. He received an M.A. in mathematics from Cambridge in 1865.

While at Cambridge, he joined a philosophical discussion group. There, he became interested in promoting the wide development of the human mind. He was soon told, however, that harsh economic reality would prevent his ideas from being carried out. Britain's productive resources, it was said, could never allow the mass of the people sufficient leisure for education. This disillusioning episode appears to have first turned Marshall's attention to economics.

At the time, British economics was dominated by the so-called classical school. Marshall had great respect for the classical writers. Initially, he saw his own work as simply using his mathematical training to strengthen and systematize the classical system. It was not long, however, before he was breaking new ground and developing a system of his own. By 1890, when he brought out his famous *Principles of Economics,* he had laid the foundation of what is now called the neoclassical school.

Attempting to explain the essence of his approach, Marshall included this passage in the second edition of his *Principles:*

> In spite of a great variety in detail, nearly all the chief problems of economics agree in that they have a kernel of the same kind. This kernel is an inquiry as to the balancing of two opposed classes of motives, the one consisting of desires to acquire certain new goods, and thus satisfy wants; while the other consists of desires to avoid certain efforts or retain certain immediate enjoyment. . . . In other words, it is an inquiry into the balancing of the forces of demand and supply.

Marshall's influence on economics, at least in the English-speaking world, was enormous. His *Principles* was the leading text for decades, and the modern student can still learn much from reading it. As a professor at Cambridge, he taught a great many of the next generation of leading economists. Today the neoclassical school he founded continues to dominate the profession. It has received many challenges but so far has weathered them all.

THE LAW OF DEMAND

Law of demand The law that the quantity of a good demanded by buyers tends to increase as the price of the good decreases and tends to decrease as the price increases, other things being equal.

The analysis begins with the **law of demand,** which says simply that, in the market for any good, the quantity of that good demanded by buyers tends to increase as the price of the good decreases and tends to decrease as the price increases, other things being equal. This law corresponds so closely to what common sense tells us about the way markets work that we could simply state it without further elaboration. But a few additional comments will ensure that it is properly understood.

Effective Demand

Effective demand The quantity of a good that purchasers are willing and able to buy at a particular price.

First, what is meant by *quantity demanded*? It is important to understand that the quantity demanded at a given price means the **effective demand**—the quantity purchasers are willing and able to buy at that price. The effective demand at a particular price may be different from the quantity consumers want or need. I may *want* a new Jaguar XJ-6; but given my limited financial resources, I am not willing actually to offer to buy such a car at its current price of $20,000. My want does not count as part of the quantity demanded in the market for Jaguars. Similarly, I might *need* corrective dental surgery to avoid premature loss of my teeth, but I might be very poor. If I were unable to pay, and no other person or agency were willing to pay, my need would not be counted as part of the quantity demanded in the market for dental services.

Other Things Being Equal

Second, why is the phrase *other things being equal* attached to the law of demand? The reason is that a change in the price of a product is not the only thing that affects the quantity of that product demanded. If people's incomes go up, they are likely to increase the quantities they demand of a great many goods, even if prices do not change. If people's basic tastes and preferences change, the quantities of things they buy will change. If their expectations about future prices or their own future incomes change, they may change their spending patterns even before those price and income changes actually take place.

Above all, in the law of demand, the "other things being equal" condition indicates that the prices of other goods remain unchanged. What really counts in determining the quantity demanded of some good is its price *relative* to the prices of other goods. If the price of gasoline goes up and consumers' incomes and the prices of all other goods go up by the same proportion, the law of demand does not suggest any change in the quantity of gasoline demanded. But if the price of gasoline goes up 10 percent while the price of everything else goes up 20 percent, an increase can be expected in the quantity of gasoline demanded, because its relative price has fallen.

Why?

Now that the meaning of the law of demand is clear, we can ask why it works. Three explanations are worth considering.

First, when the price of a good falls while the prices of other goods remain unchanged, we are likely to substitute some of that good for other things. For example, if the price of fish falls while the price of meat remains the same, we are likely to put fish on the menu a few of the times when we would have used meat had the price of fish not changed.

Second, when the price of a good changes, other things being equal, our effective purchasing power changes even though our income measured in money terms does not. For example, if the price of clothing rises while nothing else changes, we will feel poorer, very much as if a few dollars a year had been trimmed from our paycheck or allowance. Feeling poorer, it is likely that we will buy a bit less of many things, including clothing.

Third—and this reason is not quite distinct from the other two—when the price of a good falls, new buyers who did not use a product at all before are drawn into the market. There was a time, for example, when tape recorders were playthings for the rich or technical tools for businesses. Today, they can be bought very cheaply. Rich people are not buying ten or twenty tape recorders apiece at the lower prices, but sales have gone up ten- or twentyfold because many people are buying them who never had entered that market at all before.

Exceptions to the Law

Are there exceptions to the law of demand? Are there cases in which an increase in the price of a good causes people to use more of it? Theoretically, such exceptions are possible, although in practice they are quite rare. One kind of exception can occur if the change in the price of a good has such a strong impact on effective purchasing power that it causes a radical change in people's whole pattern of consumption. Imagine a family that lives in Minnesota and habitually spends January each year vacationing in Florida. One year, the price of home heating fuel jumps dramatically. The family reacts by turning down the thermostat a little, but the fuel bills for September through December still go up so much that the family cannot afford to take its Florida vacation in January. Yet, staying at home, even though it is cheaper than going to Florida, requires the family to burn more fuel than during the previous winters, when it left the house unheated for that month. The total effect of the rise in fuel prices is therefore an *increase* in the consumption of the product.

Perhaps other rare kinds of exceptions to the law of demand are also possible. The point is, though, that we have to think so hard to come up with examples that we end up being more convinced than ever of the validity of the law.

Demand Schedules and Curves

The law of demand, like so many other economic ideas, can usefully be illustrated with numerical tables and graphs. Suppose, for example, that we want to study the operation of the law of demand in the market for wheat.[1] One way to express the relationship between the price of wheat and the quantity of wheat demanded by all buyers in the market is in the form of a table like that given in Exhibit 3.1a.

From the first line of the table, we learn that when the price of wheat is

[1]In this chapter, we ignore a number of federal government policies—price supports, acreage controls, and so on—that affect the price, quantity supplied, and quantity demanded of wheat.

Exhibit 3.1
A demand schedule and a demand curve for wheat
Both the demand schedule and the demand curve show the quantity of wheat demanded at various possible prices. Both show, for example, that when the price is $2 per bushel, the quantity is 2 billion bushels per year.

(a) Demand schedule

Price of Wheat (dollars per bushel)	Quantity of Wheat Demanded (billions of bushels per year)
$3.20	1.4
3.00	1.5
2.80	1.6
2.60	1.7
2.40	1.8
2.20	1.9
2.00	**2.0**
1.80	2.1
1.60	2.2
1.40	2.3
1.20	2.4
1.00	2.5
.80	2.6

(b) Demand curve

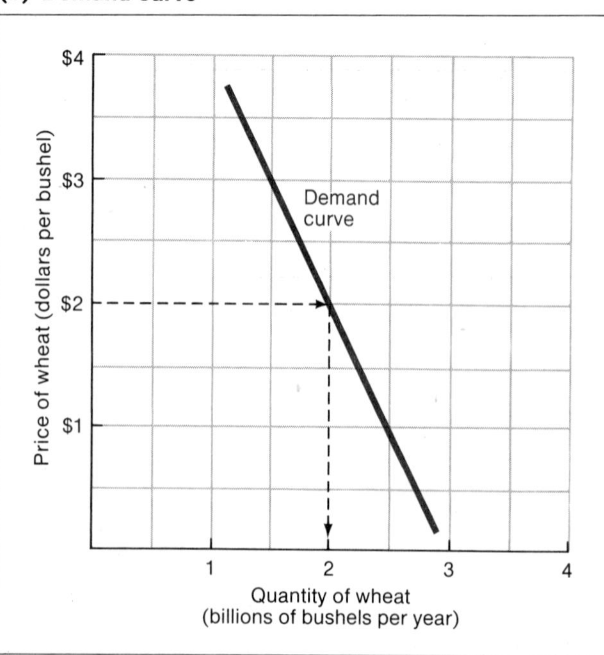

\$3.20, the quantity demanded per year will be 1.4 billion bushels. Reading further, we see that as the price decreases, the quantity demanded increases. At \$3 per bushel, buyers are willing and able to purchase 1.5 billion bushels per year; at \$2.80, the quantity demanded is 1.6 billion bushels. The complete table is called the **demand schedule** for wheat.

Demand schedule A table showing the quantity of a good demanded at various prices.

The information given by the demand schedule can be expressed just as easily in graphical form. This is done in Exhibit 3.1b. The diagonal line of the graph is called the **demand curve** for wheat. Suppose that we want to use the demand curve to determine what quantity will be demanded when the price is \$2 per bushel. Beginning at \$2 on the vertical axis, we follow across as shown by the arrow until we reach the demand curve. We then go down from that point to the horizontal axis, where we read off the answer—2 billion bushels per year. This, of course, is the same answer given in the tabular demand schedule.

Demand curve A graphical representation of the relationship between the price of a good and the quantity of it demanded.

Movements along the Demand Curve

To repeat what has been said before, the demand curve shows how the quantity demanded changes in response to a change in price, *other things being equal*. When a change in the quantity of wheat demanded occurs as a result of a change in the price of wheat, acting alone, that change is represented graphically as a movement along the demand curve for wheat. If something other than the price of wheat changes, a different graphical representation is required.

Consider Exhibit 3.2. The demand curve labeled D_1 is the same as that shown in Exhibit 3.1. It is based on certain assumptions about household income, the prices of other goods, and buyers' expectations about future changes in price. Given those assumptions, the quantity demanded at a price

Exhibit 3.2
A shift in the demand curve for wheat

The effect of a change in the price of wheat, other things being equal, is represented by a movement along the demand curve for wheat, as from Point A to Point B along Demand Curve D_1. The effect of a change in something other than a change in the price of wheat (say a change in household income) must be represented by a shift in the entire demand curve, as from the position D_1 to the position D_2.

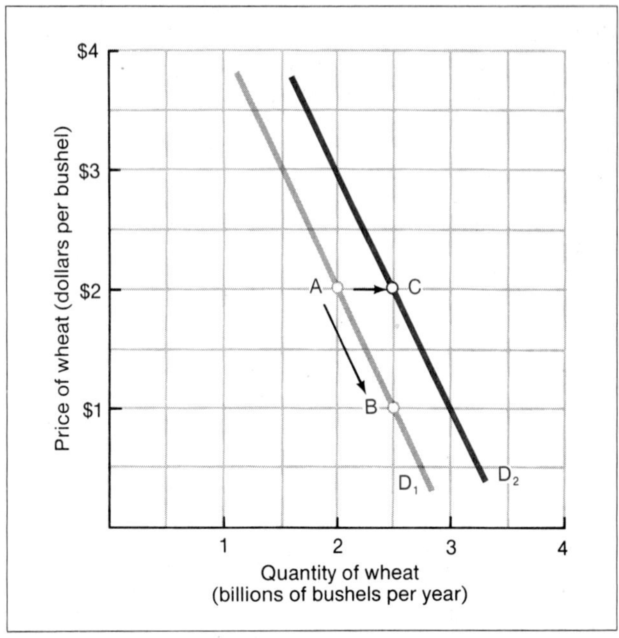

of \$2 per bushel will be 2 billion bushels per year, as at Point A on Demand Curve D_1. A fall in the price from \$2 per bushel to \$1 per bushel, other things being equal, will cause the quantity demanded to increase to 2.5 billion bushels per year. This change in price is represented by a movement along Demand Curve D_1 from Point A to Point B.

Shifts in the Demand Curve Return now to Point A. Suppose that the price does not change but that something else changes—say, household income rises. A sufficiently large increase in household income could cause consumers to demand an additional half billion bushels per year, even without a change in the price of wheat. This change is represented by a movement from Point A to Point C in the diagram—a movement *off* Demand Curve D_1 rather than along it. With household income established at its new, higher level, changes in *price* would now cause movements up or down along the new demand curve, D_2, which passes through Point C and lies everywhere to the right of the old demand curve, D_1. The new demand curve indicates that, whatever the price of wheat, the quantity demanded, given the new, higher level of household income, will be larger than it would have been at the same price, given the old level of income.

A similar story could have been told if the prices of other goods or buyers' expectations, rather than income, had changed. The general point to be established is this: When the demand for some good changes for a reason *other* than a change in the price of the product itself, the change is represented graphically by a *shift* in the entire demand curve to a new position.

It is a rather widely established convention among economists to refer to a shift in a demand curve as a *change in demand.* The phrase *change in quantity demanded* refers to a movement along a given demand curve.

Normal and Inferior Goods Economists use some special terms in discussing the sources of shifts in demand curves. Changes in income are one source of such shifts. When a rise in buyers' incomes causes the demand curve for a good to shift to the right (as happened in Exhibit 3.2), the good is called a **normal good.** People tend to reduce their consumption of some goods when their incomes go up. Such goods, called **inferior goods,** are those goods for which there are more desirable but also more costly substitutes. Hamburger and intercity bus travel are examples. An increase in buyers' incomes causes the demand curve for an inferior good to shift to the left.

Normal good A good for which an increase in the income of buyers causes a rightward shift in the demand curve.

Inferior good A good for which an increase in the income of buyers causes a leftward shift in the demand curve.

Substitutes and Complements The position of the demand curve for a good may also be affected by changes in the prices of other, closely related goods. For example, salads can be made from lettuce or from cabbage. An increase in the price of lettuce is likely to cause not only a decrease in the quantity of lettuce demanded (represented graphically by a movement up and to the left along the lettuce demand curve) but also an increase in the demand for cabbage (represented graphically by a shift to the right of the entire cabbage demand curve). When an increase in the price of one good causes an increase in the demand for another good, those two goods are said to be **substitutes** for one another. Photographic film and flashbulbs tend to be used together. If the price of film were to rise, we would expect not only a decrease in the quantity of film sold but a decrease in the demand for flashbulbs also. The

Substitutes A pair of goods for which an increase in the price of one causes an increase in the demand for the other, other things being equal.

effect of the change in the price of film is represented graphically as a movement along the film demand curve and as a leftward shift of the flashbulb demand curve. When an increase in the price of one good causes a decrease in the demand for another good, the two goods are said to be **complements.**

Complements A pair of goods for which an increase in the price of one causes a decrease in the demand for the other, other things being equal.

SUPPLY

The next step in the analysis of markets will be to examine the relationship between the price of a good and the quantity of it that suppliers are willing and able to provide for sale. Everyday experience suggests that, in order to induce sellers to increase the quantity of a good supplied, it is necessary, other things being equal, to offer them a higher price. When this is true, the supply curve for the good in question slopes upward. Exhibit 3.3 shows a **supply schedule** and a corresponding upward sloping **supply curve** for wheat.[2]

Supply schedule A table showing the quantity of a good supplied at various prices.

Supply curve A graphical representation of the relationship between the price of a good and the quantity of it supplied.

Why exactly is the supply curve for wheat expected to slope upward? There are a number of possible reasons, any or all of which may operate in a particular case. For one thing, a higher price gives farmers a greater incentive to devote more of their time and energy to wheat production. In addition, it may

[2]Exceptions to the rule that supply curves slope upward are not so rare as exceptions to the rule that demand curves slope downward. A few examples of negatively sloped supply curves will occur later in this book. For the present, however, we will stick to upward sloping curves.

Exhibit 3.3
A supply schedule and supply curve for wheat
Both the supply curve and supply schedule for wheat show the quantity of wheat supplied at various prices. An increase in the price of wheat induces farmers to supply a greater quantity of it. This is partly because they have an incentive to devote more time and energy to the crop, partly because they substitute wheat for other crops grown previously, and partly because new resources (and even new farmers) may be drawn into wheat production.

(a) Supply schedule

Price of Wheat (dollars per bushel)	Quantity of Wheat Supplied (billions of bushels per year)
$3.20	2.6
3.00	2.5
2.80	2.4
2.60	2.3
2.40	2.2
2.20	2.1
2.00	2.0
1.80	1.9
1.60	1.8
1.40	1.7
1.20	1.6
1.00	1.5
.80	1.4

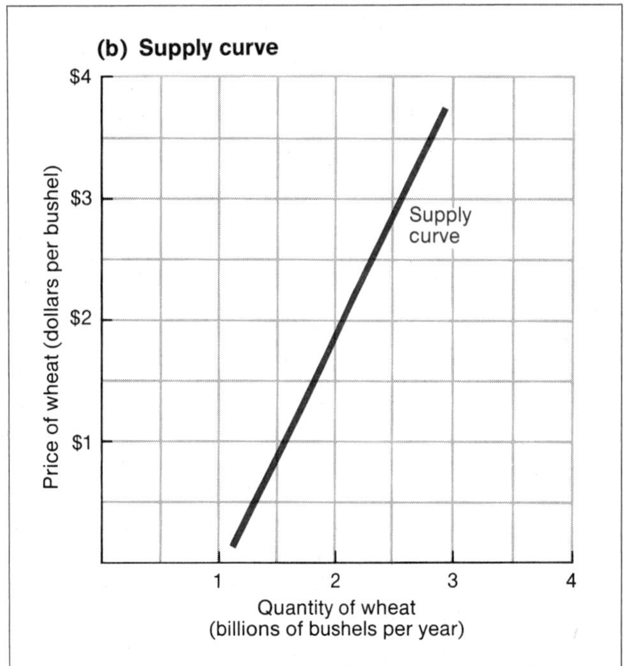

induce them to substitute wheat for other crops they had been producing Finally, the higher price may make it possible to attract resources into wheat farming from other lines of production, perhaps even leading to the establishment of new farms.

Shifts in Supply Curves

As in the case of demand, changes in the quantity supplied of a good, represented by movements along a given supply curve, are distinguished from changes in the supply of a good, represented by shifts in the supply curve. A change in the quantity supplied comes about as the result of a change in the price of the good, other things being equal. A shift in the supply curve requires a change in some other factor affecting supply.

One thing that can produce a change in the supply of a good is a change in production technology. If new technology permits more output to be produced from the same quantity of inputs, the supply curve will shift to the right. A second factor that can cause a change in supply is a change in the price of inputs used to produce a good. If input prices go up, for example, suppliers will probably want a higher price than before in order to offer the same quantity of output for sale. This effect is represented by a leftward shift in the supply curve. Finally, the supply curve for one good can be shifted as the result of a change in the price of another good, other things being equal. For example, a rise in the price of soybeans might well cause the supply curve for wheat to shift to the left, as farmers pull land out of wheat production and plant it in the newly profitable soybeans. Some examples of shifting supply curves will be given later in this chapter.

THE INTERACTION OF SUPPLY AND DEMAND

Market Equilibrium

Chapter 2 showed how the market transmits information in the form of prices to the people who are potential buyers and sellers of any good. Taking the price of the good into account, together with the other knowledge they possess, these buyers and sellers form plans. Each one decides to enter the market and buy or sell a certain number of units of the good.

Commonly, large numbers of buyers and sellers formulate their market plans independently of one another. When buyers and sellers of some particular good actually meet and engage in the process of exchange, some of them may find it impossible to carry out their plans. Perhaps the total quantity of planned purchases will exceed the total quantity of planned sales at the expected price. In this case, some of the would-be buyers will find their plans frustrated and will have to modify them. Perhaps, instead, planned sales will exceed planned purchases. Then, some would-be sellers will be unable to sell all they had expected to and will have to change their plans.

Sometimes no one will be disappointed. Given the information that market prices have conveyed, the total quantity of the good that buyers plan to purchase may exactly equal the quantity that suppliers plan to sell. The separately formulated plans of all market participants may turn out to mesh exactly when tested in the marketplace, and no one will have frustrated expectations or be forced to modify plans. When this happens, the market is said to be in **equilibrium.**

Market equilibrium A condition in which the separately formulated plans of buyers and sellers of some good exactly mesh when tested in the marketplace, so that the quantity supplied is exactly equal to the quantity demanded at the prevailing price.

If we have supply and demand schedules for a market, we can describe more exactly the conditions under which that market will be in equilibrium. Take the market for wheat as an example. In Exhibit 3.4, Columns 1 to 3 give the supply and demand schedules. Reading down Column 2, we see how much wheat producers will plan to sell at each price. Reading down Column 3, we see how much wheat buyers will plan to purchase at each price. Comparing the two, it does not take long to discover that only when the price is $2 do the separately formulated plans of buyers and sellers exactly mesh. Thus $2 per bushel is the price at which this market is in equilibrium. If all buyers and sellers make their market plans in the expectation that the price will be $2, none of them will be disappointed, and none will have to change plans.

Shortages

What if, for some reason, buyers and sellers expect the market price to be something different from $2? Suppose, for example, that a price of $1 per bushel somehow becomes established in the market. Column 2 of Exhibit 3.4 tells us that, at this price, producers will plan to supply wheat to the market at the rate of 1.5 billion bushels per year. Column 3 tells us that buyers will plan to purchase at a rate of 2.5 billion bushels per year. When the quantity demanded exceeds the quantity supplied, the difference between the two is called an

Exhibit 3.4
Supply and demand in the market for wheat

When the quantity of a product demanded exceeds the quantity supplied, there is an excess quantity demanded, or shortage, of the product. A shortage puts upward pressure on the price of the product. When the quantity supplied exceeds the quantity demanded, there is an excess quantity supplied, or surplus, of the product. A surplus puts downward pressure on the price. Only when the price of wheat here is $2 per bushel is there no shortage or surplus and no upward or downward pressure on price. At $2 the market is in equilibrium.

Price per Bushel (1)	Quantity Supplied (billions of bushels) (2)	Quantity Demanded (billions of bushels) (3)	Shortage (billions of bushels) (4)	Surplus (billions of bushels) (5)	Direction of Pressure on Price (6)
$3.20	2.6	1.4	—	1.2	Downward
3.00	2.5	1.5	—	1.0	Downward
2.80	2.4	1.6	—	0.8	Downward
2.60	2.3	1.7	—	0.6	Downward
2.40	2.2	1.8	—	0.4	Downward
2.20	2.1	1.9	—	0.2	Downward
2.00	2.0	2.0	—	—	Equilibrium
1.80	1.9	2.1	0.2	—	Upward
1.60	1.8	2.2	0.4	—	Upward
1.40	1.7	2.3	0.6	—	Upward
1.20	1.6	2.4	0.8	—	Upward
1.00	1.5	2.5	1.0	—	Upward
.80	1.4	2.6	1.2	—	Upward

Excess quantity demanded The amount by which the quantity of a good demanded exceeds the quantity supplied when the price of the good is below the equilibrium level.

Shortage As used in economics, an excess quantity demanded.

excess quantity demanded or, more simply, a **shortage.**[3] In the case of wheat, the shortage (shown in Column 4 of the exhibit) is 1 billion bushels per year when the price is $1 per bushel.

In most markets, the first sign of a shortage is the depletion of inventories of the product available for sale. If inventories run out entirely, or if the market is for a good or service that cannot be stored in inventory at all, a queue of potential buyers may form. Under such circumstances, either sellers take the initiative to raise prices or buyers take the initiative to offer higher prices in the hope of getting part of the available quantity. In either event, the shortage puts upward pressure on price.

As the price of the product rises, producers begin to plan to sell more and buyers begin to plan to purchase less. The higher the price, the smaller the shortage. When the price of wheat in Exhibit 3.4 reaches $2 per bushel, the shortage is entirely eliminated. With its elimination, there is no further upward pressure on prices. The market is in equilibrium.

Surpluses

Suppose that, for some reason, the price of wheat becomes established at a level higher than the equilibrium price, say at $3 a bushel. At this price, according to Exhibit 3.4, producers will plan to sell 2.5 billion bushels per year, but buyers will plan to purchase only 1.5 billion bushels. When the quantity supplied exceeds the quantity demanded, there is an **excess quantity supplied** or a **surplus.** As Column 5 of the exhibit shows, the surplus of wheat is 1 billion bushels per year when the price is $3 a bushel.

Excess quantity supplied The amount by which the quantity of a good supplied exceeds the quantity demanded when the price of the good is above the equilibrium level.

Surplus As used in economics, an excess quantity supplied.

When there is a surplus of the product, some producers will be disappointed, since they will not be able to make all their planned sales at the expected price. Inventories of unsold goods will begin to accumulate. Although the details may vary from market to market, the generalization can be made that a surplus puts downward pressure on the product price. Exhibit 3.4 shows that as the price falls, the quantity supplied decreases and the quantity demanded increases. Gradually, the surplus is eliminated until, when the price reaches $2 per bushel, the market returns to equilibrium.

Graphical Presentation

A graphical presentation of the material just covered will help reinforce the points made. Exhibit 3.5 shows both the demand curve (taken from Exhibit 3.1) and the supply curve (taken from Exhibit 3.3) for wheat. With both curves on the same diagram, the quantity demanded and the quantity supplied at any price can be directly compared. The distance from the vertical axis to the demand curve measures the quantity demanded, and the distance from the vertical axis to the supply curve measures the quantity supplied. It follows that the horizontal gap between the two curves measures the surplus or shortage at any price.

As we saw when working through the numerical example for this market, a surplus tends to put downward pressure on the price, and a shortage tends to

---

[3]We introduce two equivalent terms—*shortage* and *excess quantity demanded*—in order to make it clear that economists use the term *shortage* in a somewhat narrower sense than it is used in everyday speech. In this book, the word *shortage* will be used most of the time when it is clear that the economic meaning is intended. But sometimes, to avoid possible ambiguity, the more precise term *excess quantity demanded* will be used instead. The same considerations apply to the terms *surplus* and *excess quantity supplied.*

Exhibit 3.5
Supply and demand in the market for wheat
In this diagram, a surplus or shortage is indicated by the horizontal distance between the supply and demand curves. A surplus puts downward pressure on price, and a shortage puts upward pressure on it, as indicated by the arrows following the supply and demand curves. The market is in equilibrium at the point where the supply and demand curves intersect. Compare this diagram with the table in Exhibit 3.4.

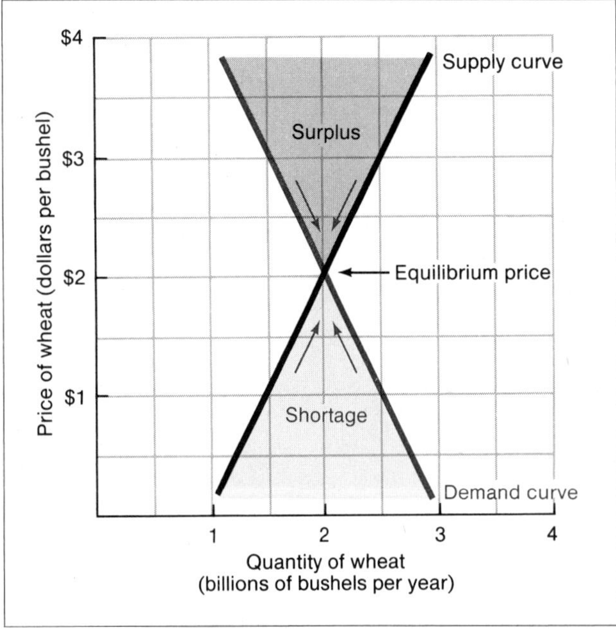

put upward pressure on it. These pressures result from the actions of frustrated buyers and sellers, who must change their plans when they find they cannot buy or sell the quantities they had intended at the price they had expected. The pressures are indicated by the arrows pointing along the supply and demand curves toward equilibrium.

There is only one price where neither upward nor downward pressure is in force—the price of $2 per bushel, the point where the supply and demand curves intersect. There is neither shortage nor surplus at that point. The quantity that buyers plan to purchase exactly equals the quantity that suppliers plan to sell. Both can carry out their plans exactly as intended, and the market is in equilibrium.

Changing Economic Conditions

When underlying economic conditions change, supply and demand curves can shift to new positions. These shifts upset the plans of buyers and sellers, who may have adjusted to some previous market equilibrium, and they bring about changes in prices and quantities. The following example describes an episode that is typical of the way markets work every day. Particular attention should be paid to the distinction between the kinds of changes that cause shifts in supply or demand curves and the kinds that cause movements along curves.

Case 3.1
Supply and Demand for Cobalt

Cobalt is a metal with important industrial applications in hardening turbine blades for aircraft engines, making high power magnets, cementing tungsten-carbide cutting tools, and manufacturing paints and varnishes. It is produced as a by-product of refining nickel and copper. About 60 percent of the world's output comes from the African country of Zaire.

In May 1978, cobalt was selling for under $10 per pound. By the end of 1978, the price had shot up to over $40 per pound. Many separate events, all happening at once, contributed to the sharp rise in price. Exhibit 3.6 shows how this complex tangle of events can be interpreted in terms of shifts in and movements along supply and demand curves.[4]

Let the supply and demand curves S_1 and D_1 in Exhibit 3.6a represent market conditions as of early 1978. These curves intersect at the equilibrium E_1, giving a market price of about $10 per pound. The first major shocks to hit the cobalt market came from the supply side. There was a strike in the mines of Zaire, and then fighting broke out in the mining region between government troops and Katangan rebels. These events had the effect of *shifting* the supply curve for cobalt to the left. S_2 represents the new position of the supply curve.

The decrease in supply at first created a shortage, thereby pushing up the price. Users of cobalt began to look for ways to conserve it. Allegheny Ludlum Steel, one of the largest cobalt users, developed a recycling program that cut the consumption of new cobalt 10 to 15 percent. Makers of high-fidelity audio systems began looking for designs that would substitute ceramic magnets for cobalt magnets. Conservation moves such as these correspond to a movement along Demand Curve D_1 in Part a. If nothing else had happened, the market would have reached a new equilibrium at E_2, with a price of about $25 per pound.

However, things were happening on the demand side of the cobalt market too. The aircraft industry was rapidly stepping up output to satisfy demand for its new models. Use of cobalt in paints and varnishes nearly doubled from 1977 to 1978. And a fad developed for a new type of earring held in place by powerful miniature cobalt magnets, making it unnecessary for wearers to pierce their ears. These events on the demand side of the market are represented in Part b as a shift in the demand curve from D_1 to D_2.

[4]The slopes of the supply and demand curves were chosen arbitrarily for the sake of illustration.

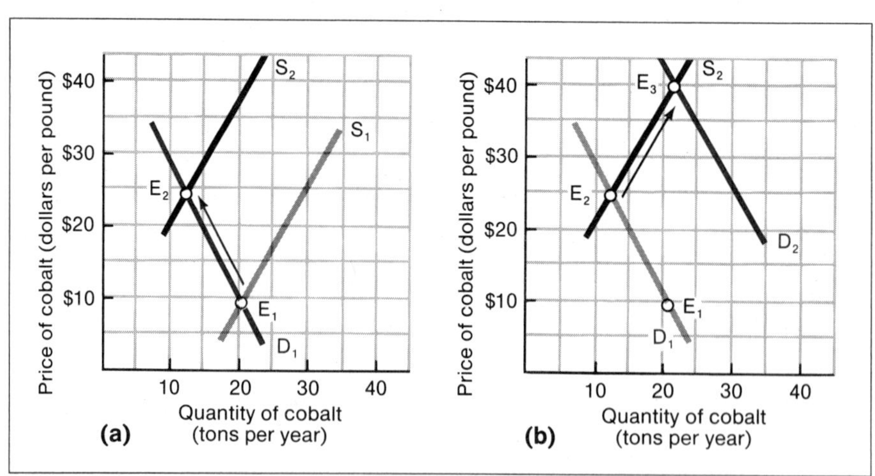

Exhibit 3.6

Changing conditions in the market for cobalt during 1978

In early 1978, cobalt was selling for about $10 per pound, represented here by the intersection between Demand Curve D_1 and Supply Curve S_1 in Part a of the exhibit. A strike and rebellion in Zaire, the world's leading producer, shifted the supply curve to the left to the position S_2. The price rose toward the point E_2 as buyers moved along Demand Curve D_1. Then a boom in the aerospace industry and other events caused the demand curve to shift to the right, as shown by D_2 in Part b of the exhibit. The price rose further as suppliers moved along the new supply curve toward its intersection with the new demand curve at E_3.

This demand shift intensified the shortage of cobalt and increased the rapidity with which the price was bid up. In response, suppliers outside Katanga did what they could to step up production. For example, Inco Ltd., the world's largest nickel producer, added new equipment that would double the amount of cobalt it could recover. These output increasing responses are represented in Part b by a movement along Supply Curve S_2 toward the final equilibrium, E_3, at a price of about $40 per pound.

Sources: Based on Agis Salpukas, "Scarcity of Cobalt Spurs Conversion," *New York Times*, December 18, 1978, and William Gilmer, Jr., "Magnetic Earrings Join Katangan Rebels as Factors in Cobalt's Recent Price Rise," *Wall Street Journal*, June 21, 1978, p. 48.

Markets in Disequilibrium

We have seen that when a market is not in equilibrium, an excess quantity demanded or supplied will put upward or downward pressure on the price. If the price is free to respond to this pressure, a new equilibrium will be established at a higher or lower price. Sometimes, though, market prices are not free to fluctuate. The forces of supply and demand must then work themselves out in some other way, as the following example shows.

Case 3.2
Coping with Gasoline Shortages: Rationing by Waiting

In the winter of 1974 and again in the spring of 1979, significant gasoline shortages struck the United States as political events in the Middle East drastically cut the supply of oil exported from that region. Because there was no immediate alternative source of oil, the supply curve for gasoline could be considered almost vertical, as shown in Exhibit 3.7.

According to this exhibit, a sufficiently high price ($2 per gallon as the graph is drawn, but this is only a guess) would have put the gasoline market in equilibrium. However, government price controls in force at the time kept the price from rising much above $1 per gallon. There was a substantial excess quantity of gas demanded; and instead of making itself visible in terms of rising prices, it made itself visible in the form of long lines at gas stations.

Exhibit 3.7
A gasoline shortage with price controls
This exhibit shows the effect of a restricted supply of gasoline when price controls are in effect. Instead of causing the price to rise toward its equilibrium level (here estimated at $2 per gallon), the shortage caused long lines to form at gas stations. The lines continued to grow until the opportunity cost per gallon of waiting in line became great enough to reduce the quantity demanded to the quantity supplied.

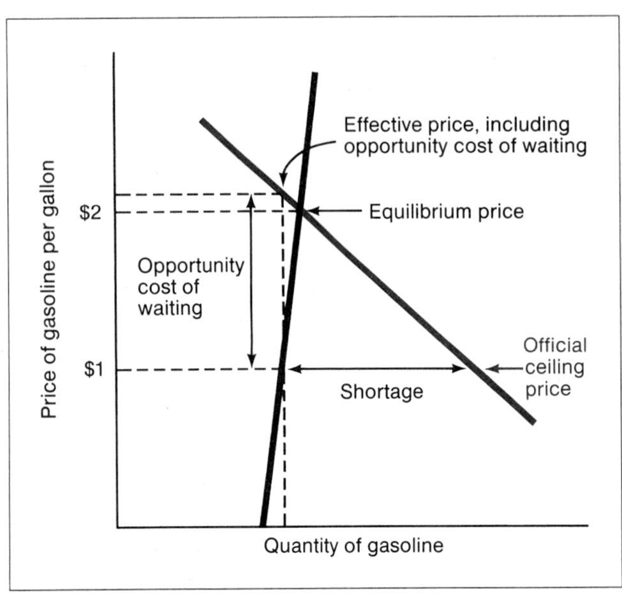

People who waited in line for gasoline had lots of time to think, and anyone who had studied a little economics could have figured out that the forces of supply and demand were still at work in a roundabout way. There were opportunity costs of waiting in line. Some people missed work. Others sacrificed valuable leisure hours. As the lines grew, the opportunity cost of waiting in them grew also, until at some point the total cost of gasoline—the money cost plus the opportunity cost of waiting—rose high enough to restrict the quantity demanded to the quantity supplied. As the exhibit is drawn, this required a total price slightly higher than the $2 per gallon to which the money price would have risen without controls. At that point, the lines stopped growing longer, and a sort of rough-and-ready equilibrium was established.

Consumers, on the average, did not gain much from price controls during these shortages. What they saved in money, they wasted in time spent in line. To get around this problem, it has been proposed that in the event of such shortages, rationing tickets limiting gas consumption to, say, two gallons per vehicle per day should be issued to motorists. People who did not use all their tickets could sell them to others who had a greater demand for gasoline. (As Exhibit 3.7 is drawn, what price do you think motorists would have been able to get for their extra rationing tickets?) Others think that the best way to handle shortages is simply to let the price rise to its equilibrium level, no matter how high it might be. As of this writing, the debate over how to handle the problem is still unresolved.

CONCLUSIONS

This completes the presentation of the basics of supply and demand analysis. The chapter will conclude with a few remarks that relate supply and demand to the role of markets as a mechanism for utilizing knowledge and that concern the scope of applicability of supply and demand analysis.

Information and Equilibrium

There is a simple connection between the idea of equilibrium and the idea of the market as a mechanism for distributing information. The connection is found in the fact that the market can be in equilibrium when, and only when, it has entirely completed its job of distributing information among buyers and sellers.

It is easy to see why this is true. First, if buyers and sellers have incomplete knowledge of prices and of other economic conditions, it is unlikely that their separately formulated market plans will exactly mesh. It may be that both buyers and sellers expect the price tomorrow to be higher (or lower) than it actually will be. It may be that buyers have one idea about what the price will be and sellers another. Whatever the case, someone is bound to be disappointed, and disappointed plans are the stuff of which disequilibrium is made.

On the other hand, if both buyers and sellers have complete and accurate knowledge of both present and future prices and market conditions, how can their plans fail to mesh? No one will plan to sell knowing that there will be no one to buy. With perfect information, people will formulate only such market plans as they know can be carried out on the expected terms, and that is what *equilibrium* means.

Saying that markets are in equilibrium only when all buyers and sellers have perfect information leads to a conclusion that may seem strange. The conclusion is that, in the real world, we can hardly ever expect to find a market in equilibrium! To paraphrase a famous saying, all people know something some of the time, and some people know a great deal all of the time, but everybody does not know everything all of the time. In real markets, prices are always being pushed this way or that by changes in underlying economic conditions. Some people learn of these changes right away, and the buying and selling they do telegraphs that information, via the price system, to others. But the market telegraph does not work with the speed of light. Before everyone who is directly or indirectly interested in what goes on in a particular market learns of some change, other changes have occurred. The whirling stream of human knowledge never quite catches up with an even more fluid reality.

Applicability

The fact that markets are never really in equilibrium is, in a sense, a limitation on the applicability of supply and demand analysis. There are other limitations too. Supply and demand analysis applies in its pure form only to markets where the number of buyers and sellers is very large and where the products offered by one seller differ very little from those offered by another. Some real world markets fit the conditions fairly well. The markets for agricultural products such as wheat are an example. But the markets for many other products do not look exactly like the idealized markets of economic theory.

For now, though, there is no need to be overly concerned with differences between the real and the ideal. The theory of supply and demand may not *exactly* fit any market at any particular moment in time; yet, in a general sense, thinking in terms of supply and demand can give extremely useful insights into the way almost all markets work. The usefulness of these tools will be proved in application as we work through this book. Fine points can be left for more advanced courses.

SUMMARY

1. The law of demand says that the quantity of a good demanded by buyers tends to change in a direction opposite to any change in price, other things being equal. By *quantity demanded,* economists mean effective demand, as distinguished from wants or needs not backed up by willingness and ability to buy. By *other things being equal,* they have in mind such things as buyers' incomes, the prices of other goods, and buyers' expectations about future price changes.
2. A change in the quantity of a good demanded that results solely from a change in the price of that good is represented graphically as a movement along a demand curve. When something other than its price changes (for example, buyers' incomes, the prices of substitutes or complements, or buyers' expectations), the result is a change in demand, represented graphically as a shift of the entire demand curve.
3. A supply curve shows the relationship between the price of a good and the quantity of it supplied, other things being equal. Unless there is some particular reason to do otherwise, economists usually draw supply curves with upward slopes. A change in the price of a good produces a change in the quantity supplied, shown by a movement along a supply curve. A change in some other factor—technology, input prices, prices of other goods—produces a change in supply, shown by a shift of the supply curve.

4. Market equilibrium is a condition in which the separately formulated plans of buyers and sellers exactly mesh, so that the quantity supplied is equal to the quantity demanded. If the price of a product is too high for equilibrium, there will be a surplus of the good, which, in turn, will tend to push the price down. If the price is below the equilibrium, there will be a shortage, which will tend to drive the price up. Equilibrium is possible only when the market has completely carried out its job of distributing information among buyers and sellers.

DISCUSSION QUESTIONS

1. The *law of demand* states that there is an inverse relationship between the price of a good and the quantity that people will be willing and able to pay for. How is this "law" like the law of gravity? How is it different? Explain.
2. Illustrate the supply of McDonald's hamburgers to an individual consumer. What is the slope of the supply curve?
3. Suppose there were a drought in the Midwest, where much of the nation's wheat is grown. What would be the impact of the drought on the demand and supply of wheat? What would happen to the price of wheat? Why? How would this be likely to affect the individual consumers of products containing wheat?
4. If you drop a marble into a bowl, it will eventually come to rest at the bottom. You can then say that the marble is at equilibrium at the bottom of the bowl. What is meant by *equilibrium*? In what ways is equilibrium in a market similar to the equilibrium of the marble? In what ways is it different?
5. If you were a wholesaler and you could see sooner than your competitors when the demand curve for the product you deal in was about to shift to the right, how could you use this advance knowledge to make money? Would you be benefiting anyone besides yourself in getting rid of the disequilibrium? Explain.
6. Suppose you read the following news item in the daily paper: "Frost in Brazil has caused a severe shortage of coffee, which has driven the price well above normal levels. The shortage is expected to persist for several years, until new coffee bushes can be planted and reach maturity." Do you think the writer is using the word *shortage* in the same sense that it has been used in this chapter? Explain.
7. Suppose that the opportunity cost of time spent waiting in line to buy gasoline were uniformly $5 per hour for all consumers. Would imposing price controls on gasoline to deal with a sudden decrease in supply then benefit anyone at all? Would it make anyone worse off than if the price were simply allowed to rise to a higher equilibrium level? Should the owners of gas stations and oil companies be counted as "anyone" in answering this question?

SUGGESTIONS FOR FURTHER READING

Breit, William, and Ransom, Roger L. *The Academic Scribblers.* New York: Holt, Rinehart and Winston, 1971, Chapter 3.

An essay on Alfred Marshall. The preceding two chapters provide useful background.

Campbell, Colin D., ed. *Wage-Price Controls in World War II: United States and Germany.* Washington, D.C.: American Enterprise Institute, 1971.

Vivid descriptions and insightful analysis of what happens when governments get serious about wage and price controls.

Marshall, Alfred. *Principles of Economics.* Various editions.

First published in 1891, this book served as the definitive treatise on economics in the English-speaking world for generations. It remains remarkably accessible to browsing, even by the beginning student. For a start, look up Marshall's treatment of the determinants of demand or his discussion (and dismissal) of cases of apparently upward sloping demand curves.

C H A P T E R **4**

THE ROLE OF GOVERNMENT IN THE ECONOMY

WHAT YOU WILL LEARN IN THIS CHAPTER

Not all economic decisions in the U.S. economy are made in the marketplace; many are also made in government at the federal, state, and local levels. This chapter provides an overview of the role of government in the economy—what distinguishes government from other actors in the economy and what the major functions of government are. It also provides an overview of how federal, state, and local governments levy taxes and what each level of government spends money on. Finally, it explains how to apply supply and demand theory to help determine who bears the real economic burden of taxation.

FOR REVIEW

Here are some important terms and concepts that will be put to use in this chapter. If you do not understand them, review them before proceeding.

- *The margin, marginal (Chapter 1)*
- *Incentives in the market economy (Chapter 2)*
- *Supply and demand analysis (Chapter 3)*

The forces of supply and demand, acting through markets, affect every significant economic decision in the U.S. economy. Nonetheless, the United States is not a pure market economy. There are other economic forces as well that affect how resources are used. By far the most important of the nonmarket forces is that of government.

As an actor on the economic stage, government differs in a number of important ways from other actors. Three characteristics in particular distinguish it from the individuals and firms constituting the market sector.

First, government can legitimately use force in economic affairs. In the private sector, firms and individuals are limited by law and custom to peaceable means of production and exchange that require the voluntary consent of everyone involved. Governments, on the other hand, are able to employ force, coercion, and involuntary expropriation in pursuit of their economic goals. When the government taxes incomes, regulates prices, drafts soldiers, or outlaws gambling, it does not require the immediate, explicit consent of the individuals taxed, regulated, conscripted, or outlawed. Although in a democracy these uses of government power are supposed to rest, at least indirectly, on the consent of the voters, they are binding on minorities and nonvoters as well. Without the use or threat of force, government could do very few of the things it does.

A second characteristic setting governments apart from other economic agents is the fact that the great bulk of goods and services produced by governments are provided to users without charge. In most cases, people do not have to pay directly for defense services, highway use, education, or police protection. Instead, they pay for these things indirectly, through taxes. In only a few cases do the taxes paid vary according to the quantity of public service consumed. The fact that governments do not charge users directly for most of their services has important implications for measuring the total contribution of government to the national product and for measuring the degree of efficiency with which government services are utilized. More on this will appear in later chapters.

A third way governments differ from other economic agents is in how they arrive at economic decisions. The system of voting and bargaining by which public decisions are made is much more complex and hard to analyze than the decision processes of private business firms and consumers. As a result, economists have not gotten as far in formulating simple rules or theories to explain resource allocation in the public sector. In the past, economists traditionally treated government decisions as givens for purposes of economic analysis and did not try to explain why one government decision rather than another was made at a particular time. In recent years, though, some progress has been made in formulating an economic theory of "public choice" to parallel the theory of private choice with which economists have traditionally worked.

Despite the peculiarities of government, market forces of supply and demand do make themselves felt to a degree even within the public sector of the economy. The principal reason is that governments have to purchase most of the inputs they require on the open market. The U.S. Department of Justice cannot hire a new clerk unless it pays at least the wage determined by supply and demand for workers with the required skills. The City of Chicago cannot buy police cars unless it pays something pretty close to what private individuals would pay for the same vehicles. The necessity of purchasing inputs at market prices makes government aware of the relative cost of various programs and helps constrain total public spending.

Of course, particular government agencies sometimes ignore the messages the market sends to them via the price system. Corrupt bidding practices, for example, result in government purchases from politically favored firms at higher than market prices. Sometimes devices such as eminent domain or the draft are used to obtain resources without paying their full market value. In such instances, the degree of market influence on government is less than usual.

A large part of the remainder of the book will be devoted to exploring the interactions between government and the private market economy. This chapter will provide some useful background material about what government does and how its expenses are paid.

WHAT DOES GOVERNMENT DO?

Some Comparisons

Just what government does varies greatly from time to time and place to place. Before looking at the functions of government in detail, and before raising the question of whether it does too much or too little or the wrong mix of things, an idea of the overall size of government is needed. Some comparisons may help.

Exhibit 4.1 gives an indication of how government has grown over time. The chart shows what has happened to federal, state, and local **government purchases of goods and services** since the early years of the century. Government purchases of goods and services (or **government purchases,** for short) include all the finished products purchased by government (everything from submarines to typewriter ribbons) plus the cost of hiring the services of all government employees (everyone from the president to the courthouse janitor). These purchases are shown as a percentage of gross national product (GNP), a measure of the economy's total output of goods and services. By this measure, government has clearly grown over time. Before World War I, government purchases averaged less than 10 percent of GNP. Except for wartime peaks, they followed a steady trend upward from about 1920 until 1970. During the 1970s, total government purchases appear to have leveled off at about 20 percent of GNP.

Government purchases of goods and services (government purchases) Expenditures made by federal, state, and local governments to purchase goods from private firms and to hire the services of government employees.

Exhibit 4.2 provides a different kind of comparison. This graph gives data for several countries on total government expenditures, including transfer payments as well as government purchases. **Transfer payments** are all payments made by government to individuals that are not in return for goods or services currently supplied. They include such things as social security benefits, welfare payments, and unemployment compensation.

Transfer payments All payments made by government to individuals that are not made in return for goods or services currently supplied. Social security benefits, welfare payments, and unemployment compensation are major forms of transfer payments.

Exhibit 4.1
Growth of government purchases in the United States

The percentage of total government purchases in GNP has grown substantially over time. In the early years of the century, government purchases averaged less than 10 percent of GNP. Government purchases hit peaks in war years and by the 1950s had grown to the present peacetime average of about 20 percent of GNP.

Sources: Data for 1929 to the present are from President's Council of Economic Advisers, *Economic Report of the President* (Washington, D.C.: Government Printing Office, 1979), Table B-1. Data for years before 1929 are from U.S. Department of Commerce, Bureau of the Census, *Historical Statistics of the United States: Colonial Times to 1970* (Washington, D.C.: Government Printing Office, 1975).

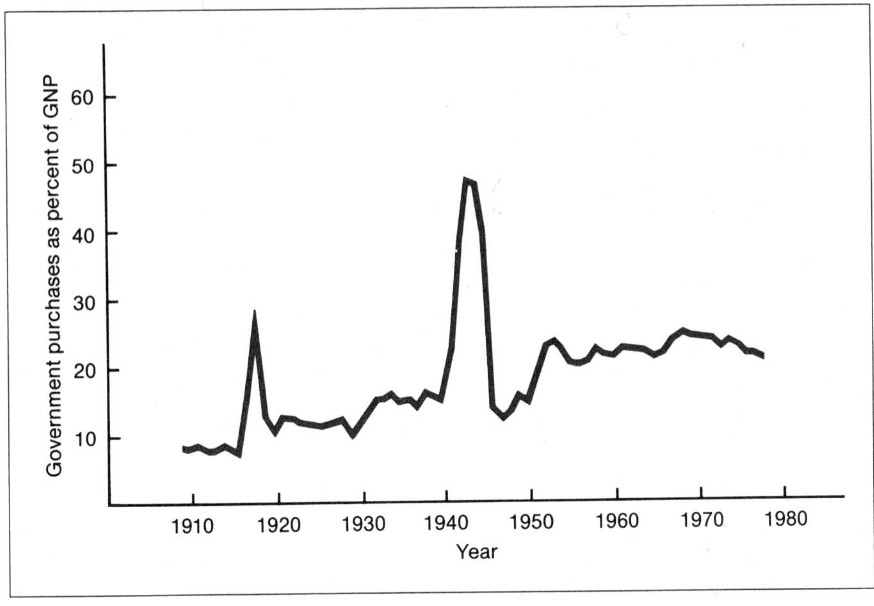

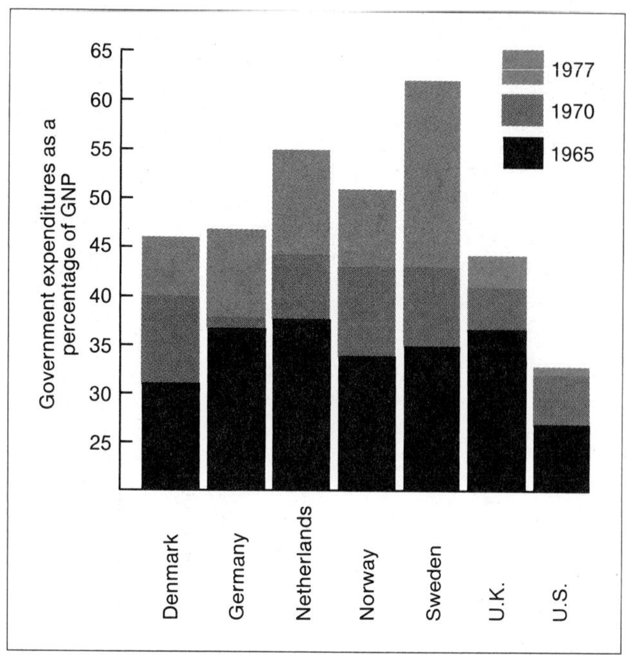

Exhibit 4.2
Total government expenditures as a percent of GNP for selected countries
The data in this graph refer to total expenditures of central and local government units, including both government purchases of goods and services and transfer payments. By this measure, the size of government relative to the rest of the economy is larger than when only government purchases are taken into account. Note that although government expenditures in the United States are growing, they are still considerably lower in relation to the size of the economy than for the other countries shown.

Source: Data from Theodore Geiger, *Welfare and Efficiency: Their Interactions in Western Europe and Implications for International Economic Relations* (Washington, D.C.: National Planning Association, 1979), Table 1–1. Used by permission. Note that the 1977 percentage for the Netherlands is actually based on 1976 data.

Using total expenditures rather than government purchases as a measure makes the public sector look somewhat larger. Government purchases plus transfer payments now equal about a third of GNP in the United States. In comparison with the advanced industrial countries of Western Europe, however, the public sector in the United States is not a particularly large percentage of GNP. In Sweden, a country with roughly the same level of per capita income as the United States, government expenditures are equal to nearly two-thirds of GNP; and in Norway and the Netherlands, government expenditures are equal to more than half of GNP.

The Functions of Government

Governments use the third to two-thirds of GNP that passes through their hands to perform a wide variety of functions. These functions can be classified under five general headings: provision of public goods, transfer of income, economic stabilization, regulation of private businesses, and administration of justice.

Public goods Goods or services having the properties that (1) they cannot be provided to one citizen without being supplied also to that person's neighbors, and (2) once they are provided for one citizen, the cost of providing them to others is zero.

Provision of Public Goods The first function of government is to provide what economists call **public goods**—goods or services having the properties that (1) they cannot be provided to one citizen without being supplied also to that citizen's neighbors, and (2) once provided for one citizen, the cost of providing them to others is zero. Perhaps the best example of a public good is national defense. One citizen cannot very well be protected against foreign invasion or nuclear holocaust without having the protection "spill over" on neighbors. Also, it costs no more to protect a single resident of a given area than to protect an entire city.

Public goods are traditionally provided by government because their special properties make it hard for private business to market them profitably. Imagine what would happen if someone tried to set up a commercially operated ballistic missile defense system. If you subscribed, I would have no reason to subscribe too and would instead play the "free rider," relying on the spillover effect for my protection. But you would not subscribe, hoping that I would, so that you could be the free rider. The missile defense company would soon go bankrupt.

Transfer of Income The second function of government consists of making transfers of income and wealth from one citizen to another. Income or wealth is usually taken from citizens by means of taxation; but sometimes, as in the case of the military draft or jury duty, it is taken by conscription of services. Benefits are distributed either in the form of direct cash payments or in the form of the free or below-cost provision of goods and services. Among the more familiar types of cash transfers are social security payments, welfare benefits, and unemployment compensation. Goods and services used for transfers include public education, public housing, fire protection, and subsidized mass transit systems. They are provided at low or zero cost on the basis of political decisions rather than at market prices on the basis of ability to pay.

From the viewpoint of economic theory, the subsidized services used as vehicles for income transfers are different from the true public goods discussed above. They are consumed individually by selected citizens and do not share the two special properties of public goods. It sometimes happens, though, that services provided primarily as transfers may be public goods in part. For example, consider the fraction of fire protection devoted to preventing general conflagration as opposed to putting out fires in individual private buildings or the fraction of public health services devoted to controlling epidemic diseases as opposed to treating individual patients.

Economic Stabilization Economic stabilization is a third major function of government. Economic stabilization policies are all policies aimed at promoting price stability, full employment, and economic growth. The government first became officially committed to a policy of stabilizing the economy at a high level of employment with the Employment Act of 1946. Almost all of Part 2 of this book will be devoted to the discussion of economic stabilization policy and the development of the theory necessary to understand it.

Regulation of Private Businesses A fourth major function of government is the regulation of private businesses. Regulatory control is exercised through a network of dozens of specialized agencies and takes a variety of specific forms. Some agencies set maximum prices at which certain products can be sold, whereas others set minimum prices. The Food and Drug Administration and the Federal Communications Commission exercise considerable control over what can be produced by the firms they regulate. Agencies such as the Occupational Health and Safety Administration and the Environmental Protection Agency regulate how things are produced. Finally, the Equal Employment Opportunity Commission exercises a major say over who will produce which goods. Regulation is a subject of widespread research and controversy.

Administration of Justice The fifth major function of government is the administration of justice. Usually, the police and courts are not thought of as part of the economic area of government; but their activities do, in fact, have important economic consequences.

Consider what happens, for example, when a judge makes a decision in a case involving an unsafe product, a breach of contract, or an automobile accident. The decision has an immediate effect on resource allocation in the particular case, because one party must pay damages to the other or make some other form of compensation. More importantly, other people will observe the outcome of the decision and, as a result, may change the way they do things. If the courts say that buyers can collect damages from the makers of unsafe products, firms are likely to design their products differently. If certain standards are set for liability in automobile accidents, car makers, road builders, and insurance companies will take notice.

In recent years, an entire field of research has opened up in the law and economics area. Although space in this book does not permit much discussion about the field, readers interested in practical applications of economic thinking may wish to pursue this area on their own or in advanced courses.[1]

One further area of economic policy combines the judicial and regulatory functions of government: the field of antitrust policy and the control of monopoly.

Overlapping Functions

The classification of government activities by function helps provide a theoretical understanding of the role of government in the economy, but it does not correspond very well to any breakdown of government activities by program or agency. Particular programs and agencies often perform a number of different functions at the same time. For example, the main business of the Defense Department appears to be the provision of a public good—national defense—but it performs other functions as well. In wartime it performs a transfer function by shifting part of the cost of wars from the general taxpayer to young lower-class males via the draft. In peacetime it provides an instrument of economic stabilization through the way it administers its huge budget for the purchase of goods and services.

A full picture of the role of government, then, comes from looking at a breakdown of its activities not only by function but also by levels, agencies, and programs.

Public Expenditures by Type of Program

Exhibit 4.3a shows the pattern of federal government expenditures in 1978. The biggest single category was income security, which includes the social security program, unemployment compensation, public assistance (welfare), and federal employee retirement and disability benefits. Income security began to take the largest share of the federal budget only in 1974. Before that, defense had been the largest category. Throughout the 1960s, defense consistently took over 40 percent of the budget, peaking at 45 percent in 1968, at the height of

[1]See, for example, Suggestions for Further Reading at the end of this chapter.

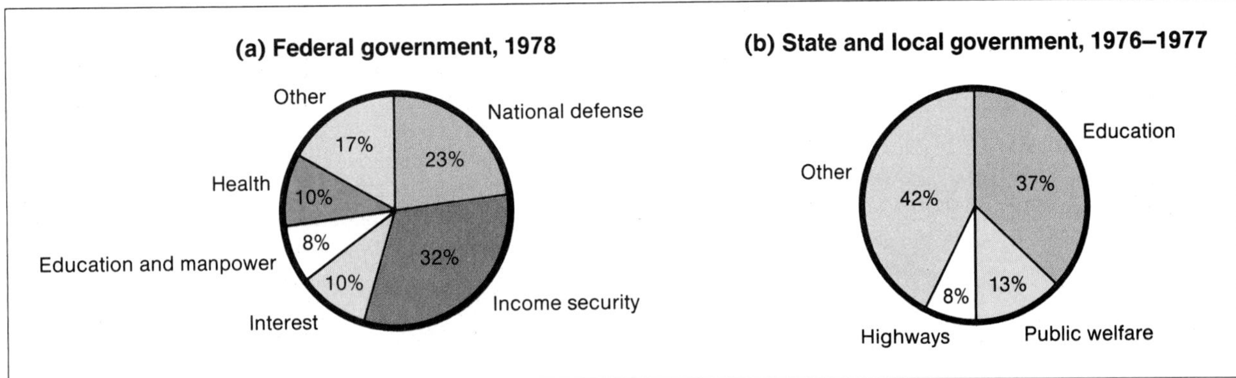

Exhibit 4.3
Patterns of government expenditure: Federal versus state and local
This exhibit shows the pattern of government expenditure at the federal, state, and local levels. The federal government bears the major burden of expenditures for national defense and income security, whereas education is by far the largest category of expenditure at the state and local levels.

Source: President's Council of Economic Advisers, *Economic Report of the President* (Washington, D.C.: Government Printing Office, 1979), Tables B-70 and B-75.

the Vietnam War. By 1978, the defense share of the budget was down to 23 percent. The other federal expenditures are largely self-explanatory.

Exhibit 4.3b shows the pattern of state and local expenditure. (State government accounted for about two-fifths of this, local government for three-fifths.) Here, by far the biggest item was education, which absorbed over a third of all expenditures. Public welfare and highways were the other largest categories.

To complete the picture, some idea of the relationship between the federal government on the one hand and state and local governments on the other is needed. Exhibit 4.4 shows that this relationship has been changing, as Washington has assumed a rapidly increasing burden of aid to state and local governments. This aid takes many forms, including job aid programs, sewage treatment construction grants, medicaid, income security programs, community development block grants, and general revenue sharing. Federal aid has been particularly concentrated in the nation's big cities. Direct federal aid to big cities increased more than tenfold between 1967 and 1977. These cities now receive more than fifty cents from the federal government for each dollar they raise from their own sources. This is more than the cities receive from their own states.

WHO PAYS FOR GOVERNMENT?

In recent years, people have become increasingly conscious of the costs as well as the benefits of a large, economically active public sector. In one sense, this is nothing new; people have grumbled about taxes ever since taxes were first invented. Nonetheless, in the late 1970s, citizens began to do more than grumble. In 1978, politicians who had paid lip service to limiting the burden of

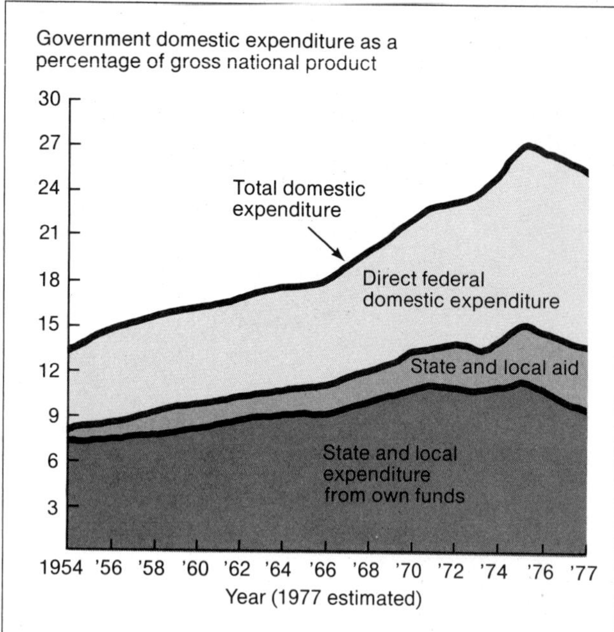

Exhibit 4.4
The changing relationship between the federal government and state and local governments
As this exhibit shows, Washington has assumed a rapidly increasing burden of aid to state and local governments in the last decade. Large cities in particular have received massive infusions of federal aid. Such cities now get more than fifty cents from the federal government for each dollar they raise from their own sources.

Source: U.S. Advisory Commission on Intergovernmental Relations, *Significant Features of Fiscal Federalism, 1976–77, Part 3: Expenditures* (Washington, D.C.: Government Printing Office, 1977).

taxes got something of a shock when voters in Alabama, Arizona, California, Hawaii, Idaho, Illinois, Massachusetts, Michigan, Missouri, North Dakota, South Dakota, and Texas imposed legal limits on state spending or taxes. Since that year of the taxpayers' revolt, economists have been paying increasing attention to the revenue side of government budgets and to the effects of taxation on the private sector. The remainder of this chapter will provide a brief tour of the economics of taxation.

What Kinds of Taxes?

We can begin by looking at the kinds of taxes that federal, state, and local governments use to raise revenue. Exhibit 4.5 gives the breakdowns. On the federal side, individual income taxes are the largest revenue raising item, although social insurance taxes and contributions have grown rapidly in recent years and are now not far behind. The corporate income tax used to be the second largest source of federal revenue, but it is now much less important than formerly.

The revenue side of the state and local government budget is quite different from that of the federal budget. State and local income taxes are in fifth place, with only 10 percent of revenues. Some states do not use the income tax at all. The largest source of revenue for state budgets is the sales tax, and for local government, property taxes are the largest item. As noted previously, an increasing share of state and local revenues comes directly from the federal government.

The Problem of Tax Incidence

Exhibit 4.5 shows the kinds of taxes paid to support various levels of government but not who really pays them. Economists refer to the question of who actually bears the burden of taxation as the problem of *tax incidence.* This

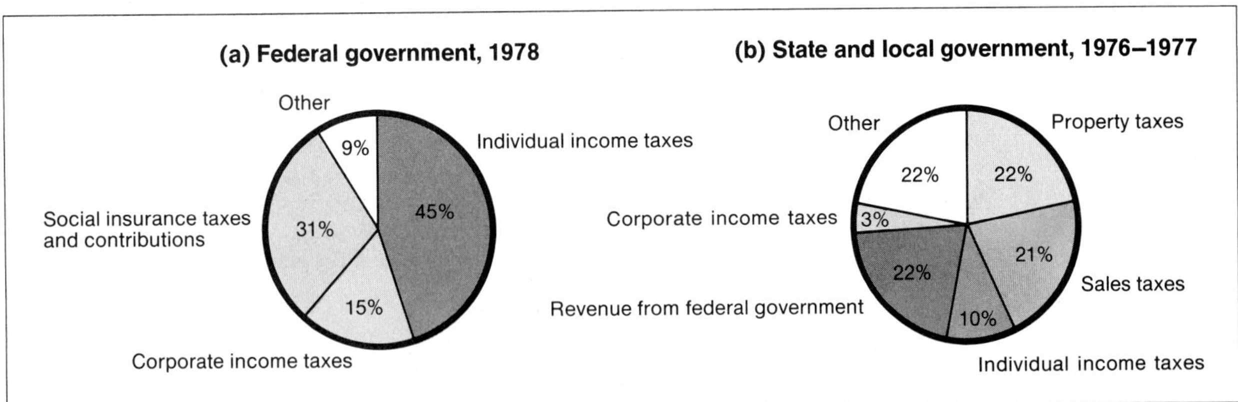

Exhibit 4.5
Sources of government revenue: Federal versus state and local
This exhibit shows the major sources of government revenue at the federal, state, and local levels. Individual income taxes and social insurance taxes are the major sources at the federal level. Local governments rely heavily on property taxes, while state governments use sales taxes and, to a lesser extent, income taxes. Notice that federal government grants are a major source of revenue for state and local governments.

Source: President's Council of Economic Advisers, *Economic Report of the President* (Washington, D.C.: Government Printing Office, 1979), Tables B–70 and B–75.

problem is not at all an easy one to solve. It is not enough just to look up the tax records of federal, state, and local governments. That would reveal only who had handed over the tax money to the authorities, not who actually bore the economic burden of the taxes. What makes tax incidence a difficult problem is the fact that the party who is obligated by law to pay the tax can often shift the burden of it to someone else.

An Illustration of Tax Incidence For a simple example, suppose a law is passed that requires all retailers to make a tax payment of ten cents to the government for each pack of cigarettes they sell. Who will bear the economic burden of this tax? A simple supply and demand analysis will provide the answer.

Look at the supply and demand curves shown in Exhibit 4.6. Without the tax, the equilibrium price of cigarettes would be twenty cents per pack, and 200 million packs per day would be sold. The tax upsets this equilibrium. In effect, the requirement of paying a ten cent per pack tax adds ten cents per pack to sellers' cost of doing business, which shifts the supply curve upward by ten cents. Buyers respond to this "artificial" shift in the supply curve in the same way they would to a genuine increase in the cost of producing cigarettes. They move up and to the left along their demand curve, cutting consumption. A new equilibrium is reached at twenty-five cents per pack—the intersection of the demand curve with the new supply curve.

Comparing the pretax with the posttax equilibrium, we see that although sellers must hand over ten cents to the government for each pack they sell, they receive only five cents per pack less than they did before the tax. Thus

Exhibit 4.6
The effects of a ten cent per pack sales tax on cigarettes
Before the sales tax is imposed, the equilibrium price for cigarettes is twenty cents per pack. The ten cent per pack sales tax can be treated as the sellers' added cost of doing business. It pushes the supply curve up by ten cents, as shown. After the shift in the supply curve, the price paid by buyers rises to twenty-five cents per pack, and the price received by sellers falls to fifteen cents. Thus, when the slopes of the supply and demand curves are equal, as shown in this exhibit, half the burden of the tax falls on sellers, and half is shifted to buyers.

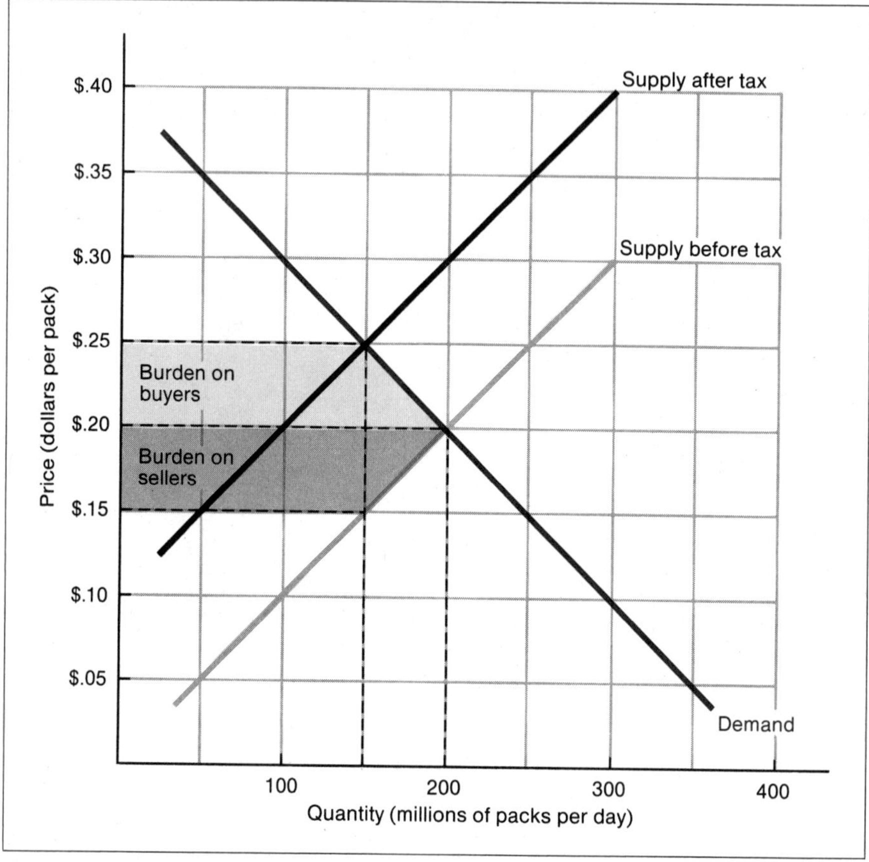

half the burden of the tax has been shifted to the buyers in the form of a price increase of five cents per pack. In the new equilibrium, the price paid by buyers is ten cents per pack more than what sellers receive after the tax.

In this example, the economic burden of the tax is divided equally between buyers and sellers, but the division need not always work out that way. If the demand curve had happened to be a little steeper and the supply curve a little flatter, the major share of the burden would have fallen on buyers. If the supply curve had been steeper than the demand curve, sellers would have borne the bigger share of the incidence of the tax. A large part of solving the puzzle of tax incidence, then, is determining just what the shapes of the supply and demand curves really are for the goods and services that are taxed.

Progressive tax A tax that takes a larger percentage of income from people whose income is high.

Overall Tax Incidence Taxes can be classified in terms of their incidence as progressive or regressive. A **progressive tax** takes a larger percentage of income from people whose incomes are high, and a **regressive tax** takes a larger percentage of income from people whose incomes are low. One of the most interesting questions about the economics of taxation is whether the overall effect of federal, state, and local taxes is progressive, regressive, or somewhere in between.

Regressive tax A tax that takes a larger percentage of income from people whose income is low.

A recent study by economist Joseph Minarik of the Brookings Institution attempts to bring together evidence on the incidence of several important kinds of taxes in an attempt to show whether the U.S. tax system as a whole is progressive or regressive. The results of his study are shown in Exhibit 4.7.

The federal income tax, as expected, is progressive. As people's incomes increase, they pay not only a higher percentage of their total income but also a higher percentage of each added dollar of income. (The percentage of each added dollar of income paid in tax is known as the **marginal tax rate.**) The social security payroll tax, in contrast, is regressive. The marginal tax rate is constant for all workers who pay the tax up to a certain maximum income ($25,900 in 1980); then it drops to zero on income above the maximum. According to Minarik's calculations, state and local taxes—including income, sales, and property taxes—are on balance slightly regressive. Adding the three

Marginal tax rate The percentage of each added dollar of income paid in taxes.

Exhibit 4.7

Tax incidence by income level in the United States, 1977

According to the data displayed in this exhibit, the U.S. tax system as a whole is neither markedly progressive nor markedly regressive over the range of income experienced by most households (66 percent of households had incomes between $5,000 and $30,000 in 1977). The progressiveness of the federal income tax offsets the regressiveness of the social security payroll tax and state and local taxes. Note that only personal contributions to social security are counted; if employer contributions were counted, the burden of this tax would be roughly doubled. The burden of state and local taxes at very low income levels is somewhat exaggerated by the presence of households whose incomes are only temporarily low.

Source: Joseph Minarik, Brookings Institution, unpublished tabulations. Reprinted by permission.

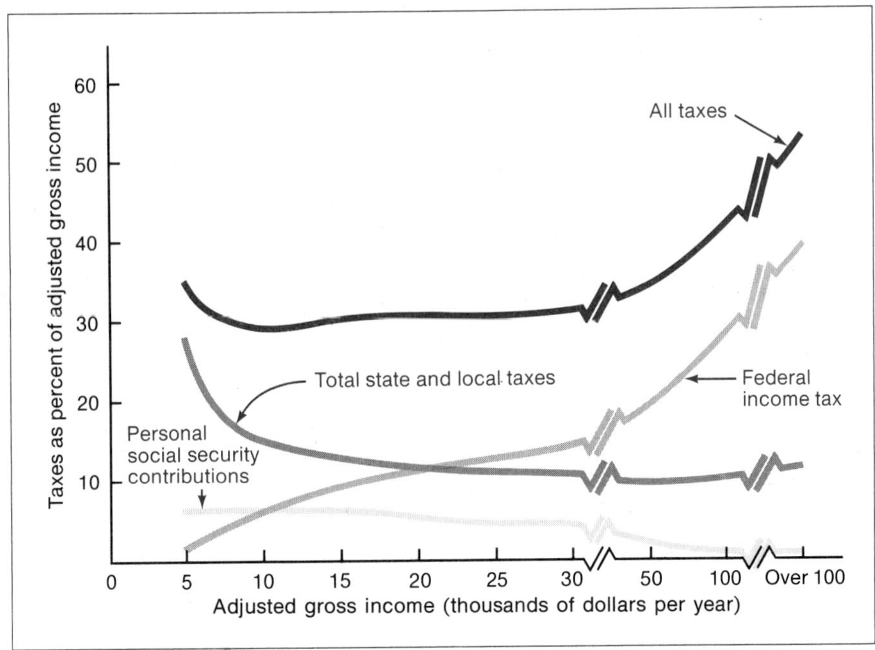

types of taxes together produces an almost flat tax schedule for the vast majority of taxpayers. It appears that the U.S. tax system as a whole is neither very progressive nor very regressive.

Incentive Effects of Taxes

Perhaps the liveliest controversy to hit the study of the economics of taxation in recent years concerns not the incidence of taxes but their effects on incentives. By far the most controversial taxes in this regard are income and payroll taxes. Let's look at both the traditional view of the incentive effects of income and payroll taxes and some recent challenges to that view.

The Traditional View Traditionally, income and payroll taxes were thought to have only minor incentive effects, because the supply curve of labor services was believed to be very steep. The reasoning behind this view is illustrated in Exhibit 4.8. That figure shows a very steep labor supply curve, indicating that the after-tax wage or salary received makes very little difference to the quantity of labor services supplied.

Two labor demand curves are also drawn. The upper one is the curve as it looks from the point of view of the employer. It shows the quantity of labor services demanded for any given level of total labor cost, including all income and payroll taxes. The lower one is the curve as it looks from the point of view of employees. It shows the after-tax earnings corresponding to each quantity of labor and each total labor cost to the employer. Employers make their decisions on how many workers to hire in terms of the upper curve; workers decide whether to accept the jobs offered in terms of the lower curve. If there were no income or payroll taxes, the two curves would coincide. As the tax rate rises, the after-tax demand curve is pushed down farther and farther from the tax-inclusive demand curve. As the figure is drawn, the quantity of labor supplied in equilibrium and the total labor cost per worker paid by employers would be virtually the same with or without the tax.

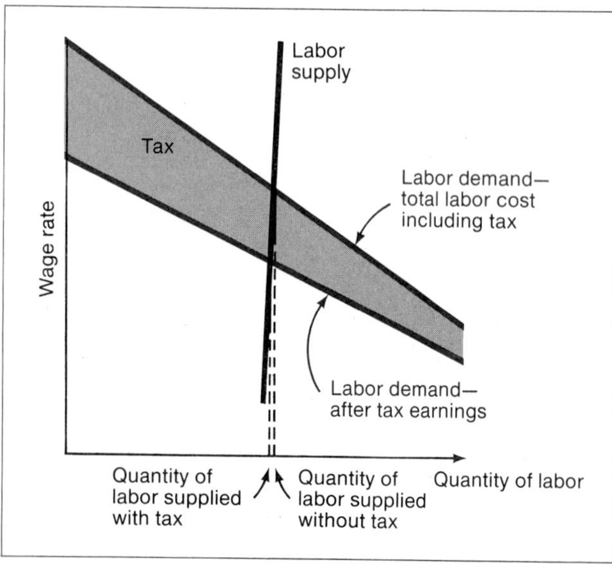

Exhibit 4.8
Incentive effects of an income tax— vertical labor supply curve
Traditionally, income and payroll taxes have been thought to have relatively minor incentive effects. The reason is that the labor supply curve, as drawn here, has been thought of as nearly vertical. Even a large gap between the employers' total labor cost (represented by the upper demand curve) and the employees' after-tax income (represented by the lower demand curve) would lead to little withdrawal of work effort by employees.

Note that with the supply curve as steep as the one shown, essentially all of the burden of the tax falls on employees. Furthermore, it makes no difference whether payroll taxes are formally paid by the employee or the employer. In 1980, for example, the social security system was financed by payroll "contributions" of 6.13 percent each from the employer and the employee. That created a 12.26 percent spread between the employer's total labor cost and the employee's after-tax earnings. The economic effect of the tax would have been no different had the employer or the employee been responsible for the entire 12.26 percent. However the responsibility for payment is divided, the economic burden of a payroll tax falls on the employee, as long as the labor supply curve is vertical, or nearly so.

The Revised View Recently, some economists have begun to question this traditional analysis of the burdens and incentive effects of income and payroll taxes. They suggest that when the income tax burden gets large enough, it may in fact begin to have significant incentive effects. One way to interpret their arguments is to draw the labor supply curve with the shape shown in Exhibit 4.9. As long as income and payroll taxes are relatively moderate, they have little incentive effect, as in the traditional analysis. But after-tax earnings eventually fall to such a small percentage of pretax earnings that people no longer find it worthwhile to work as much as before. When the after-tax demand curve falls as low as the one shown in Exhibit 4.9, incentive effects become substantial.

The Laffer Curve Under certain circumstances, the incentive effects of a tax can become so pronounced that an increase in the tax rate actually produces a decrease in the total tax revenue collected. Consider the hypothetical example of Exhibit 4.10. The vertical axis in this figure measures total income tax revenue. The horizontal axis measures the income tax rate as a percent of income. With a tax rate of zero, no revenue is collected; there is a maximum incentive to work, because workers keep everything they earn (so income is

Exhibit 4.9
Incentive effects of an income tax—curved labor supply curve
If the labor supply curve is not vertical, at least over part of its range (as drawn here), a high enough income tax rate can produce significant negative incentive effects. The high tax rate in this diagram is shown by the large gap between the tax-inclusive and after-tax demand curves. Substantially less labor is supplied with the tax than without it.

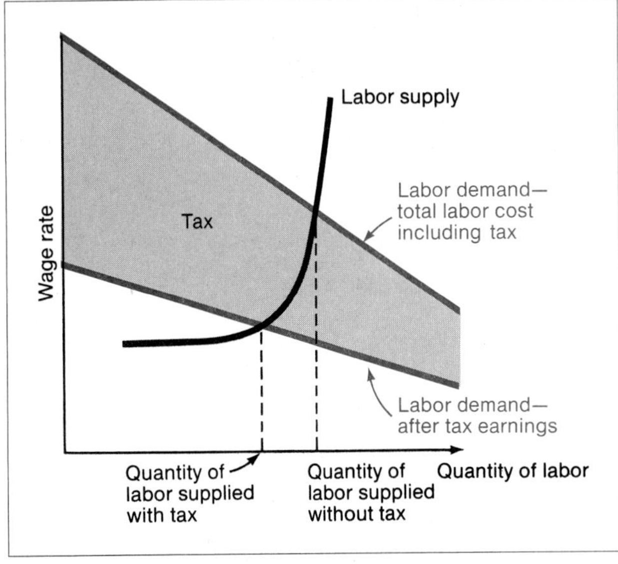

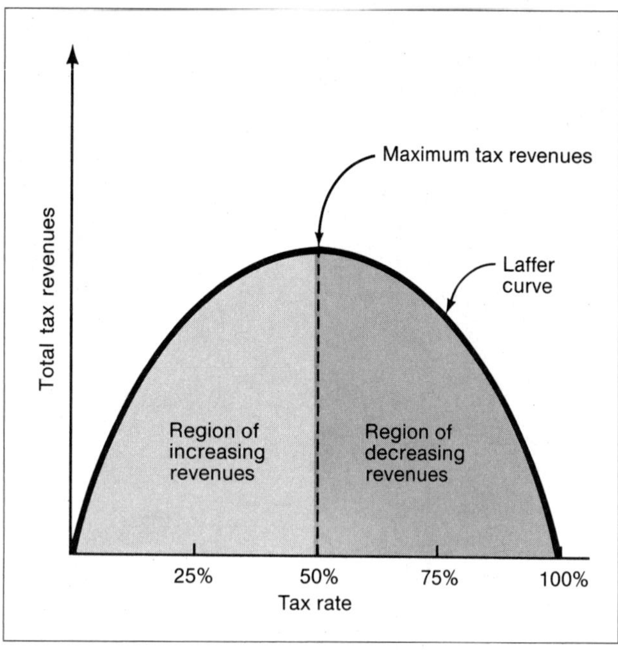

Exhibit 4.10
A Laffer curve

This Laffer curve shows the relationship thought to exist between the income tax rate and total income tax revenues. At a zero tax rate, no revenue is collected, even though incentives and total income are at their maximum. With a 100 percent tax, there is no incentive to work, so income drops to zero, and again no revenue is collected. In between, varying amounts of revenue are collected. The relationship shown is a hypothetical one. The point of maximum tax revenue need not occur at a tax rate of exactly 50 percent.

high). At the other extreme, with a tax rate of 100 percent, workers keep nothing of what they earn; there is no incentive to work, hence no income and again no tax revenue collected. In between, varying amounts of income are generated, and varying amounts of revenue are collected. At low rates, the disincentive effect is small enough that an increase in the tax rate increases total revenue. Beyond a point, however, the disincentive effect becomes large enough that an increase in the rate reduces total revenue.

Laffer curve A curve showing the relationship between a tax rate and the total revenue raised by the tax. At a zero or 100 percent tax rate, no revenue is raised; at some intermediate rate, tax revenue reaches a maximum.

The curve shown in Exhibit 4.10 has become known as a **Laffer curve,** after University of Southern California economist Arthur Laffer. Most economists accept the idea behind the Laffer curve in the abstract. There is considerable controversy, however, about just where the United States is now on the Laffer curve. Laffer and some others think that income tax rates in the United States are already so high that a reduction in tax rates would actually increase total tax revenue. But this is by no means a majority opinion among economists. There are indications that some European countries, where tax rates are higher, are experiencing substantial negative incentive effects from their tax systems. The following case study sheds some light on this problem.

Case 4.1
Incentive Effects of Income and Payroll Taxes in Europe

In 1979, the National Planning Association of Washington, D.C., published a study by Theodore Geiger of the tax and welfare systems of six European countries. One part of the study focused on the incentive effects of the high taxes required to finance the extensive welfare benefits available in most European countries. As Exhibit 4.11 shows, tax rates in Europe are considerably higher, for the average worker, than those in the United States. The percentage of income paid in taxes by the average European worker ranges from 27 percent in Germany and Norway to 35 percent in Sweden, compared with just 17 percent in the United States. Mar-

Exhibit 4.11
Average and marginal tax rates in Europe and the United States
As this exhibit shows, European workers face significantly higher tax rates than do U.S. workers. The average tax rates are based on the income and taxes of an average manufacturing worker with a family of four. The marginal tax rates are computed for the next 10 percent of income above average earnings in manufacturing.

Country	Taxes as Percent of Total Earnings	Marginal Tax Rate (percent)
Denmark	33	55
West Germany	27	34
Netherlands	31	42
Norway	27	42
Sweden	35	63
United Kingdom	26	41
United States	17	32

Source: Theodore Geiger, *Welfare and Efficiency: Their Interactions in Western Europe and Implications for International Economic Relations* (Washington, D.C.: National Planning Association, 1979), p. 28. Reprinted by permission.

ginal tax rates are even higher, ranging from 34 percent of each added dollar of income in Germany to a remarkable 63 percent of each added dollar in Sweden. The marginal tax rate for the average worker in the United States is a relatively moderate 32 percent.

In the course of his research, Geiger identified at least five perceptible negative incentive effects of these high tax rates. Most of the effects are most pronounced in Sweden, where taxes are the highest. The five incentive effects are:

1. In most of the countries studied, including the United States, there are rising pressures for a shorter workweek, longer vacations, more holidays, and new kinds of leisure (such as paid sabbaticals) for workers.
2. In the Netherlands and the Scandinavian countries especially, absenteeism rates are very high. In some large Swedish companies, absenteeism exceeds 20 percent of the labor force, partly as the result of very liberal sick leave benefits combined with high taxes on earned income.
3. In most countries, there is a perceived reduction in the difference between the after-tax disposable income obtained for work performed and the income in cash and in kind of nonworking welfare recipients. This strengthens the incentive to live on welfare.
4. High marginal tax rates foster a booming "underground economy" in several countries. Everything from repair services to legal and dental work are being done either for cash or on a barter basis. Some workers are taking leave from their regular jobs or refusing to work overtime in order to work in the underground economy.
5. In some countries, especially the United Kingdom, the tax system, together with other policies, is eroding the difference in after-tax income between skilled and unskilled workers. This is believed to be having an adverse effect on the supply of skilled workers and on the incentive to undertake certain kinds of training and education.

If the United States and Western Europe hope to maintain their high standards of living and to experience further economic growth, Geiger concluded, the interactions between tax and welfare systems on the one hand and economic efficiency on the other can no longer be neglected.

Source: Based on Theodore Geiger, *Welfare and Efficiency: Their Interactions in Western Europe and Implications for International Economic Relations* (Washington, D.C.: National Planning Association, 1979), pp. 27–30. Used with permission.

CONCLUSIONS

This chapter has explained something of the services government performs and something of who bears the costs of providing these services. But one major question not asked is *how well* the vast machinery of government does its job. This important question involves both normative and positive economics. The normative element comes in deciding what goals the government ought to pursue and the positive element in measuring how closely it meets those goals. This question of *how well* is one to which we shall return repeatedly throughout the book.

The next part of this book will introduce the analytical tools needed to determine how well the government performs its function of economic stabilization. This is one of the most important applications of economics, and in some respects it is one of the most controversial. The high rates of inflation and unemployment that the U.S. economy has experienced in the 1970s have given rise to some important new theories and important new doubts about how well the government has been doing its job. Later chapters will investigate the performance of government in the areas of the environment, energy, and international trade.

Until we get to all these later chapters, we will at least draw the preliminary conclusion that government is there and that it is important. In our theorizing, we may often speak of how markets work, as if the public sector were not there, but we will always come back to questions of government policy.

SUMMARY

1. The U.S. economy has a large and important government sector. Government purchases are nearly a quarter of gross national product, and taxes take over a third of it. But as large as government is in absolute terms, it is small as a fraction of GNP in comparison to the government sectors in many European countries.
2. Government differs from individuals and firms in several ways. Government can legitimately use force in the pursuit of its economic goals, while private individuals and firms cannot. Government gives away most of the services it produces without directly charging for them; the services are paid for indirectly through taxation. Also, political decision-making processes differ substantially from those of the private sector. Still, because government must go to markets to buy most of what it needs, market forces do exercise some influence over the public sector.
3. Five major economic functions of government are the provision of public goods, the carrying out of transfers, the stabilization of the economy, the regulation of the private sector, and the administration of justice.
4. The determination of the incidence of various kinds of taxes is a difficult problem of applied economics. The burden of many taxes can be shifted from those who bear the legal obligation of paying them to other parties. When all kinds of shifting are taken into account, it appears that the combined federal, state, and local tax systems are neither progressive nor regressive overall. Instead, the burden of taxes is shifted to some degree from middle-income groups to both the very rich and the very poor.
5. In recent years, a controversy has developed over the incentive effects of income and payroll taxes. At the tax rates experienced by workers in Europe, negative incentive effects do appear to be noticeable. A few economists believe that tax rates even in the United States are so high that cutting them would actually increase tax revenues.

DISCUSSION QUESTIONS

1. What would happen to U.S. society if we did away with the federal government? In which cases could state and local governments fill in? In which cases would they be unable to do so?
2. List the major goods and services provided by the government at different levels. Then determine the extent to which these goods are public goods. Which level of government tends to supply the most public goods? Which one the least? (Can you determine which?)
3. How can a government respond to changes in the relative prices of the goods and services it buys and provides for its constituents? How is it subject to the same forces as a business? How not?
4. Would you prefer living where income taxes are progressive or regressive? Why?
5. When a tax is imposed on cigarettes, the price paid by consumers goes up and the price received by sellers goes down. The government benefits by the amount of the difference on each pack sold. There is also a second effect of the tax; fewer packs are sold. Who benefits and who is hurt by the second effect? Does the fact that cigarettes are harmful to people influence your answer? What if they were good for people?

SUGGESTIONS FOR FURTHER READING

Buchanan, James, and Tullock, Gordon. *The Calculus of Consent.* Ann Arbor: University of Michigan Press, 1962.
The seminal treatment of the economics of public goods and public choice.

Geiger, Theodore. *Welfare and Efficiency: Their Interactions in Western Europe and Implications for International Economic Relations.* Washington, D.C.: National Planning Association, 1979.
The source of Case 4.1 and an analysis of the interactions of tax and welfare systems in Europe with the efficiency of the economic systems of which they form a part.

Musgrave, Richard A., and Musgrave, Peggy B. *Public Finance in Theory and Practice.* 2d ed. New York: McGraw-Hill, 1975.
The theory of public finance *is the economist's term for the economics of the government sector. This is one of the most widely used and authoritative treatments of the subject.*

Phelps, Edmund S., ed. *Private Wants and Public Needs.* New York: W. W. Norton, 1965.
A collection of readings on the economics of government, compiled specifically for the use of beginning students.

Posner, Richard A. *Economic Analysis of Law.* Boston: Little, Brown, 1973.
A good introduction to the economic analysis of legal issues, written primarily for beginning law students. Highly recommended for any readers who may be contemplating a career in law. After this book, the reader may want to refer to some of the more advanced papers in Henry G. Manne, ed., The Economics of Legal Relationships, *listed at the end of Chapter 2.*

PART TWO

NATIONAL INCOME, INFLATION, AND UNEMPLOYMENT

CHAPTER 5

THE CIRCULAR FLOW OF INCOME AND PRODUCT

WHAT YOU WILL LEARN IN THIS CHAPTER

This chapter will describe how the circular flow of income and product sends goods from firms to households and factor services from households to firms. At the same time, it will show how payments for these goods and services flow in the opposite direction through the economy. The idea of the circular flow will be used in two ways. First, it will give a framework for a set of important definitions and equalities. Second, it will show how the concepts of supply, demand, and equilibrium can be applied in a macroeconomic context.

FOR REVIEW

Here are some important terms and concepts that will be put to use in this chapter. If you do not understand them, review them before proceeding.

- *Equilibrium (Chapter 3)*
- *Government purchases (Chapter 4)*
- *Transfer payments (Chapter 4)*

This chapter begins putting together a theory that will explain unemployment, inflation, and economic growth and that will offer a framework for thinking about economic stabilization policy. These subjects make up the branch of economics known as **macroeconomics.** The prefix *macro* comes from the Greek word meaning "big"; but although inflation, unemployment, and economic growth are big issues in the sense of being important, that is not the reason for using the term *macro*economics. Instead, the term is applied because this branch of economics works primarily with **aggregate** economic data—any data that are grand totals for the economy as a whole. Macroeconomics is thus distinguished from **microeconomics** (*micro* meaning "small"), which studies individual prices, the behavior of individual firms and households, and so on.

Macroeconomics The branch of economics devoted to the study of unemployment, inflation, economic growth, and stabilization policy.

Aggregate A term used in economics to describe any quantity that is a grand total for the whole economy.

Microeconomics The branch of economics devoted to the study of the behavior of individual households and firms and to the determination of the relative prices of individual goods and services.

Because it will take several chapters to complete the study of macroeconomics, it is necessary to have a clear idea of the lay of the land before beginning. The best way to get an overview of the relationships among the

Circular flow of income and product The flow of goods from firms to households and factor services from households to firms, counterbalanced by the flow of expenditures from households to firms and factor payments from firms to households.

major economic aggregates is to represent them in terms of a **circular flow of income and product.** The rest of this chapter, then, will be devoted to the circular flow.

THE STRUCTURE OF THE CIRCULAR FLOW

A Simple Economy

To see the circular flow in its most basic form, begin by imagining an economy made up only of households and firms—an economy with no public sector at all. To make things simpler still, assume that households live entirely from hand to mouth, spending all of their income on consumer goods as soon as that income is received. Similarly, assume that firms sell their entire output to consumers as soon as it is produced.

The circular flow of income and product for this ultra-simple economy is shown in Exhibit 5.1. The diagram is drawn with physical goods and services

Exhibit 5.1
The circular flow in a simple economy
In this simple economy, households spend all their income on consumer goods as soon as they receive it, and firms sell all their output to households as soon as they produce it. Physical goods and factor services flow clockwise, while corresponding money payments flow counterclockwise.

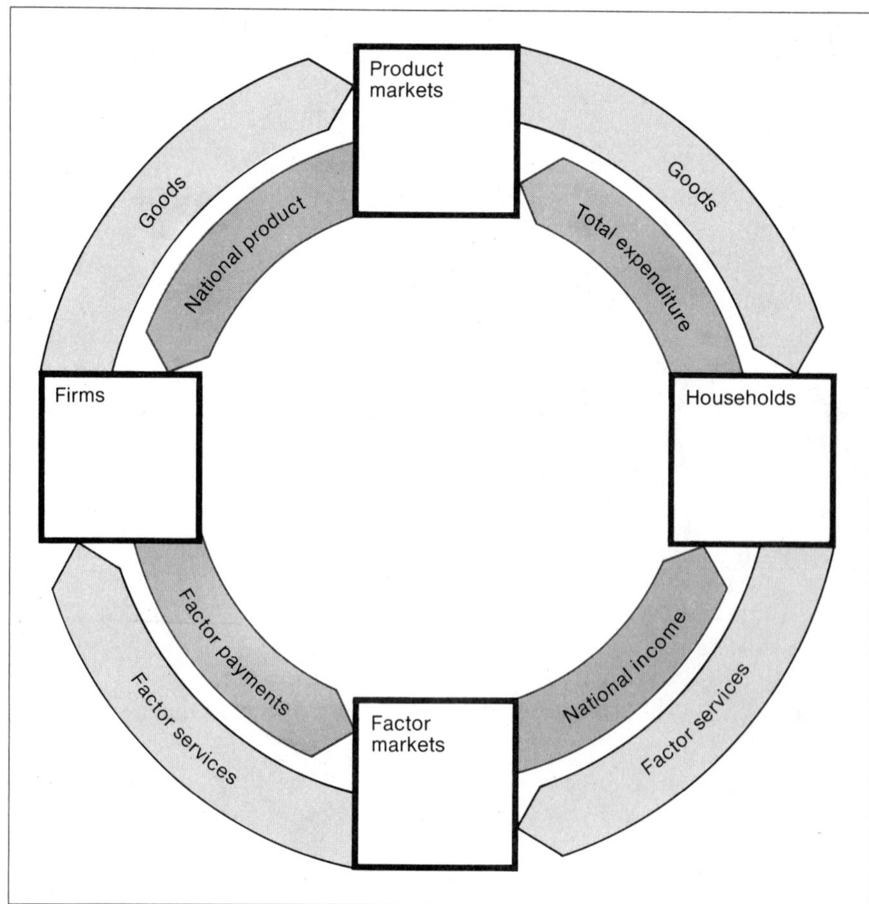

flowing clockwise and the corresponding money payments flowing counterclockwise.

Two sets of markets link households to firms in this economy. Product markets, which appear at the top of the diagram, are markets where households purchase goods and services—bread, television sets, houses, dry cleaning services, entertainment—for their own direct consumption. Factor markets, which appear at the bottom of the diagram, are the markets in which households sell to firms the **factors of production** they use in making the things sold in product markets.

Factors of production are traditionally classified as natural resources, labor, and capital. **Natural resources** include everything useful as a productive input in its natural state—agricultural land, building sites, forests, and mineral deposits, for example. **Labor** includes the productive contributions made by people working with their minds and muscles. **Capital** is all means of production created by people, including tools, industrial equipment, structures, and improvements to land.

In return for the natural resources, labor, and capital that they buy from households, firms make *factor payments* in the form of rents, wages, salaries, and interest payments. As a matter of accounting convention, when firms use land, labor, or capital that they themselves own, they are counted as "purchasing" those factors from the households that own the firms, even though no money changes hands and no explicit factor payment is made. For purposes of macroeconomic analysis, profits are thus considered an implicit factor payment from firms to the households that own them.[1]

Factors of production The basic inputs of natural resources, labor, and capital used in producing all goods and services.

Natural resources As a factor of production, everything useful as a productive input in its natural state, including agricultural land, building sites, forests, and mineral deposits.

Labor As a factor of production, the contributions to production made by people working with their minds and muscles.

Capital As a factor of production, all means of production that are created by people, including such things as tools, industrial equipment, structures, and improvements to land.

Stocks and Flows

Having said this much, let's pause for a moment to concentrate on a word used several times already. Economists call all of the things shown in Exhibit 5.1 **flows** because they are processes that occur continuously through time. Flows are measured in units per time period—for example, in dollars per year, gallons per minute, or tons per month. Measurements of flows are measurements of rates at which things are happening.

Flows Processes occurring continuously through time, measured in units per time period.

The technical language of economics distinguishes carefully between flows and stocks. A **stock** is an accumulated quantity of something existing at a particular time. (The word *stock* in this general sense has nothing to do with the stock market kind of stocks that are bought and sold on Wall Street.)

Stocks Accumulated quantities existing at a particular time, measured in terms of simple units.

For an illustration of the difference between stocks and flows, we can think of a bathtub filling. When we talk about how fast the water is running, we are talking about a *flow,* measured in gallons per minute. When we talk about how much water is in the tub at a given moment, we are talking about a *stock* measured only in gallons. Similarly, in the world of economics, we might talk about the rate of housing construction in Buffalo, New York, in terms of new units per month (the flow) as distinct from the actual number of houses in Buffalo as of January 1, 1980 (the stock).

National Income and Product

Two of the flows in Exhibit 5.1 deserve special attention and have special names. The first is **national income**—the total of all wages, rents, interest

National income The total of all incomes, including wages, rents, interest payments, and profits received by households.

[1]For certain purposes of microeconomics, profits are not considered factor payments.

National product The total value of all goods and services supplied in the economy.

payments, and profits received by households. National income is shown in the diagram as an arrow aimed at the box representing households. The second important flow is **national product**—a measure of the total value of the goods and services produced. In the diagram, national product is shown as an arrow passing from the box representing product markets to the box representing firms.

In this economy, national income and national product are equal, simply because of the way they are defined.[2] This equality can be verified in either of two ways. First, consider household expenditures as a link between national income and national product. Households are assumed to spend all of their income on consumer goods as soon as they receive it, and firms are assumed to sell all of their output to consumers as soon as it is produced. The payments made by buyers must equal the payments received by sellers, so national product must equal national income.

Alternatively, consider factor payments as a link between national income and national product. When firms receive money for the goods they sell, they use part of it to pay the workers, natural resource owners, and others who contributed factors of production to make the goods. Anything left over is profit. Factor payments, including profits, account for all the money received by firms, so total factor payments must be equal to national product. Factor payments also account for all of the income received by households, so total factor payments must be equal to national income. It again follows that national income and national product must be equal.

Saving and Investment

The circular flow shown in Exhibit 5.1 is so simple that not very much of interest can be said about it. To build a theory that will be useful for understanding the real-world economy, a few complications must be introduced.

The first change will be to drop the requirement that households immediately spend all of their income to purchase consumer goods and to permit them instead to save part of what they earn. The rate of saving by households, under this assumption, is simply the difference between national income and household consumption expenditures.

Fixed investment Purchases by firms of newly produced capital goods, such as production machinery, newly built structures, and office equipment.

Inventory investment Changes in the stocks of finished products and raw materials that firms keep on hand. If stocks are increasing, inventory investment is positive; if they are decreasing, it is negative.

Investment The sum of fixed investment and inventory investment.

The second change will be to drop the requirement that firms immediately sell all of their output to consumers. Instead, they will be permitted to sell some products to other firms and to let some accumulate in inventory before selling them to anyone. When firms buy newly produced capital goods (for example, production machinery, newly built structures, or office equipment) from other firms, they are said to engage in **fixed investment.** When firms increase the stock of finished products or raw materials that they keep on hand, they are said to engage in **inventory investment.** The rate of inventory investment can be less than zero in periods when firms are decreasing their stocks of goods or raw materials on hand. The sum of fixed investment and inventory investment will be called simply **investment.**

[2]Chapter 6 will show that the equality between national income and product does not hold precisely as these concepts are actually measured by the official statisticians of the U.S. government. It would be pointless, though, to let this statistical detail complicate all theoretical discussions. Everywhere in this chapter, and everywhere from Chapter 7 onward, the necessary simplifying assumptions are made so that national income and product *are* equal.

Circular Flow with Saving and Investment Exhibit 5.2 shows how the circular flow of income and expenditure looks when saving and investment are added. (The clockwise arrows showing the flows of goods and services have been omitted to simplify the diagram.) There are now two pathways along which expenditures can travel on their way from households to product markets. Some household income is used for consumption expenditure and reaches product markets directly. Other household income is diverted to saving, which supplies a source of funds for firms to use in making investment expenditures; this income reaches product markets indirectly.

On the way from households to firms, the flow of saving passes through a set of financial markets. These markets include a great variety of financial institutions—commercial banks, savings and loan associations, the stock and bond markets, insurance companies, and other institutions that act as intermediaries between households that save and firms that make investment

Exhibit 5.2
The circular flow with saving and investment
When saving and investment are added to the circular flow, there are two pathways by which expenditures can travel on their way from households to product markets. Some income is spent directly on consumer goods. The rest is saved and passes to firms via financial markets. The firms then use the investment expenditures in the product markets.

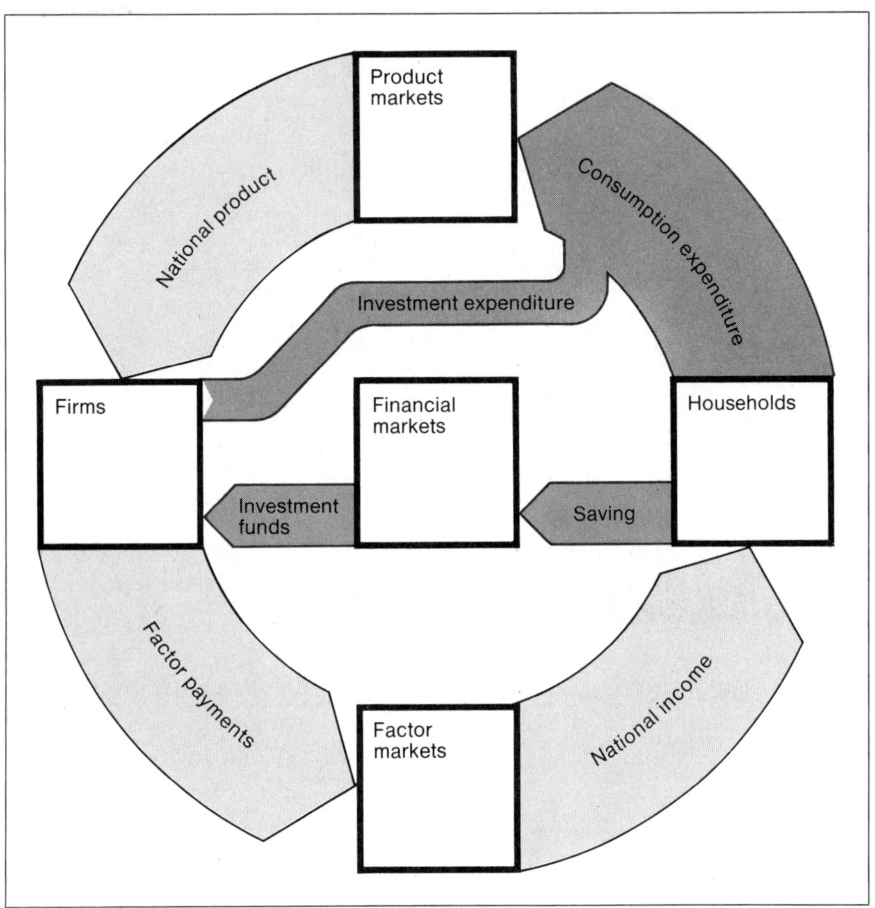

expenditures. Households supply funds to these financial markets. Firms can then borrow from financial markets to obtain the funds they need to make investment expenditures. (Chapter 11 will discuss the operation of financial markets in detail.)

Equilibrium and Disequilibrium in the Circular Flow Adding saving and investment to the circular flow raises an entirely new issue: Can total expenditure still be counted on to provide an equalizing link between national income and national product? There are now two entirely different sets of people making expenditure decisions. Households decide how much to spend on consumption, and firms decide how much to spend on investment. How can we be sure that when these two kinds of expenditures are added together, the total will just equal the total value of all goods produced? A new way of applying supply and demand analysis will help find the answers.

Aggregate Supply and Demand

Aggregate supply The total value of all goods and services supplied in the economy; identical to national product.

Aggregate demand The total value of all planned expenditures of all buyers in the economy.

The term **aggregate supply** refers to the grand total of all goods supplied by all firms in the entire economy. There is already another term for the same thing: national product. *Aggregate supply* and *national product* are two names for the total value of goods and services supplied by all firms. Following the same terminology, **aggregate demand** can be used to mean the grand total of all goods demanded for the whole economy. In defining *aggregate demand* this way, though, care must be taken in the way "demand" is used. The precise way of defining *aggregate demand* is to say that it means the total *planned* expenditures of all buyers in the economy.

In discussing supply and demand for individual goods or services, the step after defining the terms *supply* and *demand* was to explain equilibrium. The same thing can be done now by using aggregate supply and aggregate demand to explain the ideas of equilibrium and disequilibrium in the circular flow.

A Numerical Example A numerical example will make the point. Imagine an economy in which only three goods are produced: apples, milling machines, and radios. The various firms in this economy have plans to produce apples at a rate of $30,000 worth per year, milling machines at a rate of $40,000 worth per year, and radios at a rate of $30,000 worth per year. All firms are busy carrying out their plans. The result is a flow of output at a rate of $100,000 per year. This flow, which can be called either *national product* or *aggregate supply,* is detailed in lines 1 to 4 of Exhibit 5.3.

While producers are busy carrying out their plans, buyers make plans too. Consumers plan to buy apples at a rate of $25,000 worth per year and radios at a rate of $30,000 worth per year. Also, the firms that make radios are planning to buy milling machines at a rate of $35,000 worth per year in order to increase their radio-producing capacity for the future. No one is planning either to increase or to decrease the stocks of finished products held in inventory, so planned inventory investment is zero. All these buying plans are expressed in lines 5 to 11 of Exhibit 5.3. The total of all planned expenditures (consumption plus planned investment) is listed in line 11 as aggregate demand.

Comparing line 1 with line 11, *it is obvious that the plans of producers and the plans of buyers do not mesh.* Aggregate supply is not equal to aggregate

Exhibit 5.3

A numerical example of the circular flow for a simple economy

National product must always be equal to total expenditure, even when the circular flow is not in equilibrium. In the example shown here, national product (aggregate supply) exceeds total planned expenditure (aggregate demand), so unplanned inventory investment makes up the difference.

Output Resulting from Producers' Plans				
1	Total national product (aggregate supply)			$100,000
2	Apples	$30,000		
3	Radios	30,000		
4	Milling machines	40,000		
Expenditures Resulting from Buyers' Plans				
5	Total consumption expenditure		$55,000	
6	Apples	$25,000		
7	Radios	30,000		
8	Total planned investment expenditure		35,000	
9	Fixed investment	35,000		
10	Planned inventory investment	0		
11	Total planned expenditure (aggregate demand)			$90,000
Other Expenditure				
12	Total unplanned inventory investment			10,000
13	Unsold apples	5,000		
14	Unsold milling machines	5,000		
Summary				
15	Total national product			$100,000
16	Total national expenditure			100,000
17	Planned	$90,000		
18	Unplanned	10,000		

demand. There is nothing very surprising about the situation. After all, there have been no direct consultations among the various buyers and sellers when plans have been made. Each has acted on the basis of whatever knowledge has been available from the price system, plus private judgments about future trends or changes. As a result, things are not working out for everyone according to plan. The apples, radios, and milling machines are all being produced, but not all of them are being sold. After buyers have bought all they plan to, $5,000 worth of apples are left over, as are $5,000 worth of milling machines. These products cannot simply vanish into thin air. The firms that made them are putting them into inventory, even though they had not planned to do so, in the hope of selling them at some time in the future. The result is an *unplanned* inventory investment of $10,000, as shown in lines 12 to 14 of Exhibit 5.3.

An Important Equality When aggregate buying plans do not mesh with aggregate production plans, the circular flow is said to be in *disequilibrium.* Aggregate supply and aggregate demand are not equal; national product and total planned expenditure are not equal. One crucial equality does hold, though. National product is still equal to total expenditure *when both planned and unplanned expenditures are taken into account.* The reason is that goods that are produced and not sold *must* be added to inventories, whether firms planned to put them there or not. As long as unplanned inventory investment is counted as part of total expenditure—and it is—total expenditure is by definition equal to national product. In equation form:

$$\text{National product} = \text{Total planned expenditure} + \text{Unplanned inventory investment} = \text{Total expenditure.}$$

Another way to write exactly the same thing is:

$$\text{Aggregate supply} = \text{Aggregate demand} + \text{Unplanned inventory investment.}$$

Reactions to Disequilibrium In the numerical example outlined in Exhibit 5.3, aggregate demand fell short of aggregate supply. Because buyers' and sellers' plans failed to mesh, there was an unplanned accumulation of inventories. Firms would not want this unplanned rise in inventories to go on and on. In order to stop it, they would reduce their rate of output, or lower prices in order to stimulate sales, or both. These reactions would amount to a reduction in aggregate supply. The size of the circular flow would begin to shrink as the number of dollars received by firms for their products and the number of dollars paid out to workers fell.

At another time, aggregate demand might exceed aggregate supply. With total planned expenditures greater than national product, unplanned inventory depletion would take place. Firms would react in a way opposite to their reaction to an excess of aggregate supply over aggregate demand. Either they would increase output to rebuild inventories, or they would take advantage of the high level of demand to raise prices, or both. Whichever they did, the size of the circular flow would grow as incomes and expenditures rose.

Finally, it is entirely possible that when the plans of buyers and sellers were tested in the market, they would turn out to mesh. In that case, with production and planned expenditure equal, no unplanned inventory investment would occur, and no corrections would be necessary. The circular flow would be in equilibrium.

Income and Expenditure

Nothing has yet been said about national income. Go back for a moment to the situation in Exhibit 5.3. Firms are shown to be producing $100,000 worth of goods a year. To produce those goods they must make factor payments (including profits, if any) of $100,000 to households, which means that national income is also $100,000. The households receiving this income plan to buy consumer goods at a rate of $55,000 per year, which means that they plan to save at a rate of $45,000 per year. (Remember that saving plus consumption exhausts income in this simple economy.)

These household saving plans do not mesh with firms' investment plans, as shown in line 8 of Exhibit 5.3. As things actually have turned out, though, the firms have invested more than they had planned to. The actual total of their investment, including unplanned inventory investment, is exactly equal to saving. It must be. Once again, goods cannot vanish into thin air after they are produced, and unplanned inventory investment acts as the balancing item.

The Place of Government in the Circular Flow

When government enters the circular flow of income, expenditure, and product, things become slightly more complicated. Exhibit 5.4 shows how the circular flow looks when government is added. Two new pathways along which expenditures can flow from households to the product markets are opened up.

First, governments take in revenue from taxes they levy on households. Some of that revenue, as shown in Chapter 4, is immediately returned to households in the form of transfer payments. The difference between what governments take in as tax revenue and what they pay out as transfer payments is called **net taxes.** Funds thus flow from households to government as

Net taxes Total tax revenues collected by government at all levels minus total transfer payments disbursed.

Exhibit 5.4

The circular flow with government included

With government added to the circular flow of income and product, there are two new channels along which funds can flow from households to product markets. Some income is diverted to government in the form of net taxes and then used to finance government purchases. Alternatively, if the government runs a budget deficit, it may borrow from the public via financial markets and use the borrowed funds to finance its expenditures. If the government runs a budget surplus, the flow of funds along this pathway may be reversed, in which case the arrow from government to financial markets will point in the opposite direction from that shown.

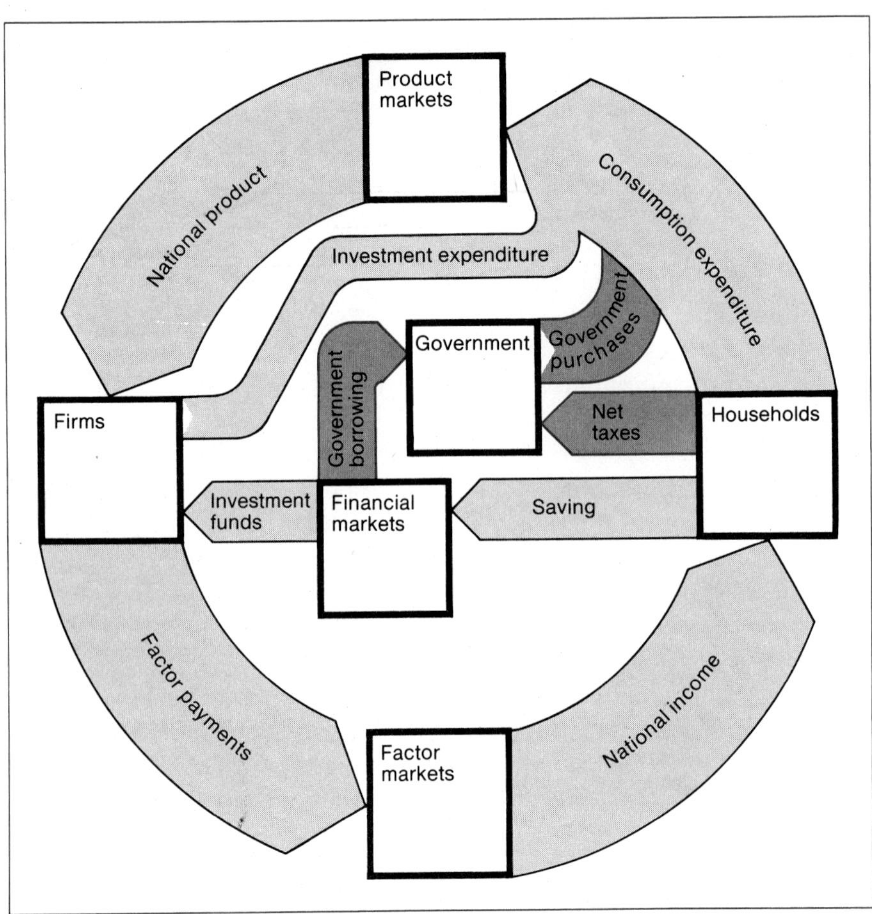

net taxes and then from government to product markets as government purchases.

Second, if government purchases of goods and services exceed net taxes, the government may need to borrow from the public through financial markets. In this case, the government budget is said to be in **deficit.** When the government runs a deficit, funds flow from households to financial markets as saving, then from financial markets to the government as government borrowing, and finally from government to the product markets as government purchases.

Deficit In referring to government budgets, an excess of government purchases over net taxes.

Surplus In referring to government budgets, an excess of net taxes over government purchases.

Sometimes, the government budget is in **surplus** rather than deficit. In that case, government's borrowing from the public is less than its repayment of past debts. The net flow of funds between government and financial markets is the reverse of what is shown in Exhibit 5.4.

Adding the Foreign Sector

The final step in constructing the circular flow of income and product is to add the foreign sector, as in Exhibit 5.5. This exhibit shows that some of the expenditures made by consumers, firms, and governments do not flow to domestic product markets but instead flow to foreign economies to pay for imports of goods and services. These expenditures are shown by the arrow labeled *imports* in the exhibit. At the same time, some expenditures on domestically produced goods and services are made by foreigners. These are shown in the exhibit by the arrow labeled *exports,* which passes from the foreign economy sector to domestic product markets.

Remember that the arrows in Exhibit 5.5 all represent flows of funds, not flows of physical goods and services. The import arrow thus shows the flow of funds out of the U.S. economy to pay for imported goods and services, and the export arrow shows the flow of funds into the U.S. economy in payment for exports of goods and services. If imports exceed exports, the U.S. economy is said to run a foreign trade deficit. This deficit must be paid for by borrowing from foreigners, hence the arrow labeled *loans from foreigners to finance trade deficit,* which points from foreign economies to the domestic financial markets. If instead U.S. exports exceed imports, the U.S. is said to run a foreign trade surplus. In this case (not shown), foreign buyers of U.S. goods have to pay for them by borrowing funds in U.S. financial markets, and the direction of the arrow is reversed.

Leakages and Injections The first section of this chapter described a highly simplified economy in which households spent all their income on consumption goods, so that all expenditures flowed directly from households to domestic product markets. As financial markets, government, and foreign economies were added, however, it was shown that in the real world, three kinds of purchases of goods and services do not originate directly in domestic households: investment (purchases of capital goods and goods for inventory by domestic firms), government purchases, and exports (purchases of domestic goods and services by foreigners). From now on, these three kinds of purchases will be referred to collectively as **injections** into the circular flow of goods and services.

Injections The part of total expenditures that does not originate from domestic households—that is, investment, government purchases, and exports.

Offsetting these injections are imports (expenditures of households, firms, and units of government on goods produced abroad), plus saving and taxes (the use of household income for purposes other than the direct purchase of goods

Exhibit 5.5
The circular flow with government and the foreign sector

This exhibit adds a foreign sector to the circular flow with government that was shown in Exhibit 5.4. Some consumption, investment, and government purchases are for goods produced abroad; this is shown as the triple arrow pointing toward the foreign sector, labeled *imports*. Some purchases of domestically produced goods and services are made by foreigners; these are shown as the arrow labeled *exports* running from the foreign sector to domestic product markets. If imports exceed exports, the excess imports must be paid for by borrowing from abroad; this is shown by the arrow labeled *loans from foreigners to finance trade deficit.* If exports instead exceed imports, there is a foreign trade surplus, and the direction of that arrow is reversed. Note that all the arrows in this exhibit represent flows of funds, not of physical goods and services. That is why the exports arrow points into the domestic economy and the imports arrow points away from it.

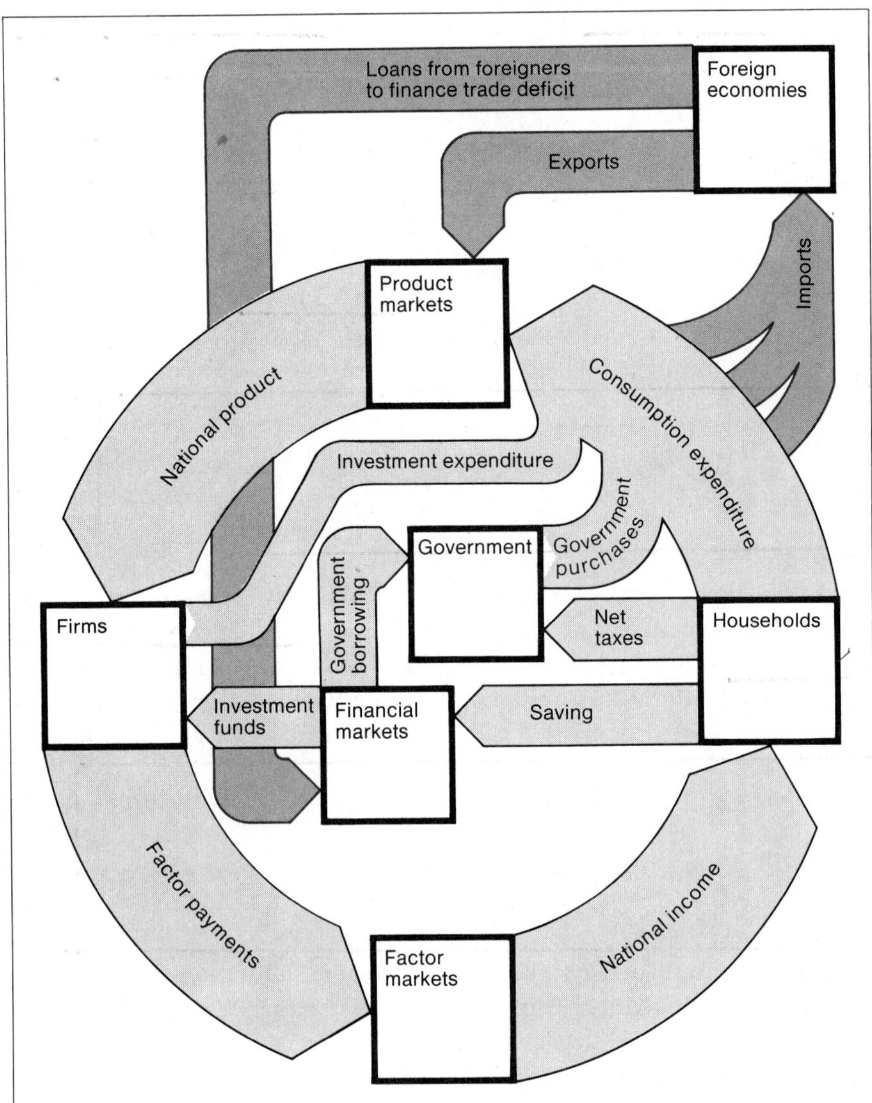

Leakages The part of national income not devoted to consumption (saving plus net taxes) plus domestic expenditures on foreign-made goods (imports).

and services). From now on, saving, net taxes, and imports will be referred to collectively as **leakages** from the circular flow.

The Equality of National Income and National Product Another numerical example will show that adding the government and foreign sectors, with their associated injections and leakages, to the economy does not disturb the fundamental equality between national income and national product on which the circular flow is based. Exhibit 5.6 shows an economy in which consumption is $70,000, investment is $22,000, government purchases are $10,000, and exports are $8,000. Of the consumption, investment, and government purchases shown, $10,000 is spent on imported goods, which cannot be counted as part of the national product of the country represented in the exhibit. National product is thus shown as the total of consumption, investment, and government purchases, plus expenditures on domestic goods by foreigners (exports), minus that part of consumption, investment, and government purchases not spent on domestic goods and services (imports). As Exhibit 5.6 is constructed, the total comes to $100,000.

Net exports Total exports minus total imports.

The production of $100,000 of national product generates $100,000 in factor payments for domestic households. As the second table in Exhibit 5.6 shows, this amount is divided among consumption ($70,000), saving ($25,000), and net taxes ($5,000). Introducing the term **net exports** to represent exports minus imports, the relationships shown in Exhibit 5.6 can be written in equation form as:

$$\begin{aligned}\text{National product} &= \text{Consumption} + \text{Investment} + \text{Government purchases} + \text{Net exports}\\ &= \text{Consumption} + \text{Saving} + \text{Net taxes}\\ &= \text{National income.}\end{aligned}$$

The Equality of Leakages and Injections It follows from the relationship between national income and national product that total injections must equal total leakages. Beginning with the equation shown above, consumption can be subtracted from both sides, and imports can be added to both sides. The result is:

$$\text{Investment} + \text{Government purchases} + \text{Exports} = \text{Saving} + \text{Net taxes} + \text{Imports}$$

or

$$\text{Total injections} = \text{Total leakages.}$$

Note that this relationship holds even though, in the numerical example of Exhibit 5.6, no individual pair of items on the leakages and injections list exactly matches up. In that example, saving exceeds investment by $3,000, imports exceed exports by $2,000, and net taxes fall short of government purchases by $5,000. The reason total injections must always equal total leakages is that injections include unplanned inventory investment as a balancing item. Suppose, for example, that beginning from the position shown in Exhibit 5.6, government purchases suddenly rise by $5,000, while planned expenditures by households, firms, and foreigners remain constant. The additional purchases made by government cannot come out of thin air; unless

Exhibit 5.6
The equality of national income and product
This numerical example shows that the equality of national income and product is maintained when the government and foreign sectors, with their associated injections and leakages, are added to the economy. National product is a measure of the goods and services produced in the domestic economy. To arrive at its total, we add consumption, investment, and government purchases of all kinds, plus foreign purchases of domestically produced goods (exports), and we subtract the portion of consumption, investment, and government purchases devoted to foreign-made goods (imports). Using the term *net exports* to stand for exports minus imports, we could say that national product equals consumption plus investment plus government purchases plus net exports. This is equal to national income, which is divided among consumption, saving, and net taxes—as shown in the second part of the table.

Consumption	$ 70,000
Plus investment	22,000
Plus government purchases	10,000
Plus exports	8,000
Less imports	−10,000
Equals national product	$100,000
Consumption	$ 70,000
Plus saving	25,000
Plus net taxes	5,000
Equals national income	$100,000

or until production of goods and services increases, they must come out of inventory. Total investment, including unplanned inventory disinvestment, thus falls by $5,000 to compensate for the rise in government purchases.

Or suppose, again beginning from the situation shown in Exhibit 5.6, that foreigners suddenly decide to buy $2,000 less of U.S. goods. Exports will fall, but the $2,000 worth of goods that otherwise would have been exported will accumulate as unplanned inventories of U.S. firms, once again maintaining the required equality.

CONCLUSIONS

This chapter has served two basic purposes. One purpose has been to establish certain key equalities among items in the circular flow of income and product. The two most important of these equalities are the equality of national income and national product and the equality of injections and leakages. The equalities hold by definition, because they are based on the concept of total investment—which includes both planned and unplanned investment.

The other purpose the chapter has served has been to introduce the concepts of equilibrium and disequilibrium in the circular flow. These concepts depend crucially on the distinction between planned and unplanned investments, which are lumped together in defining the basic equalities. To be specific, the circular flow is said to be in equilibrium when, and only when, the plans of buyers and sellers exactly mesh, so that no unplanned inventory accumulation or depletion takes place. If buyers do not demand as much as firms supply, the excess products go into inventory, whether or not firms had planned to put them there. To correct any unplanned inventory accumulation, firms must cut output or reduce prices to boost sales. Either action causes the circular flow to shrink—when this flow is measured in terms of dollars spent on products or earned in incomes. If buyers demand more than firms currently produce, goods come out of inventory, even if firms had not planned to run their inventories down. This unplanned inventory depletion causes firms to raise prices or increase output, either of which causes the volume of the circular flow to grow.

SUMMARY

1. Two of the most important elements of the circular flow are national income and national product. These two elements are linked on one side by factor payments and on the other by total expenditures. National income and national product are equal.
2. Saving and investment can be added to the circular flow without disturbing the equality between national product and total expenditure. If total *planned* expenditure is not exactly equal to national product, unplanned inventory investment (positive or negative) will make up the difference between the two.
3. *Aggregate supply* is another term for national product and *aggregate demand* another term for total planned expenditure. When aggregate supply is equal to aggregate demand, unplanned inventory investment is zero, and the circular flow is said to be in equilibrium. When aggregate supply and demand are not equal, unplanned inventory investment (positive or negative) must take place. The circular flow is then said to be in disequilibrium.
4. Adding government and a foreign sector to the circular flow of income and product does not disturb the basic equalities of the circular flow. Total injections (investment plus government purchases plus exports) must equal total leakages (saving plus net taxes plus imports). National product (consumption plus investment plus government purchases plus net exports) must equal national income (consumption plus saving plus net taxes).

DISCUSSION QUESTIONS

1. Contrast the flow of money you put into your bank account each payday with the stock of money indicated by the balance in your passbook. How are the flow and stock related? Why is one referred to as a *flow* and the other as a *stock*?
2. In the real world, who are the savers and who are the investors? Provide examples of when a person can be both a saver and an investor. Describe situations where someone is a saver but not an investor, then an investor but not a saver.
3. In what sense is the owner of a grocery store chain "investing" when the store's inventories increase? How is this similar to investment in new display freezers for the stores? How is it different?
4. Because savers and investors are not always the same people, why is it that after-the-fact savings must always equal investment? Or must they? Is this relationship true in the real world or only under certain restrictive assumptions? Explain.
5. Suppose you bought a dollar's worth of gasoline. Trace through the route this dollar might take; in fact, trace several routes it might take to go through the whole circular flow.

6. Use the circular flow diagram to analyze each of the following:
   a. The interest rate falls, and businesses borrow more money and do more investing.
   b. People decide to work less; they prefer more time off to watch ball games or take up some other leisuretime activity.
   c. Governments in the economy raise their taxes.
   d. Firms decide to lower their inventories, so they lay off 10 percent of their work force.
   e. The government increases its flow of both taxes and government spending.
7. How would the circular flow model change if there were no money in the system—that is, if all exchanges had to be barter exchanges?
8. How do unemployed workers fit into the circular flow diagram? What flows are connected to them?

CHAPTER 6

MEASURING NATIONAL INCOME AND PRODUCT

WHAT YOU WILL LEARN IN THIS CHAPTER

This chapter will explain how the various elements of the circular flow of income and product can be measured. It will describe the methods used by government statisticians to measure both nominal national product and nominal national income and show why these flows, as officially measured, correspond only approximately to the theoretical concepts in the last chapter. The chapter will explain how changes in the price level can be measured by means of price indexes, and it will introduce several specific price indexes in common use. Finally, it will show what national income and product accounts cannot measure.

FOR REVIEW

Here are some important terms and concepts that will be put to use in this chapter. If you do not understand them, review them before proceeding.

- *Government purchases (Chapter 4)*
- *Transfer payments (Chapter 4)*
- *Basic equalities of the circular flow (Chapter 5)*

The last chapter cut the circular flow of income and product into convenient pieces and gave the pieces names like *national income, investment,* and *saving*. These concepts are basic to macroeconomic theory. Because they are so important, it is useful to know how they can be measured, so the theory can be compared to what happens in the real world. This chapter will take a brief tour through some of the basics of national income accounting. The chapter is divided into two parts, corresponding to the important distinction between nominal and real measures of national income and product and their component parts. **Nominal values,** discussed in the first part, are measurements that are made in terms of the actual market prices at which goods are sold. **Real values,** discussed in the second part, are measurements that are adjusted for inflation—for changes in the price level over time.

Nominal values Measurements of economic values made in terms of actual market prices at which goods are sold.

Real values Measurements of economic values that include adjustments for changes in prices between one year and another.

MEASURING NOMINAL NATIONAL INCOME AND PRODUCT

Gross National Product

Gross national product (GNP) The dollar value at current market prices of all final goods and services produced annually by the nation's economy.

Of all economic statistics, perhaps the most widely publicized is the measure of an economy's level of total production called the **gross national product (GNP).** This statistic represents the dollar value at current market prices (the

Final goods and services Goods and services sold directly for household consumption, business investment, or government purchase. Excludes intermediate goods sold for use as inputs in the production of other goods.

nominal value) of all final goods and services produced annually by the nation's economy. **Final goods and services** are goods and services sold directly for household consumption, business investment, government purchase, or export. Intermediate goods, such as the flour used to bake bread at commercial bakeries, are not counted in GNP. To count both the value of the flour at its market price (an intermediate good) and the value of the bread at its market price (a final good) would be to count the flour twice, because the value of the flour is included in the price of the bread.

In principle, GNP could be measured directly by constructing a table that shows the quantity of each final good and service produced—massages, apples, submarines, housing units, and all the rest—multiplying these quantities by the prices at which they were sold, and adding the resulting column of figures. But that is not what national income accountants actually do. Instead, they take a shortcut based on the equality of national product and total expenditure. In practice, GNP is measured by summing the nominal expenditures of all economic units on domestically produced final goods and services. This way of measuring aggregate economic activity is known as the **expenditure approach.** Exhibit 6.1 provides an illustration of how it works, using actual 1978 data for the U.S. economy.

Expenditure approach A method of estimating aggregate economic activity by adding together the nominal expenditure of all economic units on newly produced final goods and services.

Consumption Consumption expenditures by households and unattached persons fall into three categories: durable goods, nondurable goods, and services. In principle, goods that do not wear out entirely in one year—such as automobiles, furniture, and household appliances—are considered durable, and goods that are used up in less than a year—such as soap, food, and gasoline—are considered nondurable. (In practice, the classifications are often arbitrary. All clothing, for example, is considered nondurable, whether it is a pair of stockings, which may wear out in a matter of weeks, or a woolen overcoat, which may be used for a decade.) The remaining item, services, includes things that are not embodied in any physical object when sold, such as haircuts, legal advice, and education. No distinction is made between services that are durable and those that are nondurable in their effects.

Personal consumption expenditure		$1,340.1
Durable goods	$197.5	
Nondurable goods	430.3	
Services	616.2	
Plus gross private domestic investment		345.6
Fixed investment	329.6	
Change in business inventories	16.0	
Plus government purchases of goods and services		433.9
Federal	153.8	
State and local	280.2	
Plus net exports of goods and services		−12.0
Exports	204.8	
Less imports	−216.8	
Equals gross national product (GNP)		$2,107.6
Less capital consumption allowance		−216.9
Equals net national product (NNP)		$1,890.7

Exhibit 6.1
Nominal gross national product by type of expenditure, 1978 (in billions)
Gross national product is officially estimated by the expenditure approach. This means adding together the values of expenditures on newly produced goods and services made by all economic units to get a measure of aggregate economic activity. Net national product is derived from gross national product by excluding the value of investment expenditures that merely replace worn-out or obsolete capital equipment.

Source: U.S. Department of Commerce, *Survey of Current Business*, June 1979, p. S-1.

Both the goods and the services components of consumption contain items that are produced but that do not actually pass through the marketplace on their way to consumers. One such item is an estimate of the food produced and directly consumed on farms. Another is an estimate of the rental value of owner occupied homes. (Rental payments on tenant occupied housing are included automatically.)

Investment The item called *gross private domestic investment* is the sum of all firms' purchases of newly produced capital goods (fixed investment) plus changes in business inventories. Fixed investment, in turn, is broken down into the durable equipment of producers—such as machine tools, trucks, and office equipment—and new construction—including both business structures and residential housing.

When thinking about investment, keep in mind the phrase *newly produced capital goods.* The businessperson who buys a used machine is not engaging in an investment expenditure, according to the national income accountants' definition. The machine was already counted in some previous year. Also, people who speak of making investments in land or corporate bonds are not using the word *investment* in the national income accountants' sense. Real estate and securities are not capital goods. In fact, they are not even part of the more general category, goods and services, with which the measure of GNP is concerned.

Government Purchases The contribution that government makes to GNP at the federal, state, and local levels presents a special problem for national income accountants. Ideally, this contribution should be measured in terms of the value of the services that government produces—education, national defense, police protection, and all the rest. However, since very few government services are actually sold to consumers and businesses, there are no market prices in terms of which to value them. Instead, national income accountants use government purchases of goods and services to approximate the contribution of government to GNP.

Government purchases of goods and services, as explained in Chapter 4, include the wages and salaries of all civilian and military personnel hired by government plus the purchase of all the buildings, computers, assault rifles, paper clips, and so on used by those employees. Presumably, all the government workers using all that equipment produce an output at least as valuable as the same inputs could have produced in the private sector. In any event, that is the assumption that justifies inclusion of government purchases in GNP. Note that government transfer payments are not included, since they do not represent expenditures made to purchase newly produced goods or current services.

Net Exports The final item in GNP is net exports—the difference between the nominal value of goods and services exported abroad and the nominal value of goods and services imported from abroad. Exported goods must be added in because they are products produced in the United States, even though they are bought elsewhere. Imports must be subtracted because some of the expenditures on consumer goods, investment goods, and government purchases that have already been added in were purchases of goods made abroad; and these goods should not be counted as part of national product.

Gross versus Net National Product

What makes gross national product "gross"? It is the fact that gross private domestic investment is not a measure of the actual change in capital assets and business inventories for a particular year. In the process of production, existing buildings and equipment wear out or lose their value through obsolescence. As a result, the actual increase in the stocks of capital goods and business inventories each year, called *net private domestic investment,* is less than gross private domestic investment. Although depreciation and obsolescence are difficult to measure accurately, national income accountants make an approximation called the *capital consumption allowance*.

Investment that merely replaces plant and equipment that has worn out during the year does not move the economy ahead but only keeps it standing in the same place. Gross national product is thus, in a sense, an overstatement of how much the country is getting out of the economy. To arrive at a measure of national product that includes only the actual net increase in capital goods and business inventories, the capital consumption allowance is subtracted from GNP. The resulting figure is called net national product. All told, **net national product (NNP)** is the sum of personal consumption expenditure, net private domestic investment, government purchases of goods and services, and net exports of goods and services.

Net national product (NNP) A measure of national product adjusted to exclude the value of investment expenditures that merely replace worn-out or obsolete capital goods. Officially, NNP equals GNP minus the capital consumption allowance.

National Income

The chapter will turn now to a different way of measuring what goes on in the circular flow: the income approach to national income accounting. As the name implies, the **income approach** measures the overall nominal rate of the circular flow by adding up all the different kinds of income earned by households. This is done as shown in Exhibit 6.2. The categories of income used by national income accountants differ somewhat from the theoretical classification of incomes into wages, rent, interest, and profit; and they deserve some explanation.

Income approach A method of estimating aggregate economic activity by adding together the incomes earned by all households.

Compensation of employees includes not only wages and salaries but two other items as well. The first is employer contributions for social insurance. (Chapter 4 argued that the economic burden of these taxes was borne by employees even though employers actually made the payments.) The second is other labor income, which includes various fringe benefits received by employees.

Compensation of employees		$1,301.4
Wages and salaries	$1,101.0	
Employer contributions for social insurance	94.5	
Other labor income	105.9	
Plus rental income of persons		23.4
Plus net interest		106.3
Plus corporate profits		159.5
Dividends	49.3	
Corporate profits taxes	83.9	
Undistributed corporate profits	68.8	
Plus proprietors' income		113.2
Equals national income		$1,703.8

Exhibit 6.2
Nominal national income, 1978 (in billions)
National income is officially estimated by the income approach. This means adding together the values of all income earned by households. Note that some items of income, such as the portion of corporate profits that goes to pay corporate profits taxes, are counted as "earned" by households even though households never actually receive the income.

Source: U.S. Department of Commerce, *Survey of Current Business,* June 1979, pp. S-2, S-3.

Rental income of persons includes all income in the form of rent and royalties received by owners of property. Net interest is equal to household interest income minus consumer interest payments.

Corporate profits include all income earned by the owners (the stockholders) of corporations, whether they actually receive that income or not. Dividends are the part of the income that the owners actually receive. Another part goes to pay corporate profits taxes; and a third part, "undistributed corporate profits," is retained by the corporations to use for investment purposes.

The final component of national income, proprietors' income, is a sort of grab bag of all income earned by self-employed professionals and owners of unincorporated businesses. National income accountants make no attempt to sort out which parts of this income theoretically ought to be classified as wages, rent, interest, or profit.

The Relationship between National Income and GNP

In the simplified economy of Chapter 5, national income and national product were defined in such a way that they were exactly equal. In the real world, things do not work out quite so neatly. Some adjustments must be made so that national income, as measured by the income approach, fits GNP, as measured by the expenditure approach. These adjustments are shown in Exhibit 6.3.

For one thing, net and gross national product must be distinguished from each other—a difference ignored in elementary theoretical discussions. The investment expenditures made to replace worn-out or obsolete equipment are counted as part of the business expenses of firms, so they do not show up either in corporate profits or in proprietors' income. The first step in going from GNP to national income, then, is to subtract the capital consumption allowance, leaving net national product.

Next, an adjustment must be made to reflect the fact that some of the money firms receive from sales of their product is not "earned" by owners of the firms. Instead, it is taken directly by government in payment of so-called *indirect business taxes,* which include sales taxes, excise taxes, and business property taxes paid to federal, state, and local governments. These taxes are treated differently from the corporate income tax, which is considered to be money earned by owners and then taken by government out of corporate profits. Indirect business taxes are included in the prices of goods and services,

Exhibit 6.3

Relation of national income to GNP, 1978 (in billions)

In the simple world of elementary economic theory, national product and national income are equal by definition. In the real world, certain adjustments must be made to get GNP and national income to "fit." First, the capital consumption allowance is subtracted from GNP to get NNP. Then, indirect business taxes and the statistical discrepancy are subtracted from NNP to get national income.

Source: U.S. Department of Commerce, *Survey of Current Business,* June 1979, pp. 6–7.

Gross national product	$2,107.6
Less capital consumption allowance	−216.9
Equals net national product	$1,890.7
Less indirect business taxes[a]	−185.2
Less statistical discrepancy	−1.8
Equals national income	$1,703.7

[a] Includes minor adjustments for business transfer payments and net subsidies to government enterprises.

so they count as part of net national product; but they are not included in income, so they must be subtracted when going from NNP to national income, as shown in Exhibit 6.3.

In principle, subtracting the capital consumption allowance and indirect business taxes from GNP ought to give national income, but in practice there is one further difficulty. GNP is estimated by the expenditure approach, using one set of data, and national income is measured by the income approach, using an entirely different set of data. Inevitably, no matter how carefully the work is done, there are some errors and omissions, so that the two sets of figures do not quite fit. The difference between NNP minus indirect business taxes on the one hand and national income on the other is called the *statistical discrepancy*. The discrepancy has no theoretical significance; it is simply a "fudge factor" that makes things balance.

Personal Income National income, as mentioned several times, is a measure of income earned by households, whether or not those households ever actually get their hands on the income. For some purposes, it is more important to measure what households actually receive than what they earn. The total income actually received by households is called **personal income.**

Personal income The total of all income, including transfer payments, actually received by households before payment of personal income taxes.

Exhibit 6.4 shows the steps required to transform national income into personal income. First, three items that are earned by households but not received by them are subtracted. These items are contributions for social insurance (both employer and employee), corporate profits taxes, and undistributed corporate profits. Next, transfer payments—payments received by households although not earned by them—are added. The result is personal income.

Disposable personal income (disposable income) Personal income minus personal taxes.

One further income measure is shown at the bottom of Exhibit 6.4: **disposable personal income** (or **disposable income** for short). This income is what households have left of their personal income after they pay personal taxes of various kinds to federal, state, and local governments.

This completes the discussion of the nominal side of national income accounting. The next section turns to the problem of making adjustments for changing prices.

National income		$1,703.7
Less contributions for social insurance		−164.2
Employer contributions	$94.5	
Employee contributions	69.7	
Less corporate profits taxes		−83.9
Less undistributed corporate profits		−68.8
Plus transfer payments[a]		321.2
Equals personal income		$1,708.0
Less personal taxes		−256.2
Equals disposable personal income		$1,451.8

[a]Includes government and consumer interest payments and business transfer payments.

Exhibit 6.4
National income and personal income, 1978 (in billions)
National income is a measure of all income earned by households, while personal income is a measure of the income they actually receive. To go from national income to personal income, subtract payroll taxes, corporate profits taxes, and undistributed corporate profits; then add transfer payments. If personal taxes are subtracted from this figure, the result is personal income.

Source: U.S. Department of Commerce, *Survey of Current Business*, June 1979, pp. S-2, S-3.

MEASURING REAL INCOME AND PRICES

Measuring Real GNP

The investigation of real income and prices will begin with a look at an economy much simpler than that of the United States. This will permit the presentation of the essentials in the clearest possible way before getting into practical details.

Exhibit 6.5 shows nominal GNP accounts for two years in a simple economy where only three goods are produced: movies, apples, and shirts. It indicates that nominal GNP grew from $400 in 1972 to $1,000 in 1980. But how are these figures to be interpreted? Do they mean that people really had more of the things they wanted in 1980 than in 1972? More exactly, do they mean that people had 2.5 times as much? These questions require careful answers.

A line-by-line comparison of the two years in Exhibit 6.5 shows that the figures on nominal income do not tell the whole story. The problem is that prices went up sharply between 1972 and 1980. Movies cost twice what they used to, apples three times as much, and shirts half again as much. So how much more was really produced in the second year than in the first?

We can try looking directly at the quantities of individual goods and services produced. But if we do so, we get conflicting indications: Twice as many movies and shirts were produced in 1980 as in 1972 but only half as many apples. Instead, we can approach the matter in another way, by asking how much the total value of output would have changed from 1972 to 1980 *if prices had not changed.*

This approach to the problem gives the results shown in Exhibit 6.6. There, we see that the 1980 output of 100 movies, 500 apples, and 20 shirts, which had a value of $1,000 in terms of the prices at which the goods and services were actually sold, would have had a value of only $500 in terms of the prices that prevailed in 1972. The $500 figure is a measure of *real* GNP for 1980, and it is this measure that we should compare with the 1972 GNP of $400 if we want to know what really happened to physical production in the economy between the two years. Much of the apparent growth of the economy is seen to have been due to higher prices. Thus, instead of having 250 percent more in 1980 than in 1972 (an increase from $400 to $1,000), the people in this simple economy had only about 25 percent more (an increase from $400 to $500).

Exhibit 6.5
Nominal GNP in selected years for a simple economy
In this simple economy, where only three goods are produced, nominal national income grew from $400 in 1972 to $1,000 in 1980. Prices also went up in that time, though, so people did not really have 2.5 times as much of these things in 1980.

1972	Quantity	Price	Value
Movies	50	$ 2.00	$ 100
Apples	1,000	.20	200
Shirts	10	10.00	100
1972 nominal GNP			$ 400
1980			
Movies	100	$ 4.00	$ 400
Apples	500	.60	300
Shirts	20	15.00	300
1980 nominal GNP			$1,000

Exhibit 6.6
Nominal and real GNP in 1980 for a simple economy
This exhibit shows how the numbers from Exhibit 6.5 can be adjusted to take changing prices into account. The 1980 quantities are multiplied by 1972 prices to get the value of 1980 GNP as it would have been had prices not changed. The total of 1980 quantities valued at 1972 prices is called the real GNP for 1980.

	1980 Quantity	1980 Price	Value at 1980 Price	1972 Price	Value of 1980 Output at 1972 Price
Movies	100	$ 4.00	$ 400	$ 2.00	$200
Apples	500	.60	300	.20	100
Shirts	20	15.00	300	10.00	200
Totals		1980 nominal GNP =	$1,000	1980 real GNP =	$500

Price Indexes

In the example covered in Exhibits 6.5 and 6.6, while nominal GNP in 1980 rose to a level of $1,000 (from a $400 base in 1972), real GNP in 1980 rose only to $500. The ratio of 1980 nominal GNP to 1980 real GNP provides one possible measure of the rate of the price increase between the two years. The reason for the discrepancy between 1980 nominal and real GNP is that the price level doubled between the two years. This measure of price level changes, called the **GNP deflator,** is used in the United States to adjust national income statistics. The GNP deflator can be expressed by the formula:

GNP deflator A measure of the price level equal to the ratio of current year nominal GNP to current year real GNP times 100.

$$\text{GNP deflator} = \frac{\text{Current year output valued at current year prices}}{\text{Current year output valued at base year prices}} \times 100.$$

Applying the formula to the data in Exhibits 6.5 and 6.6 gives a value of 200 for the 1980 GNP deflator. Once the GNP deflator is calculated according to this formula, it can be used to adjust nominal data for price changes. Simply divide the nominal value in question by the GNP deflator, and multiply by 100.

Exhibit 6.7 gives nominal GNP, real GNP, and the GNP deflator for the U.S. economy since 1960. At the time of writing, the base year in use for the GNP deflator was 1972. (The base year is changed every decade or so.) For years after 1972, when the GNP deflator is greater than 100, nominal GNP must be adjusted downward (deflated) to get real GNP. For years before 1972, when the GNP deflator has a value of less than 100, applying the proper adjustment yields a real GNP that exceeds nominal GNP.

The Consumer Price Index Although the GNP deflator is the most broadly based price index for the U.S. economy, it is not the most widely publicized. That honor belongs instead to the consumer price index. The **consumer price index (CPI)** differs from the GNP deflator in two ways that make it particularly useful as a measure of the impact of inflation on the general public. First, it does not take into account the changing prices of final goods and services produced by the economy, as does the GNP deflator. Instead, it considers only those goods and services that make up the "market basket" purchased by the typical urban household.[1] Second, it is calculated according

Consumer price index (CPI) A measure of the price level based on a weighted average of the prices of goods purchased by a typical urban consumer.

[1]Up until 1978, the CPI was based more narrowly on the market basket purchased only by urban wage earners and clerical workers. The new index takes into account professionals, retired persons, unemployed persons, and all other urban residents as well.

Exhibit 6.7
Real and nominal GNP and the GNP deflator, 1960–1978 (in billions)
Part a of this exhibit shows real and nominal GNP for the U.S. economy since 1960. Note that they are equal in the base year, 1972. Part b of the exhibit shows the GNP deflator, which is the ratio of current year nominal GNP to current year real GNP. By convention, this ratio is usually multiplied by 100; for example, the GNP deflator for 1975 is stated as 127, not 1.27.

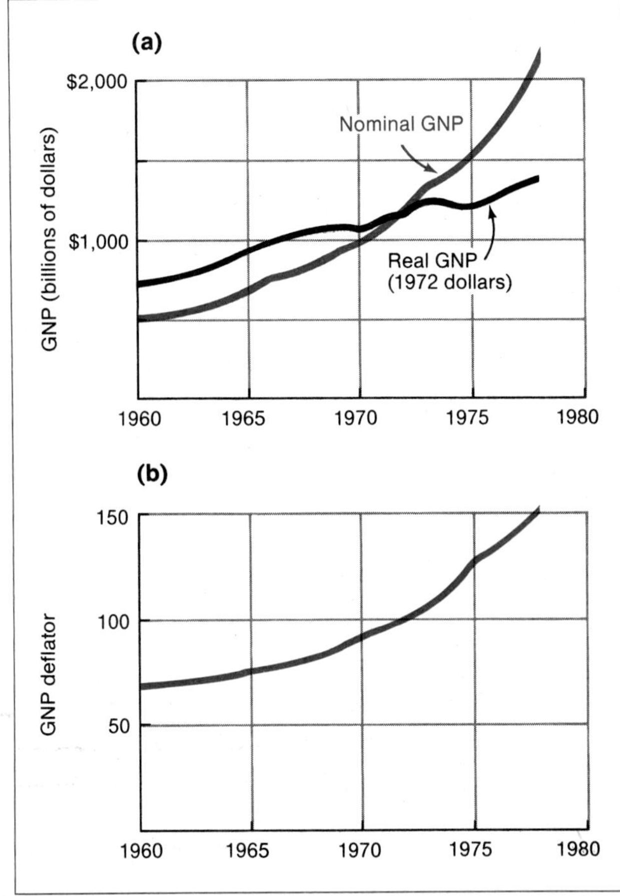

Source: President's Council of Economic Advisers, *Economic Report of the President* (Washington, D.C.: Government Printing Office, 1979), Tables B-1, B-2, B-3.

to the following formula, which does not require knowledge of quantities of output in the current period:

$$\text{Consumer price index} = \frac{\text{Base year market basket valued at current year prices}}{\text{Base year market basket valued at base year prices}} \times 100.$$

Because current price data are much easier to collect than current output data, the CPI is available each month only three weeks after the end of the month to which it applies. The GNP deflator, in contrast, is not available as rapidly; the final revised version of this index appears only several months after the close of the period to which it applies.

Comparing the CPI and the GNP Deflator Exhibit 6.8 shows how the consumer price index can be calculated using the data for the simplified economy first displayed in Exhibit 6.5. Notice that the value of the CPI, 237.5, differs from the value of the GNP deflator, 200, calculated from exactly the same underlying data. Which, if either, of the two price indexes is the true measure of change in the price level between the two years?

The reply is that neither the CPI nor the GNP deflator is *the* correct measure of change in the price level. Instead, each is the answer to a quite

Exhibit 6.8
Calculation of consumer price index for a simplified economy

The consumer price index is the base year market basket of goods valued at current year prices divided by the base year market basket of goods valued at base year prices, multiplied by 100. This exhibit shows how a CPI can be calculated using the data for the simplified economy first given in Exhibit 6.5. The 1972 output cost $400 at the prices at which it was actually sold. If it had been sold at 1980 prices, it would have cost $950. The CPI for 1980 is thus 237.5.

Good	1972 Quantity	1972 Price	Value of 1972 Quantity at 1972 Price	1980 Price	Value of 1972 Quantity at 1980 Price
Movies	50	$ 2.00	$100	$ 4.00	$200
Apples	1,000	.20	200	.60	600
Shirts	10	10.00	100	15.00	150
Totals			$400		$950

$$\text{CPI} = \frac{\$950}{\$400} \times 100 = 237.5$$

different question. The GNP deflator is the answer to the question: How much more did the 1980 output cost at the prices at which it was actually sold than it would have cost if it had been sold at 1972 prices instead? The CPI, in contrast, is the answer to the question: How much more would the 1972 output have cost if it had been sold at 1980 prices instead of at its actual 1972 prices?

Careful inspection of Exhibit 6.5 shows why the answers to the two questions are not the same. In 1972, lots of apples and not very many shirts were produced in comparison to the outputs of 1980. Yet, between the two years, the price of apples increased 300 percent while the price of shirts increased only 150 percent. Because the CPI uses base year quantities, it gives heavy weight to apples, which experienced the greatest price increase, and not much weight to shirts, which experienced only a modest price increase. In contrast, the GNP deflator uses current year quantities, thereby downplaying the importance of apples and emphasizing that of shirts.

In general, if there is a tendency for the quantities consumed of goods whose prices increase relatively slowly to grow more rapidly than the quantities consumed of goods whose prices increase relatively rapidly, the CPI will indicate more rapid inflation than will the GNP deflator. There is a slight tendency for this to be true in the U.S. economy, although the discrepancy between the two measures of inflation is not nearly so great as in the simplified numerical example.

Exhibit 6.9a shows what has happened to the CPI since 1960. Note that the Bureau of Labor Statistics uses 1967 as the base year for the CPI, whereas 1972 is used by the Department of Commerce in calculating the GNP deflator. Exhibit 6.9b shows a typical use to which the CPI can be put—namely, adjusting average weekly earnings in private nonagricultural industries for changes in the cost of living. Each year's figure for real earnings is equal to that year's nominal earnings divided by the consumer price index, then multiplied by 100. Real and nominal earnings thus cross in 1967, the base year used for the CPI.

Exhibit 6.9
Consumer price index and weekly earnings, 1960–1978

Part a of this exhibit shows what has happened to the consumer price index for the U.S. economy since 1960. Note that the CPI uses 1967 as a base year. Part b shows a typical application of the CPI—namely, adjusting average hourly earnings in nonagricultural industry for changes in the cost of living.

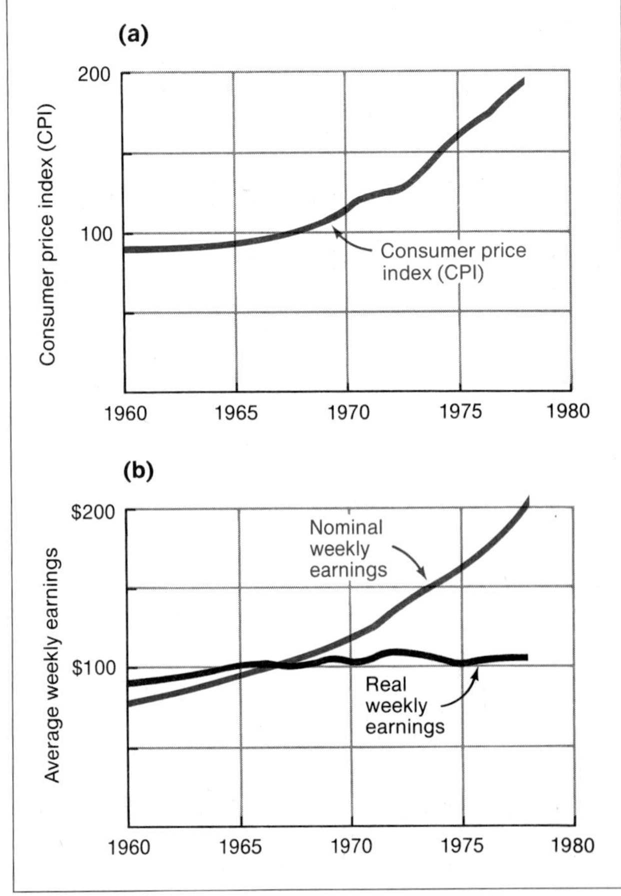

Source: President's Council of Economic Advisers, *Economic Report of the President* (Washington, D.C.: Government Printing Office, 1979), Tables B-35, B-49.

The Producer Price Index The Bureau of Labor Statistics publishes one other price index that is widely publicized—the **producer price index**. It is calculated with base year quantities, just as is the consumer price index, but the market basket of goods included is quite different. Rather than covering consumer goods, it covers a selection of producer goods bought and sold by the nation's business firms. The producer price index, in turn, is broken down into separate indexes for raw goods, intermediate goods, and finished producer goods. In 1978, the Bureau of Labor Statistics made some major methodological alterations in its treatment of price changes for producer goods; at that time, it also changed the name of the series, which it had called the *wholesale price index*. The old name continues to be used occasionally in reference to the new producer price index.

Producer price index A measure of the price level based on a weighted average of prices of crude, semi-finished, and finished producer goods bought and sold by private firms.

Like the consumer price index, the producer price index is published monthly. Because it measures the prices of inputs used to produce consumer goods, an acceleration in the rate of increase of the producer price index is widely thought to indicate worsening inflation for consumer goods a few months later.

Biases in Price Indexes It was noted earlier that changes in the relative quantities of goods produced may tend to make the consumer price index increase more rapidly than the GNP deflator. For this reason, the CPI is sometimes said to have an *upward bias*. Because it also uses base year quantities, the producer price index has a similar upward bias relative to the GNP deflator.

There is, however, a much more troublesome source of upward bias that affects all price indexes, regardless of the formulas on which they are based. This bias has its origin in quality changes rather than quantity changes. It would be highly misleading, for example, to say that the price of a new automobile increased by 300 percent between 1958 and 1978 if the 1978 car was more durable, got better gas mileage, and was significantly safer than its predecessor of a generation ago. National income accountants try to adjust the price changes of important classes of goods, such as automobiles, for changes in quality; but the adjustments are of necessity subjective, and they are widely criticized as inadequate.

Robert J. Gordon of Northwestern University is one economist who has studied the problem of quality adjustment. Although recognizing the efforts made to adjust the prices of automobiles for quality changes, he finds other major quality changes inadequately accounted for. He cites such changes in desk calculators as an example. As recently as the late 1960s, it cost more than $1,000 to buy an electromechanical desk calculator that would add, subtract, multiply, and divide. A decade later, a hand-held electronic calculator could be purchased for as little as $10. The new calculator would not only add, subtract, multiply, and divide many times faster and more quietly but would extract square roots in the bargain. Yet, because of the way the Bureau of Labor Statistics "linked" its old price series for electromechanical calculators with its new series for electronic calculators, the price decrease was understated by a factor of ten.[2]

CONCLUSIONS

We have now looked in some detail at the ways nominal and real GNP are measured. In conclusion, it will be well to give some idea of the limitations of these measurements. Several points need to be made in this connection.

First, much economic activity is not included in GNP at all. There are whole industries—gambling, bootlegging, narcotics, prostitution—whose multi-billion-dollar sales go unreported because they are illegal. Some legal economic activity also goes unreported for purposes of tax evasion. Other market activity—such as babysitting and casual yard work—goes unreported because it is too scattered to keep track of, even though the total sums involved may be quite large. The size of the underground market economy is surely large—perhaps as much as 10 percent of reported GNP. Even this does not count the enormous amount of nonmarket economic activity that takes place, including such highly valuable services as unpaid housekeeping and child care.

Second, even if real GNP did accurately measure the level of market and nonmarket economic activity, it would still not be a very good measure of welfare or human satisfaction. For example, the way income is distributed may affect the level of satisfaction. The level of real GNP per capita does not

---

[2]This example is given by Gordon in his text, *Macroeconomics* (Boston: Little, Brown, 1978), app. A-2, p. xiii. It is based on work done for his forthcoming book, *The Measurement of Durable Goods Prices*, to be published by the National Bureau of Economic Research.

directly reflect the number of families in poverty or the relative income status of upper- and lower-income groups. This is as it must be, because positive economics as a science cannot compare the relative satisfactions of different people. It cannot say what effect a redistribution of income has on "total" satisfaction. Do the recipients of government transfers gain more welfare than the taxpayers lose? There is no scientific way to tell.

Third, fewer and fewer labor hours per worker are devoted to producing real GNP as the years go by. It is plausible to think that more leisure will cause satisfaction to rise. Leisure is evidently a scarce economic good valued by workers. However, the substantial increase in the leisure of the U.S. worker in this century is not explicitly reflected in GNP calculations.

Fourth, real GNP is a measure only of currently produced goods and services. Satisfaction also comes from durable consumer goods produced in the past that are still providing services. Surely, the larger the present stock of consumer durables, the higher is satisfaction.

Fifth, the market prices at which goods are sold do not accurately reflect costs or benefits affecting third parties not directly involved in the exchange. For example, environmental pollution caused by productive activities detracts from welfare. Pollution adversely affects people who are neither buyers nor sellers of the goods whose production created it. Like several of the nonmarket goods discussed above that affect satisfaction, pollution is not entered into GNP calculations. Unlike those goods, however, pollution is a "bad"—an output with a negative value. Annual additions to the amount of pollution should, in principle, be subtracted from GNP; but practical problems make this adjustment impossible.[3]

Sixth, an increase in output does not necessarily imply an increase in welfare, even if none of the problems yet mentioned are there. An unseasonably cold winter, for example, or an epidemic of infectious disease could cause the purchases of heating fuel or medical services to rise dramatically. Yet the resulting increases in real GNP would hardly represent an increase in satisfaction! Wartime defense expenditures provide another example of the lack of direct correspondence between output and welfare. We could argue that in principle these kinds of expenditures are for the maintenance of the stock of human beings and should be treated just like investment expenditures that offset depreciation of the capital stock; that is, they should be subtracted from real GNP to get real NNP. Putting this idea into practice, however, would be difficult.

Finally, many aspects of human welfare are not related at all to the flow of economic goods and services or to the economic satisfaction obtained from them. Everyone would agree that people do not live by bread alone, but obtaining agreement about exactly what else is important would not be easy. How important are unspoiled natural areas, unalienating work, loving human contact, social justice, income equality, economic growth, and freedom? These are normative questions that each person must answer individually. The positive economist could never hope to lump these social and economic conditions into an objective measure of social welfare.

For all these reasons, then, real GNP should never be interpreted as a

---

[3]The best one can probably do is to subtract from GNP the total expenditures made solely to abate or prevent pollution. Even after such cleanup expenditures, however, enough pollution remains to adversely affect welfare.

measure of social welfare. Still, it is not completely worthless. It provides a roughly accurate picture of the economy's annual production of final goods and services, which, of course, is all that it was ever intended to do. As will be seen, it is valuable for several purposes even given its limitations.

SUMMARY

1. Official measurements of national product are made using the expenditure approach. Gross national product is obtained by adding together the values of all expenditures on newly produced goods and services. Net national product is derived from gross national product by excluding the value of investment expenditures that merely replace worn-out or obsolete capital equipment.
2. National income is officially estimated by the income approach, which means adding together the values of all income earned by households. In the real world, certain adjustments must be made to get GNP and national income to fit, even though for elementary theoretical purposes, the two are considered equal. The difference between GNP and national income is equal to the capital consumption allowance plus indirect business taxes plus the statistical discrepancy.
3. National income measures all income earned by households, while personal income measures all the income they actually receive. To go from national income to personal income means subtracting payroll taxes, corporate profits taxes, and undistributed corporate profits, then adding transfer payments. If personal taxes are subtracted from personal income, the result is disposable personal income.
4. Measurements of aggregate economic activity can be made in real terms in order to adjust for changes in prices. Real GNP means the total value of current year quantities of output evaluated in terms of the prices of some base year. The GNP deflator is the ratio of current year nominal GNP to current year real GNP.
5. Real GNP does not attempt to be a measure of welfare or satisfaction; it is only a measure of the output of goods and services. It does not do even that job perfectly because of sampling error, omitted items, and biases in price indexes. It is important to remember that a great many things contribute to overall human welfare that are not in any way measured by GNP.

DISCUSSION QUESTIONS

1. In 1967, the base year for the consumer price index, average earnings of construction workers were $154.95 per week. By November 1978, earnings in construction had reached $328 per week, but the CPI stood at 202. What were real earnings in November 1978, stated in 1967 dollars?
2. If all parents in the United States traded off child care services with their neighbors, received a wage for doing their neighbors' work, and hence did none of their own child care, what would happen to GNP as measured by national income accountants? Who, if anyone, would be better off with a situation where everyone got paid? Explain.
3. Do you think transfer payments should be included in the measure of GNP? Explain.
4. In 1933, net private domestic investment was equal to minus 6.1 billion dollars. How could this have been possible?

5. A firm gets rid of its inventory of $10,000 worth of shoes by having a sale to the public. What happens to GNP in this case? What happens to each of its components?
6. If the government increased the social security payroll deduction from 6 to 10 percent, what would happen to GNP, national income, and personal income?
7. Determine whether each of the following expenditures of an individual's own earnings is consumption, saving, investment, or something else:
   a. Purchase of a new home.
   b. Purchase of a new automobile for cash.
   c. Payment of a monthly installment on a loan.
   d. Purchase of an item of clothing for $4 plus $.20 sales tax.
   e. Purchase of common stock.
   f. Giving the individual's children a weekly allowance.
   g. Payment of tuition for additional education.
   h. A tip at a restaurant.
8. The following table shows output and prices for a simple economy in 1967 and 1977. Use the data to calculate both the CPI and the GNP deflator for 1977, using 1967 as the base year.

	1967 Quantity	1967 Price	1977 Quantity	1977 Price
Cars	1,000	$ 2,500	2,000	$ 4,000
Houses	100	20,000	150	40,000
Hospital services (total days of care)	500	100	550	250

SUGGESTIONS FOR FURTHER READING

Abraham, William I. *National Income and Economic Accounting.* Englewood Cliffs, N.J.: Prentice-Hall, 1969.
A standard text, useful for reference.

President's Council of Economic Advisers. *Economic Report of the President.* Washington, D.C.: Government Printing Office, annually.
A readily available source for national income data (and much other useful data as well).

U.S. Department of Commerce. *Survey of Current Business.* Washington, D.C.: Government Printing Office, monthly.
Recent data on national income.

U.S. Department of Commerce. *The National Income and Product Accounts for the United States, 1929–74.* Washington, D.C.: Government Printing Office, 1976.
Provides historical data on all items in the national accounts plus notes on methodology.

C H A P T E R 7

THE GOALS OF STABILIZATION POLICY AND THE PERFORMANCE OF THE U.S. ECONOMY

WHAT YOU WILL LEARN IN THIS CHAPTER

The three major goals of stabilization policy are full employment, price stability, and growth of real output. This chapter reviews the past performance of the economy in terms of each of these goals, paying particular attention to the human costs of failure to achieve each of them. The chapter concludes with a discussion of important interrelationships among the three policy goals.

FOR REVIEW

Here are some important terms and concepts that will be put to use in this chapter. If you do not understand them, review them before proceeding.

- *Production possibility frontier (Chapter 1)*
- *Marginal tax rate (Chapter 4)*
- *Stocks and flows (Chapter 5)*
- *National income and product (Chapters 5 and 6)*
- *Price indexes (Chapter 6)*

Economic stabilization policy, one of the major functions of government listed in Chapter 4, can be broken down into the pursuit of three more specific policy goals: full employment, price stability, and growth of real output.

The legal framework for the federal government's economic stabilization policy is the Employment Act of 1946, as recently amended. The original 1946 act declared simply:

> It is the continuing policy and responsibility of the federal government to use all practical means consistent with its needs and obligations and other essential considerations of national policy, with assistance and cooperation of industry, agriculture, labor and state and local governments, to coordinate and utilize all its plans, functions, and resources for the purpose of creating and maintaining in a manner calculated to foster and promote free competitive enterprise and the general welfare, conditions under which will be afforded useful employment opportunities, including self-employment, for those able, willing and seeking to work and to promote maximum employment, production and purchasing power.

In 1978, after several years of high inflation and unemployment, Congress amended the 1946 legislation with the Full Employment and Balanced Growth Act of 1978, popularly known as the **Humphrey-Hawkins Act.** This act established for the first time specific numerical goals for employment and price

Humphrey-Hawkins Act An act amending the Employment Act of 1946 by adding specific numerical policy targets for unemployment and inflation and by attempting to improve coordination of stabilization policies pursued by various branches of the federal government. Formally known as the Full Employment and Balanced Growth Act of 1978.

stability to supplement the general language of the 1946 act quoted here. The employment target, to be achieved by 1983, specifies that the unemployment rate is to be reduced to 4 percent of the labor force. (There is also a supplementary target of 3 percent unemployment for persons aged twenty-four or older.) At the same time, the rate of inflation as measured by the consumer price index is to be reduced to zero by 1988, with an interim target of 3 percent inflation to be achieved by 1983. In addition to setting these targets, the Humphrey-Hawkins Act contains provisions intended to improve the coordination of stabilization policy among the administration, the Congress, and the federal monetary authorities.

Using the Humphrey-Hawkins Act as a framework, we turn now to a discussion of each of the three goals of stabilization policy.

THE FULL EMPLOYMENT GOAL

When the Employment Act of 1946 was first passed, the memory of the Great Depression of the 1930s was still fresh in the minds of members of Congress. The goal of full employment had a simple meaning: jobs for people who wanted jobs. There was to be no repetition of the experience of the previous decade, when millions of heads of households lost jobs at which they had been steadily employed and spent years in the breadlines with little or no hope of new employment. Today, however, nearly half a century after the depression, the once-simple goal of full employment no longer seems so easy to define. The pursuit of full employment has, in fact, become a bewildering numbers game in which the human meaning of employment and unemployment is easily lost. It is important, then, to look carefully at how the official unemployment numbers are generated.

Measuring Unemployment

Classifying the Population by Employment Status The unemployment rate—probably the most widely watched statistic in the entire economy—is a measure of the stock of people unemployed as of a particular date. It is based on a breakdown of the U.S. population into a number of groups and subgroups, as shown in Exhibit 7.1.

Beginning at the left-hand side of the exhibit, the first box represents all people who are under sixteen years of age, are members of the armed forces, or are otherwise institutionalized. These people are considered not to be even potential participants in the labor force. Although people do move in and out of this group, the moves are the result of factors that are not strictly economic or even under control of the individual, such as aging, imprisonment, or discharge from the armed forces.

All people who are not in the group just described are said to be in the noninstitutional adult civilian population. This group, in turn, is divided into three groups, as shown in Exhibit 7.1. The first consists of all people who are employed. The Bureau of Labor Statistics counts as **employed** all people who work at least one hour a week for pay or at least fifteen hours per week as unpaid workers in a family business. People who have a job from which they are temporarily absent because of bad weather, labor disputes, or vacations are also counted as employed.

Employed Officially, any person who works at least one hour per week for pay or at least fifteen hours per week as an unpaid worker in a family business.

Exhibit 7.1
Classification of the population by employment status
This exhibit shows how the entire U.S. population is broken down into groups and subgroups according to employment status. People under sixteen, in the armed forces, or in institutions are considered not to be even potential participants in the labor market. Of the noninstitutional adult civilian population, only those working or actively looking for work are considered part of the labor force. The unemployment rate is the ratio of the number of unemployed to the number in the labor force.

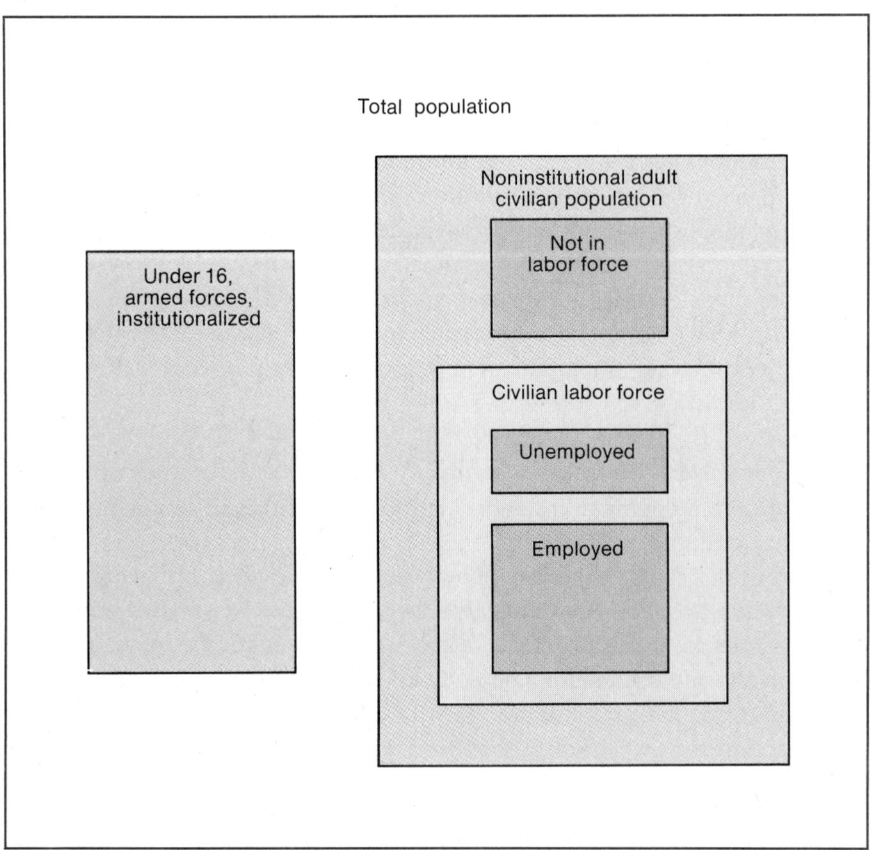

The second group is made up of the officially unemployed. In principle, to be counted as **unemployed,** one must be without a job but actively looking for one. There are, however, two exceptions. One is that people who have found a job they expect to start within thirty days are counted as unemployed even if they are not actively looking for temporary work to fill in until the job begins. In addition, people temporarily laid off from a job to which they expect to be recalled need not actively look for alternative work in order to be considered unemployed.

Unemployed Officially, any person without a job but actively looking for one.

Taken together, the employed and the unemployed constitute the **civilian labor force.** The remaining group shown in Exhibit 7.1 can thus be described as consisting of all noninstitutionalized civilians aged sixteen and older who are not in the labor force. (The box is labeled "not in labor force" for short.) These people are not counted as unemployed even though they are not employed.

Civilian labor force All members of the noninstitutionalized adult civilian population who are either officially employed or officially unemployed.

Unemployment rate The percentage of the civilian labor force not employed.

The Unemployment Rate We are now ready for a formal definition of the **unemployment rate.** Officially defined in terms of the stocks shown in Exhibit 7.1, it is simply the percentage of the civilian labor force that is not employed.

The Bureau of Labor Statistics, in cooperation with the Bureau of the Census, obtains the data needed to make unemployment measurements from a monthly sample of about fifty thousand randomly selected households. Field agents go to preselected houses and ask a series of specific questions about the job status of each member of the household. The questions include such things as: Did anyone work last week? Did anyone look for work? How long has the person been looking for work? How did the person go about looking? The result is one headline-making percentage plus a large array of supplementary tables that receive much less public attention.

Clearly, there are a lot of gray areas in the measurement of unemployment. The official unemployment rate can equally well be criticized for understating or overstating the "true" number of the unemployed. One way to bring out some of the gray areas in the measurement of unemployment is to compare the official definition of unemployment with two commonsense definitions—namely, "not working" and "can't find a job."

Unemployed versus "Not Working" The official definitions of employment and unemployment are clearly far different from the simple notions of "working" and "not working."

On the one hand, there are many people who work but who are not officially employed. Probably the largest group consists of people working full time at housekeeping and child care. These occupations are counted as employment only if done for pay; but, of course, the majority of such work is not done for pay. There also are many children under sixteen who work at least part time for pay, although they are not counted as employed. In addition, members of the armed forces are clearly working, in the normal sense of the word, as are at least some prisoners and other institutionalized individuals.

On the other hand, not everyone who is not working is unemployed. There are, of course, all those people who are not actively looking for work. There are also those temporarily absent from their jobs who are counted as employed even though they are not working. Finally, there are those working only part time but actively seeking full-time employment. Sometimes these people are referred to as "underemployed."

Unemployed versus "Can't Find a Job" The other commonsense definition of unemployment, "can't find a job," also fits the official definition only loosely. In some ways, the official definition overstates the number of people who can't find a job. As mentioned above, some people counted as unemployed actually have jobs to which they expect to be recalled or which they expect to begin within thirty days. Other people counted as unemployed could easily find some job but prefer to take their time looking for just the kind of job they want. (People who are not the only income earners in their households, for example, are likely to look longer and be more selective than those with no other income.) Still other people register as unemployed to fulfill the work requirement of certain income transfer programs even though they may not be qualified for any available work and may only go through the motions of looking. Finally, it is questionable whether the description "can't find a job" fits people who could have stayed on at their last job but quit voluntarily to look for another.

In other ways, however, the official definition of unemployment understates the number of people who can't find a job. The most important group who can't find a job but are not counted as unemployed are the so-called discouraged workers. These are people who would take a job if one were available but who do not actively look for work because they know there is little hope of finding anything suitable. The discouraged worker phenomenon is thought to be particularly prevalent among teenagers and minorities. The description "can't find a job" also fits many of those workers mentioned above who have part-time jobs but would take full-time jobs if they could be found.

The National Commission on Employment and Unemployment Statistics The problems with the official unemployment numbers are widely recognized, but there is little agreement as to how they can be corrected. In 1976, Congress established a National Commission on Employment and Unemployment Statistics to look into the question. Chaired by Sar Levitan of George Washington University, the commission has until September 1981 to issue its final recommendations.

Among the possible reforms being examined by the commission are the inclusion of discouraged workers among the unemployed and the establishment of a "hardship index" to supplement the unemployment index. The latter would attempt to measure the number of people unable to find a job that provides them with an adequate income. Some people with very low paying full-time jobs would be classified as experiencing hardship, whereas people who were officially unemployed but members of households having adequate income from other sources would be excluded from the hardship index.

The commission is also considering some changes in the definition of the noninstitutional adult civilian population. One proposal is to include military personnel in the labor force, on the ground that, in the era of the volunteer army, military service is not much different from a civilian job. Another proposal is to exclude sixteen- or seventeen-year-olds from the adult population, as officially defined.

The Unemployment Record

Whatever changes the commission may end up recommending, the Humphrey-Hawkins Act goals are supposed to be achieved in terms of the definitions in force in 1978, when the act was originally passed. Measured against the goal of a 4 percent unemployment rate for the population as a whole, the employment record of the U.S. economy is mixed at best. Exhibit 7.2 displays data for the years 1950 through 1979. In this thirty-year stretch, the 4 percent target was achieved only during the Korean War years, 1951–1953, and during the Vietnam War years 1966–1969. The target was not met for even a single year of the 1970s. In May 1975, the unemployment rate hit 9 percent, its highest level since the Great Depression.

An important part of the job in the next eleven chapters will be to build a theory capable of shedding some light on the reasons for the apparent worsen-

Exhibit 7.2
Unemployment in the United States since 1950
The Humphrey-Hawkins Act of 1978 set a 4 percent unemployment rate target for the U.S. economy, to be achieved by 1983. As this figure shows, the goal is an ambitious one. Unemployment rates below 4 percent have been achieved in only seven out of the past thirty years, during the Korean and Vietnam wars.

Source: President's Council of Economic Advisers, *Economic Report of the President* (Washington, D.C.: Government Printing Office, 1979), Table B–29.

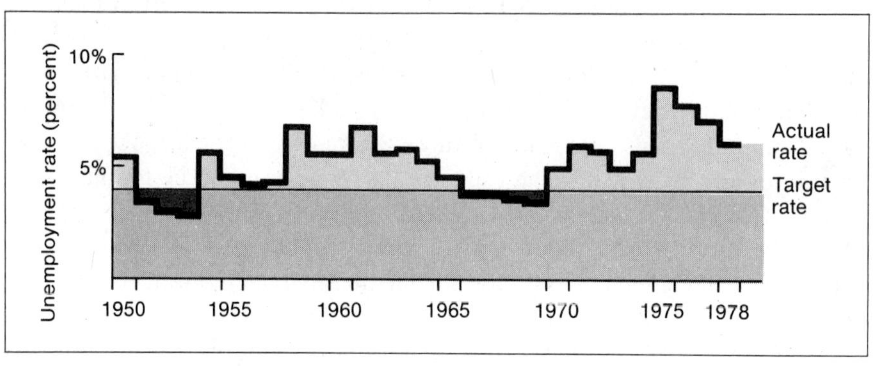

ing of the average unemployment rate during the 1970s. The same theory will also be useful in evaluating the prospects for meeting the employment goals for the 1980s set by the Humphrey-Hawkins Act.

Distribution of the Burdens of Unemployment

The burdens of unemployment, and hence the potential benefits of a full employment policy, are not at all evenly distributed over the population. Married men, for example, have a relatively low exposure to unemployment. In 1969, the best recent year for employment, married men experienced an unemployment rate of just 1.5 percent. This presumably is very nearly the minimum possible in an economy where workers are free to move from job to job when they choose. Even at the height of the 1975 recession, the unemployment rate for married men rose no higher than 5.7 percent.

Other groups in the population, however, have much higher exposure to unemployment. As Exhibit 7.3 shows, women, nonwhites, and teenagers all experience much higher levels of unemployment than married men. The unemployment rate for black teenagers exceeded 35 percent at some points in the late seventies, higher than the general unemployment rate during the worst years of the Great Depression.

Would those who now bear the greatest burden of unemployment reap the greatest benefits from a full employment policy such as that proposed by the Humphrey-Hawkins Act? According to a recent study by economists Kim B. Clark and Lawrence H. Summers of the National Bureau of Economic Research, the answer is a qualified yes.[1] Achieving the goals of the Humphrey-Hawkins Act would require a reduction of about one percentage point in the unemployment rate of "prime" workers (that is, adult males). Clark and

[1]NBER discussion paper no. 274, August 1978.

Exhibit 7.3
Unemployment rates by population subgroups
The burden of unemployment is not evenly distributed among various subgroups of the population. As this exhibit shows, women, nonwhites, and teenagers all experience much higher rates of unemployment than married men. The rates for the groups most seriously affected by unemployment are highly sensitive to changes in the overall employment picture.

Source: President's Council of Economic Advisers, *Economic Report of the President* (Washington, D.C.: Government Printing Office, 1979), Table B-29.

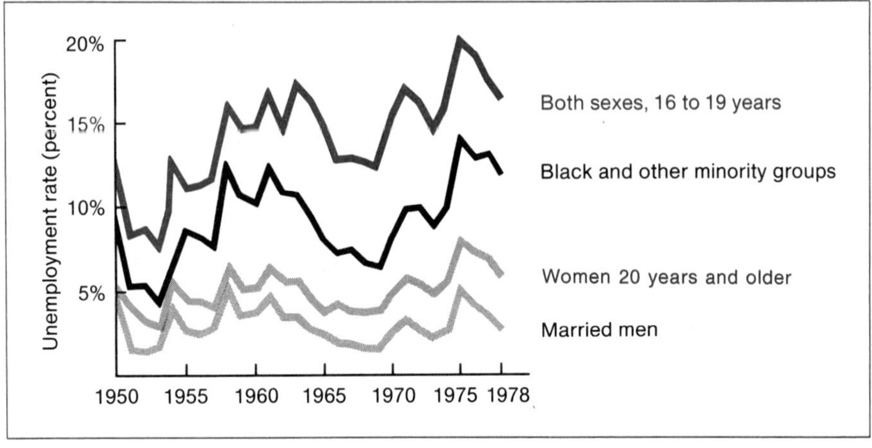

Summers indicate that such a change in the unemployment rate would be associated with approximately the following increases in employment for the groups currently experiencing the worst unemployment rates: for all male teenagers, a 4.6 percent gain in employment; for nonwhite male teenagers, a 6.3 percent gain; for all female teenagers, a 4.1 percent gain; and for nonwhite female teenagers, a 6.4 percent gain.

These employment gains would result partly from the employment of teenagers currently counted as unemployed and partly from the employment of those who would be drawn into the labor force for the first time by the greater availability of jobs. Although employment gains of the magnitude indicated by Clark and Summers would surely be welcomed, they would still leave the teenage unemployment rate as a whole over 12 percent and the rate for nonwhite teenagers over 30 percent.

PRICE STABILITY: MEASUREMENT AND PERFORMANCE

The price stability goals of the Humphrey-Hawkins Act are stated in terms of the consumer price index. As shown in Chapter 6, the CPI is an index of the prices paid for the goods and services making up the market basket of a typical urban household. The Humphrey-Hawkins Act specifies that the rate of increase of this index should slow to 3 percent per year by 1983 and to zero by 1988.

These goals appear relatively modest in historical perspective. It has been estimated that over the full century from the Civil War to the 1960s, the rate of

Exhibit 7.4
Inflation in the United States since 1950
The Humphrey-Hawkins Act of 1978 established an interim inflation target of 3 percent, to be attained by 1983. As this exhibit shows, the target is a modest one by standards of earlier years, but it would represent a significant deceleration from inflation rates prevailing in the late 1970s.

Source: President's Council of Economic Advisers, *Economic Report of the President* (Washington, D.C.: Government Printing Office, 1979), Table B–49.

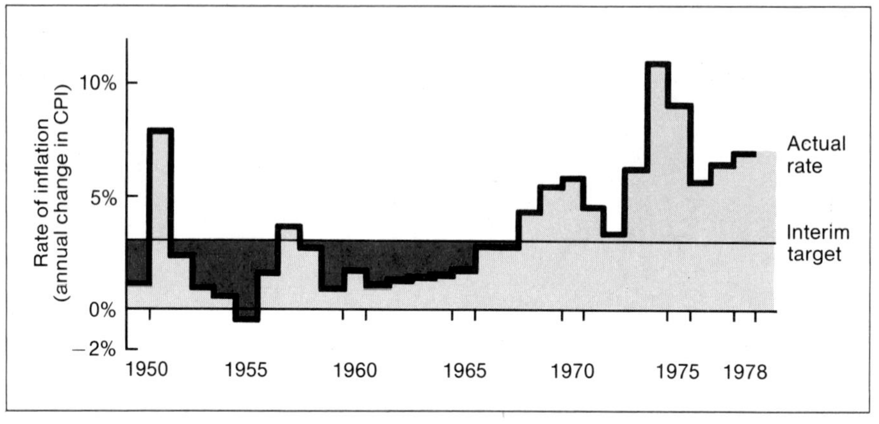

inflation averaged only about 2 percent per year. Much of that slow rate of price increase presumably was offset by unmeasured improvements in the quality of goods and services. It would not be straying far from the truth, then, to say that, historically, price stability has been the norm for the U.S. economy and inflation the exception.

However, as Exhibit 7.4 shows, several recent years have been among the exceptional ones. Although inflation exceeded the 3 percent Humphrey-Hawkins target in only two years from 1950 to 1968, it has exceeded 3 percent in every year since 1968. The inflationary experience from 1968 to the present has greatly increased the attention given to the goal of price stability by both policy makers and economists. Considerable space in the following chapters will be devoted to reviewing recent theories of inflation and policy measures proposed to deal with it.

Who Gains and Who Loses from Inflation?

As in the case of unemployment, the burdens of inflation and the potential benefits of a policy of price stability are not distributed equally among various groups in the population. Determining exactly who gains and who loses from inflation, however, is by no means an easy problem. One way to get an idea of the distributional effects of inflation is to look separately at its effects on wage and salary income, transfer payments, interest income, wealth, and taxes. After this has been done, a recent statistical study that attempts to summarize the various effects will be examined.

Wage and Salary Income Because wages and salaries rise roughly in step with prices, real income from these sources is among the areas least affected by inflation. For example, between 1968 and the end of 1978, while the consumer price index rose from its base of 100 to a level of 200, average earnings in manufacturing rose from $3.01 per hour to $6.28 per hour, slightly more than keeping pace. In a number of industries, wages are **indexed**—adjusted automatically for changes in the cost of living through escalator clauses. Not all wage and salary earners are well protected from inflation, of course; but to find the really major distributive effects of inflation, one needs to look elsewhere.

Indexing The practice of automatically adjusting wages, salaries, or other payments to compensate for changes in the price level.

Transfer Payments Over the last decade, total transfer payments have increased much more rapidly than the rate of inflation. Much of the increase, however, can be attributed to changes in social policy not directly related to inflation one way or the other. The relevant question is not whether transfer payments have increased in real terms but whether they have increased as much as they would have if price stability had been maintained.

There is no way of answering this question with certainty. In many cases, however, recipients of transfer payments appear at least as well protected against inflation as wage and salary earners. One major reason is the indexing of social security benefits, which now automatically keep pace with rising prices. In addition, an increasing proportion of all transfers are now being paid in kind (that is, in the form of free or subsidized food, housing, medical care, and so on) rather than in cash. Although the spread of in-kind transfers may not consciously have been intended to protect beneficiaries from inflation, it has had that effect.

Interest Income—Debtors versus Creditors What does inflation do to the real income of creditors, who receive interest income from bonds, mortgages, and the like, and to the real income of debtors, who pay this interest? Although the effects are somewhat more complex than for wage income or transfer payments, they are worth looking at in some detail.

The Traditional View The traditional view of the matter is that inflation injures creditors and aids debtors. Suppose, for example, that I borrow $100 from you today, promising to repay $105 next year. If there is no inflation during the year, I get use of the funds for the year, and you get a $5 increase in your purchasing power. But suppose that during the year the price level goes up 10 percent. In that case, I get the use of the funds for the year, and what is more, I get to pay you back in depreciated dollars. The $105 I give you next year will buy you only as much then as $95 will today. Your real income is negative. I, the debtor, am benefited by inflation; you, the creditor, are hurt.

Expected and Unexpected Inflation It is now recognized, however, that this traditional view of the effects of inflation on debtors and creditors is seriously incomplete, in that it does not distinguish between *unexpected* and *expected* inflation. The example just given implicitly assumes that neither I, the debtor, nor you, the creditor, expected any inflation at the time the loan was made. Suppose instead that we both had expected a 10 percent increase in the price level between the time the loan was made and the time it was repaid. You would not then have loaned me the $100 in return for a promise to repay just $105 at the end of the year. Instead, you would have insisted on a repayment of something like $115—$10 to compensate you for the decline in the purchasing power of the $100 principal plus the $5 you originally wanted as real return for relinquishing use of the funds for a year. I, in turn, would have agreed to those terms, expecting that $115 in the next year's depreciated dollars would be no more than the equivalent, in terms of real purchasing power, of the $105 I would have been willing to repay in a noninflationary world. In real terms, then, correctly anticipated inflation is neutral between debtor and creditor.

Nominal rate of interest The rate of interest measured in the ordinary way, without adjustment for inflation.

Expected real rate of interest The nominal rate of interest minus the expected rate of inflation.

Realized real rate of interest The nominal rate of interest minus the actual rate of inflation.

Nominal versus Real Interest Rates The example just given shows why it is necessary in an inflationary world to distinguish three separate interest rate concepts. The first, the **nominal rate of interest,** means the rate of interest measured in the ordinary way in current dollars. The second, the **expected real rate of interest,** means the nominal rate of interest minus the expected rate of inflation. And the third, the **realized real rate of interest,** means the nominal rate of interest minus the actual rate of inflation.

If no inflation is expected and none actually occurs, all three rates of interest are equal. If inflation does occur and is accurately anticipated, the expected and realized real rates of interest are equal, and both are less than the nominal rate. In the example given above, for instance, an accurately anticipated rate of inflation of 10 percent transformed a 15 percent nominal rate of interest into a 5 percent expected and realized real rate of interest.

If inflation does occur and is not accurately expected, the expected and realized real rates of interest will differ from one another. To extend the example, suppose that you had loaned me the $100 in question at a 15 percent nominal rate in the expectation of a 10 percent rate of inflation but that the actual rate of inflation turned out to be 12 percent. Instead of earning your expected real rate of interest of 5 percent (the 15 percent nominal rate minus 10 percent expected inflation), you would actually have earned a realized rate of interest of only 3 percent (the 15 percent nominal rate minus 12 percent actual inflation).

The distinction between nominal and real rates of interest can be used to express precisely the distributional effects of inflation as between debtors and creditors. Accurately expected inflation is neutral between creditors and debtors, because the parties will fully adjust the nominal rate of interest they agree on to take the expected inflation into account. If the actual rate of inflation exceeds the expected rate, debtors will gain at the expense of creditors, because the realized real rate of interest will fall below the expected real rate. If the actual rate of inflation falls short of the expected rate, creditors will gain at the expense of debtors, because the realized real rate will exceed the expected real rate. Note that the traditional view of inflation fits into these generalizations as a special case that applies when the expected rate of inflation is zero.

Inflation and Wealth A complete picture of the distributional effects of inflation must consider not only its effects on flows of income to individuals but also its effects on the same individuals' stocks of wealth. The effects of inflation on wealth very much depend on the form in which that wealth is held.

The one group of the population that most clearly benefited from the inflation of the 1970s consisted of those people who had most of their personal wealth tied up in their own home. In fact, most such people actually benefited in two ways. First, the market value of their houses, at least in most areas of the country, not only kept pace with inflation but outstripped it. Second, many homeowners had long-term, low-interest mortgages negotiated during the 1950s and 1960s. The unexpected increase in inflation during the 1970s benefited them as debtors, allowing them to pay off their mortgages in depreciated dollars.

People who held their wealth in common stocks, on the other hand, fared very poorly during the inflationary 1970s. This came as a major surprise. For generations, investment advisers had regarded it as dogma that corporate stocks were a sound hedge against inflation. Their reasoning was simple and persuasive. A share of common stock represents a share of ownership of the firm that issues it. If prices double, the firm's costs of doing business will double, but so should its revenues, the prices of the things it sells, the value of its plant and equipment, its profits, its dividends, and so on. The market price of the stock should thus also be expected to double, leaving the stockholder no worse off as a result of the inflation.

Somewhere toward the end of the 1960s, however, something went wrong. Inflation accelerated, but the stock market failed to respond. The reasons are complex and not yet fully understood, but the facts are clear. By the end of the 1970s, stock prices were fluctuating around an average level no higher in nominal terms than what they had reached in the mid 1960s. People who had kept their money in the stock market, on the average, lost more than half their real wealth.

Inflation and Taxes One additional topic needs to be added to the discussion of inflation and income distribution: the effect of inflation on the taxes people pay. Several kinds of taxes are worth examining separately.

Income Taxes The federal income tax, as shown in Chapter 4, is a progressive tax. As a household's nominal income rises, the household pays a higher and higher marginal tax rate. (To use the popular phrase, it moves into a higher tax bracket.) The higher tax rate applies even if the increase in nominal income represents no increase in real purchasing power but only keeps pace with the cost of living. From time to time, Congress adjusts the tax brackets to reflect rising prices; but in recent years, these periodic tax cuts have not fully compensated for inflation. Effective real income tax rates have thus risen along with the price level.

Taxation of Interest Income Interest income is subject to income tax at marginal rates up to 70 percent. Income tax is collected on the full amount of nominal interest income, regardless of what portion of the nominal rate of interest might represent only an inflation premium. The result is that when the rate of inflation rises, after-tax realized real interest rates fall even if nominal interest rates rise sufficiently to keep before-tax realized real interest rates constant.

As an example, consider a household subject to a 50 percent marginal tax rate. With no inflation, a 5 percent nominal interest rate would yield a 5 percent realized real interest rate before tax and a 2.5 percent realized real interest rate after tax. Now add 10 percent inflation, fully expected. If the nominal rate rises to 15 percent, the before-tax realized real rate will still be 5 percent, as before. But now income tax has to be paid on the full 15 percent nominal interest rate, leaving only a 7.5 percent after-tax nominal rate. Subtracting 10 percent inflation from 7.5 percent leaves a *minus* 2.5 percent after-tax realized real rate of interest. Because income tax is paid on nominal rather than real interest income, then, households receiving income in the form of interest find their real tax burdens increasing in times of inflation.

Capital Gains Taxes Households are said to earn capital gains when they buy property or financial assets and later resell them for more than the original purchase price. Capital gains are subject to income taxes, although at lower rates than ordinary income. Despite the relatively low rates at which these taxes are levied, however, they can become burdensome in times of inflation because they, like other taxes, are levied on nominal rather than real income.

Suppose, for example, a person had bought 100 shares of stock in the XYZ Corporation in 1968 at $100 per share and then sold the stock in 1978 at $150 per share. From 1968 to 1978, the price level doubled. The 1978 share price of $150 was equivalent only to $75 in 1968 dollars. In real terms, then, there was no capital gain; instead there was a capital loss. Yet a nominal capital gain of $50 per share, or $5,000 in all, would have had to be reported for income tax purposes, and tax would have had to be paid at about half the rate applicable to ordinary income.

Inflation affects many other taxes too, but the three examples just discussed are enough to give a general impression of the effects. For the economy as a whole, inflation tends to increase the fraction of real national income that flows to government in the form of taxes. For individuals, the impact of inflation on the real tax burden depends strongly on the form in which income is earned, with taxes on interest income and capital gains somewhat more strongly affected than taxes on wage and salary income.

This completes the discussion of the impact of inflation on individual items of income. It is now time to look at the overall distributional effects of inflation.

Case 7.1
Who Wins and Who Loses from Inflation?

"Inflation," said the Democratic Party platform of 1976, "is a tax that erodes the income of our workers, distorts business investment decisions, and redistributes income in favor of the rich." Party platforms are not usually the place one finds novel or radical ideas; in characterizing inflation as favoring the rich, the 1976 Democratic platform was simply expressing a rather widely held view regarding the distributional effects of inflation. Yet, according to a 1978 study by Joseph Minarik of the Brookings Institution, this conventional view may be just the opposite of the truth.

Minarik set out to evaluate the overall distributional effects of inflation, taking into account effects on wage and salary income, cash and in-kind transfers, investment income, taxes, and changes in wealth. As a data base, he had at his disposal a large computer file of responses from a Census Bureau survey of households combined with a large sample of tax returns obtained from the Internal Revenue Service. The specific question he asked was: What would be the effects on the real income of typical individuals in various income classes of a 2 percentage point increase in the rate of inflation—say from a rate of 4 percent per year to 6 percent per year? The effects, he found, depend in part on the time allowed for inflation to do its work. In general, they appeared more pronounced the longer the new, higher rate of inflation was assumed to persist.

Exhibit 7.5 summarizes Minarik's results for medium-term effects of inflation, assuming that the higher rate of inflation persists for six years. The data given in the exhibit appear to contradict the conventional notion that inflation makes the rich richer and the poor poorer. In both the short run and the long run, the very poorest families are not much affected by inflation one way or the other. Those in the income range from roughly $3,000 to $10,000 weather inflation less well, appearing to lose 1 or 2 percent of their real income when inflation accelerates. Middle-income households in the $10,000 to $20,000 range actually gain from inflation on the average. Their income is mostly in the form of wages and salaries, which keep up well with prices; and their wealth is largely invested in home ownership.

Exhibit 7.5 shows the real toll of inflation to be concentrated on households with incomes of $20,000 per year or more. Such well-to-do households are hurt by inflation in two major ways. First, a smaller portion of their wealth is in the form of housing, which held or even gained in real value during the inflationary 1970 s, and more is in the form of stocks and bonds, which performed relatively poorly. Second, they receive more income in the form of interest and capital gains and hence bear rising real tax burdens as inflation accelerates. According to Minarik's figures, a household starting with $500,000 annual income would have found its real income reduced to about $400,000 as the result of the increase in the underlying rate of inflation from the 2 percent of the 1960s to the 6 percent or more of the 1970s.

Another common belief about inflation is that it is particularly burdensome on the elderly. In another part of his study, Minarik found the belief to be well-founded. According to his figures, the adverse effects of inflation on real income start at a much lower level for those aged sixty-five and older than for younger individuals and households. An elderly person with household income of as little as $10,000

Exhibit 7.5

Effects on real income of a 2 percent increase in the inflation rate

This exhibit shows the medium-term effects on real income at different levels of a sustained 2 percent increase in the rate of inflation. Very poor households and households in the $10,000 to $20,000 income range may actually benefit slightly from inflation; households with higher incomes suffer progressively larger percentage losses in real income as a result of inflation.

Source: Adapted with permission from Joseph J. Minarik, "Who Wins, Who Loses from Inflation," *Brookings Bulletin* 15 (Summer 1978): Fig. 2, p. 9. Copyright © 1978 by the Brookings Institution, Washington, D.C.

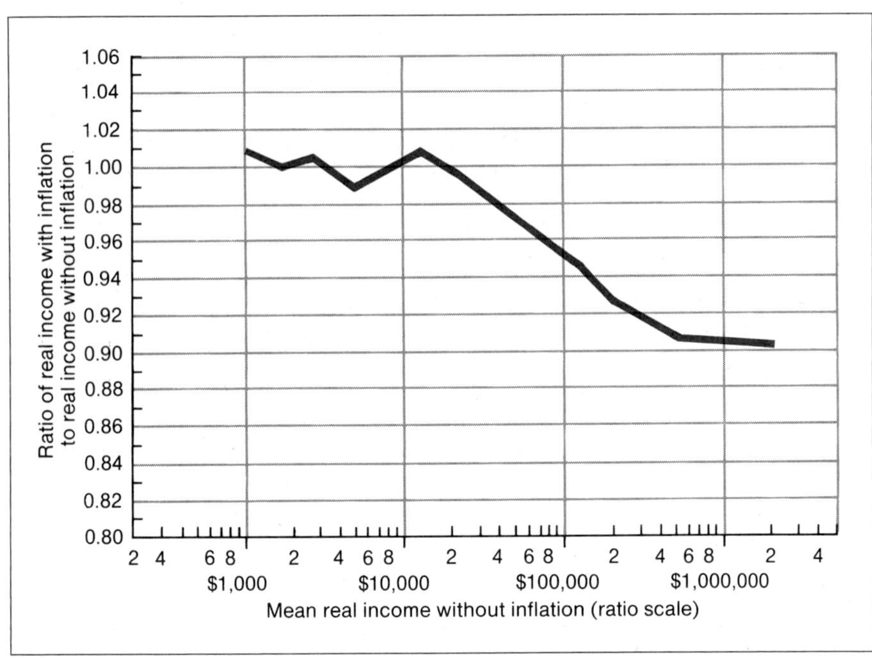

suffers about the same 10 percent loss in purchasing power from a 2 percentage point increase in the rate of inflation as does a younger household with $100,000 income. Even at income levels as low as $5,000 per year, the real income loss to the elderly was about 5 percent for each 2 percentage points added to inflation.

Source: Based on Joseph J. Minarik, "Who Wins, Who Loses from Inflation," *Brookings Bulletin* 15 (Summer 1978): 6–10.

It will be important to keep these distributional effects of inflation in mind in succeeding chapters as various theories of inflation and proposed anti-inflationary policies are discussed. For the moment, though, attention can be turned to the third major goal of macroeconomic policy—economic growth.

ECONOMIC GROWTH

Growth of Potential GNP

Economic growth means the growth of opportunities to satisfy economic wants. At any one time, economic opportunities are limited. Labor, natural resources, and capital are scarce. Their scarcity, together with the state of technological knowledge, limits production possibilities. Not all the useful goods and services desired can be produced at once.

As time passes, though, the range of possibilities expands. Capital accumulates, and new resources are found. New methods of production make it possible to get more output from each unit of input. People still will not be able to have everything at once, but they can have more things at once than before.

Growth and the Production Possibility Frontier The production possibility frontier, first introduced in Chapter 1, provides a convenient graphical method of representing economic growth. Exhibit 7.6 shows produc-

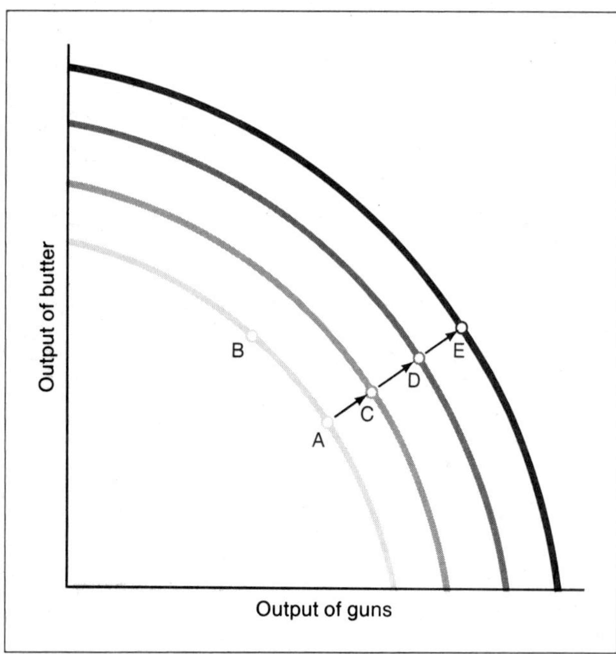

Exhibit 7.6

The process of economic growth

Economic growth can be represented as an outward expansion of the production possibility frontier. In any one year, getting more "guns" means giving up some "butter," as in a movement from B to A. Over time, however, growth could give more of both guns and butter, as in a movement from A to C, D, and E.

tion possibility frontiers for an economy producing only two goods, which will be called "guns" and "butter." In any single year, total output is constrained by the production possibility frontier. Over time, however, as new resources become available and as technology improves, the frontier expands outward. Exhibit 7.6 shows four successive production possibility frontiers, each permitting a greater potential real output.

Actual versus Potential Real Output In practice, real output may not actually expand exactly in step with the outward shift in the production possibility frontier. Remember that, in any given year, the economy may operate inside the production possibility frontier if resources are not fully employed. Economists use the term **potential real GNP** (or **potential real output**) to indicate the level of real output that the economy could achieve if resources were fully employed. If factors of production are not fully employed, actual output is said to lag behind potential output.

Potential real GNP (potential real output) The level of real GNP that the economy could, in principle, produce if resources were fully employed.

Exhibit 7.7 shows actual and potential real GNP for the U.S. economy from 1968 through 1978, as estimated by the President's Council of Economic Advisers. The figure shows potential real GNP growing at a rate of about 3 percent per year. In years when actual real GNP grows at a rate of less than 3

Exhibit 7.7
Actual and potential real GNP (billions of 1972 dollars), at seasonally adjusted annual rates
This exhibit shows actual and potential real GNP for the U.S. economy from 1968 to 1978. Over most of this period, the economy was estimated to have been operating below potential; but for two brief periods, actual output exceeded potential output. Potential real GNP is estimated to be growing at a rate of about 3 percent per year at present.

Source: President's Council of Economic Advisers, *Economic Report of the President* (Washington, D.C.: Government Printing Office, 1979), Chart 7, p. 75.

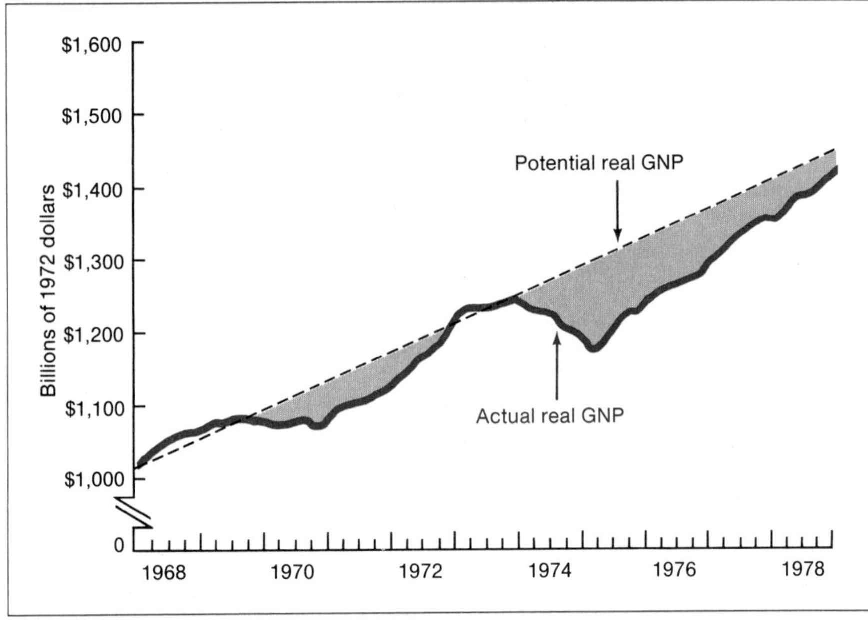

percent, or actually falls, a gap is opened up between actual and potential output. In other years, actual GNP grows more rapidly than 3 percent, and the gap narrows. Occasionally, actual real GNP rises above potential real GNP. This should not be understood to mean that the economy literally operates outside its production possibility frontier during those years. Rather, it indicates that output in these years temporarily rose above the level that could be permanently sustained with available resources.

Putting year-to-year fluctuations in actual real GNP to one side, what are the major sources of the long-run growth of potential real output? The following case study summarizes one attempt to answer this question.

Case 7.2 Sources of U.S. Economic Growth

The best-known attempt to measure the sources of U.S. economic growth is that of Edward F. Denison. His study covers the period 1929 to 1969. The U.S. economy grew at an average annual rate of 3.3 percent during these years. In the second half of the period, 1948 to 1969, the rate of growth was a bit faster—3.85 percent per year. (Note that, in both periods, output grew more rapidly than the currently estimated potential real growth rate of 3 percent.)

Exhibit 7.8 presents Denison's estimates of the relative importance of various sources of economic growth for the time span his study covered. The most important source of growth throughout the period was knowledge. Denison was not able to measure this item directly. He made direct measurements of the other sources of growth, however, and assumed that all growth that could not otherwise be explained came from advances in knowledge.

The first of the items that can be measured directly is what Denison calls "more work done." This includes the effects of population growth, changes in hours worked per week, and changes in the composition of the work force by age and sex. Next comes the accumulation of capital. Some people find the contribution of new capital to be surprisingly small in view of the importance sometimes attributed to this source of growth in theoretical discussions. Increased education is almost as important as physical capital when the whole forty years are taken into account. Since World War II, though, this item has been less important.

The four items together can be said to have brought about an outward shift of the production possibility frontier. The rest of the economic growth from 1929 to 1969 came from two sources. One source was the more efficient use of available factors of production. A major shift of surplus labor from agriculture to industry played a big role here. The other source was a small reduction in the unemployment rate.

Source: Based on Edward F. Denison, *Accounting for U.S. Economic Growth, 1929–1969* (Washington, D.C.: Brookings Institution, 1974), pp. 124–150.

Source	Percent of Growth Rate 1929–1969	1948–1969
Advances in knowledge	31.1	34.1
More work done	28.7	23.9
Capital accumulation	15.8	21.6
Increased education	14.1	11.9
Other	10.3	8.5
Total	100.0	100.0

Source: Edward F. Denison, *Accounting for U.S. Economic Growth, 1929–1969* (Washington, D.C.: Brookings Institution, 1974).

Exhibit 7.8
Sources of U.S. economic growth
This exhibit shows the relative importance of various sources of economic growth in the United States during the last fifty years. Advances in knowledge and increased education together account for 45 percent of all growth. The category "more work done" includes the effects of population growth and changes in the average workweek.

Is Economic Growth Really Desirable?

For many years, everyone thought economic growth was a good thing. The only debates about growth took place between people who thought that the present pace was good enough and those who wanted government action to increase the growth rate. Now things are different.

Today, the people who are satisfied with the record of growth and those who would like to step up the pace have been forced into a defensive alliance. On the other side are two groups. One is made up of people who think that further economic growth is impossible or will soon be so. The other is made up of those who think that further growth may be possible but who do not want it.

The growth debate raises technical issues, some of which will be discussed in the chapters on pollution, energy, and economic development. But the matter is important enough to make it worth giving at least an outline of the main issues here.

Questioning the Desirability of Growth Look first at the argument that further economic growth is not desirable whether or not it is possible. The heart of this argument is the perfectly valid proposition that GNP is not a measure of human welfare. The trouble, it is said, is that growth of GNP can be offset by a decline in the quality of life. These fears can be expressed in the form of a parable.

Imagine a peaceful little country with a per capita GNP of $100. All the GNP is produced by the women, who work the fields in the morning and gossip in the afternoon. The men do nothing but sit around and play cards and drink tea all day. Suppose now that an enterprising foreign company sets up a soap factory and puts all of the men to work. Each man can make $40 worth of soap per year. Previously there was no market for soap in this pastoral nation, but now the soap factory's boilers belch black coal smoke that soils everyone's curtains. The entire output of the soap factory is sold to local housewives, who now spend all their afternoons at the laundromat.

What has happened to the GNP of this country? As any economist will explain, it has gone up by 20 percent to $120 per capita. Farm output has not fallen, and industrial production of $20 per capita has been added. But what has happened to the level of well-being of the people of this country? They have no more to eat than before, their curtains wear out faster than before, and they are working four times as hard as before. They are, say, about one-quarter as well off as before.

Many people believe that this parable applies to the U.S. economy. They are worried not only about pollution but about values that they think will be lost as growth continues. Rapid economic growth makes skills, and hence people, obsolete before their working lives are over. Economic growth crowds out green places and covers them with asphalt. It replaces the community life of the town with the anonymity of the city. Growth is thus said to make life less worth living in ways for which more cars and microwave ovens do not fully compensate.

Separating the Issues How valid is this "quality of life" argument? Are people really becoming worse off year by year, or is that claim just romanticism? It cannot be denied that economic growth is a *potential* threat to the quality of life. As it stands, though, the argument is misleading because it

John Stuart Mill (1806–1873)

John Stuart Mill was in every respect one of the most brilliant and remarkable figures of the nineteenth century. Eldest son of the prominent economist and philosopher, James Mill, John Stuart lived an extraordinary childhood. He began his study of classical Greek at the age of three. By eight, he was reading Plato's dialogues in the original and teaching Latin to the younger members of the Mill family. His education in economics began at thirteen, under his father's tutorship, with a study of Adam Smith's work and the other classics.

This unusual upbringing was bound to produce a strong reaction sooner or later. In his early twenties, Mill went through a spiritual crisis that led him to reject many of his father's ideas. About that time, he met Harriet Taylor and began a long association with her. (Years later, after her husband's death, they were married.) Her ideas on feminism and socialism powerfully influenced Mill's thinking.

Mill published his *Principles of Political Economy* in 1848. This work is seen today as the high-water mark of the classical school, founded by Adam Smith three generations before. As a textbook and authority on economic questions, Mill's *Principles* stood unchallenged until Alfred Marshall transformed "political economy" into "economics" at the end of the century.

Mill's *Principles* is by no means limited to the narrowly technical side of economics. Mill always faced squarely the broad social implications of economic theory wherever they arose. For example, like other economists of the classical school, he believed there were not-too-distant limits to the process of economic growth. "At the end of the progressive state," he wrote, "lies the stationary state. All progress in wealth is but a postponement of this and all advance is an approach to it." Mill was not content, however, simply to describe the mechanics of growth and the technical properties of the stationary state. He wondered what a world without progress would be like. His conclusions so clearly address the concerns of our own age that they are worth quoting at length:

> I cannot . . . regard the stationary state of capital and wealth with the unaffected aversion so generally manifested towards it by political economists of the old school. I am inclined to believe that it would be, on the whole, a very considerable improvement on our present condition. I confess I am not charmed with the ideal of life held out by those who think that the normal state of human beings is that of struggling to get on; that the trampling, crushing, elbowing, and treading on each other's heels, which form the existing type of social life, are the most desirable lot of human kind, or anything but the disagreeable symptoms of one of the phases of our industrial progress. . . .
>
> If the earth must lose that great portion of its pleasantries which it owes to things that the unlimited increase of wealth and population would extirpate from it, for the mere purpose of enabling it to support a larger, but not a better or happier population, I sincerely hope, for the sake of posterity, that they will be content to be stationary long before necessity compels them to.

---

confuses two issues. One issue has to do with the size of gross national product and the other with its composition.

In Exhibit 7.9, the production possibility frontier is used to help separate the two issues. The diagram shows an economy in which the two goods produced are called "clean air" and "cars" rather than "guns" and "butter." In any single year, there is a trade-off between the two goods. More cars make the air dirtier; making fewer cars (or spending more money on each car to make them run cleaner) means having better air.

As technology improves and more capital is accumulated, the production possibility frontier shifts outward. If the actual growth path of the economy is from Point A to Point B, people will complain that the quality of life has deteriorated. It is not really economic growth that is to blame, though. Instead, the problem is the composition of output that has been chosen. Instead of moving from A to B by producing a great many new dirty cars, the economy could have grown along the path from A to C. That would have meant fewer

Exhibit 7.9
Pollution and economic growth
In any single year, there is a trade-off between cars and clean air. More cars make the air dirtier, whereas having fewer cars makes cleaner air possible. As the production possibility frontier moves outward, the choice can be made between two kinds of growth. Many new dirty cars can be made (moving from A to B), if that is what people want. Alternatively, fewer cars can be produced, and more can be spent on each car to make it run cleaner (moving from A to C instead).

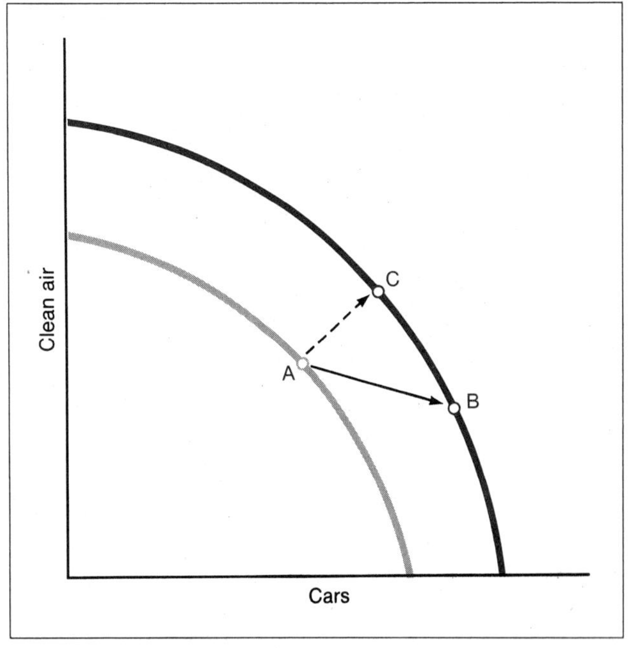

cars, each more carefully built to cause less pollution. Growth could bring more cars *and* more clean air if people chose to go that way.

Pollution is a serious problem. It cannot be brushed aside. Still, it is wrong to blame pollution on economic growth. To stop growth in order to stop pollution would be to throw the baby out with the bath water. Controlling pollution requires policies to encourage the correct composition of national product, not to control its size. Chapter 19 will take a look at a number of such policies.

Questioning the Possibility of Growth There is little point in arguing about the direction of growth if resources are being depleted so rapidly that no future growth will be possible. So is growth still possible? A look at the sources of past economic growth may help answer this question.

Refer back for a moment to Exhibit 7.8, which gives Denison's figures on the sources of U.S. economic growth over the past half century. The major sources of growth in the past are not of a nature likely to be adversely affected by possible depletion of natural resources in the future. Advances in knowledge and increased education, which together account for some 45 percent of all growth, use up relatively few natural resources. The category "more work done" takes into account the effects of population growth, which is unlikely to be as rapid in the future as in the past. But although this will slow the growth of total real income, it will not affect the rate of growth of real income per capita.

Although depletion of natural resources may impede the accumulation of capital in some forms, not all capital accumulation takes the form of such resource-intensive items as steel mills and nuclear power plants. Many recent technological developments, in fact, are resource saving. Industry, for example, is learning how to build factories that are somewhat more expensive to construct initially but that require less energy to operate once they are in place. And the trend in the important field of electronics has been to put increasingly more powerful capital devices into smaller and smaller physical packages.

It would appear, then, that most arguments about the impossibility of future economic growth rest on the fallacy of thinking of growth in purely physical terms. To be sure, if economic growth meant nothing other than endlessly piling up duplicates of the gas-guzzling cars and smoke-belching factories of the past, people might someday come up against a blank wall. But exactly because certain important natural resources are gradually being depleted, that is not the direction in which growth will proceed. Instead, it will proceed in the direction of developing new generations of capital goods and consumer goods that do their job better with fewer physical inputs and more inputs of technology and human ingenuity.

The Distributional Effects of Economic Growth

A brief explanation of distributional effects will complete the discussion of economic growth. In the long run, the distributional effects of growth in the United States appear to have been largely neutral. Workers, resource owners, and recipients of interest and profits appear each to be getting about the same sized slice of the national income pie as a century ago. As the economy has grown, the benefits have been shared by rich and poor alike.

In the context of stabilization policy, however, it is important also to consider the relatively short-term effects of economic growth. In the short run, changes in the year-to-year rate of real economic growth are closely linked to changes in employment. The faster the economy grows, other things being equal, the more jobs are created and the more rapidly the unemployment rate is reduced. In the short run, then, economic growth appears to provide the greatest benefits for those most disadvantaged by high rates of unemployment.

Besides lowering the overall unemployment rate, economic growth has the additional benefit of making it easier for people to upgrade their jobs and improve their economic circumstances. As one prominent civil rights leader has put it: "A limited-growth policy tends to freeze people to whatever rung of the ladder they happen to be on. That's OK if you're a highly educated 28-year-old making $50,000 per year as a presidential adviser. It's utter disaster if you're unskilled, out of work and living in a ghetto."[2]

CONCLUSIONS

We have described three goals of economic stabilization policy, reviewed the past performance of the U.S. economy in terms of each goal, and discussed the likely distributional effects of achieving or failing to achieve each goal. In conclusion, we will show how these goals will be used in the following chapters to develop a theory of macroeconomics that will explain past performance and, it is hoped, provide some guidance as to the policies that might improve future performance.

Even when stripped of unnecessary complexities, the theory we will introduce is too large to be bitten off and digested in a single piece. We will need to

---

[2]Margaret Bush Wilson, chairman of the National Association for the Advancement of Colored People, quoted in "Review and Outlook: The NAACP Turns a Corner," *Wall Street Journal*, January 12, 1978, p. 12.

take things one at a time. It would be convenient if we could break the whole into three separate bodies of theory, one explaining changes in unemployment, a second explaining changes in the price level, and a third explaining changes in real output. Unfortunately, that is impossible; the three goals are too closely interrelated. Any policy affecting the performance of a single goal can normally be expected to have effects on the other two as well. Instead of organizing our discussion in terms of the three policy goals, then, we will organize it in terms of the now-familiar distinction between *nominal* and *real* values. This will work as follows.

First, we will discuss the theory of what determines the size and composition of nominal national income and product and evaluate various policies that can control nominal aggregate demand. This discussion, in turn, will be divided into two sections. Chapters 8 to 10 will be devoted to matters relating to government spending and taxation policy, and Chapters 11 to 14 will be devoted to the banking system and monetary policy.

Second, once we know what determines nominal national income and product, we will look at what determines how changes in nominal national income and product are resolved into changes in employment and real output on the one hand and changes in the price level on the other. In doing this, we will rely on a simple and important relationship between nominal and real values: *The rate of growth of nominal national income and product is always equal to the rate of change of real national income and product plus the rate of inflation.* Suppose, for example, that in one year nominal GNP increases by 10 percent from $2,000 billion to $2,200 billion. This can mean that prices have not changed at all and that 10 percent more real goods and services have been produced, that real output has not changed but that there has been 10 percent inflation, that there has been 5 percent real growth and 5 percent inflation, or that there has been any other combination of a rate of growth of real output and a rate of inflation adding up to the 10 percent growth in nominal GNP. Chapters 15 to 18 will be devoted to explaining why any given change in nominal national income and product is split up in one way rather than another and to a discussion of policies through which the split can be manipulated in the hope of achieving simultaneous full employment, price stability, and balanced growth.

SUMMARY

1. The general function of economic stabilization can be broken down into the pursuit of three more specific policy goals: maintaining full employment, maintaining price stability, and maintaining steady growth of real national incomes.
2. The Employment Act of 1946 committed the U.S. government to pursue a policy of full employment, by which the act meant a job for everyone who wanted one. The Humphrey-Hawkins Act of 1978 added a specific numerical target for unemployment, namely, 4 percent of the civilian labor force, to be achieved by 1983. Such a low level of unemployment has rarely been achieved in the United States in the last thirty years, and then only during periods of war. Unemployment data suggest that teenagers, minorities, and women have been hardest hit by high unemployment rates.
3. The Humphrey-Hawkins Act also set an interim numerical goal for inflation

of a 3 percent per year change in the consumer price index, to be achieved by 1983. This goal was achieved throughout the 1950s and early 1960s; but during the 1970s, inflation exceeded the goal in every year. Recent studies of the distributional impact of inflation suggest that the burden of inflation rests more heavily on older people and on households with relatively high incomes than on younger people and households with low and moderate incomes.

4. Currently, potential real GNP in the United States is believed to be growing at a rate of about 3 percent per year—somewhat below its postwar average. While policy makers continue to regard real economic growth as a worthwhile goal, in recent years, a controversy has developed over whether rapid economic growth will be desirable or even possible in the future. The controversy raises both environmental and distributional concerns.

DISCUSSION QUESTIONS

1. It is sometimes suggested that the proper goal for employment policy would be a zero level of *involuntary* unemployment. How might one distinguish between voluntary and involuntary unemployment? What measurement problems might arise in distinguishing between the two? (Give this matter some general thought now; we will return to it in more detail in Chapter 15.)
2. Locate a recent issue of the *Monthly Labor Review*, published by the U.S. Department of Labor. Toward the back of each issue is a statistical section that will give you data with which you can update Exhibits. 7.2, 7.3, and 7.4. What progress, if any, is being made toward achievement of the goals of the Humphrey-Hawkins Act? Do you think it will be possible to reach those goals by 1983?
3. Locate a copy of a good financial newspaper, such as the *Wall Street Journal* or the *New York Times*, and find out the current interest rate on three-month Treasury bills. (Alternatively, look up this index in a recent issue of the *Federal Reserve Bulletin*.) Compare it to the current rate of inflation as measured in terms of the consumer price index. What is the current realized real rate of interest?
4. Make a list of some of the costs and benefits that past economic growth has brought to your particular area or community. Has there been too much or too little growth in your opinion? Do you think future economic growth in your area or community will bring benefits that outweigh costs? Explain.

SUGGESTIONS FOR FURTHER READING

Beckerman, Wilfred. *In Defense of Economic Growth.* London: Jonathan Cape, 1974.
A reply to the Meadows et al. doomsday book listed below.

Meadows, Dennis L., et al. *The Limits to Growth.* Washington, D.C.: Potomac Associates, 1972.
A report on a highly controversial and widely debated computer simulation study purporting to show sharp limits to economic growth in the relatively near future.

Mill, John Stuart. *Principles of Political Economy.* 1871 ed.
Excerpts available in Pelican Books edition of 1970 and many other editions. Book VI, "Of the Stationary State," contains Mill's views on the limits to growth.

President's Council of Economic Advisers. *Economic Report of the President.* Washington, D.C.: Government Printing Office, annually.
In the most recent issue, check progress made toward meeting the Humphrey-Hawkins goals. The President's Council of Economic Advisers is required by the 1978 act to report on this annually.

CHAPTER 8

THE DETERMINANTS OF PLANNED EXPENDITURE

WHAT YOU WILL LEARN IN THIS CHAPTER

British economist John Maynard Keynes made aggregate demand a key element of his economic theory. This chapter will follow his approach by looking at the determinants of each of the major components of aggregate demand. The first component, consumption expenditure, depends to a substantial extent on the level of national income. The second, planned investment expenditure, depends on the expected real rate of interest and on business expectations concerning the profitability of investment projects. Government purchases and net exports, the third and fourth determinants, depend on forces outside the scope of this chapter and will be treated as givens for the time being.

FOR REVIEW

Here are some important terms and concepts that will be put to use in this chapter. If you do not understand them, review them before proceeding.

- *Aggregate demand* (Chapter 5)
- *Planned and unplanned investment* (Chapter 5)
- *Relationships among gross national product, national income, personal income, and disposable income* (Chapter 6)
- *Real and nominal interest rates* (Chapter 7)

Chapter 5 introduced the circular flow and the ideas of aggregate supply and demand. Chapter 6 showed how national income accountants go about measuring the elements of the circular flow, including consumption, investment, government purchases, and net exports. Chapter 7 set forth a number of goals and reviewed recent macroeconomic experience in terms of them. Now it is time to put all these preliminary concepts and definitions to work and to begin developing a theory—one that will explain why national income and product are at one level rather than another in any particular year and why they have their ups and downs over time.

Some Simplifications

In economics, theory building always begins by making some simplifications in order to concentrate on essentials. One simplification that will be used throughout this discussion of macroeconomic theory is the elimination of indirect business taxes, the capital consumption allowance, and the statistical discrepancy. Getting rid of these elements of the national income accounts makes things much easier. Gross national product, net national product, and national income once again become equal by definition, as they were in the simplified circular flow diagrams of Chapter 5.

A second simplification that will be used throughout the following chapters is the omission of undistributed corporate profits. With neither indirect business taxes nor undistributed corporate profits, personal income will be equal to national income minus net taxes. (The term *net taxes,* as in Chapter 5, means all taxes—personal income tax, social insurance contributions, and corporate profits tax—minus all transfer payments.)

A third simplification will be the concentration for the time being on *nominal* values of national income, consumption, and so on—primarily a matter of taking one thing at a time. Chapters 8 to 14 will be explaining why nominal income is, say, $2 trillion rather than some other value in a certain year. Then, Chapters 15 to 18 will turn to the question of why changes in nominal income sometimes take the form of changes in prices rather than in real output.

In these early chapters, where the discussion is entirely in terms of nominal values, the term *nominal* will not be repeated every time consumption, investment, income, or whatever is mentioned. Keep in mind, though, that nominal values are meant in every case unless real values are explicitly specified.

Keynes

One further note is in order at the beginning of the discussion of macroeconomic theory—the introduction of the British economist, John Maynard Keynes, whose writings have strongly influenced macroeconomic thought since the 1930s. Although many of Keynes's particular conclusions have been challenged by contemporary economists, the fact that these challenges occur within his basic theoretical framework attests to his lasting influence. Keynes's ideas underlie all of modern macroeconomic theory as well as the contents of this book, even in places where they are not specifically acknowledged.

John Maynard Keynes (1883–1946)

John Maynard Keynes was born into economics. His father, John Neville Keynes, was a lecturer in economics and logic at Cambridge University. John Maynard began his own studies at Cambridge with an emphasis on mathematics and philosophy. His abilities soon so impressed Alfred Marshall, however, that the distinguished teacher urged him to concentrate on economics. In 1908, after Keynes had finished his studies and done a brief stint in the civil service, Marshall offered him a lectureship in economics at Cambridge, which he accepted.

Keynes is remembered above all for his *General Theory of Employment, Interest, and Money,* published in 1936, although that was by no means his first important work. Keynes's reputation as the outstanding economist of his generation lay in the departure from classical and neoclassical theory he made there. It is hardly necessary to say much about the substance of the *General Theory* in these paragraphs, because they are extensively discussed in every modern textbook on economics. It will be enough to note that its major features are a theory boldly drawn in terms of broad macroeconomic aggregates and a policy position tending toward activism and interventionism.

Keynes was no "narrow" economist. He was an honored member not only of the British academic upper class but also of Britain's highest financial, political, diplomatic, administrative, and even artistic circles. He was intimately involved with the colorful "Bloomsbury set" of London's literary-Bohemian world. He was a friend of Virginia Woolf, E. M. Forster, and Lytton Strachey; and in 1925, he married ballerina Lydia Lopokovia. He was a dazzling success at whatever he turned his hand to, from mountain climbing to financial speculation. As a speculator, he made an enormous fortune for himself, and as bursar of Kings College, he turned an endowment of £30,000 into one of £380,000.

In even the briefest discussion of Keynes, it would be unforgivable not to give his most famous quotation. Writing in the *General Theory,* he pronounced that

> the ideas of economists and political philosophers, both when they are right and when they are wrong, are more powerful than is commonly understood. Indeed the world is ruled by little else. Practical men, who believe themselves to be quite exempt from any intellectual influences, are usually the slaves of some defunct economist. Madmen in authority, who hear voices in the air, are distilling their frenzy from some academic scribbler of a few years back. . . . There are not many who are influenced by new theories after they are twenty-five or thirty years of age, so that the ideas which civil servants and politicians and even agitators apply to current events are not likely to be the newest.

Was Keynes issuing a warning here? Whether or not he had any such thing in mind, his words, forty years later, have become one of the great ironies in the history of economic ideas.

Keynes made the concept of *aggregate demand* a key element of his theory. He taught that macroeconomic analysis should begin by asking what determines each of the separate types of planned expenditure that make up aggregate demand: consumption, planned investment expenditure, government purchases, and net exports. This chapter will follow his plan by discussing each of these areas in turn.

CONSUMPTION

The Consumption Schedule

Keynes began his theory of consumption expenditure from the observation that each year, consumers spend most, but not all, their disposable personal income on personal consumption. This tendency is as clearly observable for the postwar U.S. economy as it was in Keynes's day. As Exhibit 8.1 shows,

Exhibit 8.1
Disposable personal income and personal consumption expenditures in the U.S. economy, 1950–1978
As this exhibit shows, U.S. consumers each year spend most, but not all, their disposable personal income on personal consumption. The percentage of disposable personal income devoted to consumption has remained roughly constant over the period shown.

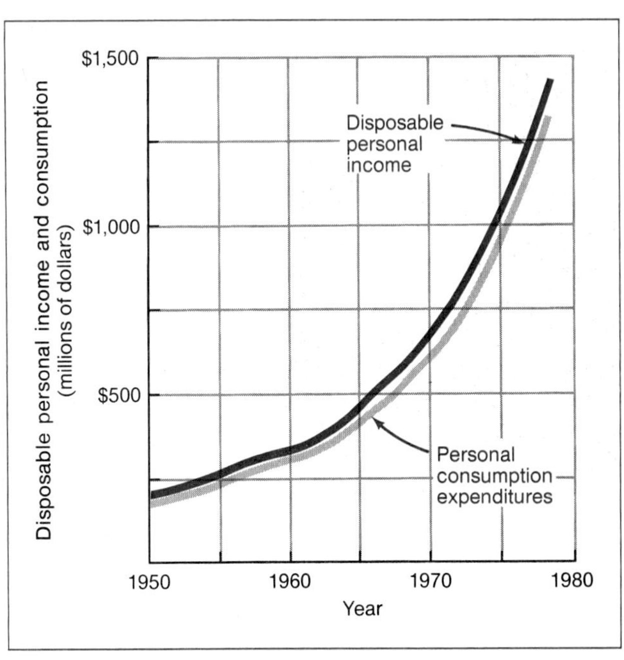

nominal disposable income in the United States grew from $205 billion in 1950 to $1,451 billion in 1978. Each year, consumers spent somewhat over 90 percent of their disposable income on personal consumption.

Reasoning on the basis of this observation, Keynes hypothesized a theoretical relationship between disposable personal income and personal consumption somewhat like the one displayed in Exhibit 8.2. This exhibit shows how consumption changes in response to changes in disposable income—not for the actual U.S. economy but rather for a simplified economy in which consumers each year devote exactly $.75 out of each $1 of added disposable income to consumption. The relationship shown in Exhibit 8.2 is known as a **consumption schedule.**

Consumption schedule A graphical or numerical representation of how nominal consumption expenditure varies as nominal income varies, other things being equal.

(a)

Nominal Disposable Income (1)	Nominal Consumption Expenditure (2)	Change in Income (3)	Change in Consumption (4)	Marginal Propensity to Consume (5)
$ 0	$ 100			
		$100	$75	0.75
100	175			
		100	75	0.75
200	250			
		100	75	0.75
300	325			
		100	75	0.75
400	400			
		100	75	0.75
500	475			
		100	75	0.75
600	550			
		100	75	0.75
700	625			
		100	75	0.75
800	700			
		100	75	0.75
900	775			
		100	75	0.75
1,000	850			
		100	75	0.75
1,100	925			
		100	75	0.75
1,200	1,000			

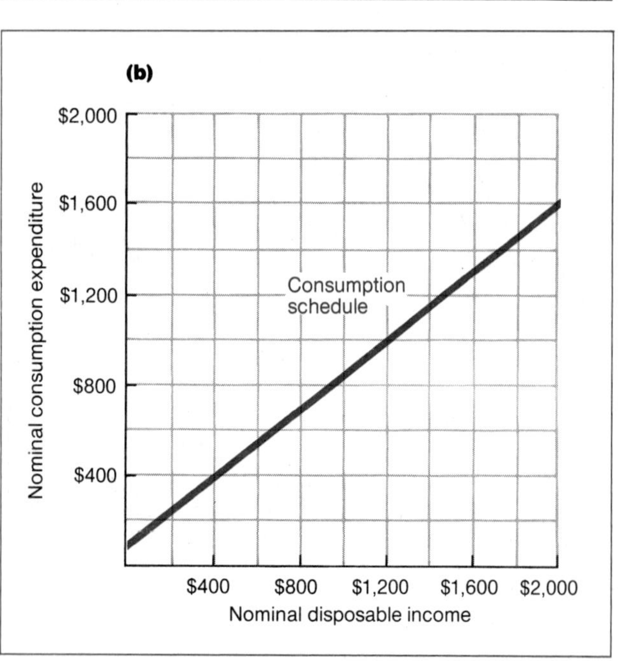

Exhibit 8.2
The consumption schedule
The table and graph both show a simple numerical example of the relationship between disposable income and consumption. The level of autonomous consumption is shown on the graph by the height of the intersection of the consumption schedule with the vertical axis. The slope of the consumption schedule is equal to the marginal propensity to consume.

Autonomous Consumption Note that the consumption schedule in Exhibit 8.2 includes a constant term. Even when aggregate disposable income is zero, aggregate consumption expenditure is equal to $100. The constant term in the consumption schedule is often referred to as **autonomous consumption.**

Autonomous consumption The level of consumption shown by a consumption schedule for a zero disposable income level.

Taken literally, the $100 level of autonomous consumption would indicate that aggregate consumption expenditures would be $100 even if aggregate disposable income were zero. In reality, of course, aggregate disposable income never falls to zero. Individual households, however, may temporarily experience zero disposable income; and when they do, they do not cut consumption expenditures to zero. Instead, they borrow or draw on past savings to maintain some minimal level of consumption. To that extent, the concept of autonomous consumption is rooted in actual consumer behavior.

Marginal Propensity to Consume Look now at Columns 1 to 4 of Exhibit 8.2a. The numbers in these columns show that whenever household income increases, some of the additional income is devoted to consumption above and beyond autonomous consumption. The fraction of each added dollar of disposable income that goes to added consumption is called the **marginal propensity to consume.**

Marginal propensity to consume The fraction of each added dollar of disposable income that goes to added consumption.

For example, a $100 increase in disposable income, from $500 to $600, raises consumption by $75, from $475 to $550. Similarly, a $100 decrease in disposable income from $500 to $400 would cause consumption to fall by $75, from $475 to $400. The value of the marginal propensity to consume for this numerical example is thus 0.75 (75 divided by 100).

In geometric terms, the marginal propensity to consume is equal to the slope of the consumption schedule. In Exhibit 8.2b, a horizontal movement of $100 in disposable income corresponds to a vertical movement of $75 in planned consumption. The slope of the consumption schedule is thus 75 divided by 100 equals 0.75, the same as the marginal propensity to consume.

Saving Schedule

Once we know the level of consumption corresponding to each level of disposable income, we can easily calculate the level of saving that corresponds to each level of disposable income. The relationship between saving and income, called the **saving schedule,** is given in numerical form in Exhibit 8.3a. The numbers in this table are calculated simply by subtracting consumption from disposable income.

Saving schedule A graphical or numerical representation of how nominal saving varies as nominal disposable income varies, other things being equal.

The saving schedule is shown in geometric form in Exhibit 8.3b. This figure can be constructed simply by plotting the numbers from Column 3 of the table. The saving schedule can also be derived directly from the consumption schedule, which is Exhibit 8.3c. The level of saving corresponding to each level of disposable income is equal to the vertical distance between the consumption schedule and the 45 degree reference line.

In the numerical example, a **dissaving**—negative saving—of $100 occurs when disposable income is zero. Saving at a zero disposable income is the negative of autonomous consumption. At the $400 level of disposable income there is a breakeven point at which neither saving nor dissaving occurs. Below that point, consumption exceeds disposable income; and above it, consumption falls short of disposable income.

Dissaving Negative saving—the difference between disposable income and consumption expenditure when consumption exceeds disposable income.

(a)

Nominal Disposable Income (1)	Nominal Consumption (2)	Nominal Saving (3)
$ 0	$ 100	–$100
100	175	–75
200	250	–50
300	325	–25
400	400	0
500	475	25
600	550	50
700	625	75
800	700	100
900	775	125
1,000	850	150
1,100	925	175
1,200	1,000	200
1,300	1,075	225
1,400	1,150	250
1,500	1,225	275
1,600	1,300	300
1,700	1,375	325
1,800	1,450	350
1,900	1,525	375
2,000	1,600	400

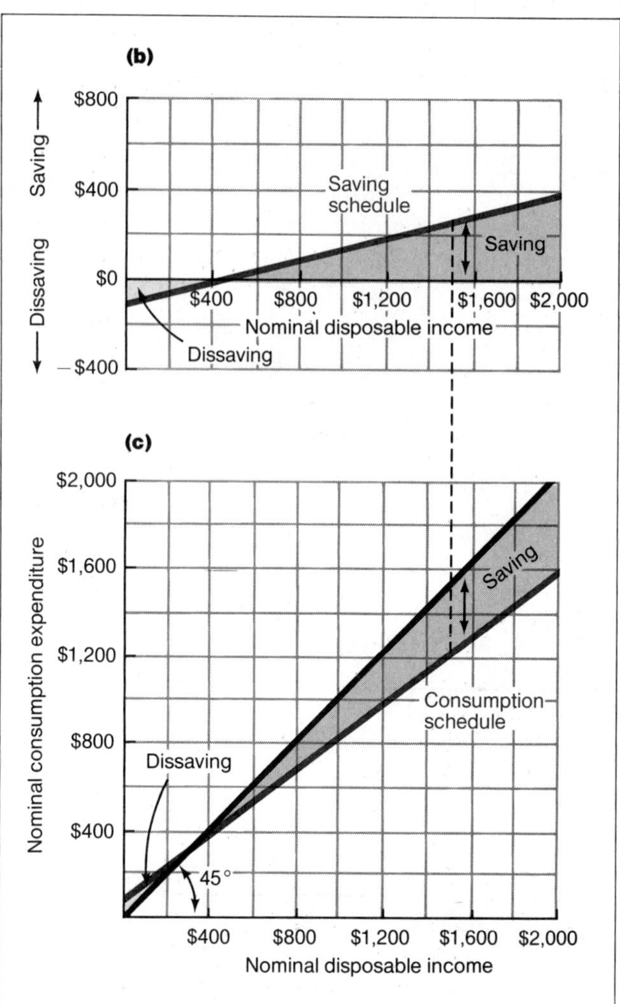

Exhibit 8.3
The saving schedule
The saving schedule shows the relationship between saving and income. In the table (Part a), saving is found by subtracting consumption from disposable income. In Part b of the exhibit, the saving schedule is given in graphical form. It could be constructed directly from the numbers in Column 3 of the table or from the consumption schedule shown in Part c.

Marginal propensity to save The fraction of each added dollar of disposable income that is not consumed.

The **marginal propensity to save** is the fraction of each additional dollar of disposable income that is not consumed. Because all disposable income is, by definition, either saved or consumed, it follows that the marginal propensity to save (MPS) is equal to 1 minus the marginal propensity to consume (MPC):

$$MPS = 1 - MPC.$$

In geometric terms, the marginal propensity to save is equal to the slope of the saving schedule, which is 0.25 in Exhibit 8.3.

Short Run versus Long Run

In practice, the marginal propensities to consume and save depend on, among other things, the time horizon under discussion. Over long historical periods, aggregate consumption expenditures have risen slightly more than $.90 for each $1 increase in aggregate disposable income. In the short run, however, people tend to change their consumption by somewhat less than $.90 out of each $1 change in income that they perceive as being only temporary. A household accustomed to a yearly disposable income of $15,000 would tend to economize somewhat on its consumption if its income dropped, in one exceptional year, to $12,000. But as long as it expected better times to return, it would tend to spend more in that year than if it expected the decline in income to be permanent.

Because this book focuses primarily on short-run problems of economic stabilization policy, the numerical examples in this and the following chapters employ a marginal propensity to consume of 0.75, which is lower than the long-run marginal propensity to consume of about 0.9. No claim is made that 0.75 is exactly the value of the marginal propensity to consume for the U.S. economy, but for the short run it is probably realistic.

Shifts in the Consumption Schedule

In working with the consumption schedule (as in many areas of economics) it is important to distinguish between movements along the schedule and shifts in the whole schedule. The consumption schedule represents the relationship between nominal consumption expenditures and nominal disposable income, other things being equal. A change in consumption brought about by a change in nominal disposable income, then, is represented by a movement *along* the schedule. A change in consumption brought about by a change in something other than nominal disposable income is represented by a *shift* in the schedule. Among the possible causes of shifts, the following are particularly important: changes in wealth, changes in expectations, changes in the price level, and changes in the rate of inflation.

Changes in Wealth The consumption decisions that a household makes are influenced not only by its current flow of income but also by its accumulated stock of wealth. Other things being equal, a household with a monthly income of $1,000 and $100,000 in the bank can be expected to spend more freely than a household living on the same monthly income and having few, if any, financial reserves. What is true for individual households is also true for the economy as a whole. Any increase in the aggregate wealth of all households, then, can be expected to produce an upward shift in the consumption schedule—that is, more consumption spending at each given level of disposable income. For example, many people hold a substantial part of their wealth in the form of corporate stocks. A rise in the average value of those stocks would increase the aggregate wealth of stockholders and would tend to produce an upward shift in the consumption schedule. A decline in aggregate wealth, other things being equal, would tend to reduce consumption and shift the consumption schedule downward.

Changes in Expectations People's consumption decisions depend not only on their current income but also on their expectations regarding their future income. Other things being equal, an increase in the expected future nominal income tends to increase present consumption expenditure, even before the increase in income is actually realized. This effect is represented by an upward shift in the consumption schedule. Similarly, a decrease in expected future income tends to depress current consumption spending. For example, if consumers feared a coming recession, in which many of them would lose their jobs and hence their sources of income, they might cut back on their consumption expenditures even before the expected decline in income actually occurred. This would be represented by a downward shift in the consumption schedule.

Changes in the Price Level All changes in nominal disposable income are represented as movements along the consumption schedule, whether they refer to changes in real disposable income with the price level constant, changes in the price level with real income constant, or some mix of the two. It is worth enquiring, however, whether a change in the price level might cause a shift in the consumption schedule as well. Two possibilities are worth considering.

First, it seems reasonable to assume that a single, permanent change in the price level, once consumers fully adjust to it, will produce a proportional change in autonomous consumption—the point at which the consumption schedule intercepts the vertical axis. Think of real autonomous consumption as the level of consumption that consumers would maintain in the hypothetical event that real aggregate disposable income fell to zero. If the price level doubles, the nominal value of autonomous consumption will also have to double in order to keep the real value of autonomous consumption constant. This implies that an increase in the price level will tend to shift the nominal consumption schedule upward.

A second effect of changes in the price level, however, tends to offset the first effect. The second effect results from the fact that many of the forms in which people hold their wealth—bank deposits, private and government bonds, life insurance, private pension rights, and so on—have values that are fixed in nominal terms. An increase in the price level thus decreases the real value of household wealth. If the price level doubles, a savings account or life insurance annuity or other savings instrument ends up with only half the purchasing power it had before. By itself, therefore, the effect of an increase in the price level on real wealth tends to cause the consumption schedule to shift downward.

In practice, it is not known which of these two effects acts more strongly on short-run consumption decisions. To simplify the discussion, this and the following chapters will assume that the two effects exactly offset one another. They will thus treat the nominal consumption schedule as not shifting either up or down in response to a single, permanent change in the price level.

Changes in the Rate of Inflation The preceding section discussed the effects of a single, permanent price level change to which consumers are fully able to adjust. Equally, if not more, important as a determinant of consumer spending are changes in the rate of inflation—that is, variations in the rate of change of the price level. Once again, two different consumer reactions to changes in the rate of inflation must be distinguished.

First, consumers tend to view increases in the rate of inflation as a sign of hard times to come. They may not expect their nominal wages and salaries to keep up with inflation, or they may expect government to fight the inflation with policies that increase unemployment and that may therefore cost them their jobs. To the extent that consumers treat inflation as a sign of hard times to come, an increase in the rate of inflation tends to depress consumer spending, thereby shifting the consumption schedule downward.

However, an increase in the rate of inflation can also have the opposite effect. When consumers see the rate edging up, they may decide to buy before prices go up still more. This anticipatory buying tends to increase consumer spending, which shifts the consumption schedule upward.

There is no way to be certain which of the two effects of inflation on consumer spending will predominate. There are indications, however, that a major shift in consumer reactions to inflation occurred during the 1970s. In the past, the "hard times" effect apparently predominated, and consumers reduced their expenditures when inflation accelerated. Today, however, the anticipatory buying effect seems to be the stronger of the two, so that news of accelerating inflation tends to stimulate, rather than depress, consumer spending.

Adjusting for Taxes

Up to this point, consumption has been discussed only in relation to disposable income. But the consumption schedule can also be adjusted for taxes and expressed in terms of national income rather than disposable income. (These chapters assume that there are no indirect business taxes or undistributed corporate profits, which means that national income is considered equal to disposable personal income plus net taxes.)

In adjustment of the consumption schedule for taxes, two separate cases will be considered. In the first case, illustrated by Exhibit 8.4, all taxes and transfers are of the **lump sum** form—that is, they do not change as income changes. Columns 3 and 4 of the table give the familiar consumption schedule in terms of disposable income, while Columns 1 and 4 show the relationship between national income and consumption expenditure.

Lump sum taxes Taxes that do not vary as income varies.

In the second case, illustrated by Exhibit 8.5, the government employs a

Exhibit 8.4
National income and consumption with lump sum taxes
Lump sum taxes are taxes that do not change when the level of income changes. This table shows how the consumption schedule can be expressed in terms of either disposable income (Columns 3 and 4) or national income (Columns 1 and 4) for an economy where all taxes are of the lump sum variety. In the simple economy on which the table is based, there are no undistributed corporate profits or indirect business taxes, so national income is equal to disposable income plus net taxes.

Nominal National Income (1)	Nominal Net Taxes (2)	Nominal Disposable Income (3)	Nominal Consumption Expenditure (4)	Nominal Saving (5)
$ 100	$100	$ 0	$100	−$100
200	100	100	175	−75
300	100	200	250	−50
400	100	300	325	−25
500	100	400	400	0
600	100	500	475	25
700	100	600	550	50
800	100	700	625	75
900	100	800	700	100
1,000	100	900	775	125
1,100	100	1,000	850	150
1,200	100	1,100	925	175

Exhibit 8.5
National income and consumption with a 20 percent income tax
With an income tax, net taxes rise as income increases. Each additional $1 of national income results in an additional $.60 of consumption, an additional $.20 of saving, and an additional $.20 of net taxes. Three-quarters of each added $1 of *disposable* income goes to consumption, but only 60 percent of each added $1 of *national* income goes to consumption.

Nominal National Income (1)	Nominal Net Taxes (2)	Nominal Disposable Income (3)	Nominal Consumption Expenditure (4)	Nominal Saving (5)
$ 100	$ 20	$ 80	$160	−$80
200	40	160	220	−60
300	60	240	280	−40
400	80	320	340	−20
500	100	400	400	0
600	120	480	460	20
700	140	560	520	40
800	160	640	580	60
900	180	720	640	80
1,000	200	800	700	100
1,100	220	880	760	120
1,200	240	960	820	140

personal income tax. Here, the amount of tax collected does change as the level of national income changes. In construction of the table, the assumption has been that everyone pays a straight 20 percent income tax, regardless of the amount of earnings. (The actual income tax is much more complicated, of course.) Again, Columns 3 and 4 give the consumption schedule in terms of disposable income, and Columns 1 and 4 give the schedule in terms of national income.

Compare the two cases. With lump sum taxes, an additional $1 of national income results in an additional $.75 of consumption expenditure and an additional $.25 in saving. With an income tax, the additional $1 of national income results in an additional $.60 of consumption, an additional $.20 of saving, and an additional $.20 of net taxes. One might say that, in the second case, there are two different marginal propensities to consume. The propensity to consume out of national income (0.6) is lower than the propensity to consume out of disposable income (0.75).

The U.S. government does make heavy use of the personal income tax, so the second of the two cases considered here is the more realistic. On the other hand, lump sum taxes simplify the job of theory building. In the chapters that follow, the simplifying assumption of lump sum taxes will be used whenever possible. When it is important for questions of policy, though, the effects of an income tax will also be discussed.

The Stability of the Consumption Schedule

So many things can produce shifts in the consumption schedule that its usefulness can be questioned. What good does it do to draw a relationship between consumption expenditure and disposable income, other things being equal, if the "other things" change so frequently?

There is some validity to this criticism. Short-run predictions of changes in consumer spending have not always proved accurate, even when forecasters have taken precautions to correct for changes in wealth, expectations, and inflation. The concern in this book, however, is not with practical forecasting techniques but rather with establishing a general theoretical understanding of important macroeconomic relationships. For present purposes, then, the consumption schedule will be treated as a reasonably stable relationship between nominal consumption expenditures and nominal disposable income. Shifts in the schedule will be introduced only when strictly necessary.

PLANNED INVESTMENT EXPENDITURE

After consumption, the second major component of aggregate demand is planned investment expenditure. Planned investment, as discussed earlier, includes both fixed investment and planned inventory investment. Total investment, as measured in the national income accounts, includes planned investment plus unplanned inventory investment. Our immediate interest is in what determines aggregate demand, so unplanned inventory investment will be ignored for the moment.

Determinants of Planned Investment[1]

The rate of planned expenditure depends on two things: the expected real rate of return on investment and the expected real rate of interest. The **expected real rate of return** is the real net annual improvement in a firm's cost or revenue that it expects to obtain by making an investment; it is expressed as a percentage of the sum invested. The expected real rate of interest is the expected real cost to the firm of borrowing funds from outside sources or the expected real opportunity cost to the firm of using its own funds. A simple example will show how these two factors enter into the decision to invest.

Expected real rate of return
The annual real net improvement in a firm's cost or revenue that it expects to obtain by making an investment; it is expressed as a percentage of the sum invested.

Suppose you are the manager of a small factory. You are worried about the rising cost of energy, so you hire a consultant who is a specialist in energy conservation. The consultant tells you that if you insulate the roof of your warehouse, you will save $1,200 per year in heating and cooling costs. The insulation will cost $10,000 to install and, once installed, will last forever. How do you decide whether to undertake this investment project?

First, you calculate the rate of return on the investment. A saving of $1,200 per year means a saving of $.12 per year for each $1 invested to install the insulation, so the rate of return is 12 percent per year. Next, you find out what the interest rate on a $10,000 loan will be. You call your banker, who says that the money is available at a nominal rate of 10 percent per year. (Neither you nor your banker expects any inflation, so that rate is also the expected real rate of interest.) You will have to pay $1,000 per year in interest charges. Even after paying the interest, you will have $200 in pure profit left from your $1,200 saving in energy costs. The investment is worthwhile, so you go ahead with it.

Perhaps you do not need to borrow money to make the investment. Instead, your firm has $10,000 or more in uncommitted cash balances left over from last year's profits. In that case, the interest rate you must use for your invest-

[1]Only the bare outlines of investment decision making are covered in this section. A more complete treatment appears in the Appendix to Chapter 8.

ment decision is the real rate those funds are now earning for you. Suppose that your uncommitted cash is invested in U.S. government bonds that pay an expected real rate of 10 percent per year. Taking $10,000 out of bonds has an opportunity cost to you of $1,000 per year in forgone interest payments, but the $1,200 saving in energy costs will more than make up for that. You still decide to put in the insulation.

This very simple example provides the basis for an important generalization. A firm will find it profitable to undertake an investment project if, and only if, the expected real rate of return on that project is higher than the expected real rate of interest. If the rate of return is equal to the rate of interest, the project will just break even, and it will be a matter of indifference whether or not it is undertaken. If the rate of interest exceeds the rate of return, the project will involve a loss and should therefore not be undertaken.

Planned Investment Schedule

The analysis of the determinants of planned investment suggests a general relationship between the expected real rate of interest and the rate of planned investment for the economy as a whole. The lower the expected real rate of interest, the greater the number of profitable investment projects. Other things being equal, then, the rate of planned investment will be higher the lower the expected real rate of interest. This relationship between interest and planned investment is shown graphically in the form of a **planned investment schedule** in Exhibit 8.6.

Planned investment schedule A graphical representation of how the rate of planned investment for the economy as a whole varies as the expected real rate of interest varies, other things being equal.

Movements along the Planned Investment Schedule Anything that causes a change in the expected real rate of interest, other things being equal, will produce a movement along the planned investment schedule. In Chapter 7, the expected real rate of interest was defined as the nominal rate of interest minus the expected rate of inflation. This definition suggests two possible causes of movements along the planned investment schedule.

First, an increase in the nominal rate of interest, with the expected rate of inflation held constant, would increase the expected real rate of interest. This would produce a movement up and to the left along the planned investment schedule. Similarly, a decrease in the nominal rate of interest, with the expected rate of inflation held constant, would produce a movement down and to the right along the planned investment schedule.

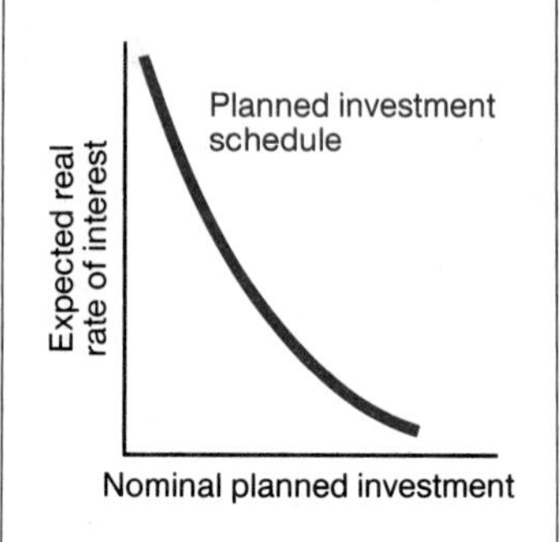

Exhibit 8.6
The planned investment schedule
The planned investment schedule shows how planned investment expenditure varies as the expected real rate of interest varies, other things being equal. The downward slope of the schedule indicates that decreases in the expected real rate of interest tend to cause increases in planned investment expenditure.

Second, an increase in the expected rate of inflation, with the nominal rate of interest held constant, would reduce the expected real rate of interest. This would produce a movement down and to the right along the planned investment schedule. Similarly, a decrease in the expected rate of inflation, with the nominal rate of interest held constant, would produce a movement up and to the left along the planned investment schedule.

Shifts in the Planned Investment Schedule A change in planned investment expenditure resulting from any cause other than a change in the expected real rate of interest is properly represented by a shift in the planned investment schedule. Such a shift can occur as the result of any factor affecting the expected real rate of return on investment projects—hence the willingness of businesses to undertake any given investment project at any given expected real rate of interest. A variety of factors can affect the expected real rate of return. For example, changes in technology might introduce attractive investment opportunities, such as computerization of production or accounting operations, that did not exist before. Or changes in the prices of inputs—for example, an increase in energy prices—might increase the attractiveness of investment projects, such as the roof insulation in the example just given, that previously would not have been considered worthwhile. Or improved expectations of the growth in demand for real output would encourage investment in increasing the capacity to supply that output. All these things would tend to cause the planned investment schedule to shift to the right, as shown in Exhibit 8.7.

Certain other kinds of developments would tend to discourage investment, shifting the planned investment schedule to the left. Pessimistic expectations about the growth of real demand would be one such factor. Another might be the introduction of government regulations limiting the price for which output could be sold, increasing production costs, or otherwise reducing the expected real rate of return on investment.

The Stability of Planned Investment

Because the rate of planned investment depends so heavily on expectations, and because expectations can sometimes change quickly, planned investment expenditure can vary considerably from year to year. As Exhibit 8.8a shows, there have been times in U.S. economic history when investment has undergone wide swings over short periods.

Exhibit 8.7
A shift in the planned investment schedule
A change in the expected real rate of interest, other things being equal, causes a movement along the planned investment schedule. A change in either the nominal rate of interest or the expected rate of inflation could cause such a change in the expected real rate of interest. Changes in other factors affecting planned investment cause shifts in the planned investment schedule. The shift shown here could be caused, for example, by an increase in business optimism or the appearance of a new technological development that makes investment more attractive at any given rate of interest.

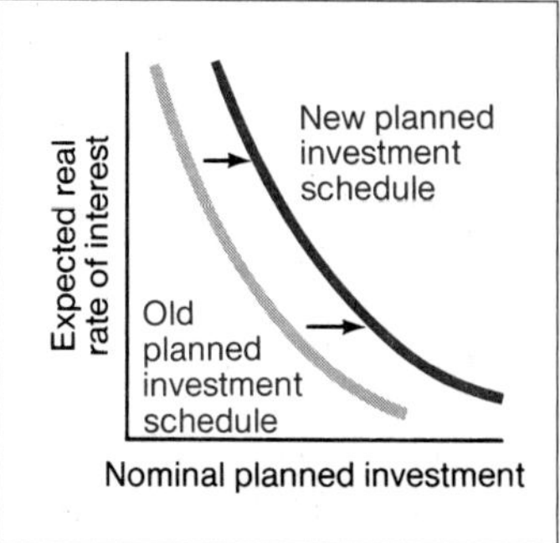

Exhibit 8.8

Investment expenditures in the U.S. economy, 1929–1978

Investment expenditure in the U.S. economy has often changed sharply from year to year. The changes shown here were caused partly by changes in interest rates and partly by changes in expected rates of return. The inventory component of total investment expenditure is particularly unstable. The data on inventory investment shown here lump together planned and unplanned inventory expenditure.

Source: President's Council of Economic Advisers, *Economic Report of the President* (Washington, D.C.: Government Printing Office, 1979), Table B–14.

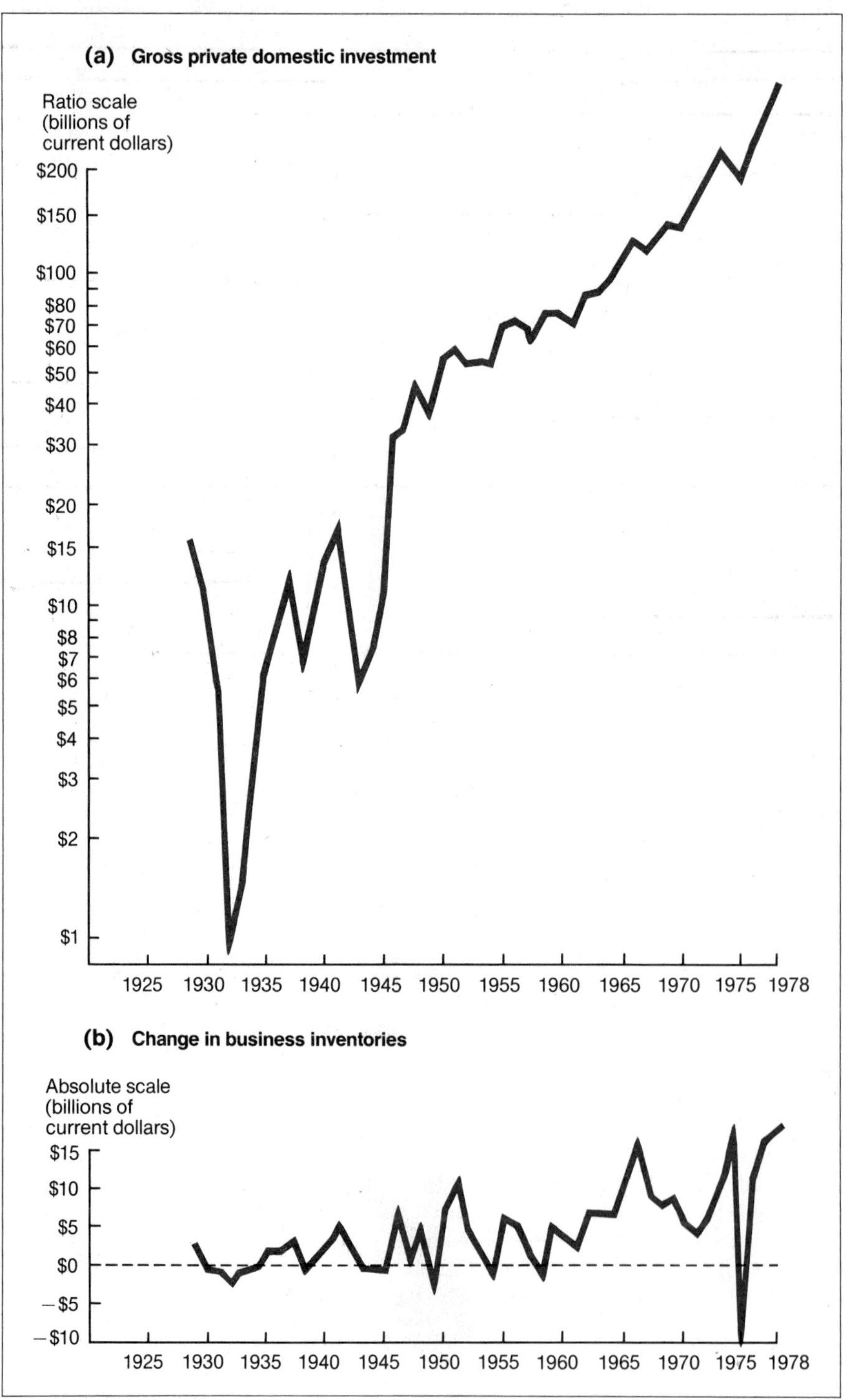

Inventory investment is a particularly unstable component of total investment expenditure, as Exhibit 8.8b shows. Unfortunately, it is impossible to distinguish statistically between year-to-year changes in *planned* inventory investment and year-to-year changes in *unplanned* inventory investment. As the theory developed in the following chapters will make clear, changes in planned inventory investment can be considered a *cause* of instability for the economy as a whole, while changes in unplanned inventory investment can be considered a *consequence* of disequilibrium originating elsewhere in the economy. Exhibit 8.8b lumps together planned and unplanned inventory investment.

OTHER TYPES OF EXPENDITURE

Government Purchases

After consumption and planned investment, the third major component of aggregate demand is government purchases of goods and services. In macroeconomic analysis, the level of government purchases traditionally is considered to be determined by political decision processes that are outside the economic system. Adhering to that tradition does not mean assuming that the legislators and executives who make spending decisions at various levels of government are wholly uninfluenced by economic considerations such as the level of national income or the rate of unemployment. It means only that these relationships, whatever they are, are too indirect and complex to put into a simple theory.

Net Exports

Net exports are the fourth and final component of aggregate demand. In the U.S. economy, they are normally only 1 or 2 percent of GNP. But that small size may understate their importance as a source of disturbances in aggregate demand, because they can be very volatile. For example, from 1975 to 1977, net exports fell from $20.4 billion to −$11.1 billion, a total swing equivalent to about 3 percent of GNP.

Because net exports appear to be of growing importance to the U.S. economy, they are included with consumption, planned investment, and government purchases in the discussion of aggregate demand. However, at this early stage in theory building, the economic determinants of the level of net exports will not be discussed. That specialized subject will be treated in Chapter 23. Meanwhile, net exports, like government purchases, will be treated as "givens"; that is, they will be considered as being determined by forces outside the scope of this analysis.

CONCLUSIONS

The objective in this chapter has been to look at the determinants of each kind of planned expenditure in order to understand how aggregate demand as a whole is determined. The chapter has shown that consumption depends on disposable income, that planned investment depends on the expected real interest rate (among other things), and that government spending and net exports can be treated as givens in an introductory discussion. Now, these relationships can be pulled together and applied—in a new chapter.

SUMMARY

1. Following the tradition of Keynesian economics, the theory building begins by looking at what determines each separate component of aggregate demand—consumption, planned investment, government purchases, and net exports.
2. The consumption schedule shows that as nominal disposable income increases, nominal consumption expenditure also increases—but not by as much as the increase in income. The fraction of each added dollar of income that is devoted to consumption is called the marginal propensity to consume. The part of disposable income that is not consumed is saved. The marginal propensity to save is equal to 1 minus the marginal propensity to consume.
3. Planned investment expenditure depends on the expected real rate of interest and the expected real rate of return on investment projects. The planned investment schedule represents the way planned investment varies as the expected real rate of interest varies, other things being equal. Other kinds of changes that affect the expected real rate of return on investment are represented graphically as shifts in the planned investment schedule.
4. For purposes of elementary theory, government purchases are considered to be determined by forces outside the scope of economic analysis. For the present, net exports are also treated as given; the discussion of their determinants is reserved for Chapter 23.

DISCUSSION QUESTIONS

1. Autonomous consumption is the level of consumption that would occur if national income were zero. Since national income will never be zero, why do we talk about autonomous consumption? In other words, what does it really mean? And how does it affect the consumption schedule? What word or expression might you use in place of *autonomous* when talking about autonomous consumption?
2. Since saving and consumption are related, is there an autonomous saving that can be related to autonomous consumption? How would you find this "autonomous saving"?
3. Suppose you unexpectedly won $1,000 in a lottery. How much of the winnings would you devote to current consumption, and how much would you save? Do you think you would spend as large a fraction of the one-time lottery prize as you would of a $1,000 increase in your annual income that you expected to be permanent? Would it surprise you to learn that some economic studies have indicated that, on the average, the fraction of windfalls spent on current consumption is less than the overall marginal propensity to consume? Explain.
4. Have you ever consciously engaged in anticipatory buying, fearing that if you did not buy some item now, its price would only be higher later? Did your fears prove justified? Would you have been better off in preparing for the coming inflation by increasing your rate of saving, thereby building a pool of funds to help you through the hard times that inflation might bring? Explain.
5. Turn back to the example of investment in roof insulation given earlier in the chapter. Assume the same facts as before, including a 10 percent nominal interest rate, with one exception: Assume that you expect a 5 percent rate of inflation over the indefinite future, with the prices of all goods and services rising at exactly the same rate. Will that make the investment more attractive or less attractive than under the assumption of price stability? Explain.

APPENDIX TO CHAPTER 8
INVESTMENT DECISION MAKING AND CAPITAL BUDGETING

read for test?

The discussion of investment decision making in this chapter used an extremely simplified example of a potential investment project that had only one possible form, an infinite life, and a uniform payback per year. This example was sufficient to get across the point that the expected real rate of interest is an important consideration in investment decision making. Clearly, though, it was too simple to give much of an idea about how investment decisions are actually made in the real world of business. In business terminology, problems like that of whether to insulate the warehouse roof are known as problems of *capital budgeting*. This appendix will introduce a few simple concepts and techniques of capital budgeting.

PAYBACK PERIOD ANALYSIS

The capital budgeting problem often takes the form of a choice among a number of alternative investment projects. When this is the case, any of a number of decision-making rules can be used. The simplest, called *payback period analysis*, can be explained by means of an example.

Suppose the Zeus Manufacturing Corporation is looking for ways to modernize its operations. Three departments have submitted proposals to the firm's manager. Project A is the installation of microfiche equipment to speed up order processing in the shipping department. This will cost $30,000 and will save the firm $15,000 a year for the foreseeable future. Project B, turned in by the machine shop, asks for an overhaul of a large stamping machine that is reaching the end of its useful life. The overhaul will cost $15,000 and will extend the life of the machine for 3 years. It will save $6,000 per year on the rental of replacement equipment. Project C is to set up a plastics molding shop, which will allow Zeus to make certain small plastic parts for itself that it now buys from subcontractors. Setting up the shop will cost $100,000, and operating expenses for the shop will be $15,000 per year. Making the parts at Zeus will eliminate the $40,000 per year now spent for the parts purchased from outsiders. There will thus be a net improvement in cash flow, after operating expenses, of $25,000 per year. The equipment in the shop will last 5 years; and in the last year, there will be an extra $5,000 cost for removing the worn-out equipment.

Exhibit 8A.1 summarizes the three projects. The figure in the net cash flow column shows the net expense (−) or savings (+) in each year of the project. The initial investment cost is listed under Year 0.

Let's see how payback period analysis can be applied to the three projects. Project A will pay back the $30,000 initial investment after 2 years of $15,000 per year improvement in net cash flow. The payback period for Project B is 2.5 years, the length of time needed to recoup the initial $15,000 at $6,000 per year. Project C has a payback period of 4 years. On the principle that time is money, Project A comes out on top. It returns the initial investment in the shortest time, so it gets top priority. Project B gets the next highest priority, and Project C will be undertaken if enough funds are left after the first two projects are taken care of.

Limitations

Payback period analysis is easy to apply, and it is widely used as a rough yardstick for ranking investment projects. Unfortunately, it has two drawbacks that limit its accuracy. One is that it completely ignores what happens after the payback period is over. The other is that it is not sensitive to variations in the timing of net cash flows

Year	Net Cash Flow	Comments
Project A		
0	−$30,000	Initial investment outlay
1	15,000	
2	15,000	
3	15,000	
4	15,000	
5	15,000	
6	15,000	Continues indefinitely
Project B		
0	−$15,000	Initial overhaul cost
1	6,000	
2	6,000	
3	6,000	
4	—	Machine scrapped
5	—	
6	—	
Project C		
0	−$100,000	Initial investment outlay
1	25,000	
2	25,000	
3	25,000	
4	25,000	
5	20,000	Includes scrapping cost
6	—	End of useful life

Exhibit 8A.1
Payback period comparisons for three investment projects
This exhibit provides the data needed for a payback period analysis of three investment projects. Two years are required for Project A to pay back its $30,000 initial investment. The payback period for Project B is 2.5 years, and for Project C it is 4 years.

within the payback period itself. These drawbacks can be illustrated by an extension of the previous example.

Suppose that Zeus has modernized its shipping department and overhauled its stamping machine. Now it is ready to take on the plastics shop project. Three different suppliers sell the equipment needed. Supplier X sells the equipment on the terms given earlier. Supplier Y charges the same initial price, and its equipment performs just as well. What is more, Supplier Y offers to repurchase the worn-out equipment for $15,000 at the end of the sixth year of the project. Supplier Z offers a slightly different type of equipment. The initial price is the same, but the annual operating cost is $20,000 rather than $15,000. Knowing that the added operating cost puts it at a disadvantage, Supplier Z offers to pay the entire cost of operating the equipment for the first year and to match Supplier Y's offer to repurchase the worn-out equipment at the end of the sixth year. In addition, it agrees to send its own workers to handle the job of removing the equipment.

The first and second columns of the table in Exhibit 8A.2 summarize the offers of Suppliers X, Y, and Z in terms of net cash flows. Payback period analysis turns out not to work for comparing the three project alternatives. The payback period is exactly 4 years for all three suppliers. Clearly, though, Supplier Y's offer is better than Supplier X's. It gives the same net cash flows during the payback period and better cash flows thereafter. Supplier Z's offer seems even better than Supplier Y's. It pays back the same total amount as the other two during the first 4 years, but the distribution of the payments is weighted more heavily at the early end of the period (and time is money).

DISCOUNTING AND CAPITAL BUDGETING

To make an accurate capital budgeting decision in a case like this, we need a way to compare payments that occur at different times. The method for doing this is known as discounting.

Exhibit 8A.2

Net present value analysis of three project variants

This exhibit gives the data needed to evaluate three investment project variants using the net present value approach. Note that the three project variants all have the same payback period—4 years. They differ in terms of net cash flows after the payback period and in terms of the timing of flows within that period. The project based on Supplier Z is seen to be the most profitable, because it shows the highest net present value. A rate of interest of 10 percent per year is used in calculating the present values shown in the third column.

Year	Net Cash Flow		Discounted Net Cash Flow
Supplier X			
0	–$100,000		–$100,000
1	25,000		22,750
2	25,000		20,750
3	25,000		18,750
4	25,000		17,000
5	20,000		12,400
6	—		—
		Net present value	–$8,350
Supplier Y			
0	–$100,000		–$100,000
1	25,000		22,750
2	25,000		20,750
3	25,000		18,750
4	25,000		17,000
5	20,000		12,400
6	15,000		8,400
		Net present value	+$50
Supplier Z			
0	–$100,000		–$100,000
1	40,000		36,400
2	20,000		16,600
3	20,000		15,000
4	20,000		13,600
5	20,000		12,400
6	15,000		8,400
		Net present value	+$2,400

The Concept of Discounting

In a world where funds can be invested at a positive real rate of interest, it is always an advantage to receive a payment earlier rather than later. Consider, for example, the advantage of receiving $100 today rather than a year from now. Assume that the actual and expected rate of inflation is zero and that the nominal rate of interest is 10 percent. Investing the $100 at 10 percent interest will give not $100 but $110 a year from now. With annual compounding of interest, $100 today will be worth as much as $110 a year from now, $121 two years from now, $133.10 three years from now, and so on.

The same thing can be expressed in a different way. We can say that when the interest rate is 10 percent, $1 payable a year from now is worth only $.91 today, $1 two years from now is worth $.83 today, $1 three years from now is worth just $.75 today, and so on—assuming zero inflation. The reduced value of the future dollars is purely a result of discounting; it does not stem from a change in the price level.

We can generalize this kind of example to any time period and any rate of interest. Let V_p be the sum of money that, if invested today at r percent per year interest, will grow to the sum V_t in t years. V_p is therefore the *present value* of the sum V_t discounted t years at r percent interest. The formula for calculating the present value of any future sum is:

$$V_p = \frac{V_t}{(1 + r)^t}.$$

The Net Present Value Approach

Return now to the Zeus Manufacturing Company and its capital budgeting problem. Looking again at Exhibit 8A.2, recall that the problem was to evaluate three project variants all having the same payback period. These variants can now be compared by using what is called the *net present value approach* to capital budgeting. This approach is based on the discounting formula given above.

The first step in applying the net present value approach is finding the interest rate to be used. This rate must reflect the opportunity cost of capital to the firm. If the firm plans to borrow money to finance the project, the interest rate should be the nominal rate charged by the lender.[1] If the firm plans to use its own funds to finance the project, the interest rate should be the nominal rate that could have been earned had the funds been invested outside the firm. In this case, assume that the proper interest rate is 10 percent.

The second step is calculating the present value of each year's net cash flow. These figures are shown in the third column of Exhibit 8A.2. Finally, the discounted net cash flows for each project (including the initial negative cash flow, which represents the project's initial cost) are added up. The sum for each project variant is called the net present value of that variant. Any project that shows a positive net present value is profitable to undertake. The variant with the highest net present value is the most profitable.

Comparison of the Two Approaches

Comparison of the net present values of the three variants shows why the payback period by itself is not always an adequate guide. If the equipment for the plastics molding shop is purchased from Supplier X, the net present value of the project is negative. This means that if the cost of capital is 10 percent per year, it will be better to continue to buy plastic components from subcontractors at a cost of $40,000 per year than to set up an internal shop. With the deal offered by Supplier Y, the added cash flow from selling the used equipment in Year 6 is just enough to make the net present value positive. The company will be ahead by $50 if it buys equipment from Supplier Y and produces its own plastic components. Finally, the net present value approach shows how very attractive Supplier Z's offer is. Simply by changing the time pattern of net cash flows within the payback period, the gain to Zeus from undertaking the project jumps from $50 to $2,400. The firm's final decision, then, is to build the shop and buy the equipment from Supplier Z.

SUGGESTIONS FOR FURTHER READING

These suggested readings apply collectively to Chapters 8 to 10; many of them cover topics overlapping more than one of the chapters.

Blinder, Alan S. *Fiscal Policy in Theory and Practice.* Morristown, N.J.: General Learning Press, 1973.

An in-depth study of fiscal policy.

Breit, William, and Ransom, Roger L. *The Academic Scribblers.* New York: Holt, Rinehart and Winston, 1971.

Chapter 7 of this book is on Keynes and his work; Chapter 8 is on Alvin Hansen, an early follower of Keynes in the United States; and Chapter 9 is on Paul Samuelson.

Gordon, Robert J. *Macroeconomics.* Boston: Little, Brown, 1978.

Chapter 3 provides a compact, intermediate level treatment of the material covered here in Chapters 8 to 10.

---

[1]The nominal rate is used because the figures in Exhibit 8A.2 are given in nominal terms. Alternatively, the figures in the exhibit could be deflated to take expected inflation into account, and the calculations to be described could then be made in terms of the expected real rate of interest.

Heilbroner, Robert L., and Bernstein, Peter L. *A Primer on Government Spending.* 2d ed. New York: Random House, 1970.
A view of fiscal policy as it looked before the discomforts of the 1970s struck.

Keynes, John Maynard. *The General Theory of Employment, Interest, and Money.* New York: Harcourt, Brace, & World, 1936.
Not all of this classic will be intelligible to the beginning student, but it repays browsing. Use the table of contents as a guide.

President's Council of Economic Advisers. *Economic Report of the President.* Washington, D.C.: Government Printing Office, annually.
Each report has a useful section on fiscal policy that can be looked up in the table of contents.

C H A P T E R **9**

THE MULTIPLIER THEORY OF NATIONAL INCOME DETERMINATION

WHAT YOU WILL LEARN IN THIS CHAPTER

Chapter 8 discussed the determinants of each of the major components of aggregate demand—consumption, planned investment, government purchases, and net exports. This chapter takes the next step in theory building by showing how knowledge of these determinants makes it possible to discover the level of nominal national income for which the circular flow is in equilibrium. Any shifts in the components of aggregate demand will be shown to result in changes in the equilibrium level of nominal national income.

FOR REVIEW

Here are some important terms and concepts that will be put to use in this chapter. If you do not understand them, review them before proceeding.

- *Aggregate supply and demand (Chapter 5)*
- *Equilibrium and disequilibrium in the circular flow (Chapter 5)*
- *Injections and leakages (Chapter 5)*
- *Consumption, saving, and investment schedules (Chapter 8)*

Chapter 5 showed that the circular flow could be in equilibrium only when aggregate demand was equal to aggregate supply—that is, only when total planned expenditures were equal to total national product. If planned expenditures exceeded national product, buyers' attempts to purchase more than was currently being produced would lead to unplanned decreases in business inventories. Firms would react to these decreases by increasing output or by raising prices, thereby causing the level of the circular flow—as measured in nominal terms—to increase. If planned expenditures fell short of national product, business inventories would accumulate at a rate faster than planned, and firms would react by cutting production or lowering prices so the nominal level of the circular flow would drop.

These are the ideas on which the Keynesian theory of national income determination is based. All that need be done now is to add a bit more precision by making use of the detailed analysis of planned expenditure developed in the last chapter.

THE AGGREGATE DEMAND AND SUPPLY SCHEDULES

Aggregate Demand Schedule

Aggregate nominal demand schedule A graph showing the relationship between aggregate nominal demand (the nominal value of total planned expenditure) and nominal national income.

The first step in constructing a theory of nominal income determination is to prepare an **aggregate nominal demand schedule**—a schedule that shows what the nominal level of total planned expenditure will be for each possible level of nominal national income. Exhibit 9.1 indicates how such a schedule can be built up from the separate consumption, investment, government purchase, and net export components discussed in the previous chapter.

(a)

Nominal National Income (1)	Nominal Consumption Expenditure (2)	Nominal Planned Investment (3)	Nominal Government Purchases (4)	Nominal Net Exports (5)	Nominal Total Planned Expenditure (Aggregate Demand) (6)
$ 100	$ 100	$100	$150	$25	$ 375
200	175	100	150	25	450
300	250	100	150	25	525
400	325	100	150	25	600
500	400	100	150	25	675
600	475	100	150	25	750
700	550	100	150	25	825
800	625	100	150	25	900
900	700	100	150	25	975
1,000	775	100	150	25	1,050
1,100	850	100	150	25	1,125
1,200	925	100	150	25	1,200
1,300	1,000	100	150	25	1,275
1,400	1,075	100	150	25	1,350
1,500	1,150	100	150	25	1,425
1,600	1,225	100	150	25	1,500

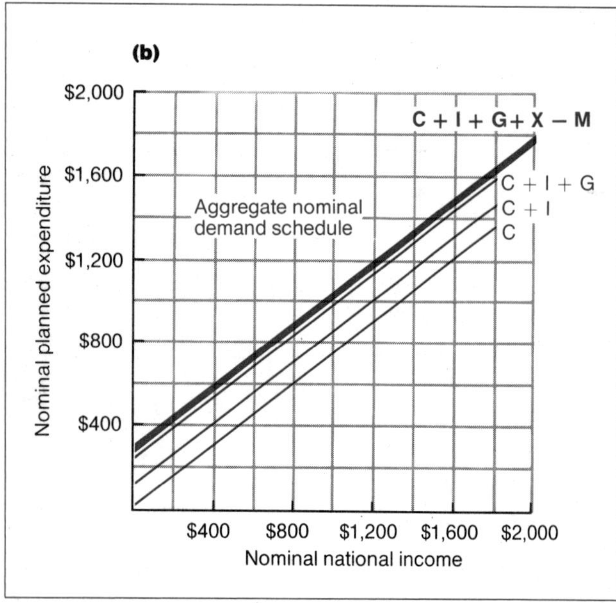

Exhibit 9.1

Construction of the aggregate nominal demand curve
Aggregate nominal demand is the nominal value of all planned expenditures. This exhibit shows how an aggregate nominal demand schedule can be built up from the separate components of consumption, planned investment, government purchases, and net exports. In the simplified economy represented in this exhibit, consumption is the only element of expenditure that varies as nominal national income varies. The slope of the aggregate demand schedule is thus equal to the marginal propensity to consume of 0.75.

Look first at the tabular form of the aggregate nominal demand schedule in Exhibit 9.1a. The consumption schedule in Column 2 is based on an assumed marginal propensity to consume of 0.75, an autonomous consumption of $100, and lump sum net taxes of $100. Interest rates and business conditions are assumed to yield the $100 of planned investment expenditure shown in Column 3. This component of expenditure is assumed not to vary as nominal income varies. Nominal government purchases (Column 4) and net exports (Column 5) are also assumed not to vary. Aggregate nominal demand (Column 6) is equal to the sum of consumption, planned investment, government purchases, and net exports.

The procedure for constructing the graphical form of the aggregate nominal demand schedule, shown in Exhibit 9.1b, is as follows: First, a set of axes is drawn with nominal national income on the horizontal and nominal planned expenditure on the vertical. Next, the consumption schedule is drawn in—adjusted for taxes so that it is stated in terms of national income (as given in Column 2 of the table). This schedule is labeled C in Exhibit 9.1b.

Then, planned investment expenditure is added. Given the shape and position of the planned investment schedule and the rate of interest, planned investment is fixed and does not change as national income changes. A line, labeled C + I, is thus drawn parallel to the consumption schedule, separated from it by a distance equal to the level of planned investment.

The next component of aggregate demand to be added is government purchases, which are assumed to be constant at $150. Adding this component gives a new line, labeled C + I + G. Net exports are assumed in this exhibit to have a constant value of $25, which means that exports (X) exceed imports (M) by that amount. Adding this component gives the aggregate demand schedule line, labeled C + I + G + X − M.

Note that if imports had exceeded exports, net exports would have been negative. In that case, the line labeled C + I + G + X − M would lie below rather than above the line C + I + G.

Aggregate Supply Schedule

Chapter 5 introduced the term *aggregate nominal supply* to refer to the total nominal value of goods and services produced by the economy. The term, it was pointed out, is a synonym for *nominal national product*. Making use of this relationship of aggregate nominal supply and nominal national product allows an **aggregate nominal supply schedule** to be introduced to show the level of nominal national product associated with each level of nominal national income.

Aggregate nominal supply schedule A graph showing the relationship between aggregate nominal supply (nominal national product) and nominal national income. The schedule has the form of a 45 degree line passing through the origin.

In this simplified economy, there are no indirect business taxes, capital consumption allowances, or statistical discrepancies. As a result, there is no distinction between gross and net national product; and national product is, by definition, equal to national income. This means that the aggregate supply schedule is extremely easy to draw. Because the level of nominal national product associated with any given level of nominal national income is equal to that level of nominal national income, the aggregate supply schedule is simply a straight 45 degree line (see Exhibit 9.2). It can easily be checked that each point on the schedule is equally far from the horizontal axis (national income) and the vertical axis (national product).

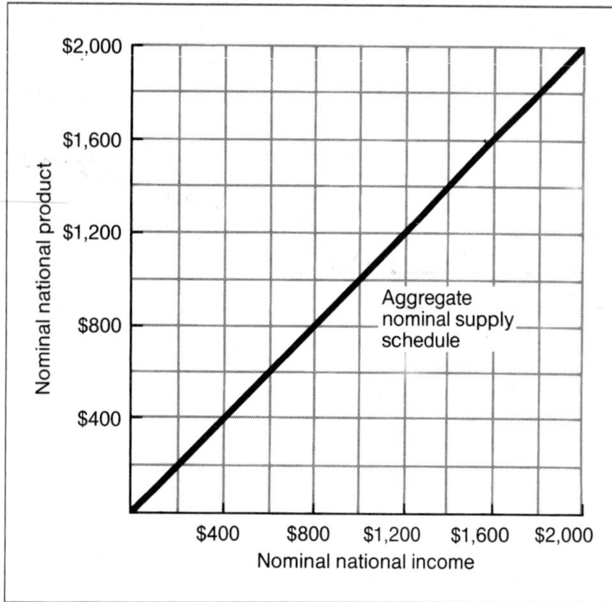

Exhibit 9.2
The aggregate nominal supply curve
Aggregate nominal supply is another term for *nominal national product.* Given the simplifying assumptions used in these chapters (no indirect business taxes, capital consumption allowances, or statistical discrepancies) nominal national product and nominal national income are, by definition, equal. The aggregate nominal supply curve, which shows the relationship between aggregate nominal supply and nominal national income, is thus a 45 degree line passing through the origin, as shown here.

FINDING THE EQUILIBRIUM LEVEL OF NOMINAL NATIONAL INCOME

The Keynesian Cross

Taken together, the aggregate nominal supply and demand schedules make it possible to determine the equilibrium level of nominal national income. Drawing the aggregate nominal supply and demand schedules together on the same diagram, as in Exhibit 9.3, gives a figure that economists call the **Keynesian cross.** A diagram much like this was used by early followers of Keynes to show how the equilibrium level of national income is determined.

Keynesian cross A figure formed by the intersection of the aggregate nominal demand and aggregate nominal supply schedules.

From Chapter 5, we know that the circular flow will be in equilibrium only when total planned expenditure (aggregate demand) is equal to national product (aggregate supply). The point of intersection of the two schedules that comprise the Keynesian cross shows exactly which level of national income permits aggregate supply and demand to be equal. That point, which corresponds to a nominal national income of $1,200 in Exhibit 9.3, is the equilibrium point.

It is easy to see that no other level of nominal national income can represent equilibrium in the circular flow. If national income were lower than the equilibrium level, say $1,000, planned expenditure (aggregate demand) would exceed national product (aggregate supply). There would be unplanned depletion of business inventories equal to the vertical distance between the aggregate demand schedule and the aggregate supply schedule, as shown in Exhibit 9.3. Firms would try to restore inventories to their planned levels by increasing production and/or prices. That increase would in turn cause nominal national income to rise until equilibrium was reached.

If, on the other hand, nominal national income were to be higher than the equilibrium level, say $1,500, then planned expenditures would fall short of national product. The unsold goods would go to unplanned inventory invest-

Exhibit 9.3
Using the Keynesian cross to determine equilibrium national income
The aggregate nominal supply and demand schedules drawn on one diagram form a figure called the Keynesian cross. This figure provides a simple way to determine the equilibrium level of nominal national income, given the assumptions concerning planned expenditure on which the aggregate demand curve is based. Any national income higher than the equilibrium level would result in excess aggregate supply, unplanned inventory accumulation, and downward pressure on nominal national income. Any national income below the equilibrium level would result in excess aggregate demand, unplanned inventory depletion, and upward pressure on nominal national income.

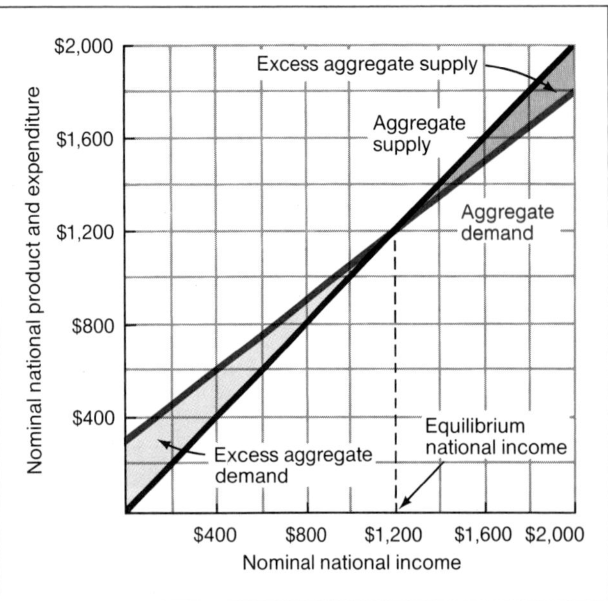

ment equal to the gap between the aggregate demand schedule and the aggregate supply schedule. Firms would react to the unplanned buildup in inventories by cutting production and/or prices. The cutback would cause nominal national income to fall until equilibrium was restored.

A Numerical Example

The same story is told in Exhibit 9.4, which gives numerical values for nominal national income, planned expenditure, and other variables that correspond to the Keynesian cross diagram of Exhibit 9.3. The table confirms that $1,200 is the only level of national income that allows equilibrium in the circular flow. Column 5 shows that national income tends to move toward equilibrium whenever it is at any level other than $1,200.

Leakage-Injection Approach

The leakage-injection approach to determining the equilibrium level of nominal national income is an alternative method for arriving at the same conclusion reached with the aid of the Keynesian cross. It uses the saving schedule rather than the consumption schedule as its starting point.

Exhibit 9.5 illustrates the use of this approach. Columns 2 to 5 of Part a show how national income is divided into consumption, saving, net taxes, and imports. Saving, net taxes, and imports are all leakages from the circular flow. In Part b, a diagonal line is drawn to show how total leakages vary as national income varies. The slope of the line representing total leakages is equal to the marginal propensity to save.

Columns 7 to 9 of Part a show planned injections: planned investment, government purchases, and exports. Under the simplifying assumptions adopted earlier, none of these is assumed to vary as nominal national income varies. The planned injections line in Part b is thus perfectly horizontal. These

Exhibit 9.4

Finding equilibrium nominal national income: A numerical example

This exhibit gives a numerical example of the determination of equilibrium nominal national income, based on the same assumptions that underlie Exhibit 9.3. At every level of nominal national income except the equilibrium level, aggregate supply either falls short of aggregate demand, causing unplanned inventory depletion, or exceeds aggregate demand, causing unplanned inventory accumulation. Unplanned inventory depletion stimulates firms to raise output or prices or both, causing nominal national income to increase; unplanned inventory accumulation causes firms to cut output or prices or both, causing nominal national income to decrease.

Nominal National Income	Nominal Planned Expenditure (Aggregate Demand)	Nominal National Product (Aggregate Supply)	Unplanned Inventory Change	Tendency of Change in National Income
$ 100	$ 375	$ 100	−$275	Increase
200	450	200	−250	Increase
300	525	300	−225	Increase
400	600	400	−200	Increase
500	675	500	−175	Increase
600	750	600	−150	Increase
700	825	700	−125	Increase
800	900	800	−100	Increase
900	975	900	−75	Increase
1,000	1,050	1,000	−50	Increase
1,100	1,125	1,100	−25	Increase
1,200	1,200	1,200	0	No change
1,300	1,275	1,300	25	Decrease
1,400	1,350	1,400	50	Decrease
1,500	1,425	1,500	75	Decrease
1,600	1,500	1,600	100	Decrease

injections represent planned expenditures on domestically produced final goods and services that do not originate in domestic households.

The point in Part b where the injections and leakages schedules cross denotes the equilibrium level of nominal national income. At that point, planned injections are equal to total leakages. Under the saving approach, then, nominal national income is in equilibrium when, and only when, saving plus net taxes plus imports are equal to planned investment plus government purchases plus exports.

A careful comparison of Exhibits 9.5 and 9.3 reveals that the gap between the leakage and injection schedules at any level of nominal national income is exactly equal to the gap between the aggregate nominal demand and supply schedules at the same level of nominal national income.

CHANGES IN NOMINAL NATIONAL INCOME AND THE MULTIPLIER EFFECT

Expenditure Changes

A great many economic factors can affect the level of planned expenditure. The aggregate demand schedule singles out the effects of changes in national income on planned expenditure. The effects of these changes are represented by movements along a given aggregate demand schedule.

Other factors also influence planned expenditure. Changes in consumer

(a)

Nominal National Income (1)	Consumption (2)	Saving (3)	Net Taxes (4)	Imports (5)	Total Leakages (6)	Planned Investment (7)	Government Purchases (8)	Exports (9)	Total Planned Injections (10)
$ 100	$ 100	−$100	$100	$25	$ 25	$100	$150	$50	$300
200	175	−75	100	25	50	100	150	50	300
300	250	−50	100	25	75	100	150	50	300
400	325	−25	100	25	100	100	150	50	300
500	400	0	100	25	125	100	150	50	300
600	475	25	100	25	150	100	150	50	300
700	550	50	100	25	175	100	150	50	300
800	625	75	100	25	200	100	150	50	300
900	700	100	100	25	225	100	150	50	300
1,000	775	125	100	25	250	100	150	50	300
1,100	850	150	100	25	275	100	150	50	300
1,200	925	175	100	25	300	100	150	50	300
1,300	1,000	200	100	25	325	100	150	50	300
1,400	1,075	225	100	25	350	100	150	50	300
1,500	1,150	250	100	25	375	100	150	50	300

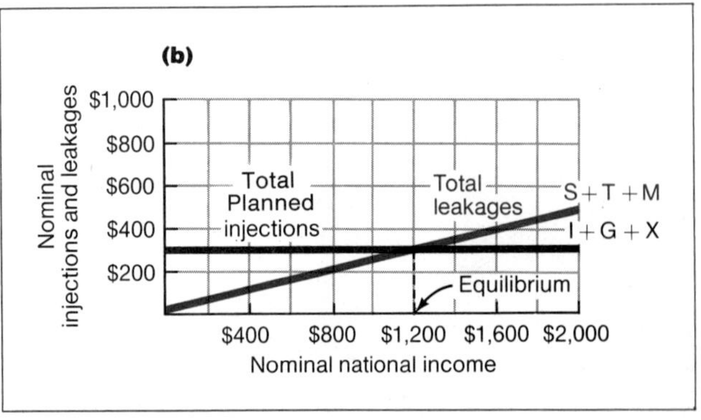

Exhibit 9.5
The injection-leakage approach to national income determination

This exhibit shows how the equilibrium level of nominal national income can be determined by finding the point where planned injections to the circular flow (planned investment plus government purchases plus exports) are equal to total leakages from the circular flow (saving plus net taxes plus imports).

expectations, in wealth, or in the rate of inflation cause the level of autonomous consumption to vary. Changes in the expected real rate of interest or the expected real return on investment projects cause the level of planned investment to vary. Changes in policy cause the government purchases component of planned expenditure to vary, and changes in the world economy affect the volume of net exports. All the changes in planned expenditure that arise from reasons other than changes in national income must be represented by shifts in the aggregate demand schedule.

Consider Exhibit 9.6, which shows the effects of a $100 increase in planned expenditure at all levels of income. For the moment, it does not matter whether this increase originates in the consumption, investment, government purchases, or net export component of aggregate demand. The effect in any case is to shift the aggregate nominal demand schedule upward by $100, from the position AND_1 to the position AND_2.

The Multiplier Effect

What happens to the equilibrium level of national income when the planned expenditure schedule shifts upward by $100? The immediate effect is that planned expenditure exceeds national product, so that inventories start to be

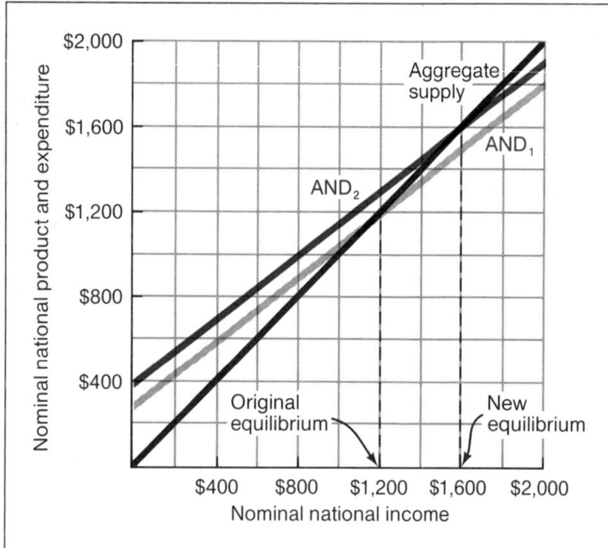

Exhibit 9.6
The multiplier effect of a shift in the aggregate demand schedule

A shift in the aggregate nominal demand schedule produces a more than equal change in equilibrium nominal national income. This is known as the multiplier effect. Here, a $100 upward shift in the aggregate nominal demand schedule produces a $400 increase in equilibrium nominal national income. The ratio of the change in equilibrium income to the original shift in demand, known as the simple multiplier, thus has a value of 4 in this example.

Paul Anthony Samuelson (1915–)

In 1970, the Swedish Academy of Sciences awarded its Nobel Memorial Prize in Economics to MIT Professor Paul Samuelson. In doing so, the academy announced that "Professor Samuelson's extensive production, covering nearly all areas of economic theory, is characterized by an outstanding ability to derive important new theorems and to find new applications for existing ones. By his contributions, Samuelson has done more than any other contemporary economist to raise the level of scientific analysis in economic theory." The multiplier theory of national income determination is just one of dozens that has been refined, restated, and sharpened by Samuelson's penetrating mind.

Samuelson began his task of raising the level of scientific analysis in economic theory early in his career. His doctoral dissertation at Harvard, written when he was just twenty-six, was boldly entitled *Foundations of Economic Analysis.* (Contrast this with the narrow, ultraspecialized topics of most dissertations!) Published in 1947, the *Foundations* immediately became—and to a great extent remains—the definitive statement in modern mathematical dress of much of neoclassical economics.

In the nineteenth century, leading economists had seen their major theoretical statements go on to become textbooks to future generations. Alas, Samuelson's *Foundations* could not serve that purpose. One must already be well educated in economics and mathematics even to read it. Something had to be done to bring the advances in economic theory made during the 1930s and 1940s into the college classroom. Samuelson solved the problem with his famous *Economics.* That book was based on the simple assumption that beginning students did not need to be taught a different *kind* of economics than the kind economists wrote in their own professional journals. What they needed was a lucid, step-by-step presentation. The formula was so successful that Samuelson's *Economics* sold millions of copies as it went through a total of eleven editions.

On policy issues Samuelson ranks as a liberal and an activist. He derides the laissez-faire market economy as a "system of coercion by dollar votes." Unlike many like-minded colleagues, however, Samuelson did not move to Washington during the Kennedy-Johnson years. He was called on frequently for his opinions and advice, but he resisted service on the Council of Economic Advisers. Although much sought as a lecturer and writer of popular articles, Samuelson remains fundamentally an economist's economist. "In the long run," he has said, "the economic scholar works for the only coin worth having—our own applause."

depleted at a rate of $100 per year. Firms react to this unplanned inventory depletion by increasing output and/or prices. Nominal national income rises to its new equilibrium level of $1,600.

Notice what has happened: A $100 upward shift in the aggregate demand schedule has induced a $400 increase in equilibrium nominal income. This ability of a given shift in aggregate demand to create a larger increase in equilibrium national income is the famous **multiplier effect,** a central pillar of Keynesian macroeconomics.

Multiplier effect The ability of a $1 shift in the aggregate nominal demand schedule to induce a change of more than $1 in the equilibrium level of nominal national income.

Round by Round One way to view the multiplier effect is to imagine the effects of the initial upward shift in aggregate demand percolating down through the economy "round by round." Suppose that the original shift is caused by a $100 per year increase in the rate of autonomous consumption expenditure. In response to the $100 increase in demand, firms raise their prices and/or output enough to cause a $100 increase in nominal national product. The increase in national product results in $100 of additional nominal income for some people in the form of higher profits, wages, rents, or interest payments. All of what has happened so far can be called the first-round effect of the shift in aggregate demand.

The second round consists of tracing the effects of the $100 in new income generated by the first round. Given an assumed marginal propensity to consume of 0.75, the people who receive this income will spend $75 of it on consumer goods and services. This spending will cause firms to step up output by $75 more and generate $75 in new factor payments and income.

In the third round, three-quarters of the $75 is spent, which generates $56.25 more of nominal national product, factor payments, and income. In the fourth round, $42.19 is added, in the fifth round $31.64 is added, and so on until the increments become too small to worry about. When all the increments to income induced by the original $100 upward shift in the aggregate nominal demand function are added together, the total is:

$$\$100 + \$75 + \$56.25 + \$42.19 + \ldots = \$400,$$

just as expected. This round-by-round version of the multiplier effect is summarized in Exhibit 9.7.

Exhibit 9.7
The multiplier effect, round by round
This exhibit shows the round-by-round multiplier effects of an initial $100 upward shift in the aggregate nominal demand schedule. Each increase in aggregate nominal demand produces an equal increase in nominal national income. Each $1 increase in nominal national income in turn produces $.75 of new consumer demand under the action of the assumed marginal propensity to consume of 0.75. In total, the infinite series of rounds produces a $400 increase in aggregate nominal demand and nominal national income. In comparing this exhibit with Exhibit 9.6, note that the original $100 increase in aggregate demand corresponds to the upward shift in the aggregate demand schedule, whereas the subsequent increases in aggregate demand correspond to movements along the new schedule.

Round	Change in Aggregate Demand	Change in National Income
1 (initial change)	$100.00	$100.00
2	75.00	75.00
3	56.25	56.25
4	42.18	42.18
5	31.64	31.64
6	23.73	23.73
7	17.79	17.79
8	13.35	13.35
9	10.00	10.00
10	7.50	7.50
All later rounds	22.56	22.56
Totals	$400.00	$400.00

The Multiplier Exhibit 9.7 shows quite clearly that as income increases in response to the original upward shift in the aggregate demand schedule, national income "catches up" with planned expenditure. For each $1 increase in nominal national income, output increases by $1, but expenditure increases by only a fraction of $1. The fraction is equal to the marginal propensity to consume. At the new equilibrium, the difference between planned expenditure and national income is eliminated.

Simple multiplier The ratio of an induced change in the equilibrium level of nominal national income to an initial shift in the aggregate nominal demand schedule. Using MPC to stand for the marginal propensity to consume, the value of the simple multiplier is given by the formula:

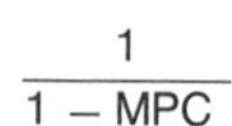

$$\frac{1}{1 - \text{MPC}}.$$

The ratio of the induced increase in national income to the original increase in planned expenditure is called the **simple multiplier.**[1] Its value depends on the fraction of each added $1 of income that goes to added planned expenditure. More precisely, the simple multiplier is given by the formula:

$$\text{Simple multiplier} = \frac{1}{1 - \text{MPC}},$$

where MPC stands for the marginal propensity to consume.

Because the marginal propensity to save is equal to 1 minus the marginal propensity to consume, the formula for the simple multiplier can also be written as:

$$\text{Simple multiplier} = \frac{1}{\text{MPS}}$$

where MPS stands for the marginal propensity to save. Whichever way the formula is written, the simple multiplier is larger the larger the marginal propensity to consume and smaller the larger the marginal propensity to save.

CONCLUSIONS

The multiplier effect plays a central role in Keynesian economic theory and economic policy analysis. The central implication of the simple multiplier is that even small changes in planned expenditure will have magnified effects on the national economy. Early Keynesian economists saw the instability of planned expenditure, magnified by the multiplier effect, as an explanation for the cycle of boom and bust that had plagued capitalist economies since the nineteenth century. They also saw in the multiplier effect the key to a new policy for economic stabilization. This part of their analysis is important enough that a separate chapter is devoted to it.

SUMMARY

1. For a given aggregate demand schedule, the circular flow can be in equilibrium at only one level of nominal national income. The equilibrium condition is that planned expenditure and national product must be equal. If planned expenditure exceeds national product, there will be unplanned depletion of inventories and upward pressure on income. If national product exceeds planned expenditure, there will be unplanned accumulation of inventories and downward pressure on national income.
2. The injection-leakage approach to the determination of the equilibrium level of nominal national income shows that equilibrium can occur only

[1]An algebraic derivation of the multiplier formula is given in the Appendix to Chapter 10.

when planned injections (planned investment plus government purchases plus exports) are equal to total leakages (saving plus net taxes plus imports). In equation form:

$$S + T + M = I + G + X.$$

3. A shift in the aggregate demand schedule changes the equilibrium level of nominal national income. According to the multiplier effect, the induced change in equilibrium nominal national income will be larger than the initial shift in planned expenditure. The ratio of the change in income to the shift in planned expenditure is known as the simple multiplier.

DISCUSSION QUESTIONS

1. It is possible to analyze the determinants of national income and product with either the circular flow or the Keynesian cross. Which do you prefer? Why? Does each contribute some insights of its own? Explain.
2. Explain the "round-by-round" effect of the multiplier by using the circular flow model.
3. If you expected a depression in the near future, would it be to your advantage to save in order to prepare for it? What would happen if we all tried to save a larger fraction of our income than usual to prepare for an expected depression?
4. If planned saving exceeds planned investment, will gross national product increase or decrease? Suppose you know the government's budget is exactly in balance. Now can you answer the question? What else, if anything, do you need to know?
5. What would be the size of the simple multiplier if the marginal propensity to consume were 0.5? 0.75? 0.8? 0.9? 0.95?
6. In what ways are the Keynesian cross and the supply and demand diagram of previous chapters similar, and in what ways are they different?
7. What changes in the economy would force a movement along the aggregate demand curve? What changes would result in a shift of the curve?
8. Suppose that consumers suddenly increase their marginal propensity to consume from 0.75 to 0.80. What effect will the increase have on the aggregate demand curve? Trace the impact of this change using the Keynesian cross diagram.

CHAPTER 10

FISCAL POLICY AND THE MULTIPLIER THEORY

WHAT YOU WILL LEARN IN THIS CHAPTER

This chapter applies the multiplier theory of national income determination to some important practical problems of economic stabilizaton policy. It shows how taxes and government purchases can be adjusted in an attempt to achieve a level of nominal national income judged compatible with the goals of full employment, price stability, and real economic growth. In addition to discussing the use of discretionary changes in taxes and government purchases for stabilization purposes, the chapter also looks briefly at certain built-in automatic stabilizers contained in the economy. The chapter ends with a review of the long-standing controversy about the economic burden of the national debt.

FOR REVIEW

Here are some important terms and concepts that will be put to use in this chapter. If you do not understand them, review them before proceeding.

- *Laffer curve (Chapter 4)*
- *Goals of stabilization policy (Chapter 7)*
- *Multiplier theory (Chapter 9)*

The multiplier theory, introduced in the previous chapter, shows how shifts in aggregate demand cause changes in the equilibrium level of national income. This chapter applies the theory to shifts in aggregate demand produced by changes in the levels of net taxes or government purchases. The control of aggregate demand through these changes is known as **fiscal policy.**

Fiscal policy The collective term for the policies that determine the levels of government purchases and net taxes.

In this chapter, as in the last two, the discussion continues in nominal terms. This is quite natural, in that government budgets are ordinarily cast in nominal terms. However, it should be kept in mind that manipulating the level of nominal national income is only an intermediate policy goal. The ultimate policy goals of full employment, price stability, and the growth of real output are affected only indirectly by changes in the nominal level of national income.

These changes can take the form of changes in either real output (with accompanying changes in employment) or the price level—or some combination of the two. When fiscal policy is used to stimulate aggregate demand and drive up the level of nominal national income, policy makers naturally hope that all or most of the expansion will take the form of job-creating increases in real output. Part of the expansion of nominal income, however, may also take the form of unwanted inflation. Similarly, when fiscal policy is used to moderate aggregate demand and slow the growth of nominal income, it is hoped that most of the slowdown will take the form of a reduction in the rate of inflation. However, some of it may also take the form of a slowdown in real economic growth, possibly accompanied by a rise in unemployment.

It will be several chapters yet before we have assembled all the pieces of macroeconomic theory needed to determine exactly what part of a change in nominal income will take the form of changes in real output and what part will take the form of changes in the price level. For the time being, we should keep in mind that the manipulation of nominal aggregate demand is a powerful but imperfect means of achieving full employment, price stability, and real economic growth.

FISCAL POLICY IN ACTION

The Target Level of Nominal National Income

We turn now to the matter of applying fiscal policy once it has been decided what level of nominal national income is most likely to promote the goals of full employment, price stability, and economic growth. That level of income, whatever it is, can be referred to as the **target level of nominal national income** (or the **income target** for short).

Target level of nominal national income (income target) The level of nominal national income judged by policy makers to be most nearly compatible with the goals of full employment, price stability, and real economic growth.

If, at any time, the equilibrium level of nominal national income is equal to the target level, no active fiscal policy is called for. To see fiscal policy in action, we need to look at the more interesting cases in which equilibrium nominal income either falls short of or exceeds the income target.

A Contractionary Gap Consider the case shown in Exhibit 10.1. As the aggregate supply and demand curves are drawn, they determine an equilibrium level of nominal national income of $800. Suppose policy makers consider $800

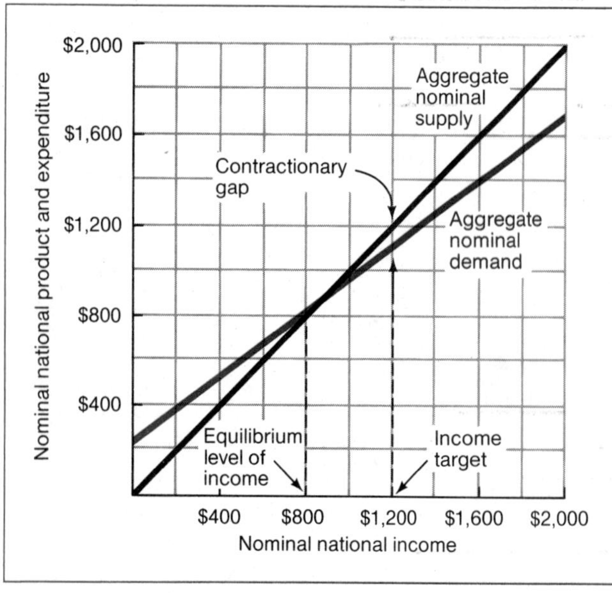

Exhibit 10.1
A contractionary gap
A contractionary gap is said to occur whenever planned expenditure (aggregate demand) is less than national product (aggregate supply) at the target level of national income. Under this condition, the equilibrium level of nominal national income is below the target level. If national income were at the target level, unplanned inventory accumulation would put downward pressure on the level of income and cause it to contract.

too low and set their target instead at $1,200. With the planned expenditure schedule shown, $1,200 cannot be the equilibrium level of income, because planned expenditures will fall short of national product by $100 if income is at the target level.

Whenever planned expenditure is less than national product at the target level of income, there is a **contractionary gap.** The size of the gap represents the rate of unplanned inventory accumulation that will take place at the target level of income with the given aggregate demand schedule. Geometrically, the gap is measured by the vertical distance between the aggregate demand and supply schedules at the target level of national income. The word *contractionary* refers to the fact that unplanned inventory accumulation tends to cause the level of nominal national income to fall if income is at the target level.

Contractionary gap The difference between planned expenditures and national product at the target level of national income when aggregate supply exceeds aggregate demand at that level.

An Expansionary Gap Alternatively, the equilibrium level of nominal national income may be higher than the target level. Such a case is shown in Exhibit 10.2, where the aggregate demand schedule is $200 higher than the one shown in Exhibit 10.1. Now planned expenditures will exceed national income at the target level of national income. Instead of unplanned inventory accumulation and a contractionary gap at the target income, there is unplanned inventory depletion and an **expansionary gap.**

Expansionary gap The difference between planned expenditures and national product at the target level of national income when aggregate demand exceeds aggregate supply at that level.

When such a gap exists, nominal national income is again not in equilibrium at the target level. If national income were to be at the target level, unplanned inventory depletion would cause the circular flow, measured in nominal terms, to expand.

Filling a Contractionary or Expansionary Gap

When there is an expansionary or contractionary gap in the economy, fiscal policy can be used to fill it. In the case of a contractionary gap, consumption, planned investment, government purchases, and net exports combined are not great enough to equal national income at the target level. Policy makers can try

Exhibit 10.2

An expansionary gap

An expansionary gap is said to occur whenever planned expenditure (aggregate demand) is greater than national product (aggregate supply) at the target level of national income. Under this condition, the equilibrium level of nominal national income is above the target level. If national income were at the target level, unplanned inventory depletion would put upward pressure on the level of income and cause the circular flow to expand.

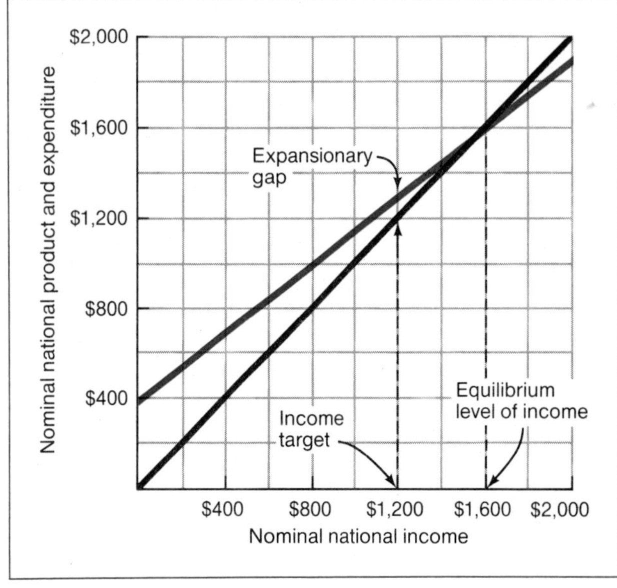

to fill the gap directly by increasing government purchases or indirectly by stimulating consumption through reduced taxes. In the case of an expansionary gap, consumption, planned investment, and government purchases are together so great that they exceed national income at the target level. Policy makers then try to eliminate the gap by cutting government purchases or discouraging consumption with a tax increase.

Injection-Leakage Approach Chapter 9 introduced the injection-leakage approach as an alternative way of determining the equilibrium level of national income. This approach sheds additional light on the process of eliminating expansionary and contractionary gaps. According to the approach, in equilibrium, saving plus net taxes plus imports must equal planned investment plus government purchases plus exports.

When there is a contractionary gap, leakages exceed planned injections at the target level of nominal income. Unless fiscal policy intervenes, the difference is taken up by unplanned inventory investment, which holds nominal national income below the target level. Fiscal policy can close the gap by adding to injections with government purchases or by reducing leakages through a cut in net taxes.

When there is an expansionary gap, saving plus net taxes plus imports fall short of planned investment plus government purchases plus exports at the target level of nominal national income. Fiscal policy can bring the two into balance either by increasing leakages in the form of taxes or by reducing injections in the form of government purchases.

In outline, this is how fiscal policy works. Now we turn to an examination of the details of multiplier theory.

Government Purchases Policy

We begin with a simple case in which the government fills a contractionary gap by increasing government purchases. In Exhibit 10.3a, initial conditions are represented by the aggregate nominal demand curve AND_1. The consumption schedule on which this curve is based assumes a marginal propensity to consume of 0.75, autonomous consumption of \$100, and lump sum taxes of \$100. Interest rates and business conditions generate \$100 of planned investment expenditure, and government purchases are \$50. Net exports are \$25; that is, exports exceed imports by \$25. The result is an initial equilibrium nominal national income of \$800. There is a contractionary gap of \$100, measured vertically at the target level of national income.

Policy makers want to fill the contractionary gap, and one way to do so is by increasing government purchases. To illustrate: Suppose policy makers authorize spending an extra \$100 to accelerate the completion of a stretch of interstate highway. If the policy is to work, this added spending must be paid for not by increased taxes but instead by borrowing from the public. The consequences of the increased spending can be considered from three viewpoints: round by round, aggregate supply and demand, and injection-leakage.

Round by Round First, we can take a round-by-round approach. Spending \$100 on the highway project creates \$100 in new income for the construction workers, which raises total national income in the first round from \$800 to

Exhibit 10.3
Use of fiscal policy to fill a contractionary gap
This exhibit illustrates the use of fiscal policy to fill a contractionary gap and move equilibrium nominal national income to the target level. Part a illustrates this process with the Keynesian cross and Part b with the injection-leakage approach. In both cases, a $100 increase in government purchases results in a $400 increase in equilibrium nominal national income.

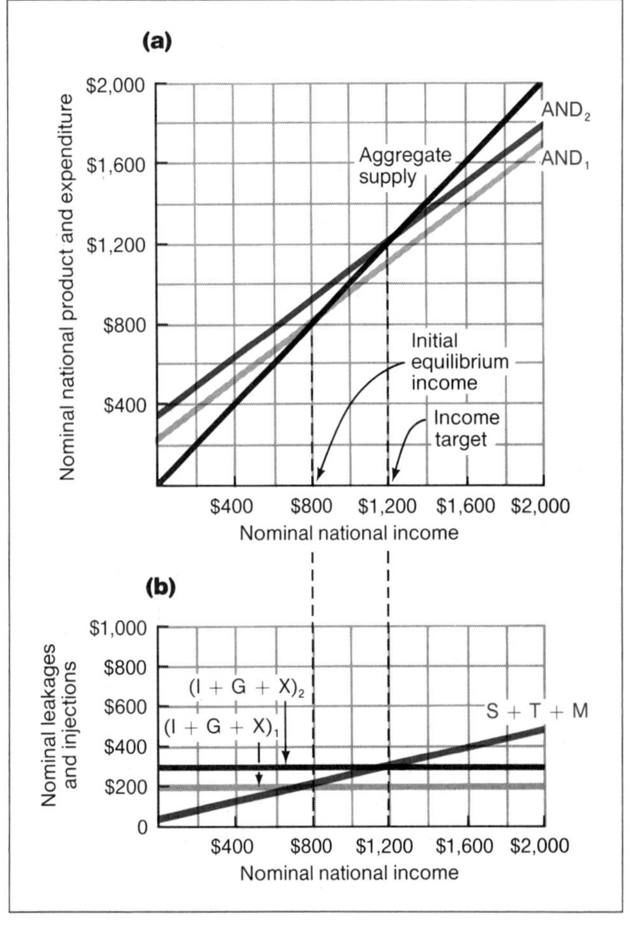

$900. Given a propensity to consume of 0.75, the workers save one-quarter of their income and spend the rest on, say, clothing. This expenditure generates $75 of new income for clothing workers and retailers, which raises total income to $975 in the second round. In the third round, clothing workers spend three-quarters of their new income on something else, which adds $56.25 more to the stream of income and expenditure. As further rounds progress, the target level of $1,200 national income is approached more and more closely.

Aggregate Supply and Demand Approach Instead of taking the round-by-round approach, we can refer to Exhibit 10.3a, which shows the effects of the increased government purchases in terms of the Keynesian cross. The decision to spend $100 on the highway project shifts the aggregate demand schedule upward by $100 to the position labeled AND_2. At the initial level of national income, $800, planned expenditures exceed national income and hence national product by $100. This added demand initially causes inventories to decline unexpectedly. In response, firms either step up output or raise prices or both, which sends nominal national income and product upward. The unplanned depletion of inventories is not eliminated entirely until the new equilibrium level of nominal national income is reached—at the point where the new aggregate demand schedule intersects the aggregate supply schedule. This new equilibrium occurs at the target income of $1,200.

Injection-Leakage Approach Finally, we can consider the effects of increased government purchases in terms of the injection-leakage approach. In Exhibit 10.3b, increased government purchases shift the injection schedule upward by $100, from $(I + G + X)_1$ to $(I + G + X)_2$. At the $800 income level, planned investment, government purchases, and exports add up to more than total leakages, so that inventories are unexpectedly depleted and incomes begin to rise. With a marginal propensity to save of 0.25, $.25 in new saving results from each $1 of added income. By the time national income reaches $1,200, saving rises by enough to finance the added government purchases, and equilibrium is restored.

The Multiplier Whichever approach we use, we come to the same conclusion: When government purchases are increased while taxes, planned investment, net exports, and the consumption schedule remain unchanged, equilibrium nominal national income changes by an amount equal to the change in government purchases times the simple multiplier. In this case, where the change in government purchases is $100 and the simple multiplier is 4, the change in equilibrium income is:

$4 \times \$100 = \$400.$

Net Tax Policy

Instead of stimulating aggregate demand by increasing government purchases or moderating it by cutting purchases, fiscal policy authorities can instead manipulate demand by raising or lowering net taxes. Net tax policy is potentially as capable of filling a contractionary or expansionary gap as government purchase policy, but the chain of effects through which it operates is sufficiently different to warrant a separate discussion.

Net Taxes and Consumption Expenditure The major difference between the two types of fiscal policy is that changes in government purchases are themselves changes in aggregate demand, whereas changes in net taxes operate on aggregate demand only indirectly—through changes in consumption expenditures. The immediate effect of a $1 tax cut is a $1 increase in the part of national income left to households as disposable income. The effect of this change on aggregate demand depends on the marginal propensity to consume. If the marginal propensity is 0.75, as assumed in the recent examples, a $1 tax cut produces a $.75 increase in consumption expenditure, other things being equal.

Geometrically, this initial effect of a tax cut appears as an upward shift in the aggregate nominal demand schedule. With a marginal propensity to consume of 0.75, each $1 cut in taxes shifts the demand schedule up by $.75. (A $1 increase in net taxes would cut $1 from disposable income, which in turn would cut consumption expenditure by $.75 and shift the aggregate demand schedule downward by that amount.) Once the aggregate demand schedule has shifted, the multiplier process takes over. The $.75 in new first-round consumption expenditure stimulated by each $1 cut in net taxes becomes someone's second-round income. Three-quarters of this second-round income is spent on further consumption, which generates third-round income, and so on. Equilibrium is reestablished only when the economy has moved along the new, higher aggregate nominal demand curve to the point where it intersects the aggregate nominal supply curve.

The Net Tax Multiplier The change in equilibrium nominal national income produced by a change in taxes is equal to the simple multiplier times the amount of the shift in the aggregate demand curve produced by the tax change. This shift is opposite in direction to the tax change (up for a tax cut, down for a tax increase) and equal in magnitude to the amount of the tax change times the marginal propensity to consume. With a marginal propensity to consume of 0.75, the simple multiplier has a value of 4. A $1 tax cut shifts the aggregate demand curve up by $.75. Multiplying this by 4 gives an increase in equilibrium nominal national income of $3. Similarly, a $1 tax increase shifts the aggregate demand curve down by $.75, which produces a $3 fall in equilibrium nominal national income.

This analysis of the effects of a change in taxes can be used to define the **net tax multiplier**—the change in equilibrium nominal national income resulting from a $1 change in net taxes. The net tax multiplier is negative, because a change in taxes causes an opposite shift in the aggregate demand curve. It is also smaller than the simple multiplier, because the size of the shift in the aggregate demand curve produced by each $1 change in disposable income is equal only to $1 times the marginal propensity to consume. Using MPC to represent the marginal propensity to consume, MPS to represent the marginal propensity to save, and 1/MPS to represent the simple multiplier, the formula is:

Net tax multiplier A multiplier showing how much equilibrium nominal national income will change in response to a change in net taxes. The formula for the net tax multiplier is −MPC/MPS.

$$\text{Net tax multiplier} = -\frac{\text{MPC}}{\text{MPS}}.$$

The complete algebraic derivation of the net tax multiplier is given in the Appendix to Chapter 10.

Taxes and Transfers A final comment on net tax policy: The term *net taxes,* as explained earlier, means taxes collected by government minus transfer payments. The net tax multiplier thus applies to changes in transfer payments as well as to changes in taxes paid. A $1 increase in transfer payments is a $1 decrease in net taxes, and a $1 decrease in transfer payments is a $1 increase in net taxes. With a marginal propensity to consume of 0.75, a $1 increase in transfer payments can be expected to produce a $3 increase in equilibrium nominal national income. This is the result of applying the net tax multiplier of −3 to the change in net taxes of −$1.

The Balanced Budget Multiplier

The initial discussion of government purchase policy examined the effects of a change in the amount of government purchases, other things (including net taxes) being equal. In the example of the effects of a $100 increase in government purchases, it was assumed that the added purchases were paid for by borrowing, not by new taxes. If the added government purchases were financed by increased taxes instead, what would be the effect on equilibrium national income?

This is a question that can easily be answered once the separate effect of each half of such a fiscal policy is known. Assuming a marginal propensity to consume of 0.75, a $100 increase in government purchases (other things being equal) tends to increase equilibrium nominal national income by $400. A matching $100 increase in net taxes (assuming the same marginal propensity to consume and other things being equal) tends to decrease equilibrium nominal national income by $300. Thus the tax increase partly, but not entirely, cancels out the expansionary effect of the increase in government purchases. Putting the halves together results in equilibrium nominal national income increasing by $100.

Balanced budget multiplier A multiplier showing how much equilibrium nominal national income will change in response to a change in government purchases matched dollar for dollar by an offsetting change in net taxes. The value of the balanced budget multiplier is always 1.

The change in equilibrium nominal national income resulting from a $1 change in government purchases matched by a $1 change in net taxes is sometimes called the **balanced budget multiplier.** This multiplier is equal to the sum of the simple multiplier and the net tax multiplier. With the formula for the former 1/MPS and the formula for the latter −MPC/MPS, the following is the expression for the balanced budget multiplier:

$$\text{Balanced budget multiplier} = \frac{1}{\text{MPS}} - \frac{\text{MPC}}{\text{MPS}}.$$

Since MPS = 1 − MPC, it simplifies to:

$$\text{Balanced budget multiplier} = \frac{\text{MPS}}{\text{MPS}} = 1.$$

The balanced budget multiplier is thus equal to 1 not only when the marginal propensity to consume is equal to 0.75, as in the example, but no matter what the value of marginal propensity to consume is. In short, an increase in government spending, accompanied by an equal increase in net taxes, all other things being equal, produces a dollar-for-dollar increase in equilibrium nominal national income.

The Multipliers Compared

Three multipliers have now been introduced. With a marginal propensity to consume of 0.75, there is a simple multiplier of 4, a net tax multiplier of −3, and a balanced budget multiplier of 1. If the marginal propensity to consume were 0.8, the simple multiplier would be 5, the net tax multiplier would be −4, and the balanced budget multiplier would be 1.

However, these multipliers should be interpreted with caution. A change in government spending is the most powerful tool of fiscal policy, in the sense that it takes advantage of the full value of the simple multiplier. That power does not mean, though, that a change in government spending is necessarily the best way to eliminate an expansionary or contractionary gap. Any of the three policies can be as effective as the others, so long as a big enough change in taxes or in the balanced budget is used. It is time now to look beyond the multiplier at some other topics in fiscal policy.

DISCRETIONARY FISCAL POLICY AND AUTOMATIC STABILIZERS

Discretionary Policy

Up to this point, it has been assumed that policy makers are free to adjust taxes and government purchases as they please, for no other purpose than to manipulate aggregate nominal demand. Policy actions of this type are known as **discretionary fiscal policy.** The following two case studies illustrate this type of fiscal policy.

Discretionary fiscal policy Changes in the levels of taxes, transfers, or government purchases made for the specific purpose of economic stabilization.

Case 10.1
The Kennedy Tax Cut

Probably the most famous example of discretionary fiscal policy was the Kennedy tax cut. John F. Kennedy assumed the office of president in January 1961 in the middle of a recession. He had been elected on a promise to "get the country moving again," and he brought to Washington a group of economic advisers firmly committed to the active use of fiscal policy.

At first, the emphasis of the new administration was primarily on the spending side of fiscal policy. The president issued orders aimed at stepping up federal expenditures by speeding highway fund allocations and accelerating procurement activities. He also submitted a package of new spending proposals to Congress.

By the next year, the economy seemed to be making considerable progress. Presidential advisers thought that the administration's national income target, aimed high enough to ensure full employment, would be achieved by the end of 1963. But contrary to these forecasts, the expansion slowed. By June 1962, the president decided to use more stimulus. On June 7, 1962, he announced that he favored a tax cut of some $10 billion.

Kennedy's tax cut proposal did not get quick treatment from Congress. Long delays resulted from congressional demands to couple the tax cut to reforms in the tax structure and changes in expenditure policy. As it turned out, Kennedy did not live to see his great tax cut enacted. But in February 1964, his successor, Lyndon Johnson, finally signed the Kennedy tax cut into law. This tax cut is now considered a famous test case of fiscal policy. The actual effects of the 1964 tax cut will receive further attention in Chapters 14 and 17.

Kennedy's tax cut, conceived during a recession, was clearly meant to fill a contractionary gap, raising output and employment. The next example concerns a proposal to use discretionary fiscal policy to deal with an expansionary gap.

Case 10.2
President Carter and the Budget Deficit

When Jimmy Carter took office as president in 1977, the economy was still recovering from its worst postwar recession. For a time, the new administration pursued an expansionary fiscal policy, as would be expected under the circumstances. During 1978, however, inflation began to accelerate ominously. By midsummer of that year, the consumer price index was rising at an annual rate of nearly 10 percent. Consumer demand was much stronger than forecasters had predicted, and it began to appear that the economy was facing an expansionary gap.

Part of the traditional Keynesian prescription under such conditions is a dose of contractionary fiscal policy—and that is just what the president opted for in his budget proposals for fiscal year 1980, as announced in January 1979. Despite Republican demands to cut taxes and liberal Democratic demands for more generous funding for social programs, the new budget contained no tax cuts and an increase in spending less than enough to compensate for inflation. (That is, the budget called for a decrease in real federal expenditures.) Taking both taxes and expenditures into account, the fiscal 1980 budget aimed for a deficit of under $30 billion, the lowest in six years.

Automatic Stabilizers

Although discretionary fiscal policy is what makes the headlines, not all fiscal policy is of a discretionary nature. Some policy changes occur automatically, without any positive action taken by Congress or the White House. Although ignored in the simplified examples up to this point, where lump sum taxes were assumed, these automatic changes are quite important in practice. For example, many kinds of taxes—including corporate and personal income taxes, payroll taxes, and sales taxes—automatically increase as the level of nominal national income increases. Also, many kinds of transfer payments tend to decrease as nominal national income increases. Unemployment benefits are a case in point.

Automatic stabilizers Changes in taxes, transfers, and government purchases that occur automatically as nominal GNP rises or falls.

Because these nondiscretionary changes in taxes and transfer payments tend to have a contractionary influence when the economy is expanding and an expansionary influence when it is contracting, they are called **automatic stabilizers.** In effect, these stabilizers reduce the value of the simple multiplier for the economy. Because of them, the economy is less sensitive than it otherwise would be to unexpected changes in planned investment, government purchases, autonomous consumption expenditure, and net exports.

Automatic stabilizers are not by themselves enough to guarantee full employment and price stability. They do, however, provide a useful supplement to discretionary fiscal policies. Consider President Carter's 1980 budget proposal, for example. Under the circumstances prevailing at the beginning of 1979, either a tax increase or a restriction on government purchases, or both, were needed to achieve the desired reduction in the budget deficit. If both the tax increase and the spending restraint had required new legislation, cutting the budget deficit would have been difficult politically. However, because nominal income was growing rapidly, the administration could count on an automatic tax increase. As a result, political resources could be reserved for the battle to restrain spending.

FISCAL POLICY AND THE NATIONAL DEBT

This chapter so far has drawn a very symmetrical picture of fiscal policy. If the economy is in a slump, the government cuts taxes or increases expenditures; the resulting deficit acts as an injection of new demand into the circular flow, and national income and product are boosted toward their target level. If the economy is overheated, with inflation and tight job markets, spending is cut or taxes are raised; enough of this results in a surplus, which withdraws demand from the circular flow and cools off the economy.

One might get the impression from this picture of fiscal policy that periods of deficit and surplus in the federal budget would more or less balance out over a period of years. In practice, though, this is not how things work. As Exhibit

Exhibit 10.4
Government expenditures and revenues, 1950–1978
Since 1950, the federal budget has been in deficit much more often than it has been in surplus. The cumulative deficit adds to some $388 billion against a cumulative surplus of only about $17 billion.

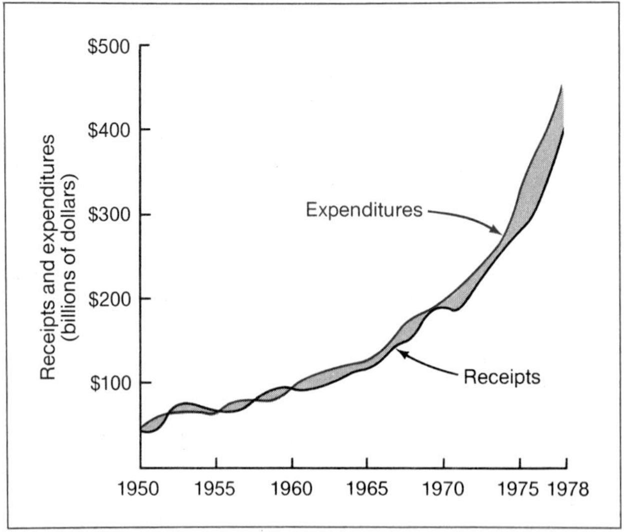

Source: President's Council of Economic Advisers, *Economic Report of the President* (Washington D.C.: Government Printing Office, 1979), Table B-70.

10.4 shows, deficits have been much more common than surpluses. Since 1950, in fact, the federal budget has been in deficit for twenty-four years and in surplus for only five years. The cumulative deficit adds to some $388 billion against a cumulative surplus of only about $17 billion.

As far back as the 1930s, when the Keynesian idea of using discretionary fiscal policy for the purpose of economic stabilization was first gaining popularity, fiscal conservatives became worried about the asymmetry of fiscal policy and issued a warning: If the government keeps spending more than it takes in, it will run up endlessly accumulating debts. Eventually, this may lead to fiscal disaster. They also raised the following questions: Can the government perpetually spend beyond its means any more than can a private household? Should the government be required to balance its budget each year, financing all programs on a pay-as-you-go basis, in order to avoid eventual bankruptcy? And even if the debts are paid on time, so that bankruptcy is avoided, does financing today's spending programs with borrowed money place an unfair burden on future generations?

Almost half a century after Keynes, these questions are still being asked. President Carter, running for office in 1976 (a year in which the federal deficit reached a record setting $66 billion), was able to score political points by promising that his administration would work toward a balanced budget. In the late 1970s, political support began to grow for passage of a constitutional amendment that would severely limit discretionary fiscal policy by requiring the federal government to balance its budget. Did these political developments represent the last gasp of an economic conservatism fifty years out of date, or did they instead represent a justified disenchantment with the results of several decades of deficit spending? The debate is likely to continue for years to come, so it will be worthwhile looking at the economic arguments advanced by each side.

In Defense of Deficit Spending

To fiscal activists, the important thing is to provide the right amount of stimulus or restraint each year to move toward the goals of full employment, price stability, and economic growth. If this requires running budget deficits more often than surpluses, then so be it. There is no reason to make controlling the size of the national debt a separate, fourth goal of policy. No one is hurt if the national debt grows, so nothing should be sacrificed in order to keep it small. Four arguments underlie this position.

Trend of the National Debt The first argument given for not being concerned with the size of the national debt is that the trend of the debt, in relation to gross national product, has been steadily down, not up. This is shown clearly by Exhibit 10.5. If ever the national debt was a burden, it was at the end of World War II. In 1945, it stood at an all-time high of 118 percent of GNP. By the mid-1970s, it had been reduced to less than a quarter of that level in comparison to the enormously larger national product.

The Power of Taxation A second argument for not being concerned with the size of the national debt is that the federal government never need worry about bankruptcy, no matter how large its debt becomes. The federal debt is backed by the federal power of taxation, which is enormous. As long as the power of taxation exists, people will continue to loan the government money to refinance the debt as it becomes due, confident that they in turn will be repaid on time, in full and with interest.

We Owe It to Ourselves The third argument is that the size of the national debt is not a matter of serious concern because it is a debt that U.S. citizens owe largely to themselves. It is a mere bookkeeping entry that can be cleared by shuffling funds from one account to another with no net drain on the real resources of the country. From the point of view of the circular flow, interest payments on the national debt are only transfer payments.

Can't Build Today's Houses with Tomorrow's Bricks Finally, it is said that there is no reason to be concerned that the national debt will put an unfair burden on future generations. Even if those in authority want to do so, the

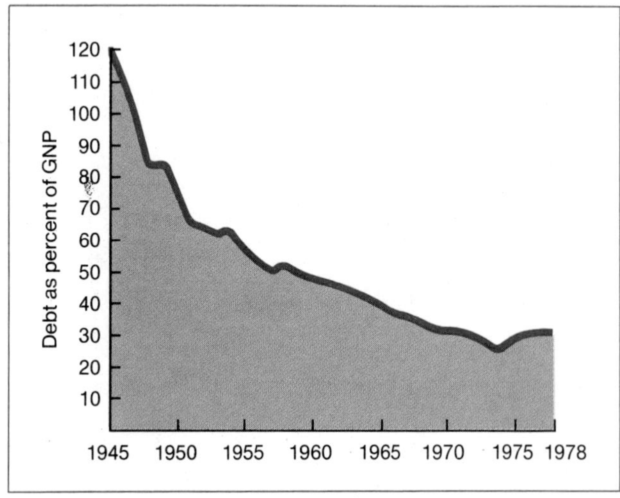

Exhibit 10.5
Federal debt held by the public as a percent of gross national product, 1945–1978
Despite the persistence of the federal deficit, the accumulated national debt has grown less rapidly than GNP. By 1974, the deficit had been reduced to less than a quarter of its wartime share of GNP. Since then, it has grown slightly.

Source: President's Council of Economic Advisers, *Economic Report of the President* (Washington, D.C.: Government Printing Office): 1978, Table B-69; 1979, Table B-70.

argument goes, today's houses cannot be built with tomorrow's bricks. Real goods and services, that is to say, cannot be transferred from the future to the present. No matter how government spending is financed today, annual real income consists of the real goods and services presently produced—no more and no less. The same has been true at every time in the past and will be true at every time in the future.

Beware False Comparisons Taken together, these arguments add up to a warning not to make false comparisons between the national debt and the debts of individual families or private firms. Individuals and private firms can go bankrupt if their debts get larger than their ability to repay. Repayments of private debts (unless they are debts to people within the same family or firm) are not mere bookkeeping entries but instead are real flows of purchasing power from those within to outsiders. Thus private debts do represent a real burden on the future consumption or investment capacity of the unit that incurs them. But none of these things, it is said, hold true for the national debt.

Reservations about Deficit Spending

Although acknowledging that the four arguments for deficit spending are valid as far as they go, modern fiscal conservatives nonetheless have grave reservations about the wisdom of unlimited deficit spending and limitless growth of the national debt. They raise four points of their own.

Reversal of the Trend First, although recognizing the downward postwar trend of the national debt in relation to GNP, they are alarmed by the apparent break with the trend that occurred in the late 1970s. Although the debt had by then fallen to a postwar low in relation to GNP, the size of the deficit itself—which measures the rate at which new debt is accumulated—reached a postwar high. Over the four years 1975–1978, the average federal deficit was more than 3 percent of GNP, compared with an average of just 0.7 percent over the previous twenty-five years. Furthermore, although the debt had fallen to a relatively low level, interest rates had risen to historic highs, so that the proportion of GNP needed to service the debt was as high in the 1970s as at the end of World War II.

Limits to Taxation Second, those people who are concerned about the size of the national debt are skeptical of assurances that taxes can be raised without limit to repay debts. On a theoretical level, the concept of the Laffer curve (see Exhibit 4.10) suggests that because of the disincentive effect of taxes, the power to raise tax rates does not always guarantee the power to increase tax revenues. On a more practical level, there are the examples of cities like New York and Cleveland, which have already found their taxing power insufficient to repay past debts on schedule. The federal government does have one power that makes it more able to meet debt payments than state and local governments, but it is not the power of unlimited taxation. Instead, it is the power to create money. This power, discussed in coming chapters, does indeed guarantee that the federal government need never default on its debts; but in the long run, use of this power can impart an inflationary bias to stabilization policy.

Rising Foreign Share of the Debt Third, fiscal conservatives reject the notion that national debt payments have no economic impact because they are mere costless transfers from one group of people to another. For one thing, because of administrative costs and the disincentive effect of taxes, no transfer is truly costless. Each dollar in debt repayment imposes an opportunity cost of more than a dollar on someone.

On a more practical level, it is no longer as true as it once was that the national debt is something U.S. citizens owe to themselves. Between 1968 and 1978, the share of the U.S. national debt held by other countries increased from about 6 percent to nearly 25 percent. In 1977, essentially all of the federal deficit was financed by other countries; and in 1978, for the first time, the federal government began going directly to foreign financial markets to sell U.S. government securities denominated in German marks and Swiss francs. The federal government may have the power to print new dollars to repay the domestic portion of the national debt, but it cannot print marks or francs.

Possible Burdens on Future Generations Fourth, critics of excessive deficit spending are not convinced that borrowing to finance government spending imposes no burden on future generations. True, it is literally impossible to build today's houses with tomorrow's bricks. But future generations can be burdened in other ways. For one thing, as mentioned above, they can be burdened with the necessity of exporting some of those future bricks to pay off borrowing from abroad. In addition, heavy government borrowing today may indirectly cause real national product to be lower in the future than it otherwise would have been. The reason is that the government and private firms must compete in financial markets for the same pool of funds created by savers. At some point, government borrowing may begin to crowd out the private investment on which future economic growth depends. (More on this subject will appear in later chapters.)

To summarize, modern fiscal conservatives are willing to accept the arguments used in defense of deficit spending by fiscal policy activists, but only up to a point. The national debt—at least that part of it held by people within the United States—is indeed not strictly comparable to private debts. The federal government is admittedly not in danger of literal bankruptcy. Nonetheless, there is a danger that excessive short-run reliance on deficit spending as a means of promoting full employment may in the long run threaten the ability of the economy to achieve price stability and real economic growth.

CONCLUSIONS

The discussion of stabilization policy has now been carried about as far as it can be on the basis of the multiplier theory alone. Already, the discussion of the controversy over the national debt has had occasion to mention money and the federal government's power to control its supply. Monetary policy is, in fact, the second side of stabilization policy, and it is as important as fiscal policy. The next three chapters will discuss the banking system and monetary policy. Then, Chapter 14 will take a fresh look at what this chapter has explained and will discuss the interactions between monetary policy and fiscal policy.

SUMMARY

1. If the equilibrium level of nominal national income is different from the target level, there is a gap between total planned expenditure and national product measured at the target level of income. If the equilibrium level of income is lower than policy makers want it to be, a contractionary gap is said to exist. If the equilibrium level of nominal income is too high, the gap is said to be expansionary.
2. One way to fill a contractionary gap is by increasing government purchases without increasing net taxes. When such purchases are increased while net taxes, planned investment, and the consumption schedule remain unchanged, equilibrium nominal national income changes by an amount equal to the change in government purchases times the simple multiplier.
3. A contractionary gap can also be filled by cutting net taxes without changing government purchases. When net taxes are changed while government purchases, planned investment, autonomous consumption, and the marginal propensity to consume remain unchanged, equilibrium nominal national income changes in the direction opposite to the change in taxes by an amount equal to the change in net taxes times the net tax multiplier.
4. An increase in government spending accompanied by an equal increase in net taxes—with planned investment, autonomous consumption, and the marginal propensity to consume unchanged—produces a dollar-for-dollar increase in equilibrium nominal national income. The balanced budget multiplier is thus equal to 1.
5. Changes in taxes, transfers, or the level of government purchases made for the specific purpose of achieving the goal of economic stabilization are called discretionary fiscal policy. In addition to discretionary fiscal policy, other changes in taxes, transfers, and even government purchases occur automatically as the level of national product varies. Examples are changes in income taxes and unemployment benefits. These are called automatic stabilizers.
6. At least since the 1930s, there has been a running controversy between fiscal conservatives, who would like to see the federal government balance its budget at least most of the time, and fiscal activists, who think that persistent deficit spending is no real cause for worry. The issue centers largely on whether the national debt (and the repayment of it) imposes a real burden, present or future, on the economy. The fiscal activists have succeeded in establishing that naive fears of national bankruptcy are based on misleading analogies between private debt and the national debt. But fiscal conservatives counter that in the long run, excessive government borrowing and indebtedness can pose a threat to economic growth and price stability.

DISCUSSION QUESTIONS

1. Is the target level of national income always the level of national income at which there will be equilibrium?
2. Should the major tool of fiscal policy be changes in government spending or changes in taxation? Justify your position.
3. Use the circular flow to trace the effect of government spending in closing a contractionary gap.
4. What importance does the size of the marginal propensity to consume have for the effectiveness of fiscal policy in closing both inflationary and deflationary gaps?

5. Explain why a given change in government spending has a greater impact on the economy than does the same change in taxation.
6. If there were a contractionary gap, would there be some advantage to simply paying workers to dig ditches and then fill them in? Under what circumstances would this policy be beneficial?
7. Who pays the cost and who receives the benefits of (a) increased government spending and (b) increased taxes? Does your answer to this question differ now from what it would have been just after you read Chapter 4?
8. Do you think that there is an expansionary gap in the economy right now (as you are taking this course)? A contractionary gap? How can you tell? What is the government doing about the gap if there is one?
9. Evaluate the following possible rule for the conduct of fiscal policy: Set the level of government purchases by looking at the actual economic merit of spending projects without considering macroeconomic effects. Then, if the resulting budget does not provide the right amount of macroeconomic stimulus, aim for the target level of national income by adjusting net taxes upward or downward as required. Is this rule compatible with active use of discretionary fiscal policy?
10. Would a rule requiring the federal government to balance its budget every year completely preclude the use of discretionary fiscal policy for stabilization purposes? Explain. Would a rule requiring the budget to be balanced on average each five years be a reasonable way of compromising the concerns of fiscal activists and conservatives?

APPENDIX TO CHAPTER 10
AN ALGEBRAIC APPROACH TO INCOME DETERMINATION AND THE MULTIPLIER

All the theoretical propositions illustrated with graphs and numerical examples in the last three chapters can also be expressed in terms of elementary algebra. Begin with the consumption schedule. Using a for the constant term in the schedule (autonomous consumption), b for the marginal propensity to consume, C for nominal consumption expenditure, T for net taxes, and Y for nominal national income, the consumption schedule can be written:

$$C = a + b\,(Y - T). \qquad \textbf{10A.1}$$

Note that the expression (Y − T) that appears in the right-hand side of this expression represents nominal disposable income.

With the consumption schedule as a basis, the aggregate nominal demand (AND) schedule is put together by adding planned investment (I), government purchases (G), and exports (X) and subtracting imports (M). This gives:

$$AND = C + I + G + X - M. \qquad \textbf{10A.2}$$

Substituting in Equation 10A.1:

$$AND = a + b(Y - T) + I + G + X - M. \qquad \textbf{10A.3}$$

It is convenient to rewrite this equation by grouping the constant terms, so that it becomes:

$$AND = (a - bT + I + G + X - M) + bY. \qquad \textbf{10A.4}$$

The term in parentheses in Equation 10A.4 represents the constant term, or vertical intercept, of the aggregate nominal demand schedule; and b, the marginal propensity to consume, represents its slope.

This equation can now be used to determine the equilibrium level of nominal national income. The theory set forth in Chapter 9 showed that for the economy to be in equilibrium, national income must be equal to planned expenditure, so that there is no unplanned inventory accumulation or depletion. This equilibrium condition can be written:

$$Y = AND. \qquad \textbf{10A.5}$$

Substituting Equation 10A.4 into Equation 10A.5, the equilibrium condition becomes:

$$Y = (a - bT + I + G + X - M) + bY. \qquad \textbf{10A.6}$$

Solving Equation 10A.6 for Y then gives this formula for the equilibrium value of nominal national income:

$$Y^* = \frac{1}{1-b}(a - bT + I + G + X - M). \qquad \textbf{10A.7}$$

The asterisk after the Y in this formula is a reminder that the equation holds only for the equilibrium value of nominal national income.

Equation 10A.7 can now be applied to solve a number of problems.

Problem 1 Use Equation 10A.7 to derive the formulas for the simple multiplier, the net tax multiplier, and the balanced budget multiplier.

Solution The simple multiplier was defined in Chapter 9 as the ratio of an induced change in the equilibrium level of nominal national income to an initial shift in the aggregate nominal demand schedule. In algebraic terms, a shift in the aggregate nominal demand schedule means an increase or decrease in the intercept term $(a - bT + I + G + X - M)$. For ease in notation, let A represent this intercept term:

$$A = (a - bT + I + G + X - M). \qquad \textbf{10A.8}$$

Equation 10A.7 then becomes:

$$Y^* = \frac{1}{1-b}A \qquad \textbf{10A.9}$$

Suppose now that this constant term changes from an initial value of A_0 to a new value, A_1, thereby producing a shift in the aggregate nominal demand schedule of $A_1 - A_0$. This increases the equilibrium value of nominal national income from

$$Y_0^* = \frac{1}{1-b}A_0$$

to a new value of

$$Y_1^* = \frac{1}{1-b}A_1.$$

The simple multiplier, as the ratio of the change in equilibrium income to the shift in the aggregate nominal demand schedule, can now be calculated as follows:

$$\text{Simple multiplier} = \frac{Y_1^* - Y_0^*}{A_1 - A_0}$$

$$= \frac{(A_1 - A_0)/(1-b)}{A_1 - A_0} = \frac{1}{1-b}.$$

This is exactly the result given in Chapter 9, except that b is used in place of MPC to represent the marginal propensity to consume.

Once this simple multiplier is established, finding the net tax multiplier is easy. Suppose that net taxes change by an amount ΔT. From Equation 10A.8, it is apparent that the resulting shift in the aggregate nominal demand schedule will be $\Delta A =$

$-b\Delta T$. The change in equilibrium income can be found by applying the simple multiplier to the shift in the aggregate demand curve, which gives:

$$\Delta Y^* = \frac{1}{1-b}\Delta A = -b\frac{1}{1-b}\Delta T.$$

Simplifying the last expression on the right:

$$\Delta Y^* = \frac{-b}{1-b}\Delta T.$$

The net tax multiplier is thus equal to $-b/(1-b)$, as given in the text.

Finally, to get the balanced budget multiplier, the simple multiplier is added to the net tax multiplier:

$$\text{Balanced budget multiplier} = \frac{1}{1-b} - \frac{-b}{1-b} = 1.$$

Problem 2 Suppose that $a = 100$, $b = 0.75$, $T = 100$, $I = 100$, $G = 150$, $X = 50$, and $M = 25$. What is the equilibrium value of aggregate nominal demand?

Solution Simply substitute the various values into Equation 10A.7. This gives:

$$\begin{aligned} Y^* &= \frac{1}{(1-0.75)}[100 - 0.75(100) + 100 + 150 + 50 - 25] \\ &= 4(\$300) \\ &= \$1{,}200. \end{aligned}$$

Compare this result with Exhibits 9.3 and 9.4, which provide graphical and numerical solutions to the same problem.

Problem 3 Suppose that, initially, all variables and constants have the values given in Problem 2 but that the government adopts a target value for nominal national income of $1,600. Assuming no change in taxes, how much will government purchases have to be in order to reach the income target?

Solution Substitute the known values for a, b, T, I, X, and M into Equation 10A.7, leaving G as the unknown. Use the target income of $1,600 in place of Y*. This gives:

$$1{,}600 = 4[100 - 0.75(100) + 100 + 50 - 25 + G].$$

Solve for G as follows:

$$\begin{aligned} 1{,}600 &= 600 + 4G \\ 4G &= 1{,}000 \\ G &= 250. \end{aligned}$$

CHAPTER 11

COMMERCIAL BANKS AND OTHER FINANCIAL INTERMEDIARIES

WHAT YOU WILL LEARN IN THIS CHAPTER

This chapter provides an introduction to the financial sector of the economy. It explains how banks, thrift institutions, insurance companies, pension funds, and securities markets operate as financial intermediaries to channel funds from savers to investors. Because banks will play a particularly important role in the subsequent analysis, the balance sheets of U.S. commercial banks are discussed here in some detail. The chapter also introduces the Federal Reserve System, which plays an important role in regulating the U.S. commercial banking system and in conducting monetary policy.

FOR REVIEW

Here are some important terms and concepts that will be put to use in this chapter. If you do not understand them, review them before proceeding.

- *Circular flow of income and product (Chapter 5)*
- *Nominal and real interest rates (Chapter 7)*

This chapter is the first of four devoted to the financial sector of the U.S. economy. This sector consists of a set of markets that provide the monetary and financial arrangements necessary to facilitate the production and distribution of real goods and personal services.

Financial Intermediaries The chapter focuses on the important institutions in the financial sector that are known as **financial intermediaries** because of their role in channeling funds from savers to investors. Financial intermediaries include commercial banks, savings and loan associations, insurance companies, securities markets, and a number of other institutions. They are a necessary part of the economy because the needs of individual lenders and individual borrowers do not necessarily match in terms of quantity of funds, time horizons, or attitudes toward risk.

Financial intermediary Any financial institution that performs the function of channeling funds from savers to investors.

The job of financial intermediaries is to reconcile the diverse interests of lenders and borrowers. For example, intermediaries can pool the funds of many small savers and use the proceeds to make large loans. They can tap the steady stream of funds flowing through the checking accounts of households and firms (funds that remain in these accounts for only a few days or weeks at a time) and use them as a basis for extending long-term loans. And, as will be shown, they can reconcile the needs of people who want to borrow in order to undertake somewhat risky investments with the needs of people who want to find relatively risk-free uses for their savings.

Financial Intermediaries in the Circular Flow Exhibit 11.1 shows the place of financial intermediaries in the circular flow of income and product. This exhibit is similar to Exhibit 5.4, except that it has additional arrows to show flows both into and out of the markets in which financial intermediaries operate. The large arrow from households to financial markets indicates that households are net lenders; but, as the small arrow from credit markets to households indicates, they do some borrowing. Nonfinancial firms, on the other hand, are net borrowers, although they do provide loanable funds to financial markets in lesser amounts than their borrowings, as shown by the smaller arrow. Similarly, the government sector is on the average a net bor-

Exhibit 11.1
The circular flow with financial intermediaries
This diagram of the circular flow of income and product features the role of the financial intermediaries that operate in the economy's financial markets. Their role is to channel funds from savers to investors. Households are net savers, as shown by the large arrow; but they also do some borrowing. Businesses are net borrowers, but they also do some saving. Units of government run deficits (borrow) more often than they run surpluses (save).

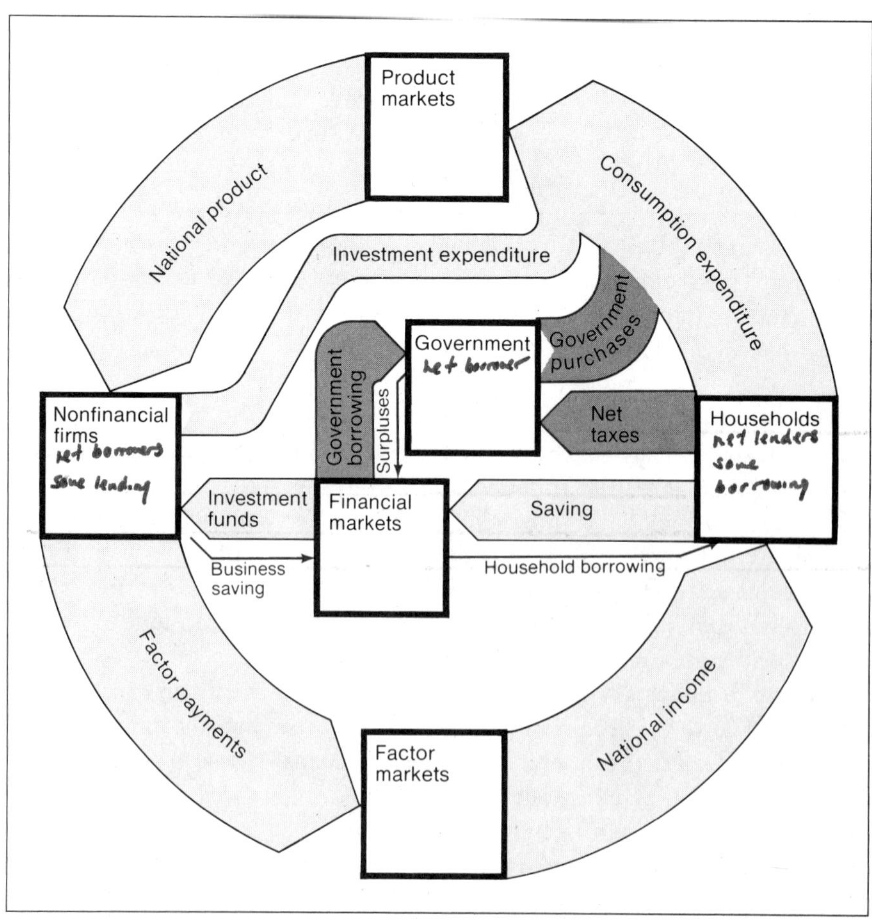

rower, because government budget deficits tend to be larger and more common than surpluses. However, the units of government that do run budget surpluses are a source of funds to financial markets.

Now that the general introduction to the function of financial intermediaries has been given, the chapter will consider the various major classes of intermediaries one by one. It will begin with commercial banks.

COMMERCIAL BANKS

Commercial banks are financial intermediaries that accept a wide variety of deposits from firms and households and in turn make loans to the public in a wide variety of forms. They are, in many respects, the most important and least specialized financial intermediaries. The best way to get an idea of how commercial banks operate is to look at their total balance sheet. This will make it clear just where the funds handled by banks come from and where they go.

A Balance Sheet for Commercial Banks

Exhibit 11.2 shows the total balance sheet of the more than 14,000 commercial banks existing in the United States as of July 25, 1979. These banks range from giants such as California's Bank of America ($79 billion in deposits) and New York's Citibank ($63 billion) to small-town "mom and pop" banks with less than $1 million in deposits.

Assets and Liabilities Like all balance sheets, the total balance sheet of these commercial banks is divided into two columns. The left-hand column lists all the banks' **assets**—all the things to which the banks hold legal claim. The right-hand column shows the banks' **liabilities**—all the claims held against the banks by outsiders—and their **net worth**—the difference between assets and liabilities. Net worth represents claims against the banks' assets by the owners of the banks.

Assets All the things to which a bank, other firm, or household holds legal claim.

Liabilities Financial claims against a bank, other firm, or household by outsiders.

Net worth The assets of a bank, other firm, or household minus its liabilities.

Exhibit 11.2
Total balance sheet for U.S. commercial banks as of July 25, 1979 (billions of dollars)

This total balance sheet shows the assets and liabilities of U.S. insured commercial banks as of July 25, 1979. Reserves and other cash items are, for the most part, non-interest-bearing assets. Bank earnings come largely from loans and securities. Three types of deposits—demand deposits, savings deposits, and time deposits—are shown separately. As in the case of all balance sheets, total assets are equal to total liabilities plus net worth.

Assets		Liabilities	
Reserves and other cash items	$ 160.8	Demand deposits	$ 369.6
Loans	875.9	Savings deposits	219.1
Securities	277.0	Time deposits	423.5
Miscellaneous assets	69.4	Borrowing from Federal Reserve	1.2
		Other borrowing	268.9
		Total liabilities	$1,282.2
		Net worth	100.8
Total assets	$1,383.0	Total liabilities plus net worth	$1,383.0

Source: *Federal Reserve Bulletin,* August 1979, Table A12, and September 1979, Table A16.

Because of the way the terms are defined, the right-hand and left-hand columns exactly balance—hence the name *balance sheet.* For all balance sheets, whether of banks or of any other financial unit or aggregate, it must always be true that

Assets = Liabilities + Net worth.

Commercial Bank Assets On the asset side of the balance sheet, the first line lists the banks' reserves and other cash items. This line includes a number of cash items. The first item is vault cash—coins and paper money that banks keep in their own vaults. The second item is balances that small banks keep on deposit with larger correspondent banks and that banks belonging to the Federal Reserve System keep as reserve deposits with the Federal Reserve. (More will be said about the Federal Reserve shortly.) The final item is certain miscellaneous categories of assets in the process of collection.

Historically, the reason banks maintained reserves of cash or deposits that could quickly be converted to cash was that, at any moment, some depositors might want to withdraw some of their funds from the bank. This could be done either by writing a check to someone who would deposit it in another bank or by walking up to the teller's window and asking for currency. In the U.S. commercial banking system today, however, the quantity of reserve-type assets that banks hold is generally not left to the judgment of individual bankers but instead is controlled by federal and state bank regulators. As the next chapter will show in detail, the power to regulate bank reserves is now an important tool of macroeconomic policy, superseding the historical use of reserves as a cushion against withdrawal of deposits.

Loans are the next (and largest) asset item on the commercial bank balance sheet. The loans that banks make to firms and to individuals are their major source of income. Borrowers use commercial bank loans for such diverse needs as financing business inventories, buying consumer durables, and constructing and purchasing new homes.

Next after loans on the balance sheet come securities. These also are income-earning assets for banks. Banks buy many bills, notes, and bonds issued by federal, state, and local government units, as well as some securities issued by private firms.

The miscellaneous assets shown on the last line of the left-hand side of the balance sheet include some smaller income-earning assets, along with the value of the banks' own buildings and equipment. Total assets of all commercial banks as of July 25, 1979, were $1,383 billion.

Demand deposits Commercial bank deposits that depositors can withdraw by writing checks; commonly known as checking accounts.

Savings deposits Deposits at commercial banks or thrift institutions subject to withdrawal at any time upon presentation of a passbook.

Time deposits Deposits at commercial banks or thrift institutions subject to withdrawal without penalty only at the end of a specified period.

Commercial Bank Liabilities The first item on the right-hand side of the total commercial bank balance sheet is **demand deposits.** They represent the total value of the balances in the checking accounts of all the banks' customers. They are the banks' liabilities because they represent funds to which the depositors have legal claim. Depositors can withdraw these funds at any time, on demand, by writing checks.

Savings deposits and time deposits, the next two items on the balance sheet, are bank liabilities that are not directly subject to withdrawal by check. **Savings deposits** can be withdrawn at any time upon presentation of a passbook. **Time deposits,** which earn higher interest rates for depositors, must be held for a specified period (ranging from thirty days to ten years) until they mature. If withdrawals are made before maturity, depositors must pay a substantial penalty in terms of forgone interest.

Additional liabilities include amounts borrowed from the Federal Reserve, from the banks' own foreign branches, from other financial institutions, and from nonfinancial firms. Federal Reserve borrowings are listed separately in Exhibit 11.2; the rest are lumped together in the "other borrowings" entry.

All these deposits, together with nondeposit bank borrowing, came to $1,282 billion as of July 25, 1979. This sum is less than that of the banks' total assets. In principle, if all the assets were converted to cash and all the liabilities were paid off, $100.8 billion would be left over. This amount represents the banks' net worth—the total value belonging to the banks' various owners.

THE FEDERAL RESERVE AND BANKING REGULATION

We have already had occasion to mention the Federal Reserve System (Fed for short). The Fed is the central banking system of the United States. It provides banking services to the federal government and to member commercial banks, and it administers a number of crucial regulations dealing with the activities of commercial banks. The Fed's regulatory powers permit it to control the volume of commercial bank demand deposits and currency in the economy. This power makes the Fed a major participant in macroeconomic stabilization policy. (The macroeconomic functions of the Fed will be discussed in detail in the next three chapters.)

Structure of the Fed

The Federal Reserve System was established in 1913 as an independent agency of the federal government—not under the direction of the executive branch. The original intent of making the Fed independent was to prevent the Treasury Department from manipulating monetary conditions for political ends. In practice, the monetary actions of the Fed and the fiscal actions of the Treasury are usually coordinated. The chairman of the Federal Reserve Board of Governors, the secretary of the Treasury, and the chairman of the President's Council of Economic Advisers meet weekly to discuss national economic policy. It would thus be more accurate to say that the Fed serves as an equal partner in determining government policy than to say that it acts as an independent agent.

The Twelve Federal Reserve Banks The overall organizational structure of the Federal Reserve System is shown in Exhibit 11.3. At its heart are the twelve District Federal Reserve banks. Ten of these banks have branches, and the total number of branches is twenty-four. Each of the twelve regional banks is a separate corporation chartered by the federal government and owned by its stockholders. The stockholders are the commercial banks in the district that are members of the system. Although the Federal Reserve banks are owned by their stockholders, they are not typical of privately owned corporations because profit seeking is not one of their goals. Any earnings of Federal Reserve banks over and above their operating expenses and the fixed dividends that go to their member banks are passed on to the Treasury.

Primary control of each of the twelve Federal Reserve banks lies with a

Exhibit 11.3
Organization of the Federal Reserve System
The Federal Reserve System, or Fed, acts as the central bank for the United States. It provides banking services to commercial banks and government and regulates the activities of commercial banks.

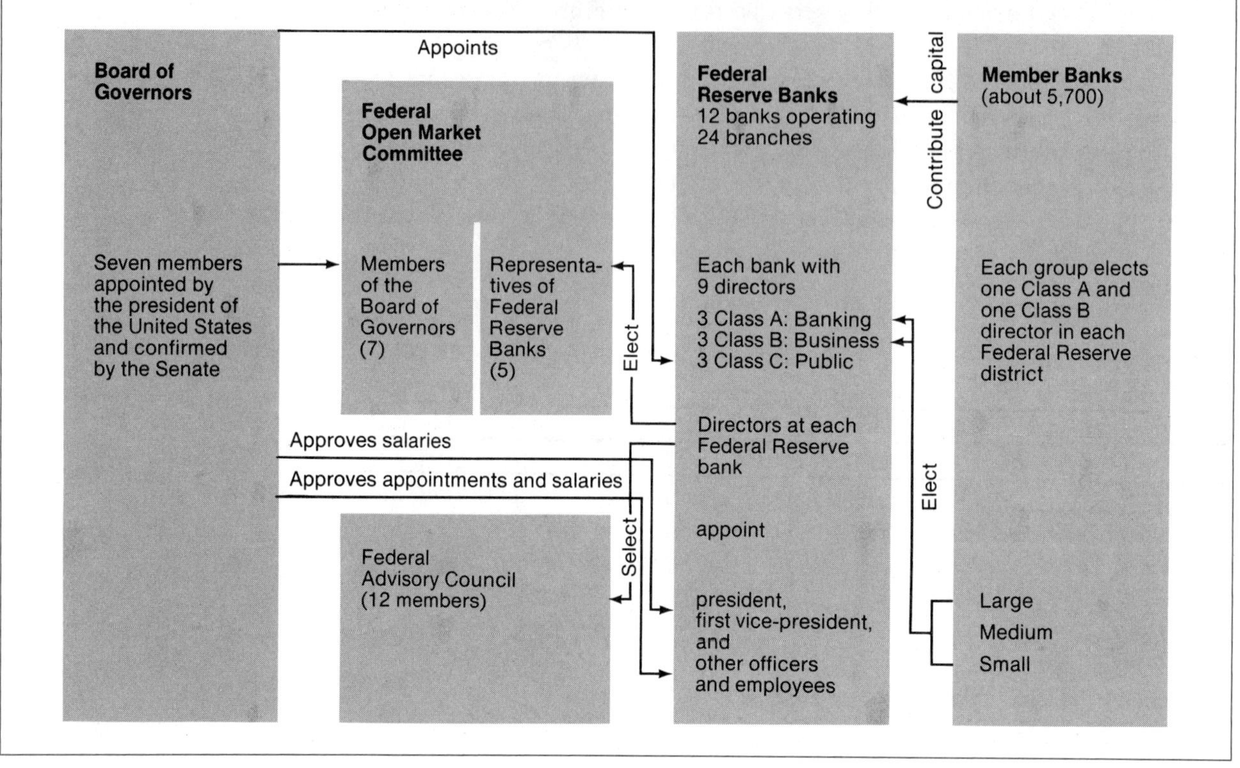

nine-member board. Of the nine, six are elected by the member bank stockholders, and the remaining three are appointed by the Fed's own Board of Governors. Each board is responsible for the policies of its own bank and for appointing bank officers.

The Federal Reserve banks perform several important functions in the banking system. They carry out policy decisions, examine and supervise the state-chartered member banks in their district, and provide banking services for the U.S. Treasury and other government agencies. They also provide banking services to their member banks. These services include clearing checks, handling commercial banks' reserve deposit accounts, making loans to member banks, and providing currency for member banks. In addition, Federal Reserve banks issue Federal Reserve notes, which form a major part of the country's stock of currency.

The Board of Governors The highest policy-making body of the entire Federal Reserve System is its Board of Governors. The board, which acts as a supervisor of the twelve Federal Reserve banks, has seven members who are appointed by the president and confirmed by the Senate. Each governor serves a single fourteen-year term and devotes full-time service to the business of the

Federal Reserve System. One term expires every other year. The present chairman of the board is Paul Volcker, former president of the Federal Reserve Bank of New York.

The Federal Open Market Committee A special Fed committee decides on the overall strategy of monetary policy and on how open market operations, involving purchases and sales of government securities, will be used to implement that policy. The Federal Open Market Committee is composed of the seven members of the Board of Governors plus five district Reserve bank presidents. The president of the Federal Reserve Bank of New York is a permanent voting member; the other four seats rotate among the remaining eleven district banks. The Open Market Committee meets ten times each year to decide on a general strategy for changes to be made in the Fed's security holdings. Actual transactions are carried out through the open market trading desk of the Federal Reserve Bank of New York.

Member Banks Many, but not all, commercial banks are members of the Federal Reserve System. National banks—those that have obtained charters from the federal government—are required to be members. Banks chartered by the states may or may not be members. As Exhibit 11.4 shows, only about a third of all banks are members of the Fed. They tend to be the larger banks, however, controlling almost three-fourths of all commercial bank assets and deposits.

Banks belonging to the Federal Reserve System are entitled to certain membership privileges. They can acquire loans, currency, and financial advice from their district Federal Reserve bank; and they can use the Fed's check-clearing facilities and transfer funds over its teletype wires. Free access to these facilities allows the large member banks to sell so-called correspondent services, such as check clearing, to smaller banks, particularly nonmembers. Member banks also earn a fixed dividend on the stock they are required to own in the Federal Reserve System.

Exhibit 11.4

Number of banks and total assets as of June 1978

Commercial banks in the United States may be chartered either by the federal government (national banks) or by the individual states. National banks must belong to the Federal Reserve System, but state banks need not be members. Only a minority of all banks are members, but member banks are larger than nonmember banks on the average. They hold nearly three-fourths of all bank assets.

	Number of Banks	Percent of Total	Total Assets (in billions of dollars)	Percent of Total
National banks	4,616	31.4	$ 671.2	55.2
State member banks	1,005	6.8	217.4	17.9
Total member banks	5,621	38.2	$ 888.6	73.1
Nonmember banks	9,077	61.8	326.5	26.9
Total banks	14,698	100.0	$1,215.0	100.0

Note: Totals may not agree because of rounding.
Source: *Federal Reserve Bulletin*, November 1978, Table A17.

There are, however, some serious disadvantages to Fed membership. Most importantly, member banks are required by the Fed to keep a larger fraction of their deposits—and, in effect, their assets—in the form of non-interest-bearing reserves than are nonmember banks in most states. This larger reserve requirement represents an implicit tax on Fed membership. Member banks are also subject to more stringent regulations regarding capital, assets, mergers, branches, holding companies, and officers than are nonmember banks.

Especially for smaller banks, the dollars-and-cents disadvantages of membership in the Fed outweigh the advantages. As a result, the percentage of banks maintaining membership in the Federal Reserve System has fallen continuously in recent years. Between 1950 and 1978, the percentage of banks that were members declined from 49 to 38, while the percentage of bank assets held by members fell from 85 to 73. This membership attrition has taken two forms. Most new banks have chosen nonmember status, and an increasing number of member banks have voluntarily withdrawn from the system. For national banks, withdrawal requires obtaining a state charter.

As will be shown in the next chapter, this decline in Federal Reserve membership has weakened the Fed's control over monetary policy. Various bills have been introduced into Congress to alleviate the problems caused by the decline in membership. Final details have not been settled as of this writing.

The Fed's Balance Sheet

Exhibit 11.5 shows a consolidated balance sheet for the twelve Federal Reserve banks. Government securities are by far the largest item on the asset side. Loans to member banks are small by comparison, but they are listed separately because they are important for policy purposes. These loans are extended to member banks to permit them to satisfy reserve requirements.

Federal reserve notes, which constitute almost all of the nation's supply of currency, are the largest liability of the Federal Reserve System. The next largest is reserves kept on deposit with the Fed by member banks. Other liabilities include deposits of the Treasury and of foreign central banks and a number of smaller items.

Exhibit 11.5
Consolidated balance sheet of the twelve Federal Reserve banks as of July 25, 1979 (billions of dollars)
The Federal Reserve banks have liabilities to the general public, in the form of Federal Reserve notes, and to member banks, in the form of reserve deposits. Their main assets are government securities.

Assets		Liabilities and Net Worth	
Securities	$117.4	Federal Reserve notes	$105.8
Loans to member banks	1.2	Member banks' reserve deposits	29.6
Other assets	31.1	Other liabilities and net worth	14.2
Total	$149.7	Total	$149.7

Note: Subtotals may not add to totals due to rounding.
Source: *Federal Reserve Bulletin*, August 1979, Table A12.

The Federal Deposit Insurance Corporation

No discussion of banking regulation would be complete without at least a brief mention of another federal agency—the Federal Deposit Insurance Corporation (FDIC). This agency was established in 1933 to protect depositors from bank failures. Deposits are now insured by the FDIC up to $40,000 per depositor per bank.

By insuring depositors against loss in the event of bank failure, the FDIC actually plays an important role in preventing such failure. As the balance sheet given in Exhibit 11.2 shows, commercial banks do not have enough cash on hand, or enough assets that are easily converted to cash, to honor the demands of depositors if all depositors try to withdraw their funds at once. Depositors know this, but ordinarily they are not concerned, because they also know that only a few people are likely to want to withdraw funds on any given day—and, in any event, these withdrawals are on the average balanced by new deposits.

However, if a rumor got started that an uninsured bank was in financial difficulty, more depositors than usual might want to withdraw their funds, and fewer than usual would make new deposits. This tendency would make the rumor self-fulfilling; drained of deposits and with reserves exhausted, the bank would fail. In the days before deposit insurance, such failures were not infrequent; and during the Great Depression, they threatened to engulf the entire banking system.

Today, with 98 percent of banks members of the FDIC, deposit insurance short-circuits the mechanism by which rumors of bank failure cause actual bank failure. Depositors no longer need run in panic to be first in line to withdraw their funds from a weak bank. Even if the bank does fail, they will get a refund from the FDIC.

NONBANK FINANCIAL INTERMEDIARIES

Banks are by no means the only financial institutions active in the economy. Many other institutions—including savings and loan associations, pension funds, insurance companies, and securities markets—perform some, although not all, of the same functions that banks do. In particular, these institutions function as go-betweens for savers with funds to lend and investors with the need to borrow. Because they perform this function, they too are considered financial intermediaries.

Thrift Institutions

The most familiar group of financial intermediaries, after commercial banks, are the so-called **thrift institutions.** They include savings and loan associations, mutual savings banks, and credit unions.

Thrift institutions Nonbank financial intermediaries primarily serving the interests of small savers and nonbusiness borrowers; thrift institutions include savings and loan associations, mutual savings banks, and credit unions.

Thrift institutions originally developed to serve the needs of small savers and nonbusiness borrowers; and to a large extent, this is the function they continue to serve. Unlike commercial banks, which are owned by shareholders, almost all thrifts are owned by their depositors. When savers make deposits, they are technically buying a "share" that gives them a voice in management as well as a claim against the assets of the institution. In practice, savings and loan associations and mutual banks are normally operated by professional managers, with little input from members. But many credit unions, especially small ones, encourage active participation by members and may have only part-time or unpaid managers of their own.

Home Mortgages Savings and loan associations and mutual savings banks play a crucial role in the national economy as the major source of home mortgage loans.[1] In 1978, for example, these two types of institutions held $408 billion out of a national total of $750 billion in home mortgage debt. These home mortgages, together with some multi-family residential and commercial mortgages, constitute some 80 percent of thrift institution assets.

Because thrifts are so important as sources of mortgage money, the home construction industry is very sensitive to flows of funds into and out of them. Like commercial banks, thrifts are legally limited by federal regulations concerning the rate of interest they can pay on savings and time deposits, although thrift institutions are generally allowed to pay a quarter percentage point higher interest rates than commercial banks. In periods of rapid inflation and in periods when the economy is booming and aggregate loan demand is high, nominal interest rates can rise well above the deposit rate ceilings. When this happens, depositors in thrift institutions are tempted to withdraw their funds and use them instead to buy high-yield securities such as Treasury bills and notes or shares in money market mutual funds. This withdrawal of funds from financial intermediaries is known as **disintermediation.**

Disintermediation The large-scale withdrawal of funds from financial intermediaries by depositors in search of higher interest rates obtainable elsewhere.

Large-scale disintermediation can have a devastating effect on the housing market. Without mortgage money, people cannot buy homes. Without buyers, homes are not built, workers are laid off, and unemployment rises. In 1974–75, a severe bout of disintermediation caused a virtual collapse of residential construction activity. This collapse contributed significantly to unemployment, which in 1975 reached its highest level since the Great Depression.

Efforts to Limit Disintermediation Largely as a result of that experience, new regulations were enacted in mid-1978 to help discourage disintermediation. In particular, thrift institutions were permitted to offer six-month certificates of deposit (CDs) in $10,000 minimum denominations. They were allowed to pay to holders of the CDs an interest rate of one-quarter percentage point more than the interest rate on six-month Treasury bills. (Commercial banks were allowed to offer such certificates at a rate equal to the Treasury bill rate—that is, one-quarter point lower than the rate for thrifts.) This new type of deposit not only protected thrift institutions from disintermediation but allowed them to acquire additional deposits. Within nine months after they were introduced, the new certificates had grown to represent 15 percent of deposits at savings and loans and mutual savings banks. It is estimated that about half these funds would have been diverted from thrifts without the high-yield certificates.

By early 1979, in fact, federal regulators became concerned that the high-yield CDs had been too successful and decided that the housing industry needed some cooling off. In March, the rules governing the new certificates

[1]Credit unions differ from other thrift institutions in that they usually make small-denomination short-term loans to members for appliances, vacations, automobiles, and the like rather than mortgage loans.

were modified to make them slightly less attractive to depositors, in part by taking away the quarter-point premium that thrifts had been allowed to pay. But at the same time, the regulators were coming under increased public pressure to allow commercial banks and thrift institutions to pay higher interest rates on deposits other than these special ones. The pressure came particularly from groups representing elderly and retired persons, who need the high nominal interest rates to protect their savings against accelerating inflation. In mid-1979, the rate ceilings on savings deposits at commercial banks and thrifts were raised by one-quarter percentage point, and a new four-year CD with a rate ceiling tied to the yield on four-year Treasury notes was authorized. Further modifications in the regulations regarding interest paid on deposits at thrift institutions can be expected in the future.

The Insurance Industry

The insurance industry is really two industries. One part of the business of an insurance company is selling protection against risk. The other is operating as a financial intermediary.

Risk Protection Insurance companies sell protection against risk on the principle that although exposure to risk is inherently unpredictable for any single individual, it is highly predictable for large numbers of individuals. No family, for example, can be certain that its house will not burn down during the coming year. An insurance company, however, can predict quite accurately, on the basis of past experience, that (say) one in every thousand houses in a given type of neighborhood will burn down each year. Knowing this, it can sell insurance. Each family pays a premium each year equal to a thousandth of the value of its house, and the pool of funds thus collected is used to compensate the unlucky one family in a thousand whose house burns down.

Today, one can buy insurance against risks of almost any kind. Fire insurance, automobile accident insurance, and health insurance are the most common types. All of them protect the buyer against losses that might never occur but that would be very costly if they did.

Life insurance is a very important kind of insurance. Superficially, it differs somewhat from the other kinds of insurance mentioned in that the risk it appears to insure against—death—is something certain to befall everyone. On closer examination, however, it turns out that what life insurance really does is protect the buyer against the risk of *premature* death. Although everyone can be certain of dying sometime, death during any single year is a risk, not a certainty—much like the risk of having a house burn down.

Pensions and annuities are closely related to life insurance. They are arrangements under which a person pays in a premium each year up to a given age, say sixty-five years, and then receives a fixed sum each year until death. (A common variation for married couples is to arrange to have the payment continue until the death of both people.) In a sense, pensions and annuities insure people against the risk that they will live too long. Pension premiums and benefits are based on participants' average life expectancy at retirement. Those who die sooner than expected will, in a sense, not get their money's worth out of the program. But those who live longer than expected will receive payments totaling more than the value of the premiums they paid in.

Insurance Companies as Financial Intermediaries This picture of what insurance companies do is, of course, an extremely simplified one. If the companies actually paid out benefits as rapidly as they took in premiums, they would not be able to cover administrative expenses, let alone make a profit. In part, insurance companies allow for administrative expenses and profit by charging premiums that are somewhat higher than the level dictated by the exact probability of risk. (In the earlier example, this would mean collecting from each purchaser of a fire insurance policy somewhat more than a thousandth of the value of the insured home.) But insurance companies and pension funds have another important source of income as well—namely their operations as financial intermediaries.

Insurance companies are able to operate as financial intermediaries because all insurance involves an element of saving. The reason is that premiums are collected before benefits are paid out, which generates in the meantime a pool of funds controlled by the insurance company. In the case of life insurance and pension funds, the lag between receipt of premiums and payment of benefits is often particularly long, which gives these companies billions of dollars to put to work in financial markets. The assets of life insurance companies alone are nearly as large as the assets of thrift institutions.

These vast quantities of funds are put to work principally through the purchase of securities such as corporate stocks and bonds. Insurance companies and pension funds also often buy commercial mortgages and sometimes invest directly in real estate. Certain types of life insurance policies also permit policyholders to take out personal loans from these companies at advantageous interest rates.

Securities Markets as Financial Intermediaries

The chapter has frequently mentioned government and corporate securities—bills, bonds, stocks, mortgage notes, and the like—without mentioning a further important class of financial intermediaries—the markets in which such securities are bought and sold. These institutions too play an important role in channeling savings from households to business and government borrowers. Conceptually, the securities markets can be divided into two classes—primary and secondary.

Primary Markets Primary securities markets are those in which new borrowing takes place. Suppose, for example, General Motors wants to build a new assembly plant or testing facility. It might finance the project with a bank loan, but it has an alternative that is often more attractive: It can sell newly issued bonds or stocks to the public. Bonds are a promise to repay a fixed nominal amount at a later date, with periodic interest payments to be made in the meantime. Stocks represent a share in the ownership of the firm, including the right to receive part of future profits in the form of dividends.

A corporation seeking to raise money through the sale of stocks or bonds does not normally approach individual households directly. Instead, it uses the services of brokers and underwriters—specialists in putting individuals and firms with funds to loan in touch with companies wishing to sell newly issued bonds and stocks. Brokers and underwriters thus act as financial intermediaries. Since the purchaser of the new securities may itself be a bank, thrift institution, or insurance company, the funds involved may pass through a chain of two or more financial intermediaries on their way from the original saver to the ultimate borrower.

Secondary Markets When most people think of securities markets, however, it is not these primary markets that they have in mind. Instead, they think of highly publicized institutions such as the New York Stock Exchange or American Stock Exchange. These exchanges are *secondary* markets; they stand in relation to the primary markets discussed above exactly as used car dealers stand in relation to new car dealers. The sellers in secondary security markets are typically not themselves issuers but instead are savers or financial institutions who own and now wish to sell stocks or bonds issued by firms or government units at some time in the past.

Strictly speaking, then, secondary security markets are not financial intermediaries. Rather than channeling money from savers to investors, they permit savers to exchange "used" securities for money or money for securities. Indirectly, however, these markets are very important to the operation of the economy's system of financial intermediaries. They give households, banks, thrift institutions, insurance companies, pension funds, and all the rest a much-needed flexibility in their financial operations.

A corporation makes a long-term financial commitment when it issues a new bond or share of stock, but the buyer need not make an equally long-term commitment. Because the secondary market with its network of brokers is always there, the buyer can resell the security tomorrow, obtaining cash to spend or buying some different kind of asset instead.

CONCLUSIONS

This chapter has wandered rather far from macroeconomic policy—but for a reason. Commercial banks and other financial intermediaries play a crucial role in regulating the circular flow of income and product, which is what macroeconomic policy seeks to stabilize. The focus here has been on their functions in channeling funds from savers to investors. The next chapter will look at the function of banks as creators of money and at the Federal Reserve as the regulator of the money supply.

SUMMARY

1. Financial intermediaries are institutions that channel funds from savers to investors. They are a necessary part of the circular flow of income and product because the needs of individual lenders and borrowers do not necessarily match in terms of quantity of funds, length of commitment, and degree of risk.
2. Commercial banks are the least specialized and most important class of financial intermediary. They accept demand deposits, savings deposits, and time deposits from households and firms and earn income by making loans and purchasing securities. Banking practices are regulated by the Federal Reserve System and by other federal and state regulatory bodies. One of the

most important Federal Reserve regulations is that member banks must maintain non-interest-bearing reserves equal to specified percentages of deposits.

3. A number of nonbank financial intermediaries also operate in the U.S. economy. They include thrift institutions, insurance companies, pension funds, and organized securities markets. Each plays an important role in channeling funds from savers to investors.

DISCUSSION QUESTIONS

1. Do you have a checking or savings account in a local commercial bank? If so, go to that bank (and if not, go to any convenient commercial bank) and ask for a copy of its most recent balance sheet. Compare the balance sheet for your bank with the consolidated commercial bank balance sheet shown in Exhibit 11.2.
2. Go to your library and look at a recent issue of the *Federal Reserve Bulletin*. Use the data in the section of tables at the back of the issue to update the commercial bank balance sheet shown in Exhibit 11.2. Also examine the detailed breakdowns of loans, securities, and so on into particular subcategories.
3. Do you maintain an account at a local savings and loan association, mutual savings bank, or credit union? If so, see if you can obtain a copy of that institution's balance sheet. (If not, obtain the balance sheet of any convenient thrift institution.) Compare it to the balance sheet for the commercial bank that you obtained for Question 1.
4. What kinds of insurance do you carry: Health insurance? Auto insurance? Life insurance? If it is convenient, call your insurance agent and ask for a copy of your insurance company's balance sheet. What kinds of assets and liabilities does it hold? Compare this balance sheet to that of a commercial bank.
5. Go to your library and find a recent copy of the business section of the *Wall Street Journal* or the *New York Times*. Look carefully through the ads and the columns and tables relating to stock and bond markets. Which items refer to secondary markets? (Hint: The Dow-Jones Industrial Average is one such item. It is an average of industrial stock prices on the New York Stock Exchange, which is a secondary market.) Which items refer to primary markets? (Hint: Look for individual advertisements mentioning the sale of new stocks or bonds, or look for daily or weekly columns discussing new issues in the stock and bond markets.)

SUGGESTIONS FOR FURTHER READING

Boone, Louis E., and Kurtz, David L. *Contemporary Business*, 2d ed. Hinsdale, Ill.: Dryden Press, 1978, chaps. 14–17.

Provides an elementary treatment of money and banking, financial management, securities markets, risk management, and insurance, all from a business point of view.

Campbell, Colin, and Campbell, Rosemary. *An Introduction to Money and Banking*, 3rd ed. Hinsdale, Ill.: Dryden Press, 1978.

Chapter 4, which deals with government securities, and Chapters 5 to 8, which deal with commercial banks, parallel the treatment of this chapter but offer much more detail.

Malkeil, Burton G. *A Random Walk Down Wall Street.* New York: W. W. Norton, 1977.

A delightful, provocative, thoroughly readable introduction to the world of Wall Street; a must for anyone interested in the stock market.

Miller, Roger Leroy. *Economic Issues for Consumers.* St. Paul, Minn.: West Publishing, 1975.

Chapter 7 treats credit markets, and Chapter 13 treats insurance; both presentations are from a consumer point of view.

CHAPTER 12

THE SUPPLY OF MONEY

WHAT YOU WILL LEARN IN THIS CHAPTER

This chapter is about money—what it is, how it is created by the banking system, and how the Fed controls the quantity of it in circulation. The first section examines the thorny problem of how to define and measure the stock of money in the economy. The next, through a series of examples based on a simplified banking system, shows how commercial banks create money on the basis of reserves supplied by the Fed. The final section discusses the policies used by the Fed to control the money supply and shows why these policies are not always completely reliable.

FOR REVIEW

Here are some important terms and concepts that will be put to use in this chapter. If you do not understand them, review them before proceeding.

- *Humphrey-Hawkins Act (Chapter 7)*
- *Assets, liabilities, and balance sheets (Chapter 11)*
- *Currency, demand deposits, time deposits, and savings deposits (Chapter 11)*
- *Commercial banks and thrift institutions (Chapter 11)*
- *Federal Reserve System (Chapter 11)*

Chapter 11 emphasized the role of banks and thrift institutions as financial intermediaries. In that capacity, they play a crucial role in channeling investment funds from savers to investors, thereby lowering transaction costs and facilitating the circular flow of income and product. The chapter also introduced the Federal Reserve System, concentrating on its regulation of banks in their role as financial intermediaries. But there is much more to be said about the role of banks and the Federal Reserve System in the economy. In fact, the most important function of these institutions is one that has not been mentioned yet.

To be specific, nothing has yet been said about the role of banks and the Federal Reserve System in the creation of money. In fact, no formal definition of *money* has been given. This chapter will fill the gap by explaining what money is, where it comes from, and how its supply is controlled by the Fed. The next two chapters will then return to the theory of national income determination, showing how monetary policy is used side by side with fiscal policy in pursuit of the goals of economic stabilization.

MONEY AND ITS FUNCTIONS

Money Anything that serves as a unit of account, a medium of exchange, and a store of purchasing power.

Money can best be defined in terms of what it does. It serves as a means of payment, a store of purchasing power, and a unit of account. Its physical form is of secondary importance; gold, cowrie shells, paper currency, and electronic bookkeeping records have all been found serviceable at various times and places because each has served these three central functions.

Means of Payment As a means of payment, money keeps transaction costs low and makes it possible to avoid the inconvenience of barter. Because it performs this function, we do not have to find out what the dentist wants for dinner before we get our teeth fixed. Instead of taking a dozen eggs or a side of bacon with us, we take money; and the dentist stops off at the supermarket on the way home to pick up whatever looks good.

Store of Purchasing Power As a store of purchasing power, money makes it possible to arrange economic activities conveniently through time. Income and expenditures thus need not be synchronized exactly. Instead, a stock of money can be kept on hand to dip into if expenditures run ahead of income or to add to if income runs ahead of expenditures.

Unit of Account Finally, as a unit of account, money makes it possible to measure and record economic stocks and flows in consistent terms. Movies, apples, and shirts cannot be added together to get gross national product; but dollars' worth of movies, dollars' worth of apples, and dollars' worth of shirts can be added up to get GNP measured in dollars.

Money as a Liquid Asset

Economists refer to all the things of value that people own as assets. A typical household's assets might include a house, a car, other personal possessions, maybe a few stocks or bonds, and, of course, some money. All assets serve to one degree or another as stores of purchasing power, because they can be sold and the proceeds can be used to buy something else.

Money, however, has two important properties that no other asset has to the same degree. First, money itself can be used as a means of payment without first having to be exchanged for something else. Second, it never experiences a gain or loss in nominal value. The nominal value of a house or a bond or a share of corporate stock can go up or down for any number of reasons, but the nominal value of a dollar is always a dollar. The constancy of the nominal value of money is a consequence of the fact that money is itself the unit of account in terms of which nominal values are defined.

Liquid Description of an asset that can be used as a means of payment or easily converted to a means of payment without risk of gain or loss in nominal value.

Because it can be used directly as a means of payment, and because its nominal value never changes, money is said to be **liquid.** No other asset is as liquid as money, although some assets can be exchanged for money quickly and easily, with little danger of a change in their nominal value, and are thus fairly liquid.

MEASURING THE QUANTITY OF MONEY

For purposes of economic policy, it is important to know not only what money is but also how much money there is in the economy at any time. In all modern economies, the quantity of money in circulation is controlled by government. Failure to supply a sufficient quantity of it can have a depressing effect on real output and employment. Indeed, some economists believe that the Great Depression in the United States was seriously aggravated by an inadequate supply of money. Flooding the economy with excessive quantities of money, however, can undermine the goal of price stability; the runaway inflation afflicting much of Latin America is blamed by many economists on irresponsible monetary expansion.

The postwar U.S. economy has escaped both major depressions and Latin American style inflation in part at least because the quantity of money has been kept within reasonable bounds. Nonetheless, as shown in Chapter 7, the record of U.S. stabilization policy in recent years is not all that might be desired. If performance is to be improved, better monetary policy will have to play an important role in achieving the improvement. And because the money supply cannot be controlled if it cannot be measured, the problem of measuring the quantity of money is becoming more important now than ever before.

Traditional Approaches to Measuring the Money Supply

Money as Currency plus Demand Deposits Traditionally, just two kinds of assets have been viewed as being perfectly liquid and thus suitable to be counted as part of the economy's stock of money. The two are currency and demand deposits.

Currency Coins and paper money are defined as **currency.** It is presently issued by two institutions of government—the Federal Reserve System and the Treasury—and it represents their monetary obligations, or IOUs, to the public. Today, currency consists almost entirely of Federal Reserve notes and Treasury coins.

Currency Coins and paper money.

Paper money and coins are no longer backed by any intrinsically valuable commodity. Neither the Federal Reserve nor the Treasury will now give anything in exchange for a $10 bill or a dime other than another $10 bill or dime—another promise to pay. Until 1934, the government issued gold coins and paper currency redeemable in gold. Until the mid-1960s one could readily obtain silver coins and "silver certificates" (dollar bills redeemable in silver), but they were gradually phased out. The few surviving silver certificates can no longer be turned in for metallic silver, and the remaining silver coins are mostly lodged in collections. We now have a currency whose value is based purely on the public's faith in its ability to exchange the currency for all kinds of goods and services.

Demand Deposits Demand deposits are bookkeeping entries at commercial banks. They represent monetary obligations of the banks to their depositors. Depositors can go to their banks and exchange these deposits for currency on demand (hence the name), but more commonly they write checks payable to other parties. A check is an order to the banking system to move funds from the account of one depositor to the account of another.

M_1 The sum of currency plus demand deposits is one of the most widely used measures of the economy's total money supply, traditionally known as **M_1**. Only currency and demand deposits belonging to the nonbank public are counted as M_1. Those owned by commercial banks, the Treasury, and the Federal Reserve are excluded.

M_1 The measure of the money supply, defined as currency plus demand deposits.

Money as Savings Deposits and Time Deposits Demand deposits are not the only kinds of deposits accepted by commercial banks. As shown in the last chapter, savings deposits and time deposits are also important. Conventional savings deposits are less liquid than demand deposits in that checks cannot be written on them. Time deposits, also known as certificates of deposit, are less liquid still, in that depositors can withdraw their funds without penalty only when the deposit "matures" at the end of a specified period.

M_2 M_1 plus savings and time deposits at commercial banks.

Because they are not perfectly liquid, savings and time deposits have not traditionally been counted as part of M_1. However, because they do serve as a partial substitute for demand deposits, those at commercial banks have been included in a second measure of the money supply, known as M_2. **M_2** is defined as M_1 plus savings and time deposits at commercial banks but excluding certain large certificates of deposit available only in denominations of $100,000 or more.

Other Monetary Aggregates Adding savings and time deposits at thrift institutions to M_2 gives a measure of money known as M_3. Still broader definitions of M also exist, all the way up to M_7. Exhibit 12.1 shows the major monetary aggregates as of June 30, 1978. Instead of going into the details of these broad aggregates, however, the chapter will now turn to some innovations

Exhibit 12.1
Major monetary aggregates as traditionally defined as of June 30, 1978
This exhibit shows the major monetary aggregates as of June 30, 1978, according to the traditional definitions in use by the Fed at that time. M_1 and M_2 are the most commonly used definitions; but, as the exhibit shows, they exclude many highly liquid assets, such as savings balances at thrift institutions and large certificates of deposit.

Aggregate	Components	Amount as of June 30, 1978 (billions of dollars, not seasonally adjusted)
M_1	Currency	$ 92.9
	Plus: Demand deposits at commercial banks	258.8
	Total	$ 351.7
M_2	M_1	$ 351.7
	Plus: Savings balances at commercial banks	223.8
	Time deposits at commercial banks	352.8
	Less: Negotiable certificates of deposit (CDs) at large banks	−86.3
	Total	$ 842.0
M_3	M_2	$ 842.0
	Plus: Savings balances at thrift institutions	275.8
	Time deposits at thrift institutions	317.4
	Total	$1,435.2
M_4	M_2	$ 842.0
	Plus: Negotiable CDs at large banks	86.3
	Total	$ 928.3

Source: "A Proposal for Redefining the Monetary Aggregates," *Federal Reserve Bulletin* 65 (January 1979): 18.

in financial institutions that are making it necessary to rethink the definition of money altogether.

Financial Innovations and New Approaches to Measuring Money

During the 1970s, a number of banking innovations were introduced. These innovations have had the cumulative effect of blurring the distinctions among some kinds of deposits while sharpening the distinctions among others. They have rendered the traditional measures of the money supply increasingly obsolete.

NOW Accounts One major innovation was the introduction of NOW (Negotiable Order of Withdrawal) accounts, first in New England and then in New York. NOW accounts are interest-bearing savings accounts on which the depositors are permitted to write checks. They are currently available only to individuals. They are offered not only by commercial banks but also by thrift institutions such as savings and loan associations and mutual savings banks. For transaction purposes, they are perfect substitutes for the traditional demand deposits. Credit unions have been offering similar interest-bearing accounts subject to withdrawal by a check-like instrument—the credit union share draft account.

Other Checking-Saving Hybrids In states where NOW accounts are not available, other banking arrangements have had similar effects in blurring the distinction between savings and demand deposits. For example, in late 1978, banks were authorized to offer automatic transfer service (ATS), under which funds could be transferred from depositors' savings accounts to their checking accounts as needed to cover checks. A depositor with both ATS savings and checking accounts at a bank offering ATS enjoys essentially all the advantages of a NOW account. In addition to ATS, many banks and thrift institutions also offer depositors the service of transferring funds from one account to another on request by telephone or according to a prearranged schedule for payment of regular bills.

Recent Developments As banking innovations proliferated, disputes arose between banks and thrift institutions. Each felt that some of the innovative banking practices were permitting the other to invade what had long been protected territory. Banks resented arrangements allowing depositors to write checks on their thrift accounts, and thrifts resented arrangements like ATS that in effect allowed banks to pay interest on demand deposits. Furthermore, some of the innovations were of dubious legality under regulatory laws prohibiting interest on checking accounts—laws that had been written many years before.

In April 1979, after a flurry of lawsuits, a federal appeals court issued a decision declaring many of the new hybrid checking-savings arrangements illegal under existing statutes after January 1, 1980. The court recognized that the services being offered might be useful ones but declared that Congress would have to rewrite the laws so they could be introduced in a more orderly way. As of this writing, the drafting of new legislation has just begun. Although it seems safe to say that many of the new services now being offered will continue to be permitted, the exact form they will take is not yet settled.

Changes in Savings and Time Deposits While the innovations discussed above tended to blur the distinction between savings and demand deposits, other changes in banking regulations during the 1970s tended to sharpen the distinction between savings and time deposits. Banks and thrift institutions were authorized to offer time deposits with longer maturities in return for higher interest rates, and penalties for early withdrawal from these deposits were significantly stiffened. These changes made time deposits even less liquid than they had been.

New Definitions of Money As a result of all these changes, economists increasingly have come to consider the traditional definitions of M_1 and M_2 less useful than they were formerly. M_1 has lost its meaning as the sole measure of funds available for use as a means of payment. The rigid distinction between commercial banks and thrift institutions has become less significant. And it has begun to make less sense to lump savings and time deposits together in measuring M_2.

As a result, it is now recognized that new definitions are needed. A recent set of recommendations by the Federal Reserve Board staff indicates the likely nature of the new definitions, although the details of the new definitions are still subject to change as of this writing.

Under the staff recommendations, M_1 would be replaced by a measure consisting of currency plus all deposits subject to withdrawal by check, including conventional demand deposits, NOW accounts, ATS accounts, share draft accounts, and whatever other similar accounts might be introduced not only at commercial banks but also at savings and loan associations, mutual savings banks, and credit unions. This new total would attempt to capture, in a single number, all funds available for immediate use as a means of payment—that is, all funds serving as money in the full functional sense of the term.

M_2, as proposed, would be equal to the new M_1 plus savings accounts not subject to check at both banks and thrift institutions. Time deposits at both banks and thrifts would be added to the new definition of M_2 to get a revised M_3. Exhibit 12.2 shows the proposed monetary aggregates as of June 30, 1978.

Near-Monies

Currency, demand deposits, savings deposits, and time deposits are only four of a great many kinds of assets held by households and firms. Some of the other assets are sufficiently liquid that they are known as **near-monies.**

Near-monies Assets that are less than perfectly liquid but still liquid enough to be reasonably good substitutions for money.

Short-Term Securities and Money Market Funds Short-term securities issued by the U.S. government and its agencies, such as 90-day and 120-day Treasury bills, are one important category of near-money. If these securities are held to maturity, they carry no risk of gain or loss in nominal value; and even if they are sold before maturity, there is little risk. For small investors, the securities come in inconveniently large denominations, usually $10,000; but even this problem is overcome by the so-called money market mutual funds. These funds buy large pools of large denomination liquid securities and then sell individual investors small shares in the pool. Most funds even permit shareholders to write checks against their balances. By mid-1979, money market mutual funds had grown to some $25 billion.

Exhibit 12.2
Proposed redefinitions of major monetary aggregates
This exhibit shows the major monetary aggregates for June 30, 1978, as they would look according to a new set of definitions proposed by the Federal Reserve staff in early 1979. Notice that the new definition of M_1 would include all deposits subject to check, including NOW accounts and ATS accounts. The broadened definition of M_2 would include savings accounts at both banks and thrifts but exclude bank time deposits, which traditionally have been included in M_2. Details of the new definitions are still subject to change at the time of this writing.

Proposed Aggregate	Components	Amount as of June 30, 1978 (billions of dollars, not seasonally adjusted)
M_1	Current M_1	$ 351.7
	Plus: NOW balances	3.3
	Credit union share drafts	.6
	Demand deposits at thrifts	.9
	ATS savings[a]	.0
	Less: Demand deposits of foreign commercial banks and official institutions	−11.2
	Total	$ 345.0[b]
M_2	Proposed M_1	$ 345.0
	Plus: Savings balances at all depository institutions[c]	494.3
	Total	$ 839.3
M_3	Proposed M_1	$ 345.0
	Plus: All savings and time deposits (including large time deposits) at all depository institutions[c]	1,154.2
	Total	$1,499.2

[a]Including payment order accounts (POA) at savings and loans, if the current Federal Home Loan Bank Board proposal is adopted. ATS savings were first offered on November 1, 1978.
[b]Total does not equal the sum of the above components because of miscellaneous adjustments to it.
[c]Excludes all NOW, ATS, POA (if introduced), and credit union share draft balances.
Source: "A Proposal for Redefining the Monetary Aggregates," *Federal Reserve Bulletin* 65 (January 1979): 17.

The Federal Funds Market As nominal interest rates have risen to record levels in recent years, money managers at financial institutions and large corporations have become increasingly careful not to let more than a bare minimum of liquid assets sit idle in currency or non-interest-bearing bank accounts. Specialized credit markets that enable financial and nonfinancial firms to earn interest on idle balances for periods as short as twenty-four hours have grown. One such market for overnight loans to banks from other banks and thrift institutions is called the **federal funds market.** The name comes from the use of this market by banks that borrow reserve deposits held at the Federal Reserve from one another. However, in recent years, the scope of the market has greatly expanded; and, as will be shown later in the chapter, it now plays a major role in monetary policy.

Federal funds market A credit market in which banks can borrow funds from one another and from thrifts for periods as short as twenty-four hours.

Repurchase agreements Arrangements under which financial and nonfinancial firms sell securities subject to agreement to buy them back, often as soon as the next day.

Repurchase Agreements Another very short-term market is that in which securities are bought and sold under so-called **repurchase agreements.** In a typical repurchase transaction, a bank might sell a million dollars' worth of Treasury bills to a corporation with an agreement to buy them back the next day at a slightly higher price, representing an interest payment for the bank's overnight borrowing. (At a 10 percent nominal interest rate, one day's use of a million dollars is worth $277.) The corporation thus puts idle funds to work for a short period, and the bank has the use of them in the meantime. By mid-1979, such borrowing had increased to $45 billion.

Money market mutual funds and repurchase agreements with nonbank customers have such a high degree of liquidity that some economists think they too should be included in one or another of the measures of the money supply.

Credit and Credit Cards

In their efforts to make transactions ever more convenient for their customers, bankers have succeeded in blurring not only the distinction between money and near-money but also the distinction between money and credit. A case in point is the "plastic money" that almost everyone carries around in purses and billfolds these days—Master Charge cards, Visa cards, and all the rest. But money and credit cards are different things, and it is important to understand why.

What distinguishes a credit card both from money and from near-money is that it is not a store of purchasing power. Instead, it is just a document that makes it easy for its holder to obtain a loan. When you go into a store, present your credit card, and walk out with a can of tennis balls, you have not yet paid for your purchase. What you have done, instead, is borrow money from the bank that issued the credit card. Simultaneously, you have instructed the bank to turn over the proceeds of the loan to the merchant. Later, the bank will send money to the merchant, thus paying for the tennis balls; and later still, you will send money to the bank to pay off the balance on your credit card account.

Although credit cards are not a form of money, a discussion of them is not entirely out of place here. The reason is that credit cards allow households to *economize* on the use of money. If people use credit cards, they do not have to keep as much cash in their billfolds or as large a balance in their checking accounts as they otherwise would. In this strictly limited sense, it is not altogether wrong to think of credit cards as "plastic money."

THE CREATION OF MONEY BY THE BANKING SYSTEM

The chapter has so far emphasized the importance of the supply of money for stabilization policy and has discussed in some detail the problem of how the quantity of money is to be measured. It turns now to the important matter of how the quantity of money is controlled by the Federal Reserve.

Although currency is issued directly by the Fed, demand deposits—the most important component of the money supply, however measured—are issued by commercial banks. The Fed's control over the money supply is thus inherently indirect, and it is exercised primarily through its powers to establish reserve requirements and to determine the outstanding amount of member bank reserves. To understand how this control works, we must first understand how money, in the form of demand deposits, is created by the commercial banking system.

A Simplified Banking System

To keep things simple, we will take a vacation from certain complexities of real-world financial markets in this section. Once the major principles governing the supply of money are made clear, we will reintroduce some of the complexities in a discussion of monetary policy.

Our simplified banking system is comprised of just ten banks, all of which are identical in every respect. The liabilities of these banks consist entirely of demand deposits, which are also the only form of money in the system. There is no currency, and the banks have zero net worth. On the other side of the banks' balance sheets, only three kinds of assets are found. The first is reserves, which consist entirely of non-interest-bearing deposits with the Federal Reserve System. In addition to reserves, the banks hold two kinds of interest-bearing assets—loans and U.S. government securities.

Regulation and Required Reserves The banks in our simple system are subject to regulation by an equally simplified version of the Federal Reserve System. The only assets of this simplified Fed are U.S. government securities, and the only liabilities are its member banks' reserve deposits. All banks are members, and all member bank demand deposits are subject to a uniform **required reserve ratio** of 10 percent. This means that they are required to hold ten cents in reserves for each dollar of deposits.

Required reserve ratio The fraction of each type of deposit that the Federal Reserve System requires member banks to hold in the form of non-interest-bearing assets.

Balance Sheet Equilibrium Like any other firms, our simplified banks want to earn the maximum possible profit for their shareholders. The source of their income is interest earned on securities and loans. To maximize profits, then, they want to expand their loans and security holdings to the greatest extent possible. Given the choice between holding assets in the form of non-interest-bearing reserves or interest-bearing loans and securities, they choose loans and securities. They thus tend to expand their loans and securities to the greatest extent they can without violating their required reserve ratio. In doing so, they try to avoid holding any **excess reserves**—reserves in excess of the required amount. A bank that has expanded loans and security holdings to the maximum extent possible is said to have its balance sheet in equilibrium.

Excess reserves Reserves held by member commercial banks in excess of required reserves.

Balance Sheets To further set the stage for our discussion of the banking system's creation of money, we can fill in some numbers in the balance sheets of our simplified commercial banks and of the simplified Fed. Each of the ten member banks will start from the following equilibrium balance sheet position:

Representative Member Bank Balance Sheet

Assets			Liabilities	
Reserves:		$ 10,000	Demand deposits	$100,000
Required	$10,000			
Excess	0			
Loans		45,000		
Securities		45,000		
Total assets		$100,000	Total liabilities	$100,000

The simplified Fed will begin with a balance sheet that looks like this:

Simplified Federal Reserve Balance Sheet

Assets		Liabilities	
U.S. government securities	$100,000	Member bank reserve deposits	$100,000

The Process of Deposit Creation The stage is now set in such a way as to give the Fed control of the quantity of reserves at member banks. This in turn makes it possible for the Fed to control the quantity of money supplied by the banking system in the form of demand deposits. Suppose, for example, that the Fed decides to increase the quantity of money available to the economy. Here is how it might typically proceed.

Open market operation A purchase of securities from the public or a sale of securities to the public made by the Federal Reserve for the purpose of altering the quantity of reserves available to member banks.

An Open Market Purchase Injecting New Reserves The easiest way for the Fed to set in motion an expansion of demand deposits is through an **open market operation**—an open market purchase in this case. To be specific, suppose the Fed's Open Market Committee directs the Federal Reserve Bank of New York to buy $10,000 in securities from a member of the public.

The Fed pays for these securities with a check—a special check drawn on itself, not on one of its member commercial banks. The seller of the securities deposits this special Federal Reserve check in his or her local commercial bank account. To keep track of things, we will call this bank the Albany National Bank. That bank in turn deposits the check in its account with the Federal Reserve bank, at which point the objective of injecting $10,000 of reserves into the system has been accomplished. After all this has taken place, the balance sheets of the Fed and the Albany National Bank now look like this:

The Fed

Assets		Liabilities	
U.S. government bonds	$110,000 (+10,000)[a]	Member bank reserve deposits	$110,000 (+10,000)

Albany National Bank

Assets			Liabilities	
Reserves at Fed		$20,000 (+10,000)	Demand deposits	$110,000 (+10,000)
Required	$11,000 (+1,000)			
Excess	9,000 (+9,000)			
Loans		45,000		
Securities		45,000		
Total assets		$110,000 (+10,000)	Total liabilities	$110,000 (+10,000)

[a]Here and in subsequent balance sheets, changes are shown in parentheses.

Notice how the $10,000 in new reserves at the Albany National Bank is distributed between required reserves and excess reserves. Deposits have gone up by $10,000, which means that the bank must hold $1,000 more in required reserves. The other $9,000 is not required to be held as reserves, so it is listed as excess reserves. The bank is no longer in equilibrium; it can increase its income by putting those reserves to work. What happens when it does is the subject of the next section.

Making a New Loan Suppose that the Albany National Bank decides to put its $9,000 to work by making a new loan of $9,000. It does this simply by crediting $9,000 to the checking account of the borrower, James Anderson. At the moment the loan is completed, the balance sheet of the bank will look like this:

Albany National Bank

Assets			Liabilities	
Reserves		$ 20,000	Demand deposits	$119,000
Required	$11,900			(+9,000)
	(+900)			
Excess	8,100			
	(−900)			
Loans		54,000		
		(+9,000)		
Securities		45,000		
Total assets		$119,000	Total liabilities	$119,000
		(+9,000)		(+9,000)

The bank now has $9,000 in new assets (loans) matched by $9,000 in new liabilities (the increase in the borrower's demand deposits). Required reserves have increased sufficiently to maintain a level of 10 percent of deposits. The bank still has excess reserves of $8,100, but it does not make further new loans, because it knows that the situation is only temporary. Anderson did not borrow $9,000 just to leave it sitting idle in his checking account; he borrowed it to buy a car.

Checking Away the Proceeds of the Loan Anderson pays for the car by writing a check on his account in the Albany National Bank. The dealer from whom he buys the car—Joyce Barnard—has her account at the Bethel National Bank, another member of the Federal Reserve System.

When Barnard deposits Anderson's Albany Bank check in her Bethel account, the Bethel National Bank sends it to the Fed for collection. The Fed credits $9,000 to Bethel's reserve account and debits (subtracts) $9,000 from Albany's reserve account. Then it puts the check itself (the actual piece of paper) in the mail so the Albany National Bank can eventually forward it to Anderson for his personal records. When all these transactions have taken place, the balance sheets of the two banks look like this:

Albany National Bank

Assets			Liabilities	
Reserves		$ 11,000	Demand deposits	$110,000
		(−9,000)		(−9,000)
Required	$11,000			
	(−900)			
Excess	0			
	(−8,100)			
Loans		54,000		
Securities		45,000		
Total assets		$110,000	Total liabilities	$110,000
		(−9,000)		(−9,000)

Bethel National Bank

Assets			Liabilities	
Reserves		$ 19,000 (+9,000)	Demand deposits	$109,000 (+9,000)
Required	$10,900 (+900)			
Excess	8,100 (+8,100)			
Loans		45,000		
Securities		45,000		
Total assets		$109,000 (+9,000)	Total liabilities	$109,000 (+9,000)

No further changes take place in the Fed's balance sheet totals.

Now we can see why the Albany National Bank could not loan out more than its initial $9,000 of excess reserves. It knew that the new $9,000 deposit it created by the loan was not likely to stay there for long. As soon as the check cleared, Albany lost $9,000 in total reserves. Its required reserves went down by only $900 (10 percent of the amount of the loss in deposits), so the $8,100 of the excess reserves that Albany had immediately after making the loan was needed to make up the difference.

Buying Securities When all transactions were completed, the Albany National Bank ended up with $10,000 more in deposits and $10,000 more in assets. But that is not the end of the story. The $8,100 in excess reserves that the bank lost did not disappear from the banking system. The Bethel National Bank's excess reserves rose by exactly the same amount that Albany's fell. Bethel gained $9,000 in deposits and $9,000 in reserves, of which only $900 were required reserves. The remaining $8,100 became excess reserves for Bethel.

Although the Albany National Bank has now returned to a state of balance sheet equilibrium, the Bethel National Bank is out of equilibrium. To increase its earning assets to the maximum, it must put its excess reserves to work. It could, like Albany, make a new loan, but it decides instead to buy $8,100 in securities. It purchases these securities from a private dealer and pays for them by writing a check on its own account. The seller then deposits the check in the Cooperstown National Bank. This time we omit Bethel's intermediate balance sheet showing the situation after the securities are bought but before the check is cleared. After the check has been cleared through the Fed, here is what Bethel's and Cooperstown's balance sheets look like:

Bethel National Bank

Assets			Liabilities	
Reserves		$ 10,900 (−8,100)	Demand deposits	$109,000
Required	$10,900 (no change)			
Excess	0 (−8,100)			
Loans		45,000		
Securities		53,100 (+8,100)		
Total assets		$109,000	Total liabilities	$109,000

Cooperstown National Bank

Assets			Liabilities	
Reserves		$ 18,100 (+8,100)	Demand deposits	$108,100 (+8,100)
Required	$10,810 (+810)			
Excess	7,290 (+7,290)			
Loans		45,000		
Securities		45,000		
Total assets		$108,100 (+8,100)	Total liabilities	$108,100 (+8,100)

The Multiple Expansion of Deposits We really do not have to trace much farther the effects of the Fed's initial injection of $10,000 of new reserves into the commercial banking system. A clear pattern is beginning to emerge. Bank A received a deposit of $10,000, of which it set aside 10 percent as required reserves and used the remainder to finance a loan of $9,000. Bank B received a deposit of $9,000, of which it set aside 10 percent as required reserves and used the remainder to finance securities purchases of $8,100. Bank C received a deposit of $8,100, of which it put aside $810 as required reserves. It used the remaining $7,290 to finance either loans or securities purchases. (The examples above show that it makes no difference which.) Each bank makes new loans and/or securities purchases equal to 90 percent of the deposit it receives, thereby generating new deposits for the next bank in line. Total new deposits generated by the initial injection of $10,000 of new reserves is thus equal to the sum of the infinite series $10,000 + $9,000 + $8,100 + $7,290 + $6,561 + $5,905 + ··· = $100,000. The whole process is referred to as the multiple expansion of deposits by the commercial banking system.

A Shortcut Just to check what we have learned, we can go back to the beginning and look at the effects of the injection of new reserves using a shortcut method based on the consolidated balance sheet for all ten member banks. The initial purchase by the Fed of $10,000 in securities from a member of the public puts $10,000 in new reserves into the banking system. The first bank to get those reserves does not hold on to all of them; it holds only the required portion (10 percent) and passes the remainder on to some other bank. Another 10 percent of these reserves come to rest as required reserves in the second bank, another 10 percent of the remainder in the third, and so on.

The multiple expansion of deposits continues in this way until all reserves have eventually come to rest as required reserves in one bank or another. But no matter how often the reserves are passed from hand to hand, the total increase in the quantity of reserves in the banking system remains $10,000. Total deposits have to rise by enough to convert all of the initial $10,000 of excess reserves into required reserves. With a 10 percent required reserve ratio, this takes $100,000 in new deposits. In the eventual equilibrium position, the consolidated balance sheet for the ten identical member banks looks like this:

Consolidated Balance Sheet of All Commercial Banks (Final Position)

Assets			Liabilities	
Reserves		$ 110,000 (+10,000)	Demand deposits	$1,100,000 (+100,000)
Required	$110,000 (+10,000)			
Excess	0			
Loans and securities		990,000 (+90,000)		
Total assets		$1,100,000 (+100,000)	Total liabilities	$1,100,000 (+100,000)

Contraction of the Money Supply

If the Fed withdraws reserves from the simplified banking system, the whole process works in reverse. Suppose, for example, that the Fed begins by selling $1,000 in securities to a member of the public. The seller pays for the securities with a check drawn on the Denver National Bank. Denver loses $1,000 in deposits and $1,000 in reserves. That leaves it $900 short of required reserves, as the following balance sheet shows (assuming the same initial balance sheet for the Denver bank as for all the banks in the previous examples):

Denver National Bank

Assets			Liabilities	
Reserves		$ 9,000 (−1,000)	Demand deposits	$99,000 (−1,000)
Required	$9,900 (−100)			
Excess	−900			
Securities		45,000		
Loans		45,000		
Total assets		$99,000 (−1,000)	Total liabilities	$99,000 (−1,000)

In order to meet its legal reserve requirements, the Denver National Bank must somehow obtain $900 in new reserves. One obvious way to do this is to sell $900 in securities. When someone writes a check to pay for these securities, another bank, say the Englewood National Bank, loses $900 in deposits and $900 in reserves, leaving it with an $810 shortfall from required reserves. Englewood in turn sells securities to meet its requirements, and the operation of the multiple contraction process continues until it causes a total loss of $10,000 in deposits.

The Money Multiplier

Money multiplier The ratio of the quantity of money to the total reserves in a banking system. Various money multipliers can be defined, depending on the definition of money used. For the U.S. banking system, the money multiplier is the M_1-to-total-reserves multiplier.

We will conclude our analysis of the simplified banking system by drawing an important generalization from both the expansionary and contractionary examples just given: In every case, the ultimate change in total demand deposits (and hence in the total money supply) in the simplified commercial banking system must be equal to the initial change in reserves divided by the required reserve ratio. The ratio of the change in the money supply to the initial change in reserves can be called the **money multiplier** for the banking system. (More precisely, it can be called the demand-deposits-to-total-reserves multiplier.)

In the simplified banking system, the formula for the money multiplier is:

$$\text{Money multiplier} = \frac{1}{\text{Required reserve ratio}}.$$

With the required reserve ratio of 0.10 used in the examples, the money multiplier is 10. Hence the $10,000 injection of new reserves results in a $100,000 expansion of the money supply, and a $1,000 withdrawal of reserves results in a $10,000 contraction.

INSTRUMENTS AND PROBLEMS OF MONETARY POLICY

We turn now from the simplified banking system to the real world. On the surface, everything looks similar. Demand deposits still make up the most important part of the money supply, although not all of it. The Fed still has the power to control bank reserves and to impose reserve requirements on member banks, although not all banks are members. And changes in the total reserves of the banking system still result in multiple expansions or contractions of the money supply.

On closer examination, however, the actual banking system of the United States differs from that of the simplified economy in a number of details, which, taken together, crucially affect both the methods and the success of the Fed in controlling the nation's money supply.

Instruments of Monetary Policy

The Federal Reserve System has three major instruments of monetary policy. The first, already illustrated for the simplified banking system, is the open market operation. These purchases and sales of securities are carried out by the Federal Reserve Bank of New York—the city in which the major securities markets are located—under the direction of the Federal Open Market Committee. By use of open market operations, the Fed can inject new reserves directly into the banking system or withdraw reserves from it.

Changes in Required Reserve Ratios Changes in required reserve ratios are the second major instrument of monetary policy. Such changes do not inject or withdraw reserves but instead change the quantity of demand deposits and other deposits that can be supported by the basis of a given quantity of reserves. Although no such example was given, it is easy to work out what would have happened in the simplified banking system if the required reserve ratio had been changed to something other than 10 percent. In the real world, the situation is complicated by the fact that there are many different required reserve ratios for different kinds and sizes of deposits. Exhibit 12.3 shows the required reserve ratios in force for member banks as of late 1978. (The Fed does not determine reserve requirements for nonmember banks.) Changes in reserve requirements are used less frequently than open market operations, but they are no longer as rare as they once were.

Changes in the Discount Rate The third major instrument of monetary policy is one that was not available to the imaginary Fed of the simplified banking system. In the simplified system, banks experiencing a deficiency in required reserves immediately had to reduce their loans outstanding or sell

Exhibit 12.3

Required reserve ratios for member banks as of November 30, 1978

The Fed requires member banks to hold reserves against deposits in amounts that vary according to the size and type of deposit. This table shows reserve requirements in force as of November 30, 1978. Reserve ratios are changed periodically as an instrument of monetary policy. A change in the reserve requirements does not change the total quantity of reserves held by the banking system, but it does change the portion that banks are allowed to count as excess reserves.

Demand Deposits[a]					Savings Deposits	Time Deposits[b]
0–1	Over 1–10	Over 10–100	Over 100–400	Over 400		
7%	9.5%	11.75%	12.75%	16.25%	3%	1–8%

[a] Deposit intervals are in millions of dollars. Requirement schedules are graduated, and each deposit interval applies to that part of the deposits of each bank.
[b] Varies according to maturity date and size of deposit.
Source: *Federal Reserve Bulletin*, December 1978, Table A–9.

Discount rate The rate of interest charged by the Federal Reserve to member banks for reserves borrowed from the Fed.

securities. In practice, however, banks very commonly smooth over temporary reserve deficiencies by borrowing reserves. They can borrow from one another via the federal funds market mentioned earlier in the chapter. More importantly for present purposes, however, member banks can also borrow from the Fed itself. The Fed charges a rate of interest on these borrowed reserves that is known as the **discount rate.** By raising the discount rate, it discourages banks from borrowing reserves and thus reduces the total quantity of reserves in the system. By lowering the discount rate, it permits the quantity of borrowed reserves to rise. Changes in the discount rate thus constitute the Fed's third major policy instrument.

Practical Problems of Monetary Policy

The Fed has relied on these three major tools of monetary policy to control the growth of the money supply for many years, but only relatively recently has it begun to publicize its monetary growth targets in advance. Beginning in 1975 and continuing through 1978, the Fed adopted the practice of announcing to Congress once every three months a target growth rate range for M_1, M_2, and M_3. These targets covered the year ahead, so that the horizon for the targets also moved ahead each quarter.

The Humphrey-Hawkins Act of 1978 somewhat changed the Fed's procedure for announcing targets. Now it is required to announce each February its objectives for growth of the main monetary aggregates over the current calendar year. In July, it must update these objectives and announce tentative objectives for the following year. It is also required to explain how the monetary objectives tie in with the broader objectives of stabilization policy as expressed in the *Economic Report of the President* issued each year by the administration.

But despite the variety of policy instruments available, and despite the carefully announced targets, monetary policy in practice is a far more imprecise affair than in the simplified economy described earlier in this chapter. The real world is full of many problems and pitfalls not yet mentioned. As a result, the Fed, even with the best of intentions, has had only mixed success meeting the monetary policy objectives that it has set for itself. The rest of the chapter will look at some of the reasons for this problem.

Variations in Money Multipliers

The key to control over the money supply in the simplified banking system was a fixed money multiplier, equal to the reciprocal of the required reserve ratio on demand deposits. In the real world, the closest equivalent to this multiplier is the so-called M_1-to-total-reserves multiplier (the M_1 multiplier for short). As the name implies, this multiplier is the ratio of M_1 to total reserves of the commercial banking system. It is more complicated and subject to more variation than the money multiplier of our simple banking system.

Structure of Reserve Requirements One major reason for the greater complexity of this real-world money multiplier is that required reserve ratios vary from one bank to another and from one kind of deposit to another. Refer back for a moment to Exhibit 12.3. As that exhibit shows, some reserves must be used to support deposits that are not counted as part of M_1. Other things being equal, the greater the ratio of savings and time deposits to demand deposits at banks, the lower the M_1 multiplier. In addition, Exhibit 12.3 shows that reserve requirements on demand deposits are graduated. Other things being equal, a shift of demand deposits from banks with high reserve requirements to banks with low reserve requirements tends to push up the M_1 multiplier.

Nonmember Banks A second major reason for variations in the M_1 multiplier is the existence of nonmember banks and thrift institutions. Thrifts offer savings and time deposits that compete with those offered by commercial banks. Nonmember banks offer demand deposits that count as part of the money supply but are not subject to the required reserve ratios set by the Fed. Hence shifts in deposits among member banks, nonmember banks, and thrifts are also a source of variability in the money multiplier.

Excess Reserves Yet a third reason for variability in the M_1 multiplier is the fact that real-world banks, unlike those in the simplified banking system, cannot always keep their excess reserves exactly at zero. Even using the federal funds market, which efficiently channels reserves from banks with surpluses to banks with deficits, banks sometimes find it hard to keep up with unexpected deposit flows. Excess reserves, while only a small amount on average, do show some variation over time.

Currency The Fed allows its member banks to count currency on hand (so-called vault cash) as reserves, which means that when individuals or firms withdraw money from their banks in the form of currency, they drain total reserves from the banking system. When this happens, a multiple contraction of the money supply takes place unless the Fed offsets the shift with an injection of new reserves.

In addition, currency is a form of money that is not a liability of the commercial banking system and thus is not itself subject to reserve requirements. Even if the Fed maintains the level of reserves, the larger the fraction of their money balances people choose to hold as currency, the larger the M_1 multiplier.

Recent Variations in the M_1 Multiplier In combination, these four considerations make the money multiplier (M_1 to total reserves) significantly variable. Exhibit 12.4 gives some idea of this variability in the United States over recent years. Since 1969, the multiplier has varied from 7.7 to 8.7. The quarter-to-quarter changes have been sharp enough to create problems for the Fed's control of the money supply. Whenever the money multiplier changes, the money supply changes unless the Fed quickly steps in to adjust member bank reserves by an offsetting amount.

Other Money Multipliers This section has focused on the money multiplier defined in terms of M_1, but the multiplier would be variable regardless of the particular monetary aggregate in terms of which it was defined. In fact, if the money supply were defined to include all balances available for use as a means of payment, as has been proposed, new sources of variability would be introduced. To maintain some element of stability, various proposals have been advanced in Congress and at the Fed to subject nonmember banks and checkable deposits at thrifts to uniform reserve requirements of some sort. As of this writing, final details of the new regulations have yet to be resolved.

Open Market Operations and the Federal Funds Rate

We see, then, that both the quantity of reserves and the money multiplier are subject to variations arising from forces beyond the direct control of the Fed. In an effort to offset these effects and stabilize the money supply, the Fed continuously carries out open market operations, injecting or withdrawing reserves from the system as needed.

The Federal Funds Rate Target To do so, it needs a day-to-day operating target for conducting open market operations. Throughout most of the 1970s, the manager of the open market trading desk at the New York Federal Reserve Bank—who has the responsibility for the day-to-day conduct of open market

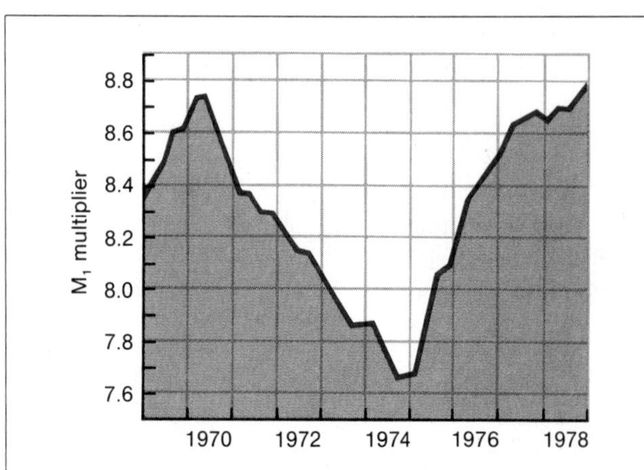

Exhibit 12.4

Variations in the money multiplier (M_1 to total reserves), 1969–1978 (seasonally adjusted)

As this exhibit shows, the M_1-to-total-reserves money multiplier for the U.S. economy is subject to substantial variation from quarter to quarter. Such variation results from shifts of funds from one type of deposit to another, variations in the public's demand for currency, variations in excess reserves, and other factors. The series has been adjusted to correct for the influence of regulatory changes in required reserve ratios.

Source: Data from Board of Governors of the Federal Reserve System, Banking Section.

operations—was instructed to target the federal funds rate within a range specified by the Federal Open Market Committee. The committee chose the funds rate range that it believed would be consistent with its economic objectives, including short-run money growth. If money growth appeared to be departing from objectives, the manager was supposed to vary the funds rate operating target within this range, raising it when money appeared to be growing too rapidly and lowering it when money growth seemed too slow. With the prospect of more pronounced or sustained variations in money growth, the committee adjusted its specified federal funds rate range.

By targeting the federal funds rate, which balances the demand for short-term funds by banks wanting to avoid reserve deficiencies with the supply of such funds by banks with temporary excess reserves, the Fed was able to offset certain kinds of disturbances to the money supply. For example, Treasury operations, vault cash movements, foreign currency transactions, or delays in check clearing can have substantial impacts on reserve availability. An unexpected drain of reserves from the banking system will quickly produce a rise in the federal funds rate, as banks faced with reserve deficiencies try to borrow to cover them. To keep the funds rate from rising above its target rate, the Fed's trading desk would supply additional reserves. These reserves would replace those that had been drained from the system, thereby helping to keep the money supply on an even keel. Later, if reserves flowed back into the system, the federal funds rate would tend to drop, and the trading desk would take this as a signal to siphon off the excess.

By targeting the federal funds rate, the Fed could also, at least in some instances, offset changes in the money multiplier. For example, a shift of demand deposits from accounts with low reserve requirements to accounts with high reserve requirements tends to raise the average required reserve ratio and depress the money multiplier. Needing more reserves to support the existing volume of deposits, banks attempt to borrow reserves in the federal funds market, sending the funds rate upward. To keep the rate from rising, the Fed's trading desk would supply additional reserves—whatever was required to keep the fall in the money multiplier from causing an unwanted decline in the money supply.

Criticism of the Federal Funds Rate Target Although the federal funds rate served as a trustworthy guide to open market operations in the circumstances just mentioned, during the 1970s many economists became strongly critical of the Fed's reliance on it. The reason was that there were other circumstances in which the federal funds rate could give misleading signals that could lead the Fed to destabilize the money supply unintentionally.

Suppose, for example, that beginning from a situation in which the money supply was right where the Fed wanted it, there was suddenly a surge in the demand for loans and thus for money to carry out the associated transactions. Banks would respond to this rise in loan demand by converting their excess reserves, if any, into loans and by attempting to borrow additional reserves via the federal funds market. With a given supply of reserves, the federal funds rate would be driven up.

If the Fed responded to the increase in the federal funds rate as usual, it would begin buying securities from the public to inject new reserves into the system. This would succeed in keeping the funds rate down but would also accommodate the unexpected rise in demand for loans and deposits, allowing the money supply to rise. And that is just what the Fed would not want.

But, one might well ask, if the Fed did not want the money supply to rise in response to an increase in the demand for loans, why did it not just raise its target rate for federal funds? The reason is that at the time a change in the federal funds rate occurs, the Fed cannot always tell why it is occurring. It cannot immediately distinguish federal funds rate changes that arise from variations in the money multiplier or in the level of reserves from those that reflect changes in the demand for loans and deposits.

As a result, say the critics, the Fed did not always react with sufficiently prompt or sufficiently large adjustments to its federal funds rate target. Instead, it sometimes allowed the funds rate to lag behind the course of events for as long as several months at a stretch, during which time the growth of the money supply got seriously out of line with the Fed's own objectives for money growth, as shown in Exhibit 12.5.

Exhibit 12.5a shows annual targets for recent years and compares them with actual performance for the same one-year periods. Exhibit 12.5b shows quarterly growth rates of M_1 and M_2 over the same span of years. No great significance can be attached to occasional quarterly departures of the actual growth rates from the announced target ranges. However, persistent failure to stay within the targets, as when the growth rate of M_1 exceeded its target ceiling for eight successive quarters from late 1976 through the fall of 1978, is more of a cause for concern. This episode was blamed, at least in part, on use of the federal funds rate as an operating target. What the Fed should do, the critics said, was to forget about the federal funds rate and instead concentrate directly on controlling the quantity of reserves in the system.

Recent Changes in Operating Procedures The Fed's usual response to these criticisms was to point to the instability of the money multiplier and to contend that rigid pursuit of a reserves target would lead to excessive volatility in the federal funds rate, often resulting from only temporary changes in money demand. Such volatility, it said, would in turn destabilize credit markets, because other short-term interest rates tend to move together with the federal funds rate.

During 1979, however, the Fed encountered new difficulties in controlling money growth. As Exhibit 12.5 shows, the growth rate of both M_1 and M_2 dropped below their target ranges in the first quarter. The decline in the growth rate of M_1 resulted in part from the introduction of ATS accounts at the end of 1978, but despite the continued, though diminishing, effect of such accounts, the monetary aggregates began to grow rapidly again in the second quarter of 1979. By the third quarter, both M_1 and M_2 were growing at annual rates several points in excess of the announced targets.

Faced with these circumstances, on October 6, 1979, the Fed announced a major change in its operating procedures. The new procedures deemphasize the federal funds rate as a day-to-day guide to policy. Increased emphasis is placed instead on controlling the supply of member bank reserves, even though this will mean much larger daily variations in the federal funds rate than in the past. How well the new procedures will work is not yet clear as of this writing.

Exhibit 12.5

Monetary growth rate targets and performance, 1976–1979

This exhibit compares recent growth rates of M_1 and M_2 with the target growth ranges announced by the Fed. Part a compares annual target growth ranges with actual annual growth rates for the same periods. Part b shows quarterly data for money growth rates. Although little significance need be attached to occasional quarterly deviations from the target ranges, persistent failure to meet the targets is a more serious cause for concern.

Source: Data from *Federal Reserve Bulletin*, various issues.

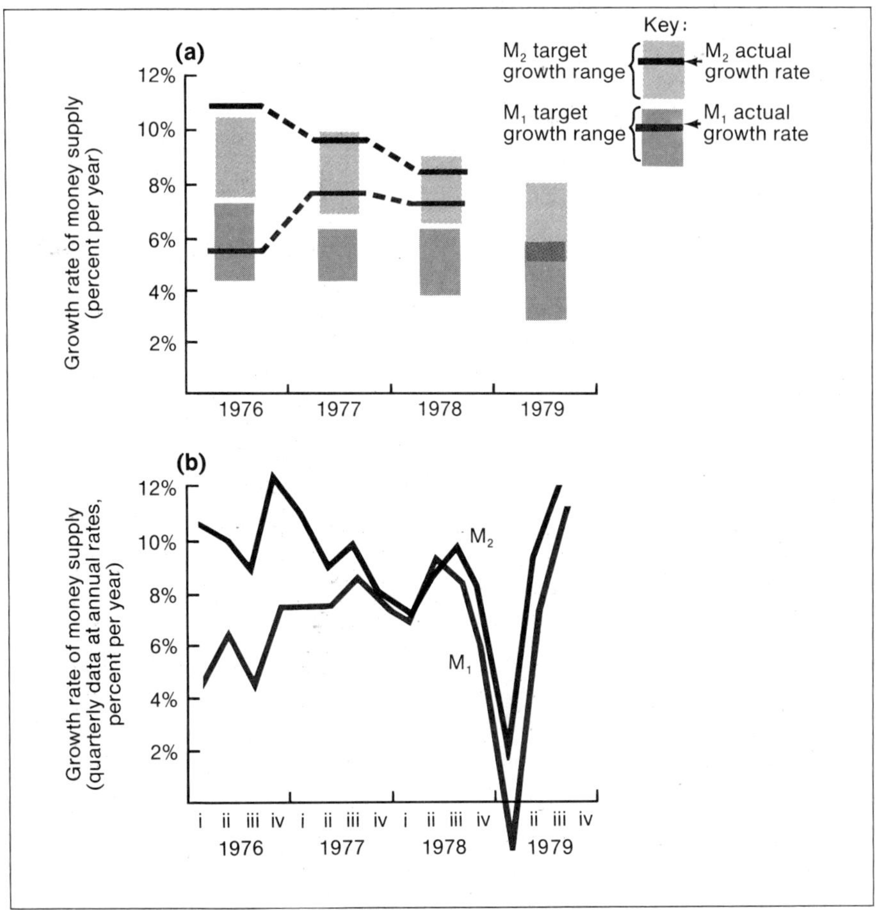

CONCLUSIONS

This chapter has examined in some detail a few questions concerning the supply of money: how the money supply can be measured, how money is created by the commercial banking system, and how the Fed attempts to exercise control over the money supply. Now it is time to return to a theme sounded briefly at the beginning of the chapter—the relationship between monetary policy and the goals of full employment, price stability, and economic growth. It is the importance of money to these goals of stabilization policy, after all, that justifies the attention to technicalities in this chapter.

The next chapter will turn from the supply side of the money market to the demand side. Chapter 14 will examine the effect of variations in money demand and supply on nominal national income and product. Chapters 15 to

18 will show how monetary and fiscal policy together affect the success or failure of stabilization policy as a whole.

SUMMARY

1. Money is defined in terms of what it does. As a unit of account, it allows us to keep accounts and measure aggregate economic magnitudes. As a means of payment, it allows us to escape the inconvenience of barter. And as a store of purchasing power, it helps us arrange our economic activities in an orderly way through time.
2. One traditional definition of money, M_1, includes currency plus demand deposits at commercial banks. Another definition, M_2, adds savings and time deposits at banks to this total. In addition to the money included in M_1 and M_2, there are other highly liquid assets, such as deposits at savings and loan associations, short-term government securities, credit union shares, money market mutual fund shares, and repurchase agreements. Recent innovations in banking practices have made it necessary to rethink the traditional definitions of money.
3. In a simplified banking system, an injection of new reserves sets off a multiple expansion of deposits and the money supply. Each bank receiving new reserves makes loans or buys securities equal to its excess reserves. In that way, it passes along part of the reserves to the next bank in line. The process continues until deposits have risen enough to convert all the new reserves into required reserves. The ratio of money to reserves is known as the money multiplier.
4. In the actual U.S. banking system, the Federal Reserve System has available three main instruments of monetary policy: open market operations (buying and selling securities on the open market), changes in required reserve ratios, and changes in the discount rate (the rate charged to member banks for loans of reserves).
5. The Fed's instruments of monetary policy do not give it precise control of the money supply. A major reason is that the money multiplier can change for reasons not under direct control of the Fed. Shifts of funds from one type of bank to another, from banks to thrifts, from one type of deposit to another within banks, and from deposits to currency can all affect the money multiplier. So can changes in banks' excess reserves. In addition, shifts of funds from member bank deposits to currency can alter the total reserves available to the banking system.
6. A further factor that may have made it difficult for the Fed to control the money supply in recent years was its practice of using the federal funds rate as a guide to day-to-day open market operations. According to critics, the federal funds rate can give misleading signals when demands for loans and deposits change unexpectedly. In October 1979 the Fed moved to deemphasize control of the funds rate and to emphasize instead the direct control of reserves.

DISCUSSION QUESTIONS

1. List the functions that money performs in the economy, and illustrate them with examples of how you yourself have used money for each purpose. Have you ever used something other than money for any of the three purposes?

2. Do you have an account at any bank or other financial institution? If so, is your account part of M_1? Of M_2?
3. Is it possible that with increased use of credit cards we will eventually do away with currency and demand deposits? Explain. Would we be doing away with money if this did occur?
4. Go to your library and look in the back of any issue of the *Federal Reserve Bulletin*. Where the recent banking data are reported, find the current values for currency, demand deposits, and time deposits at commercial banks. Use these values to update Exhibit 12.1. Next, examine the data given for M_1 and M_2 and the definitions of these quantities. Is the Fed still using traditional definitions, or has it modified them?
5. Using the same starting position given in the text for the simplified banking system, work through the multiple expansion (or contraction) process for the following policy actions:
   a. An injection of $5,000 in new reserves via an open market purchase.
   b. A withdrawal of $500 in new reserves via an open market sale.
   c. A selective reduction in the required reserve ratio for the Albany National Bank only—from 10 percent to 8 percent. (Assume that once the expansion process gets underway, no one ever deposits new reserves in the Albany bank but uses only the other nine banks.)
   d. A general reduction in the required reserve ratio for all banks from 10 percent to 8 percent.
6. Go to your library and obtain copies of the *New York Times* business section or the *Wall Street Journal* for recent Fridays. Usually, these Friday papers contain short news items or columns reporting weekly changes in the money supply, which the Fed announces each Thursday. What is happening to the money supply? What comments do the papers make regarding Fed policy? Are any comparisons of actual and target money growth given?

SUGGESTIONS FOR FURTHER READING

"A Proposal for Redefining the Monetary Aggregates," *Federal Reserve Bulletin* 65 (January 1979): 13–42.
An analysis of recent changes in financial practices and proposed ways of redefining the monetary aggregates in response to them.

Board of Governors of the Federal Reserve System. *The Federal Reserve System: Purposes and Functions,* 6th ed. Washington, D.C.: Government Printing Office, 1974.
A short introduction to the structure and functions of the Fed.

Campbell, Colin, and Campbell, Rosemary. *An Introduction to Money and Banking,* 3rd ed. Hinsdale, Ill.: Dryden Press, 1978.
Chapters 9, 13, 14, and 15 parallel the discussion in this chapter but add considerably more detail.

Federal Reserve Bulletin, monthly.
Each issue contains the most recent monetary data, which can be used to update the tables and charts in this chapter.

President's Council of Economic Advisers. *Economic Report of the President.* Washington, D.C.: Government Printing Office, annually.
Check the table of contents for the part of the report pertaining to monetary policy.

Simpson, Thomas D. *Money, Banking, and Economic Analysis.* Englewood Cliffs, N.J.: Prentice-Hall, 1976.
A somewhat more advanced treatment of the material covered by Campbell and Campbell's Introduction to Money and Banking.

C H A P T E R **13**

THE DEMAND FOR MONEY AND THE MONEY MARKET

WHAT YOU WILL LEARN IN THIS CHAPTER

This chapter discusses the determinants of the quantity of money that people wish to hold at any given time—that is, people's demand for money. People value money for its liquidity, but because money normally earns no interest, the nominal rate of interest represents an opportunity cost of holding it. The relationship between the demand for money and the rate of interest can be used to draw a demand schedule for money. This schedule can be combined with the supply of money to show how equilibrium is established in the money market.

FOR REVIEW

Here are some important terms and concepts that will be put to use in this chapter. If you do not understand them, review them before proceeding.

- *Nominal and real interest rates (Chapter 7)*
- *Liquidity (Chapter 12)*
- *Control of the money supply by the Fed (Chapter 12)*
- *Net present value approach to asset valuation (Appendix to Chapter 8; optional)*

Chapter 12 defined money, discussed the various things that serve as money and near-monies in the U.S. economy, and explained how the supply of money is determined. This chapter turns first to the determination of the demand for money and then to the interaction of the supply and demand for money in the money market. It will lay the groundwork for the discussion of the interaction of monetary and fiscal policy in Chapter 14.

THE DEMAND FOR MONEY

Portfolio Balance

In discussing the demand for money, as in dealing with other subjects in economics, it is important to distinguish between stocks and flows. The demand for money is the demand for a stock. The question is not one of how much money people would like to spend per day or month—that would be a flow of money—but rather of how large a share of their total wealth people would at any time like to hold in the form of money, as opposed to other forms such as securities, real estate, and consumer durables.

Portfolio balance The idea that people try to maintain a balance among the various kinds of assets they own—including money, consumer durables, stocks, and bonds—shifting from one kind of asset to another as economic conditions change.

Economists find it useful to talk about the demand for money in terms of the concept of **portfolio balance.** A *portfolio* is simply the collection of assets of all kinds that a person owns. Balancing the portfolio means adjusting the proportions of currency, checking account funds, savings deposits, securities, real estate, and so on to best suit the interests of the portfolio holder.

Liquidity and the Demand for Money

The reason people want to hold at least part of their portfolio in the form of money is that money is liquid. As Chapter 12 explained, liquidity means that money can be used directly as a means of payment and that holding it involves no risk of gain or loss of nominal value. These two aspects of liquidity provide the motives for holding at least part of any portfolio in the form of money.

Transactions motive A motive for holding money arising from the convenience of using it as a means of payment for day-to-day transactions.

The Transactions and Precautionary Motives The most familiar reason for holding money is that it is a quick and convenient way to purchase things. With money on hand, it is not necessary to borrow or to sell some less liquid asset every time a purchase is made. This reason is often called the **transactions motive** for holding money. Generally speaking, people's demand for money for transactions purposes is expected to increase as their nominal incomes increase, other things being equal.

Precautionary motive A motive for holding money arising from its usefulness as a reserve of liquid funds for use in emergencies or in taking advantage of unexpected opportunities.

In addition to holding enough money to take care of normal weekly or monthly purchases between paychecks, people may also want to keep some highly liquid reserves on hand for emergency use or to take advantage of unexpected opportunities. Some writers distinguish this from the transactions motive for holding money by calling it the **precautionary motive.** Both the transactions and the precautionary motives arise primarily from the use of money as a means of payment.

The Speculative Motive In addition to serving as a means of payment, money also protects its holder against any possible loss of nominal value. If portfolio holders have reason to think there may be a decline in the market price of other assets they might hold—such as stocks, bonds, or real estate—it will pay them to hold money instead, at least temporarily. If the expected drop in the nominal value of the other assets does materialize, they will have avoided a possible capital loss. If no further declines are expected, they can purchase the other assets at a bargain price.

Speculative motive A motive for holding money arising from its fixed nominal value, when the nominal value of alternative assets is expected to decline.

Keynes called this the **speculative motive** for holding money, because people holding money for this reason are speculating that the price of other assets will fall. The term has stuck, despite the fact that, in practice, it is difficult to compartmentalize the demand for money into transactions, precautionary, and speculative components.

The Opportunity Cost of Holding Money Offsetting the advantages of holding money—its usefulness as a means of payment and its fixed nominal value—is a major disadvantage. To hold money, one forgoes the opportunity to earn interest. When it is narrowly defined to include only currency and commercial bank demand deposits, money pays no interest at all. Even when it is more broadly defined to include such things as NOW accounts and ATS accounts, the interest paid on transaction-type deposits is less than that available on nonmonetary assets.

The proper measure of the opportunity cost of holding money is the nominal rate of interest that could be earned on other assets. As Chapter 7 showed, the nominal rate of interest is equal to the expected real rate of interest plus the expected rate of inflation. Normally, the nominal rate of interest exceeds the expected rate of inflation. Holders of interest-bearing assets thus expect to earn a real return even after allowing for the expected decline in the purchasing power of their funds. Using the nominal rate of interest to represent the opportunity cost of holding money, then, reflects both the lost opportunity to earn a real return and the lost opportunity for protection from expected inflation.

The Demand for Money in a Two-Asset Economy

In order to bring out more clearly some of the essential features of the demand for money, it will be useful to introduce a simplified economy in which there are only two financial assets available to portfolio holders. These assets are money (in the narrow sense of non-interest-bearing currency and demand deposit balances) and long-term bonds.

The Price of Bonds and the Rate of Interest A short digression on the subject of bonds is needed at this point. Bonds are simply IOUs of firms and units of government. They have been mentioned several times without explanation of one of their important features—the relationship between the price of a bond and the rate of interest.

In the United States, long-term corporate bonds are typically issued in denominations of $1,000. The issuing firm promises to pay the bondholder a certain sum per year for a certain number of years (usually twenty to thirty years) until maturity and, upon maturity, to repay the initial $1,000. The annual sum the bondholder receives until maturity is set according to the nominal rate of interest prevailing at the time the bond is issued. If the interest rate is 8 percent, the annual payment on a $1,000 bond will be $80; if the interest rate is 10 percent, the payment will be $100; and so on.

As Chapter 11 showed, there are active secondary markets in which bonds of this type can be bought and sold. The original purchaser need not hold the bond until maturity. There is no guarantee, however, that the bond can be sold in the secondary market "at par"—that is, at its original purchase price of $1,000. Instead, the price at which the bond can be resold depends on what has happened to the interest rate between the date of issue and the date of resale.

To illustrate: Suppose a certain firm issues a twenty-five-year bond at a time when the nominal interest rate on such bonds is 10 percent, agreeing to pay $100 per year for twenty-five years plus $1,000 on maturity. The original purchase price is $1,000. A year later, the original buyer wants to sell the bond; but in the meantime, the nominal interest rate has gone up to 12.5 percent. That means brand new $1,000 bonds are scaled to pay $125 per year to their purchasers, so no one is willing to buy last year's bond with the $100 payment unless its price is cut to approximately $800—since $100 is 12.5 percent of $800. The original buyer of the bond with the $100 annual payment suffers a capital loss of $200 in selling the bond.

If, instead, the interest rate had fallen, say to 5 percent, new bonds would be paying only $50 per year. In that case, the old bond carrying a $100 annual payment could be sold at a premium in the secondary market—for roughly $2,000, in fact.

Actually, there is a little bit more to calculating how much a bond is worth on the secondary market, because we have not taken into account the fact that all bonds are worth the same $1,000 amount at maturity regardless of the annual payment the bondholder receives in the meantime. That is why the prices in the above examples are stated as approximations. However, as long as we stick to long-term bonds for which the date of maturity lies in the rather distant future, the price of the bond is determined almost entirely by the interaction of the size of the annual payment and the nominal interest rate. In any event, the important thing to remember is this: *A rise in the nominal rate of interest depresses the price of bonds in the secondary market, and a fall in the nominal rate of interest raises the price of bonds in the secondary market.*[1]

Portfolio Balance in the Simple Economy The quantity of money demanded by the inhabitants of the simplified economy depends on how they decide to balance their portfolios between money and bonds. Two factors can be expected to influence their decision.

First, the higher the nominal income in the simplified economy, the greater the desired quantity of money. The reason is the transactions motive. People's purchases increase when their income increases, so their demand for money also increases.

Second, the higher the nominal rate of interest, the lower the desired quantity of money. There are two reasons for this. One is that a high nominal rate of interest means a high opportunity cost to holding money; holders of money could be earning a high income by holding bonds instead. Second, relative to what has been experienced in the past and what is expected in the future, the higher the rate of interest, the lower the price of bonds. If the price of bonds is perceived as low, people will be inclined to hold more bonds relative to money in the hope that their price will go up and they can be resold for a capital gain. Conversely, if the interest rate is low, the price of bonds will be high and people are likely to be reluctant to hold them for fear the price will drop and they will be stuck with a capital loss. In this situation, people will be inclined to hold more of their portfolio in money. The speculative motive for holding money is thus seen to influence people's decisions regarding the balance of their portfolios between bonds and money.

A Money Demand Schedule The quantity of money demanded, then, increases as the nominal interest rate falls and as nominal income increases. The relationship among the amount of money demanded, the interest rate, and the level of nominal income that prevails in a given economy in a given period is known as that economy's **money demand schedule.** Exhibit 13.1 shows what that schedule might look like for the simplified economy. The entries in Exhibit 13.1a give the quantity of money demanded when the interest rate is that indicated at the left-hand border of the table and the level

Money demand schedule A schedule showing the quantity of money that people desire to hold in their portfolios given various values for the nominal interest rate and the level of nominal income.

[1]Readers who worked through the Appendix to Chapter 8 can calculate precisely the market value of any bond—given the current rate of interest, the annual payment, the number of years until maturity, and the face value at maturity—by using the net present value approach illustrated in Exhibit 8A.2.

(a)

Nominal Interest Rate (Percent)	Level of Nominal National Income					
	$200	$400	$600	$800	$1,000	$1,200
2	$120	$240	$360	$480	$600	$720
4	60	120	180	240	300	360
6	40	80	120	160	200	240
8	30	60	90	120	150	180
10	24	48	72	96	120	144
12	20	40	60	80	100	120
14	17	34	51	68	85	102
16	15	30	45	60	75	90

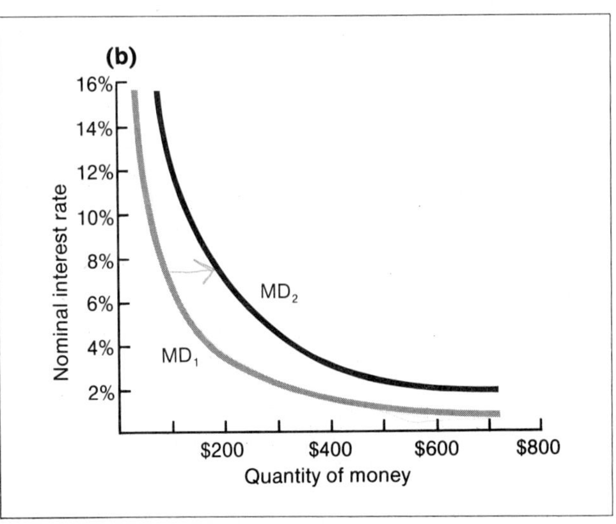

Exhibit 13.1
Money demand schedule for a hypothetical economy
The table and diagram show how the quantity of money demanded varies as the nominal interest rate and the level of nominal income vary in a simplified economy like the one used in these numerical examples. The entries in the body of the table show the quantity of money demanded at the nominal interest rate corresponding to the row and the nominal income corresponding to the column. Each column of the table can be graphed to get a money demand curve like that shown in Part b of the exhibit. The curve MD_1 assumes income to be fixed at $600. A rise in income to $1,200 would shift the money demand curve to the position MD_2.

of nominal national income is that shown at the top of the table. For example, when the interest rate is 10 percent per year and the level of nominal national income is $600, the quantity of money demanded is $72.

Exhibit 13.1b gives the money demand schedule in graphical form. At any given level of income, the relationship between the quantity of money demanded and the interest rate can be shown by a downward-sloping curve that looks much like an ordinary demand curve. For example, the curve labeled MD_1 shows the way money demand varies as the interest rate varies when income is $600. This curve is drawn from the data in the $600 column of the table in Part a. A change in the level of income would produce a shift in the money demand curve. For example, if income were to increase to $1,200, the money demand curve would shift to the position labeled MD_2 in the figure. The data given in the last column of the table indicate that when income doubles, the quantity of money demanded at any particular level of the interest rate doubles.

Income Velocity As Exhibit 13.1 is constructed, the ratio of money demanded to nominal income is constant for all levels of income, given a particular rate of interest. For example, when the nominal interest rate is 6 percent, money demand is $1 for each $5 of nominal income. When the interest rate rises to 12 percent, $1 of money is demanded for each $10 of income, and so on.

Sometimes, instead of speaking in terms of the ratio of money demanded to nominal income, economists use its reciprocal. The ratio of nominal income to money demanded is known as the **income velocity of money.** It measures the rate at which money circulates—that is, the number of times each year that the money stock turns over in carrying out transactions involving final goods and services.

Income velocity of money (velocity) The ratio of nominal income to the quantity of money.

In the simplified economy, velocity depends only on the nominal rate of interest. In the real world too it is strongly influenced by the nominal rate of interest; but as the following case study shows, other factors also influence velocity.

Case 13.1
The Demand for Money, Velocity, and Nominal Interest Rates in the U.S. Economy

Exhibit 13.2a presents the relationship between the demand for money (M_1) as a fraction of nominal GNP and the nominal rate of interest on three-month Treasury bills. Exhibit 13.2b shows the relationship between the income velocity of money and this interest rate. Because the income velocity of money is measured here as the ratio of nominal GNP to M_1 (the reciprocal of the ratio shown on the horizontal axis in Exhibit 13.2a), the two parts of the figure are mirror images of one another, showing the same relationship from two points of view.

At first glance, the relationships shown are much as would be expected. As nominal interest rates have risen over the last thirty years, the demand for money as a fraction of GNP has fallen, and the income velocity of money has risen. A closer inspection of the exhibits shows, however, that the relationships have not been completely stable. Compare, for example, the lines drawn through the points representing 1968, 1969, and 1970 with those drawn through 1976, 1977, and 1978. In Part a, the later line lies significantly to the left of the earlier one; and in Part b, the later line lies significantly to the right. It appears that the relationship of velocity and money demand to the nominal rate of interest has shifted over time.

What has caused the shift? In part, it has presumably been caused by the various banking innovations mentioned in the last chapter. NOW accounts and other liquid assets not counted as part of M_1 can be used as means of payment. Increased use of these accounts has decreased the quantity of currency and demand deposits that households and firms need to hold for any given interest rate and level of nominal income. Also in part, the shift has been attributed to adjustments of firms' cash management practices to chronically high interest rates. After very high nominal interest rates were first experienced in 1973 and 1974, corporate money managers became much more interested and skilled than before in using such devices as repurchase agreements to put idle cash balances to work for periods as short as twenty-four hours. Once the relevant techniques were learned and the relevant markets developed, these frugal cash management practices tended to persist even in years like 1976, when nominal interest rates temporarily dropped. Finally, the shift has been brought about in part through new applications by both financial and nonfinancial firms of information processing systems, which have allowed money holders to keep exact track of their available funds and thereby have reduced the demand for money balances relative to the volume of transactions.

Exhibit 13.2
Velocity and interest rates in the U.S. economy, 1950–1978
Part a of this exhibit traces the relationship between the demand for money (M_1) as a fraction of GNP and the nominal rate of interest on three-month Treasury bills from 1950 to 1978. Part b shows the relationship between the income velocity of money (measured as the ratio of GNP to M_1) and the same interest rate. The two graphs are mirror images—alternative ways of looking at the same underlying relationship. Note that there has been an apparent shift in the relationship; most of the points up to 1975 lie within the broad shaded band in each part of the figure; but the points for 1976, 1977, and 1978 lie outside this band.

Source: *Federal Reserve Bulletin*, various issues.

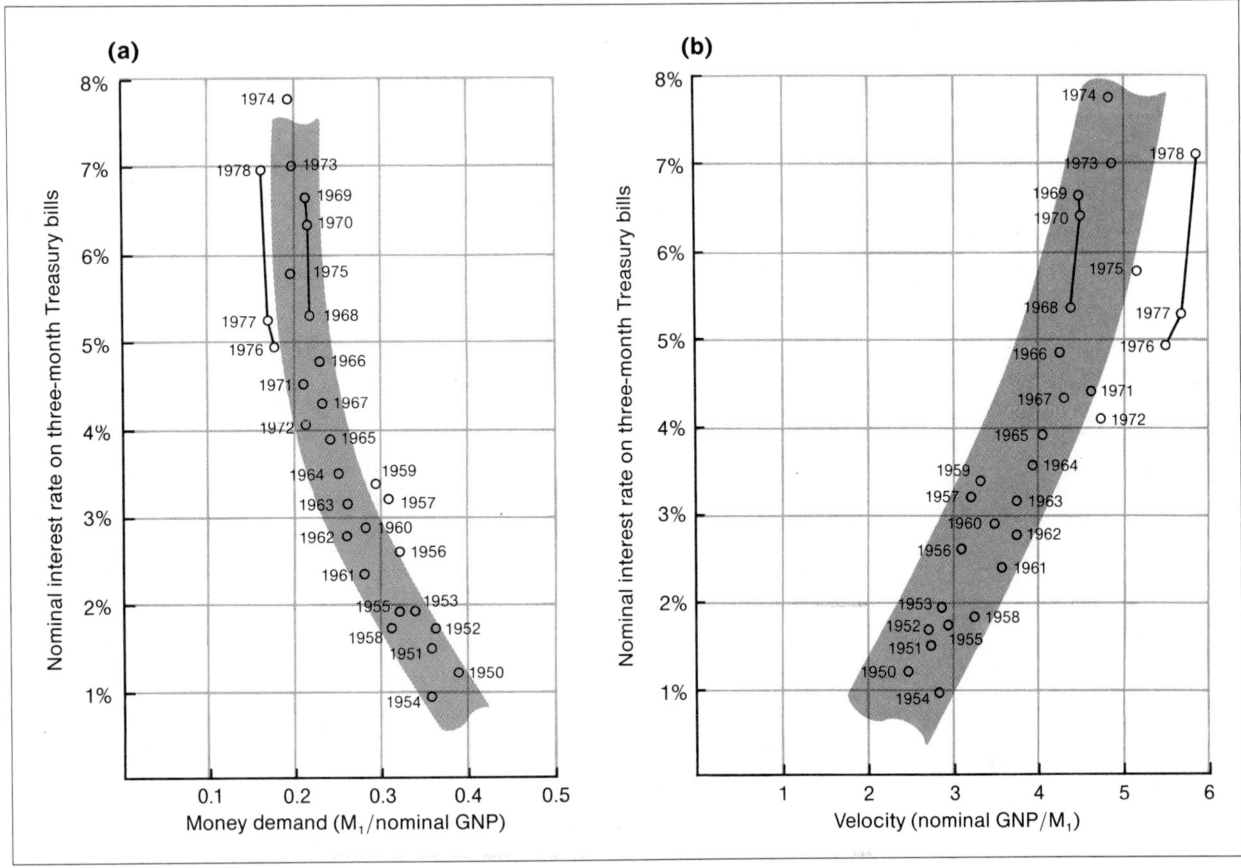

EQUILIBRIUM AND DISEQUILIBRIUM IN THE MONEY MARKET

Now that both the supply and the demand for money have been analyzed, the next step will be to put the two together and investigate the nature of equilibrium and disequilibrium in the money market. Exhibit 13.3 shows the basic diagram that will be used to do this. It contains a downward-sloping demand curve for money (taken from Exhibit 13.1) and a money supply curve; and it uses an assumed national income of $1,200. The money supply curve is simply a vertical line; it reflects an assumption that in the simple economy the money

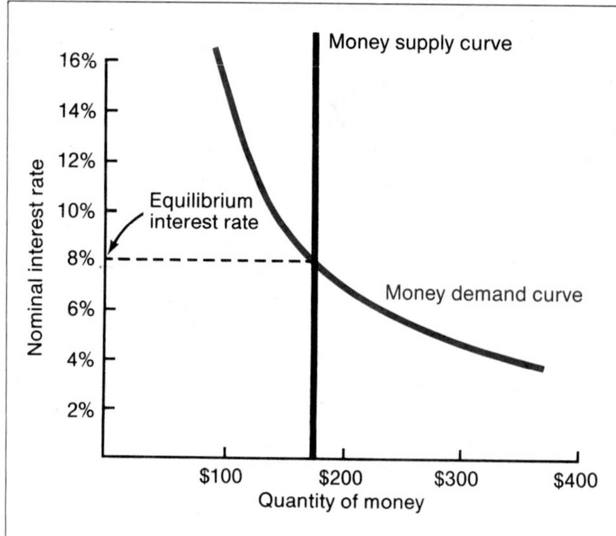

Exhibit 13.3
Equilibrium in the money market
The money demand curve in this diagram is based on the data given in Exhibit 13.1, and it uses an assumed nominal national income of $1,200. The money supply curve assumes a quantity of money supplied of $180. The equilibrium nominal interest rate is 8 percent. At any higher interest rate, an excess quantity of money supplied would put downward pressure on the interest rate. If the interest rate were below equilibrium, there would be an excess quantity of money demanded and upward pressure. Both money supply and money demand are measured in stock terms.

supply is determined solely by Federal Reserve policy and is not directly affected by changes in economic conditions. As Exhibit 13.3 is drawn, the quantity of money supplied is assumed to be $180.

It is important to remember that both the demand for money and the supply of money are measured in terms of stocks, not flows. The supply represents the stock in existence at a given time, and the demand represents the stock that people desire to hold in their portfolios under given conditions.

Equilibrium

It is apparent from the diagram that there is only one nominal rate of interest, 8 percent, at which the stock of money that people want to hold is equal to the stock of money supplied by the banking system in accordance with Federal Reserve policy. At any higher rate of interest, there would be an excess quantity of money supplied.

Reactions to an Excess Supply of Money At an interest rate of 12 percent, for example, the excess quantity supplied would be $60. This quantity reflects the fact that people do not want to hold as much money in their portfolios as the Federal Reserve has caused the banking system to put into circulation.

Individual asset holders react to an excess quantity of money supplied by using their excess money to buy other assets. Given the high interest rate, they are particularly attracted to the idea of replacing some of the money in their portfolios with bonds. However, although some individual asset holders can successfully reduce the quantity of money in their portfolios by buying bonds, not all asset holders can do so at once. Every time someone takes money out of his or her portfolio to buy a bond from someone else, that money ends up in the portfolio of the seller.

No matter how much money is churned around from portfolio to portfolio in pursuit of bonds, every cent of the fixed stock of money supplied by the banking system has to be in someone's portfolio at each moment. What occurs as a result of all this churning is not a fall in the money stock but a rise in the price of bonds. This rise in bond prices means a fall in the nominal rate of interest on bonds. As the interest rate falls, the excess quantity of money supplied is reduced, not because the extra money disappears but because the amount of money that people desire to keep in their portfolios rises until it catches up with the quantity of money supplied. Soon the nominal interest rate reaches its equilibrium level, and the excess demand is entirely eliminated.

Reactions to an Excess Demand for Money If the interest rate were for some reason below the equilibrium level, there would be an excess quantity of money demanded, and a process opposite to that just described would occur. People would want to sell bonds in order to get the greater quantity of money they would prefer to hold at the low interest rate. This would not increase the total supply of money available in the system, but it would depress the price of bonds—which in turn would raise the interest rate until equilibrium were restored.

Equilibrium in the money market thus associates one and only one nominal interest rate with a given quantity of money and a given nominal income. The reactions to excess supply and demand just discussed play a critical role in the adjustment of the money market to two important types of disturbances, as will now be shown.

Effects of a Change in Money Supply

The first step will be to examine the effects of an increase in the money supply resulting from an open market purchase of securities from the public by the Federal Reserve. Suppose that initially the money supply is $180, as shown by the money supply curve MS_1 in Exhibit 13.4. A nominal national income of

Exhibit 13.4

Effects of an increase in the money supply

Initially, a money supply of $180 puts the money supply curve in the position MS_1. An open market purchase of $20 by the Federal Reserve has the immediate effect of moving the money supply curve to MS_2. That is not the end of the story, however. With a money multiplier of 9.0, the money supply reaches $360 ($MS_3$) before the deposit expansion process works itself out completely. The new equilibrium nominal interest rate is 4 percent.

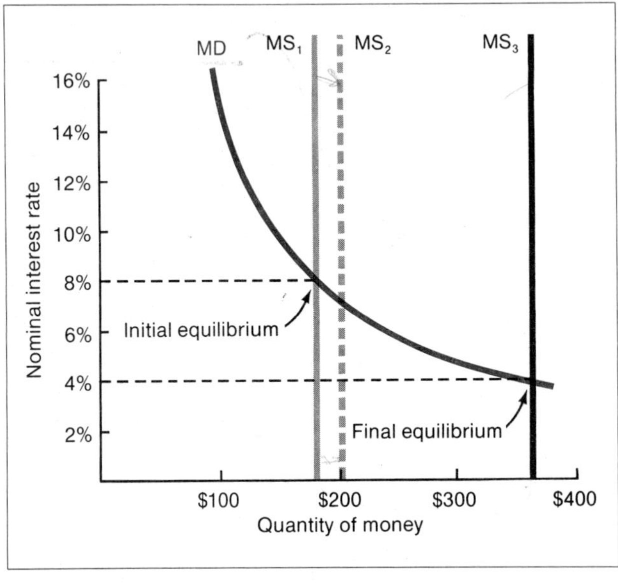

\$1,200 gives the money demand curve MD. The equilibrium interest rate is 8 percent, and the money multiplier is 9.0.

Imagine that the Federal Reserve makes an open market purchase of \$20 worth of government securities, paying for them with one of its own checks. The immediate effect of this purchase is to increase the money supply by \$20 and to raise bond prices slightly and lower the rate of interest slightly.

If this were the end of the story, the money supply curve would be put in the position indicated as MS_2, and the market would be put in a new equilibrium at the intersection of that curve with the money demand curve. But this is not the end of the story. As soon as the original Federal Reserve check is deposited in the bond seller's bank, the total reserves of the banking system go up by \$20 to a new level of \$40. This sets off the process of deposit expansion described in Chapter 12; and by the time the reserves-to-money multiplier has worked itself out, the money supply will reach \$360. This will shift the money supply curve all the way to the position MS_3.

New Equilibrium Now there will be a large excess quantity of money supplied. Asset holders will not desire to hold the new money at the old interest rate and will try to reduce their money holdings. It is likely that some excess money balances will be spent on physical assets, including consumer durables; and it is certain that some will be spent on bonds. As before, the actions of portfolio holders will bid up bond prices and lower interest rates. When the interest rate falls low enough (to 4 percent as this example is constructed), the quantity of money demanded will rise enough to reestablish equilibrium. In the new equilibrium, total money balances outstanding will be larger than initially, and the nominal interest rate will be lower.

Effects of an Increase in Income

In looking at the money market effects of an increase in the money supply, we assumed that nominal income remained unchanged throughout. Now we will look at the effects of a change in nominal income, assuming that the money supply will remain fixed. This will complete the groundwork for the next chapter, where the two types of changes will be considered in combination.

A Shift in the Money Demand Curve Exhibit 13.5 sets the scene for exploring the effects of a change in nominal income. Suppose that initially the economy is in equilibrium with a money supply (MS) of \$180, a nominal income (MD_1) of \$600, and an interest rate of 4 percent. At this interest rate, the desired quantity of money holdings is \$180, just equal to the money supply—as of course it must be in equilibrium.

Now suppose that, for some reason, nominal income rises to \$1,200. The increase in income causes the money demand curve to shift to the new position, MD_2. With the money supply still at \$180, this means a very substantial excess quantity of money demanded. To meet the increased demand for money, portfolio holders will have to sell some of their earning assets, especially bonds. This will depress the price of bonds and raise the nominal interest rate.

As the nominal interest rate rises, the desired ratio of money to income falls, since the higher interest rate raises the implicit cost of holding money balances. When the nominal interest rate rises high enough, the desired quantity

Exhibit 13.5

Effects of an increase in national income

Initially, a nominal income of $600 puts the money demand curve at MD_1. The equilibrium nominal interest rate is 4 percent with the money supply at $180. If an increase in nominal income to $1,200 shifts the money demand curve to MD_2, the interest rate will have to rise to 8 percent to restore equilibrium.

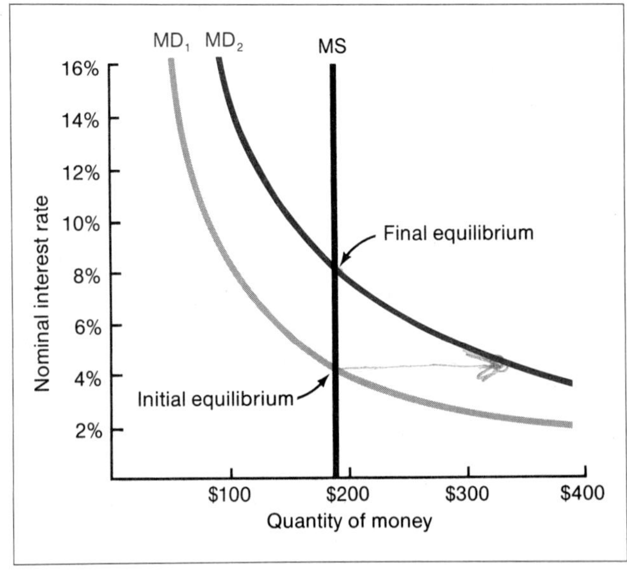

of money will fall to $180, entirely eliminating the excess quantity of money demanded. This will happen at an interest rate of 8 percent for the current example. Therefore, the new equilibrium rate of interest is 8 percent.

CONCLUSIONS

This completes the initial discussion of the supply and demand for money. The important next step—to apply this theory to the problem of national income determination—is the aim of the next chapter. That chapter will show how the inclusion of the money market in the analysis of national income determination leads to some important modifications of the multiplier theory and sets the stage for the discussion of inflation and unemployment.

SUMMARY

1. The collection of various assets a person owns (money, real estate, consumer durables, bonds, stocks, or whatever) is called a portfolio. Portfolio holders try to maintain a balance among the various kinds of assets they own, shifting from one to another as economic conditions change. As nominal income rises, people tend to want more money in their portfolios to satisfy their transactions demand. As the nominal rate of interest rises, people tend to want less money in their portfolios, because the opportunity cost of holding money increases and because their speculative demand for money decreases.
2. A downward sloping money demand curve can be drawn to indicate, in graphical form, how the quantity of money demanded changes as the interest rate changes, given some level of nominal income. An increase in the level of nominal income shifts this curve to the right, and a decrease shifts it to the left.

3. If the money supply is assumed to be fully controlled by Federal Reserve policy, the money supply curve can be represented by a vertical line. Together, the money supply and money demand curves associate one and only one nominal rate of interest with each quantity of money supplied and each level of nominal income. With nominal income unchanged, an increase in the money supply must be followed by a fall in the nominal rate of interest, other things being equal. With the money supply unchanged, an increase in nominal income causes the nominal rate of interest to rise, other things being equal.

DISCUSSION QUESTIONS

1. List the items that you might consider part of your portfolio. Is your portfolio basically similar to the one discussed in the text? In what ways is it similar? In what ways is it different?
2. Which is most important in determining your own demand for money—the transactions motive, the precautionary motive, or the speculative motive? Explain.
3. If the interest rate paid on savings deposits were increased, would you change your portfolio? Would you invest more or less in a savings account? Explain.
4. What is the average balance in your checkbook during a typical month? How much currency do you carry on a typical day? The sum of these two figures will give the quantity of money demanded. In order to get a point on your demand for money schedule, a price is needed. What price should be used?
5. Evaluate the following statement: It is at best a mere metaphor, and at worst seriously misleading, to speak of the money "market." Money cannot be bought and sold; it is just the means of payment we use in buying and selling everything else. Since it cannot be bought and sold, it cannot have a true market.
6. Do you know what the interest rate is on three-month Treasury bills at the time you are reading this chapter? Try to find out.

SUGGESTIONS FOR FURTHER READING

Campbell, Colin, and Campbell, Rosemary. *An Introduction to Money and Banking,* 3rd ed. Hinsdale, Ill.: Dryden Press, 1978.
Chapters 16, 17, and 18 parallel the discussion of this chapter but offer additional details.

Goldfield, Stephen. "The Case of the Missing Money." *Brookings Papers on Economic Activity,* 1976, No. 4.
A summary of the debate over the leftward shift in the money demand curve during 1974 and 1975.

Porter, Richard D.; Mauskopf, Eileen; and Simpson, Thomas D. "Financial Innovation and the Monetary Aggregates." *Brookings Papers on Economic Activity,* 1979, No. 1.
An analysis of the effects of innovations in corporate cash management techniques and the use of repurchase agreements on the demand for money.

CHAPTER 14

THE INTERACTION OF MONEY AND THE MULTIPLIER

WHAT YOU WILL LEARN IN THIS CHAPTER

This chapter ties together the analysis of fiscal and monetary policy given in previous chapters. First, it shows how the two policies interact to establish simultaneous equilibrium in the money market and the circular flow. Next, it shows how the effects of fiscal policy actions are modified when monetary reactions to fiscal policy are taken into account. Finally, after discussing the basic tools of fiscal and monetary policy analysis, the chapter introduces some important controversies concerning the relative importance and effectiveness of fiscal and monetary policy.

FOR REVIEW

Here are some important terms and concepts that will be put to use in this chapter. If you do not understand them, review them before proceeding.

- *Real and nominal interest rates (Chapter 7)*
- *Fiscal policy (Chapter 10)*
- *Supply of money (Chapter 12)*
- *Demand for money (Chapter 13)*

This chapter ties together the multiplier analysis of Chapters 8 to 10 with the analysis of the financial sector presented in Chapters 11 to 13. In doing so, it makes a transition from what economists call partial equilibrium analysis to what they call general equilibrium analysis.

The difference between the two lies in the role played by the "other things being equal" assumption. In **partial equilibrium analysis,** it is said that if Event X occurs, the effect on Market Y will be Z, provided that the equilibrium of other markets is not disturbed. In **general equilibrium analysis,** in contrast, it is said that if Event X occurs, the effect on Market Y will be Z, provided that other markets also adjust fully to the event in question.

Partial equilibrium analysis
An approach to the study of markets along the lines of: If Event X occurs, the effect on Market Y will be Z, provided that the equilibrium of other markets is not disturbed.

General equilibrium analysis
An approach to the study of markets along the lines of: If Event X occurs, the effect on Market Y will be Z, provided that other markets also adjust fully to the event in question.

So far, the multiplier theory and the theory of money have been examined only from the partial equilibrium point of view. Chapter 10, for example, analyzed the effect of a change in fiscal policy on the equilibrium level of the circular flow without considering the possible effects that the change might have on the demand for money, on the nominal interest rate, and on the level of planned investment. Similarly, Chapter 13 looked at the effect a change in the money supply would have on the equilibrium nominal interest rate without considering the possible effect of such an act of monetary policy on the level of nominal national income or the position of the money demand curve.

This chapter will also look at fiscal and monetary policy, but now using the general equilibrium approach. After delineating some basic principles, it will turn to important controversies surrounding the relative strength and effectiveness of monetary and fiscal policy.

THE INTERACTION OF MONEY AND NATIONAL INCOME

The Conditions for General Equilibrium

The chapter begins by showing what the economy looks like when the circular flow and the money market are simultaneously in equilibrium. Consider Exhibit 14.1, which shows two main channels of interaction (represented by large arrows) between money and the level of nominal national income. Each of these channels requires some comment.

Nominal Income and Money Demand The first interaction runs from the level of nominal national income, as determined by aggregate supply and demand, to the position of the money demand curve. As shown in the last chapter, the quantity of money demanded depends both on the nominal rate of interest and on the level of national income. A change in the nominal interest rate produces a movement along a given money demand curve, whereas a change in nominal national income produces a shift in the money demand curve. In order to put the money demand curve in its proper position, then, it is necessary to know the equilibrium level of nominal national income.

Nominal Interest, Real Interest, and Investment The second channel of interaction runs from the money market to the aggregate demand schedule by way of the effect of interest rates on the level of planned investment. Low interest rates encourage investment; and investment, in turn, is an important component of aggregate nominal demand. It is necessary to be careful in analyzing this interaction, because supply and demand in the money market are brought into equilibrium by the *nominal* rate of interest, whereas the level of planned investment expenditure is determined by the *expected real* rate of interest. This is no problem so long as the expected rate of inflation is zero, because with no inflation expected, the nominal rate of interest and the expected real rate of interest are equal. Such a case is shown in Exhibit 14.1. The first part of this chapter will assume zero expected inflation. Later, however, the chapter will consider the important case where inflationary expectations are not zero, so that the nominal and expected real rates of interest diverge.

Finding the Equilibrium Values The money market and the circular flow can be in equilibrium simultaneously only if a certain pair of values for the interest rate and nominal national income prevail. Let the required level of nominal national income be Y and the required interest rate be r. (The r stands for both the nominal and the expected real rate of interest, which are equal under the present assumption of zero expected inflation.) Then the value of r must be just right to induce the level of planned investment needed to put

Exhibit 14.1
A general equilibrium view of national income determination
The money market and the circular flow can both be in equilibrium at once only if a certain pair of values for the interest rate and nominal income prevail. The large arrows in this figure show how the interest rate and nominal national income interact. The equilibrium interest rate helps determine the position of the aggregate demand curve through its effect on planned investment spending. The level of nominal national income helps determine the interest rate through its effect on the position of the money demand curve.

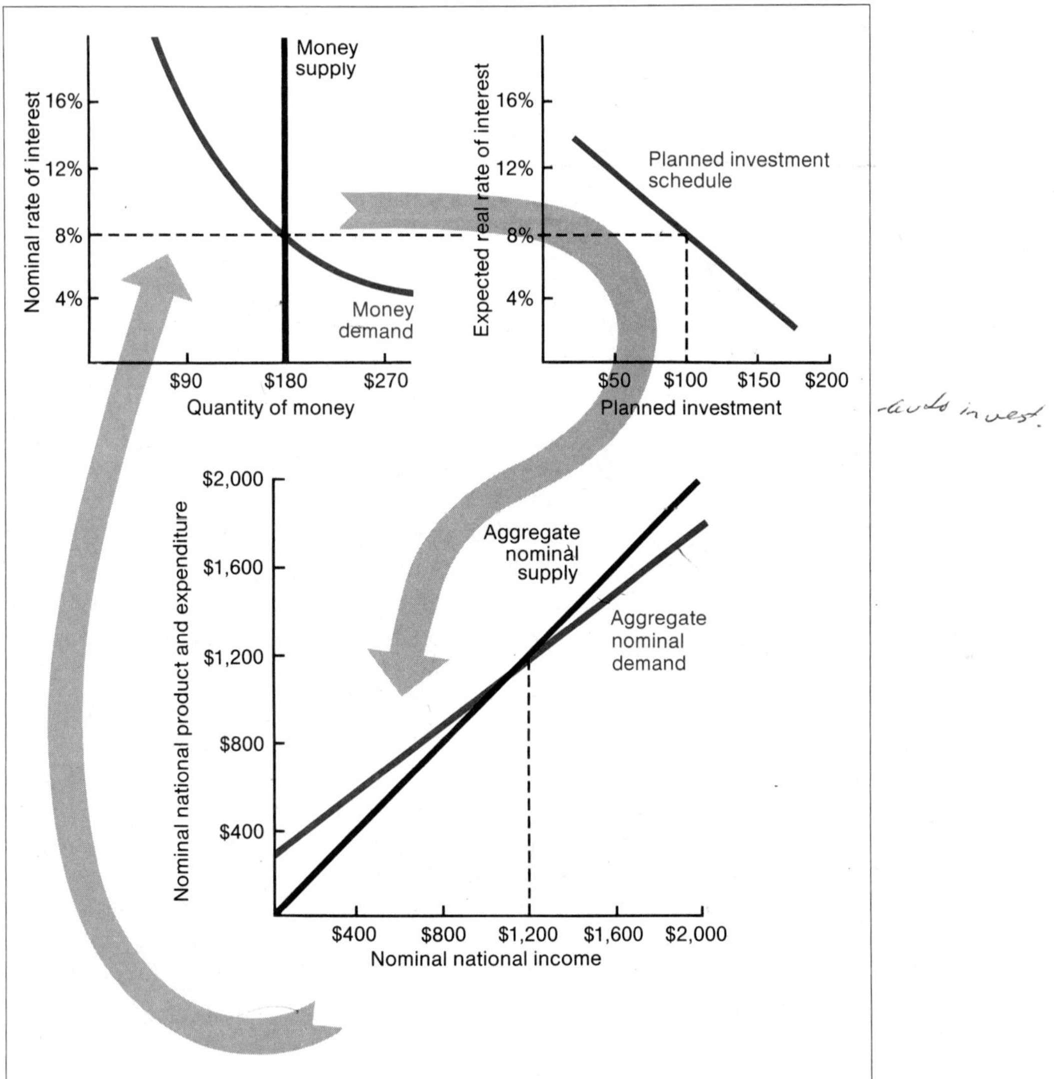

equilibrium nominal national income exactly at the level Y, and the value of Y must be just right to put the money demand curve in the position needed to keep the equilibrium interest rate at r.

As Exhibit 14.1 is drawn, an interest rate of 8 percent and a nominal national income of $1,200 are called for. The aggregate demand schedule is drawn on the assumptions that autonomous consumption is $145, the marginal propensity to consume is 0.75, government purchases are $75, net exports are $25, and net taxes are $60. Planned investment must therefore be $100 in order for equilibrium nominal national income to be $1,200. A check of the planned investment schedule reveals that an interest rate of 8 percent is just what is needed to encourage that amount of planned investment.

Turning to the money market, where a money supply of $180 is assumed, the money demand curve must be in exactly the position indicated in Exhibit 14.1 for the equilibrium rate of interest to be 8 percent. This position, which corresponds to a nominal national income of $1,200, verifies that r = 8 percent and Y = $1,200 are an equilibrium pair for the interest rate and nominal national income.

The Equilibrium Is Unique For any given set of assumptions about autonomous consumption, the marginal propensity to consume, government purchases, net taxes, net exports, the money supply, and the position of the planned investment schedule, there is just one pair of values for the interest rate and nominal national income that permits both the money market and the circular flow to be in equilibrium. Thus, equilibrium values of nominal national income and the interest rate are unique.

To see this, assume momentarily that one of the values is different, and then show that this does not permit both markets to be in equilibrium. Suppose, for example, that the interest rate were only 4 percent, while all underlying economic conditions were the same as before. The planned investment schedule in Exhibit 14.1 shows that a 4 percent interest rate would cause planned investment to rise to $150. With planned expenditure $50 higher than before, equilibrium nominal national income would rise by $200 to $1,400 under the impact of the multiplier effect. Thus an interest rate of 4 percent requires an equilibrium nominal national income of $1,400.

The money market part of Exhibit 14.1 shows that 4 percent cannot be the equilibrium rate of interest when the money demand curve is in the position shown and the money supply is $180. The money demand curve would have to shift to the left to make 4 percent the equilibrium rate of interest. But an increase in nominal national income from $1,200 to $1,400 would shift the curve not to the left but to the right. There is no way that 4 percent can be an equilibrium rate of interest when the level of nominal national income is $1,400, given the assumed money supply. There is also no way that the equilibrium level of nominal national income can be anything but $1,400 when the rate of interest is 4 percent. Given the assumed underlying economic conditions, it is necessary to conclude that when the interest rate is 4 percent, there is no value of nominal national income that permits both the money market and the circular flow to be in equilibrium.

The same reasoning could be repeated for any value of r other than 8 percent and any value of Y other than $1,200. This pair of equilibrium values for nominal national income and interest rate is unique.

A Revised Look at the Effects of Fiscal Policy

Chapter 10 discussed the effects of three kinds of changes in fiscal policy: changes in government purchases, changes in net taxes, and matched changes in government purchases and taxes under a balanced budget policy. Each of these kinds of fiscal policy must now be reconsidered from the point of view of general equilibrium analysis. For purposes of comparison with what follows, recall the conclusion reached in Chapter 10 about the effects of a change in government purchases: When government purchases are increased while taxes, planned investment, and the consumption schedule remain unchanged, equilibrium nominal national income will change by an amount equal to the change in government purchases times the simple multiplier.

Effects of a Change in Government Purchases Beginning with government purchases, assume that the economy is initially in equilibrium with interest rate r and nominal national income Y. Then assume that fiscal policy makers decide to increase government purchases by $100, with no accompanying change in taxes. Consider the effects of this fiscal policy as they work their way through the economy.

The first effect of the increase in government purchases is to shift the aggregate demand schedule upward by $100. Planned expenditure now exceeds national product at the initial income level. This causes unplanned depletion of inventories, to which firms respond by increasing output and/or raising prices. The level of nominal national income begins to rise.

Money Market Effect As nominal national income rises, the change in fiscal policy begins to affect the money market. The increase in nominal national income causes the money demand curve to shift rightward. In Exhibit 14.2 this is shown as a shift from the initial position of the money demand curve, MD_1, toward a new position, MD_2. The money demand curve shifts because when incomes rise, people tend to want more money in their portfolios. Because the money supply does not increase, people's attempts to get more

Exhibit 14.2
The crowding out effect

An increase in government purchases causes nominal national income to rise via the multiplier effect. The increase in income shifts the money demand curve from its initial position, MD_1, to the new position, MD_2. The equilibrium interest rate rises from r_1 to r_2. An amount of private investment equal to ΔI is "crowded out."

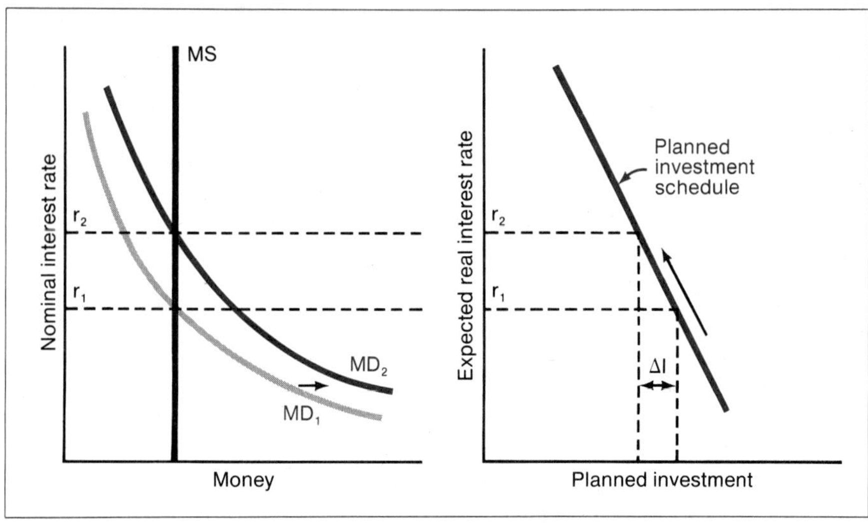

money by selling bonds simply drives down the price of bonds and drives up the rate of interest. Altogether, then, the effect on the money market of the increase in government purchases is to push up the rate of interest.

The Crowding Out Effect Attention can now be shifted from the money market to the planned investment schedule, also shown in Exhibit 14.2. Increased money demand has driven up the nominal rate of interest. With zero inflation expected, as assumed, the expected real interest rate rises in step with the nominal rate. Firms find it more costly to undertake fixed investment projects and to increase inventories of raw materials or finished goods. They therefore reduce their planned investment expenditures, shown by a movement upward and to the left along the planned investment schedule. This decrease in planned investment expenditures, as an indirect effect of an increase in government purchases, is called the **crowding out effect.** The amount of investment crowded out is labeled ΔI in the exhibit.

Crowding out effect The tendency of expansionary fiscal policy to cause a drop in private planned investment expenditure as a result of a rise in the interest rate.

Exhibit 14.3 shows what happens in terms of aggregate supply and demand. The original position of the aggregate demand curve is shown as AND_1. Considered in isolation, the increase in government spending would have pushed the schedule all the way up to the position AND_2. When the crowding out effect is taken into account, though, it is apparent that the upward shift in aggregate demand is less than the amount of increase in government purchases. If ΔG stands for the increase in government purchases and ΔI for the amount of investment crowded out, the upward shift is reduced to ΔG − ΔI. This puts the final position of the aggregate demand curve at AND_3.

Looking at Exhibits 14.2 and 14.3 together now, notice that both income and the interest rate have changed. The new equilibrium interest rate, r_2, and the new equilibrium nominal national income, Y_2, are higher than they were to begin with. Government purchases and private consumption are higher than initially, but private investment is lower.

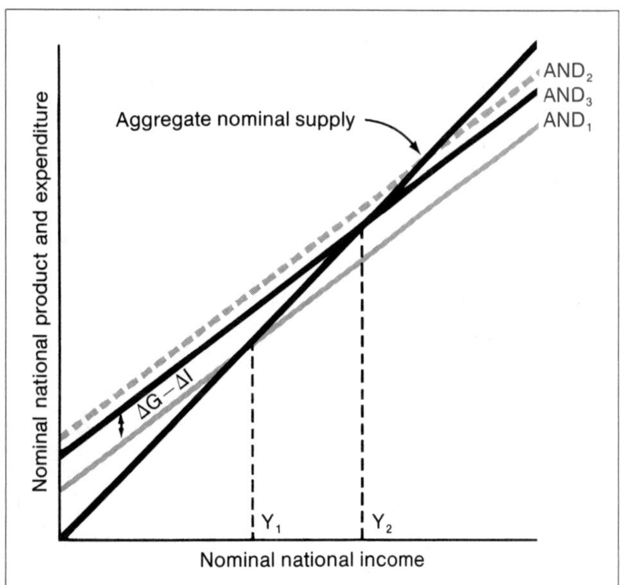

Exhibit 14.3
The crowding out effect in terms of aggregate supply and demand
Here the crowding out effect is shown from the perspective of aggregate supply and demand. Taken by itself, the increase in government purchases (ΔG) would have pushed the aggregate demand curve from AND_1 to AND_2. The crowding out effect chops ΔI off private investment, however, so the actual shift is only from AND_1 to AND_3, a distance equal to ΔG − ΔI.

Crowding Out and the Multiplier Because an increase in government purchases crowds out some private investment, nominal national income does not rise by the full amount of the simple multiplier times the increase in government purchases. This fact does not, however, directly contradict the conclusion reached in Chapter 10 and repeated above. The trouble is that the earlier conclusion, which was based on partial equilibrium analysis, included the assumption that planned investment would not change when nominal national income changed. The general equilibrium approach taken here shows that that assumption is invalid. This makes it necessary to modify the way the multiplier theory is applied to the analysis of fiscal policy. The multiplier must now be applied not just to the change in government purchases but rather to the change in government purchases minus the induced change in private planned investment expenditure.

The new way of applying the multiplier theory to the analysis of fiscal policy can be put in the form of a simple equation. Using the symbol ΔY to represent the change in nominal national income resulting from a change in government purchases, ΔG, and using $(1/1 - MPC)$ to stand for the multiplier:

$$\Delta Y = \frac{1}{1 - MPC}(\Delta G - \Delta I).$$

Other Fiscal Policies The crowding out effect applies to other types of fiscal policy as well as to changes in government purchases. When taxes are lowered, or when the level of government purchases is increased while the budget is kept in balance, nominal national income rises. This pushes interest rates up and crowds out some investment. The result is that the overall effectiveness of these fiscal policies is somewhat less than would be predicted by the simple applications of the tax multiplier or balanced budget multiplier outlined in Chapter 10.

It must also be remembered that when taxes are raised or government purchases lowered, as might be done to eliminate an expansionary gap from the economy, the crowding out effect works in reverse. The contractionary impact of fiscal policy is somewhat diminished, because as incomes fall, the demand for money and the interest rate fall too. These effects stimulate new planned investment expenditure, somewhat offsetting the downward shift in the aggregate demand schedule that the contractionary policy produces.

A Revised Look at the Effects of Monetary Policy

Chapter 13 described the effects of a change in the money supply from a partial equilibrium point of view, taking into account only what happens in the money market. This section will reconsider the effects of changes in the money supply in a general equilibrium context, taking into account the interaction of money and the multiplier theory of income determination.

An Open Market Purchase To be specific, suppose that the Federal Reserve initiates an expansion of the money supply through an open market purchase of bonds. It will not be necessary to give separate consideration to the expansion of the money supply by the use of other instruments of monetary policy because the effects are very little different from those of an open market operation.

Chapters 12 and 13 analyzed initial effects of the open market purchase. The open market purchase creates an increase in commercial bank reserves, and banks are induced to begin the process of deposit expansion. When the expansion is complete, the money supply will have increased by an amount equal to the expansion in the reserves times the money multiplier. This is indicated in Exhibit 14.4 by the shift in the money supply curve from the position MS_1 to the position MS_2.

As the money supply expands, people find that they have more money than they want to hold in their portfolios at the original rate of interest. They attempt to reduce these holdings by buying other assets, including bonds. This tends to push the price of bonds up and the interest rate down. In the diagram, the process is represented by a movement along the original money demand curve, MD_1, toward its intersection with the new money supply curve, MS_2.

Income and Expenditure Effects As the interest rate begins to fall, business executives are encouraged to increase their level of planned investment, which is indicated by a movement down and to the right along their planned investment schedule. The increase in investment expenditure shifts the aggregate nominal demand schedule upward, as shown in Exhibit 14.5. Planned expenditure now temporarily exceeds nominal national income; and by the familiar multiplier process, nominal national income begins to increase.

As this income increases, the money market is once again affected. Now the money demand curve begins to shift to the right, moving toward the position

Exhibit 14.4
Money market and investment effects of an increase in the money supply
An increase in the money supply shifts the money supply curve from MS_1 to MS_2. The immediate effect of this shift is a movement down along the money demand curve, MD_1, toward its intersection with the new money supply curve. The interest rate then falls and planned investment expenditure rises, which stimulates nominal national income through the multiplier effect. The rise in income in turn shifts the money demand schedule to a new position, MD_2, which cuts short the fall in the interest rate—and a new equilibrium is established.

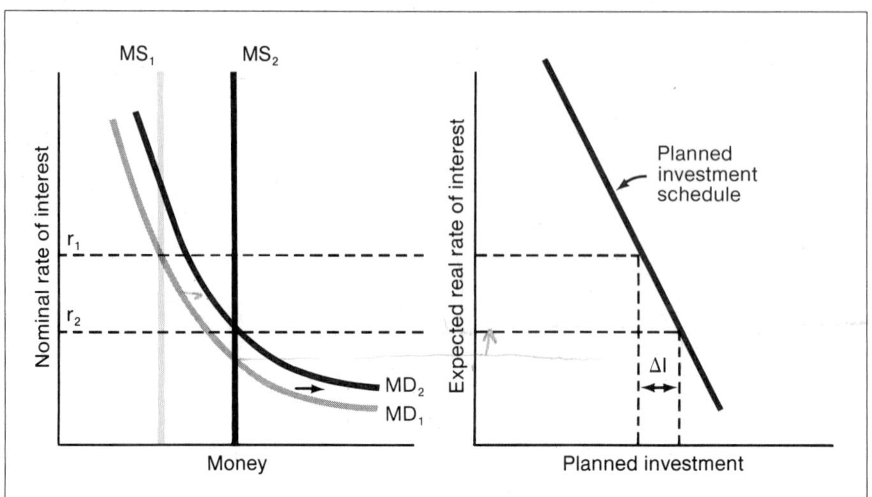

Exhibit 14.5
The effect of an increase in the money supply on aggregate demand and nominal national income
An increase in planned investment spending, caused by an increase in the money supply, shifts the aggregate demand curve upward. The amount of the shift is equal to the change in investment, ΔI. A new equilibrium is established, with nominal national income increasing from Y_1 to Y_2.

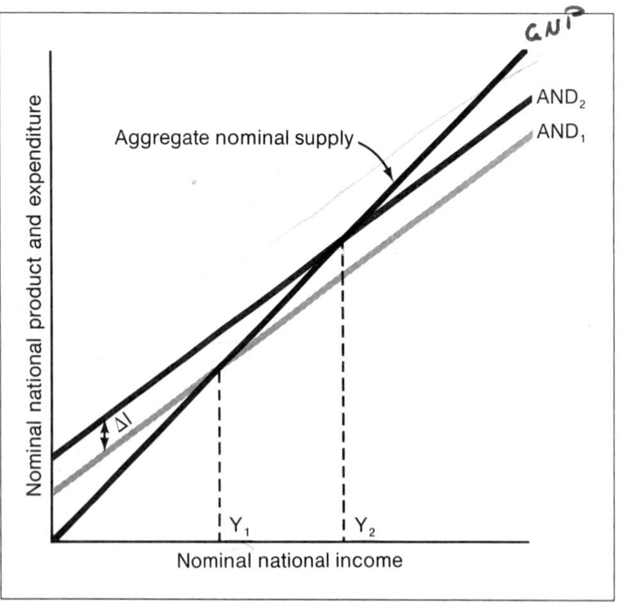

marked MD_2 in Exhibit 14.4. This shift cuts off the fall in the interest rate, and a new equilibrium interest rate is established where MD_2 and MS_2 intersect.

Once this interest rate is established, planned investment stops expanding. The aggregate nominal demand schedule comes to rest at a new equilibrium position, AND_2, as shown in Exhibit 14.5. That means the new equilibrium level of nominal national income will be higher than it was before the increase in the money supply.

In short, general equilibrium analysis shows that an increase in the money supply will result in new equilibrium values for both the interest rate and nominal national income. With zero inflationary expectations, as assumed, both the nominal interest rate and the expected real interest rate will be lower than before the monetary expansion took place, and the level of nominal national income will be higher.

Accommodating Monetary Policy

Now that the separate effects of fiscal and monetary policy have been described, it is not difficult to envision how the two policies might be used in combination. Although not every possible combination of policies will be discussed here, one case is important enough to deserve at least a brief mention: the case of accommodating monetary policy.

The Fed is said to pursue an **accommodating monetary policy** when, in the face of expansionary fiscal policy, it expands the money supply in an attempt to keep interest rates stable. To see why the Fed might want to do this, consider what happens when the government increases its purchases without raising taxes in order to stimulate aggregate demand. It must finance the deficit by selling bonds to the public. This depresses the price of bonds, thereby raising the nominal interest rate. The increase in the interest rate is unwelcome—for two reasons. First, with unchanged inflationary expectations, it raises the expected real rate of interest and crowds out some private invest-

Accommodating monetary policy A policy under which the Federal Reserve System expands the money supply in an attempt to keep interest rates from rising when the Treasury sells bonds to cover a budget deficit.

ment. This partially negates the intended stimulative effect of the increased government purchases. Second, it makes it more expensive for the Treasury to raise the money needed to finance the deficit. By making open market purchases of bonds at the same time the Treasury is selling new bonds to finance the deficit, the Fed keeps the interest rate from rising, thereby "accommodating" the Treasury.

But, of course, by feeding new reserves to the banking system, the Fed's actions cause the money supply to expand. In effect, the combined actions of the Fed and the Treasury mean that the government is paying for its purchases with newly created money.

In times gone by, governments did not always bother with such niceties as bonds and open market purchases when they wanted to spend more than they collected in taxes. Instead, they just cranked up their presses and printed new currency. In remembrance of this ancient custom, economic journalists to this day sometimes refer to the combination of deficit spending and accommodating monetary policy as "deficit finance via the printing press."

CONTROVERSIES OVER MONETARY POLICY

The analysis of the interactions of monetary and fiscal policy just worked through may appear to be perfectly straightforward and perhaps not particularly exciting. Yet some of the major economic controversies of the twentieth century revolve around the ideas presented in the preceding pages. Taking things in historical sequence, the so-called Keynesian-monetarist controversy will be the first one looked at.

The Keynesian-Monetarist Controversy

Keynes's general theory of employment, interest, and money was intended to be "general" in the sense that it would take into account both monetary and fiscal influences on the economy.[1] However, in the first years after the publication of Keynes's book, it was not the general theory as a whole that dominated the thinking of the economics profession. Instead, some followers of Keynes tended to place a one-sided emphasis on planned expenditure and to downplay the role of money in the economy. Early followers of Keynes interpreted the experience of the Great Depression as justifying the view that "money doesn't matter." They attributed the fact that monetary policy had failed to prevent both the 46 percent decline in nominal income and the increase in the unemployment rate to 25 percent of the labor force that occurred between 1929 and 1933 not to poor conduct of monetary policy but to its ineffectiveness. The fact that the Great Depression did not end until World War II had brought on a massive increase in government spending appeared to support this view.

After the war, many of the early Keynesians forecasted a new depression and economic stagnation. They thought that private investment opportunities would dry up with the disappearance of wartime government spending. Experience proved them wrong. The United States and the countries of Western Europe experienced rapid postwar recovery. Central banks in most of

---

[1]John Maynard Keynes, *The General Theory of Employment, Interest, and Money* (New York: Harcourt, Brace, & World, 1936).

the major economies pursued "easy" monetary policies during these years, and inflation was a more widespread problem than depression. Those countries that succeeded in controlling inflation did so only by orthodox monetary policies. Economists began to wonder if perhaps money mattered after all and began to look once again at the general theory as a whole.

The Monetarists. The reaction against the one-sided theories of the early Keynesians received major support during the 1950s and 1960s from a group of economists working under the intellectual leadership of Milton Friedman of the University of Chicago. Friedman's empirical research led him to think that monetary policy had had a much greater influence on the course of economic events than the Keynesians were willing to admit. It appeared to be possible to

---

In October 1976, Milton Friedman received the Nobel Memorial Prize in economics, becoming the sixth American to win or share in that prize. Few were surprised. The main surprise was that this most original and influential of economists had had to wait in line so long! The explanation is that Friedman has built his career outside the economics establishment—built it, in fact, by challenging virtually every major establishment doctrine.

Friedman was born in New York in 1912, the son of immigrant garment workers. His hard-working parents sent him across the river to Rutgers University in New Jersey, where Friedman came under the influence of Arthur Burns, then a young assistant professor. From Burns, Friedman learned the importance of empirical work in economics. Statistical testing of all theory and policy prescriptions became a key characteristic of Friedman's later work. From Rutgers, Friedman went to the University of Chicago for an M.A. and then east again to Columbia University, where he got his Ph.D. in 1946. With his degree in hand, he returned to Chicago to teach. There, he became the leading member of the "Chicago School," which provides the main intellectual counterweight to the Eastern Establishment in U.S. economics today.

Milton Friedman (1912–)

If one were to single out the theme that underlies all of Friedman's work, it would be his conviction that the market economy works—and works best when left alone. This can be seen in his best-known work, *A Monetary History of the United States.* Written with Anna Schwartz, the work challenges two major tenets of orthodox Keynesian economics: first, the idea that the market economy is inherently unstable without the guiding hand of government, and second, that monetary policy had been tried and found useless as a cure for the Great Depression. Friedman and Schwartz found both beliefs to be the opposite of the truth. "The Great Depression," Friedman later wrote, "far from being a sign of the inherent instability of the private enterprise system, is a testament to how much harm can be done by mistakes on the part of a few men when they wield vast power over the monetary system of the country."

Friedman strongly favors a hands-off policy by governments in almost every area, not just in monetary matters. The trouble, in his view, is not that government is evil by nature but rather that so many policies end up having the opposite of their intended effects. "The social reformers who seek through politics to do nothing but serve the public interest invariably end up serving some private interest that was no part of their intention to serve. They are led by an invisible hand to serve a private interest." Transport regulation, the income tax, public education, agricultural subsidies, and housing programs are among the many policy areas where Friedman believes the government has done more harm than good and where a free competitive market would do better.

Today, Friedman continues to take on new challenges. He promotes his ideas before congressional committees, in professional journals, in his *Newsweek* column, and in face-to-face debate with his colleagues. Economics has never had a more respected heretic.

explain even the Great Depression in terms of faulty monetary policy—especially the 25 percent decrease in M_1 that the Fed permitted between 1929 and 1933. Because of the emphasis they gave to monetary phenomena, Friedman and his followers became known as **monetarists.**

Monetarists Economists who believe that movements in the money supply are the primary causes of ups and downs in business activity.

The economics profession did not immediately become converted to monetarism. In fact, the 1960s were in some respects the heyday of Keynesian policy, as such prominent Keynesians as Walter Heller, James Tobin, and Gardner Ackley left their academic posts to join the Council of Economic Advisers under Presidents Kennedy and Johnson. Nonetheless, the ideas of the monetarists proved influential in persuading the Keynesians to return to the idea of a general theory in which monetary and fiscal policy played co-equal roles.

Monetarism versus Keynesianism: Unresolved Issues Today, the theoretical gap between monetarism and Keynesian economics has been narrowed but not altogether eliminated. The analysis presented in the first part of this chapter can be used as a framework for discussing some of the important unresolved issues, including the following:

1. What is the relative importance of monetary and fiscal policy in determining nominal national income?
2. How are the effects of monetary policy actions transmitted through the economy?
3. To what extent is monetary policy a determinant of the rate of inflation, in both the long run and the short run?
4. What kind of monetary and fiscal policies are best suited to achieve the goals of economic stabilization?

The first two of these issues will be discussed in the remainder of this chapter. The third and fourth will be left for Chapters 15 to 18.

How Large a Crowding Out Effect? The debate over the relative importance of monetary and fiscal policy as determinants of nominal national income is, to a considerable extent, a debate over the importance of the crowding out effect. Exhibit 14.6 shows why. Suppose that the money demand curve has the shape shown by MD_1, indicating that the demand for money is not very sensitive to changes in the interest rate. If this is the case, the portfolio adjustments required when the money demand curve shifts relative to the money supply curve (as when nominal income changes) or when the money supply curve shifts relative to the money demand curve (as in the conduct of monetary policy) will bring about large changes in the rate of interest. Suppose that at the same time the planned investment schedule is relatively flat, like the curve I_1, so that a change in the rate of interest will induce a large change in planned investment expenditure.

Taken together, the curves MD_1 and I_1 tend to give the sort of results expected by monetarists. An expansion of government purchases leads to a large increase in the rate of interest, a large drop in private investment spending, and hence a large crowding out effect. Also, an increase in the money supply leads to a large decline in the rate of interest and a large increase in investment spending. Therefore, given curves of these shapes, fiscal policy tends to be relatively ineffective and monetary policy relatively effective.

Exhibit 14.6
Alternative views of monetary and fiscal policy effectiveness.
If the money demand curve has a shape like MD_1 while the planned investment schedule is shaped like I_1, monetary policy will tend to be more effective than fiscal policy. A change in the money supply will have a big impact on planned expenditure, while fiscal policy will be severely hampered by the crowding out effect. On the other hand, a money demand schedule like MD_2 with a planned investment schedule like I_2 will give the advantage to fiscal policy. Changes in the money supply will have little impact on investment spending, and the crowding out effect will be small.

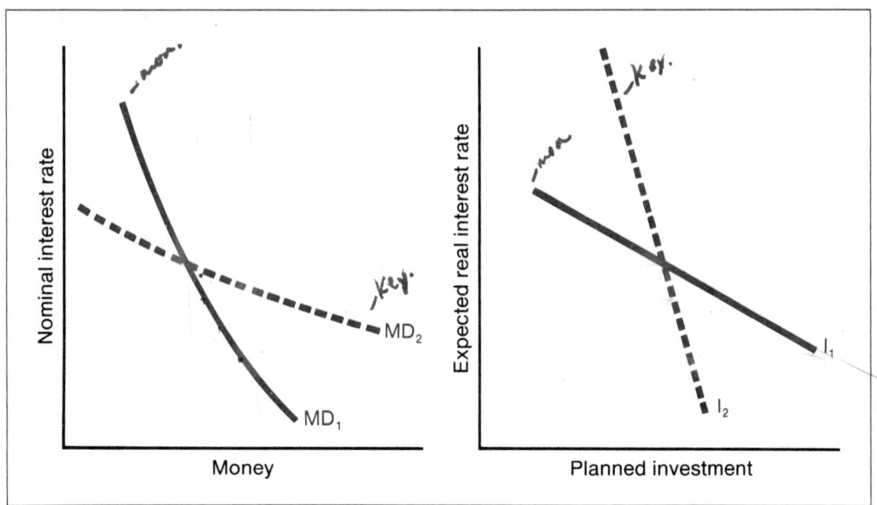

On the other hand, if the money demand curve has the shape MD_2 and the planned investment schedule the shape I_2, the situation is reversed. Fiscal policy will have relatively little impact on interest rates; and interest rates, in turn, will have relatively little impact on private investment. Changes in taxes or government purchases will then operate on aggregate nominal demand without much hindrance from the crowding out effect. At the same time, the economy will become much less sensitive to changes in the money supply. The world will behave more like a Keynesian would expect it to.

The Transmission Mechanism In addition to disagreeing about the size of the crowding out effect, monetarists and Keynesians continue to disagree about the nature of the mechanism by which the effects of monetary policy are transmitted through the economy.

Keynesians tend to emphasize the chain of causation running from changes in monetary policy to changes in interest rates to changes in planned investment spending. This is the transmission mechanism emphasized so far in the chapter. Keynesians also suggest that there may be a secondary chain of causation running from a decrease in interest rates to an increase in stock prices and, hence, via an increase in wealth, to an increase in consumer spending.

Monetarists, without disagreeing that interest rates and planned investment play an important role in transmitting the effects of monetary policy, tend to emphasize that changes in the money supply affect the economy in many other ways as well. In particular, they point out that it can be very misleading to think in terms of a world in which money and bonds and perhaps stocks are the only assets that people hold in their portfolios—however convenient such a two- or three-asset economy may be as an expositional device for writers of textbooks.

Instead, when the Fed injects new money into the economy—more money than people initially want to hold—those who first receive the new money are likely to try to rebalance their portfolios by purchasing a broad variety of assets. These assets might include not only bonds of various types and maturities as well as stocks, but also productive capital equipment, housing, and even consumer durables. Increased demand for all these assets tends to drive their prices up, which in turn stimulates construction firms to build more houses, corporations to issue new stock and purchase new capital equipment, and durable goods makers to increase production to replace depleted inventories. The effects of expansionary monetary policy are thus transmitted through a great variety of channels, including some that are not adequately reflected in market interest rates, to many parts of the economy. The implication is that monetary policy may thus be more effective than the traditional Keynesian transmission mechanism would imply.

Evidence Not surprisingly, a number of attempts have been made to bring empirical evidence to bear on the Keynesian-monetarist controversy. These efforts have succeeded in narrowing, although not entirely closing, the gap between the two schools of thought. The following case studies represent two of a number of possible approaches to evaluating the relative importance of fiscal and monetary policy as determinants of nominal national income. One approach, discussed in Case 14.1, is to look at critical policy episodes when monetary and fiscal policy move in opposite directions. Unfortunately, this happens too infrequently to provide conclusive answers. The alternative approach, discussed in Case 14.2, is to use modern econometric techniques to sort out monetary from fiscal influences in periods when the two policies have worked in the same direction.

Case 14.1
Two Critical Episodes in Economic Policy

During the 1960s, there were two important policy episodes in which monetary and fiscal policy moved in opposite directions. Both have been interpreted as favoring the monetarist position in regard to the relative power of fiscal and monetary policy.

The first episode occurred in the second half of 1966. In that year, the Federal Reserve became worried about possible overheating of the economy and suddenly cut the growth of the money supply from 6.4 percent per year to zero. During the same period, the federal budget swung from surplus to deficit. President Johnson, who did not believe in the need for restraint, was angered by the Fed's policy. He called William McChesney Martin, then the Federal Reserve Board chairman, down to the LBJ Ranch for consultation. Martin flew down but remained unpersuaded. Champions of the Fed's independence from political control have picturesquely dubbed this episode "the Fed's finest hour." The outcome of the finest hour was the mini-recession of early 1967, which apparently indicated that the restrictive monetary policy outweighed the effect of the rising federal deficit.

The second episode also occurred during the Johnson administration, but this time the lineup of forces was reversed. In mid-1968, Congress, at the request of the administration, passed a 10 percent income tax surcharge to cool off the economy. The surcharge swung the federal budget very sharply from a strong deficit position to a strong surplus position. This time, the Federal Reserve feared "fiscal overkill" and continued through the end of 1968 to maintain a very rapid rate of monetary expansion. The outcome of the episode was that the tax surcharge failed to have its intended restraining effect on the economy. The growth of nominal GNP did not decline. This too is cited by monetarists as a demonstration of the relative importance of monetary policy.

Case 14.2
A Monetarist Analysis of the 1964 Tax Cut

Case 10.2 recounted the history of the Kennedy tax cut of 1964. More than any other single episode of macroeconomic policy, the expansion that followed this tax cut bolstered the reputation of the Keynesian economists. Yet some skeptics have remained unconvinced. One of these is Richard T. Froyen of the University of North Carolina. In 1974, he published an article challenging the Keynesian conclusion that the expansion of 1964 and 1965 could be explained only by the tax cut. Froyen pointed to the fact that monetary policy was also expansionary in the period surrounding the tax cut. In one statistical test, he showed that some 92 percent of the growth in GNP from January 1964 to mid-1965 could be explained by looking at monetary policy and government purchases alone, without taking taxes into account at all.

In another test, he compared his monetarist approach with two of the most elaborate Keynesian studies to see which would have best predicted the effects of the tax cut if predictions had been made at the end of 1963 using all three methods. He found that one of the Keynesian studies did a slightly better job than his monetarist approach and that the other one did much worse.

Froyen concluded that accelerating rates of monetary growth provide a plausible alternative explanation of the economic expansion that followed the tax cut. It would be wrong, in his view, to interpret this dramatic episode as confirming the Keynesian view of how the economy works. Instead, it seems to offer little conclusive evidence one way or the other. The debate goes on.

Source: Based on Richard T. Froyen, "Monetarist Econometric Models and the 1964 Tax Cut," *Economic Inquiry* 12 (June 1974): 159–168.

Inflationary Expectations and the Effects of Monetary Policy

As the debate between monetarists and Keynesians continues, other controversies that do not always exactly parallel this older one have developed. Take, for example, the issue of the effects of monetary policy in a world of nonzero inflationary expectations. The analysis of these effects involves elements about which there is fairly broad agreement among economists, but at the same time it serves to illustrate some new areas of controversy.

Inserting a Wedge Up to this point, to simplify the analysis, it was assumed that the expected rate of inflation in the economy was zero. This simplification conveniently made the nominal interest rate equal to the expected real interest rate, but it clearly came at some cost in terms of realism. In what follows, it will be worth sketching at least roughly the way the theory can be modified to take inflationary expectations into account.

Turn first to Exhibit 14.7. This exhibit shows how the expected rate of inflation can be represented as a wedge between the nominal rate of interest, which appears on the vertical axis of the money market diagram, and the

Exhibit 14.7
Inflationary expectations and interest rates
If the expected rate of inflation is not zero (zero was assumed earlier in this chapter), the nominal interest rate will differ from the expected real interest rate by an amount equal to the expected rate of inflation. The expected rate of inflation can thus be pictured as a "wedge" between the nominal interest rate, appearing on the vertical axis of the money market diagram, and the expected real rate of interest, appearing on the vertical axis of the planned investment diagram.

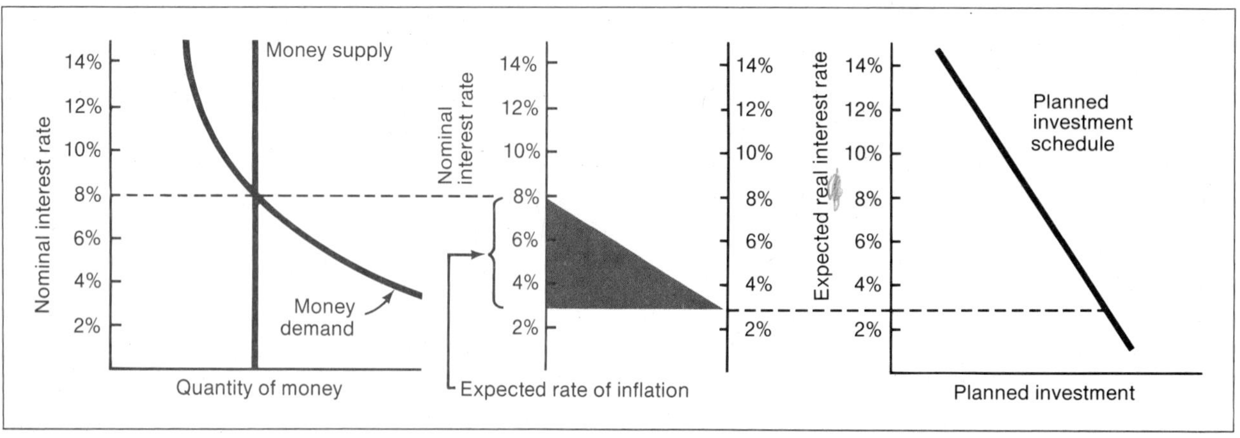

expected real rate of interest, which appears on the vertical axis of the planned investment curve. The figure is drawn on the assumption of a 5 percent per year expected rate of inflation. That brings an 8 percent nominal interest rate down to a 3 percent expected real rate. A lower expected rate of inflation would insert a thinner wedge between the two rates and a higher expected rate of inflation a fatter one.

How Large a Wedge? It would be simple enough to modify Exhibits 14.1, 14.3, 14.4, and 14.6 to take into account any given level of inflationary expectations. To do so, it would be necessary only to add a wedge of the kind shown in Exhibit 14.7. But how large a wedge? That is to say, what determines the expected rate of inflation at any one time? Economists are not altogether in agreement as to the answer.

Adaptive Expectations One hypothesis is that people form their expectations of future inflation primarily on the basis of the rate of inflation experienced in the immediate past. If inflation is rapid, people expect rapid inflation to continue; if prices are stable, they expect continued price stability. This is known as the **adaptive expectations** hypothesis, because it says that people's expectations about inflation adapt fairly quickly to what has recently happened to the price level.

Adaptive expectations Expectations about the rate of inflation or other future economic events formed primarily on the basis of experience in the recent past.

Rational Expectations Clearly, the adaptive expectations hypothesis makes a lot of sense, in that all it really says is that people tend to learn from experience. Some economists argue, however, that this hypothesis may be too restrictive. In forming their expectations about inflation, these economists say, people may not look only at the past rates of inflation that reflect the outcome of past economic policy. They may look also at policies presently being pursued or likely soon to be introduced and may try to judge the effects of these policies on the price level. Their judgments about the future effects of current and future policies are then combined with their lessons of past experience to form expectations about the future rate of inflation.

This view of how expectations are formed has come to be known as the **rational expectations** hypothesis, because it emphasizes the rational sifting and weighing of all available indications of how the price level might move in the future.

Rational expectations Expectations about the rate of inflation or other future economic events based on a rational weighing of all available evidence, including evidence on the probable effects of present and future economic policy.

Monetary Policy, Expectations, and Interest Rates The fact that inflationary expectations change in response to changing economic conditions and policies makes it necessary to modify the analysis of the effects of monetary policy on interest rates. Under the simplifying assumption of zero inflationary expectations used earlier in the chapter, expansionary monetary policy led to a new equilibrium in which both nominal and real interest rates were lower. In the real world, however, things are not always so simple.

Long-Term Effects Imagine, for example, that the economy is initially in an equilibrium with zero inflationary expectations and the nominal and real rates of interest both at 4 percent. Suppose that the Fed then undertakes a sustained, rapid expansion of the money supply, stimulating the growth of nominal GNP. Some of this growth will presumably take the form of growth of real output; but in the present case, suppose that nominal GNP grows too rapidly for real GNP to keep up. The difference between the growth of nominal and real GNP must be made up by inflation.

Initially, no inflation is anticipated; but as inflation continues, it comes to be expected. This drives a wedge between the nominal rate of interest and the expected real rate of interest. If inflation is rapid enough and continues long enough, the wedge will grow large enough to begin pushing up the nominal rate of interest. If, say, everyone comes to expect 6 percent per year inflation as the long-term norm, the initially assumed 4 percent nominal rate of interest surely cannot be maintained. The nominal rate would in principle rise to 10 percent, enough to restore the expected real rate to its original 4 percent. The conclusion, then, is that if the money supply is continuously expanded sufficiently to produce sustained inflation, the long-term effect will be to raise, not lower, nominal interest rates.

Short-Term Effects As a long-term proposition, this conclusion is now widely accepted. The short-term effects of monetary policy on interest rates are less settled, however, and depend in part on whether one emphasizes adaptive or rational expectations.

With purely adaptive expectations, the short-term effects of monetary expansion might well be exactly as represented earlier in this chapter: Both the nominal and real interest rates would be depressed. Only later, after the actual rate of inflation accelerated, would more rapidly rising prices begin to be reflected in expectations and in a higher nominal rate.

Rational expectations, however, introduce new possible short-term effects of policy changes. For example, under the Humphrey-Hawkins Act, the Fed is supposed to announce its plans for monetary expansion up to a year in advance. If it were possible to predict exactly the effects on the rate of inflation of the Fed's policy, borrowers and lenders would begin to take that amount of inflation into account from the day the announcement was made. If the announcement implied a higher than previously expected rate of inflation, nominal interest rates would jump upward immediately, even before the announced policy was put into effect. With full adjustment of the nominal rate, the expected real rate of interest might not change at all.

In practice, perfect forecasting of inflation is not possible. Highly paid professional "Fed watchers" try to guess the significance of every speech made by the Federal Reserve chairman, every minute variation in the federal funds rate, and every week's data on the monetary aggregates. More often than not, however, these Fed watchers cannot even agree among themselves. The short-run effects of monetary policy remain difficult to forecast.

CONCLUSIONS

In tying together fiscal and monetary policy, this chapter has rounded out the discussion of the determination of nominal national income and product. As the discussion of monetary policy and inflationary expectations made clear, it is time now to turn to the question of how the growth of nominal income is split up between inflation and the growth of real income. Only when we have thoroughly investigated that question will we be able to make a judgment as to what fiscal and monetary policy can and cannot hope to accomplish in promoting full employment, price stability, and economic growth.

SUMMARY

1. Analysis of the interaction between money and the multiplier requires moving from partial equilibrium analysis to general equilibrium analysis. What happens in the money market affects aggregate demand because any change in the interest rate changes planned investment expenditure. What happens to aggregate demand affects the money market, because movements in nominal national income shift the money demand curve.
2. The money market and the circular flow can both be in equilibrium at once only if a certain pair of values for the interest rate and nominal income prevail. With the money supply, autonomous consumption, the marginal propensity to consume, net taxes, and the position of the planned investment schedule given, the equilibrium values for nominal national income and the interest rate are unique.
3. An increase in government purchases has a somewhat weaker impact on the equilibrium level of nominal national income than a simple application of the multiplier theory predicts. The reason is that any growth in nominal income shifts the money demand curve to the right and pushes up the interest rate. This in turn crowds out some private investment, partially offsetting the increase in government purchases.
4. If the expected rate of inflation is assumed not to change, an increase in the money supply has the initial effect of depressing the nominal and the expected real rate. This stimulates planned investment, and aggregate demand increases. As nominal national income rises, the money demand schedule shifts to the right, limiting but not completely cancelling out the

fall in the interest rate. In the new equilibrium position, the interest rate will be lower and the level of nominal national income higher than before the monetary expansion.

5. Keynesian and monetarist economists have long debated the relative effectiveness of monetary and fiscal policy and the transmission mechanisms through which they influence the economy. The inflationary experience of the 1970s has added new elements of controversy—for example, over the role played by inflationary expectations in determining the effects of monetary policy.

DISCUSSION QUESTIONS

1. Suppose that you wanted to study the effect of a variation in rainfall on the prices of three agricultural products: corn, soybeans, and hogs. Do you think a general equilibrium approach or a partial equilibrium approach would give you more insight into the problem? Explain.
2. Use the theory presented in this chapter to trace the effects of a tax increase. What happens to national income, the interest rate, investment, and consumption?
3. Use the theory presented in this chapter to trace the effects of an increase in required reserve ratios on demand deposits. What happens to national income, the interest rate, investment, and consumption?
4. Suppose there is a contractionary gap in the economy. For the sake of discussion, assume that the government can with equal ease bring national income up to its target level by using expansionary monetary policy or by increasing government purchases. Suppose that the government also has a long-term goal of promoting rapid economic growth. Can you think of any reason for the government to use one policy rather than the other? Explain.
5. Would you say that the chairman of the Federal Reserve Board of Governors is one of the four most powerful people in the United States? Would your opinion have been the same before you read this chapter? Before you started this course?
6. Suppose that the Fed decided on a policy of pegging the nominal interest rate at some level, r, by smoothly expanding or contracting the money supply. (This policy could be represented graphically by drawing a horizontal rather than a vertical money supply curve.) Assume zero inflationary expectations. How would the policy affect the effectiveness of fiscal policy? What would happen to the crowding out effect? (Bonus question: Suppose the Fed attempted to peg the nominal interest rate in the face of rising inflationary expectations. What do you think would happen?)

APPENDIX TO CHAPTER 14 **THE ELEMENTARY ALGEBRA OF MONEY AND INCOME DETERMINATION**

This appendix is a continuation of the Appendix to Chapter 10, which developed a simple algebraic version of the multiplier theory. It adds no new theory to what has been presented in the body of Chapter 14. Nonetheless, readers who feel comfortable with elementary algebra may find the approach presented here useful in consolidating their understanding of the general theory of nominal income determination.

Throughout this appendix, the expected rate of inflation is assumed to be zero, as in the first part of the chapter.

AGGREGATE DEMAND

The basic equation for aggregate nominal demand or planned expenditure is:

$$AND = C + I + G + X - M. \quad \textbf{14A.1}$$

In the Appendix to Chapter 10, the C in this equation was replaced with a consumption schedule, which was written as:

$$C = a + b(Y - T), \quad \textbf{14A.2}$$

where a and b were constants representing autonomous consumption and the marginal propensity to consume, and Y − T stood for nominal disposable income. Now, I in Equation 14A.1 will also be replaced with a simple planned investment schedule:

$$I = c + dr, \quad \textbf{14A.3}$$

where I stands for planned investment and r for the interest rate, and where c and d are constants. The constant d, which is the reciprocal of the slope of the planned investment schedule, will have a negative value, because planned investment increases as the rate of interest falls.

Putting together Equations 14A.1, 14A.2, and 14A.3, the following general expression for the aggregate demand schedule is arrived at:

$$AND = a + c + b(Y - T) + dr + G + X - M. \quad \textbf{14A.4}$$

MONEY DEMAND

For a general equilibrium analysis of nominal income determination, a money demand schedule is also needed. The one used earlier, in Chapter 13, gave a money demand curve in the shape of a rectangular hyperbola. (Exhibit 13.1, for example, is based on the formula MD = 1.2Y/r.) To retain this kind of money demand schedule would involve the use of quadratic equations and would unnecessarily complicate the arithmetic, so it is replaced with a linearized money demand schedule written as:

$$MD = e + fY + gr, \quad \textbf{14A.5}$$

where MD stands for the quantity of money demanded, r for the interest rate, and Y for income and where e, f, and g are constants. The constant g is the reciprocal of the slope of the money demand schedule. It is negative because the quantity of money demanded decreases when the interest rate rises.

The reader is cautioned that this linear formulation of the money demand function has certain drawbacks. One is that, except for a certain central range of the variables, algebraic solution of the equilibrium equations (to be presented below) may produce negative values for income or the interest rate. Such negative values have no reasonable economic meaning. Care will be taken to keep within the safe range of values in the examples.

NUMERICAL VALUES

The constants in these equations can be replaced with representative numerical values to show how the algebraic formulations of planned expenditures and money demand can be put to work. Using $a = 100$, $b = 0.75$, $c = 200$, $d = -500$, $e = 80$, $f = 0.2$, and $g = -400$, Equations 14A.4 and 14A.5 can be rewritten as:

$$AND = 300 + 0.75(Y - T) - 500r + G + X - M \quad \textbf{14A.6}$$

and

$$MD = 80 + 0.2Y - 400r. \quad \textbf{14A.7}$$

EQUILIBRIUM CONDITIONS

As shown in the text of Chapter 12, the economy as a whole can be in equilibrium only when both the money market and the circular flow are in equilibrium. Money market equilibrium requires that money supply equal money demand, and equilibrium in the circular flow requires that national product be equal to planned expenditure. These equilibrium conditions can be written as:

$$MS = MD \qquad \textbf{14A.8}$$

for the money market, where MS stands for the money supply, and

$$Y = AND \qquad \textbf{14A.9}$$

for the circular flow.

Substituting Equations 14A.6 and 14A.7 into Equations 14A.8 and 14A.9:

$$MS = 80 + 0.2Y - 400r \qquad \textbf{14A.10}$$

and

$$Y = 300 + 0.75(Y - T) - 500r + G + X - M, \qquad \textbf{14A.11}$$

which simplifies to:

$$Y = 1200 - 3T + 4(G + X - M) - 2000r. \qquad \textbf{14A.12}$$

Equilibrium in the economy is possible only for pairs of values for r and Y that simultaneously satisfy Equations 14A.10 and 14A.12.

POLICY VARIABLES

Besides r and Y, there are five variables in Equations 14A.10 and 14A.12 for which numerical values have not yet been specified. Two of these values are X (exports) and M (imports). The problems that follow will be simplified by the assumption that imports equal exports, so that the two just cancel out and can be ignored. The remaining three variables are G (government purchases), T (net taxes), and MS (the money supply). These are collectively referred to as policy variables, because they stand for the elements of the economy that are under the direct control of the government. The following problems will show how the manipulation of these variables can be used by policy makers in their attempts to hit their economic targets.

Problem 1: Government policy makers set their policy variables at the values $G = 150$, $T = 100$, and $MS = 300$. Apply Equations 14A.10 and 14A.12 to determine the equilibrium values of r and Y.

Solution: Equation 14A.10 becomes:

$$300 = 80 + 0.2Y - 400r,$$

and Equation 14A.12 becomes:

$$Y = 1200 - 300 + 600 - 2000r.$$

Simplifying and setting the equations equal to zero:

$$220 - 0.2Y + 400r = 0$$
$$1500 - Y - 2000r = 0.$$

The usual methods for solution of simultaneous equations give the pair of values $r = 0.10$ and $Y = 1{,}300$ as the equilibrium levels for interest rate and national income.

Problem 2: Using the solution to Problem 1 as a starting point, assume that the authorities want to raise the equilibrium level of national income to a target level of $1,400, using monetary policy alone. How much will the money supply have to be increased to accomplish this objective?

Solution: Substitute Y = 1,400, G = 150, and T = 100 into Equation 14A.12 in order to find the required equilibrium value for r.

The substitution gives:

$$1400 = 1200 - 300 + 600 - 2000r,$$

which simplifies to:

$$100 - 2000r = 0.$$

The solution to this last equation is r = 0.05.

Next, substitute the equilibrium values Y = 1,400 and r = 0.05 into Equation 14A.10 in order to determine the money supply necessary to give a 0.05 rate of interest when national income is $1,400. This gives:

$$MS = 80 + 0.2(1400) - 400(0.05) = 340.$$

The solution to the problem, then, is that the money supply must be increased by $40—from $300 to $340—in order to raise national income to $1,400.

Problem 3: Using the solution to Problem 1 as a starting point, show that an increase of $50 in government purchases will be more effective in raising the equilibrium level of national income if the Fed pursues an accommodating monetary policy than if it leaves the money supply unchanged.

Solution: An accommodating monetary policy is one that expands the money supply enough to keep the interest rate unchanged—in this case equal to 0.10. Substitute the values T = 100, G = 200, and r = 0.10 into Equation 14A.12 to get the new value that equilibrium national income will reach if accommodating monetary policy is pursued. Without going into details, the new equilibrium Y with accommodating monetary policy is $1,500. (Further substitution of Y = 1,500 and r = 0.10 into Equation 14A.10 shows that the money supply would have to be increased to $340 to achieve this result.)

Without accommodating monetary policy, the new values of Y and r are found by going through the same steps outlined in the solution to Problem 1, using G = 200. Again without going into details, the solution turns out to be Y = 1,400 and r = 0.15. Substitution of the new, higher value of the interest rate into the investment schedule (I = 200 − 500r) shows that $25 of the original $150 in private planned investment is crowded out by the $50 increase in government purchases. This accounts for the lower equilibrium value of Y when accommodating monetary policy is not used.

SUGGESTIONS FOR FURTHER READING

Friedman, Milton, and Heller, Walter J. *Monetary versus Fiscal Policy.* New York: W. W. Norton, 1969.
A classic debate on the subject of this chapter.

Gordon, Robert J. *Macroeconomics.* Boston: Little, Brown, 1978, chaps. 4, 5.
A more advanced treatment of the material covered in this chapter.

Samuelson, Paul A. "Monetarism Objectively Evaluated." In *Readings in Introductory Economics,* edited by John R. McKean and Ronald A. Wykstra. New York: Harper & Row, 1971, pp. 120–132.
One Nobel Prize winner's evaluation of the work of another.

CHAPTER 15

UNEMPLOYMENT AND INFLATION: SOME TRADITIONAL ANSWERS

WHAT YOU WILL LEARN IN THIS CHAPTER

This chapter is the first in a section of four chapters devoted to inflation and unemployment. It introduces four traditional theories that attempt to explain how a given change in nominal national income and product affects employment, the price level, and real output. The theories are the quantity theory, the Keynesian theory, the Phillips curve theory, and the cost-push theory. None of them is in itself complete, but each contains an important element of truth.

FOR REVIEW

Here are some important terms and concepts that will be put to use in this chapter. If you do not understand them, review them before proceeding.

- *Goals of stabilization policy* (*Chapter* 7)
- *Theory of nominal income determination* (*Chapters* 8 *to* 14)

Chapter 7 introduced full employment, price stability, and economic growth as the major goals of macroeconomic policy. The seven chapters since then, however, have been concerned only indirectly with these policy goals. They have been devoted primarily to the question of what determines the level of *nominal* national income and product. Fiscal and monetary policies, the two main weapons in the government's macroeconomic policy arsenal, have been portrayed as determining nominal income and product instead of acting directly on employment, prices, and growth.

This chapter will discuss how a given change in the level of nominal national income and product is translated into specific effects on employment, prices, and real output. As pointed out earlier, the percentage rate of change in nominal GNP must always be equal, by definition, to the percentage rate of change in real GNP plus the percentage rate of inflation. If fiscal and monetary policy combine to bring about a nominal GNP growth rate of, say, 10 percent per year, it clearly makes a great deal of difference whether the rate is 8 percent real growth and 2 percent inflation or 2 percent real growth and 8 percent inflation.

The chapter starts by reviewing some traditional theories of the relationships among real and nominal income, inflation, and unemployment. Although none of these traditional theories is in itself sufficient to explain the complex macroeconomic events of the 1970s, each contains valid pieces.

Chapters 16 and 17 will show how these pieces can be fitted together to provide a comprehensive understanding of recent macroeconomic experience in the United States. Finally, Chapter 18 will review the subject and discuss a number of suggestions and recommendations regarding the future course of economic stabilization policy.

THE QUANTITY THEORY

The Income Velocity of Money

The first of the four traditional theories—the quantity theory—is also the oldest. It begins with the observation that as the circular flow of income and product churns around during the year, any given dollar, whether a dollar bill or a dollar's worth of demand deposits, is used again and again to conduct first one person's business and then another's. Chapter 13 introduced the *income velocity of money*—the average number of times each dollar is used for income generating purposes during a year. The income velocity of money is given by the formula:

$$V = \frac{Y}{M_1},$$

where V stands for velocity, Y for nominal national income, and M_1 for the quantity of money (defined traditionally to include currency and commercial bank demand deposits).

This formula can be rewritten by breaking down nominal national income into the product of two separate elements—real income (y) and the price level (P), which gives:

$$V = \frac{Py}{M_1}.$$

The equation can be further rewritten to isolate the element of price on the left-hand side, giving:

$$P = \frac{M_1V}{y}.$$

The Quantity Theory Itself

So far, no theory has been stated. All that has been done is to rewrite the definition of velocity. To turn the definition into a theory, two additional assumptions must be made. One is that the income velocity of money is at least approximately constant and is determined by customary and institutional factors. The other is that the level of real income is determined entirely by "real" factors such as population, technology, productivity, and capital stock. With both assumptions in place, the relationship $P = M_1V/y$ says that in a country with some predetermined level of real income, the price level is proportional to the quantity of money in circulation. It also follows that a given rate of growth of the money supply, with real income constant, will result in an equal rate of inflation.

Does It Work? Does the quantity theory of prices work—in the sense of providing a valid basis for scientific predictions about the relationship between prices and money? It appears that at least one prediction based on the theory is borne out by a surprisingly broad range of examples. The prediction is that if an economy is exposed to a sustained, rapid increase in its money supply, the result will be sustained, rapid inflation. The following case study suggests how widely this generalization applies.

Case 15.1
The Quantity Theory and the Collapse of the Cowrie System in West Africa

As early as the eighth century, the economic system of West Africa passed beyond the stage of primitive barter and became monetarized. The monetary unit was the cowrie shell. These shells were portable, easily identified, difficult to counterfeit, and scarce—which made them suitable as a medium of exchange, a store of value, and a unit of account. As an eighteenth century Dutch writer reported:

> What we call money being arbitrary, and its nature and value depending on tacit convention betwixt men, these shells, in several parts of Asia and Africa, are accounted current money, with a value assigned to them. This is established by a reciprocal consent, and those who are pleased to show a contempt of them do not reflect that shells are as fit for a common standard of pecuniary value as either gold or silver.[1]

But cowries were not everywhere as scarce as in West Africa. As commerce with Europe began to develop, English, Dutch, Portuguese, and French traders began to import them into the region from Europe and the Orient. For a time, the increase in the quantity of cowries apparently did not exceed what was needed to finance an expanding real volume of trade; but after about 1850, things got out of hand. Between 1850 and 1892, the price of an ox rose from 9,000 cowries to 60,000 and the price of kola nuts from 2,000 cowries to 50,000. At such price levels, cowries became impractical as a unit of currency; too many hours of labor would be required simply to count them. The cowrie system collapsed. Even today, however, cowries are reported in use as currency for small transactions in very rural areas in West Africa.

Source: Based on Okonwo A. Nwani, "The Quantity Theory in the Early Monetary System of West Africa, with Particular Emphasis on Nigeria, 1850–1895," *Journal of Political Economy* 83 (February 1975): 185–193. © 1975 by the University of Chicago. Used by permission.

Hyperinflation The example of the cowrie currency is only one of hundreds of similar episodes in world history. In this century, probably the most infamous inflation was that which occurred in Germany after World War I. Between 1919 and 1923, the quantity of money in circulation increased by a multiple of nearly 10 billion. This increase in the money supply, aided by an increase in velocity, pushed the price level up by a factor of more than 10 billion. At the height of the inflation, it was said to have taken a larger basket to carry one's money to the store than to carry one's groceries home. Very rapid and sustained inflation of this sort is called **hyperinflation.**

Hyperinflation Very rapid and sustained inflation.

Quantity Theory in the Short Run The quantity theory of prices is recognized as the leading theory of hyperinflation. For the purposes of short-term stabilization policy with which this book is primarily concerned, however, the quantity theory in its crude form is inexact at best.

One problem is that velocity is not really a constant. As shown in Chapter

[1] *A Voyage to the Island of Ceylon by a Dutch Gentleman* (London, 1754), as quoted in Okonwo A. Nwani, "The Quantity Theory in the Early Monetary System of West Africa, with Particular Emphasis on Nigeria, 1850–1895," *Journal of Political Economy* 83 (February 1975): 186.

13, it tends to vary in the same direction as changes in interest rates. Interest rates, in turn, are affected by both monetary and fiscal policy. This does not necessarily negate the monetarist proposition that the money supply is the major factor determining the level of nominal national product, provided that the changes in velocity are minor and reasonably predictable. But velocity sometimes changes unpredictably, which significantly complicates the use of the quantity theory for short-term forecasting.

Furthermore, even granting the monetarist view of the relationship between money and nominal national product, there remains the problem of how a given change in nominal national product will be split up between changes in prices and changes in real output. In the long run, changes in real output tend to be dominated by such factors as population growth, capital formation, and technological change, which are reasonably predictable. But in the short run, changes in real output depend strongly on changes in the unemployment rate. Thus another reason that the quantity theory of prices cannot be used for short-run purposes is that it does not provide a theory relating short-run changes in employment and real output to short-run changes in nominal national product.

These matters will be raised again in the next three chapters. For the moment, however, it is enough to conclude that the crude quantity theory contains a part of the key to the inflation-unemployment puzzle, but only a part. Another theory is presented now.

UNEMPLOYMENT, INFLATION, AND THE KEYNESIAN CROSS

Keynesian Theory

During the first two postwar decades, when periods of high unemployment alternated with periods of inflation, most economics textbooks featured a theory of unemployment and inflation that was based on simple Keynesian multiplier analysis. For want of a better term, this theory can be called the "crude Keynesian theory."

Exhibit 15.1 contains a Keynesian cross diagram of the familiar kind. Notice, though, that one significant change has been made. A point on the horizontal axis has been labeled "full employment national income." That label replaces the indication of a "target" level of national income that some of the earlier diagrams contained.

To get a theory of unemployment and inflation from this diagram, we can reason as follows: First, suppose that consumption, planned investment, and government spending are just sufficient to put the aggregate demand schedule at the level of AND_1. In this position, it intersects the aggregate nominal supply schedule exactly at the "full employment" level of nominal national income. By assumption, when equilibrium nominal national income is at this level, just enough goods will be demanded to keep everyone who wants a job busy. (To put it less casually, just enough goods will be demanded to keep all but 5 to 6 percent of the labor force at work, as measured by official statistics.)

Contraction of Nominal Demand Causes Unemployment Next, suppose that because of an error in policy or some unexpected change in private consumption or planned investment, the aggregate demand schedule slips to

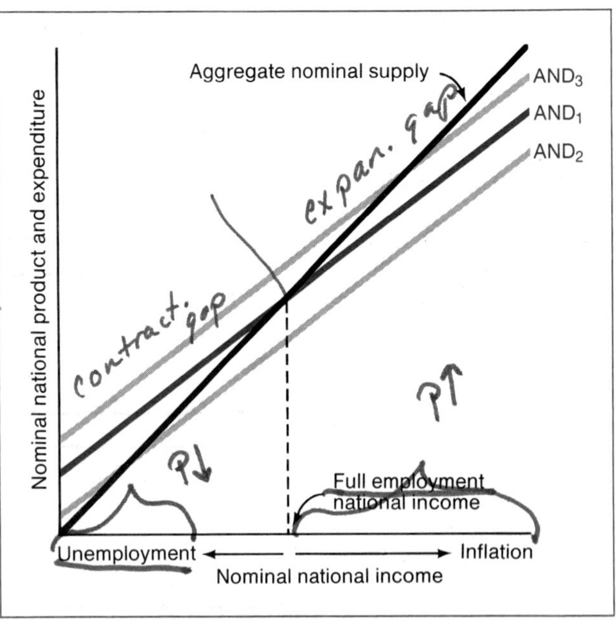

Exhibit 15.1
Inflation and the Keynesian cross
The crude Keynesian theory of inflation is based on this Keynesian cross diagram and some additional assumptions. When the aggregate demand curve is in position AND_1, it is assumed that real GNP will be sufficient to keep everyone employed. If the aggregate demand curve shifts to AND_2, it is assumed that the resulting fall in nominal GNP will take the form of reduced real output and increased unemployment. If the aggregate demand curve shifts to AND_3, it is assumed that all of the subsequent increase in nominal GNP will take the form of a price increase.

the level marked AND_2. This move creates a contractionary gap. Applying the multiplier theory, one can predict that this downward shift in planned expenditure will be followed by a downward movement of nominal national income. Now, one more crucial assumption is added. The assumption is that in the short run, at least, all or most of the downward movement of nominal national income below the full employment level will take the form of a fall in real income and product, and not much, if any, will take the form of a decline in prices. Because the lower level of real output requires fewer workers to produce it, the economy will experience a period of relatively high unemployment and price stability.

Expansion of Nominal Demand Causes Inflation Finally, assume that for one reason or another the aggregate nominal demand schedule shifts upward, reaching the position labeled AND_3 in Exhibit 15.1. This high level of planned expenditure produces an expansionary gap. In accordance with the multiplier theory, nominal national income rises. Remember, though, that everyone, or almost everyone, who wants a job now has one. It is not physically possible to squeeze more than a little extra real output from the economy above the full employment level. The rise in nominal national income that the multiplier theory requires can take place only in the form of an increase in the price level. As a result, the expansionary gap brings on a period of very low unemployment and inflation of the general price level.

Does It Work?

Like the crude quantity theory, the crude Keynesian theory has considerable intuitive appeal if applied in the proper time and place. In particular, the theory provides a fairly plausible reading of the record of inflation and unemployment in the United States from 1951 to 1969. Nonetheless, it cannot be judged entirely satisfactory for several reasons.

First, proponents of this theory have always had difficulty explaining why downward movements in nominal national income affect real output so much more strongly than they affect prices, at least in the short run. A number of hypotheses have been advanced by various authors, but none of them has ever been universally accepted. Also, it has sometimes been difficult to rationalize the various hypotheses in terms of microeconomic theory.

Second, where expansionary gaps are involved, the crude Keynesian theory tells us at most how much prices will rise but not how fast. Because inflation is by nature a matter of speed of change in the price level, the theory is thus seriously incomplete.

Finally, and clearly most seriously, the crude Keynesian theory is altogether unable to explain how high (and even rising) unemployment can occur simultaneously with high (and even rising) rates of inflation. For this reason, the theory has lost even its intuitive appeal as an explanation of unemployment and inflation in the 1970s.

THE PHILLIPS CURVE

Early Empirical Work

Economists place a strong emphasis on empirical work—work based on real-world data—as well as on abstract theorizing. Sometimes a single empirical study can suggest a whole new direction for a theory to take. A well-known research paper by British economist A. W. H. Phillips, outlined in the following case study, had such an impact.

Case 15.2
A. W. H. Phillips and the Phillips Curve

In 1958, A. W. H. Phillips published the results of some attempts he had made to test the simple hypothesis that wage rates tend to rise faster when unemployment is low than when it is high. The data he had available covered a very long period in the economic history of Great Britain, stretching from 1861 to 1957. The statistical evidence he assembled seemed to support the idea that the rate of change in money wages can be explained by the level of unemployment.

Phillips presented his results in a series of charts, one of which is reproduced here as Exhibit 15.2. This diagram contains a curve that represents the average relationship between unemployment and the rate of change of wages during the period 1861 to 1913. The points scattered near the curve show wage and unemployment data for the years 1948 to 1957. The fit of the modern years in Phillips's study to the curve calculated on much earlier data is remarkably close.

Source: A. W. H. Phillips, "The Relationship between Unemployment and the Rate of Change of Money Wage Rates in the United Kingdom, 1861–1957," *Economica* New Series 25 (November 1958): 283–299.

Phillips curve A curve showing the relationship between the rate of inflation and the level of unemployment. Inflation, usually placed on the vertical axis of such a figure, can be measured in terms of either the rate of change in wages or the rate of change in a price index.

Since the publication of Phillips's article, curves like the one in Exhibit 15.2 have come to be called **Phillips curves.** In recent years, the term *Phillips curve* has been broadened to include similar curves drawn on diagrams where the vertical axis measures the rate of change of prices (that is, the rate of inflation) instead of the rate of change of wages. Recent data for the United States will be presented in a Phillips curve framework in Chapter 17.

Exhibit 15.2
One of A. W. H. Phillips's original Phillips curves for the British economy
In 1958, A. W. H. Phillips published an influential paper that looked at the relationship between unemployment and the rate of change in wages over a long period in Great Britain. He found that data from the period 1948 to 1957 fit rather closely a curve based on data from the period 1861 to 1913, as shown here. Curves like this have since come to be called *Phillips curves.*

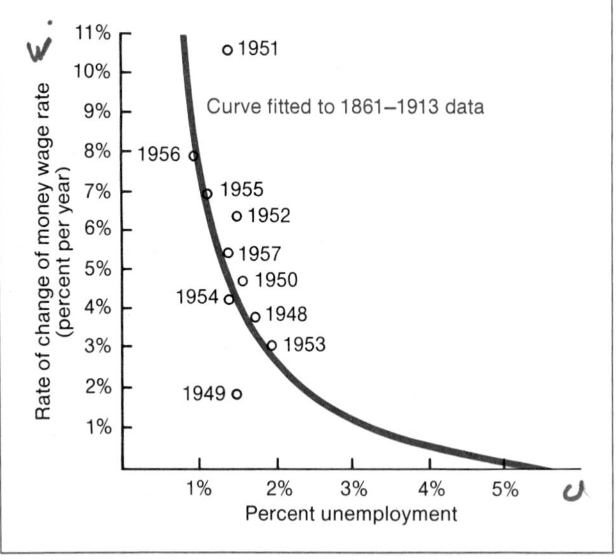

Source: A. W. H. Phillips, "The Relationship between Unemployment and the Rate of Change of Money Wage Rates in the United Kingdom, 1861–1957," *Economica* New Series 25 (November 1958): 283–299. Reprinted by permission.

Interpreting the Phillips Curve

Like the crude quantity theory and the crude Keynesian theory already examined, the intuitively appealing concept of the Phillips curve is open to serious misinterpretation when applied to economic policy. One tempting but misleading interpretation is to regard the curve as a menu of alternatives from which policy makers can choose a preferred compromise between the evils of inflation and unemployment.

A. W. H. Phillips was an economist whose reputation was based largely on a single paper published on the right topic at the right time. In the late 1950s, the relationship between inflation and unemployment ranked as the major unsolved problem of macroeconomic theory. The curves that Phillips drew in his famous article in *Economica* suggested a simple, stable relationship between inflation and unemployment. Phillips's paper offered little by way of a theoretical explanation of the relationship, but his curves became the peg on which all future discussion of the problem was hung. Almost immediately, every article on inflation and unemployment became a discussion of what was the shape of the Phillips curve, what point on the Phillips curve was best as a policy target, how the Phillips curve could be shifted, and so on. Today, the term is so well established that Phillips's name enjoys a sort of immortality even though his own interpretation of the famous curve has fallen into disrepute.

Phillips was born in New Zealand, but he made London his base for most of his academic career. He taught at the London School of Economics during the 1950s and 1960s until moving to the Australian National University in 1967. Phillips was originally trained in electrical engineering, and this training seems to have influenced his approach to economic problems, which has been characterized as "scientistic." In the mid-1950s he was suggesting the use of an "electric analog machine or simulator" as an aid to the study of economic dynamics. This idea perhaps foreshadowed the intensive use of electronic computers in contemporary economic research.

A. W. H. Phillips (1914–1975)

The Phillips Curve as a Menu Suppose, for example, that the president and the Council of Economic Advisers were presented with data that suggested the Phillips curve shown in Exhibit 15.3. It can easily be imagined that if the administration were a Democratic one, strongly influenced by union labor or sympathetic to the plight of the unemployed, it might pursue expansionary policies and aim for a point high up and to the left, such as the point marked D in the figure. In contrast, a Republican administration, dominated by conservative businesspeople and bankers, might aim for a point such as R, near the intersection of the Phillips curve and the horizontal axis.

Shifts in the Phillips Curve The trouble with interpreting the Phillips curve as a policy menu is that it may not stand still while the diners enjoy their meal. As the 1960s progressed, economists in the United States began to notice that inflation-unemployment points for recent years did not fit the Phillips curves they had plotted using data from the 1950s. It became common to speak of an upward drift in the Phillips curve. The menu seemed to be getting less appetizing as time went by. If the upward drift had been entirely spontaneous, policy makers could simply have been told to make the best of disappointing circumstances and still choose the point they liked best from the new, higher Phillips curve. However, to the extent that the shifts in the Phillips curve have been caused by the particular policies chosen to move the economy along a supposedly fixed curve, the idea of the Phillips curve as a policy menu needs to be reevaluated altogether.

Chapter 17 will explore further the way in which the choice of particular inflation and unemployment goals determines the position and rate of drift of the Phillips curve. Modern theories of inflation that economists are now developing do have a place for the Phillips curve, but the place is not quite the one that early interpreters had in mind.

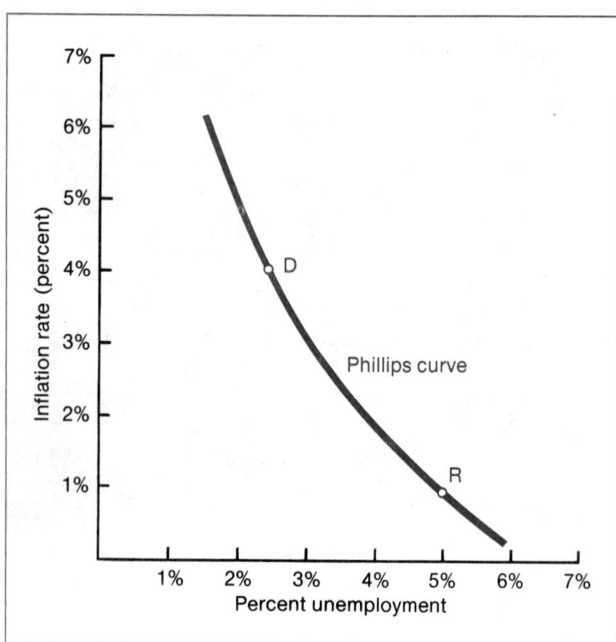

Exhibit 15.3
The Phillips curve as a policy menu
The Phillips curve is sometimes misleadingly interpreted as a policy menu offering a fixed trade-off between inflation and unemployment. If the curve for the U.S. economy had the shape shown here, it could be imagined that Democrats would want to choose a point like D, where low unemployment would be "bought" at the price of high inflation, while Republicans might prefer a point like R. Unfortunately for this interpretation, the Phillips curve is not stable. Policies designed to produce movements along it can cause it to shift to a new position.

THE COST-PUSH THEORY

Demand-Pull Inflation

All three of the theories looked at so far share the common element that inflation is touched off by a rise in aggregate demand. In the quantity theory, the excessive aggregate demand results from an injection of new money into the economy. In the Keynesian theory it is represented by a shift in the aggregate demand schedule to a position high enough to produce an expansionary gap. And according to the Phillips curve analysis, inflation does not become serious until demand has risen enough to produce a shortage of labor. Because all these theories single out a rise in aggregate demand as the initial cause of a rise in the price level, they are collectively referred to as **demand-pull theories of inflation.**

Demand-pull inflation Inflation that is initially touched off by an increase in aggregate demand.

Cost-Push Inflation

In the course of the 1950s and 1960s, economists began to realize that serious inflation could occur even when there was considerable slack in overall demand and a substantial level of unemployment. None of the demand-pull theories adequately explained this possibility, and it became increasingly popular to speak of a new kind of inflation, called **cost-push inflation.**

Cost-push inflation Inflation that is initially touched off by a spontaneous rise in wages, profit margins, commodity prices, or other elements of cost during a period of slack aggregate demand.

The Wage-Price Linkage The most commonly heard version of the cost-push theory runs something like this. Suppose that, initially, the economy is enjoying a period of relative price stability and moderate, but not unusually low, unemployment. Then it comes time for some powerful labor union in an important basic industry (say the steel industry) to renegotiate its contract with employers. Through aggressive bargaining and perhaps the threat or actual occurrence of a strike, the union wins a very generous raise for all its members.

Suppose the rise in wages is so high that it cannot be fully offset by increases in output per labor hour. If so, the cost of making a ton of steel goes up. Citing the increase in cost as justification, the steel companies raise their prices. Steel is used to make cars, refrigerators, apartment buildings, and hundreds of other things, so costs rise in all these other industries. The makers of the goods using steel all raise their prices, again citing the rise in costs as justification. The increase in the price of steel has now become a general increase in the price level.

As other union contracts expire, the bargaining becomes tougher and tougher. For one thing, the leaders of the auto workers, coal miners, teamsters, and so on have put their reputations on the line with their rank-and-file union members, who expect them to do as well as the steelworkers did. On top of that, union negotiators are now able to point to the rise in the cost of living as additional justification for giving their workers a fat wage package. The cost-push mechanism is now in full swing, and the initial spark has touched off an inflationary wage-price spiral.

Adherents of the cost-push theory of inflation point out that, over time, the average price level tends to move together with unit labor costs—that is, with the average cost of labor per unit of output. This is particularly true when volatile food and energy prices are excluded. Because unit labor cost is just average wages divided by output per worker, cost-push theorists stress that upward pressure on wages tends to cause upward pressure on prices, assuming that productivity remains constant.

Other Versions of the Cost-Push Theory Another version of the cost-push theory holds that the process need not start with a rise in wages. Other powerful economic interests may touch off the first spark. For example, it is often suggested that some large, highly concentrated industry like the automobile industry may initiate the cycle by unilaterally raising its prices simply to increase profits, even though there is no justification for the increase in terms of rising costs or rising demand. The resulting inflation is then called **profit-push inflation** to distinguish it from the **wage-push inflation** of the first scenario.

Profit-push inflation A variety of cost-push inflation in which a spontaneous increase in profit margins is the initial source of price increases.

Wage-push inflation A variety of cost-push inflation in which a spontaneous increase in nominal wage rates is the initial source of price increases.

Finally, the cost-push cycle may be touched off by a rise in the price of important basic commodities, such as oil or wheat. The initial source of commodity price rises may lie altogether outside the U.S. economy. It may involve such uncontrollable elements as Arab politics or the weather in Russia. Nonetheless, once underway, commodity price increases can spread throughout the economy by the cost-push mechanism, producing **commodity inflation.**

Commodity inflation A variety of cost-push inflation in which a spontaneous increase in commodity prices is the initial source of general price increases.

Does It Make Sense?

Does the cost-push theory of inflation make sense? The answer is that, like the other theories examined, it contains an element of truth; but that element is subject to strict qualifications. These qualifications are worth reviewing in detail.

drawbacks;

The Cost-Push Illusion The first qualification is the distinction between genuine cost-push inflation on the one hand and the **cost-push illusion** on the other. Because of the cost-push illusion, ordinary demand-pull inflation may look like cost-push inflation to those who are actually caught up in it. Milton Friedman uses a vivid example to illustrate the illusion. His story is based on a much longer parable told by A. A. Alchian and W. R. Allen.

Cost-push illusion The phenomenon that demand-pull inflation often looks like cost-push inflation to those caught up in it, because inventories cushion the immediate impact of demand on prices at each link in the chain of distribution from producers to retailers.

Case 15.3
The Cost-Push Illusion

Let us suppose in a country in which everything else is fine all of a sudden there is a great craze for increasing the consumption of meat, and all the housewives rush to the butchers to buy meat. The butchers are delighted to sell them the meat. They do not mark up the prices at all; they just sell out all the meat they have but they place additional orders with the wholesalers. The wholesalers are delighted to sell the meat. They clean out their inventories. They go back to the packing houses. The packing houses ship out their meat. The price is the same but the packing houses send orders to their buyers at the cattle market: "Buy more beef!" There is only a fixed amount of cattle available. And so the only thing that happens is that in the process of each packer trying to buy more beef, he bids up the price. Then a notice goes from the packer to the wholesaler. "We are very sorry, but due to an increase in our costs we are required to increase the price." A notice goes from the wholesaler to the retailer. And the retailer finally says to the customer when she comes in to complain that the beef has gone up: "I'm terribly sorry, but my costs have gone up." He's right. But what started the increase in costs all the way up and down the line? It was the housewife rushing in to buy the meat.

Source: Based on Milton Friedman, *Unemployment versus Inflation?* Institute for Economic Affairs Occasional Paper No. 44 (London: Institute for Economic Affairs, 1975), pp. 34–35. Originally appeared in Armen A. Alchian and William R. Allen, *University Economics: Elements of Inquiry,* 3rd ed. (Belmont, Calif.: Wadsworth, 1972). Used by permission.

The point of this example is that what is true for individuals is not necessarily true for the economy as a whole. Each person may raise prices only reluctantly and only when placed under severe pressure by a rise in wages and costs. But where does the pressure come from? It comes from an increase in demand, according to the critics of the cost-push theory of inflation.

What keeps the true cause of inflation from being evident to everyone is the existence of inventories at each link in the chain from producer to consumer. The initial impact of an increase in demand is a decline in inventories, first at the retail level, then at the wholesale level, then at the factory level, and so on. As businesspeople at each link in the chain increase their orders to replenish stocks, the process eventually reaches someone who cannot respond by pulling goods out of the inventories of the next person in line. This person may be the packer who has to buy beef at auction, the importer who has to bid for raw materials on world commodity markets, or the employer who can find new workers only by bidding them away from other jobs. Sooner or later, the rise in demand encounters the inescapable fact of the scarcity of resources, and then a price rise starts getting passed back up the chain of distribution.

The Direction of Causation A second qualification to the cost-push theory is also related to the question of the direction of causation. As mentioned above, the price level tends, over time, to move closely together with unit labor costs. Yet this does not necessarily mean that changes in wages are causing changes in prices. The wages employers are willing to pay workers are closely related to the value, at current market prices, of the output produced per hour by those workers. Even if the physical quantity of output produced per hour does not increase, an increase in the price of that output can provide a basis for raising wages. Thus wages rising to keep up with price increases, which themselves were caused by increases in demand, could produce the observed close relationship between the price level and unit labor costs.

Monopoly Power

A third qualification to the cost-push theory of inflation hinges on the concept of monopoly power. Economists say that a firm has **monopoly power** whenever it is able to raise the price of its product without losing all, or nearly all, its customers to competitors. Applied to the labor market, a union can be said to have monopoly power if it is able to obtain a substantial increase in the wages of its members without a serious loss of jobs to nonunion workers.

Monopoly power A seller's power to raise the price of a product without losing all, or nearly all, customers.

Most accounts of cost-push inflation depend on monopoly power to set the cost-price spiral in motion. Clearly, a union or a firm would not make the initial push in wages or prices if it did not think it could gain an advantage by doing so. Without monopoly power, making such a push would result only in a loss of jobs or sales to competitors. About the only exception to the rule that cost-push inflation has to begin in a relatively monopolistic part of the economy is commodity inflation set in motion by bad weather, which in turn leads to rising prices in the agricultural sector.

According to a well-established proposition of microeconomic theory, other things being equal, prices (or wages) will be higher in a market where sellers have substantial monopoly power than in a market where there is a high degree of competition. For any given degree of monopoly power, though, there will be a level beyond which prices cannot profitably be raised. In nontechnical language, this is a matter of charging all that the market will bear. Once the profit-maximizing equilibrium price (or workers' welfare-maximizing wage) is reached, the price (or wages) in a monopolistic market, although high, will stop rising.

Here, then, is the confusion that must be avoided. Monopoly power can cause high prices and wages, but there is no reason to expect it to cause steadily rising prices and wages. It follows that a firm or labor union with firmly established monopoly power is no more likely suddenly to push its prices or wages above the prevailing equilibrium level than one that operates in a fully competitive manner. Only a sudden increase in the degree of a firm's or union's monopoly power could cause the sudden increase in prices or wages needed to touch off the mechanism of cost-push inflation. No evidence has been found of any substantial increase in the monopoly power of either business or labor that could account for the acceleration of inflation over the last fifteen years.

Relative Prices Even if a sudden increase in monopoly power as a source of cost-push inflation could be identified, one more qualification would still be needed. Assume for the sake of discussion that some major union (make it the steelworkers again) wins a sudden large increase in wages. The increase is caused by the election of a new union leader, who is determined to bargain much more aggressively than the old one. The question is why this should cause a general increase in prices and wages, rather than just an increase in steel prices and steelworkers' wages relative to those in other sectors of the economy. That is, why will the increased prices and wages in the steel industry not be offset by lower prices and wages elsewhere?

Think of it this way. When the price of steel goes up, either the quantity of steel sold will be reduced, or the buyers of steel will have to spend more than before to buy the unchanged quantity. Very probably both will happen. If the quantity of steel produced falls, some steelworkers will be laid off. They will have to hunt for work elsewhere, and the presence of these new job seekers will tend to depress wages outside the steel industry. If buyers of steel spend more to purchase steel, they will have less left over to purchase other things. The demand for and prices of other goods will thus tend to fall. Instead of a general wage-price spiral, then, all the economy will experience is a shift in relative prices. The price of steel will go up, and the prices of other things will go down. As measured by a general price index, no significant inflation will occur.

This argument suggests that in order to have true cost-push inflation, something must prevent the smooth adjustment of relative prices and wages. Suppose that prices and wages in other sectors did not fall when steel prices and wages went up. Other sectors of the economy would not be able to absorb the newly laid off steelworkers, so they would have to stay home and draw unemployment. Real output would drop, and unemployment would rise. Price indexes would go up because steel prices would be higher and no other prices would be lower.

Cost-Push Summary All these qualifications together greatly narrow the range of circumstances in which the cost-push theory of inflation can be made to work. First, all those cases of demand-pull inflation that masquerade as cost-push inflation as a result of the cost-push illusion or as a result of wages rising to catch up with previous price movements must be eliminated. Second, there must be some factor or combination of factors that touches off the wage-price spiral. A rise in international commodity prices might be sufficient, but the simple presence of monopoly power is not by itself enough. Third, there must be some reason for inflexibility of wages and prices in all sectors of the economy, so that wage and price increases in one sector are not simply offset by wage and price declines elsewhere. These qualifications do not entirely undermine the validity of the cost-push theory, but they do indicate that we have quite a bit more work to do before we know how to apply it properly.

CONCLUSIONS

Each of the four traditional theories of inflation and unemployment presented in this chapter has something to recommend it. Each seems to fit the facts in some particular time or place. None is a completely general theory of inflation and unemployment, however. The theories are like the separate pieces of a puzzle not yet put together.

Putting together the unemployment-inflation puzzle is perhaps the most important single job for economists today. The job is by no means finished, but little by little the outlines of a picture are beginning to emerge. Perhaps the most fascinating feature of the emerging picture is that it appears to have room for all the pieces. As the modern theories of unemployment and inflation are developed in the next two chapters, it will be found that, properly qualified and interpreted, none of the four theories of this chapter directly contradicts any other. Taken together, there is reason to hope that they form a theory that can help policy makers guide the economy back toward full employment and price stability.

SUMMARY

1. The crude quantity theory of prices has a very long tradition in economic thought. It is based on the assumption that the velocity of money is a constant, so that prices are proportional to the money supply when real output is given. This theory appears to work fairly well during episodes of hyperinflation; but for practical short-run applications, a more sophisticated theory of velocity and real output is needed.
2. The crude Keynesian theory of inflation and unemployment is based on the usual Keynesian nominal income determination theory, plus a few other assumptions. One assumption is that there is a particular level of nominal income associated with full employment. A second assumption is that below this level, movements in nominal income take the form only of movements in employment and real output, with prices unchanged. A third assumption is that above the full employment level, movements in nominal income take the form of pure price movements. The crude Keynesian theory does not allow for the possibility that high rates of inflation and unemployment may occur at the same time.
3. A Phillips curve shows the relationship between inflation rates and unemployment rates for an economy. If the Phillips curve were stable, it would

provide a "menu" from which policy makers could choose according to their tastes. However, the curve is not stable. It turns out that its position is partly determined by the very policies that government authorities pursue when they try to choose a particular point on the curve.

4. The idea of cost-push inflation was introduced to explain how prices could rise when there was substantial slack in employment and aggregate demand. According to the theory, inflation can be touched off by spontaneous increases in profits, prices, or wages. In applying the cost-push theory, it is very important to distinguish between genuine cost-push inflation and the cost-push illusion.

DISCUSSION QUESTIONS

1. Milton Friedman writes, "Long-continued inflation is always and everywhere a monetary phenomenon that arises from a more rapid expansion in the quantity of money than in total output."[2] Why does he add the qualifying phrase *long-continued?* Can short-term inflation have other sources?
2. The crude Keynesian theory implies a sharply kinked, L-shaped Phillips curve. Explain why.
3. Some people maintain that unemployment is a painful human tragedy while inflation is just a matter of dollars chasing dollars. What sort of choice would such a person make if faced with a Phillips curve "menu" (assuming, for the sake of discussion, that the menu were a stable one)? Do you think that inflation, like unemployment, also affects people? If inflation is not "about people" but only "about dollars," why is it studied in an economics course?
4. Assume that in a country where everything else is fine, there is suddenly an outbreak of hoof and mouth disease that sharply decreases the supply of beef cattle. Would the resulting rise in the price of beef be true cost-push inflation? Trace this kind of inflation through the marketing chain for beef. At what points would it look different from demand-pull inflation? At what points would it be hard to tell the difference?

---

[2]Milton Friedman, *Monetary Correction*, Institute for Economic Affairs Occasional Paper No. 41 (London: Institute for Economic Affairs, 1974), p. 10.

CHAPTER 16

A CLOSER LOOK AT UNEMPLOYMENT

WHAT YOU WILL LEARN IN THIS CHAPTER

This chapter explores some key relationships among the goals of full employment, price stability, and real economic growth. Changes in the unemployment rate are analyzed in terms of flows of individuals into and out of employment, unemployment, and the civilian labor force. These changes in turn are shown to be associated with changes in the growth rate of real output. A theory of job search that relates changes in the unemployment rate to changes in the average duration of unemployment is introduced. The final section of the chapter surveys a number of alternatives for permanently lowering the rate of unemployment.

FOR REVIEW

Here are some important terms and concepts that will be put to use in this chapter. If you do not understand them, review them before proceeding.

- *Stocks and flows (Chapter 5)*
- *Employment, unemployment, and the civilian labor force (Chapter 7)*
- *Humphrey-Hawkins Act (Chapter 7)*
- *Potential real GNP (Chapter 7)*

The goals of economic stabilization policy, as mentioned repeatedly in this book, are full employment, price stability, and economic growth. In manipulating aggregate nominal demand through the use of fiscal and monetary policy, government authorities attempt indirectly to advance these goals. Their efforts, however, are not always successful. Sometimes, attempts to promote economic growth and employment through expansionary monetary and fiscal policy result largely in undesired acceleration of inflation. At other times, attempts to restrain inflation by dampening aggregate nominal demand slow real economic growth, increase unemployment, and have little of the hoped-for effect on the price level. In order to judge when fiscal and monetary policy are and are not likely to have their desired effects, we clearly need to know more than we yet do about the interrelationships among full employment, price stability, and real growth. This chapter will focus on how unemployment is affected by changes in the rate of inflation and the rate of real economic growth. It will pave the way for the discussion of the dynamics of inflation in the next chapter.

UNEMPLOYMENT, JOB SEARCH, AND INFLATION

Sources of Changes in the Unemployment Rate

In Chapter 7, the unemployment rate was defined as the ratio of two stocks of workers—those officially counted as unemployed to those officially counted in the civilian labor force. Changes in the unemployment rate thus occur as the result of flows into and out of the underlying stocks. Exhibit 16.1 shows the major employment flows connecting the important employment stocks originally shown in Exhibit 7.1. (For simplicity, flows into and out of the noninstitutional adult civilian population are ignored.)

Employment Flows Look at flows into and out of the civilian labor force in the exhibit. Flows into the labor force, labeled as *entries,* can be either successful or unsuccessful. A successful entrant finds a job immediately; an

Exhibit 16.1
Unemployment stocks and flows

This exhibit shows the relationship between major stocks and flows within the noninstitutional adult civilian population. When new jobs are created, they can be filled either by workers previously unemployed or by workers just entering the labor force. Sometimes, new workers enter the labor force without immediately finding work; this is called unsuccessful entry. Workers quitting or losing their jobs may either become unemployed or leave the labor force directly.

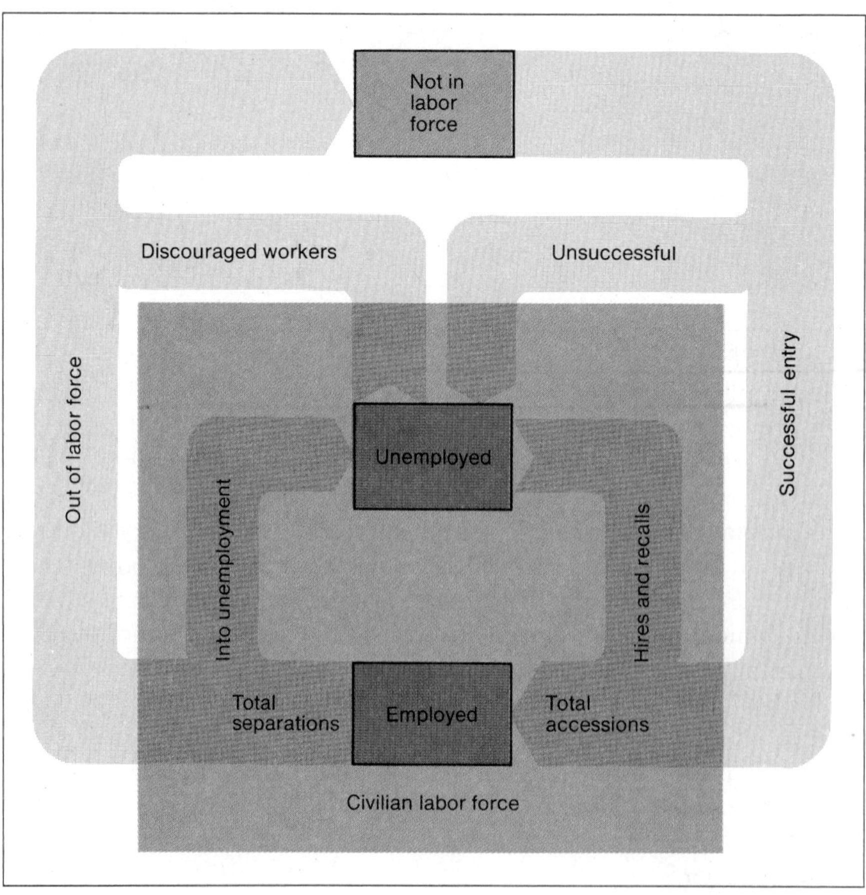

unsuccessful entrant begins actively looking for a job but does not immediately find one and thus becomes officially unemployed.

Two kinds of flows out of the labor force are also shown in the exhibit. First, people can quit or lose their present jobs and not look for others. Second, discouraged workers can stop looking for a job after a period of unemployment during which they have never found one. In either case, once they stop looking for a job, they are considered to have left the labor force.

Next, turn to the flows into and out of employment. A person can become employed either by being hired for a new job or by being recalled to a former job. Hires plus recalls are shown in the diagram as *total accessions.* There are also a number of ways to leave employment. They include being fired, being laid off, quitting, or retiring. The sum of all of these ways is shown as *total separations.*

Finally, turn to the flows into and out of unemployment. Additions to the stock of the unemployed occur whenever people enter the labor force unsuccessfully or whenever they are separated from a job and begin immediately to look for a new one. Subtractions from the stock of the unemployed occur when unemployed job searchers find jobs or when they stop looking and leave the labor force. The number of unemployed people grows or shrinks depending on whether additions to the number exceed or fall short of subtractions from it.

The Unemployment Rate versus the Employment Rate A careful study of the stocks and flows shown in Exhibit 16.1 reveals a peculiarity of the unemployment rate that has not yet been mentioned: Increases in the number of jobs supplied by the economy are not necessarily reflected in decreases in the unemployment rate. The reason is that the unemployment rate is measured as a percentage of the number of people in the labor force, not as a percentage of the entire working age civilian population. When the economy expands and new jobs are created, not all of those jobs are filled by people who were previously unemployed. The knowledge that more jobs are available also draws more people into the labor force. Some of the new entrants fill some of the jobs, but others do not immediately find jobs and therefore become unemployed. Because expansion of the economy draws more people into the ranks of both the employed and the unemployed, the unemployment rate does not necessarily fall.

This possibility has led some observers to suggest that the unemployment rate, widely publicized though it is, is not always a very good measure of the country's macroeconomic performance. Consider, for example, the six-month period from April through September 1978. The unemployment rate in the United States started this period at 6 percent and ended it at exactly the same level. During the period, the number of unemployed persons increased by 19,000. Those figures indicate that the economy was doing poorly in terms of the employment goal of macroeconomic policy. But other figures tell quite a different story. The total number of people employed, for example, increased by a healthy 1,067,000 over the period. The economy was in fact expanding rapidly in terms of both employment and real output, and the only major policy worry was an accelerating rate of inflation.

In order not to be misled by the official unemployment index, many economists recommend shifting the focus of policy from the unemployment rate to the employment rate. The **employment rate** measures the number of

Employment rate The ratio of the number of people employed to the number of people in the noninstitutional adult civilian population.

people employed as a percentage of the entire noninstitutional adult civilian population rather than as a percentage of the labor force. Between April and September 1978, the employment rate rose from 59.2 percent to 59.5 percent, correctly signaling the direction in which the economy was moving.

Okun's Law

The employment stocks and flows represented in Exhibit 16.1 are helpful in understanding an important relationship between unemployment and real economic growth. The relationship is known as **Okun's law,** after Arthur Okun, a member of the Kennedy-Johnson Council of Economic Advisers at the time he originally proposed the relationship.

Okun's law A rule of thumb according to which for each three percentage points by which real economic growth exceeds (or falls short of) the growth rate of potential real GNP in any year, the unemployment rate will tend to fall (or rise) by one percentage point.

Okun's law is based on the concept of potential real output introduced in Chapter 7. In the long run, potential real output tends to grow as the result of population growth, growth of labor force participation, and growth of output per worker. In the early 1960s, when Okun formulated his law, potential real output was growing at a rate of about 4 percent; but recent estimates suggest that it has slowed to about 3 percent.

As long as actual real output follows the growth path of potential real output, Okun said, the rate of unemployment does not change. Changes in the unemployment rate thus tend to be associated with deviations of the actual

---

Arthur Okun (1928–   )

Arthur Okun is one of the best known of a generation of "new economists" who dominated economic policy making during the Kennedy and Johnson administrations of the 1960s. In 1961, the young associate professor left Yale to join the "New Frontier" as a staff economist on the President's Council of Economic Advisers. In 1964, he became a full member of the council and eventually, in 1968–69, its chairman. When Johnson left office, Okun stayed in Washington as a senior fellow of the Brookings Institution, a position that permitted him to combine research with active public affairs involvement.

Okun's name is perhaps most widely heard in connection with his famous "law" relating changes in unemployment to changes in real national product. This noteworthy empirical generalization was first formulated in a paper, "Potential GNP, Its Measurement and Significance," written for the American Statistical Association in 1962. In this paper, Okun tried to answer the question of how much output the economy could produce under conditions of full employment. Because of his concern for "the enormous social cost of idle resources," he found this question a central one for economic policy.

During the time Okun was on the Council of Economic Advisers, "growthmanship" was at its height in the economics profession. Okun saw rapid economic growth as crucial to avoiding the waste and extravagance of unemployment. "The economy loses ground if it stands still," he wrote. He added:

> Unless the growth of output keeps pace with our ever-expanding potential, the unemployment rate tends to rise. The nation needs continually to set new records in production and sales. Its economy needs to grow bigger and better than ever before—because its labor force, capital stock, technology, and managerial and organizational resources are always getting bigger and better.

Okun's recent work reflects the change from the optimistic growth oriented 1960s to the problem-ridden, inflation dominated 1970s. Okun contributed to the understanding of chronic inflation and has proposed a variety of initiatives to combat it, including the reduction of sales and payroll taxes and the provision of tax rewards for wage-price restraint. In 1979, Okun was awarded the Seidman Foundation prize for his impact on public policy.

growth rate of real output from the growth rate of potential output. Using actual data for the postwar U.S. economy, Okun found that for each one percentage point that the growth rate of real output fell short of the growth rate of potential output in a given year, unemployment tended to rise by approximately a third of a percentage point. Similarly, for each one percentage point by which the growth rate of real output exceeded the growth rate of potential output, unemployment tended to fall by a third of a percentage point. Assuming the growth rate of potential real GNP to be 3 percent, then, the unemployment rate would be expected to drop by one percentage point in a year when actual real output grew at 6 percent and to rise by one percentage point in a year when the growth rate of real output was zero.

A major reason that more than a one percentage point increase in the growth of real GNP is required to produce a one percentage point drop in the unemployment rate is that real growth not only provides new jobs for those who would otherwise be unemployed but also draws additional workers into the labor force. Some of these new workers take jobs immediately, and some become unemployed for a time while they look for jobs. The measured unemployment rate thus fails to fall point by point with the rise in the growth rate of real output.

The Duration of Unemployment

The picture of the state of the job market given by the unemployment and employment rates together is more complete than the picture given by the unemployment rate alone, but it is still incomplete in one important respect. Nothing has yet been said about the average *duration* of unemployment.

An economy in which each worker was out of work for about five weeks of each year would have an unemployment rate of about 10 percent; so would an economy in which 10 percent of the labor force was out of work for the entire year while the other 90 percent experienced no unemployment at all. The social implications of unemployment in the two economies, however, would clearly be quite different. The long-term unemployment of even a few people is of much more concern politically than the frequent occurrence of very short spells of unemployment for a large number of workers.

As might be expected, unemployment in the U.S. economy presents a mixed picture in terms of duration. Exhibit 16.2 gives data for ten recent years. In 1969, the best year shown, more than half of those unemployed at any one time had been out of work for under five weeks, and only one in twenty had been out of work for over six months. Even in years of high unemployment, such as 1975, short spells of unemployment are more common than long ones.

Frictional Unemployment Economists refer to the portion of unemployment accounted for by people spending relatively short periods between jobs as **frictional unemployment.** The presence of frictional unemployment is the major reason that the policy goal called full employment can never mean a zero rate of unemployment. Frictional unemployment is present in good times as well as bad. Each month, many people voluntarily quit their jobs to look for better ones. This keeps the measured unemployment rate up, but it is nothing to worry about. Quite the contrary. A normal level of frictional unemployment is a sign of a healthy economy—the means by which workers become matched with better jobs.

Frictional unemployment That portion of unemployment accounted for by people spending relatively short periods between jobs.

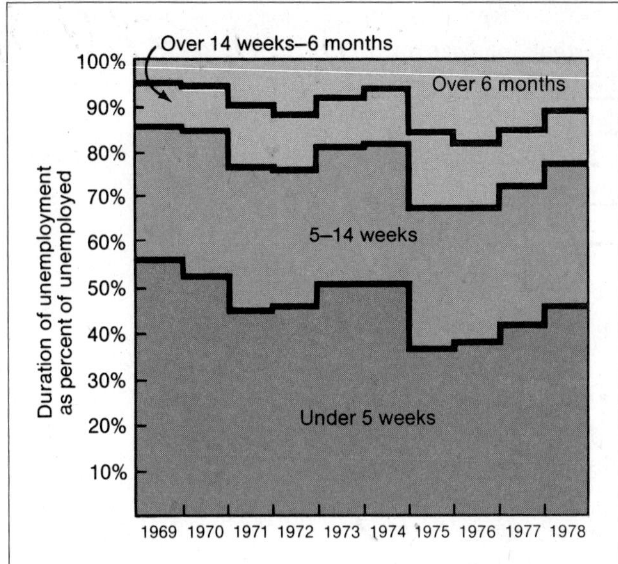

Exhibit 16.2

Duration of unemployment spells, 1969–1978

As this exhibit shows, there is considerable variation in the length of unemployment spells experienced by unemployed workers. In times of lower overall unemployment, over half of all unemployed workers are out of work for under five weeks, and only 5 percent are out of work for over six months. In years of peak overall unemployment, the proportion of those out of work for half a year or more approaches 20 percent; but even so, well over a third are unemployed for under five weeks.

Source: President's Council of Economic Advisers, *Economic Report of the President* (Washington, D.C.: Government Printing Office, 1979), Table B-31.

Dual labor market The division of the labor market into a primary sector, containing good jobs with established firms, and a secondary sector, containing low-paid, unstable jobs with marginal firms.

Dual Labor Market More serious policy problems are raised by the minority of workers who spend long periods in the ranks of the unemployed or who become unemployed frequently. According to one often heard theory, these workers are victims of a **dual labor market**. The idea is that the primary sector of the labor market contains high-wage jobs with large, profitable firms. These jobs are likely to be unionized, to offer more opportunities for advancement, and to be less affected by the ups and downs in business activity. The secondary sector of the labor market, in contrast, contains low-paying jobs with marginal firms, which are held by unorganized workers with unstable work patterns. These are largely dead-end jobs offering few opportunities for advancement. They are heavily hit by cyclical swings in unemployment.

Because secondary sector jobs are unattractive, workers who are not qualified for primary sector jobs typically have short periods of employment, often because they quit rather than because they are laid off. These periods alternate with long periods of vainly trying to find something better. The special policy problems raised by unemployment in the secondary labor market will be examined later in the chapter.

Unemployment and Job Search

We have seen that the unemployment rate depends on the balance between flows of workers into and out of the stock of the unemployed. The balance is a rather delicate one, as flows into and out of unemployment are quite large in comparison with the number of workers unemployed at any one time. Depending on the time of year, some 4 to 6 percent of all workers experience a change in employment status each month. It follows that anything that happens to change even slightly the average length of time a worker remains unemployed can have a very significant impact on the measured rate of unemployment. The tendency for the average duration of unemployment to move closely together with the unemployment rate is shown clearly in Exhibit 16.3.

Exhibit 16.3
The unemployment rate and the average duration of unemployment, 1969–1978

The unemployment rate and the average duration of unemployment tend to move closely together over time. In 1969, when the unemployment rate was at the very low level of 3.5 percent, the average duration of unemployment spells was under 8 weeks. The average duration of unemployment reached a peak of 15.8 weeks in 1976, one year after the unemployment rate reached its peak of 8.5 percent, largely because the recovery of 1976 benefited the short-term unemployed more quickly than the long-term unemployed.

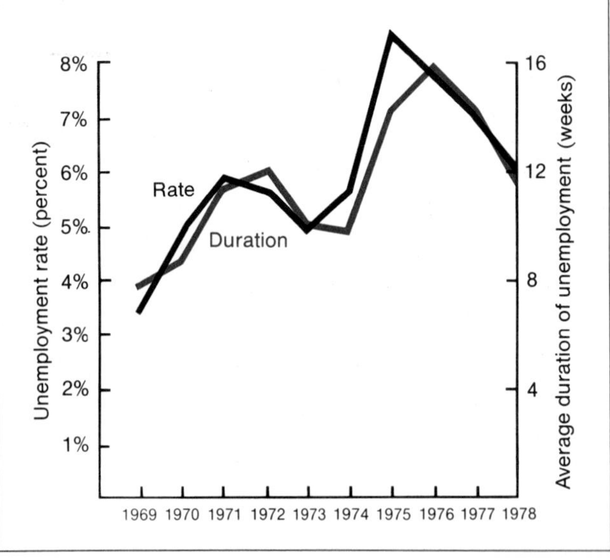

Source: President's Council of Economic Advisers, *Economic Report of the President* (Washington, D.C.: Government Printing Office, 1979), Tables B–29, B–31.

For this reason, much recent work on the theory of unemployment has focused closely on the process of job search as a key to the average duration of unemployment and hence to the measured unemployment rate. There are many variations of the job search theory of unemployment, and new ideas are still being put forth and tested. Certain basic assumptions, though, are shared by almost all economists working in this field.

Information One basic assumption underlies all job search theories: the notion that workers looking for jobs and employers looking for workers operate without complete information of one another's needs or requirements and without complete information about future economic trends. The job search process is essentially a matter of putting the labor market to work as a mechanism for distributing information.

Consider an individual unemployed worker who is looking for a new job. At the start of the job search, he or she knows that "somewhere out there" are a number of employers looking for workers. The first necessity is to find out who and where these employers are and what their jobs are like.

The jobs will not all be equally good. For one thing, some will pay better wages than others. In addition, some will offer pleasant surroundings and some will not, some will be near and others far, and some will be stimulating and others dull. To keep things simple, the discussion will deal only with wage differences among jobs; but the job seekers themselves will, of course, make mental adjustments in wage offers to allow for nonwage advantages and disadvantages of any job.

The worker, then, sets out to sample the available jobs. Common sense indicates that people will not automatically take the first job offered. To play it safe, even after getting one job offer, they often will check a few more potential employers to see if something better will turn up. On the average, the larger the number of jobs they include in their sample, the better will be the best wage offer they come across.

The Reservation Wage

There is a limit, however, to the length of time people will search for a job when jobs are available. That limit can be expressed in terms of a reservation wage. A person's **reservation wage** is the wage (adjusted for nonmonetary advantages of the job, as always) below which he or she will not accept an offer. A person who has a reservation wage of $150 per week, for example, will reject any offer of $149 a week or less and take any job that offers $150 a week or more.

Reservation wage The wage (adjusted for nonmonetary advantages and disadvantages of a job) below which a person will not accept a job offer.

People's reservation wages tend to decline the longer their job search continues. There are at least two reasons for this. First, the people may initially be very optimistic, overestimating their own worth in the eyes of potential employers, and then gradually become more realistic as the hoped-for top-level offers do not materialize. Second, even if unemployment insurance is available, long periods without work tend to cut into people's savings, and financial pressure to get back to work increases. Empirical studies confirm the idea that reservation wages decline as the job search period lengthens.

Determining the Duration of Unemployment

The idea of repeated sampling to find the best job offer plus the idea of a declining reservation wage offers a simple theory of the duration of unemployment. Exhibit 16.4 gives a graphical presentation of the theory. An upward-sloping curve is drawn in the diagram to show that, on the average, a worker can find a better job offer by spending more time in the job search. A downward-sloping curve is drawn to show how the worker's reservation wage falls as time goes on. The two curves come together the first time the worker gets a job offer that meets that worker's reservation wage. This takes five weeks on the average as the figure is drawn. The worker takes the job, and the period of unemployment is at an end.

Two things should be stressed about this figure. First, the curves express averages for workers of similar skills and experience. Individual workers may, simply by good luck, find offers meeting their reservation wage on the first or second try. Others, less lucky, may have to look longer than average before they find something they will accept. Second, the positions of the curves, and hence

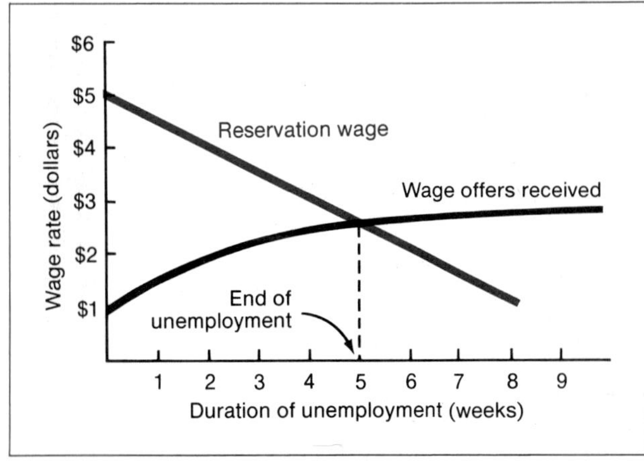

Exhibit 16.4
Determination of the average duration of unemployment

The longer people search for jobs, the better, on the average, will be the best wage offers they uncover. At the same time, the longer they search, the lower their reservation wages tend to fall. In this exhibit, the duration of unemployment is determined by the intersection of the reservation wage curve and the wage offer curve. It indicates the point at which people first receive job offers that meet their reservation wage.

the average length of the job search, may be very different for workers at different skill levels. In particular, for workers in the secondary labor market, wage offers received are likely to be very low. At the same time, hope for something better, even if unrealistic, keeps the reservation wage from falling very rapidly. This can stretch out the period of unemployment to many months.

Job Search and Inflation

The job search theory just outlined, simple though it is, provides many useful insights into what happens to unemployment when economic conditions change. For example, if the number of job seekers increases while other things (including the number of job openings) remain unchanged, there will be more competition for the available jobs. Each unemployed person will, on the average, have to search longer before finding an acceptable job that some other worker has not found first. The average duration of unemployment and the unemployment rate will thus rise. On the other hand, if the number of job openings increases while other things (including the number of job seekers) remain unchanged, it will be easier for the average worker to find an acceptable job. The duration of unemployment and the unemployment rate will fall. Variations such as these in the number of job openings and the number of job seekers play an important role in causing ups and downs in the unemployment rate from month to month and year to year.

The job search theory also proves very helpful in understanding the effects of inflation on unemployment. Because these effects will play a central role in the discussion of the dynamics of inflation in the next chapter, it will be worthwhile to look at them in some detail here.

The Effects of Unexpected Inflation From earlier discussions of financial markets, we are already familiar with the notion that unexpected inflation can produce effects that are quite different from those produced by expected inflation. This is as true in the case of job markets as it is in the case of financial markets. We begin by looking at the effects of unexpected inflation on the process of job search.

Imagine an economy in which neither prices nor wages have been changing in the recent past and in which neither is expected to change in the immediate future. Suppose that under these initial conditions, the average duration of unemployment is five weeks and the measured unemployment rate is 5 percent. Suddenly, out of the blue, all prices and nominal wages begin to rise. What will happen?

Look at things from the point of view of the unemployed job seekers. By assumption, they do not expect prices to go up. It does not occur to them that during the period they work at their new jobs, it will cost them more to live than before. Also by assumption, they do not know that wages in general have gone up, so they do not immediately reconsider their own estimates of their value to potential employers. Unexpected inflation thus has no initial effect on their reservation wages. What does happen is that before they have searched very long, they get nominal wage offers that look pretty good. Operating on their own, with incomplete information, job seekers are likely to consider such high wage offers to be isolated pieces of good luck. They will quickly accept the jobs.

No individual job seeker realizes, of course, that many other job seekers are also experiencing "good luck" and taking under five weeks, on the average, to find jobs. The decrease in the average duration of the job search shows up as a drop in the measured unemployment rate. The conclusion is that unexpected inflation causes unemployment to fall.

The Effects of Expected Inflation It will not take too long, of course, for workers to catch on to what is happening. Unexpected inflation then becomes expected inflation. The effects of expected inflation are quite different.

Expected inflation, unlike unexpected inflation, does cause reservation wages to rise. If wages and prices begin rising by, say, 5 percent per year, and job seekers know it, it is easy to see what they will do. Expecting prices to be higher than before, they will reestimate the level of the nominal wage they will need to keep up with the cost of living. Also, expecting wages to be higher than before, they will know that the first high nominal wage offer they get is not an isolated bit of good luck but part of a general trend. They will not need to grab at that job because later offers may be even better.

In fact, if inflation is fully expected by all workers and employers, it will have no real impact on the labor market. Workers will know that by waiting they will get better nominal wage offers but that the cost of living will be going up just as fast as the wage offers. Employers will know that the higher nominal wages they have to pay each year will be entirely offset by the prices they will get for the products they sell. No one will be any better off or any worse off than if neither prices nor wages changed at all. Job seekers will behave no differently than they would if prices and wages were stable.

The Effects of False Expectations There is a third case to consider—that in which people falsely expect prices to rise when in fact they are remaining stable. If wages and prices stopped rising but workers still expected them to go up by 5 percent a year, the search for jobs would become more difficult. People would raise their reservation wages, thinking that they needed the extra money to cover a higher cost of living. They would expect average nominal wage offers to rise also, but these offers would not rise. The workers, operating in isolation from one another, might well think that they were just having uncommonly bad luck. For a while, at least, they would keep looking for jobs that met their expectations. Eventually, they would either really get lucky and find one or become discouraged and lower their reservation wages to realistic levels. Meanwhile, though, the average duration of their job search would have risen, and so would the measured unemployment rate.

The Natural Rate of Unemployment

Some important generalizations can be drawn from the preceding discussion of the effects of inflation on job search and unemployment. First, job search theory suggests that a higher rate of inflation than workers expect tends to shorten the average duration of unemployment and lower the unemployment rate. If the actual rate of inflation is lower than expected, in contrast, the duration of unemployment lengthens and the unemployment rate rises. In the middle lie all cases where the expected and actual rates of inflation are just equal. This middle ground includes the special case where the actual and expected rates of inflation are zero—that is, the case of price stability.

The case of fully anticipated inflation, when the price level changes neither more nor less rapidly than it is expected to, provides an important benchmark for economic policy. To emphasize its importance, a special term will be used to refer to the rate of unemployment that prevails when the actual rate of inflation equals the expected rate of inflation. That rate is called the **natural rate of unemployment.** It is natural not in the sense that it is a god-given constant beyond the influence of economic policy. Instead, it is natural in the sense that it is the rate of unemployment that prevails when everyone knows what is going on and no one is fooled. Because it is the rate of unemployment that prevails when everyone has accurate knowledge of market conditions, it can also be called the equilibrium rate of unemployment. The term *natural rate,* however, is too well-established to abandon.

Natural rate of unemployment The rate of unemployment that would prevail if the expected rate of inflation were equal to the actual rate of inflation.

The Phillips Curve and the Natural Rate of Unemployment

Chapter 15 introduced the Phillips curve to represent the trade-off between inflation and unemployment. The curve contained an element of truth, but it seemed to shift over time. The job search theory of unemployment now offers an explanation of why the Phillips curve can shift from one year to another.

Consider Exhibit 16.5, in which three Phillips curves are sketched. Each curve represents the short-run trade-off between unemployment and inflation for a given expected rate of inflation. On each curve, unemployment is at the natural rate (here assumed to be 5 percent) when the actual and expected rates of inflation are equal.

If people expect the rate of inflation to be 2 percent, but in fact inflation accelerates to 3.5 percent, the economy will move up and to the left along the middle Phillips curve, from Point A to Point B. If people expect the rate of inflation to be 4 percent, but in fact it slows to 3.5 percent, the economy will

Exhibit 16.5

Expected inflation and the shifting Phillips curve

The position of the Phillips curve depends on the rate of expected inflation, and the rate of unemployment depends on the relationship between the expected rate of inflation and the actual rate. With expected inflation at 2 percent, for example, an acceleration of actual inflation to 3.5 percent would lower the unemployment rate, moving the economy from Point A to Point B. Unemployment is at the natural rate whenever actual and expected inflation are equal. Because expectations eventually catch up to any sustained rate of inflation, the long-run Phillips curve is vertical at the natural rate of unemployment.

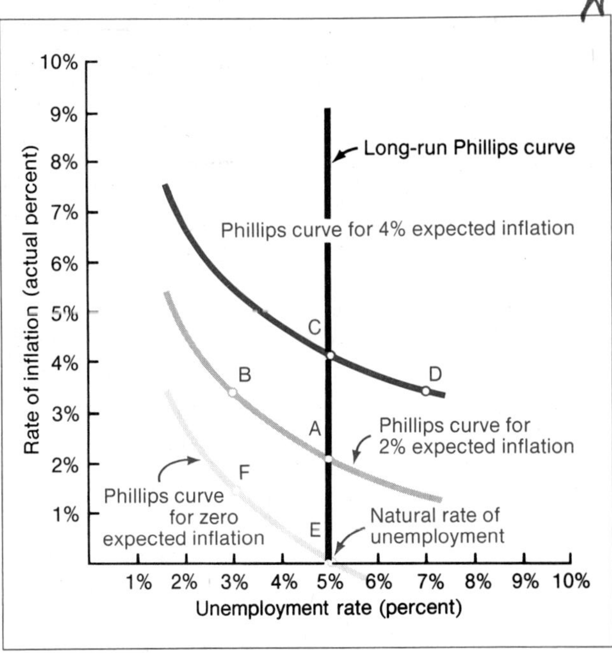

move down and to the right along the top Phillips curve, from Point C to Point D.

Suppose that the economy had experienced a long period of price stability, so that the actual and expected inflation rates were both zero. In that case, the bottom Phillips curve would provide a short-run menu from which policy makers might choose. They might, for example, get unemployment down to 3 percent if they were willing to tolerate a bit of inflation, moving from Point E to Point F.

Shifts in the Phillips Curve They could do that only in the short run, however. After a while, people would notice that prices were going up. They would begin to expect them to continue to do so. As soon as that happened, the Phillips curve would begin to shift upward, and the policy menu would suddenly begin to look less appetizing. At any point in time, the position of the Phillips curve thus depends on the expected rate of inflation. Notice that each Phillips curve in Exhibit 16.5 passes through the point corresponding to the natural rate of unemployment and the expected rate of inflation.

The Phillips Curve in the Long Run Once it is understood how the Phillips curve shifts in response to changing inflationary expectations, it becomes apparent that Phillips curves of the usual kind are essentially short-run phenomena. Movements along a given Phillips curve can take place only so long as the actual rate of inflation changes while the expected rate of inflation remains unchanged. In the long run, however, any given rate of inflation, if maintained over a period of time, will come to be expected. Economists do not all agree about the mechanisms through which people adjust their expectations of inflation or about the speed of those adjustments, but they do agree that adjustments eventually take place. In the long run, then, the unemployment rate will tend to return to its natural rate as soon as the adjustment of expectations to the actual rate of inflation is complete. This tendency is represented in Exhibit 16.5 by a long-run Phillips curve that is perfectly vertical. In the long run, there is no trade-off between inflation and unemployment.

LOWERING THE NATURAL RATE OF UNEMPLOYMENT

To refer to a certain rate of unemployment as "natural" is not to endorse that rate of unemployment as desirable. In fact, if the ambitious goals of the Humphrey-Hawkins Act (discussed in Chapter 7) are to be achieved, it appears that the present natural rate of unemployment of 5 to 6 percent will have to be lowered. Unless it is lowered, there is no possibility that the 4 percent unemployment target for 1983 can be reached simultaneously with the 3 percent annual inflation target.

The task of lowering the natural rate of unemployment is made all the more difficult by changes that have been taking place in the composition of the U.S. labor force. In particular, from 1957 to 1977, the percentage of teenagers in the labor force increased from 17 percent to 24 percent and the percentage of women from 31 to 40 percent. Both of these groups tend to enter and leave the labor force more frequently than others and to experience higher rates of unemployment while in the labor force. These demographic shifts in the composition of the labor force alone have been variously estimated to have increased the natural rate of unemployment by one-half to one full percentage point.

In order to lower the natural rate of unemployment, then, special attention will have to be paid to improving access to the job market for women and teenagers, as well as to attacking the sources of unemployment for adult males. In part, this is likely to require the government to rethink a number of present policies that have the undesired side effect of increasing the natural unemployment rate. In addition, continued efforts to improve the effectiveness of policies designed specifically to provide jobs for the unemployed will be required. To give an idea of the magnitude of the task of lowering the natural rate of unemployment, the next section will examine a number of particularly important areas of employment policy.

Policies Tending to Raise the Natural Rate of Unemployment

Minimum Wage Laws For years, economists have argued that minimum wage laws, rather than easing the plight of the poor, increase unemployment and throw more people into poverty. The usual explanation of this perverse effect is that some people may have reservation wages lower than the minimum wage rate but cannot legally be offered jobs at such low wages. This is not the whole story about the effects of minimum wage laws, however. They have another effect as well: the discouragement of on-the-job training. This effect may help explain the particularly high rate of teenage unemployment.

To see how this works, consider a hypothetical example. John Jones, a seventeen-year-old high school dropout, approaches the Atlas Company for a job. Jones is completely untrained, but he still claims to be worth $3.50 an hour and is in fact worth that much. The Atlas Company offers him his choice of two jobs—that of messenger, paying $3.50 per hour, and that of machinist's assistant. Unfortunately, the Atlas personnel manager explains, a lot of his time in the second position would be spent learning about machines and not really producing very much. The company can therefore afford to pay him only $2.50 per hour for that job. Jones realizes the advantages of on-the-job training and takes the lower-paying job. Within a year, he is promoted to a machinist first class and is earning $6 per hour.

Now introduce a legal minimum wage of $3 per hour. The Atlas Company can still offer Jones the messenger job but not the machinist assistantship. The company would lose money paying him $3 per hour in that position and is legally barred from paying $2.50. Jones takes the messenger job but soon finds it boring and quits to look again for something better.

This example shows how minimum wage laws can contribute to a vicious cycle of teenage unemployment. Employers expect unstable work behavior from teenagers and tailor available jobs accordingly. The teenage workers themselves are turned off by the dead-end jobs thus created and shift aimlessly from one employer to another. One direction to move in lowering the natural rate of unemployment would be to get rid of minimum wage laws and replace them, if need be, with other types of income assistance programs having a less serious disincentive effect.

Empirical estimates of the effects of minimum wages on the unemployment rate vary. In a 1977 survey of the problem, Phillip Cagan estimated that the overall unemployment rate was increased by 0.45 to 0.63 percentage points from 1956 to 1974 as a result of minimum wage legislation.[1] Whatever the exact size of the impact over all, a number of investigators agree that the primary impact has been on teenage unemployment rates and on those of black teenagers in particular.

Unemployment Compensation Unemployment compensation is a second government policy that, although not intended to raise the unemployment rate, does tend to have that effect. The major reason is that it lowers the opportunity cost to unemployed workers of job seeking. This, in turn, allows the workers to maintain a higher reservation wage.

Consider, for example, the case of a worker who earned gross pay of $600 per month and took home about $450 after federal income taxes, state income taxes, and social security taxes. Without unemployment compensation, the opportunity cost of being unemployed would be $450 per month. With unemployment compensation, the worker would typically receive benefits equal to 50 percent of his or her gross pay, or $300 per month in this case. These benefits are nontaxable for most workers. The opportunity cost of remaining unemployed is thus reduced to $150 a month.

Levels of unemployment benefits vary from state to state. Some workers would receive a lower level of benefits than in the above example, but it is not uncommon for the level of benefits to approach, or even exceed, 100 percent of take-home pay. There might, for example, be other income earners in the household, putting the worker in a higher income tax bracket. The worker might live in a state where dependents' allowances are given in addition to the basic unemployment benefits. And the worker might have significant work related expenses, such as commuting, meals away from home, or special clothing, that would be saved while he or she was unemployed. Any of these things would lower the opportunity cost of unemployment. In combination, they could eliminate it altogether.

Economists have known for a long time that unemployment compensation could potentially increase the unemployment rate. Recently, they have paid increasing attention to measuring the magnitude of the effect. The following case study reports one recent attempt at measurement.

Case 16.1
The Effects of Unemployment Compensation on the Unemployment Rate and the Duration of Unemployment

In 1976, government field workers conducted a special population survey designed to collect data on previous work experience, earnings, and job-seeking activities of the unemployed. These data subsequently became the basis of a study of determinants of job search behavior conducted by John Barron of Purdue University and Wesley Mellow of the U.S. Bureau of Labor Statistics. The sample covered by the survey included 3,188 individuals, of which 31 percent were currently receiving unemployment benefits. Earnings from prior jobs averaged $192 per week, of which benefits replaced an average of 47 percent.

[1] Phillip Cagan, "The Reduction of Inflation and the Magnitude of Unemployment," in *Contemporary Economic Problems*, ed. William Fellner (Washington, D.C.: American Enterprise Institute, 1977), pp. 35–36.

Barron and Mellow found that job seekers currently receiving unemployment benefits remained unemployed an average of 7.7 weeks longer than those who had received no benefits and did not have applications for benefits pending. They concluded that the unemployment rate of 7.4 percent that prevailed at the time of the May 1976 survey was 1.3 percentage points higher than it would have been in the absence of unemployment compensation, which translates into absolute numbers as about 1,230,000 additional unemployed workers.

Interestingly, however, not all of those 1,230,000 people would actually have found jobs if it had not been for unemployment insurance. Instead, Barron and Mellow found, about half of them would have withdrawn from the labor force. This implies that the unemployment rate significantly overstates the impact of unemployment compensation on jobs and production. The employment rate would in this case provide a more accurate measure.

Source: Based on John Barron and Wesley Mellow, "The Determinants of Current Search Effort and Subsequent Labor Force Status," paper prepared for the Employment and Training Administration, U.S. Department of Labor (Research Grant No. 91-18-77-26), December 1978.

Seasonal Effects The Barron and Mellow study focused on the effects of unemployment insurance on flows of people out of unemployment. But unemployment insurance can also have an effect on flows of workers into unemployment. One way it does this is by providing a hidden subsidy to seasonal, cyclical, and casual employment.

Consider the construction industry, for example. Construction costs are lower in the summer than in the winter because of the weather, so firms have a natural incentive to employ seasonal labor. However, in the absence of unemployment compensation, there would be an offsetting disincentive. Workers would be reluctant to go into the building trades, where they would work fewer weeks per year, unless their hourly wage rate when employed were higher than for steady work. Thus it might pay construction firms to hire workers on a steady work basis at a lower wage and absorb the added expense of the special equipment and materials needed for winter construction.

With unemployment compensation, the picture is different. Workers need not be paid such a high premium to enter a seasonal occupation if they will get supplemental benefits from the state during the months they are laid off. Hence, employers will not adapt their construction methods to year-round work.

The seasonal component of unemployment averages around three-quarters of a percentage point. Considering that similar effects hold true with respect to the incentives firms have for scheduling work over the course of the business cycle, or over periods of temporary high demand, the impact of unemployment compensation on the rate of unemployment would be quite substantial.

Work Registration Requirements Work registration requirements are another government policy believed to contribute significantly to the high natural rate of unemployment in the United States. These regulations require recipients of certain kinds of welfare benefits to register for work and to take jobs if they become available. The idea, of course, is to move people off the welfare rolls and into productive employment. Ironically, however, work registration requirements can have the effect of increasing the measured unemployment rate even if they are highly successful in achieving their intended objective.

It is easy to see how this can happen. Suppose that in a certain city, a new work registration rule is passed; it applies to a thousand individuals who otherwise would have been counted as not in the labor force. (They may, for example, have been so-called discouraged workers.) With the rule in effect, they all troop down to the state employment office once a week, and this effort gets them reclassified as in the labor force. Through diligent placement efforts, assume that five hundred of them actually get jobs. That is a wonderful accomplishment. The employment rate for the community has gone up. Nonetheless, the *unemployment* rate has gone up too, because the unemployment rate among the new registrants, which is 50 percent, is higher than the unemployment rate among those previously in the labor force.

The effects of work registration requirements on unemployment have been investigated empirically by Kenneth Clarkson of the University of Miami and Roger Meiners of Texas A&M University. They find the effects to be quite substantial. They estimate, for example, that of the average of 7.2 million officially unemployed persons in 1976, fully 2 million were work registrants under the food stamp and Aid to Families with Dependent Children programs. If these 2 million had remained outside the labor force, as Clarkson and Meiners believe they otherwise would have, the measured unemployment rate for that year would have been only 5.7 percent rather than 7.7 percent.[2]

Policies Intended to Reduce Unemployment

We turn now from policies that have the unintended side effect of raising the unemployment rate to policies that are specifically intended to lower it. They include programs of job placement, manpower training, and public employment.

Job Placement Job placement programs are designed to match workers to suitable jobs, thereby shortening the period of job search for unemployed workers. To the extent that ignorance on the part of both workers and employers is a barrier to job search and thus a cause of unemployment, job placement programs undoubtedly help. For that matter, there are large numbers of private job placement agencies, both profit making and nonprofit, that also presumably contribute to the reduction of unemployment.

But job placement has its limitations. For teenagers and other low-skill workers, the major limitation is that the jobs for which unemployed workers are qualified are often jobs they do not wish to take or to keep very long if they do take them. Merely plugging unemployed workers into secondary sector jobs as fast-food servers or hospital orderlies does not solve the problem of high quit rates and turnover that makes unemployment rates high in the first place.

A 1977 study of the Work Incentive (WIN) program, a job placement program for welfare beneficiaries conducted by the U.S. Department of Labor, came to these conclusions regarding the limitations of job placement: "Four months after job entry, more than half [of those placed] had left. Of those who had left, half had quit, almost one-third had been laid off, and others had been fired."[3] Furthermore, the study found that "women who went through WIN

---

[2]Kenneth W. Clarkson and Roger E. Meiners, "Institutional Changes, Reported Unemployment, and Induced Institutional Changes," *Carnegie-Rochester Conference Series on Public Policy* 10 (1979): 205–236.

[3]U.S. Department of Labor, *The Work Incentive Program and Related Experiences*, R&D Monograph 49, Employment and Training Administration (Washington, D.C.: Government Printing Office, 1979), p. 21.

and did not get work at the end had become markedly more dependent on welfare than they were when they started."[4]

Manpower Training Manpower training programs attempt to overcome the problem of pure job placement programs by upgrading the skills of the unemployed to qualify them for jobs they will want to keep once they find them. Unfortunately, although the idea is attractive, these programs have proved difficult to administer successfully. Some programs have failed spectacularly by offering training that turned out upon completion to be of no real use in the job market.

Partly as a result of early failures, more attention is now given to integrating job placement and manpower training more closely. One approach is to offer wage subsidies to encourage private employers to offer on-the-job training. Employers might normally be reluctant to offer training for fear the worker would go elsewhere once trained. The subsidy is designed to overcome this reluctance. Some very encouraging results have been reported from pilot programs, but it remains to be seen whether they can be duplicated on a national scale.

Public Employment Public employment is a major alternative to job placement and manpower training programs. Unlike the latter, which aim to fit unemployed workers into existing private sector jobs, public employment creates new jobs geared to the skills of the unemployed. At its peak in 1978, the government was employing some 725,000 workers under the Comprehensive Employment and Training Act, commonly known as CETA. This made CETA the largest such program since the days of the Great Depression. Public employment programs, however, tend to encounter certain difficulties; and CETA is no exception.

One difficulty is getting the right mix between the employment and the training aspects of the jobs. It is expensive to offer jobs with a large component of meaningful training. More jobs per dollar can be created, in the short run, by hiring workers to shovel snow and pick up roadside trash. But if this is done, the programs make no real contribution to the long-term problem of unemployment.

The other problem that public employment programs appear inevitably to encounter is the problem of displacement—that is, of the use of workers hired under the public employment program to do jobs that would have been performed by other federal, state, and local government workers anyway. To the extent that displacement occurs, the program creates no new jobs and in fact becomes little more than a program by which the federal government supplements state and local government payrolls. In the early years of the CETA program, displacement occurred on massive scales in some localities. In Buffalo, New York, for example, CETA employees accounted for a third of the entire city hall work force in 1978. It appears likely that many of these CETA jobs displaced jobs that would otherwise have been filled by non-CETA employees. In the same year, New York City used CETA funds to rehire three thousand city workers who had been laid off shortly before for budgetary reasons.

[4]Ibid., p. 23.

Congress has continually tinkered with the rules of CETA in an effort to keep the program focused on its original purpose of providing meaningful training and employment for the hard core unemployed. As yet, however, no one appears to have come up with just the right formula.

CONCLUSIONS

The analysis in this chapter still leaves an uncomfortable gap between the natural rate of unemployment at 5 to 6 percent and the rate of unemployment of 4 percent or so traditionally considered to represent full employment. There appear to be three alternative ways to close the gap, but none of them is without drawbacks.

First, the government could pursue conventional monetary and fiscal policies aimed at keeping the current level of unemployment as far below the natural rate as possible. The drawback of this approach, as will be explained more fully in the next chapter, is that it may necessitate abandoning the goal of price stability; and in the long run, it may not work at all.

Second, the government could pursue the whole range of policies designed to lower the natural rate of unemployment. The problem here is that job placement, training, and public employment alone are not likely to be enough. Yet taking the axe to unemployment insurance and minimum wage laws is likely to conflict with other economic and political goals.

The third alternative appears to be simply to learn to live with a fairly high measured rate of unemployment. The cost would be abandoning the unemployment rate as a major indicator of the success of macroeconomic policy. In part, its place in macroeconomic policy might be taken by the employment rate, which many people believe to be a more meaningful indicator. And in part, the problems of high teenage, minority, and women's unemployment would cease to be considered as *macro*economic problems at all. Instead, they would become *micro*economic problems to be grouped with such problems as poverty, disability, and old age.

No clear choice among these alternatives has yet been made.

SUMMARY

1. The unemployment rate measures the percentage of workers in the civilian labor force who are not employed. In periods when both the labor force and the number of employed workers are expanding, the unemployment rate may give misleading signals about the state of the economy. For this reason, some economists prefer to emphasize the employment rate, which is the percentage of workers in the noninstitutional civilian adult population who are employed. During 1978, for example, a rising employment rate correctly signaled rising economic activity while the unemployment rate remained unchanged.
2. Changes in the unemployment rate tend to be associated with changes in the growth rate of real output. According to Okun's law, for each three percentage points by which real economic growth exceeds (or falls short of) the growth rate of potential real GNP in any year, the unemployment rate will tend to fall (or rise) by one percentage point.

3. The unemployment rate is closely correlated with the average duration of unemployment. Anything that affects the process of job seeking thus has an important impact on the unemployment rate. Workers look for a job until they find one that meets their reservation wage—a process that takes several weeks on the average. In periods when inflation proceeds at a rate faster than people expect it to, this period of job search tends to be shortened. In periods when inflation is slower than expected, the period of job search tends to stretch out. The rate of unemployment that prevails when no one is fooled by the rate of inflation is called the natural rate of unemployment.
4. The theory of job search helps explain why the short-run Phillips curve shifts from time to time. The position of the Phillips curve depends on the expected rate of inflation, since unemployment equals the natural rate whenever actual and expected inflation are equal. The actual rate of unemployment at any time depends on the relationship between the actual and expected rates of inflation.
5. To call one particular rate of unemployment natural is not to say that it is a good thing. The natural rate for the U.S. economy in the 1970s appears to be 5 percent or more, high enough to be considered a significant social problem. Sometimes, government efforts to help the poor and the unemployed have the side effect of keeping the natural rate of unemployment high. Minimum wage laws and unemployment compensation do this. Job placement programs, manpower training, and public employment have been tried as methods of lowering the natural rate, but none of them has yet proved entirely satisfactory. In the end, we are faced with the fact that lowering the natural rate of unemployment involves some very difficult trade-offs.

DISCUSSION QUESTIONS

1. Try using the wage offer curve and reservation wage curve to explain how inflation affects the measured level of unemployment. How does expected inflation affect each curve? How does unexpected inflation affect each curve?
2. What do you think determines people's expected rate of inflation? Do you think it is reasonable, as a rough rule of thumb, to say that people expect this year to be just what it was last year? Explain. What do you expect the rate of inflation to be next month? Next year? Make a note of your answer, and check yourself a month and a year later.
3. Suppose that unemployment compensation were simply abolished. What would that do to measured unemployment? What would it do to the reservation wage curve in Exhibit 16.4? What would it do to the natural rate of unemployment? What would it do to the position of the short-run Phillips curves in Exhibit 16.5?
4. Consider this plan for the reform of unemployment compensation. The level of unemployment payments for unemployed persons would remain exactly the same as it is now, but unemployment payments would continue for six weeks after each person began a new job. What do you think that would do to the unemployment rate? Why?

SUGGESTIONS FOR FURTHER READING

Cagan, Phillip. "The Reduction of Inflation and the Magnitude of Unemployment." In *Contemporary Economic Problems,* edited by William Fellner. Washington, D.C.: American Enterprise Institute, 1977.
A survey of problems of lowering the natural rate of unemployment.

Clarkson, Kenneth, and Meiners, Roger. "Institutional Changes, Reported Unemployment, and Induced Institutional Changes." *Carnegie-Rochester Conference Series on Public Policy* 10 (1979): 205–236.
A detailed analysis of the effects of work registration requirements on the measured unemployment rate. Begins with a useful review of explanations for why the unemployment rate is as high as it is.

Feldstein, Martin. "The Economics of the New Unemployment." *Public Interest,* No. 33 (Fall 1973): 3–42.
Somewhat dated, but still a good, readable presentation of the causes of the rising natural rate of unemployment.

Friedman, Milton. *"Unemployment versus Inflation? An Evaluation of the Phillips Curve.* London: Institute for Economic Affairs, 1975.
An explanation of the Phillips curve in terms of job search theory.

Phelps, Edmund S., et al. *Microeconomic Foundations of Employment and Inflation Theory.* New York: W. W. Norton, 1970.
A seminal collection of papers on the new unemployment theory. Most of them are rather technical, but there is a good introductory essay by Phelps.

Williams, Walter E. "Government Sanctioned Restraints That Reduce Economic Opportunities for Minorities." *Policy Review,* No. 2 (Fall 1977): 7–30.
Williams is especially critical of minimum wage laws and their impact on minority teenage unemployment.

CHAPTER 17

THE DYNAMICS OF INFLATION

WHAT YOU WILL LEARN IN THIS CHAPTER

This chapter explores the dynamic interaction between inflation and unemployment. It shows how persistently expansionary monetary and fiscal policy can hold unemployment below the natural rate for an extended period of time, but only at the expense of accelerating inflation. It also shows why, when the policy brakes are applied after a period of accelerating inflation, the economy may temporarily experience the worst of both worlds—a high rate of inflation together with rising unemployment. The theory of inflationary dynamics developed here will be applied to the interpretation of recent macroeconomic experience in the United States.

FOR REVIEW

Here are some important terms and concepts that will be put to use in this chapter. If you do not understand them, review them before proceeding.

- *Theory of nominal income determination (Chapters 8 to 14)*
- *Adaptive and rational expectations (Chapter 14)*
- *The Phillips curve (Chapters 15 and 16)*
- *Okun's law (Chapter 16)*

The subject of inflation has entered the discussion at many points in the last several chapters. Controlling inflation has been presented as a major goal of economic policy. The effects of inflation on financial markets and the job search process have been examined in some detail. What has not yet been done in any systematic way, however, is to explain what determines the rate of inflation itself. What determines which part of a given growth rate of nominal GNP will take the form of real output growth and which part the form of inflation? Why did the average annual rate of inflation take such a big jump in the 1970s in comparison with all previous peacetime experience? And once the genie of inflation is out of the bottle, why is it so difficult to get it back in?

The suspicion that these questions have been put off because economists just do not know the answers is in a sense correct. Rapid peacetime inflation is only a little over ten years old in this economy, and explaining the phenomenon has required some very serious rethinking of previous economic theory.

What is more, it is not only economists who have needed time to adjust their thinking to chronic inflation. Consumers, business managers, and government decision makers have been adjusting too. People have now come to view inflation as the norm rather than the exception. Expecting inflation, they plan to protect themselves from it. The reactions of the economy to expected inflation are thus very different from its initial reaction to unexpected inflation. This has been a complicating factor in the search for an adequate theory.

Nonetheless, the fact that economists may not yet know all the answers is no reason to avoid giving a progress report. Despite disagreements on details, virtually all modern theories of inflation contain certain elements in common. In an introductory treatment such as this, it will be enough to concentrate on these common elements and leave the details to be worked out as time goes by.

THE EFFECTS OF ACCELERATING INFLATION

The fundamental insight on which modern theories of inflation are based is that it is not so much the rate of inflation itself as changes in it that affect employment and real output. This insight will be put to work first by an examination of the case of accelerating inflation. The examination will make use of four building blocks for a theory of inflation developed in previous chapters.

Building Blocks for a Theory of Inflation

The first building block is the theory of nominal income determination developed in Chapters 8 through 14; this theory explains the effects of monetary and fiscal policy on nominal income, national income, and product.

Second, at all times, the rate of growth of nominal national product must be equal to the growth rate of real output plus the rate of inflation. With this rule and with a given rate of change of nominal national product, the job of a theory of inflation becomes simply that of determining how the given rate of change in nominal national income will be split up between change in real output and change in prices. Will a 10 percent increase in nominal GNP come out as a 3 percent gain in real output and 7 percent inflation? As no inflation and a 10 percent gain in real output? As 12 percent inflation and a 2 percent drop in real output? The outcome must lie somewhere along this spectrum of possibilities.

The third building block is the rule of thumb referred to as Okun's law. This law offers a useful relationship between the rate of growth of real output and changes in the unemployment rate. According to Okun's law, the unemployment rate will remain unchanged in any year in which actual real output grows at the same rate as potential real output. At present, the growth rate of potential real output appears to be approximately 3 percent per year. Deviations from this long-run trend are associated with changes in the unemployment rate. More specifically, for each three percentage points by which real economic growth exceeds (or falls short of) the long-run trend in any year, the unemployment rate will tend to fall (or rise) by one percentage point.

The fourth and final building block is the Phillips curve, which was developed in Chapter 16 in terms of a job search theory of unemployment. The Phillips curve links the unemployment rate to the difference between the expected and actual rates of inflation.

With these building blocks at hand, we turn now to an analysis of accelerating inflation.

Expansionary Policy from a Standing Start

Exhibit 17.1 shows a short-run Phillips curve representing a "standing start" equilibrium position for the economy. A standing start means that:

1. The unemployment rate is equal to the natural rate of unemployment (assumed to be 5 percent) and has not changed during the current year.
2. There is currently no inflation and no expected inflation.
3. The current growth rate of nominal national product is 3 percent per year, just equal to the 3 percent rate of growth of potential real GNP resulting from changes in productivity and in the size of the labor force.

As shown in Chapter 16, the short-run Phillips curve always passes through a point corresponding to the natural rate of unemployment and the expected rate of inflation. In this case, the expected rate of inflation is zero and the natural rate of unemployment 5 percent, so the Phillips curve passes through Point A in Exhibit 17.1.

Assume that the government takes fiscal or monetary policy action sufficient to increase the growth rate of nominal output from its initial 3 percent per year to 10 percent per year. As aggregate nominal demand increases in response to the policy stimulus, a familiar train of events gets underway. Expenditures increase, and firms unexpectedly find their inventories falling. Some respond by stepping up output, others by raising prices, and still others by doing a little of both.

Effects on the Labor Market Soon the effects of the expansionary policy begin to be felt in the labor market. The firms that are stepping up their output attempt to recruit new workers. Some offer higher nominal wages, knowing that the rising level of demand will let them recoup these wages in higher

Exhibit 17.1
The effects of expansionary policy from a standing start
This exhibit shows the effects of expansionary monetary or fiscal policy beginning from a standing start position at Point A. Initially, the actual and expected rates of inflation are assumed to be zero, and both real and nominal output are assumed to be growing just at the 3 percent trend rate of growth of potential real GNP. Expansionary policy is then assumed to accelerate the rate of growth of nominal output to 10 percent per year. This moves the economy up and to the left along the short-run Phillips curve to Point B. Total real growth is 9 percent, including 3 percent growth of potential output plus 6 percent growth associated with the drop in unemployment. Adding 1 percent inflation makes a total of 10 percent. Point B′ is not far enough along the Phillips curve to account fully for the 10 percent nominal growth. Point B″ is too far.

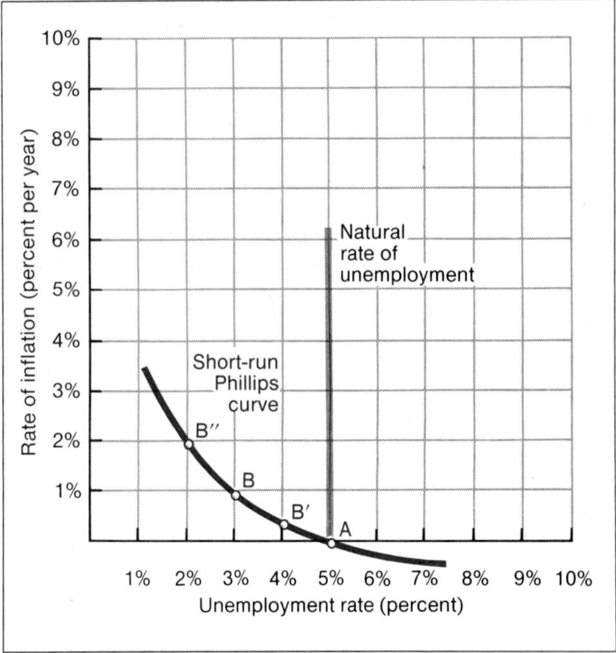

prices and expanded sales volume. Job seekers consider themselves luckier, on the average, in finding good offers. They are not expecting any inflation, so they have not raised their reservation wages. The average duration of unemployment drops, and the economy begins to move away from Point A—up and to the left along the short-run Phillips curve.

How Far along the Phillips Curve? How far along the Phillips curve will the economy move in response to this initial dose of expansionary policy? To answer this question, two of the building blocks listed at the beginning of this section must be called on. The first is the rule that the growth rate of nominal output must equal the sum of the growth of real output and the rate of inflation. And the second is Okun's law, which explains that the decline in unemployment as the economy moves to the left along the Phillips curve will be accompanied by an increase in the growth rate of real output.

In the present example, a 10 percent growth rate of nominal national income is assumed. The economy must thus move up and to the left along the Phillips curve until that entire 10 percent nominal growth rate is accounted for by the sum of three items: (1) the 3 percent annual rate of growth of potential real GNP; (2) the additional growth of real GNP associated, according to Okun's law, with the decline in the unemployment rate; and (3) the rate of inflation. As Exhibit 17.1 is drawn, this accounting requires the economy to move to Point B, where the unemployment rate has fallen from 5 percent to 3 percent and the rate of inflation has risen from 0 to 1 percent. At Point B, the assumed 10 percent growth rate of nominal national product is split up as follows: 3 percent is accounted for by the long-run growth trend of potential real GNP; another 6 percent is converted to real growth by the two percentage point drop in the unemployment rate (three percentage points are added to real growth for each one point drop in unemployment, according to Okun's law); the remaining 1 percent takes the form of inflation, as shown.

No other combination of inflation and unemployment is possible under the assumed conditions. Suppose, for example, that the economy moved only to Point B′, with the unemployment rate falling only one percentage point and the rate of inflation a little under 0.5 percent. The one percentage point drop in the unemployment rate would add 3 percent to the underlying 3 percent growth rate of potential real GNP, giving a 6 percent growth rate of real GNP in all. Adding in the 0.5 percent inflation rate gives a total growth rate of nominal output at Point B′ of just 6.5 percent, not enough to account for the entire 10 percent growth of nominal output assumed to have been induced by monetary and fiscal policy. Point B′, then, is not far enough along the Phillips curve.

Suppose, on the other hand, that the economy moved past Point B all the way to Point B″. To reach B″, the unemployment rate would have to fall from 5 percent to 2 percent, and the rate of inflation would have to increase from 0 to 2 percent. The three percentage point drop in the unemployment rate would, according to Okun's law, add nine percentage points to the 3 percent underlying growth rate of potential real GNP, for a 12 percent growth rate of real output in all. Adding the 2 percent inflation rate prevailing at Point B″ to the 12 percent rate of real growth gives a 14 percent growth rate of nominal output. But monetary and fiscal policy have been assumed to be sufficient to permit only a 10 percent growth rate of nominal output. Point B″ is thus too far along the Phillips curve under the assumed conditions.

To repeat, only one combination of inflation and unemployment is possible once the growth of nominal output, the initial rate of unemployment, and the expected rate of inflation are given.

Repeated Applications of Expansionary Policy

We now have a simple but powerful set of tools for judging the effects of macroeconomic policy. Chapters 8 through 14 showed how fiscal and monetary policy affect nominal national income and product. Now the Phillips curve, assisted by Okun's law, shows how any given growth rate of nominal output will be split up between changes in real output and changes in the price level. These tools will be applied now to determining the effects of repeated application of expansionary monetary and fiscal policy.

The Deteriorating Trade-off In the example just given, acceleration of the growth rate of nominal output to 10 percent from a standing start produced a two percentage point drop in the unemployment rate at the cost of just 1 percent inflation. Policy makers would have every reason to be very pleased with those results. They would be so pleased, in fact, that they would surely want to try another dose of the same medicine. In the second year, unfortunately, a further 10 percent expansion of nominal GNP would not be split up so favorably between inflationary and real output effects—for two reasons.

First of all, to keep real output growing at the same 9 percent rate as in the first year, it is not enough just to keep unemployment at a low level. Instead, a further drop in the unemployment rate is required. Yet the farther to the left the economy moves along the Phillips curve, the steeper the curve gets—which means that a bigger shot of unexpected inflation is needed to give each additional percentage point reduction in unemployment.

What is more, in the second year of expansionary policy, the government no longer has the advantage of a standing start. People have experienced some inflation, although mild, and some of them may be alert enough to realize that continued expansionary policy will bring more. Once people come to expect inflation, the short-run Phillips curve begins to shift upward. That too makes the inflation-unemployment trade-off less attractive than in the first year.

Continuous Acceleration It follows, then, that although a second year of expansionary policy is likely to produce some further gain in both employment and real output, the cost in terms of inflation will be higher than before. In subsequent years, the trade-off will get less favorable still. Soon it will not be enough just to repeat the original policy of 10 percent growth of nominal output. Nominal output will have to expand faster and faster just to keep unemployment from rising. The economy will then have reached the situation shown in Exhibit 17.2. Each year, the growth rate of nominal output has to be stepped up just to keep even with the upward drift of the short-run Phillips curve and ever-accelerating inflation.

A Generalization All this information can be put in the form of an important generalization: To keep unemployment below the natural rate for a sustained period requires a continuous acceleration of inflation. A case study will show the principle in action.

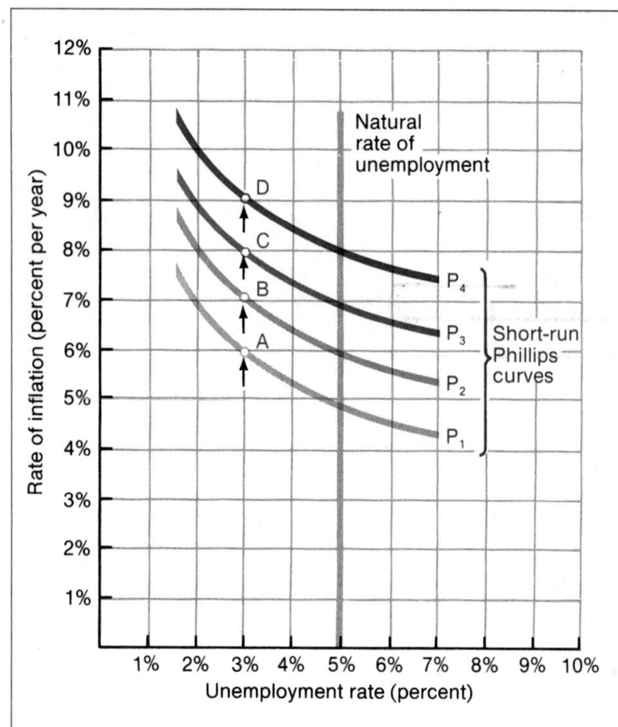

Exhibit 17.2
The effects of prolonged acceleration
To keep unemployment below the natural rate for a sustained period requires a continuous acceleration of the rate of inflation. The actual rate of inflation must always be higher than the expected rate. Here, as rising inflationary expectations push the Phillips curves up from P_1 to P_4, an accelerating growth of nominal output holds the economy to the path marked by Points A, B, C, and D in successive years.

Case 17.1
Acceleration in the Kennedy-Johnson Era

John Kennedy came to the presidency in 1960 with the declared intention to get the country moving again after two recessions late in the Eisenhower administration. Lyndon Johnson, who succeeded him, was equally determined to pursue an expansionary policy. Economists are still debating the relative importance of the Kennedy tax cut, heavy defense spending, and accelerating monetary growth; but there is no doubt that, in combination, these policies were as expansionary as anyone could have wished. The result was what Johnson proudly called "the longest peacetime [sic] expansion in American history."

Exhibit 17.3 shows the unemployment-inflation record for the economy during the Kennedy-Johnson era. The pattern is just what theory would lead us to expect. Expansionary policy at first produced substantial gains in employment with little inflation penalty. From the year of the 1964 Kennedy tax cut on, though, each successive reduction in unemployment was accompanied by a bigger jump in prices. By the end of Johnson's term in office, inflation was rising higher and higher each year just to keep unemployment where it was.

INFLATIONARY RECESSION AND THE STOP-GO CYCLE

In theory, there is no limit to the number of years that unemployment can be held below its natural rate by continued acceleration. In practice, though, political pressures eventually build up to do something about inflation. The most obvious thing to do is to put on the monetary and fiscal brakes and decelerate the growth of aggregate demand in nominal terms. It is not necessary that nominal aggregate demand actually fall—just that its rate of growth be reduced.

Exhibit 17.3
The Kennedy-Johnson acceleration
The administrations of Presidents Kennedy and Johnson during the 1960s witnessed almost uninterrupted acceleration of inflation accompanied by falling unemployment. During the late 1960s, unemployment remained below its natural rate for several consecutive years.

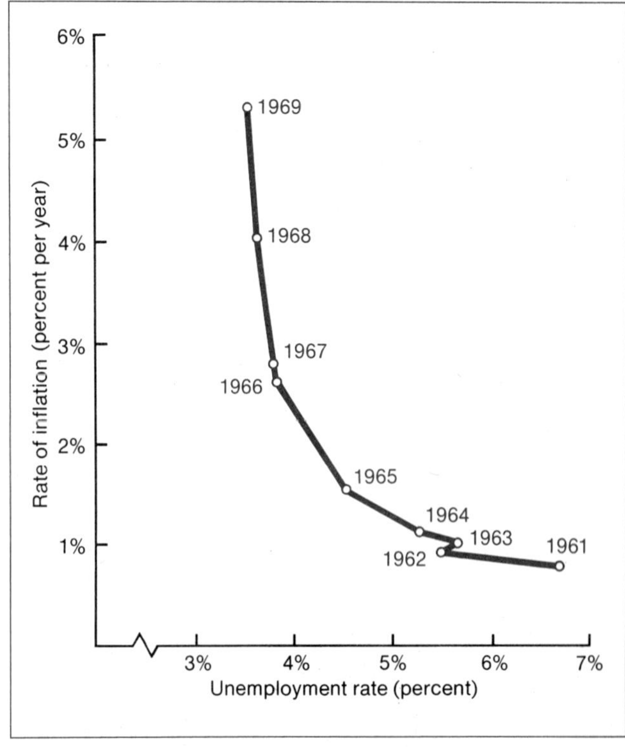

Source: President's Council of Economic Advisers, *Economic Report of the President* (Washington, D.C.: Government Printing Office, 1979), Tables B-29, B-54.

The Effects of Deceleration

As might be expected, the effects of such a deceleration are much like the initial effects of expansion, taken in reverse. As deceleration begins, aggregate demand does not grow as fast as firms have foreseen when making their production, pricing, and inventory plans. The result is unplanned inventory accumulation. As stocks of unsold goods pile up, some firms react by cutting prices (or at least raising them less than they had planned), while others cut back production.

The production cutbacks mean fewer job openings. They also mean that the firms still taking on workers are able to get the personnel they want without offering wages as high as they would otherwise have had to. Remember, though, that the deceleration is at first unexpected. Workers who have become used to low unemployment and rapid inflation initially continue to have high reservation wages as they set out to look for jobs. At first, they do not realize that conditions in the labor market as a whole have changed. Each attributes his or her difficulty in finding a job to individual bad luck. The average duration of the job search lengthens, and the unemployment rate rises.

A word should be said about the unionized sector of the labor market. Inflationary expectations play an important role in labor-management negotiations. If, as deceleration begins, both parties expect prices to continue rising as before, they are likely to agree on nominal wage increases that fully reflect that expectation. To the extent that nominal wages in unionized industries continue to rise rapidly, however, job openings in these industries become even scarcer than they otherwise would be, as demand falls off. High wage settlements in unionized industries thus make the job search prospects of the unemployed that much more difficult.

Inflationary recession A period of rising unemployment during which the rate of inflation remains high or even continues to rise.

Inflationary Recession What happens next can be called an **inflationary recession.** Unemployment goes up, real output goes down, and prices continue to rise, perhaps even faster, temporarily, than before.

Exhibit 17.4 gives a graphical interpretation. This diagram starts where Exhibit 17.2 left off, at the end of a period of accelerating inflation. The economy is initially assumed to be at Point D. Policy makers have raised the growth rate of nominal output to 12 percent. With unemployment steady, the economy experiences 9 percent inflation after allowing for the annual 3 percent growth of potential real GNP. This actual 9 percent rate of inflation continues to run ahead of the 8 percent expected rate of inflation on which Phillips curve P_4 is based.

Then the brakes are applied. To be specific, assume that contractionary fiscal and monetary policy is used to cut the growth rate of nominal output to 6 percent. Inflationary expectations, however, are still moving up. Last year, people expected an inflation rate of only 8 percent, but they experienced 9 percent. This year, they presumably expect the 9 percent to continue, shifting the short-run Phillips curve up to P_5.

With the Phillips curve at P_5, inflation would have to accelerate to 10 percent to keep unemployment from rising. The reduced growth rate of nominal output does not permit that much inflation, however. Unemployment begins to rise, and the economy moves to the left toward Point E. By the time it gets there, unemployment has risen two percentage points. The growth rate of real output drops to −3 percent. (This represents a 3 percent growth of potential GNP minus 6 percent attributable—according to Okun's law—to the two percentage point rise in unemployment.) At Point E, then, the 6 percent growth rate of nominal GNP is split up into 9 percent inflation and −3 percent real growth.

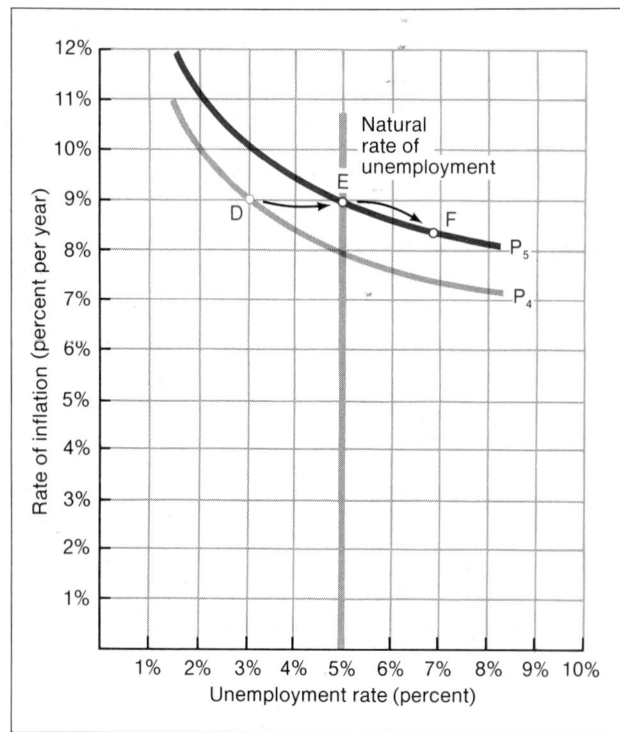

Exhibit 17.4
Inflationary recession

This exhibit, which begins where Exhibit 17.2 left off, shows how an inflationary recession is produced when the rate of growth of nominal national output is cut back after a prolonged period of accelerating inflation. In the episode shown, the rate of growth of nominal national product is cut back from 12 percent per year to 6 percent per year, while inflationary expectations, still adjusting to accelerating inflation, carry the short-run Phillips curve up from P_4 to P_5. As a result, the economy moves from Point D to Point E. Unemployment rises, and real output falls; but inflation initially continues unabated. A second year of 6 percent growth of nominal national output would result in a further increase in unemployment, but the rate of inflation would begin to decline as the short-run Phillips curve stopped shifting upward. This would move the economy to Point F.

Cost-Push Inflation During an inflationary recession, cost-push inflation becomes important. Chapter 15 showed that two conditions must be met for true cost-push inflation (as distinct from the cost-push illusion) to occur:

1. Some force that will touch off a rise in wages or prices when demand is not rising must be present.
2. Something must prevent prices and wages in competitive markets from falling when prices or wages in more monopolistic markets rise.

During inflationary recession, exactly the conditions required are present. In highly concentrated and highly unionized industries, inflationary expectations cause wages and prices to keep rising, even when demand begins to slow down. These wage and price increases mean fewer jobs in the sectors affected. Falling wages in nonunionized sectors cannot be counted on to take up the slack in employment. Any decline in wage offers that occurs while inflationary expectations continue to push up reservation wages will only lengthen the average period of job seeking and raise unemployment still further.

The cost-push theory of inflation thus comes into its own during an inflationary recession. In such a period, demand-pull and cost-push are not conflicting interpretations of the same thing. Instead, the latter occurs as an aftereffect of the former.

Continued Deceleration If the growth rate of nominal output were held to 6 percent for another year, the economy would continue to move down and to the right along Phillips curve P_5 toward Point F. Unemployment would continue to rise, and real output would continue to fall, but now the rate of inflation would begin to fall too. In subsequent years, the Phillips curve would begin to shift downward, as shown in Exhibit 17.5. This process is the mirror image of the continued acceleration shown in Exhibit 17.2.

Exhibit 17.5

Continued deceleration toward a soft landing

Continuation of deceleration, beginning from the situation shown in Exhibit 17.4, could eventually bring the economy to a soft landing, with a stabilized rate of inflation and unemployment at the natural rate. The exact path followed by the economy would depend on aggregate demand policies and on how rapidly inflationary expectations declined. Two possibilities are shown here, one ending with a soft landing at zero inflation (Point S), and the other ending at a stable 2 percent rate of inflation (Point S′).

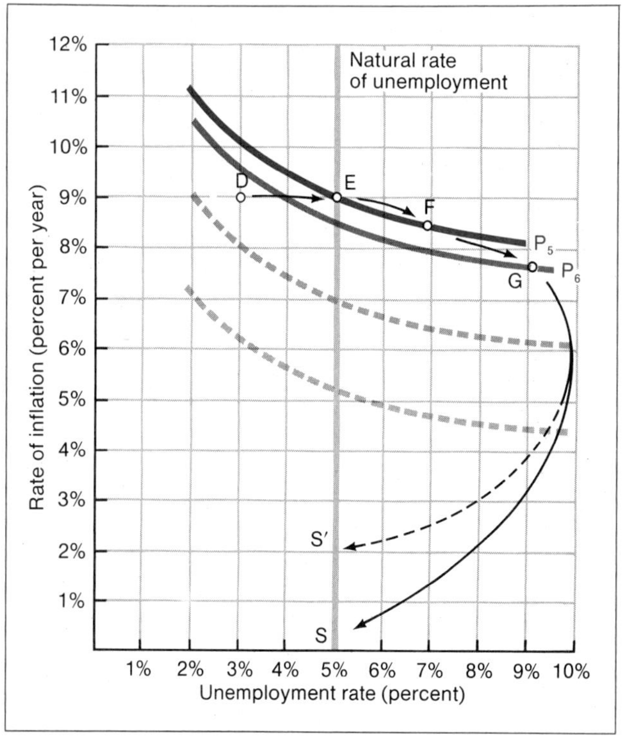

In principle, through the proper manipulation of aggregate nominal demand, the economy could after a few years be brought to a "soft landing" at some point along the long-run Phillips curve. This could happen at a zero rate of inflation (Point S in Exhibit 17.5) or at some rate of inflation greater than zero (for example, Point S'). With unemployment at its natural rate, maintaining a steady growth of nominal output would result in a steady-state rate of inflation equal to the growth of nominal output minus the growth of potential real output.

The Stop-Go Cycle

In the real world, however, it is difficult to achieve a true soft landing. Just as prolonged acceleration generates political pressure to do something about inflation, so prolonged deceleration brings pressure to do something about unemployment. It is always politically tempting to respond to these pressures by once again accelerating the growth of nominal output.

Reflation An expansion of aggregate demand after a period of high unemployment and decelerating inflation, bringing substantial short-term gains in employment with little or no inflationary penalty.

Reflation The application of expansionary policy after a prolonged period of deceleration is known as **reflation.** In the first stages of a reflation, before inflationary expectations are rekindled, it is possible to get a big drop in unemployment with little penalty in terms of inflation. In fact, if renewed expansion of aggregate demand starts while the Phillips curve is still drifting downward, the unemployment rate may fall to the natural rate while the rate of inflation is still declining. But although reflation temporarily brings the best of all possible economic worlds, unemployment cannot be cut below the natural rate without permitting inflation once again to accelerate. The economy is back to familiar territory, having completed a cycle.

Stop-go policy A cycle of acceleration, inflationary recession, deceleration, and reflation brought about by alternating political pressures to do something first about inflation and then about unemployment.

The cycle of acceleration, inflationary recession, deceleration, and reflation is popularly known as **stop-go policy.** Unlike the traditional business cycle, which economists have known about for more than a century, the origins of the stop-go cycle are more political than economic. Perhaps it can even be said that the stop-go cycle is a peculiarity of democratic politics (with a lower-case "d"—Republicans are not immune). In an election year, it is particularly difficult to resist the short-run gains of reflation or to take the initial steps to end runaway acceleration.

Inflationary Bias

To add the final touch to the discussion of stop-go, a possibility not yet considered must be mentioned. It may be that, on the average, the political system is more sensitive to the political pressures that arise from unemployment than to those arising from inflation. If this is the case, the symmetry of the stop-go pattern is destroyed. The details of what happens when an inflationary bias is added to a policy of stop-go stabilization will not be worked through here, but Exhibit 17.6 gives a sketch of the process. The economy goes into an upward spiral because the upward push that the economy is given during the acceleration phase of the stop-go cycle is longer and more vigorous than the downward push it receives during the recessionary phase.

Turning from the realm of theory to the real world, one can find some striking similarities between the hypothetical stop-go cycle of Exhibit 17.6 and recent experience with inflation and unemployment in the United States. The following case study outlines this experience.

Exhibit 17.6
Stop-go with an inflationary bias
The so-called stop-go cycle means the alternation of acceleration, inflationary recession, deceleration, and reflation, as political pressure builds up first to do something about inflation and then to do something about unemployment. If the pressures to reduce unemployment are, on the average, stronger than the pressures to control inflation, the stop-go cycle may be given an upward bias. Each time around, the cycle spirals higher, as this sketch indicates.

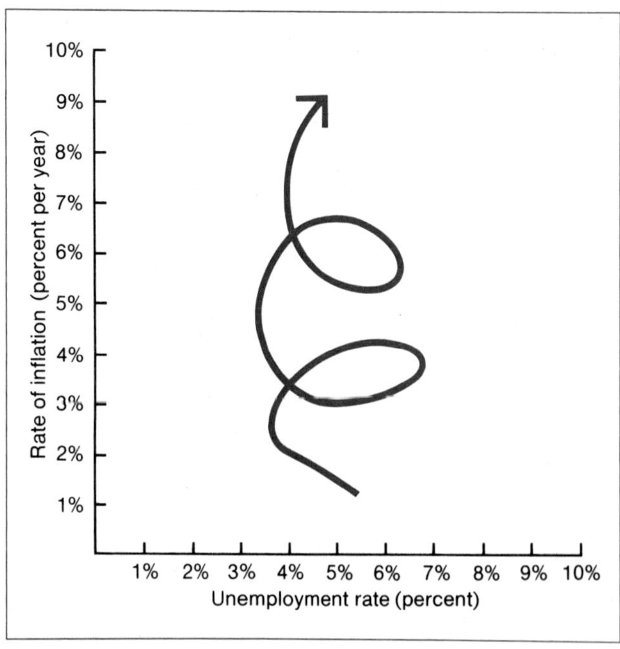

Case 17.2
Recent U.S. Experience with Unemployment and Inflation

Exhibit 17.7 presents actual data on inflation and unemployment in the U.S. economy from 1954 to 1978. One part of this record—the Kennedy-Johnson acceleration—has already been examined. Now some other features will be explored.

Exhibit 17.7
Recent U.S. experience with inflation and unemployment
Since 1954, inflation and unemployment have spiraled upward in a series of roughly circular loops. One cycle, that following the 1957 recession, was cut off before the previous peak of inflation had been reached. In 1973–74 and again in 1979, inflation reached an especially high peak because internationally generated commodity inflation was added to domestic inflationary pressures. Inflation is given as a year-to-year percentage increase in the consumer price index.

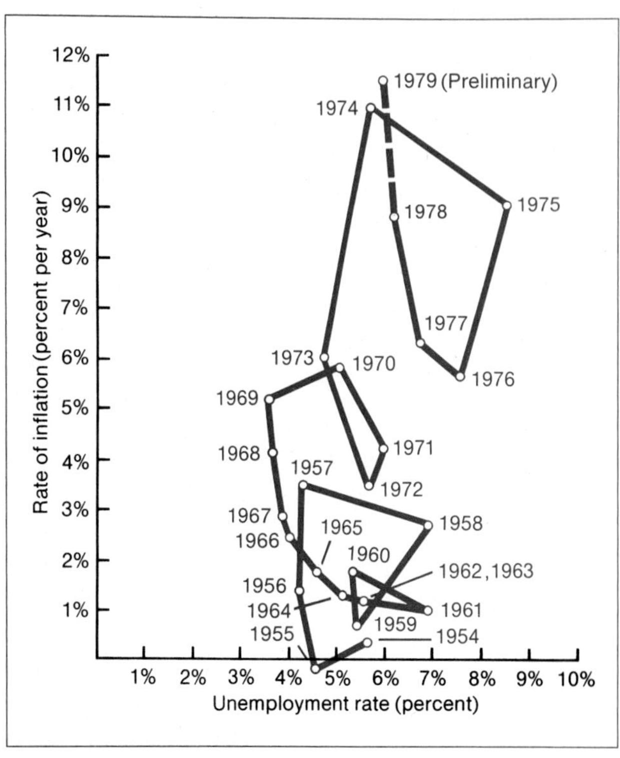

Source: President's Council of Economic Advisers, *Economic Report of the President* (Washington, D.C.: Government Printing Office, 1979), Tables B-29, B-54; 1979 data, from various published sources, are for the first three quarters.

The overall impression one gets from the figure is that of a series of roughly circular clockwise loops. Although the lengths and strengths of successive accelerations and decelerations are rather irregular, it does not take much imagination to see an upward spiral of sorts. This figure at least roughly resembles that of Exhibit 17.6.

Although the rate of inflation has drifted up over the years, it has not moved up over every single cycle. Consider the period following the recession of 1957. The recovery from this recession was very weak. The vertical line drawn between the points for 1959 and 1960, which forms the upward portion of the next loop, is shorter and farther to the right than most. This weak recovery seems to have happened because President Eisenhower had been frightened by the inflation of 1956 and 1957 and did not want to repeat the experience. Restrictive policy cut the recovery off before the previous peak of inflation was reached.

During the 1970s, in contrast, the loops in the stop-go cycle have resumed their upward drift and have become more stretched out. The acceleration of inflation from the 1972 rate to the high rate in 1974 was particularly abrupt and was aggravated by some special cost-push factors. One was a "price bulge" appearing as an aftereffect of President Nixon's experiment with wage and price controls in 1971–72. (These controls will be discussed more fully in the next chapter.) Then, in 1974, came the fourfold rise in oil prices that followed the Arab oil embargo, which added to an already pronounced element of international commodity inflation. A decline in the international value of the dollar added further inflationary pressures. Without these special factors, 1974 would still have been an inflationary year, but it is doubtful if a rate as high as 11 percent would have been reached.

The particularly sharp recession of 1974–75 resulted, as expected, in a deceleration of inflation. This deceleration lasted only through 1976, however. In 1977, the rate of inflation began to rise again, starting from a higher base than ever before. By mid-1979, the inflation rate once again exceeded 10 percent. Again, a rise in oil prices made inflation even worse than it otherwise would have been.

CONCLUSIONS

The elementary theory of inflationary dynamics presented in this chapter emphasizes certain common elements in the approaches of a wide variety of economists to inflation. Simple as it is, the theory yields some worthwhile insights into recent policy experience. The theory is incomplete in certain important respects, however; and economists disagree on just how the missing pieces ought to be filled in.

One piece of the picture that needs to be filled in more completely concerns the formation of inflationary expectations. This piece is important, since the whole theory rests on the assumption that people react quite differently to unexpected inflation than to expected inflation.

The diagrams for this chapter have been constructed with the implicit assumption of purely adaptive expectations: Each year the expected rate of inflation is shown as equal to the actual rate of inflation the year before. But although recent experience is certainly one of the major factors affecting expectations, it is an oversimplification to make it the only factor. In a more complete treatment, some attention would also have to be given to rational expectations—that is, to the fact that the formation of expectations is to some extent a forward-looking as well as a backward-looking process. Chapter 14, for example, suggested that close observers of financial markets would likely view a turn toward more expansionary policy by the Fed as a signal of future inflationary pressure.

The same can also be true of fiscal policy. Suppose, for example, that there is an election coming up next year, and the newspapers report that the president intends to pursue an expansionary policy to bring unemployment down. Rational expectation theorists say that at least some people will realize that accelerating inflation is a likely consequence and will make their economic plans accordingly. Thus, they claim, even in the near term, more of the expansion will be felt in the form of inflation and less in the form of reduced unemployment than otherwise. In their view, it is only unexpected policy actions that have strong impact on real income and employment. The importance of rational expectations theory and its policy implications are hotly debated. There will be occasion to mention the controversy again in the next chapter.

Another piece of the picture to which this chapter has given little attention concerns the interaction of the internal dynamics of inflation with external shocks to the economy and spontaneous cost-push elements. As shown in Case 17.2, such special factors, operating in years like 1974 and 1979, can significantly affect the size and timing of the swings in unemployment and inflation that occur during the stop-go cycle. There continues to be considerable debate among economists on the nature and importance of the effects on inflation of such things as oil price increases, union wage settlements, and changes in the value of the dollar in foreign exchange markets.

Finally, there has been no opportunity yet to discuss anti-inflationary policies other than traditional monetary and fiscal policy. The chapter has shown that the more firmly inflation and inflationary expectations become established, the longer and more painful is the deceleration necessary to return the economy to price stability. The next chapter will discuss a number of proposals that have been advanced to supplement traditional monetary and fiscal policy in the hope of achieving full employment, price stability, and economic growth. Many of these proposals, as we will see, are also very controversial.

SUMMARY

1. Four fundamental building blocks for a theory of inflationary dynamics are: (1) the theory of nominal income determination; (2) the rule that, at all times, the growth rate of nominal national product must be equal to the growth rate of real output plus the rate of inflation; (3) Okun's law, which says that for each three percentage points by which real economic growth exceeds (or falls short of) the growth of potential real GNP in any year, the unemployment rate will fall (or rise) by one percentage point; and (4) the Phillips curve, which specifies a short-run trade-off between inflation and unemployment for a given expected rate of inflation.
2. With a given expected rate of inflation, an increase in the growth rate of nominal output has the short-run effect of moving the economy up and to the left along the Phillips curve. In the course of this movement, unemployment falls and the growth rate of output consequently increases. The movement along the Phillips curve continues until a point is reached where the entire rate of increase of nominal national product is accounted for by the sum of (1) the growth of potential real GNP, (2) the growth of real GNP

attributable via Okun's law to the decline in the unemployment rate, and (3) the rate of inflation.

3. To keep unemployment below the natural rate requires that the actual rate of inflation be higher than the expected rate of inflation. To the extent that people tend to expect what has happened in the immediate past to continue to happen in the future, inflationary expectations tend to rise with increases in the actual rate of inflation, although with a lag. Only by continually accelerating the rate of inflation, so that expectations never catch up with actuality, can the unemployment rate be kept below the natural rate for a prolonged period.
4. An inflationary recession is the worst of both worlds. Fiscal or monetary brakes cut the growth rate of nominal output, but past inflationary experience continues temporarily to push up inflationary expectations and the short-run Phillips curve. The result is a combination of rising unemployment and high or even increasing inflation. Once people become aware that the brakes have been applied and inflation has been checked, inflationary expectations fall and eventually the economy can be decelerated to a soft landing.
5. During a prolonged period of acceleration, political pressures build up to do something about inflation. Similarly, during a prolonged deceleration, pressures build up to take action on unemployment. The result can be a stop-go cycle of alternating acceleration, inflationary recession, deceleration, and reflation. If the political system is, on the average, more sensitive to unemployment than to inflation, the stop-go cycle can be given an upward bias, sending the rate of inflation spiraling over time.

DISCUSSION QUESTIONS

1. If, after a long period of relatively steady prices, there were an increase in the growth rate of aggregate demand, why would the initial increase in prices be strictly demand-pull inflation? Why would cost-push elements not appear right away?
2. In some periods and some countries, governments have used the acceleration technique to keep unemployment low for long periods. All the time they were doing it, however, they continually issued statements to the effect that they were keeping a watchful eye on prices, that they viewed price stability as an important goal, and so on. Do you think such statements might serve any actual economic purpose? Do you think it would make any difference if the government just announced, "OK, it is our policy to keep unemployment low, so we are going to let the rate of inflation climb each year by two percentage points above what it was the year before"?
3. Suppose that some private economic research organization discovered a 100 percent accurate and reliable method of forecasting next year's rate of inflation. Why might the government want to prevent this forecast from being published? What do you think would be the effect on the shape of the short-run Phillips curve if the forecast were widely published and widely known to be accurate?
4. What effect do you think shortening the period between national elections would have on economic policy? What effect would lengthening the period have? What effect would there be if the government could call an election any time it wanted, as in some parliamentary systems? Under the last option, under what economic conditions do you think the government would most frequently decide to call an election?
5. Using a newspaper or some government source such as the *Survey of Current Business* or the *Economic Report of the President,* find inflation and unemploy-

ment statistics for 1979 and later years, if available. Include forecasts for the current year if you can find them. Plot these new data on Exhibit 17.7. Do the points fall where you expected them to? Write a paragraph interpreting the newest data.

APPENDIX TO CHAPTER 17
A SIMPLE ALGEBRAIC MODEL OF THE DYNAMICS OF INFLATION

This appendix shows how the theory of the dynamics of inflation presented in Chapter 17 can be put in terms of a simple set of algebraic equations and how these equations, in turn, can be used as the basis for a somewhat more complete graphical exposition of the theory. Either the equations or the enhanced graphical apparatus can be used to calculate the way any given growth rate of nominal national product will be split up between inflation and real growth under specified initial assumptions.

BUILDING BLOCKS

The algebraic model is based on the same four building blocks listed at the beginning of the chapter. The first of these blocks is the theory of nominal national income determination that was developed in Chapters 8 through 14. An algebraic version of this theory was presented in the Appendix to Chapter 14, but that part of the analysis will not be repeated here. Instead, the assumption will be made that the growth rate of nominal national product in any year is given as the outcome of monetary and fiscal policy decisions. The growth rate of nominal output in Year t will be represented as $\dot{Y}_t$, with the dot meaning that the quantity in question is a growth rate expressed in percent per year and with the subscript referring to the year in question.

The Phillips Curve

The second building block to be used here is the short-run Phillips curve. This curve expresses a relationship between the rate of inflation and the unemployment rate, given the expected rate of inflation. To simplify the algebra, the Phillips curve is made a straight line for purposes of this appendix. The Phillips curve equation can be written:

$$\dot{P} = \dot{P}_e + h(U - U_n), \qquad \textbf{17A.1}$$

in which $\dot{P}$ is the actual rate of inflation, $\dot{P}_e$ is the expected rate of inflation, U is the actual rate of unemployment, U_n is the natural rate of unemployment, and h is a negative constant equal to the slope of the Phillips curve.

As a further simplification, a one-year adaptive expectations rule will be used so that the expected rate of inflation in each year is equal to the actual rate of inflation in the previous year. To keep track of the years, subscripts are added, with t standing for the current year, $t - 1$ for the previous year, and so on. Finally, a value of -1 is assumed for the constant h, and the natural rate of unemployment is assumed to be 5 percent. Incorporating all these changes, Equation 17A.1 becomes:

$$\dot{P}_t = \dot{P}_{t-1} - (U_t - 5). \qquad \textbf{17A.2}$$

Exhibit 17A.1 shows how the equation just given can be used to draw in the short-run Phillips curve appropriate to any given situation. It is clear from the equation that when the unemployment rate in the current year (U_t) is equal to the natural rate of unemployment (here assumed to be 5 percent), then the actual rate of inflation ($\dot{P}_t$)

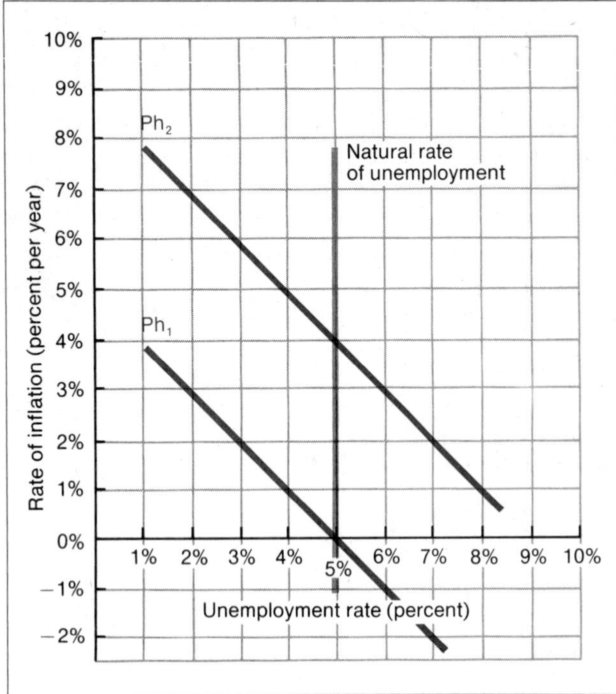

Exhibit 17A.1

Graphing the short-run Phillips curve

The simplified Phillips curve used in this appendix is a straight line with a slope of −1. A reference point for sketching the short-run Phillips curve appropriate to any year is given by the following rule: When the actual and expected rates of inflation are equal, the actual unemployment rate must be equal to the natural rate of unemployment. The Phillips curve in this appendix is further simplified by a one-year adaptive expectations assumption under which the current year's expected rate of inflation is equal to last year's actual rate of inflation. For example, Phillips curve Ph_1, shown here, reflects zero expected inflation (zero actual inflation in the previous year), and curve Ph_2 reflects 4 percent expected inflation (4 percent actual inflation in the previous year).

will be equal to the expected rate of inflation (which by assumption is the previous year's inflation rate, $\dot{P}_{t-1}$). The short-run Phillips curve for any year must thus pass through the point corresponding to the natural rate of unemployment and the expected rate of inflation. If the expected rate of inflation is 0, then the short-run Phillips curve will be in the position Ph_1 in Exhibit 17A.1. If instead the expected rate of inflation were 4 percent per year, the short-run Phillips curve would be in the position Ph_2, and so on. Thus each one percentage point increase in the expected rate of inflation shifts the Phillips curve up by one percentage point.

Okun's Law

The next building block to be added to the model is Okun's law. Okun's law provides a relationship between the rate of real economic growth and changes in the unemployment rate: The rate of real economic growth in any year will be equal to the growth rate of potential GNP (assumed to be 3 percent per year) minus three percentage points for each one percentage point by which the unemployment rate rises from its rate of the previous year. This relationship can be put in the form of an equation as follows:

$$\dot{y}_t = 3 - 3(U_t - U_{t-1}), \quad \textbf{17A.3}$$

where $\dot{y}$ stands for the rate of growth of real output and the subscripts t and $t - 1$ stand for the current year and the previous year, as before.

The final building block needed for the simple algebraic model is the rule that the growth rate of nominal output in any year is equal to the growth rate of real output plus the rate of inflation. In equation form, this can be written:

$$\dot{Y}_t = \dot{y}_t + \dot{P}_t. \quad \textbf{17A.4}$$

An alternative way to state the same relationship is to say that the growth rate of real output is equal to the growth rate of nominal output minus the rate of inflation—that is:

$$\dot{y}_t = \dot{Y}_t - \dot{P}_t. \quad \textbf{17A.5}$$

Demand Pressure Equation

The system of equations given here can be simplified by substituting Equation 17A.5 into Okun's law, as stated in Equation 17A.3, to give:

$$\dot{Y}_t - \dot{P}_t = 3 - 3(U_t - U_{t-1}). \quad \textbf{17A.6}$$

This in turn can be rewritten in the form of the following useful equation:

$$\dot{P}_t = \dot{Y}_t - 3 + 3(U_t - U_{t-1}). \quad \textbf{17A.7}$$

This equation is a version of Okun's law restated as a relationship among the rate of inflation, the rate of nominal GNP growth, and the change in the unemployment rate. In words, it says that the rate of inflation in any year will be equal to the rate of growth of nominal output minus 3 percent to allow for the growth of potential real GNP plus three percentage points for each one percentage point by which the unemployment rate increases over its level of the previous year. Equation 17A.7 will be referred to as the *demand pressure equation,* because it shows how much upward pressure is put on the rate of inflation by the growth of aggregate nominal demand ($\dot{Y}$), given the change in the unemployment rate.

The demand pressure equation, like the equation for the Phillips curve, can be represented graphically. Exhibit 17A.2 shows how. A convenient reference point for constructing the demand pressure curve appropriate to the conditions of a particular year is provided by the case in which the unemployment rate does not change from one year to the next. Inspection of Equation 17A.7 shows that if the current year's unemployment rate (U_t) is equal to the previous year's unemployment rate (U_{t-1}), the rate of inflation in the current year must be equal to the growth rate of nominal national income ($\dot{Y}_t$) minus 3 percent to allow for the trend rate of growth of potential

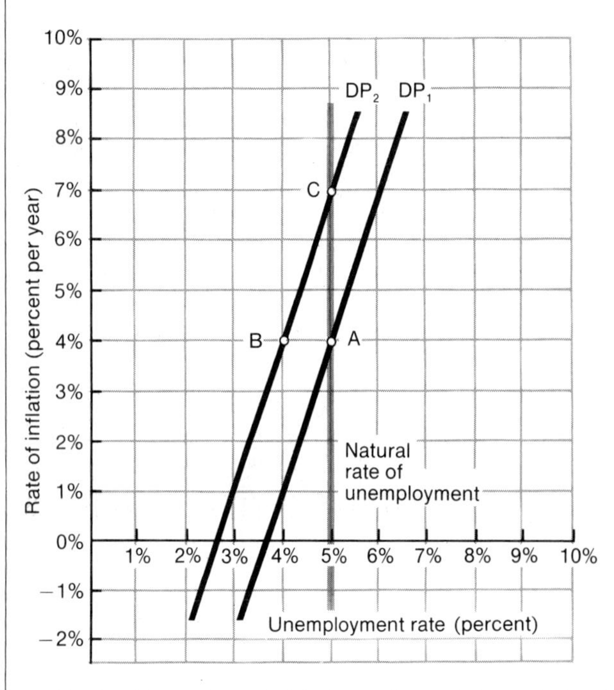

Exhibit 17A.2
Graphing the demand pressure curve
The demand pressure curve can be graphed on the same set of axes used for the Phillips curve, with unemployment on the horizontal axis and inflation on the vertical axis. The demand pressure curve has a slope of 3 because, according to Okun's law, each one percentage point drop in the unemployment rate tends to be associated with a three percentage point increase in the growth rate of real output and, hence, with a three percentage point drop in the inflation rate associated with a given rate of growth of nominal GNP. A reference point for drawing the demand pressure curve is provided by the fact that if the unemployment rate in the current year does not change from that in the previous year, the rate of inflation will be equal to the current year's growth rate of nominal GNP minus three percentage points to allow for the trend growth of real output. For example, the curve DP$_1$ applies to a year in which the growth rate of nominal GNP is 7 percent and the previous year's unemployment rate was 5 percent. It thus passes through reference Point A (5, 4). The demand pressure curve could be shifted to position DP$_2$ in Year 2 either by a decline in the Year 1 unemployment rate to 4 percent while nominal growth stayed at 7 percent (see Point B) or by an increase in the nominal growth rate to 10 percent in Year 2 with the unemployment rate in Year 1 still assumed to be 5 percent (see Point C).

real GNP. For example, the demand pressure curve DP_1 in Exhibit 17A.2 is drawn on the assumption that the unemployment rate in the previous year was 5 percent and the growth rate of nominal GNP in the current year is 7 percent. If unemployment does not change in the current year, the rate of inflation must be 4 percent (7 − 3). DP_1 accordingly passes through Point A, where the unemployment rate is 5 percent and the rate of inflation is 4 percent. Moving down and to the left along DP_1, then, the rate of inflation decreases by three percentage points for each one percentage point drop in the unemployment rate, given the growth of nominal output.

A change in either the current year's growth rate of nominal GNP ($\dot{Y}_t$) or the previous year's unemployment rate (U_{t-1}) can shift the demand pressure curve. For example, if the unemployment rate in Year 1 were to fall to 4 percent and the growth rate of nominal GNP were to remain at 7 percent, the demand pressure curve for Year 2 would shift to the position DP_2. Note that this curve passes through Point B, which corresponds to 4 percent unemployment and 4 percent (7 − 3) inflation. Thus each one percentage point decrease in the previous year's unemployment rate shifts the demand pressure curve to the left by one percentage point. Alternatively, if unemployment in Year 1 were to remain at 5 percent, the demand pressure curve could still be shifted to the position DP_2 if the growth rate of nominal GNP in the current year (Year 2) were to rise to 10 percent. This is shown by the fact that DP_2 also passes through Point C, where the unemployment rate is 5 percent and the rate of inflation is 7 percent (10 − 3). Thus each one percentage point increase in nominal output growth shifts the demand pressure curve upward by one percentage point. In short, the demand pressure curve for any year t can always be constructed by locating the point (U_{t-1}, $\dot{Y}_t - 3$) and drawing a line with a slope of 3 through that point.

Determining the Rate of Inflation and the Unemployment Rate

Equation 17A.2 (the Phillips curve) and Equation 17A.7 (the demand pressure curve) now provide a pair of simultaneous equations that can be solved for the rate of inflation and the unemployment rate in the current year, given the growth rate of nominal output as determined by monetary and fiscal policy, the rate of unemployment in the previous year, the rate of inflation in the previous year (which is assumed to be the expected rate of inflation in the current year), and the natural rate of unemployment (which is assumed to be equal to 5 percent). The following problem shows how these equations can be put to work.

Problem 1: Assume that in Year 0, the economy is in a standing start position, with $U_0 = U_n = 5$ and $\dot{P}_0 = \dot{P}_{-1} = 0$. The growth rate of real and nominal output is 3 percent per year. In Year 1, fiscal and monetary policy is used to increase the growth rate of nominal output from 3 percent to 7 percent per year. What will be the rate of inflation and the unemployment rate in that year?

Solution: Substituting the values given into Equation 17A.2 gives the following short-run Phillips curve for Year 1:

$$\dot{P}_1 = 0 + 5 - U_1 = 5 - U_1. \qquad \textbf{17A.8}$$

Substituting the given values into the demand pressure equation (Equation 17A.7) provides a second relationship between the rate of inflation and the unemployment rate:

$$\dot{P}_1 = 7 - 3 + 3(U_1 - 5) = -11 + 3U_1. \qquad \textbf{17A.9}$$

Solving Equations 17A.8 and 17A.9 by the usual methods for the solution of simultaneous equations gives the values $U_1 = 4$ and $\dot{P}_1 = 1$. The result of the policy of accelerating the growth rate of nominal GNP to 7 percent in Year 1, then, is to pull the unemployment rate 1 percent below the natural rate, to 4 percent, and to produce a rate of inflation of 1 percent. Real output growth equals 6 percent—7 percent nominal growth minus 1 percent inflation—up from 3 percent in Year 0.

This problem can also be solved graphically, as shown in Exhibit 17A.3. First graph the short-run Phillips curve, defined by Equation 17A.8, for Year 1. This gives the curve

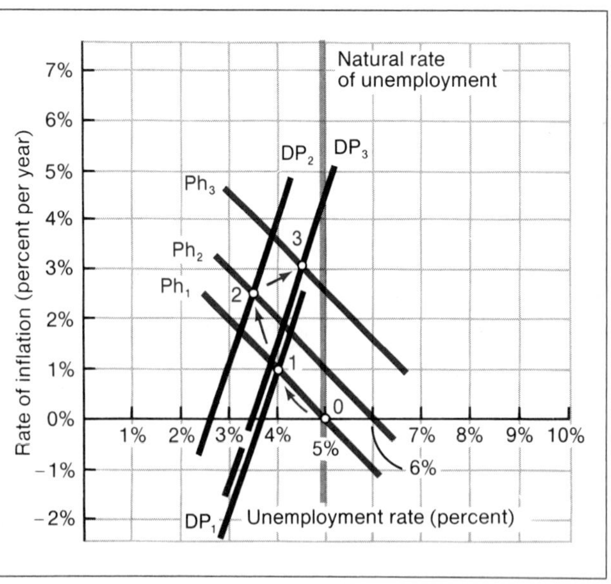

Exhibit 17A.3

Graphical solution to Problems 1 and 2

The short-run Phillips curve Ph_1 and the demand pressure curve DP_1 give the solution to Problem 1. Beginning from a standing start (Point 0), an increase in the growth rate of nominal GNP to 7 percent in Year 1 results in an inflation rate of 1 percent and a drop in the unemployment rate to 4 percent (Point 1). In the first part of Problem 2, the growth rate of nominal GNP is held at 7 percent for Year 2. The curves Ph_2 and DP_2 show that this policy brings about 2.5 percent inflation and 3.5 percent unemployment in Year 2 (Point 2). In Year 3, the growth rate of nominal GNP is cut back to 3 percent, producing a rise in unemployment, while the rate of inflation continues to accelerate (Point 3).

labeled Ph_1 in Exhibit 17A.3. Note that the curve passes through the reference point (5, 0) corresponding to the 5 percent natural rate of unemployment and the Year 1 expected inflation rate of 0 percent. Next graph the demand pressure curve, given by Equation 17A.9, for Year 1. This gives the demand pressure curve labeled DP_1 in Exhibit 17A.3. The demand pressure curve passes through the reference point (5, 4) corresponding to the previous year's (Year 0) unemployment rate of 5 percent and the 7 percent Year 1 growth rate of nominal GNP, reduced by three percentage points to allow for potential real GNP growth. The intersection of these two curves occurs at the point (4, 1)—that is, at the same 4 percent unemployment rate and 1 percent rate of inflation given by the algebraic solution for Year 1.

Problem 2: Beginning from the same standing start position assumed in Problem 1, suppose that policy makers accelerate the growth rate of nominal output from 3 percent in Year 0 to 7 percent in Year 1, keep it at 7 percent in Year 2, and then cut it back to 3 percent again in Year 3. Use the graphs of Equations 17A.2 and 17A.7 to trace the path taken by the economy in terms of inflation and unemployment.

Solution: Under the adaptive expectations assumption, the expected rate of inflation in Year 2 has risen to 1 percent. This increase causes the short-run Phillips curve to shift up by one unit to the position Ph_2 in Exhibit 17A.3. In accordance with the Phillips curve rule of thumb, it passes through the point (5, 1). At the same time, the decline in the rate of unemployment that occurred during Year 1 shifts the demand pressure curve to the left. With the growth rate of nominal output still assumed to be 7 percent, holding the rate of unemployment to 4 percent in Year 2 will not be enough to keep inflation down to its 1 percent level of Year 1. Instead, an additional 1 percent decline in the rate of unemployment will be required. The new position of the demand pressure curve is thus DP_2, and it passes through the point (4, 4) as required by the demand pressure curve rule of thumb.

The intersection of Ph_2 and DP_2 shows that in Year 2, the rate of inflation will be 2.5 percent and the rate of unemployment 3.5 percent. Keeping the growth rate of nominal output at 7 percent for a second year thus results in a less attractive trade-off between inflation and unemployment than in the first year. In Year 1, unemployment fell by a full percentage point, and the rate of inflation increased by only one percentage point. In Year 2, unemployment falls only half a percentage point, and the rate of inflation rises by a point and a half.

In Year 3, policy makers will cut the growth rate of nominal output back to 3 percent, the same rate as in Year 0. Doing so does not, however, return the economy immediately to its standing start position. Instead, it precipitates an inflationary recession, as can be discovered by drawing the Phillips curve and demand pressure curves for Year 3. Because the rate of inflation expected in Year 3 rises to the rate actually experienced in Year 2, the Phillips curve shifts up another one and a half units to the position Ph_3. At the same time, the combined effect of the decline in the unemployment rate to 3.5 percent during Year 2 and the decline in the growth rate of nominal output to 3 percent in Year 3 shifts the demand pressure curve to the position DP_3.

Substitute $\dot{Y}_3 = 3$ and $U_2 = 3.5$ into Equation 17A.7 to check that this is the correct position for the demand pressure curve. Alternatively, apply the rule of thumb given earlier, which says that DP_3 must pass through the point $(U_{t-1}, \dot{Y}_t - 3)$ or, in this case, the point (3.5, 0). The intersection of Ph_3 and DP_3 gives an unemployment rate of 4.5 percent and a rate of inflation of 3 percent for Year 3. The rates of inflation and unemployment have both risen, while the rate of real growth has fallen to zero.

Problem 3: Beginning from the position of the economy for Year 3 in the previous problem, outline a four-year program for growth of nominal output that will bring the economy to a soft landing at zero inflation and 5 percent unemployment in Year 7.

Solution: Left to the reader. (Hint: Use a graphical trial-and-error method. The solution is not unique.)

SUGGESTIONS FOR FURTHER READING

Friedman, Milton. "The Role of Monetary Policy." *American Economic Review* 58 (May 1968): 1–17.
Friedman's presidential address to the American Economic Association, considered the original statement of the "accelerationist" view of inflation presented in this chapter.

Gordon, Robert J. *Macroeconomics.* Boston: Little, Brown, 1978.
Chapter 8 of this advanced intermediate textbook gives a somewhat more detailed exposition of a model very similar to that given in this chapter and its appendix.

Spencer, Roger W. "The National Plans to Curb Unemployment and Inflation." *Federal Reserve Bank of St. Louis Review,* April 1973.
An easily readable discussion of the spiraling pattern of inflation and unemployment, which was already apparent in 1973 and has continued since then.

CHAPTER 18

FURTHER TOPICS IN STABILIZATION POLICY

WHAT YOU WILL LEARN IN THIS CHAPTER

This chapter begins with a review of the effects of fiscal and monetary policy on output, employment, and the price level discussed in Chapters 8 through 17. The review will serve as background to a debate over how the tools of fiscal and monetary policy should be used to achieve the goals of economic stabilization: Should they be used actively to fine tune the economy, or should steady-as-you-go rules be followed instead? The final section of the chapter will introduce incomes policy and indexing—two types of macroeconomic policy that go beyond traditional demand management in the effort to achieve the goals of full employment, price stability, and balanced growth.

FOR REVIEW

Here are some important terms and concepts that will be put to use in this chapter. If you do not understand them, review them before proceeding.

- *Humphrey-Hawkins Act* (Chapter 7)
- *Indexing* (Chapter 7)
- *Keynesian-monetarist debate* (Chapter 14)
- *Adaptive and rational expectations* (Chapter 14)
- *The Phillips curve* (Chapters 15 and 16)
- *Job search theory* (Chapter 16)
- *Dynamics of inflation* (Chapter 17)

The Great Depression of the 1930s had many lasting effects on economic policy and economic thought. One of those effects was to give the government increased responsibility for economic stabilization—a responsibility that was formalized in the Employment Act of 1946 and the Humphrey-Hawkins Act of 1978.

The primary focus of stabilization policy, as it has developed over the years, has been the management of aggregate nominal demand. Basically, the idea is that if the economy goes into a slump and too many people are out of work, aggregate demand can be boosted with expansionary fiscal or monetary policy, and the economy can be gotten moving again. If a boom gets too hot and prices rise too fast, putting the damper on aggregate demand is supposed to cool things off. The hope is that by judicious use of expansionary and contractionary policy the economy can be fine tuned for prosperity without inflation.

As we have seen, however, things have not worked out particularly well in recent years for the would-be stabilizers, fine tuners, and demand managers.

The degree of instability experienced in the 1970s, in fact, has seriously called into doubt the adequacy of traditional approaches to stabilization policy. This chapter will look at the sources of some of those doubts and at some new directions that economic thinking is taking in response to them. The groundwork for this discussion will be laid initially by a review of some of what has been covered in the last ten chapters.

INFLATION, UNEMPLOYMENT, AND AGGREGATE DEMAND: A RECAP

Policies Affecting Aggregate Demand

Aggregate demand means the total value of all expenditures by all buyers in the economy. The concept of demand management thus encompasses all policies that affect the consumption plans of households, the investment plans of business firms, the plans of government units regarding the purchase of goods and services, and international trade of goods and services. Demand management policies fall into two groups—fiscal and monetary.

fiscal policy

Fiscal policy acts by directly varying the volume of planned expenditures injected into the circular flow through government purchases or withdrawn from the circular flow through taxation. Fiscal policy actions in turn affect private consumption and investment decisions and lead to a multiplier effect, which magnifies the impact of changes in taxes and government purchases.

monetary policy

Monetary policy, unlike fiscal policy, does not act by directly injecting new flows of expenditures into the economy. Instead, monetary actions inject new stocks of money into the portfolios of asset holders. The effects of monetary policy actions on aggregate demand are felt indirectly as people readjust their portfolios to accommodate the changed supply of money, thereby affecting the prices of other assets, interest rates, planned investment spending, consumer durables purchases, and so on. Nonetheless, although indirect, the effects of monetary policy are potentially quite powerful.

Just how powerful monetary policy is relative to fiscal policy is still a matter of some controversy between Keynesian and monetarist economists. Despite differences in emphasis, however, both sides to the debate would agree that fiscal and monetary policy in some appropriate combination can be used to expand or contract aggregate demand, thereby altering the equilibrium level of nominal national income and product.

The Dynamics of Inflation and Unemployment

Through fiscal and monetary actions, policy makers are able to exercise considerable control over nominal national income and product. The manipulation of nominal income and product, however, is only an indirect means of pursuing the ultimate policy goals of full employment, price stability, and real economic growth. It is thus critical to know how any given change in nominal output will be split up between changes in the price level and changes in real output and employment.

The Phillips Curve The Phillips curve, first introduced in Chapter 15, serves as a framework for discussion of this problem. The curve depicts a short-run trade-off between inflation and unemployment: more jobs if more inflation is tolerated. However, the curve does not represent a stable policy menu in the long run. It does not because the rate of unemployment depends not just on the rate of inflation but on the difference between the actual rate and the expected rate of inflation. The rate of unemployment that prevails when the actual rate of inflation is equal to the expected rate is called the natural rate of unemployment, and it is presently about 5 to 6 percent.

If the rate of inflation unexpectedly accelerates from a level to which people have become accustomed, the economy will move up and to the left along the short-run Phillips curve, and the unemployment rate will fall below the natural rate. When inflation speeds up, employers offer workers fatter wage deals than they have come to expect, and workers rapidly snap up the jobs. The average duration of unemployment falls, and the unemployment rate goes down. It stays down until people find out what prices are really doing. Higher prices mean that the workers' big new paychecks do not buy any more than before. Once workers come to expect a given rate of inflation, they start taking their time again shopping around for ever higher-paying jobs, and unemployment rises again to the natural rate—unless the rate of inflation in the meantime undergoes a further acceleration.

Inflationary Recession If the government puts the fiscal and monetary brakes on aggregate demand after a period of prolonged acceleration of inflation, policy and expectations for a time work at cross purposes. As aggregate demand slows and inventories begin to accumulate, firms begin to offer fewer jobs and raise wages less rapidly than before. Individual job seekers, however, do not immediately perceive that the entire job market picture has changed. They still look for job offers matching their inflationary expectations. Because such jobs have become harder to find, the average duration of unemployment and the unemployment rate rise, even while the momentum of inflation continues to carry prices higher. The growth rate of real output slows, and the economy enters a phase of inflationary recession.

If the growth rate of aggregate demand remains slow or slows further, however, the rate of inflation eventually begins to decline. Job seekers moderate their inflationary expectations (although the revision of expectations is likely to lag behind the actual decrease in the rate of inflation). Unemployment tends to remain higher than normal for as long as inflation continues to decelerate.

Finally, if fiscal and monetary policies are applied to speed up the growth of aggregate demand after a period of declining inflation, policy and expectations again operate at cross purposes for a time. Now, however, they produce the best, rather than the worst, of both worlds. The number and quality of job offers made available increase; and workers, now accustomed to slowing inflation, eagerly accept them. The unemployment rate can fall rapidly during such a reflationary period, which means that the increase in aggregate nominal demand can be accommodated by faster growth of real output without initially rekindling inflation. If aggregate demand policy remains strongly expansionary, however, this temporary respite will give way to accelerating inflation, and the economy will have completed a full cycle of accelerating inflation with low unemployment, inflationary recession, recession with decelerating inflation, and reflation with falling unemployment.

Markets and the Distribution of Information This, then, is a rough outline of the theory of inflation and unemployment put together in the last three chapters. Now that all the pieces are in place, it can be seen how the theory builds on the fundamental insight that markets are mechanisms for distributing information. In the best of times, the plans of businesspeople, workers, and consumers do not always mesh. Some people make mistakes, while others achieve windfall gains. Lots of little errors tend to cancel one another out.

Unanticipated changes in the rate of inflation or the direction of macroeconomic policy, however, add something new to the picture. Such changes can mean that, for a while, everyone will tend to make mistakes in the same direction at once. When inflation speeds up, a great many workers will accept pay deals that turn out not to be so good after all. When inflation slows down, many firms will find themselves stuck with wage bills and price lists that are higher than they ought to be. These widespread errors give rise to the changes in unemployment that are the familiar by-products of changes in the rate of inflation.

Does the theory say, then, that people are fools? Not at all. People are smart. They learn from experience. All the theory says is that learning does not take place at the speed of light. A little time passes after actual events change their course before people adjust their plans and expectations to new conditions. In the meantime, people may be led to do things they would not do if they had complete information about economic conditions.

Policy Implications This theory of the dynamics of inflation and unemployment contains some important implications for economic policy. They were discussed in detail in Chapter 17, but it is worth listing three of them here again.

1. Unexpected increases in the rate of inflation pull the rate of unemployment below what it otherwise would be. If policy makers allow inflation to run faster and faster year after year, they can keep unemployment low for quite a while.
2. When inflation slows after a long period of acceleration, people end up in the worst of all possible worlds. Inflationary expectations generate cost-push inflation, while the slowdown of demand pushes up unemployment. The worse the inflation, the more distasteful the cure.
3. Recession cures inflation, but only slowly. After the cure is underway and the rate of inflation is falling, a quick step-up of aggregate demand (reflation) temporarily brings the best of both worlds. Until expectations adjust to the reversal of policy, there is falling unemployment without rising inflation.

The theory reviewed here can now be applied to some current policy problems.

FINE TUNING VERSUS POLICY RULES

When economists express a fear that macroeconomic policy has failed, they do not mean that it has failed to have any effect on the economy. Everyone grants that the level of aggregate demand, measured in nominal terms, has a powerful influence on economic life. Disputes about the relative importance of monetary or fiscal tools of demand management should not obscure this agreement. Instead, doubts about demand management are doubts about whether the particular policies that have been pursued have had a stabilizing effect. The fear is that the powerful tools of demand management, if misused, can have results opposite to those intended.

Much of the debate over demand management revolves around two different philosophies of how such policies should be used. Traditionally, Keynesian economists have taken an activist line. They think that the federal government should make frequent and vigorous use of both fiscal and monetary policy tools in order to fine tune the economy. That way, they hope, just the desired mix of high employment, high real growth, and price stability can be achieved. Other economists, including most of those who consider themselves monetarists, argue that attempts to fine tune usually do more harm than good. In their view, the correct policy is instead one of steady-as-you-go, governed by rules that remain unchanged over long periods.

The Case for Fine Tuning

The case for fine tuning is based on three beliefs about the economic and political system of a modern democracy like the United States. The first is the belief that, left to itself, the private economy is unstable. The second is that the tools of demand management work fairly rapidly and predictably. The third is that, with careful scientific argument and patient persuasion, government authorities can be educated to use the tools of demand management in the best long-run interest of the public at large.

The belief that the private economy is unstable has a long history. For nearly two hundred years there have been alternating periods of boom and depression in market economies. By World War II, a whole branch of economic theory, under the name of business-cycle theory, had grown up to support this view. The Great Depression reinforced the idea of instability in the minds of all those who lived through it.

The idea that fiscal and monetary policies are quick and predictable in their effects on the economy is part and parcel of the Keynesian tradition. It is supported by much of the theory presented in Chapters 8 through 14 of this book.

Then there is the idea that in a democratic nation political power will end up in the hands of politicians who will use the tools of policy wisely. This is an outgrowth of the liberal tradition as it has developed since the 1930s.

Experience with Fine Tuning The fine tuners came into their own in the Kennedy-Johnson era. Initially, their policies met with success. The years 1961 to 1969 saw one of the longest periods of expansion in the history of the United States. Since that time something has gone wrong. Economic instability has increased. A stop-go policy cycle has pushed the economy into widening swings of unemployment and inflation. It looks, then, as if at least part of the fine tuner's argument must be incorrect. Either the tools of activist monetary and fiscal policy do not work as quickly and predictably as they should, or else the tools have been badly mishandled. What do the opponents of fine tuning have to say?

The Case against Fine Tuning

Opponents of fine tuning challenge every aspect of the case just set forth. They claim that their historical studies show the private economy to be more stable than is often thought. They are skeptical that politicians have the courage to keep long-run economic goals in mind when faced, in the short run, with the need for reelection. But the most telling point in the case against fine tuning is a challenge to the idea that the effects of demand management are either quick or predictable.

Inside lag The delay between the time a policy action is needed and the time it is taken.

Outside lag The delay between the time a policy action is taken and the time its effects on the economy are felt.

Lags In recent years, economists have begun to worry more and more about lags and delays in the operation of fiscal and monetary policy. There are two major kinds of lags. First, there is the so-called **inside lag**—the delay between the time policy action is needed and the time action is taken. Second, there is the **outside lag**—the delay between the time policy action is taken and the time its effects on the economy are felt.

The inside lag has several sources. One is the time it takes to gather accurate economic statistics. During the famous episode of "the Fed's finest hour" (see Case 14.1), President Johnson would probably have resisted tight monetary policy less if he had known how fast demand was already expanding. In late 1972 and early 1973, both monetary and fiscal policies might have been tighter if people in Washington had known in time of shortages that were developing in key industries. And in 1974, restrictive policy might have been relaxed earlier if it had been known how rapidly business inventories were piling up. A second source of inside lag is the legislative process of Congress. This is particularly serious for fiscal policy. (Recall that the Kennedy tax cut—see Cases 10.1 and 14.2—took over two years to reach the statute books.) Because the Federal Reserve System is independent of Congress, the inside lag for monetary policy is probably shorter than for fiscal policy.

The causes of the outside lag for fiscal and monetary policy are not really very well understood, but it is well established that the lag is a serious one. For monetary policy, it is likely to be at least six months before the first important effects of a policy change are felt and perhaps two years before all the effects have worked through the system. It is sometimes thought that fiscal policy has a shorter outside lag, although just how much shorter is not clear.

Lags and Destabilization Monetarist economists such as Milton Friedman have long argued that the length and variability of policy lags make fine tuning very hard. You can understand this if you have ever stood under a shower when the water temperature changed. First you are scalded. When you try to adjust the taps, you find that there is a lag of a few seconds between the time you turn them and the time the water coming out changes in temperature. You overreact to the scalding and are next frozen. By the time you get the system fine tuned again, the temperature is probably back where it was in the first place. You might just as well have stepped aside and waited.

The point is that when there are lags, policy actions can have a destabilizing rather than a stabilizing effect. A policy that is intended to speed recovery from a recession may take effect only in time to make inflation worse when recovery is already underway. An action intended to cool off a boom may take hold near the bottom of the next recession, when it is least wanted.

Stability and Rational Expectations

Somewhat paradoxically, while many monetarists have argued that fine tuning works poorly because policy lags are long and variable, still other economists have recently advanced the notion that fine tuning no longer works to affect unemployment and real output because policy lags are much shorter than previously thought. The latter economists are the so-called rational expectations theorists mentioned at the end of Chapter 17.

These theorists are fond of emphasizing that people tend to respond rationally and intelligently in their own interest when they see change coming. Attempts to fine tune the real economy through demand management, however, are based at least in part on the faith that people will make mistakes when confronted with changing economic conditions. As shown above, for example, the effects of changes in aggregate demand on employment and real output occur when job seekers' inflationary expectations are out of line with the actual trend of inflation.

Economists such as Robert Lucas, a major exponent of rational expectations theory, argue that as the same patterns of policies are repeated over and over again, people tend to catch on. As the inflationary process has been described, for example, more expansionary monetary policy first has the effect of stimulating real output. Then, gradually, as the economy adjusts fully, it pushes up the rate of inflation. Lucas would argue that people have become aware of the link between monetary policy and changes in the rate of inflation, so that as soon as a change in monetary policy comes to be anticipated, they immediately adjust their inflationary expectations. Job seekers are no longer fooled into taking jobs that they would once have thought represented just isolated instances of good luck. The short-run Phillips curve is seen as shifting up more rapidly than would be the case under purely adaptive expectations, and the economy stays close to the vertical long-run Phillips curve. Unemployment and real output cease to respond to anticipated changes in monetary policy. As a result, all nominal values in the economy—wages, prices, and nominal interest

---

Robert Lucas, professor of economics at the University of Chicago, is a leading exponent of rational expectations theory. Together with such colleagues as Thomas Sargent of the University of Minnesota and Robert Barro of the University of Rochester, he has challenged many established ideas of macroeconomics.

Lucas received both his undergraduate and graduate training at the University of Chicago, but in some respects his own theories are as critical of Chicago's school of monetarism as they are of Keynesian macroeconomics. In particular, his work focuses on an assumption implicit in older theories—an assumption that people cannot see opportunities or learn to act in their own self-interest. Attempts to implement policy based on such an assumption are bound to run into trouble, Lucas thinks, because sooner or later someone will catch on. For example, although the government may for a time be able to fool workers with unexpectedly high rates of inflation, thus lowering the unemployment rate, workers will eventually come to adjust their plans for ever accelerating inflation, and the policies will no longer be effective.

While many economists remain skeptical of the specifics of the theories advanced by Lucas and his colleagues, the general attitude that underlies rational expectations theory does appear to be spreading. This attitude includes an insistence on real world testing of theories and a skepticism about the ability of traditional macroeconomic policy to fine tune the economy for full employment, price stability, and growth.

Robert Lucas (1937–)

rates—are seen as adjusting very rapidly to any shift in monetary policy that is foreseen.

A similar argument can be made for fiscal policy. Believing that neither expected monetary nor expected fiscal policy actions have any significant effect on real output or employment, rational expectations theorists explain variations in real output and employment that do occur in terms of unanticipated policy moves or outside influences not directly related to macroeconomic policy.

As yet, few economists would accept the notion that the average job seeker or home buyer makes full, rational use of all available information about the present and future course of economic policy or the notion that prices respond immediately to predictable changes in monetary policy. Nonetheless, there is little doubt that many key decision makers in the private sector—corporate economic forecasters, financial analysts, union negotiators—have learned a lot about inflation and its causes during the decade of the 1970s. Even if people are not so universally rational in their expectations as to make traditional demand management totally ineffective, enough of them have become sufficiently sophisticated to introduce additional complications into the conduct of stabilization policy.

Policy Rules as an Alternative to Fine Tuning

What do the opponents of fine tuning offer in its place? Specific suggestions vary. A common theme, though, is that demand management should be made subject to explicit long-term rules rather than being left to the discretion of policy makers.

A Monetary Growth Rule Milton Friedman has for years tried to popularize the idea of a monetary growth rule. He suggests that the Fed be required by law to keep money growth to the same steady pace year after year. Friedman thinks the constancy of the pace matters more than the specific rate but suggests that a good target would be equal to the long-run growth of potential real GNP. That would be somewhere in the neighborhood of 3 percent per year at present.

Balanced Budget Rules On the fiscal policy side, a variety of rules that would require the federal government in one way or another to maintain a balanced budget have been proposed. Not all such rules, however, have been put forward for the specific purpose of improving economic stability. Some are instead aimed primarily at placing a constraint on government spending as a share of national income. Nonetheless, some variants of a balanced budget rule might have stabilizing effects.

Full employment balanced budget rule A rule under which taxes and spending policy would be adjusted so that the federal budget would be in balance if the economy were at full employment.

The leading proposal of this kind is a rule that would require a so-called **full employment balanced budget.** Under such a rule, Congress and the president would decide the level of government purchases solely on the basis of the actual needs they see for defense, housing, health care, and so on. No attention would be paid at this stage to the macroeconomic effects of these policies. Then, having made the spending decisions, they would adjust taxes so that the budget would be in balance if the economy were at full employment. Because actual net taxes change with the size of nominal income, there would still be actual budget deficits in times of recession and surpluses in times of exceptionally high employment. Fiscal policy of an "automatic" variety would exist. This, it is hoped, would have a stabilizing effect on real output.

In contrast, it is widely feared that any stricter policy rule that required the federal budget to be in balance every year regardless of the state of the economy could have destabilizing effects. During a recession, tax revenues tend to fall and transfer payments to rise. To maintain a year-to-year balanced budget, the government would have to cut purchases as economic activity contracted, thereby further reducing aggregate demand. Such a policy would be pro-cyclical, according to the usual multiplier analysis, and hence destabilizing. (To guard against this problem, some advocates of a strict balanced budget have suggested that in years of high employment, the government could set aside a "reserve fund" for expenditure in time of recession. Such a policy would be tantamount to following a full employment balanced budget rule.)

The Growing Humility of Economic Policy Makers

As of this writing, neither the Fed nor the fiscal policy makers in Congress and the White House are inclined to bind themselves to rigid long-term policy rules. Nonetheless, there appears to be a growing realization that the government's ability to steer economic events may be somewhat more limited than it was thought to be in the heady years of the early 1960s. This changing attitude is evident from a review of recent editions of the *Economic Report of the President,* prepared each year by the President's Council of Economic Advisers. In the 1976 *Report,* President Ford's council wrote:

> There is a lesson to be drawn from past policy mistakes. The history of monetary and fiscal policies demonstrates that we have a great deal to learn about implementing discretionary policy changes. Our ability to forecast is at best imperfect, especially in an increasingly complex and interdependent world, and the difficulties in forecasting grow larger as we extend the period for which the forecast is made. . . .
>
> The proper conclusion is not that we should forswear the use of discretionary policy. . . . Discretionary policies do have an important function in our economic system. But we must be mindful of the great difficulties in successfully executing countercyclical policies.
>
> What is called for in our judgment is a steadier course in macroeconomic policies than has been followed in the past. We should set policies broadly consistent with sustainable long-term noninflationary growth and try to limit the size and duration of any policy deviations that promise short-term benefits but risk interfering with our long-run goals.[1]

Still more recently, President Carter's advisers commented in their 1979 report:

> Our ability to foresee economic developments and to design appropriate policies to deal with emerging problems over a 5-year period [as required by the Humphrey-Hawkins Act] is extremely limited. The outlook for 1979 is uncertain, the prospects for 1980 are much more so, and the probable course of later developments can be foreseen only dimly.[2]

BEYOND DEMAND MANAGEMENT

It can be seen, then, that although traditional tools of demand management are not likely to be abandoned soon, economists have become pessimistic about

---

[1]President's Council of Economic Advisers, *Economic Report of the President* (Washington, D.C.: Government Printing Office, 1976), pp. 20–21.

[2]President's Council of Economic Advisers, *Economic Report of the President* (Washington, D.C.: Government Printing Office, 1979), p. 111.

the ability of discretionary fiscal and monetary policies alone to return the economy quickly to the desired path of full employment, price stability, and balanced economic growth. Not surprisingly, they have cast about for supplementary policy tools. This section will examine two such tools—incomes policies and indexing.

Incomes Policies

Incomes policy A policy that attempts to control wages, salaries, earnings, and prices directly in order to fight inflation.

An **incomes policy** is any policy that directly controls wages, salaries, and earnings for the purpose of fighting inflation. Ordinarily, such a policy also includes direct controls on wholesale and retail prices. The United States has experimented with incomes policies, and they have become a permanent feature of economic life in many Western European countries. It will be worthwhile to look at how these policies work and why they are highly controversial.

The Theoretical Case for an Incomes Policy From a theoretical point of view, the case for an incomes policy is strongest when the policy is intended as a temporary measure to fight inflationary recession. Chapter 17 showed that when policy makers put on the brakes after a long period of accelerating inflation, the economy is thrown for a time into the worst of all possible worlds. Workers and employers base their plans on the expectation of more inflation; yet aggregate demand is actually tailing off. Wages, prices, and unemployment all rise at once—until expectations adjust to reality.

Now enters the timely use of an incomes policy. Suppose that just at the moment the fiscal and monetary brakes are put on, the government announces a program of strict price and wage controls. This is done with great fanfare and a show of grim determination to lick inflation once and for all. What is hoped is that workers and businesspeople will believe that these controls are going to stop inflation. If they do, they will revise their inflationary expectations downward much more rapidly than if they have to wait to learn from experience. This revision of expectations will get rid of the cost-push element of the inflationary recession. Workers will know that they do not have to push for high wages to beat inflation, so they will accept the controls. Firms will know that they will not have to pay higher wages, so they will keep their prices in line and concentrate on increasing their sales. The readjustment to price stability and full employment will be more rapid and less painful than it would be without an incomes policy.

Problems with Controls So much for theory. Granting that wage and price controls are helpful in squeezing the cost-push element out of an inflationary recession, does that mean that they are a cure-all for the country's economic problems? Not really. The problem is that controls can be of help in correcting past mistakes in demand management policy, but they cannot work as a substitute for sound demand management. Unfortunate things can happen if the government tries to use an incomes policy to fight inflation without also slowing the growth of aggregate demand or if it leaves controls in force after a recession is over and a new boom gets underway.

If aggregate demand rises in nominal terms, one of three things must logically happen. First, national product (aggregate supply) may rise in real terms to meet the increased nominal demand without a rise in prices. Second, prices may rise to meet the increase in nominal demand without an increase in output. Finally, neither prices nor output may rise, in which case the aggregate quantity of goods demanded will exceed the aggregate quantity of goods supplied, and there will be an overall shortage of goods. A combination of these three alternatives may sometimes occur, but no fourth alternative is logically possible.

Naturally, the first alternative is the most attractive. It will mean real economic growth without inflation. Real economic growth can come from only two sources, however. One is an increase in potential GNP, which can be hoped for at the rate of about 3 percent per year in the long run. The other is a fall in unemployment. This source of growth is temporary, because unemployment will soon reach a level below which it can fall no further. In the long run, then, real growth without inflation or shortages is possible only if demand management limits the growth of nominal GNP to the potential long-term growth rate of real GNP.

An incomes policy cannot buy real growth without inflation or shortages if that rule of demand management is not followed. All it can do is determine which of the second two alternatives will occur. If aggregate demand is allowed to run away without controls, the result is runaway inflation. If controls are applied and demand still runs away, the result is shortages, rationing, and black markets.

The U.S. Experience with Controls There have been two major experiments with wage and price controls in the U.S. economy. One was during World War II. Huge wartime government spending made it impractical to control aggregate demand. The effects of controls under wartime conditions were as predicted. Rationing was introduced, and there were widespread shortages and black markets. All this was tolerated because people felt rationing to be the fairest way to distribute essentials during the emergency. As soon as the war had been won, controls were abandoned with a sigh of relief.

The other major experiment with an incomes policy took place during the Nixon administration. This case is much more relevant to future policy and deserves a closer look.

Case 18.1
Nixon's Wage and Price Controls

On August 15, 1971, President Richard Nixon announced a dramatic new economic policy. The policy was prompted as much by international as by domestic events, but the part of the program that got the most attention was domestic. It was a strict ninety-day freeze on all prices and wages, intended to combat inflation.

The freeze later became known as Phase I of what proved to be a protracted experiment with controls. It was followed by Phase II, a full-fledged incomes policy lasting until January 11, 1973. Under Phase II, firms could raise prices to cover increases in costs but could not increase their profit margins. Wage increases were limited to 5.5 percent except in special circumstances.

Phases I and II came at the sort of time when price controls can be expected to work best. As Exhibit 18.1 shows, inflation had been on the decline for almost two years. Phase I clearly speeded the fall of inflation while it lasted, although some of the gains were lost in a post-freeze "bulge." By mid-1972, the bulge had been overcome, and the rate of inflation had fallen further.

According to recent estimates by Alan S. Blinder and William J. Newton of Princeton, the combined effect of Phases I and II was to hold the price level some

Exhibit 18.1
Inflation and the Nixon wage-price controls

The Nixon administration experimented with wage and price controls between 1971 and 1974. Controls were introduced when the rate of inflation was already falling. The initial freeze slowed inflation immediately, although it was followed by a price bulge at the start of Phase II. During Phases III and IV, in the face of rapid expansion of aggregate demand, controls failed to hold the line against inflation.

Source: President's Council of Economic Advisers, *Economic Report of the President* (Washington, D.C.: Government Printing Office, various issues).

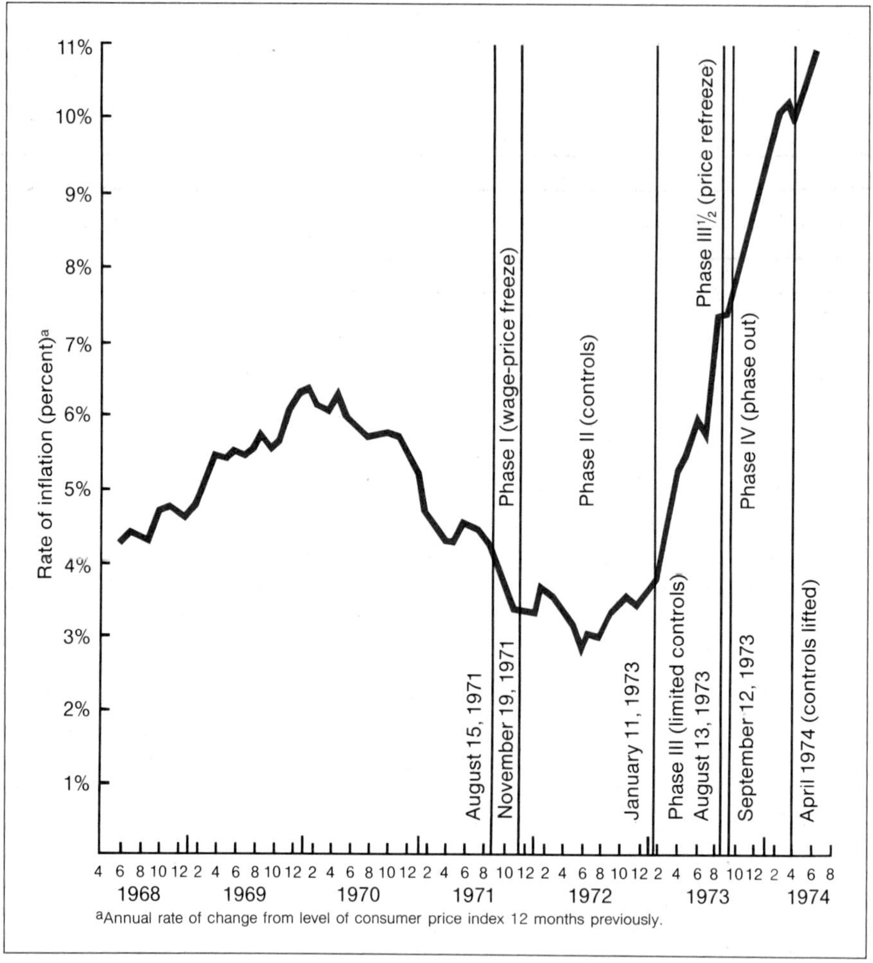

1.22 percentage points below the level it would have reached in the absence of controls.[3] This modest but measurable contribution to slowing the rate of inflation was achieved at the cost of only a few shortages, mainly in lumber. No widespread disruptions were felt.

Believing that Phases I and II had done their job, Nixon wisely followed the orthodox prescription and began to put incomes policy back on the shelf. In January 1973, Phase II was replaced by Phase III. This phase imposed slightly looser standards and emphasized self-enforcement. By the time Phase III came into effect, a strong recovery of aggregate demand was underway, and the rate of infla-

[3]Alan S. Blinder and William J. Newton, "The 1971–1974 Controls Program and the Price Level: An Econometric Postmortem," National Bureau of Economic Research Working Paper No. 279, September 1978, p. 29.

tion turned upward, as shown in Exhibit 18.1. According to Blinder and Newton, prices rose during Phase III at a rate just slightly faster than they would have if controls had never been imposed at all, indicating that some "catch up" inflation was occurring during this period. Political pressure built up to "get tough." Nixon responded in August 1973 with a refreeze of prices and wages, which came to be called Phase III 1/2.

Taken together, Phases III and III 1/2 fit the principle that controls will not work when aggregate demand is not controlled. During Phase III, when controls were weak, inflation went up at a very rapid pace. During the refreeze of Phase III 1/2 inflation was temporarily halted, but serious shortages and distortions began to show up. Contractors could not build because they could not get reinforcing bars for their concrete. Miners could not mine because they could not get the bolts they needed to strengthen their mine shafts. Publishers had to shift to expensive, high-quality paper because cheap, low-quality paper became hard to get. Firms began to hoard inventories of raw materials in fear of more shortages to come.

It was judged that the distortions of Phase III 1/2 were too great a price to pay for artificially keeping inflation down. In August 1973, Nixon switched to Phase IV, which was a phase-out; and in April 1974, Congress let the authority for controls expire altogether. According to the Blinder and Newton estimates, catch-up inflation then began in earnest. By August 1974, prices had reached the level they would have been at if controls had never been in force. What is more, catch-up inflation continued for many months thereafter. By 1975, the price level was nearly 1 percent higher than it would have been if the Nixon incomes policy had never been conceived.

The Continuing Interest in Incomes Policy The Nixon experiment with controls was a mixed success at best. As long as inflation was falling anyway, the controls appear to have helped a little—and at least provided useful political window dressing. When inflation began to rise again, they proved useless and then worse than useless. Given the record shown in Exhibit 18.1, it would be reasonable to suppose that today people would be less likely to expect controls to do any good, so their important psychological effects would be diminished. One hardly has to be a full-fledged rational expectations theorist to reach this conclusion.

Nonetheless, despite the Nixon experience, both academic economists and federal policy makers maintain a continuing interest in incomes policies. Despite the unwillingness of Congress to repeat the Nixon experiment by authorizing mandatory wage and price controls, the Carter administration embarked in late 1978 on an ambitious program of wage and price guidelines. Stripped to their essentials, the Carter guidelines, in their original form, were supposed to limit wage increases to 7 percent per year and price increases to a rate 0.5 percent less than in the immediately preceding period. The guidelines were nominally voluntary for the largest unions and corporations, but they were backed by the threat to withhold government contracts in cases of noncompliance. By mid 1979, the Carter program was in disarray, and the rate of inflation had accelerated well into double-digit territory.

TIP Meanwhile, as the rate of inflation turned up again after the 1974–75 recession, yet another kind of incomes policy began to become fashionable in academic circles: the idea of a **tax-based incomes policy** (**TIP** for short).

Tax-based incomes policy (TIP) An incomes policy employing tax incentives (penalties or rebates) to secure compliance with otherwise voluntary wage and price guidelines.

TIP exists in a number of variants, but all have in common the idea of using the tax system to provide incentives for compliance with otherwise voluntary wage and price guidelines. In the so-called "carrot" version of TIP, advocated by Arthur Okun, firms and/or workers who held their prices and wages to the level sanctioned by the guidelines would receive tax reductions or rebates to reward them for their good behavior. In the "stick" version of TIP, associated with Henry Wallich and Sydney Weintraub, tax penalties would be imposed on guideline violators. Either way, it is argued, firms and workers would have an actual financial incentive to comply with the price and wage guidelines. Nonetheless, unlike mandatory price and wage controls, firms facing exceptional supply and demand conditions in either their labor markets or their product markets would be free to establish prices and wages in excess of the guidelines if they were willing to pay the penalties or forgo the benefits specified by the particular variant of TIP that was in force. This freedom, it is said, would be sufficient to ensure that shortages, rationing, and black markets would not emerge.

Since TIP has not been tried to date, discussions of its effects and practicability remain highly speculative. Clearly, a truly comprehensive trial of TIP would require an enormous administrative apparatus—presumably nearly as big as full-fledged wage and price controls. TIP opponents argue that the administrative difficulties would be insurmountable; TIP advocates argue among themselves over whether the carrot or the stick variant would be more feasible administratively, whether TIP should apply to prices as well as wages, whether it should apply to all firms or only large ones, and so on.

One subtle but hard-to-dismiss argument even holds that the effect of TIP would be to speed rather than to slow inflation. According to this argument, any TIP policy, whether of the carrot or the stick variety, would be equivalent to a tax on wages. In a market economy, growing firms wishing to attract the added workers they need to expand output normally have to pay premium wages; under TIP, they would not only have to pay premium wages but would have to pay a tax penalty (or forgo a tax benefit) as well. By discouraging firms from expanding, TIP would slow the growth of real output. And for a given growth rate of aggregate nominal demand, slower growth of real output means more rapid inflation. TIP advocates have countered that exceptions could be made for rapidly expanding industries and firms, but to do so would clearly add considerably to the administrative burdens faced by the program.

Indexing

Given the somewhat limited success to date with incomes policy in the United States, some economists have turned to a very different kind of policy that also goes beyond demand management: the policy called indexing. As explained in Chapter 7, *indexing* means inflation-proofing wages, taxes, debts, savings, and a host of other things by using escalator clauses to adjust nominal values when prices change. It is viewed partly as a way of combating inflation and partly as a way of easing some of inflation's worst effects when it does occur.

The best-known advocate of indexing has been Milton Friedman. His program for indexing features five specific measures. The first three, which apply to government, would be compulsory:

1. Indexing income taxes. If, say, the consumer price index went up 10 percent in a year, the $5,000–$5,999 income bracket would become the $5,500–$6,599 bracket, the $6,000–$6,999 bracket would become $6,600–$7,799, and so on. Corporate income taxes would be indexed the same way.

2. Indexing capital gains for tax purposes. If you bought a house for $30,000 in 1976 and sold it for $40,000 in 1978, you would have had to declare a capital gain of $10,000. If prices had gone up by 15 percent in the meantime, though, $4,500 of that amount would be only "paper" gain, not real capital gain. Under Friedman's plan, you would pay taxes only on the remaining $5,500.
3. Indexing government bonds. U.S. savings bonds would be written so that they would pay some fixed rate of interest (say 3 percent) plus the annual rate of inflation. If the consumer price index went up by 8 percent in a year, a bond would earn 11 percent that year (3 + 8 = 11). In effect, indexed bonds would pay a guaranteed real rate of interest rather than the guaranteed nominal rate promised by ordinary bonds.

In addition to these actions by government, Friedman would hope for additional voluntary actions in the private sector. These would include:

1. Indexing private corporate bonds, mortgage loans, and perhaps even some savings deposits. This would work just like the indexing of government bonds.
2. Indexing wages and salaries. Many union contracts already have "escalator clauses" that do this. Under such contracts, if the consumer price index went up by 5 percent, wages would also rise by 5 percent more than they would have otherwise. Friedman hopes that these kinds of contracts become more widespread.

Effects of Indexing How would indexing help? Proponents argue that there would be three beneficial effects.

First, indexing would, like wage and price controls, help squeeze the cost-push element out of inflationary recession. As things are now, even when inflation slows, workers want to keep pushing wages up because they fear that they will need the higher wages to offset expected inflation. With indexing, workers would no longer have to fear inflation. If prices went up, they would be protected by escalator clauses; and if they did not go up, the protection would not be needed. There would be no need to readjust labor contracts to raise nominal wages. Indexing would thus help keep the Phillips curve from continuing to rise during an inflationary recession. A slowdown in the growth rate of aggregate nominal demand would have less of an effect on employment and more of an effect on prices than otherwise.

Second, indexing would reduce the government's temptation to let aggregate demand run out of control. As things are now, the government gains enormously by inflation. People and corporations are pushed into higher tax brackets. People are taxed for capital gains that are really only "paper" gains. And the real cost of paying off the national debt goes down, which means that people who bought government bonds in the past are forced to pay an inflation "tax" too. Friedman estimates the government's revenue from such inflation "taxes" to have been $25 billion in 1973 alone.[4] With indexing, government could not get these huge windfall gains. Policy makers would thus have less incentive to pump up aggregate demand.

Finally, indexing would relieve some of the burdens of inflation even if it

[4]Milton Friedman, *Monetary Correction*, Institute of Economic Affairs Occasional Paper No. 41 (London: Institute of Economic Affairs, 1974), pp. 14–15.

did not halt inflation altogether. Now, inflation robs people of the real value of their savings and confers windfall gains on those lucky enough to have gone into debt before inflation became reflected in high nominal rates. Inflation is a particular hardship on the elderly who are attempting to live off savings in retirement. Indexed government bonds would give them a valuable form of protection.

Prospects for Indexing Indexing is not a completely untried idea in the United States. Social security payments, federal retirement benefits, and the wages of some government workers are already indexed. Many unions, including the huge auto workers' union, have escalator clauses in their contracts. In Canada and Australia, the personal income tax is now indexed. In Argentina, the current leader, almost everything in the economy is indexed. In 1978, Congress came very close to passing a bill that would have indexed capital gains taxes, and similar legislation will doubtless be submitted again. If inflation continues in the United States, it is likely that indexing will become still more widespread here.

Not all economists, however, are convinced that indexing would always have the desirable effects predicted by its advocates. Although it might help control inflation produced by excessive inflationary expectations, it is not clear that it would work as well to control commodity inflation resulting from reductions in supplies of food, energy, or other important goods. Critics of indexing also warn that the policy creates temptations for the government to fiddle with the price indexes themselves, underreporting the true rate of inflation. Proponents of indexing reply that it is not a cure-all. It is just one of a number of ideas that may make it easier to recover from the inflationary effects of past errors in demand management and to avoid a repetition of those errors.

CONCLUSIONS

Macroeconomics as it is now known was born in the crisis of the Great Depression. Before that time, the distinction between what is now called macroeconomics and microeconomics was not as sharp as it later became. In particular, part of what made Keynes's ideas catch on was their macro quality. To the followers of Keynes, it seemed that the really important features of national economic life could be captured in a few key relationships between broad aggregate quantities. Macroeconomics meant building with big blocks labeled "consumption," "investment," "aggregate supply," "money," and so on. The demand management policies of the 1960s grew out of this macroeconomic approach.

Today, the distinction between macroeconomics and microeconomics is once more becoming blurred. One thing more than any other unites the critics of the theory and policy of the past—a belief in the great importance of understanding the detailed microstructure of economic life. This is as true of economists who are liberals as of those who are conservatives. It is as true of neo-Keynesians as it is of monetarists. And it is true of those who simply look for the truth with no labels attached.

The exciting topics of macroeconomics today are such micro questions as: How can we understand unemployment in terms of the job search decisions of individual workers? How is cost-push inflation generated in concentrated, as compared with competitive, industries? Which particular sectors of the economy are affected first and which only after a long lag when new money is injected into the economy? How do individual workers, consumers, and businesspeople form their expectations and plans for the future?

We are back, it seems, to the theme with which the book began. Economics is about people. It is not about aggregate demand or expansionary gaps or Phillips curves—except when these things are understood as expressions of the way individual people think and act and plan.

SUMMARY

1. Modern theories of inflation and unemployment place major emphasis on the role of expectations in determining how demand management policies affect the economy. When there are unexpected changes in the rate of inflation, many workers and employers make mistakes and do things they would not otherwise have done. These mistakes show up as changes in the unemployment rate.
2. If the rate of inflation climbs faster and faster each year, unemployment can be kept low for a long period. When the rate slows down, an inflationary recession is likely to result. Recession cures inflation, but only slowly. When aggregate demand first begins to grow again after a recession, unemployment may fall sharply—with little increase in inflation.
3. There are important lags in the use of fiscal and monetary policies. There is an inside lag between the time a policy is needed and the time it is enacted, and there is an outside lag between that time and the time it takes effect. If lags are long enough, attempts to fine tune the economy can have destabilizing rather than stabilizing effects. For this reason, some economists frown on fine tuning and advocate steady-as-you-go policy rules instead.
4. Incomes policies (wage and price controls) are one kind of stabilization policy that goes beyond demand management. There is good reason to believe that temporary controls may be helpful in easing the effects of inflationary recession. But an incomes policy cannot work as a substitute for good demand management.
5. Indexing seeks to fight inflation by tying the nominal values of taxes, bonds, mortgages, wages, and other things to the purchasing power of the dollar. Indexing is hoped to have three beneficial effects. It may, like wage-price controls, help squeeze the cost-push element out of inflationary recession. It may also lessen the incentive that government now has to inflate. And it may make it easier for retired and middle-class people to protect their savings against rising prices.

DISCUSSION QUESTIONS

1. In what sense does an abnormally high or low rate of unemployment indicate that the market is not performing its function of distributing information very well?
2. What specific reforms in government can you think of that would slow the inside lag of economic policy? The outside lag?
3. Herbert Stein is a relatively conservative economist who does not usually support spending large amounts of money to expand the federal bureaucracy. Yet he advocates spending large amounts of money to improve the quality of economic

statistics available to government and the speed with which they are collected. Why does he think the data gathering branch of government is so important?

4. Go to the library, and see if you can find the *Economic Report of the President* for any of the years during President Kennedy's term of office. Do you think those reports generally reflect a confidence in the ability of policy makers to fine tune the economy? Find some specific passage to contrast with the passages from the 1976 and 1979 reports quoted in this chapter.

SUGGESTIONS FOR FURTHER READING

Blinder, Alan S., and Newton, William J. "The 1971–1974 Controls Program and the Price Level: An Econometric Postmortem." Cambridge, Mass.: National Bureau of Economic Research, Discussion Paper No. 279, September 1978.
In addition to giving the numerical estimates of the impact of the Nixon controls cited in Case 18.1, this paper presents a brief history of controls and earlier econometric estimates of their effects.

Fellner, William, ed. *Contemporary Economic Problems.* Washington, D.C.: American Enterprise Institute, annually.
This annual publication of the American Enterprise Institute always includes a number of papers on problems of macroeconomic policy. Back issues, as well as the most recent one, are worth consulting.

Friedman, Milton. *Monetary Correction.* Institute of Economic Affairs Occasional Paper No. 41. London: Institute of Economic Affairs, 1974.
Friedman makes his case for indexation here.

Gordon, Robert J. *Macroeconomics.* Boston: Little, Brown, 1978.
In Chapter 12, entitled "The Monetarist-Nonmonetarist Debate on Policy Activism," Gordon argues that the debate over fine tuning versus rules is much more important than the debate over the relative effectiveness of monetary and fiscal policies. Also worth noting are Gordon's brief but generally skeptical comments on the workability of indexation as macroeconomic policy (see pages 325–326).

Pechman, Joseph A., ed. *Setting National Priorities.* Washington, D.C.: Brookings Institution, annually.
This annual publication of the Brookings Institution is principally an analysis of the federal budget, but it includes useful sections on general issues of macroeconomic policy as well.

President's Council of Economic Advisers. *Economic Report of the President.* Washington, D.C.: Government Printing Office, annually.
Mentioned several times before as a suggested reading, this important source should be consulted for the administration's latest line on the topics covered in this chapter.

PART THREE

THE THEORY OF PRICES AND MARKETS

CHAPTER 19
THE ECONOMICS OF POLLUTION

WHAT YOU WILL LEARN IN THIS CHAPTER

This chapter will explain how the problem of pollution, like other economic problems, can be treated as a problem of allocating scarce resources to their best uses. It will apply the concepts of opportunity cost, marginal analysis, and supply and demand to determine the optimal degree of pollution abatement. Then it will examine the advantages and disadvantages of various approaches to pollution abatement, including the command-and-control approach currently favored by environmental regulators and other approaches that place more emphasis on efficiency and economic incentives. Finally, it will explore briefly the normative as well as the positive economics of pollution.

FOR REVIEW

Here are some important terms and concepts that will be put to use in this chapter. If you do not understand them, review them before proceeding.

- *Opportunity cost and the margin (Chapter 1)*
- *Market justice and distributive justice (Chapter 1)*

In recent years, economists have devoted increasing attention to the interrelated problems of pollution, energy, population, and resource depletion. These problems take on an increased urgency as the planet earth seems to shrink year by year. Each year there seem to be fewer unpolluted areas remaining; each year the ratio of the earth's surface area to its population declines; and each year people burrow deeper into the planet's mines and wells to extract scarce resources that can never be replaced. What does the future hold in store for the planet?

Economics, as the science of scarcity, has much to say about pollution, energy, population, and resource depletion. The more tightly scarcity presses, the more important it is to use resources wisely. Economics can help in three ways: First, it can help formulate realistic standards of wise use against which to measure the actual allocation of resources. Second, it can help identify the sources of past and present errors in resource use. Third, it can help formulate improved policies that will make it possible to meet the challenge of the future successfully.

This chapter begins the job by discussing the problem of pollution. It puts the familiar tools of supply and demand to work in a novel way to analyze the demand for pollution opportunities. In doing so, it provides a framework for comparing several different strategies of pollution control.

Chapter 20 will attend to the problems of energy and resource depletion, and Chapter 21 will turn from the problems of industrialized countries to the problems of population and economic development faced by third world countries.

POLLUTION AS AN ECONOMIC PROBLEM

Pollution and Scarcity

Everyone has something to say about pollution. There are as many different ways of looking at the problem as there are people. Ecologists look at pollution in terms of the disruption of complex systems of plant and animal life. Politicians look at it in terms of votes. Moralists look at it in terms of good and evil. Economists too have a point of view.

From the economic point of view, pollution is a problem of scarcity. The critical scarce resource is the waste disposal capacity of the environment. That capacity is not unlimited. Air, water, and land areas can absorb human and industrial wastes to a certain extent without adverse effects. Some production by-products can be incorporated into natural cycles. Small amounts of pollutants can be diluted to imperceptible concentrations. However, the capacity for natural recycling and dilution is already smaller than the waste output of the economic system in many areas.

Once pollution has been identified as an economic problem, familiar tools of economic analysis can be applied to it. The discussion that follows will show how economic ideas such as opportunity cost, marginalism, and supply and demand can aid in understanding the problem of pollution and in finding ways to deal with it.

Trade-offs and Opportunity Costs

Economists think of environmental issues in terms of trade-offs and opportunity costs. Some trade-offs involve converting wastes from one form into another. Most methods of pollution abatement do not really get rid of wastes but merely change their physical form. Production and consumption are, after all, subject to the law of the conservation of matter. Scrubbing systems on factory smokestacks convert airborne wastes into waterborne wastes, but they do not reduce the total tonnage of wastes. Sewage treatment systems convert waterborne wastes into solid wastes, but some place must still be found to dump the sludge. Incineration gets rid of solid wastes but creates airborne wastes.

Recycling is often pictured as a way out of these trade-offs, since it converts wastes into useful substances rather than other wastes. Yet even recycling involves opportunity costs. To gather bottles and cans and remelt them or to remove usable sulfur from the smoke of burning coal and oil requires a lot of energy. This energy produces waste heat. Ultimately, recycling means trading off material pollution for energy pollution.

Of course, this does not mean that waste treatment and recycling are futile. It is just because wastes cannot be made to vanish that it is very important to release them into the environment in the least destructive way. Changing wastes from one form into another makes the maximum use of scarce environmental waste disposal capacities under a variety of local conditions.

There is also a second important set of trade-offs bearing on the pollution problem. Pollution can sometimes be reduced by substituting one product for another. It is possible, for example, to substitute unleaded for leaded gasoline. Fewer material goods and more services can be produced. Pollution can be reduced still further by giving up marketable goods and services in favor of such nonmarket goods as increased leisure and the direct enjoyment of nature through outdoor recreation.

Applications of the Marginal Principle

All these trade-offs mean a lot of decisions that cannot be made without some general standards. To economists, it seems natural to express many of the important standards in marginal terms. As an example, consider the decision of how much pollution should be tolerated. This decision, it can be shown, requires finding a balance between two margins.

The first margin is the **marginal social cost of pollution.** For a given type of pollution, this means the cost to all members of society of an additional unit of pollution. Suppose, for example, that in a community of 1,000 people, each additional pound of sulfur dioxide emitted costs each person 0.003 cent in the form of damage to painted surfaces and 0.004 cent in terms of personal discomfort. The marginal social cost of sulfur dioxide pollution in this community is thus:

Marginal social cost of pollution The total additional cost to all members of society of an additional unit of pollution.

$$1{,}000\ (0.003 + 0.004) = 7 \text{ cents per pound.}$$

For most kinds of pollution, it is likely that the marginal social cost of pollution increases as its quantity increases. A graph of the marginal cost of pollution will thus have the form shown in Exhibit 19.1. Marginal social cost begins at zero for pollution within the natural absorptive capacity of the environment. As pollution concentrations become first unpleasant and then dangerous, marginal social cost rises to a high level.

The second margin is the **marginal cost of pollution abatement,** which is the economic cost of reducing pollution of a given kind by one unit. Other things being equal, the marginal cost of pollution abatement tends to rise as the level of pollution decreases. For example, in controlling automobile

Marginal cost of pollution abatement The added cost of reducing a given kind of pollution by one unit.

Exhibit 19.1
The marginal social cost of pollution
The marginal social cost of pollution is the total additional cost to all members of society that results from a one-unit increase in pollution. At low levels of pollution, within the natural absorptive capacity of the environment, the marginal social cost of pollution may be zero. As the quantity of pollution increases, the marginal social cost probably tends to increase for most pollutants.

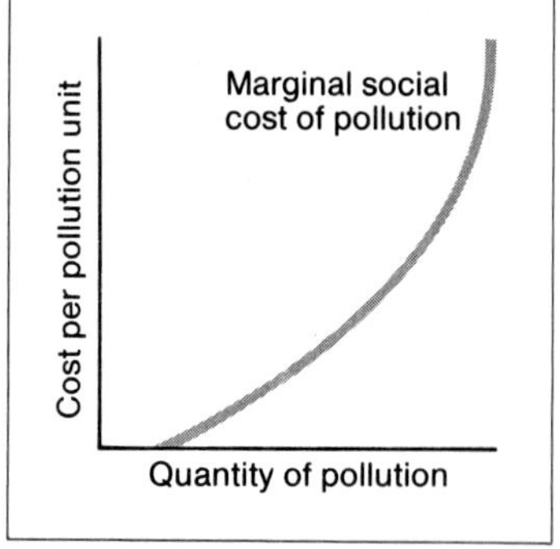

exhaust emissions, relatively cheap devices can cut pollution by half. Somewhat more complicated and expensive devices are required to cut the amount in half again, to the level of 75 percent abatement. Very elaborate and costly methods must be installed to cut it in half a third time, to 87.5 percent abatement. Given such examples, the marginal abatement cost curves are drawn with negative slopes, as in Exhibit 19.2.

The Optimal Quantity of Pollution

In Exhibit 19.3, both schedules appear in one diagram, which makes it possible to identify the point—the intersection of the two curves—where the marginal cost of abatement is equal to the marginal social cost of pollution. As far as economics is concerned, this point represents the optimal quantity of pollution. Pollution in excess of this amount represents a misallocation of resources. The damage done by additional pollution then exceeds the cost of eliminating it. Excessive abatement—that which operates to the left of the intersection point—is also wasteful. It too represents an unnecessary reduction in human welfare. If the marginal cost of pollution abatement exceeds the marginal social cost of pollution, a gain is made by trading a small reduction in environmental quality for a relatively large increase in material production.

Measurement Problems

This marginal analysis gives a simple theoretical standard for pollution control. The standard is not so easy to apply in practice, however. There are severe problems of measurement, especially on the side of social cost. Attempts to measure the social cost of pollution usually concentrate on such things as damage to property, health costs measured in terms of medical expenses and time lost from work, and the value of wildlife and crops killed. Actual estimates suffer from several defects.

First, data on the costs of pollution are at best fragmentary, and the many gaps must be filled by pure guesswork. Second, it is difficult to account for purely subjective costs, including offenses to aesthetic sensibilities and discomforts not actually resulting in damage to health. Yet these subjective costs have a very real economic value. The fact that many people spend hard-earned money to avoid the effects of pollution by leaving polluted areas shows such costs to be real. Finally, estimates of the social costs of pollution rarely give more than the average cost figures. But the marginal cost data, which are much

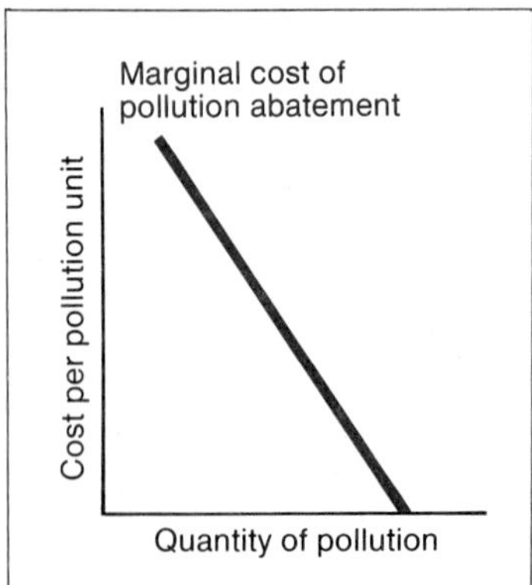

Exhibit 19.2
The marginal cost of pollution abatement
The marginal cost of pollution abatement is the added cost of reducing pollution by one unit. The marginal cost of eliminating pollution tends to increase as the percentage of all pollution eliminated increases. That gives the marginal cost of pollution abatement curve a downward slope.

Exhibit 19.3
The optimal quantity of pollution
The optimal quantity of pollution is determined by the intersection of the marginal cost of pollution abatement curve and the marginal social cost of pollution curve. To the left of that point, the benefits of further reductions in pollution do not justify the high cost of abatement. To the right of the point, the cost of abatement is less than the cost imposed on society by additional pollution.

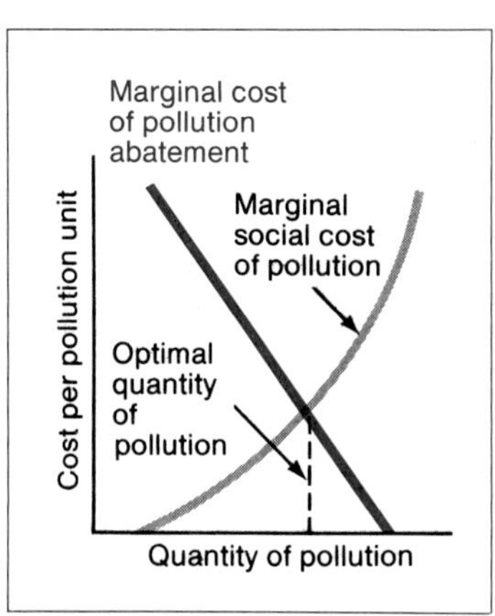

more difficult to obtain, are the really relevant data for making pollution policy decisions.

There are problems too in estimating the costs of pollution abatement. One major problem is that calculations must take into account not only the direct costs of getting rid of one form of pollution but also the social costs of any different forms of pollution that may be produced as a result. Measurement of these costs is subject to all the problems of measuring the social costs of any kind of pollution.

Nonetheless, despite the serious problems of precisely calculating marginal costs and benefits, thinking in marginal terms can often prevent serious mistakes, even when only approximate data are given. The following case study provides an illustration.

Case 19.1
New York's North River Sewage Treatment Plant: A Case of Overzealous Cleanup?

Dr. Merril Eisenbud is a prominent environmental scientist who served as New York City's first environmental protection administrator. An example he gives of apparently overzealous environmental protection can serve as an excellent illustration of the importance of marginal thinking in the environmental area.

The example concerns the North River sewage treatment plant that New York City is building in Harlem to control wastes being dumped into the Hudson River. The plant was originally designed to remove 67 percent of organic wastes of the type that rob the river of oxygen and threaten aquatic life. During the 1960s and early 1970s, however, enthusiastic politicians enacted regulations that raised the required level of cleanup for plants like the North River installation to 90 percent.

The project encountered the problem of increasing the marginal cost of pollution abatement in the process of redesigning to meet the new standards. Cleaning up the first 67 percent of the pollution would have cost about $250 million. Getting rid of the next 23 percent cost another $750 million, which raised the total cost of the installation to $1 billion.

According to Dr. Eisenbud, redesign of the plant to meet the 90 percent abatement standard also took the project into the region of a zero or near zero marginal social cost of pollution:

> What the Federal law failed to take into account, Dr. Eisenbud says, is the nature and use of the receiving water. For some water, 90 percent removal is not enough, he says, while for others it is far too much. Because the Hudson is scoured each day by tides that run as far north as Poughkeepsie and because the harbor waters getting the city's wastes are not used

for drinking or washing, the 67 percent removal standard was more than sufficient, according to all technical advisers on the project.[1]

The benefit of the additional abatement was thus effectively zero. In short, the North River project, as redesigned, went past the crossover point, where the benefits of further pollution abatement were not worth the added cost.

ECONOMIC STRATEGIES FOR POLLUTION CONTROL

Supply and Demand

Controlling pollution is a problem of economic policy. As in many other cases, supply and demand can be used to explain where the problem comes from and to compare alternative solutions.

Consider Exhibit 19.4. The marginal cost of pollution abatement curve drawn in Exhibit 19.2 is now given a new name—the demand curve for pollution opportunities. It is very easy to understand why the same curve serves both purposes. Simply ask how much a firm would be willing to pay, if necessary, for the opportunity to dump an additional unit of untreated waste directly into the environment. The answer is that it would pay any sum smaller—but not any sum larger—than the cost of pollution-free waste disposal.

So much for the demand curve. Exhibit 19.4 also shows a supply curve for pollution opportunities as a straight line lying right along the horizontal axis. The line indicates that unlimited pollution opportunities are available without paying any price at all. The equilibrium quantity of pollution is found where

[1] Michael Sterne, "Environmentalist Questions Priorities," *New York Times*, May 12, 1978, p. B-1. © 1978 by The New York Times Company. Reprinted by permission.

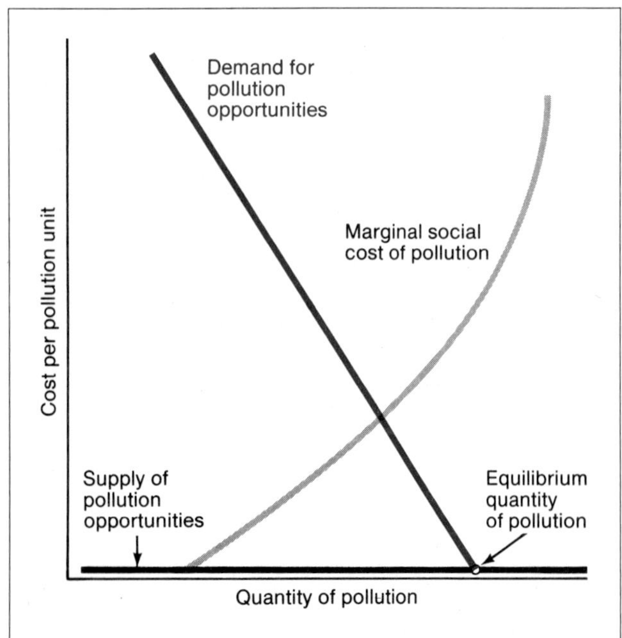

Exhibit 19.4

Supply and demand for pollution opportunities

The marginal cost of pollution abatement curve can also be called the demand curve for pollution opportunities. The position of the supply curve for pollution opportunities depends on how much firms must pay in order to discharge wastes into the environment. If they do not have to pay at all, the supply curve will coincide with the horizontal axis, as shown here, and the equilibrium quantity of pollution will be greater than the optimum quantity.

the two curves intersect. Unless the social cost of pollution is also zero (which is not the case) this equilibrium is not the optimal point. What can be done?

Command and Control

Most current government policies for controlling pollution take the so-called command-and-control approach. Congress sets up some agency with authority to control pollution of particular types or in particular areas. Sometimes, the regulators simply set a maximum amount of pollution permitted from each source and leave the choice of abatement methods up to the polluter. In other cases, the regulators specify that certain abatement procedures must be followed. Command-and-control regulations have the effect of rationing pollution opportunities. They can keep the economic system from ending up at an equilibrium like that shown in Exhibit 19.4, where there is too much pollution.

Although this approach has in many cases been effective, economists often find fault with it. For one thing, regulations can be written so rigidly that they do not give polluters enough incentive to search for the least-cost method of cleaning up their wastes. For another, regulation does not always ensure that the burden of cleaning up is efficiently allocated among various pollution sources. Critics of the command-and-control approach have suggested some alternative strategies for pollution control that use supply and demand more directly. Two important strategies are the residual charge and property rights approaches.

Residual Charges

One nonregulatory strategy for controlling pollution works by shifting the pollution opportunity supply curve with **residual charges,** which are, in effect, waste disposal taxes. Charges of a fixed amount per unit of waste are imposed on all sources of a given kind of waste. As an example, consider a residual charge on sulfur dioxide emissions. Suppose that all sources of this type of pollution had to pay a fee of $.05 per pound for all sulfur emitted into the atmosphere.

Residual charges Charges of a fixed amount per unit of waste imposed on all sources that discharge a given kind of waste into the environment.

Exhibit 19.5 shows the effect of this residual charge, which shifts the pollution opportunity supply curve up from its position along the horizontal axis to a position $.05 higher. Polluters react to the tax by moving back along their demand curve to a new equilibrium where there is less pollution. They do this because it pays them to use all pollution abatement methods that can remove a pound of sulfur from the stack gases for $.05 or less.

By raising or lowering the amount of the charge, any desired degree of pollution control can be achieved. Ideally, the charge is set so that the pollution opportunity supply curve passes exactly through the intersection of the marginal abatement cost curve (demand curve) and the marginal social cost curve. This ideal situation is shown in Exhibit 19.6. (Unfortunately, there is no easy way to determine just where the intersection is and, hence, just what the charge should be. The agency responsible for setting the rate of the residual charge is faced with the measurement difficulties mentioned above.)

Objections to Residual Charges Because pollution taxes and residual charges are likely to figure prominently in future policy debates, it will be worth taking a moment to look at some often-heard objections to them. The

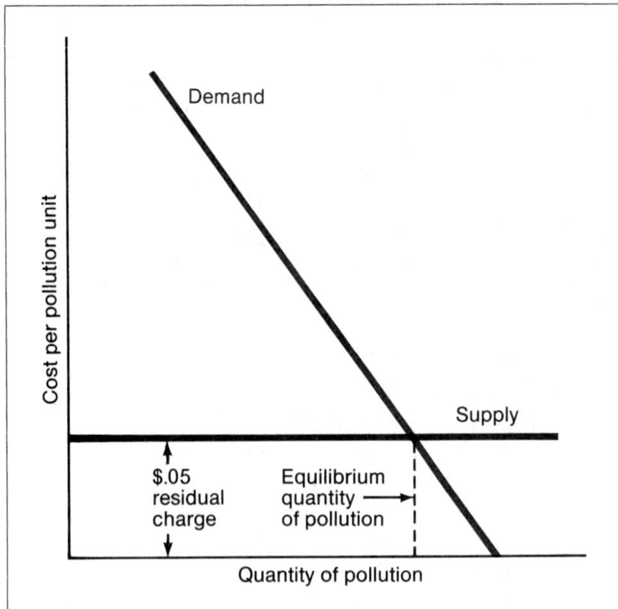

Exhibit 19.5
The effect of a residual charge
A residual charge makes it necessary for polluters to pay for the opportunity to discharge wastes into the environment. Here, the charge is set at $.05 per unit. The residual charge moves the pollution opportunity supply curve upward to the position shown and forces polluters up and to the left along their demand curve, thereby reducing the equilibrium quantity of pollution.

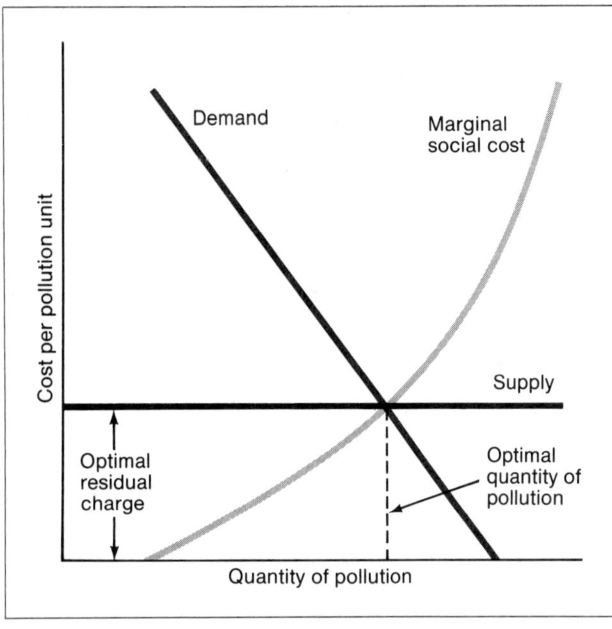

Exhibit 19.6
An optimal residual charge
Ideally, a residual charge could be set just high enough to reduce pollution by the optimal amount. Here, the supply curve for pollution opportunities cuts the demand and marginal social cost curves at their point of intersection. In practice, such fine tuning of residual charges is quite difficult.

objections come from three principal sources—industrialists, consumers, and environmentalists.

Industrialists sometimes say that residual charges impose an unfair double burden on industry, which has to pay the charge at the same time it is undergoing the expense of installing pollution abatement equipment. Consumers object that industry can pass the burden of the charge along in the form of higher product prices. Environmentalists protest that residual charges grant a license to pollute. They fear that industry will just put up the money and keep right on despoiling the environment as before. Each of these objections is discussed in the following sections.

Double Burden The double burden objection is the weakest of the three. No industry is ever forced by a residual charge to pay a double charge. Any polluter always has the option of paying the charge and making no effort at all to reduce pollution. In this case, it bears just one burden, that of the charge itself. Any money it spends on pollution abatement equipment is spent for one reason only—that it is cheaper to install the equipment than to pay to pollute. Far from being a second burden, abatement expenditures represent a way to escape from the tax and hence to reduce the total burden.

Passing on the Burden The argument that residual charges can be shifted to consumers has more truth to it. Exhibit 19.7 shows why. Let D represent the demand curve for a commodity and S_1 the market supply curve before there is any pollution control policy. These conditions give an equilibrium at E_1, with price P_1 and quantity of output Q_1. A residual charge raises the marginal cost of production. The increase is either the amount of tax paid per unit of production or the cost of the abatement equipment needed to avoid payment, whichever is smaller. This increase shifts the whole supply curve up to the new position, S_2. The vertical distance between the old and new supply curves is equal to the per unit burden of the charge. With the new supply curve, S_2, equilibrium is at E_2 with price P_2 and quantity Q_2. The difference between the new price and the old one shows the share of the burden passed along to the consumer. As the figure is drawn, this amount is about half the burden of the tax. The exact share passed on varies from product to product, depending on the shapes of the supply and demand curves.

It can be seen, then, that at least part of the burden of a residual charge can be passed along to consumers. But does this really constitute a valid criticism of the policy? A strong argument can be made that it does not. After all, someone always pays the price of pollution; different policies change only who pays for it. Under current conditions, producers and consumers of pollution-intensive goods both get a free ride. They shift the burden to innocent third parties (the victims of the pollution). If the burden is to be lifted from these third parties, why should consumers expect to be able to continue their free ride?

Exhibit 19.7
Effects of a residual charge on product price
The effects of a residual charge are shown here in terms of the supply and demand for a product produced by a firm that must pay the charge. The product supply curve is shifted up from S_1 to S_2. This causes the equilibrium price of the product to rise from P_1 to P_2. Part, but not all, of the cost increase is thus passed along to the consumer.

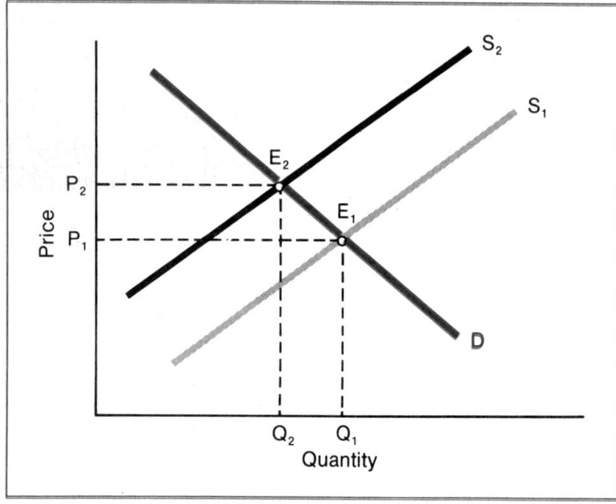

Higher prices for high pollution products are actually beneficial. They stimulate consumers to make the trade-offs that are necessary to protect the environment. If the prices of relatively dirty products rise compared to those of relatively clean products and services, consumers will shift their spending patterns accordingly. If firms cannot pass along to consumers part of the pollution taxes imposed upon them, it is not easy to see how the necessary change in consumption habits will come about.

License The third objection—that residual charges are just a license to pollute—is open to more than one interpretation. Depending on how it is interpreted, it may be wholly invalid or partially valid.

Sometimes the argument implies that residual charges have no effect on pollution, that businesses will pay the charges and carry on as before. But this is flatly incorrect, unless one is going to deny that the law of supply and demand applies to waste disposal as it does to other business activities. At other times, the license to pollute argument is meant as an objection to the fact that the taxes eliminate only part, not all, of the pollution output. In this application, too, the argument violates good economic reasoning. To eliminate all pollution regardless of cost, as some environmentalists advocate, involves greater sacrifices of material welfare than can be justified in terms of consumer satisfaction. Instead, pollution control should proceed only up to the point where the marginal cost of pollution abatement begins to exceed the marginal social cost of pollution.

A third interpretation of the license to pollute argument makes more economic sense. The problem is that no direct compensation is offered to those downwind or downstream of any pollution sources that continue polluting even after imposition of the charges. To these remaining victims, it seems unjust that a firm can legally continue to make life miserable just by paying a fee to the government. Polluters, it is argued, should pay compensation to their victims, not taxes to the government.

Pollution Control and Property Rights

Pollution as Theft The question of who should be compensated for pollution damage raises the whole issue of pollution and property rights. The basic idea is this: From the point of view of property rights, pollution is theft. If you use the air in and around my home as a dumping ground for your unwanted combustion products, you are stealing waste disposal services from me. If you use my living room as a reverberation chamber for noise from your truck or motorcycle, you are robbing me of my right to peace and quiet. As the owner, I should have the right to prevent you from using my property in these ways unless you negotiate with me in advance to buy my permission. If you do not, I should be able to bring civil or criminal action against you in a court of law.

In some respects, however, current law is stacked against property owners and in favor of polluters. Various changes have been recommended to redress the balance. It could, for example, be made easier for private citizens to initiate lawsuits when their property is attacked by pollution. At present, property owners often must wait for local governments to take legal action on their behalf. If the polluters have more pull in the statehouse or city hall than their victims do, the victims may wait in vain. Also, it could be made easier for large groups of citizens to act jointly, through class action suits or other means, to gain legal redress for damages done to them.

What would be the economic effect of laws permitting property owners to protect themselves from pollution? One possible effect would be the creation of a private market for pollution rights. In this market, people would sell pollution opportunities to firms in return for a price high enough to compensate them for the damage done. If all individuals sold pollution rights at prices equal to the marginal cost to them of pollution damage, the pollution market would look like the diagram in Exhibit 19.8. The pollution opportunity supply curve would follow exactly along the marginal social cost curve. The equilibrium quantity of pollution would be exactly the economically optimal amount.

Objections The legal protection of private property rights as a method of pollution control is open to certain practical objections. One objection is that not all environmental resources that are open to pollution damage are privately owned. Does this mean that polluters would retain unlimited opportunities to dump their wastes in public waterways, world oceans, publicly owned wilderness areas, and the like? One way to overcome the problem would be to auction off all rivers, oceans, national parks, and similar areas to private owners. The private owners could then protect them from damage. Short of this radical proposal, taxes and user charges could protect such public resources, while private law protected privately owned resources.

There is a second objection to giving private owners blanket rights to protect their property against pollution. Such a policy might result in excessive reduction in pollution levels. A potential polluter located in a densely populated area might have to negotiate pollution opportunity contracts with tens of thousands of individual small property owners before emitting even a single puff of smoke. The transaction costs of doing this would be prohibitive, even if the actual charges paid to each owner were in themselves reasonable; and just one holdout among the individual property owners could wreck the deal. To avoid these difficulties, a firm might spend far more than the economically optimal amount on pollution abatement. Some might argue, of course, that

Exhibit 19.8
Pollution opportunities with perfect protection of private property
If all property were privately owned and if polluters always had to compensate victims for damage to persons or property, a private market in pollution opportunities would be created. Ideally, the supply curve in this market would exactly coincide with the marginal social cost of pollution curve. The equilibrium quantity of pollution would then equal the optimal quantity.

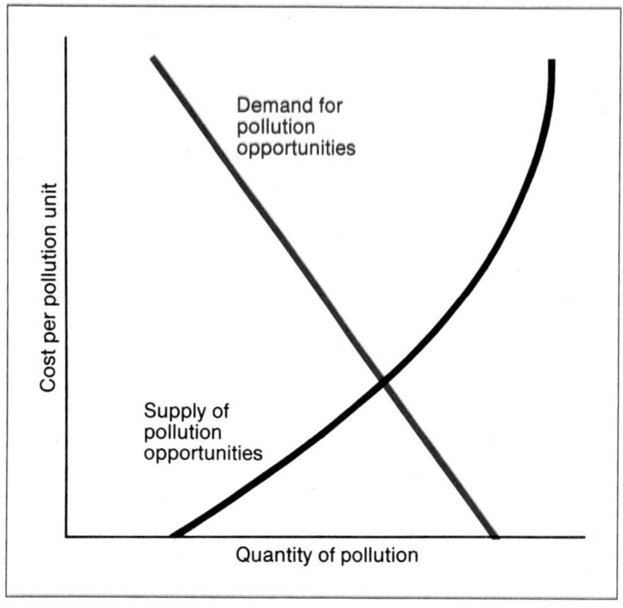

people have suffered from too much pollution for so long that it would be a pleasant novelty to suffer from too little. Speaking more practically, though, it can be conceded that the property rights approach probably works best when the impact of pollution is relatively concentrated. Some type of residual charge scheme may be a better answer when the damages are very widely dispersed.

Trends in Pollution Control Techniques

The drawbacks of the command-and-control approach to pollution abatement, compared with the theoretical elegance of the residual charge and property rights approaches, have been well known for many years. Until quite recently, however, officials engaged in the practical task of enforcing environmental protection laws were not much interested in alternatives to command and control.

Toward the end of the 1970s, however, a powerful new ingredient entered the debate over pollution control techniques. That ingredient was inflation. Everyone was concerned about rapidly rising prices, and complaints were heard increasingly often that one reason prices were going up was that environmental regulations were pushing up costs.

In some cases, regulators reacted by simply relaxing specific pollution standards that appeared to have been pushed beyond the point of optimal pollution abatement and then continuing to enforce the relaxed standards by the same command-and-control strategies. More importantly, however, some environmental officials—such as Douglas M. Costel, head of the Environmental Protection Agency—began to look seriously at new methods of enforcement that would emphasize economic incentives rather than command and control. The following case study gives an idea of some of the problems and promise of one such approach.

Case 19.2
The "Bubble" Concept in Pollution Control

The steel industry is one of the nation's dirtiest; and as such, it has been one of the hardest hit by environmental cleanup regulations. By the late 1970s, it had invested more than $6 billion in pollution control equipment, and its pollution control costs were approaching 10 percent of total operating costs. If any industry needed to find ways to clean up the air while minimizing the cost to consumers, the steel industry was it. Then, along came a brave new idea called the "bubble concept."

The bubble concept is simplicity itself. In the past, under its command-and-control strategy, the Environmental Protection Agency had been imposing specific standards on each pollution emitting piece of equipment within a plant. But that could change:

> The law now says how much pollution is allowed in the air—for example, an annual average of no more than seventy-five micrograms of particulates per cubic meter. In hope of reaching this standard, the EPA limits pollution from each source it wants to control—blast furnaces, boilers, paint sprayers, etc.—in an industrial complex. Under the bubble concept, the regulators would replace these "stack by stack" rules with a single limit applied to the whole plant. In either case, the total pollution would be the same. But by operating under an imaginary bubble, the plant's engineers would have the flexibility to find the most cost-effective mix of pollution controls to meet the standard.[2]

[2]Peter Nulty, "A Brave Experiment in Pollution Control," *Fortune*, February 12, 1979, p. 121. © 1979. Time Inc. Courtesy of *Fortune Magazine*.

One early bubble enthusiast on the industry side was John Barker, an environmental engineer for Armco Steel:

> Taking Armco's plant in Middletown as a test case, Barker found that spraying water on piles of iron ore would prevent 284 tons of particles a year (mostly dust and iron oxide) from blowing into the surrounding community. The cost per ton would be $704. By comparison, pollution-control devices on a blast furnace would reclaim 309 tons of iron oxide for $8,500 a ton, and devices on an open-hearth furnace would capture 140 tons for $35,700 a ton.[3]

Studies such as this helped convince many EPA administrators that the bubble concept was worth pursuing, but it soon became clear that there were many practical details to work out. For one thing, there is the problem that not all kinds of pollution are equally damaging. Fine particles are more damaging to lungs than coarse particles, for example. And the carcinogenic benzapyrene emitted from the steel industry's coke ovens is clearly far more dangerous per ton than mere dust of any size.

Because of this and other difficulties, the EPA to date has endorsed the bubble concept only in limited form. More than one bubble is to be placed over every plant—for example, a general bubble for particulates and a tighter bubble for carcinogens from coke ovens. No one knows yet how well the bubble concept will work out in practice or how successful bubble enthusiasts will be at overcoming the remaining bureaucratic resistance. But the whole idea is an encouraging sign that economists, environmental regulators, and industrial engineers can at least sometimes find common ground for action.

CONCLUSIONS

The main objective of pollution control, as discussed in this chapter, has been to improve the efficiency of resource allocation. A complete analysis of environmental policy should look at the normative implications of this objective as well. The discussion will conclude with a look at pollution control policies in terms of market justice and distributive justice.

By the standard of market justice, the effects of pollution control policies of almost any kind appear to be beneficial. Pollution is theft. It is a form of coercion through which producers enjoy unjustifiably high profits and consumers enjoy unjustifiably low prices. Third parties, as victims of pollution, are unwillingly forced to bear the costs without sharing in the benefits. Policies that put a price tag on pollution help to correct these injustices by making everyone pay the full cost of the things produced and consumed.

Strictly speaking, according to the standard of market justice, a policy not only should impose penalties on polluters but also should provide compensation to the victims of pollution. Policies based on enforcement of private property rights—including the right of pollution victims to sue for damages—do this, while residual charges do not.

From the point of view of distributive justice, the effects of pollution control policies are more problematical. If one's notion of distributive justice is simply increased equality of real incomes, antipollution measures may well make things worse. One would have to study carefully the exact distribution of the costs and benefits of various alternative policies in order to be certain on this point. Without such study, only conjectures can be made. These conjectures suggest, however, that low income groups might not fare well. They might bear

[3]Ibid.

a disproportionately large share of the costs of pollution control policies and might receive a disproportionately small share of the benefits.

One result of effective pollution control policies, as shown here, must be to raise the prices of goods to consumers. Low income groups spend a larger portion of their budget on material goods and devote a smaller portion to consumption of services and to saving. The burden of pollution taxes can thus be expected to rest more heavily on them in proportion to their incomes.

At the same time, it seems likely that the benefits of pollution control policies are less valuable to the poor than to the rich. Suppose that the benefits of pollution control were equally distributed in physical terms. For example, suppose that the level of air pollution were lowered just as much in low income as in high income neighborhoods. This does not mean that the benefit would be equally distributed in economic terms. Clean air and other environmental amenities are to a considerable extent luxury goods. They have a high value to those who already have a generous supply of material goods and a relatively low value to those who do not. How many pounds of beef or pairs of shoes or dollars would poor people be willing to give up in order to reduce by half the sulfur dioxide content of the air they breathed? How much would wealthy people be willing to sacrifice for the same purpose? It is easy to see that, at least beyond a certain point, pollution control policies may reflect the tastes only of the relatively well-to-do.

SUMMARY

1. Pollution can be viewed as a problem in the allocation of scarce resources. In this case, the scarce resource is the waste absorption capacity of the environment. Once this capacity is exceeded, further waste disposal must incur opportunity costs of one kind or another. If wastes are discharged untreated into the environment, the opportunity costs take the form of a less healthy and pleasant world in which to live. If costly pollution abatement techniques are used, scarce factors of production must be diverted from other uses. No policy can avoid these trade-offs altogether. The economic problem of pollution is how to balance the social cost of pollution against the economic cost of pollution abatement.
2. Supply and demand analysis can be applied to the problem of pollution control. The marginal cost of pollution abatement curve can be thought of as a demand curve for pollution. If there are no pollution controls of any kind, the supply curve for pollution opportunities is a horizontal line at zero height. The equilibrium quantity of pollution will be too high when the supply curve has that shape. All pollution control policies aim in one way or another to limit the supply of pollution opportunities.
3. The command-and-control approach to pollution abatement is, in effect, a form of administrative rationing for pollution opportunities. It has been effective in some cases, but economists often criticize it as inefficient. Residual charges are an alternate pollution control method. Under a residual charge scheme, the supply curve for pollution opportunities becomes a horizontal line at the height equal to the charge per unit of waste. Still another approach to pollution control is through the enforcement of private property rights. Ideally, if all property were privately owned and polluters had to compensate owners for all damage to persons and property, the

supply of pollution opportunities curve would coincide with the marginal social cost of pollution curve. Each approach has its advantages and its practical difficulties. For the moment, it seems worthwhile to experiment with all methods.

4. Pollution raises normative as well as positive issues. One such issue is that of compensating victims of pollution. The regulatory and residual charge approaches to pollution control do not compensate victims. Pollution control via defense of private property rights appears to be superior in this respect. Another normative question concerns the distributive impact of pollution control. In the absence of firm evidence to the contrary, it seems plausible to think that the costs of pollution control may be borne more than proportionately by the poor and that the benefits of pollution control may accrue more than proportionately to the well-to-do.

DISCUSSION QUESTIONS

1. Why has pollution become a major national policy issue only recently? Is pollution worse than it used to be? Do the cars of New York City today discharge more tons of waste each day than the horses of New York City did in 1901? Has the high standard of living in the United States actually caused more pollution, or has it made people less willing to tolerate it than they used to be? Or has it done both? Discuss.
2. Can you think of circumstances in which the marginal social cost of waste disposal for a firm is also part of its explicit private costs of production? Of its implicit private costs? Of neither its implicit nor explicit costs? Explain.
3. When does waste disposal become pollution? How do you distinguish between the two? Is the distinction a matter of positive economics or of normative economics? Explain.
4. Many environmentalists are uncomfortable with the concept of an economically optimal amount of pollution. They tend to think that less pollution is always better. Do you agree? Do you think that the difference between the environmentalist viewpoint and the viewpoint set forth in this chapter is one of values or of analysis? Explain.
5. Suppose you were a member of Congress when a bill came up to abolish all specific pollution control regulations for automobile exhausts. In place of the present regulations, there would be a residual charge of $.01 per mile placed on all driving. The charge would be reduced appropriately for drivers who could prove that their cars were equipped with effective emission control devices. Would you favor this measure? Explain. If your only objection were that $.01 per mile was too low a charge, how high would you think the rate should be?
6. Many of the Great Lakes have become seriously polluted. Among the people damaged by this pollution are the owners of lakefront property. Do you think that these owners ought to be permitted to bring suit against any company polluting the lake on which their property is located? If such suits were permitted, do you think many would be brought? Should property owners who win their cases against polluters be able to obtain a cease-and-desist order stopping all further pollution, or should they simply be awarded monetary damages? Explain.

SUGGESTIONS FOR FURTHER READING

Dorfman, Robert, and Dorfman, Nancy S., eds. *Economics of the Environment: Selected Readings.* New York: W. W. Norton, 1972.
A collection of papers by well-known economists covering the whole range of topics discussed in this chapter. Most are reprints of articles from professional journals, but none is excessively technical.

Freeman, A. Myrick, III; Haveman, Robert H.; and Kneese, Alan V. *The Economics of Environmental Policy.* New York: Wiley, 1973.

A book length, nontechnical discussion of many of the themes of this chapter, including problems of allocating common property resources and ways of putting economic incentives to work solving environmental problems.

Mills, Edwin S. *The Economics of Environmental Quality.* New York: W. W. Norton, 1978.

A thorough, up-to-date treatment of environmental problems and policies from an economic point of view. Includes a historical sketch of environmental policy in the United States and a discussion of environmental problems and policies of the rest of the world.

CHAPTER 20

THE ECONOMICS OF ENERGY

WHAT YOU WILL LEARN IN THIS CHAPTER

This chapter covers selected topics in the economics of energy. It begins by introducing a theory of the allocation of nonrenewable resources over time. It discusses both competitive markets and markets dominated by cartels. It then examines recent U.S. oil and natural gas policies in the light of this allocation theory, paying special attention to the effects of price controls and decontrol. The remainder of the chapter is devoted to the principal energy alternatives to oil and natural gas: coal, nuclear power, and solar power.

FOR REVIEW

Here is an important concept that will be put to use in this chapter. If you do not understand it, review it before proceeding.

- *Positive and normative economics (Chapter 1)*

Having discussed the economics of pollution, we turn now to another aspect of the economics of life on a small planet: the economics of energy. The availability of energy, like the availability of unlimited environmental sinks for the disposal of waste products, is something that used to be taken for granted. Today, however, energy—more than any other commodity—symbolizes the problem of scarcity. The United States now has a Department of Energy and a national debate over energy policy. Such diverse topics as inflation, military strategy, and international diplomacy cannot be discussed without bringing energy into consideration. It seems appropriate, then, to devote a chapter to the economics of energy and energy policy, beginning with nonrenewable energy sources and moving on to possible alternatives.

THE ECONOMICS OF OIL AND NATURAL GAS

The nonrenewable fossil fuels oil and natural gas are the most important current sources of energy in the United States. These fuels are being replenished by natural processes at imperceptible rates, if at all. The economics of oil and gas is thus a matter of allocation over time—of when it is best to use the limited stocks available.

The discussion will begin with the fairly well developed branch of eco-

Theory of the mine The branch of economics concerned with the allocation over time of nonrenewable natural resources.

nomics known as the **theory of the mine,** which deals with problems of this type. Although this chapter is interested primarily in nonrenewable energy resources, the theory of the mine applies equally well to nonrenewable resources other than energy.

Introduction to the Theory of the Mine

The key economic decision studied by the theory of the mine is that of when to extract and use the limited stock of resources that the mine contains. This decision involves a strict trade-off between the present and the future: What is used today cannot be used tomorrow, and what is conserved cannot be used today.

Both immediate and delayed use have advantages. Immediate use permits gratification of consumer demand without delay or permits use of the resource for investment purposes, thereby increasing tomorrow's supply of productive capital. Delayed use is advantageous because, to the extent that any of the resource is consumed today, what remains will be scarcer and hence more valuable in the future.

The Case of Competitive Markets The way resource owners handle the trade-off between present and future use depends, among other things, on the structure of the markets in which they operate. As often is true, the case of perfectly competitive markets provides a useful benchmark. Consider, for the sake of illustration, the market for natural gas, assuming for the present that the market is perfectly competitive, that the quantity of natural gas available for extraction is known, and that the cost of extracting it is zero.

Under these idealized conditions, the only decision left to gas well owners is whether to extract their gas and sell it now or to conserve all or part of it for the future. If the owners are motivated primarily by financial considerations, they can be expected to make the choice that will maximize their total wealth. Keeping the gas in the ground means holding that wealth in the form of a reserve of energy that can be expected to increase in value in the future. Extracting the gas and selling it today allows the conversion of the wealth to other forms—for example, corporate stocks or government bonds—that can be expected to earn their owners a normal rate of return on the invested capital.

It follows that the decision of when to sell the gas depends on a comparison of the market rate of return available outside the gas industry with the rate at which the price of gas is expected to increase in the future. Suppose, for example, that the market rate of return on alternative investments is 10 percent per year, that the price of gas today is $3 per thousand cubic feet (tcf), and that this price is expected to rise at the rate of 5 percent per year. Selling 1,000 tcf of gas at today's prices and investing the proceeds at 10 percent will give a gas well owner a sum of $3,300 at the end of a year. Alternatively, leaving the same 1,000 tcf of gas in the ground and selling it at $3.15 per tcf next year will yield a sum of $3,150. Under these assumed conditions, then, it will be most profitable to sell the gas today.

However, there is a limit to how much gas will be sold currently, because today's sales of gas tend to change the conditions initially assumed to prevail. For one thing, greater supplies of gas brought to market today will tend to depress the price below the assumed level of $3 per tcf. In addition, more sales today will reduce the stocks available for the future, thereby reducing future supplies and increasing the future price. As the price today falls and the expected future price rises, the expected percentage increase of next year's price over this year's price also rises. As soon as the expected rate of price increase becomes equal to the rate of return available on alternative investments, it will no longer be profitable to sell today. Any owners who have not yet sold will conserve their supplies for the future, because it will pay them to do so.

In short, when a resource exists in a known, fixed quantity and the cost of extraction is low, a competitive market will allocate that resource over time, as shown in Exhibit 20.1. The price will rise over time at a rate equal to the market rate of interest. Other things being equal, the rate of use will fall as the price rises.[1]

Some Qualifications The preceding argument puts a ceiling on the rate at which the price of a scarce resource will increase and the rate at which it will be used up. However, there are circumstances under which the rate of the price increase is less rapid than the interest rate because the rate of depletion is slower than implied. In particular, this will be the case if the resource is costly to extract or if high prices stimulate a search for new reserves or for substitutes.

If, for example, the current price of a resource is equal to the current marginal cost of extracting it, the quantity supplied will be limited by the quantity demanded at the current price rather than by the expected effect of current use on future prices. The quantity demanded may very well not be high enough to deplete the resource fast enough to push its future price up at a rate equal to the interest rate. Alternatively, if there are reserves of a resource that cannot be profitably extracted today but that can be used if the price rises

[1]If economic growth or population growth causes demand for the resource to increase as time goes by, this pattern may be somewhat modified. The rate of price increase will still not exceed the interest rate, but the rate of use can, for a time, increase before it begins to taper off.

Exhibit 20.1
Market allocation over time of a nonrenewable resource
The market price of a nonrenewable resource tends to rise over time. Supply and demand conditions limit the rate of depletion, so the price will not rise at a rate faster than the rate of interest. As the price rises, the rate of use falls, other things being equal.

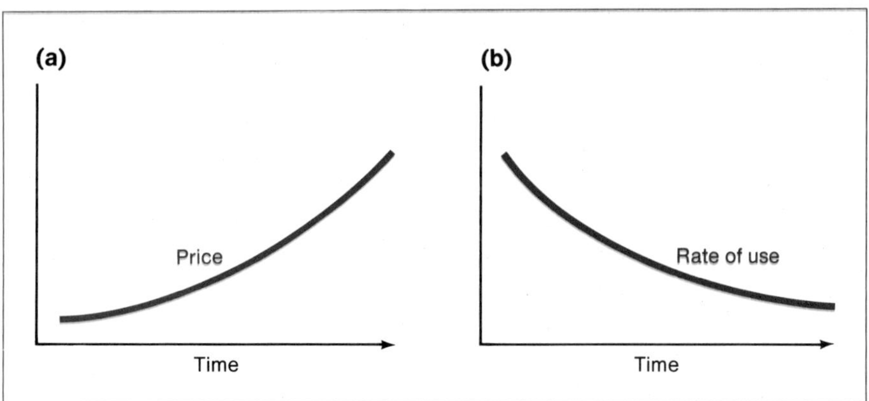

a little, the presence of those reserves will limit the rate of price increase, because it will increase expected future supply.

In practice, the usable reserves of many important resources do appear to increase quite elastically as demand and prices rise. This is partly because higher prices make it worthwhile to spend more money on exploration and partly because they make it worthwhile to exploit known low-grade reserves. Exhibit 20.2 shows how the known reserves of many important nonrenewable resources expanded between 1950 and 1970. Naturally, the rates of reserve expansion shown in the table cannot be extrapolated indefinitely into the future. They do show, however, that the assumption of absolutely fixed quantities of known reserves is a very restrictive one.

Effects of a Cartel Up to this point, it has been assumed that the markets in which nonrenewable resources are bought and sold are perfectly competitive. With the rise of the OPEC oil cartel during the 1970s, however, economists have become increasingly interested in the situation where a nonrenewable resource is controlled by a cartel rather than supplied competitively.

Under given conditions of demand and cost, a cartel tends to supply a smaller quantity at a higher price than does a competitively organized market. By reducing the quantity supplied and raising the price, the cartel benefits its members by increasing profit per unit sold. Profits are maximized at the point where marginal cost and marginal revenue are equal. Exhibit 20.3 makes the

Exhibit 20.2
The growth of reserves of nonrenewable resources, 1950–1970
In the past, known economic reserves of most (but not all) nonrenewable resources have expanded at a faster rate than those reserves have been used up. The reason is partly that new high-grade reserves are discovered and partly that higher prices and new technologies make it worthwhile to exploit reserves that were known earlier but considered to be of no commercial value. There is, however, no theoretical guarantee that reserves will continue always to grow in the future.

Ore	Known Reserves in 1950 (1,000 Metric Tons)	Cumulative Production 1950–1970 (1,000 Metric Tons)	Known Reserves in 1970 (1,000 Metric Tons)	Percentage Increase in Known Reserves 1950–1970
Iron	19,000,000	9,355,000	251,000,000	1,221
Manganese	500,000	194,000	635,000	27
Chromite	100,000	82,000	755,000	675
Tungsten	1,903	630	1,328	−30
Copper	100,000	80,000	279,000	179
Lead	40,000	48,000	86,000	115
Zinc	70,000	70,000	113,000	61
Tin	6,000	3,800	6,600	10
Bauxite	1,400,000	505,000	5,300,000	279
Potash	5,000,000	216,000	118,000,000	2,360
Phosphates	26,000,000	1,011,000	1,178,000,000	4,430
Oil[a]	75,000,000	180,727,000	455,000,000	507

[a] Thousand barrels.
Source: National Commission on Supplies and Shortages, *Government and the Nation's Resources* 16 (1976). Reprinted by permission from Stephen F. Williams, "Running Out: The Problem of Exhaustible Resources," *Journal of Legal Studies* 7 (January 1978): 166 (Table 1). Copyright 1978 by the University of Chicago Law School.

Exhibit 20.3
Comparison of a competitive market and a cartel
For the same conditions of cost and demand, producers in a competitive market will tend to supply more each period than will the same producers organized as a cartel. The competitive market produces a quantity that makes marginal cost equal to price; the cartel maximizes profits at the quantity that makes marginal cost equal to marginal revenue.

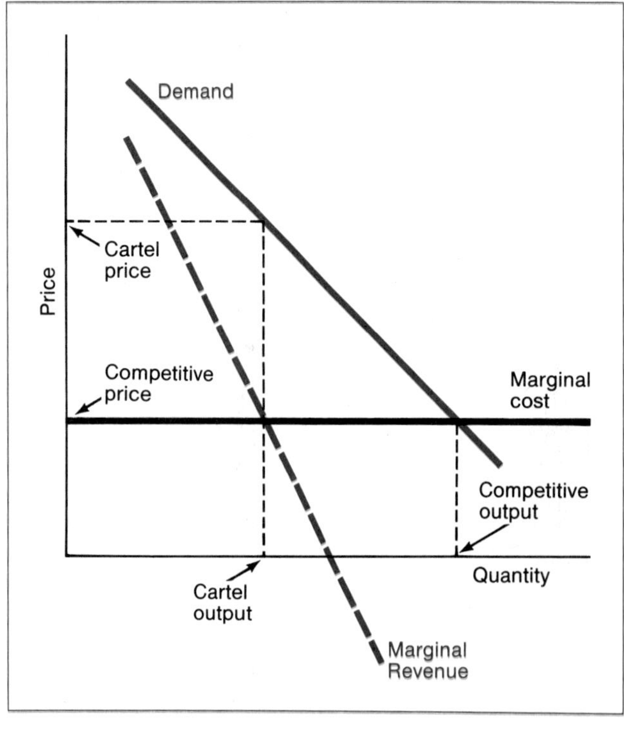

comparison between the output chosen by a cartel and that resulting from competition under the simplifying assumption of constant marginal cost.

Because they sell a smaller quantity at a higher price, cartels are more conservational than competitive markets. If, for example, a cartel were suddenly formed in a resource market that had been perfectly competitive, its first act would be to cut back production. Only in that way could the market price be raised. As a by-product of this profit maximizing action, more of the resource would be left in the second and each subsequent year than would have been the case under competition.

What is more, an additional factor may tend to make natural resource cartels even more conservational than the preceding argument implies. That factor is the possibility that the cartels will try to practice intertemporal price discrimination. According to the theory of price discrimination, cartels will cut back production most sharply in markets with the most inelastic demand, because they can get away with raising the price most in such markets. Thus, if a cartel expects future demand for its product to be more elastic than present demand, it will discriminate against present buyers by raising the price very high initially. The high price will further slow the present rate of consumption. In the case of an oil cartel, it seems reasonable to believe that present demand is in fact less elastic than demand will be in the future, because the technology of substitute energy sources is constantly improving.

Is the Market Rate of Use Optimal?

The theory of the mine shows that the market contains a built-in conservation mechanism. In effect, it transforms predictions of future scarcity into actions for present conservation, as profit maximizing resource owners opt to sell at higher future prices rather than low present prices.

But an important question remains: Might it not be wise to be more conservational still? That is, should current resource owners do future generations a favor by leaving them an even greater endowment of nonrenewable resources than what the market forces dictate? The question of obligations toward future generations raises profound normative issues. Previous generations toiled in mines, fields, and factories, enduring great hardships to accumulate the stock of capital on which present wealth depends. Many people today feel that they themselves should do no less for their own descendants. Fortunately, it is not necessary to resolve all the great ethical questions of income distribution among the generations in order to answer the narrower question of how rapidly nonrenewable resources should be used up. The reason is that the conservation of nonrenewable resources is a question not of how much wealth should be left for future generations but of what form that wealth should be left in.

Basically, there are two tangible forms in which to leave wealth to future generations. One form is capital. It can be produced in as much quantity as people want, provided they are willing to abstain from the present consumption of income and to invest the resulting saving. The other form is natural resources. They cannot be created, but they can be conserved. Even after the decision of how much total wealth to leave to the next generation is made, there is still a need to decide how much of that wealth to leave in each of the two forms. At that point, it is surely ethically acceptable for people to think of themselves and to adjust the mix in such a way that their own sacrifices are minimized.

Once the matter is put this way, it is easy to determine, at least in principle, the optimum degree of conservation of nonrenewable resources. A dollar's worth of nonrenewable resources should be extracted today and invested in durable capital goods if and only if the future value of the resulting capital is greater than the future value of the natural resources that are left in the ground. The future value of the capital can be determined by compounding the current rate of saving at the prevailing rate of return. The rule just given can thus be restated as the instruction to extract resources in the present unless the value of those resources in the future, as measured by their market price, will be likely to rise more rapidly than will the interest rate. As previously shown, a competitive market economy operates in such a way as to ensure that this rule will not be violated. If monopolistic tendencies make markets more conservational than this rule implies, people must bear a greater than necessary burden in the present for any given endowment that they choose to pass along to the future; but the error will be one of leaving too many, not too few, natural resources.

Price Controls and Renewable Resources

The preceding discussion of the allocation of nonrenewable resources, whether in a competitive market or in one dominated by a cartel, assumed that prices would adjust flexibly to the supply decisions of producers and the demand decisions of buyers. While such price flexibility does exist in world energy markets, the U.S. markets for oil and natural gas have for some years operated under price controls. The exact nature of the controls applying to the two products differ, as do the agencies involved in administering them; but oil and gas controls have two essential features in common. First, they place a ceiling, lower than the world price, on the price that is paid to domestic producers. Second, they place a ceiling on the price paid by consumers that is roughly equal to an average of the world price and the price allowed domestic producers.[2]

The Effects of Price Controls The effects of this kind of price control are shown in Exhibit 20.4. The exhibit refers to the oil market, but that for gas is analytically similar. Part a of the exhibit shows the U.S. market as it would appear in the absence of controls, using three supply curves. One fairly inelastic supply curve represents the supply of domestically produced oil. A second curve represents the supply of imported oil, which is shown as perfectly elastic. (The perfectly elastic supply curve implies that foreign producers are willing to sell unlimited quantities at the official OPEC price, shown as P_0 in

[2] For oil, the averaging of domestic and import prices is accomplished by the so-called entitlement system, under which refiners buying low-priced domestic oil are required, in effect, to pay a special tax, while refiners buying high-priced imported oil receive what is, in effect, a subsidy. For gas, the averaging is accomplished through so-called roll-in pricing, under which utility commissions permit pipeline companies to sell high-priced imported gas below cost while making up the loss by selling low-priced domestic gas above cost. Details of both regulatory programs can be found in the suggestions for further reading at the end of this chapter.

Exhibit 20.4
Effects of oil price controls
This exhibit shows, in somewhat simplified form, the effects of price controls such as those prevailing for oil in the United States in the 1970s. Part a shows how the market operates without controls. Domestic users purchase domestic supplies up to the point where the domestic supply curve crosses the import supply curve and import the remainder of their needs. Part b shows the effects of price controls that set a ceiling, P_1, on the price paid to domestic producers and a ceiling, P_2, equal to the average of the domestic price and the import price, on what can be charged to users. Under controls, the equilibrium quantity of domestic production is smaller, total domestic consumption is greater, and imports are greater than without controls.

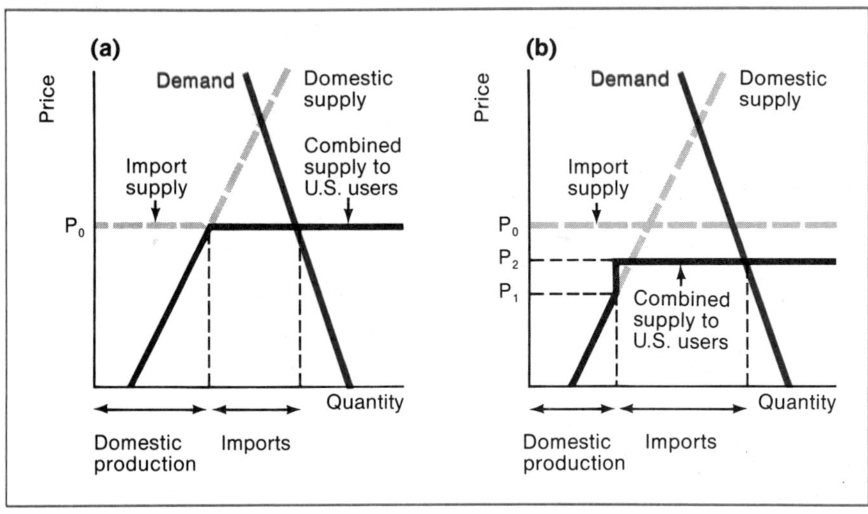

the exhibit. This is something of a simplification, but it serves as a satisfactory approximation for present purposes.) A third curve, shown as a solid line, represents the combined supply curve as it appears to U.S. users. In the absence of price controls, these users will buy from domestic producers up to the point where the domestic price begins to exceed the world price and will then begin to buy imported oil. The combined supply curve thus has a kink in it, as shown. Equilibrium occurs at the point where the demand curve intersects the combined supply curve. The quantities produced domestically and the quantities imported are shown in the diagram.

Exhibit 20.4b shows the U.S. oil market with price controls in effect. As before, P_0 is the world price of oil as set by the cartel. Domestic producers can now be paid no more than P_1, which is below the world price.[3] All oil is sold to U.S. users at price P_2, which is an average of the prices of domestic and imported oil. The combined supply curve as seen by domestic buyers is again shown by a solid line in Part b. This time it follows the domestic supply curve only up to the ceiling price, P_1, beyond which no additional domestic supplies are forthcoming. At that point, imports take over; they are bought at price P_0 but resold to domestic users at P_2. The combined supply curve as seen by U.S. users becomes horizontal at price P_2. Equilibrium is reached where this combined supply curve crosses the demand curve.

Quantities produced domestically and imported under price controls are shown in Exhibit 20.4b. Comparison with Part a of the exhibit shows that price controls decrease domestic production, increase domestic consumption, and increase total oil imports.

Moves toward Decontrol Each of these effects of controls—the decrease in domestic production, the increase in domestic consumption, and the increase in oil imports—runs contrary to professed national policy goals. In order to encourage domestic production, discourage consumption, and reduce imports, steps have recently been taken to phase out price controls on both natural gas and oil. Legislation passed by Congress in 1978, if not further modified, will gradually deregulate the price of natural gas over a period of about five years. Already, the initial phases of deregulation appear to be having a beneficial effect on the exploration for and production of natural gas. In the spring of 1979, President Carter acted under authority previously granted by Congress to begin a similar phased decontrol of domestic crude oil prices. Decontrol of oil prices will probably be accompanied by a new tax on domestic oil, which will mean that U.S. producers still will not receive the full world price. The success of the decontrol effort will depend in part on the exact nature of this tax, which is not clearly decided as yet.

Opposition to Decontrol Despite the fact that the effects of price controls seem strongly at variance with widely accepted policy goals, decontrol of oil and natural gas prices has faced—and continues to face—stiff political opposition. Setting aside such narrow considerations as regional and party rivalries within Congress, at least three economic arguments are advanced in favor of retaining controls.

---

[3]This too is a simplification. Actual price controls impose separate ceilings for various categories of oil, depending on location, time of discovery, and the recovery technology employed.

The first argument is based on the fear of inflation. As energy prices rise to the world level, they will push up the consumer price index. At a time when prices are already increasing rapidly, this idea is not welcome. Thus even some government economists who favor eventual decontrol of energy prices think any major policy change should wait until the broader problem of inflation has been solved.

The second argument against decontrol is based on the belief that the U.S. economy should not be allowed to be disrupted by the artificially high price of oil charged by the OPEC cartel. Price controls in this context are seen as shielding the domestic market from the excessive world price, thereby permitting the same high rate of energy use that could be enjoyed if the world energy market were perfectly competitive. Despite some theoretical appeal of this argument, it is not clear that a policy based on it would really work. Domestic energy prices can be kept low only at the expense of enormous payments to foreign oil producers, and these payments can be even more disruptive to the economy than high energy prices would be.

The third argument against decontrol is based on its probable distributional effects. Decontrol, it is argued, would lead to a massive transfer of income from energy users to energy producers, and the transfer would offend the sense of distributive justice of at least some policy makers. This normative argument is usually combined with the positive economic assertion that decontrol would not significantly discourage demand or encourage domestic supply. The transfer of income from consumers to producers would thus not "buy" much in the way of reduced consumption or increased production. While this is not the place to debate the normative question of whether the government should favor producers, consumers, or neither of them in its economic policies, some attention should be given to the second part of the argument—whether the supply of energy, the demand for energy, or both supply and demand are significantly elastic with respect to price.

Effects of Decontrol If demand and supply were both perfectly inelastic, price decontrol would lead only to a pure transfer from consumers to producers. If either demand or supply were not perfectly inelastic, however, the situation would be more complicated. There would still be some transfer of income from consumers to domestic producers, but there would also be a transfer from foreign producers to domestic producers and a reduction in the real cost of energy to the U.S. economy as a whole. It will be worthwhile, then, to look at least briefly at the likely supply and demand responses to higher energy prices.

Demand Price controls have protected some—but not all—U.S. energy users from the full impact of higher world prices. Where prices have risen, demand has already begun to respond. Between 1973 and 1977, total energy use in the United States increased just 0.17 percent for each 1 percent increase in GNP. This represents a radical break with the long-term trend of one-for-one energy and GNP growth.

In the consumer sector, reductions in energy use have been less dramatic, partly because price controls have shielded consumers from some price increases. Prices for heating oil, bottled gas, and coal, adjusted for inflation, rose by some 50 percent between 1973 and the end of 1978. That helped to make homeowners much more conscious of insulation, storm windows, and thermostats.

On the other hand, cutbacks in gasoline use have been disappointing, despite the fifty-five-mile-per-hour speed limit and tougher mileage standards for new cars. This is not surprising in light of the behavior of gasoline prices. As Exhibit 20.5 shows, the real price of gasoline, adjusted for inflation, was no higher at the end of 1978 than it was in 1967 and was actually lower than it was in 1957. Only after the new upsurge in world oil prices following the 1979 Iranian revolution did the price of gasoline rise above its previous peak. When gasoline prices finally did rise, the immediate result was a boom in public transportation ridership and in the demand for subcompact cars.

In sum, the available evidence indicates considerable price responsiveness of energy demand among industrial users. The potential for consumer response to higher energy prices is large, but it has not been fully tested in areas where price controls have been effective.

Supply There is mounting evidence that there are considerable reserves of fossil fuels that are not worth bringing to the market at present prices but that,

Exhibit 20.5
Gasoline prices adjusted for inflation

This exhibit shows the course of gasoline prices, adjusted for inflation, from 1957 to mid-1979. From 1957 to 1972, the trend was steadily downward; gasoline prices in current dollars rose less than 20 percent, while the consumer price index as a whole rose nearly 50 percent. The 1974 Arab oil embargo sent gasoline prices up 33 percent in a single year; but thereafter, the prices in current dollars stabilized while inflation in general accelerated. By the end of 1978, before the price of gasoline started rising again, it was as low in real terms as it had been in 1967 and actually lower than twenty years before.

The index shown in this exhibit is the ratio of the gasoline and motor oil series to the consumer price index (all items). Source: President's Council of Economic Advisers, *Economic Report of the President* (Washington, D.C.: Government Printing Office, 1979), Tables B-50 and B-51.

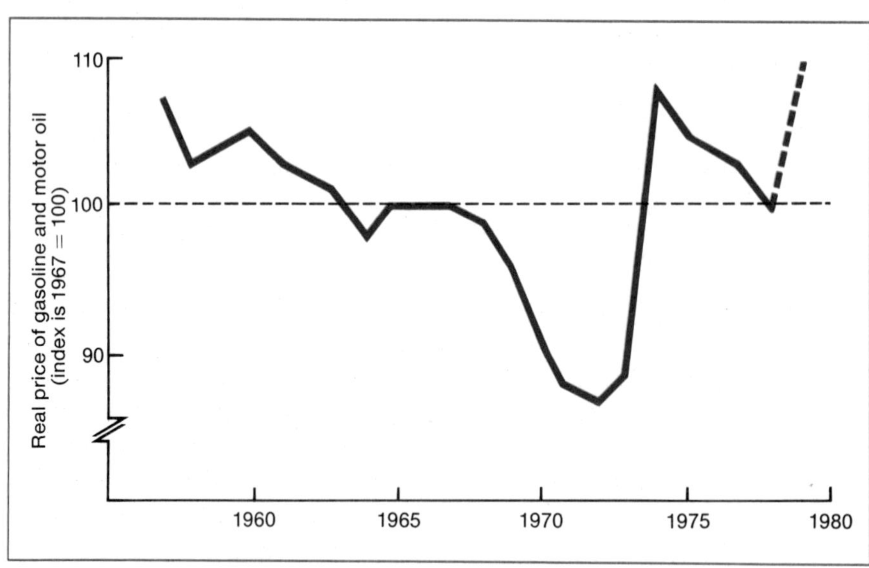

at some price, will be worth extracting. There is much debate, however, about just how much these new sources will cost to develop and which ones are likely to appear on the market first in response to rising prices.

Consider natural gas supplies, for example. In 1977, proven U.S. reserves of natural gas worth recovering at the then-prevailing price were officially calculated at 216 trillion cubic feet (Tcf). That amount was less than a ten-year supply. Yet the following other natural gas reserves were also known to exist in the United States: 300 Tcf of gas (a fifteen-year supply) trapped in coal seams, 600 Tcf (a thirty-year supply) in so-called tight sands under the Rocky Mountains, another 600 Tcf trapped in the Devonian shale formations of Ohio and neighboring states, and a stupendous 100,000 Tcf of natural gas (a theoretical five-thousand-year supply) dissolved in geopressurized brine along the Gulf Coast. No one will really know how much of all that gas can be recovered until the price rises high enough to make it worthwhile for someone to try recovering it.

No one has yet found a five-thousand-year supply of oil, but a number of more modest prospects exist for obtaining additional supplies at costs somewhat in excess of today's prices. These prospects include expanded offshore exploration, expanded use of secondary and tertiary recovery (that is, of methods for getting a higher percentage of the oil out of existing reservoirs), and the extraction of oil from tar sands and oil shale. Outside the United States, especially in China and Mexico (neither of which is a member of OPEC), there are prospects for large conventional discoveries.

The supply response to higher energy prices is by no means limited to added production of oil and gas, however. Much attention is now being given to the development of alternative energy sources. The economic prospects and problems of these sources are sufficiently different from those of oil and gas to warrant discussion in a separate section.

THE ECONOMICS OF ALTERNATIVE ENERGY SOURCES

For the immediate future, the major energy alternatives to oil and gas are coal, nuclear power, and solar power. Strictly speaking, coal and conventional nuclear power are nonrenewable energy sources like oil and natural gas, but they present rather different economic problems in that the availability of known fuel reserves is not the main barrier to their wider use. Solar power—broadly defined to include wind power, water power, and the combustion of farm and forest products (biomass)—is genuinely renewable. This section will discuss each of these alternatives in turn.

Coal

Coal, like oil and natural gas, is a fossil fuel; but unlike the latter, its use as an energy source is limited on the demand rather than the supply side. U.S. coal reserves are enormous—enough to last five hundred years at least. What is more, mining capacity already in place is not even being used fully. The major factor constraining the greater use of coal as an energy source is the cost of burning it in an environmentally acceptable way. This raises two sets of economic issues—those concerned with setting the environmental standards for use of coal and those concerned with meeting the standards.

Setting the Standards The major pollutant in coal is sulphur, which, when burned, produces sulphur dioxide. In urban areas, air pollution from unrestricted burning of coal is a major public health hazard. In agricultural and forest areas, sulphur dioxide pollution causes acid rain, which damages vegetation. And in wilderness areas, such as those of the coal-rich western states, burning coal is a threat to visibility and hence to the attractiveness of national parks and other outdoor recreation areas.

Chapter 19 discussed a number of alternative strategies for regulating air pollution, and little need be added to that discussion here. Suffice it to say that the regulation of emissions from coal combustion has until now emphasized the command-and-control approach, which is often criticized for its inefficiency. By adopting more sophisticated regulatory strategies that pay more attention to variations in local conditions and provide more incentives to employ least-cost methods of abatement, it is likely that the economic burden on coal could be eased while acceptable air quality standards are maintained.

Meeting the Standards Meanwhile, work is under way on a number of alternative technologies for the clean burning of coal. Presently, most coal is burned directly to fire boilers generating electricity, with the pollutants scrubbed out of the stack gases before they are released into the air. The major alternatives focus on preliminary conversion of coal into a clean synthetic fuel that can be burned without elaborate pollution control devices at the point of use. One technique, known as solvent refining, produces a liquid substitute for oil. Another technique bakes the coal and blasts it with air to produce a clean, flammable mixture of carbon monoxide and hydrogen known as producer gas. This gas was widely manufactured in local gasworks around the turn of the century, but it was displaced by natural gas when long-distance pipelines were built. Although producer gas is unlikely to be reintroduced in the residential market (it has a much lower energy value per cubic foot than natural gas), many industrial users are now finding it profitable to build on-site producer gas plants to meet their own needs.

Nuclear Energy

Nuclear energy, everyone's darling in the 1960s and already a major contributor to U.S. energy supplies, now faces an uncertain future. Not all the objections to this form of energy are economic. However, the economic problems of nuclear energy are, in a sense, the most threatening ones because they are producing disenchantment among its traditional friends as well as among its foes.

Because nuclear energy is used almost exclusively to produce electricity, its major competitor is coal. It is appropriate, then, to cast the discussion of the economics of nuclear power in the form of a comparison with coal.

Nuclear Power versus Coal—The Basics The basic economics of nuclear power versus coal is very simple to state: Nuclear power plants are more expensive to build but cheaper to operate.[4] According to one recent set of estimates, as of 1978, a new nuclear power plant would cost $913 per kilowatt

---

[4]Cost data given in this section, except where otherwise noted, are taken from Edmund Faltermayer, "Nuclear Power after Three Mile Island," *Fortune*, May 7, 1979, pp. 114–122.

of capacity, compared with $639 per kilowatt for coal. Once built, however, the coal plant would gulp a hundred-car trainload of fuel every two days, while the nuclear plant would consume less than half a carload of fuel per year. At 1978 prices for coal and uranium, this would make the fuel cost of nuclear power just half the fuel cost for coal.

Whether the trade-off of higher construction costs for lower fuel costs is worthwhile depends on the cost of capital and the percent of capacity at which the plant is operated. During the 1960s, the economics seems clearly to have favored nuclear power over coal. Utilities reported total generating costs per kilowatt hour, including capital costs, to be 40 percent lower for nuclear facilities of that period than for coal-fired plants of comparable age.

Today, however, the advantage is shifting. Higher interest rates and longer construction times have pushed up capital costs. Safety problems requiring more frequent shutdowns have seriously reduced the percentage of capacity at which nuclear plants have been able to operate. And although environmental regulations have increased the cost of coal-fired plants too, they have had even more of an impact on nuclear plants in that they have increased the gap in construction costs. A recent internal study by the Exxon Corporation suggests that when all of these effects are taken into account, the operating cost per kilowatt hour for plants built today is 5.07 cents for nuclear and 5.11 cents for coal—nowhere near enough of a difference to justify the enormously greater construction cost of the nuclear plant.[5] Even these figures are based on what some observers think are overly optimistic assumptions about the percentage of capacity utilization for the nuclear alternative.

Nuclear Power versus Coal—The Hidden Costs If conventional calculations such as those given above suggest that nuclear power is losing the economic advantage it once enjoyed over coal, some unconventional calculations are even more disconcerting. They focus on a number of hidden costs of nuclear power—costs that are opportunity costs from the point of view of the economy as a whole but that are not fully borne by owners of nuclear facilities or their rate payers (users of electric power). The most important of these hidden costs are in waste disposal and dismantling and in health and safety areas.

Waste Disposal and Dismantling One of the great unsolved problems of nuclear power is how to dispose of the radioactive wastes it produces. These wastes are extraordinarily toxic and must be kept isolated for thousands of years. No one really knows how the job can best be done, although there are a number of promising alternatives under exploration. Even if it is technically possible to safely dispose of nuclear wastes, however—something that many nuclear critics are willing to concede—there is no realistic way of knowing what the cost will be. The government agrees, in principle, that private nuclear utilities should be charged the full cost of waste disposal, but that is not yet being done.

A similar problem concerns the dismantling of the reactors themselves at the end of their useful life of forty years or so. Estimates of the dismantling costs range anywhere from 5 to 25 percent of the original construction costs.

---

[5]Dan Dorfman, "Nuclear Power Cost Questioned by Exxon," *Washington Post,* June 6, 1979, p. D3.

Again, no one really knows, because no big nuclear power plant has ever been dismantled. Whatever the costs, however, they are not being fully charged against nuclear power now being generated. The economic advantage of nuclear power over coal is thereby exaggerated.

Safety and Health The Three Mile Island episode of 1979 touched off a great national debate over the safety of nuclear power. Critics charged that the accident came within a hairsbreadth of a core meltdown that could have killed tens of thousands of people. Proponents of nuclear power countered that the accident injured not a single person and in fact showed that a nuclear plant could survive a much more serious combination of human errors and equipment failures than even the critics had imagined possible. This is not the place to resolve the technical arguments over nuclear safety; but however they are resolved, it is clear that after Three Mile Island, stricter safety standards will be imposed on the nuclear industry. These standards will further erode any remaining cost advantage that nuclear power holds over coal.

A further safety related issue concerns liability for nuclear accidents. Early in the nuclear power era, Congress passed the Price-Anderson Act, which set a $560 million limit on utilities' insurance liability in case of accident. Competing energy sources, in contrast, must bear full liability. The Price-Anderson Act thus constitutes another hidden subsidy of nuclear power by the government. In the wake of Three Mile Island, it is safe to say that the premiums for nuclear liability insurance, if utilities were required to carry it, would be quite substantial.

Hazards of Coal Nuclear power, to be sure, is not unique in posing health and safety hazards. Pronuclear writers often point out that coal too has major health and safety problems. The hazards to which coal miners are exposed far exceed those confronted by workers in the nuclear industry, and air pollution is a very real public health hazard in contrast to the largely speculative hazards of low-level radiation or core meltdowns. Some calculations indicate that unrestricted burning of coal might be as much as a thousand times more hazardous than widespread use of nuclear power.

There can be no doubt that a balanced economic comparison of nuclear power versus coal must take into account the full health and safety costs of both alternatives. More research needs to be done, however, before this aspect of the debate can be said to favor nuclear power conclusively. For one thing, the health and safety costs of coal mining are not hidden; they are costs that the coal industry is already bearing in its wage bills, retirement benefits, workmen's compensation premiums, and so on. As for the public health hazards of air pollution as compared with those of nuclear disasters, the question is not so much which is greater at present but which can be controlled at least cost through well-designed regulation.

Solar Energy

Solar energy represents the third major alternative to nonrenewable oil and natural gas. Solar energy—broadly defined to include wind power, hydroelectric power, alcohol, and wood—now contributes about 6 percent of the nation's total energy needs. This percentage is expected to double by the end of the century even if no major new policy initiatives are undertaken. (In 1979, the Carter administration announced plans for a Solar Development Bank, which—if created—would be the centerpiece of an effort to raise the solar contribution to 20 percent by the year 2000.) The economics of solar power can be summarized briefly under the headings of capital costs and net energy costs.

Capital Costs Replacing fossil fuels with solar power represents, even more than in the case of nuclear power, a trade-off of capital investment and operating costs. The system of dams along the Columbia River between Oregon and Washington, for example, although enormously costly to construct, produces electric power at an operating cost of around half a cent per kilowatt hour. Unfortunately, few, if any, really attractive sites remain in the United States for large-scale hydroelectric projects. For the immediate future, solar prospects appear to consist of small-scale applications that are economical given today's costs and technology and larger-scale applications that cannot yet repay their capital costs but that offer some promise for future development.

One of the best-known small-scale applications of solar energy is for residential water heating. In recent years, many companies, large and small, have begun producing practical solar hot water systems. The system produced by AMSOLHEAT, a small company in Danbury, Connecticut (see Exhibit 20.6), is typical. It uses off-the-shelf technology made economically attractive by rising energy prices. Entrepreneur Joseph Heyman of AMSOLHEAT has calculated that his sytem, which costs about $3,000 installed, can pay for itself in seven years as a replacement for electric water heating; this represents an attractive rate of return at today's interest rates.

Another example of off-the-shelf technology, once widespread and now returning to use, is low-head hydroelectric power. Low-head hydroelectric power from small dams on local streams compares to hydroelectric power from the dams of the Columbia River as a wood stove does to a 1,000 megawatt nuclear plant. Nonetheless, many small dams dating from the last century are now being put back into use with modern generating equipment.

For the future, many potentially attractive technologies exist for both large-scale and small-scale use. Wind power, photovoltaic power, and large-scale solar steam plants are in the design or pilot plant stage. All are still at least one technological generation away from being economically competitive with conventional fuels, however.

Net Energy Costs One of the most controversial aspects of solar energy sources concerns their net energy costs. Practitioners of the art of net energy analysis attempt to add up all the energy inputs needed to produce a unit of energy output from a given technology to see if more comes out than goes in. If more energy goes in than comes out, a technology clearly cannot be considered an energy "source" in the conventional meaning of the term.

Photovoltaic power is an example of a technology that is on the margin from a net energy point of view, at least given today's technology. This kind of power uses silicon wafers to convert sunlight directly into electricity. The wafers, which are manufactured by a highly energy-intensive process, have an expected life of about ten years in commercial applications. Even if located in

Exhibit 20.6

A practical application of solar power

After world oil prices began to rise in 1973, many companies began to produce domestic solar hot water heating systems. The system produced by AMSOLHEAT of Danbury, Connecticut, is typical, in that it uses off-the-shelf technology that had fallen into disuse in the 1950s and 1960s with the advent of cheap conventional fuels. At 1979 prices, the AMSOLHEAT system was calculated to save enough electricity to repay its initial cost in seven years.

Source: Courtesy of American Solar Heat Corp., Danbury, Conn.

AMSOLHEAT Introduces Free Hot Water for Two Billion Years.

Now we don't anticipate your home will be around for the projected two billion years of the sun's existence, but during the next hundred years or so isn't it reassuring to know that the price of the sun's heat will never increase (it's free), whereas the price of home fuel oil will continue to rise.

The Sun Yesterday.

Harnessing the sun's energy for productive use has been experimented with for centuries . . . with the introduction of a solar powered steam engine operating a printing press in 1878, an irrigation system in Egypt (1913) and a solar still delivering 6,000 gallons of water in the Chilean desert over 40 years ago.

Solar water heating systems have been commercially available in such countries as Australia, Israel, and Japan for a number of years. In Florida and Southern California, there was a thriving solar water heater business in the 1940's and 50's, which declined, of course, when conventional fuel became cheap and widely available.

The Sun Today.

In the 1970's, however, interest in solar heating and application in affordable systems has risen again, this time to stay, due in no small part to economic necessities rising out of the oil embargo.

Here in the Northeast, American Solar Heat Corporation (AMSOLHEAT) is proving the thesis that solar heat effectively and efficiently provides the necessary energy to heat domestic hot water.

With AMSOLHEAT's solar collectors, the sun's energy, unlike our natural resources of oil, gas and coal, is not only renewable but economically controllable so that your hot water heating bills can be reduced significantly. AMSOLHEAT customers have seen their hot water bills reduced by up to 70 per cent! With these savings, the AMSOLHEAT solar unit, priced at $1,260.00, will pay for itself within a short period of time (6 years plus).

This simple diagram tells you HOW the sun works for you.

AMSOLHEAT SOLAR PANEL
FROM SOLAR PANEL
AMSOLHEAT STORAGE TANK
TO EXISTING HOT WATER SYSTEM
TO SOLAR PANEL
COLD WATER SUPPLY
AMSOL HEAT LETS THE SUN SHINE

The heat of the sun is collected in the water of the copper pipes within AMSOLHEAT's solar panel. This water is circulated through the AMSOLHEAT storage tank in the basement which goes into your existing hot water system.

Testimonial—Mrs. Rose Heyman of Danbury, Conn., a satisfied AMSOLHEAT customer, said this of our solar panels ". . . definitely increased the amount of our hot water."

This simple panel tells you WHEN the sun is working for you.

While the roof panels are collecting solar energy and the hot water is storing in the basement tanks, this panel inside your home (installed next to your thermostat) indicates the following:

ON: When your AMSOLHEAT system is operable.

FREE HEAT: When you're getting free solar heat.

DRAIN: When the panels drain to prevent freezing.

TEMPERATURE GAUGE: Temperature of your solar panel or storage tank.

Testimonial—Barbara Wardenburg of Ridgefield, Conn., another satisfied customer, had this to say about AMSOLHEAT's panel ". . . simple enough operation so our children can see the practical application of science working to solve human problems."

This simple coupon will help you save money. CALL now 792-0077 or mail this coupon today for a free AMSOLHEAT installation estimate.

AMERICAN SOLAR HEAT CORPORATION
7 National Place
Danbury, Ct. 06810

☐ I am a homeowner tired of paying increasing prices for hot water heat.

☐ I am an architect, contractor, builder and want to know more about AMSOLHEAT products.

Name ______________________

Address ______________________

Telephone # ______________________

the sunny Southwest, more than half of the ten years would be needed just to repay the energy used in manufacturing the wafers, not counting any of the other energy used in constructing and operating the plant.

Alcohol fuel, another solar technology, has also been challenged on net energy grounds. It appears that alcohol made from grain grown in the United States by mechanized methods and produced with gas or oil fired stills consumes more energy than it yields. Alcohol cannot be entirely written off as an energy source, however. For one thing, if mixed with gasoline to make gasohol, it improves mileage and raises octane ratings, thereby contributing more than its energy value to the mix. Also, alcohol produced from raw materials other than grain or distilled using wood or crop waste as a fuel can be more energy efficient. For example, Brazil has a large program of alcohol fuel production that uses sugar cane as its raw material and burns cane waste as a fuel.

CONCLUSIONS

Perhaps the safest thing to say about the economics of energy is that it is a rapidly changing field. The prospects for oil and natural gas depend very much on supply and demand reactions to price decontrol over the next five to ten years. Nuclear power appears at the moment to be going nowhere, but existing plants contribute an indispensable one-eighth of all electric power. Coal is enormously abundant, but its wider use is being held up while cost-efficient ways are sought to overcome its environmental problems. Solar power is growing in importance but is unlikely to contribute more than a fifth of U.S. energy needs in this century. Energy economics promises to be exciting for years to come.

SUMMARY

1. According to the theory of the mine, in a competitive market, a nonrenewable resource will be depleted no faster than the rate that will cause its price to rise at a rate equal to the prevailing interest rate. Any faster rate of depletion would be self-correcting, since wealth-maximizing resource owners would begin to withhold present supplies from the market in order to sell them at higher prices later. When the market for such a resource is dominated by a cartel, the rate of depletion tends to be less than in a competitive market.
2. Price controls on oil and natural gas in the United States have partially insulated domestic markets from the effects of rising world prices. The result has been a lower rate of domestic production, a higher rate of domestic consumption, and a higher rate of imports than would have prevailed without controls. Controls on both oil and gas prices are presently being phased out.
3. The major energy alternatives to oil and natural gas are coal, nuclear energy, and solar power. All these alternatives require greater capital expenditure per unit of energy output than oil and gas if they are to meet health, safety, and environmental safeguards. From an economic point of view, all three still appear to be in the running as major energy sources for the future, although coal and solar power currently seem to be gaining at the expense of the nuclear alternative.

DISCUSSION QUESTIONS

1. Imagine that you are snowed in for the winter in a small cabin in the mountains. Your food supply consists of a sack of potatoes. There are more than enough potatoes to survive on but less than enough to eat all you want every day. How will you allocate the potatoes over the winter? Will you eat an equal amount every day? More per day at first and then gradually taper off? Fewer at first and more toward the end? What does the theory of the mine have to say about this kind of situation?
2. When this edition of this text was written, Congress had just passed legislation that was to gradually deregulate the price of natural gas over a period of about five years. Is this deregulation process proceeding on schedule, or has new natural gas legislation proved necessary since 1978?
3. Go to your library, and find a copy of the *Monthly Labor Review* or some other publication that gives a product-by-product breakdown of the consumer price index. Compare the current price index for gasoline with the price index for all goods and services for all urban consumers. Use these data to update Exhibit 20.5.
4. Is it still true, as you are reading this, that the government is subsidizing imported oil at the expense of domestic production? What has happened to the so-called entitlements program? (Hint: Use the *New York Times* index for a quick review of major energy policy changes since early 1979.)

SUGGESTIONS FOR FURTHER READING

Goodman, John C., and Dolan, Edwin G. *The Economics of Public Policy.* St. Paul, Minn.: West Publishing, 1979.

Four chapters in this book are devoted to energy-related topics. Chapter 3 deals with gasoline rationing, Chapter 7 with electric power, Chapter 9 with natural gas, and Chapter 10 with oil.

Mead, Walter J. *Energy and the Environment: Conflict in Policy.* Washington, D.C.: American Enterprise Institute, 1978.

This short monograph looks at the reasons that energy and the environment have become two of the leading political issues of the day and examines their economic relationships.

Stobaugh, Robert, and Yergin, Daniel, eds. *The Energy Future.* New York: Random House, 1979.

This study, by a group of Harvard business school professors, examines a broad spectrum of energy alternatives for the future and concludes that conservation remains the most important single hope for reducing U.S. dependence on imported oil.

Williams, Stephen F. "Running Out: The Problem of Exhaustible Resources." *Journal of Legal Studies* 7 (January 1978): 165–199.

The article begins with an exposition of the theory of the mine and concludes with an examination of some of the normative issues connected with the allocation of nonrenewable resources over time.

CHAPTER 21

THE ECONOMICS OF POPULATION AND DEVELOPMENT

WHAT YOU WILL LEARN IN THIS CHAPTER

Most of the inhabitants of the planet earth are very poor, and the numbers of the poor are increasing more rapidly than those of the more well-to-do. This chapter discusses some of the economic problems faced by the inhabitants of the less developed countries. It begins with a lesson in basic population arithmetic. Then it compares population growth trends over time in the developed and less developed countries and shows why the population problem of the less developed world is in many respects more serious than that faced in earlier times by the now developed countries. Finally, the chapter turns from the population problem itself to the problem of producing sufficient food to feed the ever-growing third world population.

FOR REVIEW

Here is an important concept that will be put to use in this chapter. If you do not understand it, review it before proceeding.

- *Sources of economic growth (Chapter 7)*

Having dealt with pollution and energy, the discussion turns now to a third major problem of life on this planet: population. How will the ever-increasing numbers of people in the world find room to live? How are they going to be fed? These are among the most pressing worldwide problems to be faced in the closing years of the twentieth century.

Unlike the problems of pollution and energy, those of food and population have largely been solved in the world's industrialized market economies. For that reason, this chapter will focus on the less developed countries, where two-thirds of the world's people already live. It begins with a brief discussion of the nature of the economic development process itself. Next, it turns to the topic of population. Finally, it reviews the status of world food production, on which the solution of the problems of development and population so heavily depend.

THREE FACES OF ECONOMIC GROWTH

Economic Development as Growth

The less developed countries that make up what is called the "third world" differ from one another and from the developed countries in many ways, but they have one conspicuous thing in common—low per capita income. No magic number divides the rich countries from the poor; there is a spectrum of degrees of poverty, as shown in the map in Exhibit 21.1. At the very bottom of

$3,001 to more than $7,000

Australia
Austria
Bahamas Islands
Bahrain
Belgium
Bermuda
Brunei
Canada
Czechoslovakia
Denmark
East Germany
Faroe Islands
Finland
France
Gabon
Greenland
Iceland
Israel
Italy
Japan
Kuwait
Libya
Liechtenstein
Luxembourg
Monaco
Nauru
Netherlands
New Zealand
Norway
Oman
Qatar
San Marino
Saudi Arabia
Spain
Sweden
Switzerland
United Arab Emirates
United Kingdom
United States
USSR
West Germany

$201 to $1,000

Albania
Algeria
Angola
Antigua
Belize
Benin
Bolivia
Botswanna
Cameroon
Chili
Colombia
Congo
Cook Islands
Cuba
Dominica
Dominican Republic
Djibouti
Ecuador
Egypt
El Salvador
French Guiana
Gambia
Ghana
Gibraltar
Gilbert Islands
Grenada
Guadeloupe

$1,001 to $3,000

Andorra
Argentina
Barbados
Brazil
Bulgaria
Costa Rica
Cyprus
Falkland Islands
Fiji
French Polynesia
Greece
Hong Kong
Hungary
Iran
Iraq
Ireland
Jamaica
Malta
Martinique
Mexico
Netherlands Antilles
New Caledonia
Panama
Poland
Portugal
Puerto Rico
Romania
Singapore
South Africa
Surinam
Taiwan
Trinidad and Tobago
Turkey
Uruguay
Venezuela
Yugoslavia

Exhibit 21.1
Gross national product per capita, 1977 (in 1977 U.S. dollars)
The countries of the world exhibit an enormous range in per capita incomes. There is no sharp dividing line between the developed and less developed countries. Here, four groups are distinguished. The most poverty stricken countries are those with incomes of less than $200 GNP per capita. Those with per capita incomes of less than $1,000 are also very poor, but many are experiencing promis-

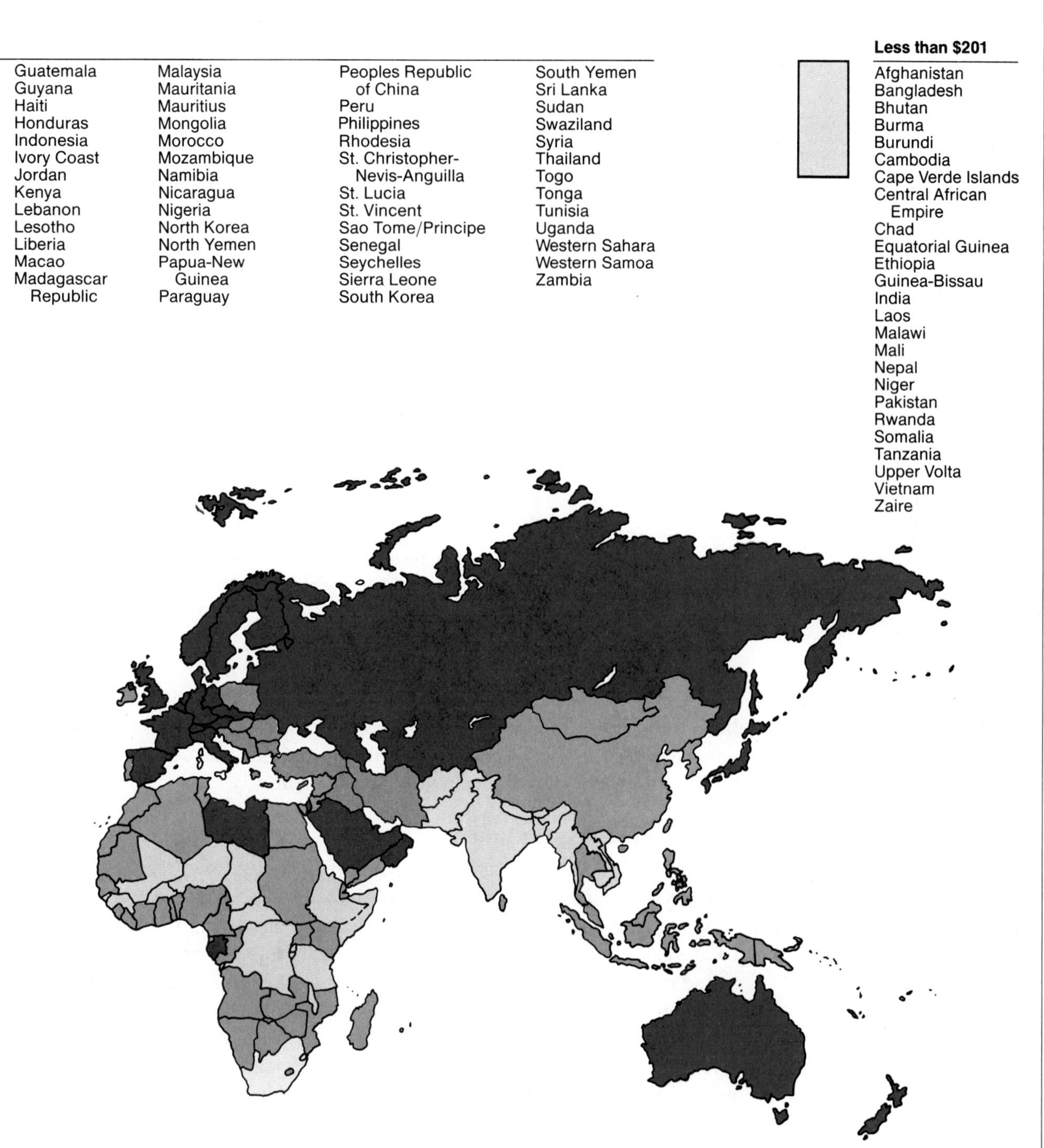

ing self-sufficient economic growth. Countries in the $1,000 to $3,000 range belong in the less developed category in some respects; but in other ways, they more closely resemble the countries with more than $3,000 per capita GNP. This last group includes the oil-rich countries of the Middle East as well as the industrialized countries of Europe and North America.

Source: Adapted from U.S. Central Intelligence Agency, National Foreign Assessment Center, *Handbook of Economic Statistics* (Washington, D.C., 1978), Figure 1, p. 1.

the spectrum are the poorest of poor countries—those with per capita GNP of less than $200 per year. These countries are found in southern Asia, from Afghanistan to Vietnam, and in a band through central Africa reaching from Guinea on the west coast to Tanzania on the east. The map also distinguishes countries with per capita GNP in the range of $201 to $1,000, clearly in the less developed group but somewhat better off. A third group, in the $1,001 to $3,000 range—including much of Latin America as well as such countries as Portugal, Yugoslavia, and Taiwan—straddles the ill-defined border between developed and less developed status. Countries with still higher levels of per capita GNP include the truly developed countries as well as the somewhat anomalous oil-rich countries of the Middle East.

To draw these distinctions in terms of per capita incomes implies that economic development equals economic growth. That is the traditional view of the matter, and it is a view that still has much truth to it. Economic growth can occur without bringing a better life to everyone, but it is hard to see how a better life for all can come without at least some growth. This is especially true for the least developed countries that have less than $200 of GNP per capita.

Much of development economics, then, focuses on ways to enable a country to grow. Growth oriented development studies usually emphasize capital accumulation as the great key. Capital accumulation has accounted for only about 15 percent of economic growth in the United States in recent years; but it is more important for less developed countries, which have a great shortage of capital. Typically, saving and investment are only 5 to 7 percent of GNP, compared to over 15 percent in the United States and 35 percent in Japan and the Soviet-type economies. Without capital accumulation, it is difficult to put unemployed and underemployed people to work. Without capital it is equally difficult to improve the level of education or to take advantage of imported technology. Yet, although capital accumulation and growth are important, they are not the whole story of economic development.

Development as Industrialization

The developed countries are not only richer than the less developed countries; they are also more highly industrialized. Developed countries typically have between a fifth and a quarter of their populations engaged in industry. In the less developed countries, the proportion is likely to be 10 percent or less. A second interpretation of economic development, then, is that it means industrializing, just as the advanced countries have done in the past.

The view that development means industrialization, like the view that development means economic growth, has much truth to it. The less developed countries have large and growing urban populations. Only industrialization offers them much hope of employment. As incomes rise in a developing country, the demand for manufactured goods increases rapidly. It makes sense to meet many of these needs with domestic sources of supply. Many less developed countries have valuable raw materials that they now export for processing; these materials could be processed domestically instead. Still, despite all this, the importance of industrialization to development should not be exaggerated.

For one thing, an overemphasis on industrialization may cause resources to be wasted on ill-conceived showcase projects. Not every less developed country needs a steel mill and an automobile plant. Even small-scale industrial projects may be inappropriate if they mean building an exact replica of some plant originally designed for Manchester or Milwaukee, where relative factor scarcities and other market conditions are completely different.

What is more, an overemphasis on industrialization can lead to the neglect of other development objectives. The third face of economic development shows why.

Development as Depauperization

It is a widely shared opinion that a major goal of economic development should be a better life for the poorest of the poor—the people at the low end of the income distribution in the poorest countries. They are the true paupers—lacking adequate food, often lacking all access to medical care, and not infrequently lacking even the most primitive shelter.

Development economists once were confident that the benefits of growth and industrialization would automatically trickle down to the poorest of the poor. Unfortunately, this optimism may not be justified, as the research of Irma Adelman and C. T. Morris has shown.[1] Their work focuses on the range of development from sub-Saharan Africa to the poorest countries of South America—that is, from about $100 to $500 per capita income. In these countries, development tends to bring both relative and absolute impoverishment to the poorest 60 percent of the population. At very low levels of development, there appears to be no trickling down at all. The poor begin to benefit only after an intermediate level of development has been reached.

Adelman and Morris have concluded that the policies needed to benefit the poor are different from those needed to maximize growth rates. The ideas of development as growth or industrialization, they say, should be replaced with the idea of **depauperization**—the provision not only of the necessary material basis for life but also of access to education, security, self-expression, status, and power. Depauperization stresses the removal of social, political, and spiritual deprivation as much as physical deprivation. It has as much to do with equity as with growth.

Depauperization Economic development of a kind that benefits the poorest of the poor, providing them not only with the material necessities of life but also with access to education, status, security, self-expression, and power.

Two Strategies

The choice of development goals strongly influences the strategy that can best promote the development process. The Soviet Union represents one extreme. For early Soviet planners, development meant industrialization above all else. Through high rates of saving, they sacrificed consumption to achieve rapid growth. Through collectivization, they sacrificed the growth of agriculture to achieve the growth of industry. Eventually, the benefits of successful industrialization began to trickle down to the population at large. Initially, though, living standards declined, and the overall distribution of income shifted in favor of industrial workers and against peasants.

Even where industrialization as an end in itself is not made a higher priority than overall growth, the benefits of development may be spread unevenly. Many less developed countries suffer from what is called a **dual economy.** In such an economy, a modern, Westernized industrial sector provides high wages for better educated workers and a tax base to pay a middle class of civil

Dual economy An economy that is sharply divided into a modern, westernized industrial sector capable of rapid growth and a traditional rural sector that remains stagnant.

[1]Irma Adelman and C. T. Morris, *Society, Politics, and Economic Development* (Baltimore: Johns Hopkins University Press, 1967).

servants. Meanwhile, a secondary, traditional sector remains largely untouched. Sometimes, the overall growth rate of GNP can be maximized by concentrating available development resources on the modern sector, at least in the short run. Often also foreign aid and the investments of multinational corporations are concentrated on the modern sector of dual economies.

There is a second kind of development strategy that contrasts with the industry-first approach. It emphasizes redistribution and mass education first and growth later. Redistribution in the context of less developed countries means most importantly the redistribution of land ownership. Education means mass education in literacy and general knowledge, rather than just specialized training for participation in the modern sector. If this strategy works, redistribution can provide the basis for rural development and education the basis for the growth of broadly based, labor-intensive industry. Adelman and Morris cite Israel, Japan, South Korea, Singapore, and Taiwan as countries that have successfully followed this strategy. China should probably be added to the list. In the last century, U.S. economic development followed this strategy much more than did economic development in Europe.

POPULATION AND DEVELOPMENT

Whatever development strategy they choose, all less developed countries face certain common problems that they must somehow solve. None is more serious than the problem of population growth. As background for a discussion of population problems in the less developed countries, here is a review of some basic population arithmetic.

Population Arithmetic

For a population to increase, it is obvious that more people must be born than die each year. (In this section and in what follows, immigration and emigration are ignored.) The number of people born into a population per thousand per year is the **crude birthrate** for that population. The number who die per thousand per year is the **crude death rate.** The difference between the two is the **rate of natural increase.**

Crude birthrate The number of people born into a population per thousand per year.

Crude death rate The number of people in a population who die per thousand per year.

Rate of natural increase The current growth rate of a population calculated as the crude birthrate minus the crude death rate.

Exhibit 21.2 shows crude birthrates, crude death rates, and rates of natural increase for a selection of countries, according to the latest available data. In interpreting data such as these, it sometimes helps to translate rates of natural increase into population doubling times. This is done in the last column of the table. The faster the rate of natural increase, the shorter the period of time required for the population to double in size.

Growth Curves A population that grew indefinitely at a constant rate of natural increase would double each time a fixed number of years elapsed. It would reach 2, 4, 8, 16, 32, 64 (and so on) times its original size, following the same sort of growth path as that followed by the value of a sum of money invested at compound interest.

Normally, however, living populations are not able to grow exponentially without limit. Suppose that bacteria are allowed to multiply in a glass jar of nutrient, or a population of fruit flies is allowed to grow in a glass cage or room of fixed size, or a breeding pair of dogs is introduced on an island previously inhabited only by rabbits. Under such conditions, the growth of the population of bacteria, fruit flies, or dogs typically follows the kind of S-shaped growth

Exhibit 21.2
Birthrates, death rates, and the rate of natural increase of the population for selected countries (most recent available data)
The rate of natural increase for a population is found by subtracting the current death rate per thousand from the current birthrate per thousand. If the rate of natural increase is greater than zero, it can also be expressed as the number of years that would be required for the population to double if that rate were to continue.

Country	Crude Birthrate	Crude Death Rate	Rate of Natural Increase	Doubling Time of Population (years)
Honduras	47	12	35	20
Mexico	41	7	34	20
Algeria	48	14	33	21
Nigeria	50	18	32	22
Ghana	48	17	31	22
Pakistan	44	14	30	23
Somalia	48	20	28	25
Brazil	36	8	28	25
Haiti	42	16	26	27
Ethiopia	50	25	25	28
Afghanistan	50	27	23	30
Yemen	48	25	23	30
Thailand	32	9	23	30
Argentina	22	9	13	53
China	20	8	12	58
Japan	15	6	9	77
USSR	18	10	8	87
Czechoslovakia	19	12	7	99
United States	15	9	6	116
France	14	10	4	173
Italy	13	10	4	173
Sweden	12	11	1	693
United Kingdom	12	12	0	—
West Germany	10	12	−2	—

Source: Reprinted by permission from *1979 World Population Data Sheet* (Washington, D.C.: Population Reference Bureau, 1979).

curve shown in Exhibit 21.3. At first, the population will expand at the exponential rate. The biological characteristics of the species in question determine the population doubling time under optimal conditions. Sooner or later, though, the population will begin to fill up its jar or cage or island or whatever. Then, under more crowded conditions, the time needed to double

Exhibit 21.3
Typical S-shaped curve of population growth
A living population cannot grow indefinitely in a finite environment. Under laboratory conditions, populations of bacteria or fruit flies or other organisms tend to follow S-shaped growth curves such as the one shown here. In the long run, it seems inevitable that the growth curve of human population will also begin to decrease.

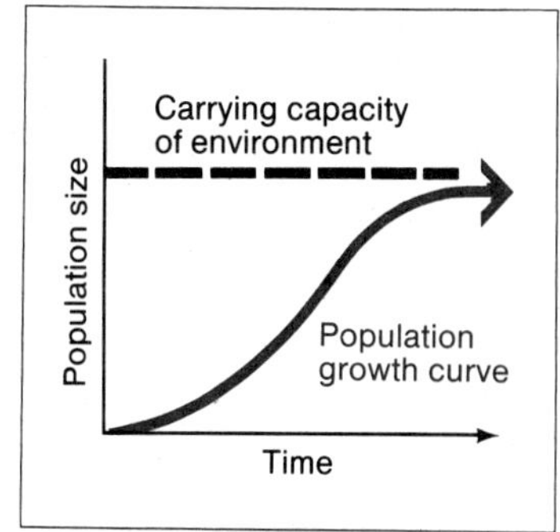

the population will increase. Eventually, overcrowding will bring population growth to a halt.

Must the growth of human population also be subject to this S-curve pattern? In the long run, it surely must. Estimates of the maximum human population of earth vary widely, but no one doubts that there is some finite ceiling. (One admittedly fanciful estimate places the limit as high as 20 million times the present world population. This would require people to live 120 to the square meter in a two-thousand-story building covering the entire earth. Even that limit would take only 890 years to reach at the present growth rate of world population!)

In the short run, though, the growth of human population has not followed the simple S-curve pattern. In fact, over as long a period as any kind of population estimates can be made, the world rate of natural increase has been accelerating, not slowing down. World population has doubled in about the last forty-five years and would double again in the next thirty-five if the current growth rate were to continue. The last preceding doubling of population took about eighty years, from 1850 to 1930. The doubling before that took some two hundred years. It is hard to imagine that this trend will continue. There are now indications that the world is reaching the bend in the population growth curve and that world population growth, for the first time, is beginning to slow.[2]

Population Equilibrium

There can be no doubt that in the long run the level of human population is headed for an equilibrium state in which births will just balance deaths. The really interesting question is: What will that equilibrium look like? Let's explore some possibilities.

First, imagine a market economy in which people earn money to buy the necessities of life only by selling factor services. The population begins to approach some fixed limit to population growth defined, for example, by the food supply. Income is distributed unequally in this society. As population nears the ceiling, the price of food rises relative to the wage rate. The lowest income groups find their standard of living reduced, and this eventually affects their birth and death rates. At some point, an excess of deaths over births will occur among the poorest classes. This will be accompanied by a balance between births and deaths for those living just at the margin of subsistence. An excess of births will be possible only among the well-to-do. When enough people have finally been pushed down to or below the margin of subsistence, population growth as a whole will cease. The result can be called a marginal subsistence equilibrium for population.

This equilibrium assumes great inequality. It implies affluence for a few against the backdrop of destitute masses whose members are continuously replenished by the excess children of the rich driven down into poverty. If the assumption of inequality is removed, the result is a second type of population equilibrium, which can be called the absolute subsistence equilibrium. Under

---

[2]For example, Donald J. Bogue and Amy Ong Tsui, in "Zero World Population Growth," *Public Interest*, no. 55 (Spring 1979): 99–113, go so far as to declare the once-feared population bomb a dud. Between 1968 and 1975, they report, fertility declined in 103 countries having a total population of 3.2 billion and increased or was unchanged in only 45 countries with a total population of 749 million.

this solution, as crowding begins to lower the living standards of a population, taxes and transfers are used to divide the burden equally among all. This equality permits population growth to go on longer; no one is starved or crowded to the point of being unable to reproduce until everyone reaches that point. The total number of people living in poverty in the absolute subsistence equilibrium is greater than in the marginal subsistence equilibrium.

Population projections like these were what once caused economics to be called the "dismal science." As long ago as 1798, Thomas Malthus forecast a marginal subsistence population equilibrium for humanity that would come about through the operation of the law of diminishing returns, as a growing population caught up with a fixed supply of agricultural land. According to Malthus's theory, only the landlords, who owned the means of producing precious food, would escape eventual poverty. Even the capitalists would eventually be ground down and their profits reduced to zero.

Malthus's prophecy has not come true for Great Britain, the United States, or other advanced industrial countries. These countries have instead achieved, or nearly achieved, a nonsubsistence population equilibrium with low birthrates, low death rates, and high living standards. The process by which this equilibrium has been achieved is a good illustration of how economic and demographic processes interact.

Thomas Robert Malthus was born in England in 1766 and received what was, for his time, a radical upbringing. His father was an admirer of Rousseau and Condorcet, and one of his tutors was imprisoned for expressing the wish that the French revolutionaries would invade and liberate England. Malthus studied at Cambridge, took holy orders, and became a curate.

In 1793, a book appeared that had a great impact on the circles in which young Malthus moved. The book was *Enquiry Concerning Political Justice and Its Influence on Morals and Happiness* by the anarchist and socialist, William Godwin. As a result of many lively debates over this book and subsequent essays by Godwin, Malthus decided to write down his own view that population growth constituted an insurmountable barrier to a society of absolute equality and abundance. This writing appeared as *An Essay on the Principle of Population* in 1798.

The heart of Malthus's argument was the doctrine that population tended to grow in geometric progression (2, 4, 8, 16, and so on) while the means of subsistence grew only in arithmetic progression (2, 4, 6, 8, and so on). As population increased, increasingly less fertile land would have to be brought into cultivation. Population would outstrip food production, and wages would be driven down to the subsistence level.

Famine, vice, misery, and war could be avoided only if people engaged in "moral restraint"—later marriages with fewer children per family. Schemes such as the Poor Laws or subsidized housing for the poor were worse than useless, according to Malthus. They simply encouraged population growth and led to an actual deterioration of conditions.

Malthus's views influenced Darwin in developing his survival of the fittest doctrine in the nineteenth century. More than anyone else, it was Malthus who was responsible for earning political economy the name of the "dismal science." Not everyone has interpreted the man in such a negative light, however. John Maynard Keynes placed Malthus firmly in "the English tradition of humane science . . . a tradition marked by a love of truth and a most noble lucidity, . . . and by an immense disinterestedness and public spirit."

Thomas Robert Malthus (1766–1834)

The Demographic Transition

In a preindustrial society, birthrates and death rates are both very high, and the rate of natural increase of population is low. With industrialization and economic development, per capita incomes begin to rise. The first demographic effect of rising income is a reduction in the death rate brought about by better nutrition, better hygiene, and better medical care. With the birthrate remaining high, the drop in the death rate increases the rate of natural increase. Population enters a phase of very rapid growth.

If there are sufficient natural resources and enough investment in new capital, economic growth can outstrip population growth. Per capita income then rises. This has happened in all the major industrialized countries of the world. In these countries, rising per capita incomes have eventually caused the birthrate to fall. Population growth has then slowed, and population equilibrium has been approached.

Demographic transition A population cycle that accompanies economic development, beginning with a fall in the death rate, continuing with a phase of rapid population growth, and concluding with a decline in the birthrate.

The whole cycle, from falling death rates to rapid population growth to falling birthrates and equilibrium is called the **demographic transition.** Exhibit 21.4 provides a graphical view of the demographic transition. Part a represents the course of the crude birthrate and death rate over time. Part b shows what happens to the rate of natural increase as it first rises and then falls. Part c shows the familiar S-curve pattern of population growth that results from the demographic transition. The human population growth curve shown in Part c differs in an important respect from that of flies in a jar or dogs on an island; it levels off at an equilibrium population below the biologically maximum level set by subsistence requirements.

The crucial part of the demographic transition is the fall in birthrates produced by rapid economic development. Demographers do not completely understand the mechanisms that bring about this decline. In large part, it is probably caused by increasing urbanization. Traditionally, a large number of children is an economic asset to a farm family, because children can contribute to production from an early age. In the city, children tend to be an economic burden. There is no guarantee of remunerative jobs for them, and

Exhibit 21.4
The demographic transition
In a preindustrial society, both birthrates and death rates are high, so that population growth is slow. The first effect of economic development is a drop in the death rate. This brings on a period of rapid population growth. As economic development continues, the birthrate begins to fall. Population growth decelerates and eventually may fall to zero.

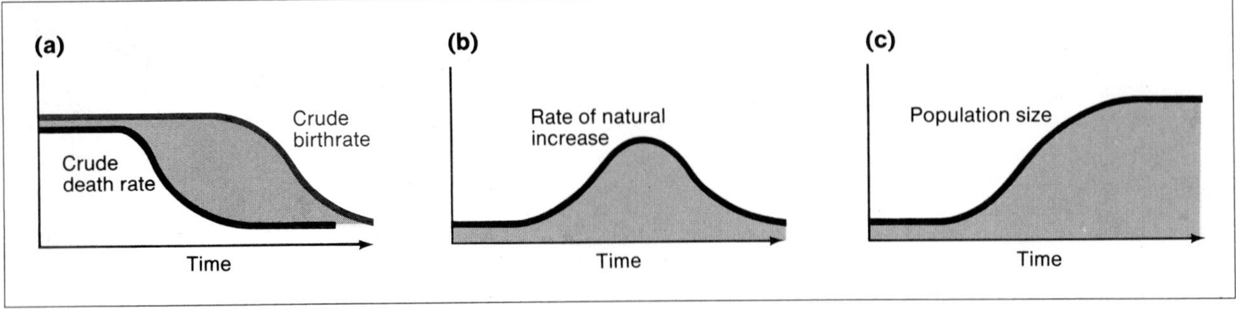

their food, clothing, and housing cannot be produced at home. More subtle changes in life-styles and attitudes toward family life, which occur as income rises, also seem to be involved in the demographic transition.

Net Reproduction

To complete the demographic transition and approach an equilibrium population takes many decades. To understand why the transition takes so long, one needs to know more about population growth than crude birthrates and crude death rates alone can offer.

Crude birthrates and death rates can be misleading because they depend on both the underlying reproductive behavior of a population and its age structure. A more direct measure of reproductive behavior is the **net reproduction rate** for a population—the average number of daughters born to each female child in the population over her lifetime. If the net reproduction rate is equal to 1, then the population is, in the long run, just replacing itself. If it is greater than 1, then the population has a long-run tendency to grow. If it is less than 1, it has a long-run tendency to shrink.

Net reproduction rate The inherent long-term growth rate of a population, measured as the average number of daughters born to each female child over her lifetime.

In the short run, the rate of natural increase in a population may be positive even when the net reproduction rate is 1 or less. In particular, this will happen when population growth has been slowing in the recent past. The present situation in the United States provides a case in point. The U.S. net reproduction rate is now less than 1, but it has fallen to that level only recently. The elderly people now in high mortality brackets are members of the relatively small generation born around the turn of the century. People in the high fertility range are members of the much larger generation who were born immediately after World War II. The disproportion in the size of the generations causes the crude death rate to be lower—and the crude birthrate to be higher—than will be the case in the long-run equilibrium. If there is no further change in reproductive behavior, and if the net reproduction rate remains slightly less than 1, it will take some forty to sixty years for the rate of natural increase to fall to 0. Only at that point will the demographic transition in this country be complete.

The Population Trap

Birthrates, death rates, economic growth, and income levels are in very delicate balance during economic development. Countries that develop successfully undergo a process called the demographic transition. During that process, rising income levels first depress death rates, causing population growth rates to accelerate, and then depress birthrates, causing population growth to slow.

Exhibit 21.5 shows what happens to per capita income and population growth, assuming steady economic growth, during the demographic transition. In Part a, the vertical axis measures the level of per capita income. When income is below Level B, people are so poor that death rates are high, and when it is above A, people are prosperous enough that birthrates are low. (Of course, things are really more complicated than this. There are not really any sharp cutoff levels of income, but this simple assumption makes the point.) In Part b, the vertical axis measures growth rates of total GNP and population. Note that population growth never exceeds the growth of GNP. The curve of per capita income in Part a always moves upward, although it rises less rapidly in the zone between A and B while the demographic transition is under way.

Exhibit 21.5
The demographic transition and economic growth
Here, the effects of the demographic transition are shown in terms of economic growth and population growth. It is assumed that death rates begin to fall once per capita income reaches Level A and that birthrates begin to fall once per capita income reaches Level B. During the transition, population growth speeds up and per capita income growth slows. Economic growth always stays above population growth, however.

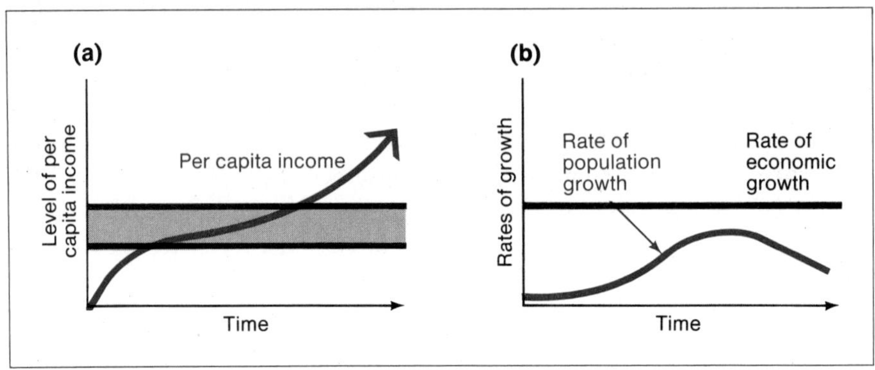

Can today's less developed countries complete this process as the developed countries have done? It is to be hoped that they can, but it is by no means certain. There is a real danger that they will get caught in a **population trap,** which will abort their attempt to make it through the demographic transition.

Population trap A situation in which the rate of population growth rises above the rate of economic growth, halting the growth of per capita income and aborting the demographic transition.

Exhibit 21.6 shows schematically how a country can fall foul of the population trap. Suppose that such a country begins development normally, as did the country represented in Exhibit 21.5. This time, though, either population growth is more rapid or economic growth is slower. At Time T, population growth begins to exceed the growth of income, and per capita income starts to fall. Instead of completing the demographic transition, the country falls back into a subsistence equilibrium with birth and death rates both high and per capita income stagnant.

Exhibit 21.6
The population trap
If at some point during the demographic transition the rate of population growth exceeds the rate of economic growth, a country may be caught in a population trap. As this exhibit is drawn, the country enters the trap at Time T. At that point, per capita income begins to fall and the demographic transition is aborted.

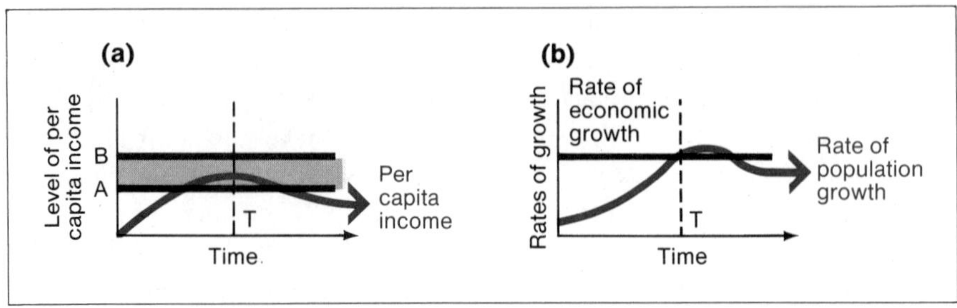

Escaping the Population Trap In the nineteenth century, when Western Europe and North America were industrializing, death rates fell only slowly—and only after living standards had already begun to improve. Population growth rates did not rise above 1 percent per year in most cases. Today, modern death control techniques have reached almost every corner of the globe, no matter how poor. That makes it more difficult for today's less developed countries to escape the population trap. During the nineteenth century, the U.S. economy experienced growth rates of GNP in the range of 3.5 to 4.5 percent per year. Growth rates in that range are no longer good enough for less developed countries, where population itself can grow as fast as 3.5 percent per year. Any growth rate for GNP slower than 6 to 7 percent per year gives little hope for escaping the population trap just by outrunning it. Countries like South Korea or Taiwan may make it, but those like Haiti, Chad, or Dahomey, where per capita incomes are already falling, will not.

The only other way to escape the population trap is to bring down the birthrate while per capita incomes are still low. Although headway has been made in some countries, serious problems remain elsewhere, as the examples in the following three-part case study show.

Case 21.1
Three Experiments in Population Control

Saying that less developed countries need to bring population growth under control is one thing; accomplishing the feat is another. Here is a report on population programs in three of the largest countries of the third world. Each has made major efforts, but the results are not uniformly encouraging.

Pakistan. Few countries have a more serious population problem than Pakistan. Development planners were thus delighted when, in 1973, Pakistan was chosen as the laboratory for a massive experiment in the "inundation" approach to family planning. Using $58 million in U.S. aid as well as local resources, the plan was literally to flood the countryside with condoms and birth control pills at a price so low—2.5 cents for a month's supply—that even the poorest people could afford them. The flood of birth control devices was to be followed by teams of "continuous motivators," who were to visit each household three or four times a year to give encouragement and instruction.

Today, the program appears to be a total failure. The birthrate has gone up, not down. Only 9 percent of fertile couples in the country have ever tried birth control, and only 6 percent practice it regularly. Why the failure? Poor administration is part of the reason, but the real flaw in the program was its assumption that families *wanted* to have fewer children. In rural Pakistan, each child, male and female, begins to contribute positively to the support of the family as early as the age of four by tending goats or chickens, running errands, or driving a bullock cart. And in this conservative Moslem society, children are a source of social prestige. The condoms were turned into children's playthings or melted down by contractors to make caulking material.

India. India, a neighbor of Pakistan, faces a population problem of much the same magnitude. Under the leadership of former Prime Minister Indira Gandhi and her controversial son, Sanjay, however, India adopted a very different approach to birth control. To make certain that families stayed on the birth control track once they got on it, the government emphasized sterilization and insertion of IUD's as the main birth control techniques. An elaborate program of incentives and disincentives was devised to persuade married men to undergo sterilization. The incentives included transistor radios; the disincentives included disqualification for government housing for men not willing to accept sterilization after two children. When even this program proved unequal to the task of getting the birthrate down to a level of 25 per 1,000, the government turned to outright coercion. At a rate of a million a month, men were herded into sterilization clinics.

It soon became apparent, though, that the Gandhi policy had gone too far. After a period of nationwide political disruption, Gandhi was swept out of office by India's voters, who feared and detested the birth control program. Under the new government, birth control efforts collapsed, and the birthrate began to creep up again. It has already risen to 35 per 1,000 from its low of 33 in 1977 and is likely to reach 40 soon unless the government takes strong action—something that is now almost impossible politically.

Indonesia. Meanwhile, on the Indonesian island of Bali, a population program is achieving heartening success. In the tiny village of Banjar Kangin, for example, 218 of the village's 243 fertile couples are practicing some form of birth control. At monthly town meetings, each man is asked what he has done about birth control that month—and then the next month's supply of condoms and pills is handed out.

Why the contrast? Several things appear to contribute to it. For one thing, the Hindus of Banjar Kangin have much more open and permissive attitudes toward sex than do the Moslem Pakistanis. (But even Moslem areas of Indonesia do better than Pakistan.) For another, the administrative structure of the village is much stronger. But perhaps most important of all is that the village economic structure is such that children are perceived as liabilities, not assets. Even with these successes, though, Indonesia's population is expected to soar from 132 million in 1978 to 215 million in 2000.

Source: The descriptions of the programs in Pakistan and Indonesia are based on Bill Peterson, "Battling the Birth Boom—Small Wins, Big Failures," *Washington Post,* May 19, 1978, p. A-1. India's story is based in part on Barry Kramer, "The Politics of Birth Control," *Wall Street Journal,* May 8, 1978, and in part on William Borders, "Birth Control Slows in India," *New York Times,* February 6, 1978, p. A-2.

FOOD AND DEVELOPMENT[3]

Hunger

The aspect of economic development that causes the greatest concern of all is the problem of hunger. Hunger comes in varying degrees. People are said to be undernourished if they suffer from a quantitative lack of calories. They are said to suffer from malnutrition if the food they do get contains insufficient protein and other nutrients, even if energy requirements are met. Undernourishment leads to actual starvation. In recent years it has been a major problem in the countries just south of the Sahara in Africa; in India, Bangladesh, and Sri Lanka in Asia; and in Bolivia, Haiti, and El Salvador in the Americas, to list only a few. Malnutrition is much more widespread and has long-run effects that are hardly less devastating. A protein insufficiency in the diets of young children and breast-feeding women is especially dangerous, because it retards brain development. People who survive a malnourished childhood are likely to suffer from lethargy and lack of productive ability in later life. These are hardly the traits required for the labor forces of poor countries struggling to achieve development.

Accurate statistics on world hunger are hard to come by. Definitions vary, and the governments of some of the worst-hit countries are reluctant to supply information. Some who have studied the problem believe that as many as

[3]This section draws on many points in the useful survey, *World of Hunger,* by Jonathan Power and Anne-Marie Holenstein (London: Temple Smith, 1976). Used by permission.

two-thirds of the world's population may suffer from undernourishment or malnutrition in some form. The data in Exhibit 21.7 are based on much more conservative methods of estimation, but they still show an appallingly serious problem.

Hunger and Population

The relationship between hunger and population is complex. It is natural to think of overpopulation causing hunger, with a Malthusian growth of numbers of people outstripping food production. Hunger can be a spur to population growth, too, however. Malnutrition leads to high infant mortality. High infant mortality in turn leads to the desire to have a large family, so that at least some children will survive. Perhaps the relationship between malnutrition and desired family size is part of the reason why birthrates have fallen earliest in those countries that have distributed the benefits of development widely among their populations.

When the world food problem is presented as a race between production and growth of demand, the results are sobering. Information presented at the World Food Conference in 1974 placed seventy-one less developed countries in three groups according to food and population trends during the period 1953–1971. In twenty-four of these countries, the rate of increase in food production fell short of population growth. In an additional seventeen, the rate of increase of food production exceeded the rate of population growth but fell short of the growth rate of domestic demand. Because rising incomes permitted people to eat more, these countries had to increase food imports (or decrease food exports), thereby making things harder yet for the countries in the first group. In the thirty remaining countries, the growth rate of food output exceeded the growth rate of demand, but even some of these countries

Exhibit 21.7
Estimated numbers of people with insufficient protein/energy supply, by regions, 1970

According to the relatively conservative estimates reported in this table, some 388 million people had less than minimum standards of nutrition in 1970. Some observers think that nearly two-thirds of the world's population may suffer from malnutrition to some extent.

Region	Population (billions)	Percentage below Lower Limit	Number below Lower Limit (millions)
Developed regions	1.07	3	28
Developing regions (excluding Asian centrally planned economies)	1.75	20	360
Latin America	0.28	13	37
Far East	1.02	22	221
Near East	0.17	20	34
Africa	0.28	25	68
World (excluding Asian centrally planned economies)	2.83	14	388

Source: Jonathan Power and Anne-Marie Holenstein, *World of Hunger* (London: Temple Smith, 1976). Reprinted by permission.

experienced regional problems because of maldistribution within their borders.[4]

What can be done about the world food problem? The remainder of this section will examine some possible approaches.

Food Aid

In 1954, the U.S. Congress passed the Agricultural Trade Development and Assistance Act, commonly known as PL480. This act has been the heart of world food aid efforts. During the 1960s, the United States gave up to 84 percent of all world food aid. The less developed countries were able to rely on food aid for 30 to 45 percent of their food imports.

Under Title 1 of PL480, food was sold on favorable terms to governments. Under Title 2, food went free to governments and to the United Nations World Food Program. Title 2 food aid was aimed at the especially underprivileged and at disaster relief. At the same time the populations of less developed countries were benefiting from PL480, U.S. farmers were also benefiting. The program was thus a combination of idealism and self-interest, but the combination for a long time seemed to work well.

Despite the very substantial benefits to countries receiving food aid, PL480 and the food aid programs of other governments have had their critics. It is important to realize why food aid alone is not likely to provide a long-run answer to the world food problem.

First of all, U.S. food aid is a somewhat uncomfortable mixture of charity and self-interest. As such, it is liable to disruption from the self-interest side. In periods when U.S. farmers produce large grain surpluses, voters and consumers are happy to see the surpluses given away. In the early 1970s, however, a combination of circumstances caused U.S. food surpluses suddenly to disappear. This put upward pressure on domestic food prices, and exports began to meet opposition from consumer groups. By 1974, the amount of food delivered under aid programs fell to a third of its 1972 level. PL480 thus proved least reliable just when it was needed most.

There is a second serious problem in the tendency of some receiver governments to rely on food aid as a substitute for domestic agricultural development. In some cases, the motivation has been political. Necessary agricultural reforms would have threatened the privileges of entrenched ruling classes, so U.S. aid seemed like an easy way out. In other cases, food aid has disrupted domestic markets. It has, for example, kept prices low in the less developed countries; this is fine for the landless poor, but it greatly reduces incentives to farmers. Sometimes, the effect of food aid on relative prices has made the growth of nonfood cash crops more attractive than food crops.

Finally, some critics of food aid are unhappy about the standards by which recipients have been selected. Food aid recipients have often been chosen more with political than with nutritional considerations in mind. As a result, say the critics, too small a portion of total food aid has gone to the countries where hunger and malnutrition are the most serious.

---

[4]Preliminary Assessment of the World Food Situation, World Food Conference, 1974, UNIE/Conf. 65/Prep./6. Data also presented as Table 7 in Power and Holenstein, *World of Hunger*, pp. 41–43.

Need for Rural Development

Throughout the world, less developed countries are urbanizing rapidly—far more rapidly than today's developed countries did at comparable stages of their own growth. The reasons for this urbanization are complex. Partly the modernity and the promise of a better life in the city attract people. Partly the problem is education systems that do not emphasize agricultural topics. Whatever the causes, cities are not able to meet the aspirations of all those who arrive in them. Urban unemployment rates are very high. Many people who are employed work in tertiary services—from shining shoes to hustling—that contribute little to economic development or to the development of the individuals. Huge shantytowns surrounding third world cities are the rule rather than the exception.

Current rates of urbanization far exceed the potential for industrial development in most poor countries. One study calculated that, just to keep urban unemployment from rising in a typical less developed country, industrial output would have to grow at 18 percent per year.[5] Even in Brazil, which has had outstanding success with industrialization and urban development, industrial growth has run at only 15 percent per year. To get rid of the 20 to 25 percent unemployment common in cities of less developed countries, industry would have to grow at something like 30 to 35 percent per year for a decade.

When urban unemployment and the food problem are considered together, it is not surprising that many development economists believe that the real hope for the less developed countries lies in the countryside. The hope is to hold people on the land and to make them productive there within a meaningful community structure. If the third world nations can do that, they may be able to feed themselves, distribute what little they have more equitably, meet the nonmaterial aspirations of their populations, and retain their independence. That, at least, is what the advocates of rural development say. They all recognize that there are problems, though.

Technological Problems Rural development does not mean just the introduction of new agricultural methods. It also means the growth of small-scale industry in villages and towns, which is necessary to meet local needs and provide employment for those whom even the most ambitious land reform program would leave landless. Is the technological basis for such development available?

In some respects, technological progress has been remarkable. The most talked-about development is the appearance of new, high-yield varieties of wheat and rice. Under laboratory conditions, these new varieties can triple food output per acre. They provide the best hope for less developed countries to escape from the sheer shortage of land.

Unfortunately, high-yield wheat, rice, and other grains cannot just be stuck in the ground and expected to do their magic. The secret of their success lies in their ability to absorb huge quantities of fertilizer. If ordinary varieties of grain are overfertilized, they produce only luxuriant growth of stems and leaves or

---

[5]David Turnham, *The Employment Problem in Less Developed Countries* (Paris: Organization for Economic Cooperation and Development, 1971), as cited by Power and Holenstein, *World of Hunger*, pp. 74–75.

William Arthur Lewis (1915–)

Theodore W. Schultz (1902–)

In October 1979, the Royal Swedish Academy awarded the Nobel Memorial Prize in Economic Science jointly to two men noted for their work in the economics of development. The two—Sir William Arthur Lewis, professor of economics at Princeton University, and Theodore Schultz, professor of economics at the University of Chicago—had never worked together directly. Their writings, however, shared a common theme: the importance of the agricultural sector in the development process, and the hazards of a development strategy overemphasizing industrialization.

Lewis was born on the island of St. Lucia in the British West Indies. He was educated in London and lectured at the University of London from 1938 to 1948. Before coming to Princeton in 1963, he served for several years as vice-chancellor of the University of the West Indies and was knighted by Queen Elizabeth for this work. The author of a number of books on development and development planning, he is best known for *The Theory of Economic Growth,* published in 1955. Lewis has served as an adviser to the governments of many developing nations, to the British government, and to the United Nations. It was this practical experience in particular that led him to recognize the central importance of agriculture in the economies of the less developed countries.

Theodore Schultz grew up on a farm in South Dakota in a community of German settlers. In 1930, he received a Ph.D. from the University of Wisconsin; in that same year, he joined the faculty at Iowa State College. During the 1930s and 1940s, Schultz worked to make agricultural economics a branch of general economics that would benefit from advances in other parts of the discipline. The numerous New Deal farm programs of the period provided many opportunities for research, and he published a series of books on U.S. agricultural policy. At the same time, he developed an interest in the process of economic growth—in particular, the contribution of investment in human capital to growth and development. This line of research led eventually to the publication, in 1964, of his book *Transforming Traditional Agriculture.* In this book, he argued that traditional farmers were efficient in the use of whatever resources they had available and would quickly adopt new methods of production when given the chance to do so. The popularity among third-world farmers of the new, high-yield crop varieties stands as a case in point.

Both men continue to be active scholars and advocates of their common point of view. The Nobel award will no doubt act as a further spur to their work in the economics of agricultural development.

seedheads so heavy that they break the stalk of the plant. With high-yield varieties, extra fertilization produces growth where it is needed. Without such fertilization, the new varieties actually produce less than traditional crops. (In many cases, heavy use of pesticides and irrigation is needed as well.)

As the use of high-yield varieties has spread, less developed countries have become more dependent on imported fertilizers. They now produce barely half their own fertilizer needs. What is worse, fertilizer production depends critically on oil. This is particularly true of nitrogen fertilizers, which make up half the total used. These are made almost entirely from natural gas and petroleum products. The "green revolution" has been extremely hard hit by high oil prices, because outside the Middle East, few less developed countries have their own oil supplies.

Rural industrial development faces technological problems that are, if anything, greater than those faced by agricultural development. Western industrial research has developed technology designed to use cheap capital and save expensive labor. The opposite conditions prevail in rural areas of the third world. Too little research has gone into the development of simple but sophisticated labor-intensive ways of doing things.

Institutional Problems A number of institutional problems also threaten rural development. Chief among them are the problem of land reform and the problem of supplying credit to rural areas.

Advocates of rural development support land reform, which involves buying (or sometimes confiscating) the large holdings of absentee landlords and distributing the land in the smallest feasible parcels among those who actually till the soil. The effects of land reform, if it works, are threefold. First, a small landowner has a greater incentive than a tenant farmer to improve the land and introduce better production techniques. Second, wide distribution of ownership means wide distribution of the product, with all the benefits this is believed to bring. Third, land reform can lead to more stable rural community structures, which help stop the rush to the city. They also help provide the dignity and sense of personal worth that are part of the process of depauperization.

Many countries have carried out thorough land reforms, but many others have not. Two problems hold back further land reform. One major problem is political. The land-owning classes often dominate the political structures of less developed countries and are reluctant to relinquish their hold. The second problem is economic. Under some circumstances, technological considerations may make it more productive to consolidate land holdings into bigger farms to realize economies of scale. To some extent, land reform can involve a trade-off between growth and depauperization.

The other major institutional weakness that holds back small-scale rural development is a weakness of credit markets. In many less developed countries, small farmers have no access to banks and other modern credit facilities. They must rely on local money lenders or merchants, who charge extremely high interest rates.

High-yield crops have made the credit problem more serious than ever. The green revolution can actually work against the small farmer. Higher yields drive land rents up and put downward pressure on output prices. The new varieties cannot be used without expensive fertilizers and pesticides, but buying these goods puts the small farmer more at the mercy of the money lender. Thus, if land reform is carried out without credit reform, it can in fact retard the introduction of new techniques.

CONCLUSIONS

The tone of much of this chapter has been pessimistic. There is no doubt that the problems of the less developed countries will be very difficult to surmount and that some countries will fail. There is every doubt of the ability and the will of the industrialized countries to carry the burden of development. Nonetheless, there are places where things are going right rather than wrong. It is fitting to end this chapter with one of these success stories.

Case 21.2
Daniel Benor's Agricultural Revolution

In India, Turkey, Thailand, Nepal, Sri Lanka, and Indonesia, Daniel Benor, a slender, balding Israeli, is producing a remarkable agricultural revolution. His revolution, sponsored by the World Bank, is quite different from the highly technological green revolution that has been so widely publicized. And it works. Small farmers are doubling and tripling their crop yields wherever the system is tried.

Benor's program is deceptively simple. It is based on what he calls the "T&V" (training and visitation) system of passing information from top experts to farmers in the field. The key link in the system consists of a network of village level extension workers whose responsibility it is to pass carefully limited and digestible doses of information along to a limited group of farmers. The extension worker visits each assigned village on a regular schedule, each week to two weeks. The emphasis is on such labor-intensive basics as proper spacing, weeding, and the use of the most promising seeds.

Even more importantly, in some cases, the program guards against misuse of the green revolution technologies. Take insecticides, for example. In the Gujarat area of India, cotton is the principal crop. The hybrid variety most widely grown responds well to good fertilization and care, but it is vulnerable to insect pests. The farmers' instinctive reaction was to spray heavily with insecticides. They sprayed so heavily, in fact, that they not only increased costs but upset the entire regional ecology. The pest problem actually got worse, not better.

Benor's solution to this problem was to put his T&V system to work teaching farmers when *not* to spray. He trained special "scouts," armed with magnifying glasses, to count the number of pests per plant. The fields would be sprayed only when a threshold—say twenty pests per plant—was reached. As soon as the number started to decline, spraying stopped. Using this simple approach, one agricultural cooperative of two hundred members increased its profits by a third in a single year. Elsewhere, the same principle is applied to prevent overfertilization.

Benor has become a hero to Asian farmers. Traditional development specialists were skeptical of his method at first, but it has now been so widely validated that they too are convinced of its effectiveness. World Bank President Robert S. McNamara, once a skeptic, is now one of Benor's biggest boosters. Countries all over the world are now eager to try the T&V system in the hope that as agricultural yields rise, the race between population and food may one day be won by food.

Source: Based on Hobart Rowen, "Poorest of Poor's Crop Yield Soars," *Washington Post,* November 12, 1978, p. K–1.

SUMMARY

1. Economic development is a complex phenomenon, a major part of which is sheer economic growth—increasing the size of GNP as a whole. Development also means industrialization. In countries that have already developed, industry has grown more rapidly than agriculture. In extreme cases, such as that of the Soviet Union, the agricultural sector has actually been stripped of resources to aid the more rapid growth of industry. A third aspect of economic development is depauperization—not only growing but distributing the benefits of growth to the poorest classes. An industry-first growth strategy may hamper depauperization.
2. A population grows whenever its crude birthrate exceeds its crude death rate. In a finite environment, living populations cannot grow indefinitely. If the birthrate does not fall to the death rate, overcrowding will force the death rate up to the birthrate. Population growth in developed countries has undergone a process known as the demographic transition. In preindustrial society, both birth and death rates were high. As industrialization began, death rates fell and a period of rapid population growth began. Economic growth was even more rapid than population growth, however, so per capita incomes rose. This brought birthrates down and reduced the rate of population growth.

3. Virtually all less developed countries face serious population pressures. Modern death control techniques have been introduced to all corners of the globe, no matter how poor. Where birthrates are still high, population growth rates are more rapid than they ever were during the demographic transition in developed countries. If the growth rate of GNP does not keep up with the growth of population, a country may be caught in a population trap. In order to complete the demographic transition successfully, many countries will have to find a way of lowering birthrates while per capita incomes are still at a very low level.
4. Some observers believe that as many as two-thirds of the world's people suffer from undernourishment or malnutrition in some form. In many developing countries, population growth is outstripping food production, thereby making the problem worse. In the past, food aid has been an important stopgap measure, but food aid alone is not the long-run solution. Rural development is needed if less developed countries are to be able to feed themselves. Technological advances, including high-yield grains, provide a potential basis for rural development. Economic and institutional problems remain, however. Some way must be found to provide the fertilizers, pesticides, and capital needed to make the best use of high-yield grains. Land reform and credit reform are also necessary parts of successful rural development.

DISCUSSION QUESTIONS

1. In what ways are the problems faced by the less developed countries similar to the problems faced by the United States one hundred or two hundred years ago? In what ways are they different? Will today's less developed countries follow a similar path to economic development, or is a different route more promising? Explain.
2. In early phases of industrialization, urbanization seems to be a major factor in bringing birthrates down. Today, birthrates are still falling in the United States, even though the degree of urbanization is no longer changing rapidly. What other factors do you think are at work causing the continued decline in birthrates?
3. Less developed countries are short on capital. Foreign firms are often willing to invest in such countries. Is foreign investment a good way for the countries to solve their capital shortage? What are the advantages and disadvantages to the countries of such foreign investment?
4. Less developed countries tend to have less equally distributed incomes than do developed countries. Why do you think this is so? Why does development sometimes increase rather than reduce inequality?
5. Do you see any similarity between the dual economy of some less developed countries and the dual labor market that some economists believe exists in the United States?
6. People in the United States eat huge quantities of meat. Each pound of meat requires up to ten pounds of grain to produce. It is sometimes said that the world food problem could be solved in part simply by people eating less meat. Suppose that this advice were taken to heart, and meat consumption in the United States were cut in half, with more bread eaten instead. Would the grain thus saved ever actually reach the hungry poor in the developing countries? If so, explain how shifts in market prices and changes in supply and demand conditions would operate to get it there. If not, explain why the market would fail to move the grain in the desired direction.
7. It is sometimes said that it is pointless to give money to developing countries to buy food, because this money will just end up lining the pockets of Kansas farmers without doing the less developed countries themselves any real good. Is this concern wholly justified, partly justified, or wholly unjustified? Why?

SUGGESTIONS FOR FURTHER READING

Bogue, Donald J., and Ong Tsui, Amy. "Zero World Population Growth." *Public Interest*, no. 55 (Spring 1979): 99–113.
A report on recent declines in fertility in many countries that are disproving some of the more pessimistic population forecasts made only a few years ago. The authors suggest that the "population bomb" may turn out to be a dud.

Ehrlich, Paul, and Ehrlich, Ann. *Population, Resources, and Environment.* 2d ed. San Francisco: W. H. Freeman, 1972.
A good introduction to population arithmetic, the debate over optimal population size, and population control techniques.

Johnson, D. Gale. *World Food Problems and Prospects.* Washington, D.C.: American Enterprise Institute, 1975.
A survey of the world food outlook from the perspective of 1975.

Meier, Gerald M., ed. *Leading Issues in Economic Development.* 3rd ed. New York: Oxford University Press, 1976.
A good introduction to the field of development economics.

PART FOUR
THE WORLD ECONOMY

CHAPTER 22

INTERNATIONAL TRADE AND COMPARATIVE ADVANTAGE

WHAT YOU WILL LEARN IN THIS CHAPTER

This chapter introduces some important microeconomic principles of international trade. It shows how worldwide efficiency and productivity can be enhanced when every country specializes in producing and exporting the goods that it can produce at lower opportunity cost than its trading partners. At the same time, it explains why not every individual in every country will necessarily gain from international trade, even though, on the average, consumers in all countries will gain. The possibility that some consumers or workers may be harmed by changes in patterns of international trade lies at the root of most political controversies over trade policy.

FOR REVIEW

Here are some important terms and concepts that will be put to use in this chapter. If you do not understand them, review them before proceeding.

- *Opportunity cost (Chapter 1)*
- *Distributive justice (Chapter 1)*

Up to this point, economics has been studied solely within the context of a single national economy. A whole area of economic theory—the theory of international trade—has received hardly a mention.

The first question to be asked about this area of economics is why a separate theory of international trade is necessary. Does it really make that much difference that buyers and sellers in certain markets live on opposite sides of national boundaries? The answer is that the differences between international and national markets are small enough that most of the familiar tools of analysis apply to both; yet there are enough differences to require that the tools be applied in new ways and to new problems. A separate body of theory is therefore justified.

From a microeconomic point of view, the distinguishing feature of international markets is that finished products tend to move more easily in them than do factors of production. Land, with its natural resource deposits and associated climate factors, is the most immobile of factors. Labor also tends to be fairly immobile because of cultural, political, and linguistic barriers. Capital tends to be the most internationally mobile factor of production, but even it does not move as unrestrictedly between countries as within.

Factor immobility matters because it causes persistent differences in relative and absolute costs of production among nations. With factors immobile, goods that make intense use of labor tend to be cheaper in countries where labor is relatively abundant, agricultural commodities tend to be cheaper in countries with good climates, and so on. Were factors more mobile, countries with high labor costs would hire more foreign workers until their costs for labor-intensive products had fallen. Countries with bad growing conditions would import soil and sunlight to equalize the costs of agricultural production. In general, internation differences in production costs would be minimized.

From a macroeconomic point of view, the main point distinguishing international from national economics is the fact that different countries have different currencies, which fluctuate in value relative to one another. Different currencies make it possible for countries to pursue independent macroeconomic policies. This can mean inflation in one country and deflation across its border, differences in economic growth rates, and a variety of other things. When it comes to studying problems of international currency markets and the balance of payments, these differences become crucial.

This chapter will discuss the microeconomic aspects of international trade. Then, Chapter 23 will turn to the macro view of international economics.

THE THEORY OF COMPARATIVE ADVANTAGE

The study of international trade from a microeconomic point of view must begin with the theory of comparative advantage. In a sense, international trade theory starts here historically as well as logically. The theory of comparative advantage was first clearly set forth by David Ricardo early in the nineteenth century. Ricardo wanted to show why it would be to England's advantage to maintain active trade with other countries. To do so, he used an example very much like the following.

An Example

Imagine two countries called (for the sake of the example) Norway and Spain. Both have farms and offshore fishing beds, but the moderate climate of Spain makes both the farms and the fishing beds more productive. The number of labor hours required to produce a ton of each product in the two countries is shown in Exhibit 22.1. For simplicity, only labor costs are considered in this example. Other costs can be thought of as proportional to labor costs. Also, per unit labor costs are assumed to be constant for all levels of output.

Absolute advantage In international trade theory, the ability of a country to produce a good at lower cost, measured in terms of factor inputs, than its trading partners'.

Exhibit 22.1 reveals two kinds of differences in the cost structure of the two countries. First, both fish and grain require fewer labor hours to produce in Spain. Spain is thus said to have an **absolute advantage** in the production of both goods.

	Spain	Norway
Fish	4	5
Grain	2	5

Exhibit 22.1

Labor hours per ton of output in Spain and Norway

The figures in this table show the number of labor hours required to produce each ton of fish and grain in Spain and Norway. Spain has an absolute advantage in the production of both goods. Norway has a comparative advantage in fish, and Spain has a comparative advantage in grain.

David Ricardo, the greatest of the classical economists, was born in 1772. His father, a Jewish immigrant, was a member of the London stock exchange. Ricardo's education was rather haphazard, and he entered his father's business at the age of fourteen. In 1793, he married, abandoned strict Jewish orthodoxy, and went into business on his own. These were years of war and financial disturbance. The young Ricardo developed a reputation for remarkable astuteness and quickly made a large fortune.

In 1799, Ricardo read *The Wealth of Nations* and developed an interest in questions of political economy. In 1809, his first writings on economics appeared. They were a series of newspaper articles on "The High Price of Bullion," which appeared the next year as an influential pamphlet. Several other short works added to his reputation in this area. In 1814, he retired from business to devote all his time to political economy.

Ricardo's major work is *Principles of Political Economy and Taxation,* first published in 1817. This work contains, among other things, a pioneering statement of the principle of comparative advantage as applied to international trade. With a lucid numerical example, Ricardo shows why it is to the mutual advantage of both countries for England to export wool to Portugal and to import wine in return, even though both products can be produced at absolutely lower costs in Portugal.

But international trade is only a sidelight of Ricardo's *Principles.* The book covers the whole of economics as then known, beginning with value theory and progressing to a theory of economic growth and evolution. Ricardo, like his friend Malthus and his later follower John Stuart Mill, held that the economy was growing toward a future "steady state." In this state, economic growth would come to a halt, and the wage rate would be depressed to the subsistence level.

Ricardo's book was extraordinarily influential. For more than half a century thereafter, much of economics as written in England was an elaboration of or commentary on Ricardo's work. The most famous of all economists to fall under the influence of Ricardo's theory and method was Karl Marx. Although Marx eventually reached revolutionary conclusions that differed radically from any views Ricardo held, his starting point was Ricardo's labor theory of value and method of analyzing economic growth.

David Ricardo (1772–1823)

Second, there are differences in the opportunity costs between the two countries. Consider the cost of each good in each country not in terms of labor hours but in terms of the other good. In Norway, producing a ton of fish means forgoing the opportunity to use five labor hours in the fields. A ton of fish thus has an opportunity cost of one ton of grain there. In Spain, producing a ton of fish means giving up the opportunity to produce two tons of grain. In terms of opportunity costs, then, fish is cheaper in Norway than in Spain, and grain is cheaper in Spain than in Norway. The country in which the opportunity cost of a good is lower is said to have a **comparative advantage** in producing that good.

Comparative advantage In international trade theory, the ability of a country to produce a good at a lower opportunity cost, in terms of other goods, than its trading partners'.

Pretrade Equilibrium If no trade takes place between Norway and Spain, equilibrium in fish and grain markets in the two countries will be established independently. This example has simplified things by ignoring all costs but labor costs and by assuming these costs to be constant. In pretrade equilibrium, the ratio of the price of fish to the price of grain in each country will thus be equal to the ratio of labor inputs needed to produce the goods. In Norway, where a ton of grain and a ton of fish both take the same labor to produce, the price of fish will be equal to the price of grain. In Spain, where a ton of fish takes twice as much labor to produce as a ton of grain, the equilibrium price of fish will be twice the price of grain.

Suppose that each country has 1,000 labor hours available for the production of fish and grain. The way these labor hours are divided between the two products in each country depends on demand and consumer tastes. Suppose that demand conditions are such that in Norway 100 tons of grain and 100 tons of fish are produced, while in Spain 350 tons of grain are grown and 75 tons of fish are caught. The quantities produced and consumed in pretrade equilibrium are noted in Exhibit 22.2.

The Possibility of Trade The stage is now set to consider the possibilities for trade between Norway and Spain. A superficial look at labor costs in the two countries might suggest that there were no possibilities for trade. Norwegians might like to get their hands on some of those cheap Spanish goods, but why should the Spanish be interested? After all, couldn't they produce everything at home more cheaply than it could be produced abroad? If so, how could they gain from trade? But a closer analysis shows that this superficial view is incorrect. Absolute advantage turns out to be unimportant in determining patterns of trade. Only comparative advantage matters.

To see that possibilities for trade between the two countries do exist, imagine that an enterprising Norwegian fishing party decides to sail into a Spanish port with a ton of its catch. Spanish merchants in the port will have been used to giving 2 tons of grain, or its equivalent, for a ton of fish. The Norwegians will have been accustomed to getting only 1 ton of grain for each ton of fish. Any exchange ratio between 1 and 2 tons of grain per ton of fish will seem more than normally attractive to both parties. For instance, a trade of 1.5 tons of grain for a ton of fish will make both the Spanish merchants and the Norwegian fishing party better off than they would have been had they traded only with others from their own country.

Gains from Specialization The opening of trade between Spain and Norway will soon begin to have an effect on patterns of production in the two countries. In Norway, farmers will discover that instead of working five hours to raise a ton of grain from their own rocky soil, they can fish for five hours instead and trade their catch to the Spaniards for 1.5 tons of grain. In Spain, people will find it is no longer worth their while to spend four hours to catch a ton of fish. Instead, they can work just three hours in the fields. The 1.5 tons of grain that they grow will get them a ton of fish from the Norwegians. In short, the Norwegians will find it worth their while to specialize in fish, and the Spanish will find it worth their while to specialize in grain.

Suppose now that trade continues at the rate of 1.5 tons of grain per ton of

	Spain	Norway	World Total
Fish	75	100	175
Grain	350	100	450

Exhibit 22.2

Pretrade equilibrium outputs of fish and grain in Spain and Norway

If Spain and Norway do not engage in trade, each country will have to meet all its needs from its own resources. The quantities of goods each produces will depend on the strength of domestic demand. The relative prices of the two goods in each country will be determined by their labor costs, as shown in Exhibit 22.1.

Exhibit 22.3
Posttrade production and consumption of fish and grain in Spain and Norway
This table assumes that Spain and Norway have traded fish for grain at the rate of 1.5 tons of grain per ton of fish. Both countries have become entirely specialized. When this table is compared with the table in Exhibit 22.2, it is clear that consumers in both countries have the same amount of the product they export and more of the product they import than they did in the absence of trade. Also, total world production of fish has risen from 175 to 200 tons, and total world production of grain has risen from 450 to 500 tons.

		Spain	Norway	World Total
Fish	Production	0	200	200
	Consumption	100	100	200
Grain	Production	500	0	500
	Consumption	350	150	500

fish until both countries have become completely specialized. Spain no longer produces any fish, and Norway no longer produces any grain. Norwegians catch 200 tons of fish, half of which is exported to Spain. The Spanish grow 500 tons of grain, 150 tons of which are exported to Norway. Exhibit 22.3 summarizes this posttrade situation.

A comparison of this table with Exhibit 22.2 reveals three noteworthy things. First, Norwegians are better off than before; they have just as much fish to eat and 50 tons more grain than in the pretrade equilibrium. Second, Spaniards are also better off; they have just as much grain to consume as ever—and more fish. Finally, total world output of both grain and fish has risen as a result of trade. Everyone is better off, and no one is worse off.

Generalized Mutual Advantage The principle of mutual advantage from international trade is perfectly general. It applies to any situation where one country has a comparative advantage over another in producing some good. Wherever there is a comparative advantage, international specialization can increase both consumption in each trading country and world output as a whole.

A complete analysis of international trade would add many details. It would have to allow for cases in which only one country or neither country became fully specialized and for cases in which the constant cost assumption did not hold. No part of the more detailed theory, however, would undermine the basic conclusion: International trade and specialization promote world economic efficiency and generate mutual advantages to all trading nations.

PROTECTIONISM AND TRADE POLICY

Free Trade Challenged

There is a strong theoretical case that free international trade promotes world efficiency and consumer welfare. Nonetheless, many nations pursue policies that actively thwart such trade. Policies that interfere with international trade are referred to by the general term **protectionism.** The most common protectionist policies are the imposition of **tariffs,** which are taxes levied on imported goods, and **import quotas,** which are limitations on quantities imported. The U.S. government imposes tariffs and quotas on a number of goods.

Protectionism Policies of shielding domestic industry from foreign competition.

Tariff A tax levied on imported goods.

Import quota A limitation on the quantity of a good that can be imported in a given time period.

The sections that follow will look at some of the more commonly heard arguments in favor of protectionism. Some of them are altogether false. Others are partly valid in terms of positive economics. Still others focus primarily on normative considerations.

Cheap Foreign Labor One common argument against free trade sees a threat in imports from countries where wages are lower than in the country being considered. At the same time, though, workers in the low-wage countries fear competition from the country that is backed by heavy capital investment. If one argument were true, both ought to be. If both were true, then trade must be making everyone worse off.

Fortunately, both arguments are false. It is exactly such differences in factor supplies and comparative costs that create opportunities for mutual advantage. The fallacious cheap foreign labor argument implies that trade is best conducted with countries differing as little as possible from one's own. The theory of comparative advantage suggests, in contrast, that trade with such countries is likely to offer the least benefit. There is sometimes (but not always) an element of truth in the cheap foreign labor argument if it is applied to specific groups of workers, as will be shown below. But applied to average standards of living, as it often is, it is false.

Infant Industries The famous infant industry argument is a second weapon in the protectionist arsenal. It runs like this: Suppose a certain country has a comparative disadvantage in the production of automobiles but wishes to establish a domestic auto industry. To do so, it prohibits imports. This permits the domestic auto industry to expand and mature. Production costs fall, and efficiency increases. Eventually, the country achieves a true comparative advantage in cars. At that time, consumers will recoup the losses they suffered while the industry was growing up.

This sequence of events is not, in fact, wholly impossible. Nonetheless, it does not justify protection. If the present value of future gains to consumers more than offsets near-term losses, the auto industry ought to be able to grow without protection. It can borrow money to cover short-term operating losses while it competes with cheap foreign auto makers. Eventually, when the industry matures and gains its comparative advantage, it can pay off the loans and have some money left over. No special protection is needed to ensure the emergence of a domestic auto industry.

Suppose, though, that such borrowing will not be profitable for the auto industry. That, then, will be a sign that the future gains are so small or so distant that they do not offset current losses. In that case, to protect the industry is to promote misallocation of resources over time. Sometimes it is suggested that imperfections in the credit market may make it difficult for an infant industry to borrow the funds it needs to finance expansion. But if true, this at most creates a case for government sponsored loans to the infant industry. It still does not constitute a case for tariffs.

Terms of Trade A third well-known protectionist theory is the terms-of-trade argument, which has some respectable basis in positive economics. The argument applies to a country that exercises monopoly or monopsony power in the international market. For example, suppose that the United States is the world's largest exporter of wheat and the largest importer of textiles. Restricting wheat exports and textile imports drives the world market price of wheat up and the world market price of textiles down. If the price movement is great enough, the improved terms of trade more than compensate for the decrease in the volume of trade.

The terms-of-trade argument is valid (at least as a possibility) as it stands. Two things should be noted about it, however. First, it does not quite challenge the doctrine of comparative advantage head-on. What it really says is that by clever market manipulation, a country may be able to get a larger share of the gains from trade than it would if international markets operated unrestrictedly. Second, it cannot be applied to both sides of a market at once. If all countries try to play the terms-of-trade game, all of them lose; and for one to play it openly invites mutually self-defeating retaliation.

Macroeconomics Another partially valid protectionist argument suggests that trade may not be beneficial in times of macroeconomic disequilibrium. The basic idea is this: When a country is experiencing widespread unemployment, cutting off imports in a key sector may increase domestic employment. This may prime the pump, putting the economy on the road to macroeconomic recovery at the expense of only small microeconomic losses. The best rejoinder to this argument is that there are more sophisticated tools of macroeconomic policy that can do the same job with less microeconomic damage.

International Trade with More than One Factor of Production

The discussion up to this point has been limited to an economy in which there is only one factor of production—labor. Removing this assumption has some interesting implications. A modification of the earlier Spain-Norway example will illustrate some of them.

Assume from now on that fishing requires a relatively large capital investment per worker and farming a relatively small one. In the accepted terminology, fishing is said to be capital intensive and farming labor intensive. Assume, as before, that in the absence of trade, the opportunity cost of fish will be higher in Spain than in Norway. The theory of comparative advantage still applies, regardless of the number of factors of production under consideration. International trade will still make it possible for total world production of both fish and grain to increase. It will still enable the quantities of both goods available for consumption in both countries to increase. But now, a new question arises concerning the gains from trade. How will they be distributed within each country?

Internal Distribution To answer this question, one must look at what happens in factor markets as trade brings about increasing specialization in each country. In Norway, production shifts from farming to fishing. As grain production is phased out, large quantities of labor and relatively small quantities of capital are released. The shift in production thus creates a surplus of labor and a shortage of capital. Factor markets can return to equilibrium only when wages fall relative to the rate of return on capital. Only then will fisheries adopt relatively more labor-intensive methods of production. Meanwhile, in Spain, an opposite process occurs. The shift from fishing to farming depresses the rate of return on capital and increases the wage rate. This causes Spanish farmers to use more capital per worker than before.

These changes in relative factor prices determine how the gains from trade are distributed among the people of each country. Spanish workers and Norwegian ship owners will gain doubly from trade. They will gain first because trade increases the size of the pie (the total available quantity of goods) and second because the factor price shifts give them a relatively larger slice of the larger pie. For Norwegian workers and Spanish farm owners, in contrast, one of these effects works against the other. They still benefit from the growth of the pie, but they get a relatively smaller piece of it than before. They may or may not end up better off on balance as a result of the trade.

Suppose that the comparative advantage in the pretrade situation were large and the difference in factor intensity between the two countries were small. Norwegian workers and Spanish farm owners would then still gain from trade in an absolute sense, even though they would lose ground relative to others in their own country. If conditions were not so favorable, however, they could end up absolutely worse off than before trade began.

The Importance of Mobility The preceding section considered only two broadly defined factors of production—labor and capital. What was said there applies even more forcefully to narrowly defined factors of production. If one thinks in terms not of labor in general but of farmers and fishermen and in terms not of capital in general but of boat owners and tractor owners, then it becomes even more likely that trade will have a strongly uneven impact on incomes. The more specialized and less mobile the factors of production are, the more relative factor prices will shift as a result of trade and the more likely it will be that some specific groups will be harmed by trade.

Take an example nearer to home than that of Norwegian farmers and Spanish fishers. Consider instead the effects on the U.S. economy of increased imports of Chinese textiles. The impact of increased textile imports can be divided into three parts. First, all consumers in the United States will benefit because textiles will be cheaper than before. Second, the Chinese will increase their purchases of U.S. goods. This will benefit workers in U.S. export oriented industries. Finally, U.S. textile workers and manufacturers will suffer a decreased demand for their products.

Those with relatively mobile skills or assets can escape most of the impact by moving to other industries. For example, a truck driver working for a textile firm can switch to hauling peaches, or a plant making shirt boxes can switch to making shoe boxes. Some workers, however, are less mobile because of their personal circumstances or the specialization of their skills. They are likely to suffer a loss of income that will more than offset the benefits they receive as consumers from cheaper textiles. Imagine, for example, a middle-aged highly specialized spinning machine operator who has all his savings tied up in a house in a small textile town. He will derive slim consolation from being able to buy a cheap Chinese raincoat to wear on his weekly visits to the unemployment office.

In aggregate terms, the loss to the group adversely affected is more than offset by the gains to others in the economy. But this fact is not likely to make much impression on unemployed textile workers. They will see free trade as a threat and will campaign for protection. The government will then have a hard political decision to make. Which group of interests should it look after? How much weight should it place on the widespread gains from trade and how much on the complaints of particular people who do not share in those gains? Is there any way to reconcile these conflicting interests?

Balancing Gains and Losses These are questions of normative economics. If the people who lose from free trade are more deserving than those who gain, then the principle of distributive justice may call for protection. Protection will not necessarily advance distributive justice, however. The immediate impact points in that direction, but a number of things must be taken into account before a balanced judgment can be made.

First, to protect textiles would benefit textile workers. Suppose that these workers were relatively low paid and had lower than average mobility. If the idea of distributive justice emphasized support for the incomes of low paid workers, the impact of a protectionist policy would be beneficial.

Second, the tariff or quota would also benefit the owners of other factors used in the textile industry. These owners would include stockholders, other investors, executives, and owners of real estate in textile communities. On the average, ownership of nonlabor resources tends to be concentrated in the hands of people with relatively high incomes. It is hard to say whether these other factor owners would gain more or less from protection than workers would. That could be discovered only by empirical study. But it is very likely that this part of the impact, considered separately, would tend to increase inequality.

Third, protecting textiles would hurt consumers at large by raising textile prices. Again, it is hard to be sure about the distributional impact without a detailed study of whether high or low income groups tend to spend the greater share of their incomes on textile products. A seat-of-the-pants guess is that the pinch of higher textile prices would be felt more keenly by low income groups.

Finally, even if it is determined that the benefits of protection are concentrated on groups meriting special consideration and adverse effects are concentrated on less meritorious groups, one difficulty remains. The dollar losses to those harmed by protection will be greater in aggregate than the benefits to those helped. Does the gain in equality, if any, more than offset the loss in efficiency? In short, protecting a certain industry may improve things from the point of view of distributive justice, but this result is far from certain.

Alternative Policies

Suppose, for the sake of argument, that the distributional impact of protecting textiles is positive. Suppose even that this favorable result outweighs the necessary loss in efficiency. Does this mean protectionism should be supported? Not yet. Before any definite conclusion can be reached, the policy of protection must be compared with any alternative policies that may have the same distributive effects. One such alternative may be to subsidize the retraining and relocation of textile workers who lose their jobs. Another may be simply to offer these workers cash compensation.

How do these alternatives rate? In terms of efficiency, they are not perfect, but probably they are better than tariffs or quotas. In terms of distributive justice, they seem to offer two advantages. One is that benefits are more precisely concentrated on the people who want to get them. The other is that the tax burden required to fund the alternative program is likely to be distributed more equitably than the burden of high textile prices would be.

CONCLUSIONS

The debate over the merits of free trade versus protectionism has gone on for centuries. Adam Smith himself—with his doctrine that a highly developed division of labor depends on the widest possible market—was one of the early advocates of free trade. Since his time, protectionism has never been widely popular in the economics profession. Among politicians and the general public, however, the pendulum has swung back and forth several times. There have been great eras of free trade alternating with severe tariff wars. At present, free traders appear to be somewhat on the defensive, as the following case study suggests.

Case 22.1
The Wall Street Journal Polls Protectionist Sentiment

In 1978, at a time when people in the United States were becoming increasingly concerned about the ability of U.S. goods to compete in world markets, the *Wall Street Journal* conducted a two-part survey of U.S. attitudes toward protectionism and free trade. In one part, a Washington based survey research firm contacted 209 randomly selected persons by telephone. In the second part, the *Wall Street Journal* staff selected a sixteen-member panel of people thought to have representative views for an intensive two-hour discussion.

The telephone survey revealed clear doubts about U.S. competitiveness: 56 percent of the respondents thought U.S. economic power was declining, while only 6 percent thought it was increasing; 46 percent thought the quality of foreign products was improving, while just 21 percent thought it was declining. (However, by a narrow margin of 34 to 28 percent, those polled thought the quality of U.S. goods was still superior.)

Faced with this perceived decline in competitiveness, respondents to the poll favored protectionist measures: 58 percent thought the government should take action to restrict the quantity of foreign-made products sold in the United States, while just 32 percent favored free trade. Asked specifically about tariffs, 64 percent favored increases, and only 26 percent did not.

The in-depth panel revealed some of what lay behind the differences in opinion. As might be expected, union members and officials tended to be protectionists. The president of a Steelworkers local undoubtedly spoke for many unionists when he said: "I think foreign trade is good, but we're going to have to keep it competitive and not let foreign products cost us jobs. It puts our people on welfare, which means you people who work in nonunion places will have to support my people. So I think the idea is maybe to tax the imports to make them competitive."

Among younger adults and professional people, however, free trade sentiment apparently tends to prevail. A foreign exchange dealer on the panel characterized protectionist measures as a "costly luxury." If certain industries could not compete, he saw no sense in supporting them artificially. People working in those industries should shift to other occupations. A further source of antiprotectionist feeling was concern over inflation. "As a consumer," one panelist said, "my first criterion in purchasing is quality and price, and I just won't allow myself to look at that label and see where it's made."

Source: Based on Richard J. Levin, "Losing the Lead?" *Wall Street Journal,* April 17, 1978, p. 1. Used by permission of the Wall Street Journal,

SUMMARY

1. A country is said to have a comparative advantage in the production of any good that it can produce at a lower opportunity cost than that of its trading partners. Trading nations can realize mutual benefits if each specializes in products for which it has a comparative advantage. Such specialization can give consumers in each country more of all goods than they would have without international trade.
2. Some arguments against free trade are based on considerations of positive economics. Of these, the cheap foreign labor and infant industry arguments have little merit. The terms of trade argument establishes that a country with monopoly or monopsony power in international markets can gain by imposing tariffs on imported goods—but only if its trading partners do not retaliate. Trade restrictions are sometimes used to combat domestic unemployment in periods of macroeconomic disturbance, but conventional tools of macro policy are likely to be better for such a purpose.
3. Other protectionist arguments emphasize normative considerations. In a world of multiple factors of production, many of which are highly specialized, certain groups of workers or capitalists can gain by the exclusion of foreign competition. However, their gains are more than offset in dollar terms by losses to some of their fellow citizens.

DISCUSSION QUESTIONS

1. Suppose you learned that Vladimir Horowitz, the great pianist, was also an amazingly proficient typist. Knowing this, would it surprise you to learn also that he hired a secretary to type his correspondence even though he could do the job better and faster himself? What does this have to do with comparative advantage?
2. Turn to Exhibit 22.1. Suppose that new, high-yield grains were introduced in Norway and that the number of labor hours needed to grow a ton of grain there were cut from 5 hours to 2.5 hours. What would happen to trade between Norway and Spain? Would it still pay for Norwegians to import their grain from Spain? If the labor hours per ton of grain in Norway fell all the way to 2, what would happen to the pattern of trade?
3. One of the people interviewed in the *Wall Street Journal* poll (see Case 22.1) made the following statement: "We may still be No. 1, but I don't think we will be much longer. The Common Market, Japan, Russia, all areas of the world are catching up. . . . It's no longer economical for us to produce anything." On the basis of what you have learned about the principle of comparative advantage, do you think it is really possible to reach a point in time when it is no longer economical to produce anything—that is, when it is economical to import everything?
4. Suppose you, a convinced advocate of free trade, became president of the United States. Would your policy be to cut off all U.S. tariffs and quotas at once, or would you bargain with your trading partners, saying that you would cut U.S. tariffs only if they cut their own tariffs? Why would a mutual reduction be better than a one-sided reduction?
5. Simple trade theory suggests that countries will export goods in which they have a comparative advantage and import goods in which they have a comparative disadvantage. In fact, countries often import the same kinds of goods they export. For example, most countries that are big exporters of automobiles are also big importers of automobiles. Why do you think that happens?

SUGGESTIONS FOR FURTHER READING

Ricardo, David. *Principles of Political Economy and Taxation.* London, 1817. (Available in a modern paperback edition from Pelican Books, 1971.)
Chapter 7, "On Foreign Trade," is generally credited with being the first clear exposition of the theory of comparative advantage.

Snider, Delbert A. *Introduction to International Economics.* 6th ed. Homewood, Ill.: Richard D. Irwin, 1975.
A useful basic text on international trade theory, covering in depth the topics treated in this chapter.

CHAPTER 23

THE BALANCE OF PAYMENTS AND THE INTERNATIONAL MONETARY SYSTEM

WHAT YOU WILL LEARN IN THIS CHAPTER

This chapter introduces the world of international monetary economics. First, it explains how international transactions can be organized into simplified balance of payment accounts. Next, it shows how exchange rate movements can be interpreted in terms of supply and demand. Then, it discusses the major factors influencing supply and demand curves in foreign exchange markets in both the long run and short run. Finally, it examines problems of international monetary policy and evaluates the advantages and disadvantages of alternative sets of rules for the international monetary game.

FOR REVIEW

Here are some important terms and concepts that will be put to use in this chapter. If you do not understand them, review them before proceeding.

- *Instruments of monetary policy (Chapter 12)*
- *Portfolio balance (Chapter 13)*
- *Tariffs and quotas (Chapter 22)*

Of all the economic news that makes the headlines, that involving the balance of international payments is probably the least understood. Even well-informed people who have a basic understanding of what is going on and who read news reports of inflation and unemployment may have only the haziest idea of how the international monetary system works.

There was a time when this relative ignorance of international monetary affairs could be explained by the sheer strength and self-sufficiency of the U.S. economy. This was especially true during the first two decades following World War II, when the United States was less dependent on foreign trade than any of its major trading partners. The country consistently exported more than it imported, and its goods set standards for quality and technology in a broad range of world markets. Furthermore, the U.S. dollar was the undisputed world standard of value. But in recent years all this has been changing. During the 1970s, U.S. readers began being exposed to the same kind of economic news that had long been familiar to readers in other countries, and policy makers began struggling to find the right response to developments.

Consider, for example, the three-year period from 1976 through 1978. During that period, the U.S. balance of exports and imports swung from its traditional surplus position to a series of record breaking deficits. The U.S.

dollar lost 16 percent of its value against a weighted average of the currencies of trading partners—and lost much more than that in relation to certain key currencies. The West German mark, for example, gained more than a third in value, rising from \$.38 in June 1976 to \$.53 by September 1978. These events are detailed in Exhibit 23.1. Although the balance of payments recovered to the point of showing a small surplus in the first quarter of 1979 and the value of the dollar was stabilized, the international monetary events of 1978 left a strong impression on the U.S. public. A Gallup poll taken in November 1978 showed that keeping up the value of the dollar was the number 1 foreign policy concern of those polled. It outranked even such traditional concerns as

Exhibit 23.1

Recent trends in the balance of payments and in currency values

In the late 1970s, international monetary developments were very much in the news. During 1977 and 1978, the U.S. balance of payments shifted from its traditional surplus position to that of a sharp deficit. The value of the dollar fell in relation to a weighted average of the values of the currencies of major U.S. trading partners, and the value of certain strong currencies—most notably the West German mark—rose to record levels.

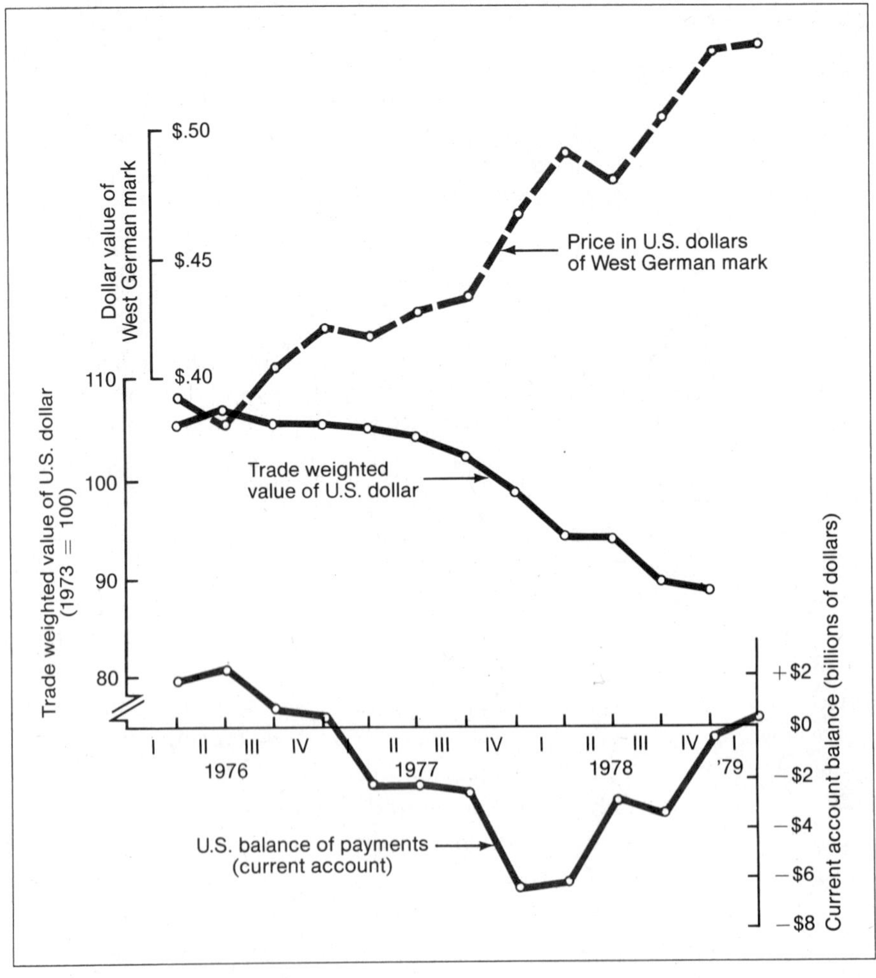

securing adequate energy supplies, containing communism, and defending the security of U.S. allies.[1]

Against the background of the just mentioned world events, this chapter faces the difficult job of explaining in a few short pages a subject that is worthy of a whole book. It will try to accomplish this goal by limiting objectives, sticking to the basics, and omitting all but a bare minimum of technicalities.

THE BALANCE OF PAYMENTS AND FOREIGN EXCHANGE MARKETS

Any discussion of an economy's balance of international payments is complicated by the fact that thousands of different kinds of international payments are made every day. Payments for goods and services exported and imported are probably the first that come to mind, but there are many others. Equally important are long- and short-term loans made to finance imports and exports and payments made in connection with purchases or sales of assets such as securities or real estate in international markets. In addition, governments and private individuals make many kinds of unilateral transfer payments to residents of other countries. They include outright gifts, pension payments, and official foreign aid. Finally, the U.S. Federal Reserve System and foreign central banks engage in many important kinds of official transactions with each other. The complexities of international payments are too great to be tackled all at once. They are best explained step by step, beginning with simplified situations in which only limited kinds of payments take place.

Foreign Exchange Markets and the Current Account

The first category of international payments to be discussed is that of payments on **current account**—payments for imports and exports of goods and services plus private payments and government transfer payments. For the moment, it is assumed that no other kinds of transactions occur among the citizens of the various countries of the world.

Current account The account whose transactions include imports and exports of goods and services plus international unilateral transfer payments.

Current account payments in international trade differ from otherwise similar payments within a country in one important respect: The two countries have different national currencies. Because of this, each international transaction involves a visit to the **foreign exchange market**—the whole complex of institutions (including banks, specialized foreign exchange dealers, and official government agencies) through which the currency of one country can be exchanged for that of another.

Foreign exchange market The whole complex of institutions—including banks, specialized foreign exchange dealers, and official government agencies—through which the currency of one country can be exchanged for that of another.

Suppose, for example, that a West German clothing importer wants to buy a shipment of Levis. The importer plans to finance the purchase with West German marks held in a Frankfurt bank account. However, the U.S. manufacturer wants to be paid in dollars, which can be used to meet payrolls and buy materials in the United States. The German's bank sells the necessary quantity of marks on the foreign exchange market, receiving dollars in return. The dollars are then forwarded to the U.S. manufacturer to pay for the Levis.

---

[1]Survey by the American Institute of Public Opinion (The Gallup Poll) for the Chicago Council on Foreign Relations, November 17–26, 1978, reported in *Public Opinion* 2 (March–May 1979):24.

The Supply and Demand for Foreign Exchange Meanwhile, thousands of other people in the United States and Germany are also buying and selling dollars and marks for their own purposes. The overall activity in the foreign exchange market, like that in any other market, can be characterized in terms of supply and demand curves, such as those shown in Exhibit 23.2. This market, as drawn, shows the supply and demand for dollars, with the price (the exchange rate) in terms of marks per dollar. But it could equally well have been drawn to show the supply and demand for marks, with the price in dollars per mark. The ratios of dollars to marks and marks to dollars are two ways of expressing the same thing; there is just one exchange rate.

Look first at the demand curve for dollars that appears in this market. Under the assumption that only current account transactions take place, the shape and position of the demand curve depends on how German demand for U.S. goods varies as the exchange rate varies, other things being equal. It is easy to see that the demand curve will normally be downward sloping, as drawn. Suppose, for example, that Levis sell in the United States for $10 a pair. At an exchange rate of 2 marks per dollar, German consumers would have to pay 20 marks per pair. They might buy a total of, say, 1 million pairs per year, thereby generating a demand for $10 million in the foreign exchange market. If the exchange rate fell to 1.8 marks per dollar while the U.S. price remained unchanged, German consumers would be able to buy Levis more cheaply—for 18 marks per pair. At the lower price, the Germans would presumably buy a greater quantity, say 1.25 million pairs. The demand for dollars on the foreign exchange market would thus increase to $12.5 million.

Elastic demand The situation where quantity changes by a larger percentage than price along the demand curve, so that total revenue increases as price decreases.

The supply curve for dollars in Exhibit 23.2 is drawn with an upward slope, indicating that more dollars will be supplied to the foreign exchange market as the price of dollars, in terms of marks, rises. This will be the case whenever U.S. demand for German goods is **elastic**—that is, whenever a 1 percent change in the price of German goods causes a greater than 1 percent change in the

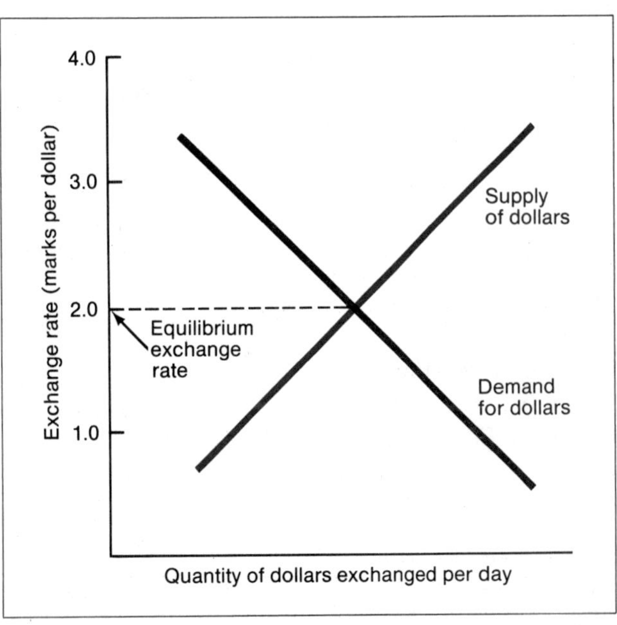

Exhibit 23.2
The foreign exchange market: Elastic demand for foreign goods
In this exhibit, the foreign exchange market is represented in terms of supply and demand curves for the dollar, with the price (exchange rate) stated in terms of the West German mark. The demand curve slopes downward because a lower exchange rate for the dollar, other things being equal, makes U.S. goods cheaper for Germans. That situation stimulates the export of goods, and more dollars are demanded to pay for them. The upward slope of the supply curve drawn here results from an assumed elastic demand in the United States for German goods. An increase in the exchange rate makes imports cheaper for people in the United States; and with elastic demand, they spend more total dollars on the larger quantity of goods.

quantity demanded. An example will show why the slope of the dollar supply curve depends on the elasticity of U.S. demand for German goods. Suppose that a certain model of the German BMW automobile has a price of 20,000 marks. At an exchange rate of 2 marks per dollar, the car would sell for $10,000 in the United States (not including shipping costs and other charges). If 5,000 BMWs per year were sold at that price, U.S. buyers would have to supply $50 million to the foreign exchange market in order to get the 100 million marks needed to pay the German manufacturer. Suppose that the exchange rate rose to 2.5 marks per dollar, so that U.S. buyers could get the car for just $8,000 (a 20 percent decrease in the dollar price). In keeping with the assumption of an elastic demand for BMWs, assume that the quantity imported would rise by 50 percent to 7,500 per year as a result of the change in the dollar price. In order to obtain 7,500 cars at 20,000 marks per car and an exchange rate of 2.5 marks per dollar, U.S. buyers would have to supply $60 million to the exchange markets. The quantity of dollars supplied to the foreign exchange markets would have increased in response to an increase in the price of the dollar in terms of marks, as shown in the diagram.

Supply with Inelastic Demand for Foreign Goods If U.S. demand for foreign goods were **inelastic** rather than elastic, the supply curve of dollars on the foreign exchange markets would have a negative slope, as shown in Exhibit 23.3. An inelastic demand means that a 1 percent change in the U.S. price of German goods would cause less than a 1 percent change in the quantity demanded. The BMW example can easily be changed to illustrate this. Suppose that when the exchange rate rises from 2 to 2.5 marks per dollar (bringing the U.S. price of BMWs down by 20 percent from $10,000 to $8,000), only 500 additional cars are sold (just a 10 percent increase). To get the German currency needed to buy 5,500 cars at 20,000 marks per car and an exchange rate of 2.5 marks per dollar, U.S. buyers would have to supply only

Inelastic demand The situation where quantity changes by a smaller percentage than price along the demand curve, so that total revenue decreases as price decreases.

Exhibit 23.3

The foreign exchange market: Inelastic demand for foreign goods

In this exhibit, the foreign exchange market is shown as it might look with inelastic demand by the United States for German goods. Here, when the exchange rate goes up, German goods become cheaper for people in the United States, as before. However, because the quantity demanded changes by a smaller percentage than the change in price, fewer dollars are needed to purchase the increased quantity of imports. The quantity of dollars supplied in exchange for marks thus decreases as the price of dollars in terms of marks increases.

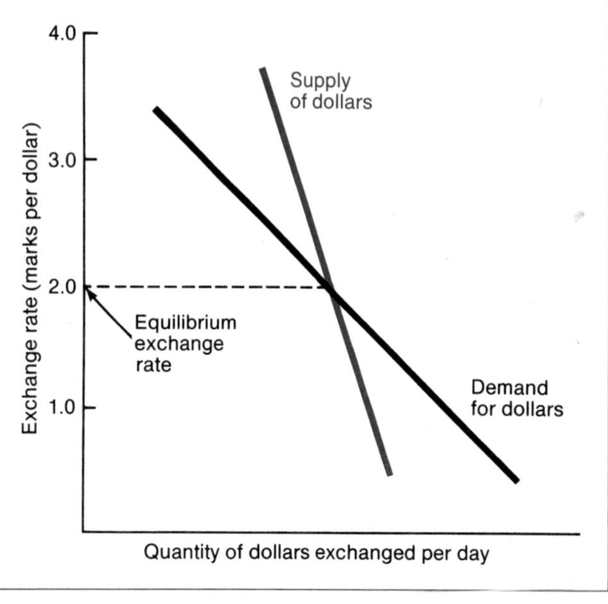

$44 million to the foreign exchange markets. An increase in the price of dollars in terms of marks would thus reduce the supply of dollars.[2]

Equilibrium—Current Account Only It is now possible to show how equilibrium is maintained in the foreign exchange markets in a world where the only international transactions are those that take place on current account. As Exhibit 23.4 is drawn, the foreign exchange market is initially in equilibrium at an exchange rate of 2 marks per dollar. Suppose that some change in current account payment occurs—say that individuals or government agencies in the United States increase transfer payments to Germany. To get marks that they can give to the German recipients of the transfers, the U.S. donors must give up more dollars on the foreign exchange markets. This is shown in the exhibit as a shift in the dollar supply curve from S_1 to S_2. The shift in the supply curve initially creates an excess supply of dollars, which tends to depress the exchange rate. As the rate falls, U.S. goods become cheaper for Germans to buy, which encourages a greater demand for dollars. This situation is represented by a movement down along the demand curve. At the same time, German goods become more expensive for U.S. buyers, which decreases somewhat the quantity of dollars supplied. This situation appears as a downward movement along the new dollar supply curve.

As the figure is drawn, the supply and demand for dollars come into equilibrium again at an exchange rate of 1.8 marks per dollar. The results of the increase in U.S. transfer payments to Germany have been the depression of the exchange rate, the stimulation of U.S. exports of goods and services, and the discouragement of U.S. imports of goods and services.

[2] As long as the negatively-sloped supply curve intersects the demand curve from the left as the price rises—as shown in Exhibit 23.3—the foreign exchange markets will function normally. It is theoretically possible, however, that the demand curve could be so steeply sloped that the supply curve would cross it from right to left as the price of the dollar, in terms of marks, increased. The complications that would arise in this situation will be discussed later in the chapter.

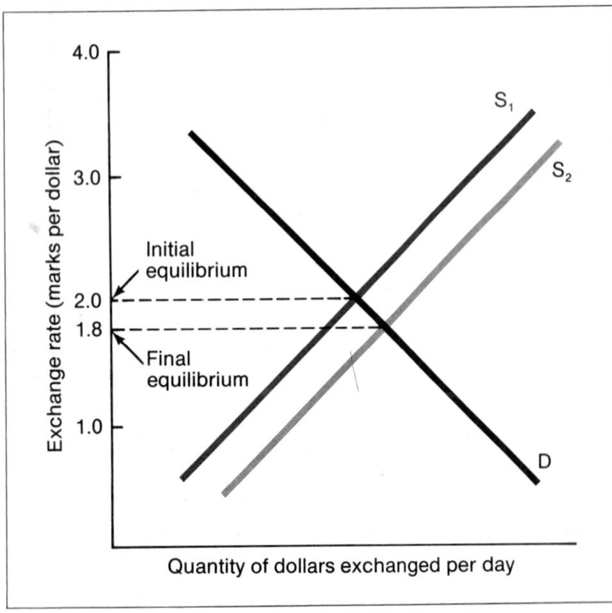

Exhibit 23.4

Maintaining equilibrium in the foreign exchange market

When only current account transactions are taken into account, the process by which equilibrium is maintained in the foreign exchange market is very simple. Suppose that an increase in transfers from the United States to Germany shifts the supply curve for dollars to the right, from S_1 to S_2. This situation creates an excess supply of dollars and puts downward pressure on the exchange rate. As the exchange rate falls, Germans are induced to spend more on U.S. goods and people in the United States spend less on German goods. The exchange rate reaches a new equilibrium at 1.8 marks per dollar.

In the terminology of foreign exchange markets, the dollar is said to **depreciate** when its price falls in terms of foreign currency, as in the example above. Seen from the German point of view, a fall in the price of the dollar in terms of marks is equivalent to a rise in the price of marks in terms of dollars. At the same time the dollar depreciates, then, the mark can be said to **appreciate** against the dollar.

Depreciation A fall in the price (exchange rate) of the currency of one country in terms of the currency of another country.

Appreciation A rise in the price (exchange rate) of the currency of one country in terms of the currency of another country.

Foreign Exchange Markets with Current and Capital Accounts

Current account transactions are not the only ones that take place among residents of different countries. International lending and borrowing and international sales and purchases of assets are just as important in determining exchange rates. A U.S. company, for example, might obtain a short-term loan from a London bank to finance the purchase of a shipload of beer for import to the United States. The Brazilian government might get a long-term loan from Citibank of New York to help finance construction of a hydroelectric project. A U.S. millionaire might open an account in a Swiss bank. An oil-rich Middle Easterner might purchase Iowa farmland or stock in a U.S. corporation.

All these transactions, and others like them, are called transactions on **capital account.** Purchases of U.S. assets by foreigners and borrowing by those in the United States from foreigners create flows of dollars into the United States and are thus called **capital inflows.** These inflows contribute to the demand for dollars in foreign exchange markets. Purchases of foreign assets by U.S. residents or loans by U.S. residents to foreigners create flows of dollars away from the United States and are thus called **capital outflows.** These outflows contribute to the supply of dollars in foreign exchange markets.

Capital account The account whose transactions include all international borrowing and lending and all international purchases and sales of assets for investment purposes.

Capital inflow Purchases of domestic assets by foreigners and borrowing by domestic residents from foreigners.

Capital outflow Purchases of foreign assets by domestic residents and borrowing by foreigners from domestic sources.

Relationships between Current and Capital Accounts When only current account transactions are considered, equilibrium in foreign exchange markets requires that imports of goods and services and unilateral transfers to foreign residents and governments be financed only by exporting goods and services and by unilateral transfers from abroad. Once capital account transactions are introduced, however, new means of financing these transactions are available. Imports of goods and services can now be paid for either by exports or by capital inflows—that is, by borrowing from foreigners or by selling assets to foreigners. Similarly, a country can export more goods and services than it imports, so long as it provides its trading partners with the means to pay for them by making loans to or buying assets from the trading partners.

Consider the hypothetical case shown in Exhibit 23.5. In the year for which these accounts are drawn up, the United States is shown as importing more goods and services than it exports and running a current account deficit of $30 billion. (All flows of dollars away from the United States are shown as −, and all flows of dollars toward the United States are shown as +.) At the same time, however, borrowing from foreigners plus sales of U.S. assets to foreigners (capital inflows) exceed loans to foreigners plus purchases of foreign assets (capital outflows) by $30 billion. The United States thus has a $30 billion capital account surplus that exactly balances the current account deficit.

It is not necessary to draw a new set of foreign exchange supply and demand curves to take both current and capital transactions into account. There are

Exports	+$120	
Imports	−150	
Unilateral transfers	0	
Current account deficit		−$30
Sales of U.S. assets to foreigners and borrowing from foreigners	+$60	
Purchases of foreign assets and loans to foreigners	−30	
Capital account surplus		+$30

Exhibit 23.5

Hypothetical balance of payments accounts: Current and capital accounts only (billions of U.S. dollars)

In a world where the only international transactions are those taking place on current and capital accounts, any current account deficit must be balanced by a capital account surplus and vice versa. In this hypothetical example, the United States is shown importing more than it exports, thereby running a current account deficit. This deficit is financed by a capital inflow—that is, by borrowing from abroad or by sales of U.S. assets to foreigners. Note that all outflows of dollars are listed with a minus and all inflows with a plus.

still just one supply curve of dollars, one demand curve for dollars, and one exchange rate for the dollar in terms of any other currency (such as the German mark). However, there are now additional sources of shifts in the supply and demand curves. Consider, for example, the effects of a rise in U.S. interest rates, other things being equal. One immediate effect is to make U.S. securities more attractive than before to foreign buyers. Their increased demand for dollars with which to buy these securities shows up as a rightward shift in the demand for dollars in the foreign exchange markets, which tends to cause the dollar to appreciate against the mark. Similarly, a rise in German interest rates, other things being equal, causes a rightward shift in the supply curve for dollars, which tends to cause the dollar to depreciate against the mark.

The Official Reserve Account

One important category of international transactions has yet to be explained: the sales and purchases of foreign currency reserves held by the Federal Reserve in the United States and the corresponding central banks of other countries. These sales and purchases are not included in the current account because they are not made to pay for imports or exports or to make unilateral transfers. They are not included in the capital account, because they are not necessarily made for investment purposes. Often, sales and purchases of foreign currency reserves by central banks are made instead to offset an excess supply or demand of dollars or other currencies, thereby preventing or moderating exchange rate fluctuations that would otherwise take place. These sales and purchases are referred to as transactions on the **official reserve account.**[3]

Official reserve account The account whose transactions include purchases and sales of reserves of foreign currency by central banks.

An example of how official reserve transactions might affect exchange rates appears in Exhibit 23.6. This diagram begins with the same scenario as did Exhibit 23.4: Initially, the market is in equilibrium at an exchange rate of 2 marks per dollar. This is shown by the intersection of D_1 and S_1. Next, an increase in U.S. transfer payments causes a rightward shift in the dollar supply

[3]In practice, it is impossible to distinguish clearly between central bank transactions made for investment purposes and those made for purposes of intervention in the foreign exchange markets. For example, when the Saudi Arabian government buys U.S. securities, it may be acting from ordinary business motives—looking for a good investment for its oil earnings—and at the same time may recognize and welcome the fact that the action helps stabilize the value of the dollar. In what follows, however, the focus is on the intervention motive for reserve account transactions.

Exhibit 23.6
Official intervention in the foreign exchange market
This exhibit begins with the same scenario shown in Exhibit 23.4. Starting from an exchange rate of two marks per dollar at the intersection of D_1 and S_1, an increase in transfers from the United States shifts the dollar supply curve to the right, to S_2. That shift creates a surplus of dollars and puts downward pressure on the exchange rate. To prevent the exchange rate from falling, the U.S. or German government begins official reserve purchases of dollars. These purchases shift the demand curve for dollars to the right, to D_2, until the demand curve intersects the new supply curve at the old exchange rate.

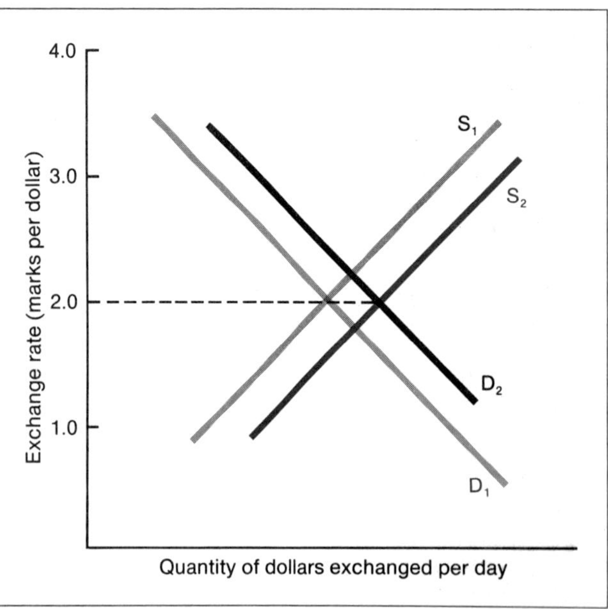

curve to S_2, which creates an excess supply of dollars at the original exchange rate. Normally, this would cause the dollar to depreciate against the mark. Instead of permitting the exchange rate to fall, however, the Federal Reserve could decide to use some of the German marks it holds as part of its foreign currency reserves to purchase the surplus dollars. Alternatively, the German central bank might sell marks in order to build up its reserves of dollars, or both central banks might act together, coordinating their efforts. In any event, the transactions would show up on the exchange market diagram as a rightward shift in the demand curve for dollars. As Exhibit 23.6 is drawn, sufficient official reserve purchases of dollars are made to shift the demand curve all the way to Position D_2. The entire excess supply of dollars is thus soaked up, and the exchange rate does not change.

Relationships of the Three Accounts

Once the official reserve account is introduced, it no longer need be true, as in Exhibit 23.5, that the capital account deficit or surplus will exactly offset the current account deficit or surplus. However, the total of the current account, capital account, and official reserve account balances must add to zero. The reason is that every purchase of a dollar on the foreign exchange markets by one party must correspond to a sale of a dollar by some other party, and all sales and purchases appear in one or another of the three accounts.

Exhibit 23.7, which shows the main elements of the U.S. balance of payments accounts for 1977, illustrates the relationships among the current, capital, and official reserve accounts. In that year, the United States ran a current account deficit of $15.2 billion. Rather than being offset by a capital inflow, this deficit was compounded by a $19 billion capital account deficit. The capital account deficit was the result of a much more rapid increase in U.S. holdings of foreign assets than of foreign holdings of U.S. assets. The combined balance of payments deficit on current plus capital accounts was

Merchandise exports	$120.0	
Merchandise imports	−151.1	
Net exports of services	20.6	
Net unilateral transfers	−4.7	
Current account deficit		−$15.2
Purchases of foreign assets and loans to foreigners	−$34.4	
Sales of assets to foreigners and borrowing from foreigners	15.4	
Capital account deficit		−$19.0
Change in foreign official reserve holdings of U.S. assets	$35.4	
Change in U.S. official reserve holdings of foreign assets	−0.2	
Surplus on official reserve account		+$35.2
Statistical discrepancy		1.0
Grand total	0	0

Totals may be off slightly because of rounding.
Source: President's Council of Economic Advisers, *Economic Report of the President* (Washington, D.C.: Government Printing Office, 1979), Table B–97.

Exhibit 23.7
U.S. balance of payments accounts, 1977 (billions of U.S. dollars)
This exhibit shows, in simplified form, the actual U.S. balance of payments accounts for 1977. In that year, the United States ran both a current account deficit and a capital account deficit. The deficits were offset by transactions on the official reserve account, chiefly purchases of dollars by foreign central banks.

thus $34.2 billion. The deficit was offset by transactions on the official reserve account, where foreign central banks made some $35.4 billion of dollar purchases.

In principle, the sum of the current, capital, and reserve accounts shown in Exhibit 23.7 should be exactly zero. However, statistical sources and techniques are imperfect, and the items therefore do not quite balance. The total of the various errors and omissions in the three accounts, which is $1 billion for 1977, appears in the table under the heading "statistical discrepancy."

THE DETERMINANTS OF EXCHANGE RATES

So far, only the mechanics of exchange rate determination have been discussed; exchange rates, like other prices, are determined by supply and demand. The next step is to look beyond the supply and demand curves for a theory explaining why, at any particular time, the curves intersect at one exchange rate rather than another. Once that step has been taken, the next section will discuss the important policy issues of how and why governments use reserve transactions to intervene in foreign exchange markets.

The Long Run: Purchasing Power Parity

Purchasing power parity theory (of exchange rates) The theory holding that the price of a unit of Currency A in terms of Currency B will, in the long run, tend to be equal to the ratio of the price level in Country B to the price level in Country A.

The leading theory of exchange rate determination in the long run is the so-called **purchasing power parity theory.** According to this theory, the price of a unit of Currency A in terms of Currency B (that is, the exchange rate) will, in the long run, tend to equal the ratio of the price level in Country B to the price level in Country A.

In a world where all goods and services were traded internationally, with no transportation costs or other barriers to trade, the purchasing power parity theory would presumably hold exactly. Suppose, for example, that the U.S. and

German domestic price levels are such that $100 will buy exactly twice as large a market basket of goods in the United States as can be bought for 100 marks in Germany. The purchasing power parity theory will then imply that the exchange rate must be 2 marks per dollar. If a dollar could be exchanged for more than 2 marks, U.S. consumers would all try to turn in their dollars and do their shopping in Germany. Their attempt to do so would immediately drive the price of the dollar back down to 2 marks. Similarly, if a dollar could be purchased for less than 2 marks, Germans would try to turn in all their marks for dollars and shop in the United States. This would quickly push the price of the dollar up to 2 marks. In such a world, in fact, the expressions "100 dollars" and "200 marks" would simply be different names given in Germany and the United States to equal-sized lumps of abstract purchasing power.

In practice, exchange rates do not always reflect purchasing power parities exactly. According to a study by economist Irving B. Kravis, for example, in 1978, $1 in the United States had as much purchasing power as 3.12 marks in Germany, even though the official exchange rate was 2.08 marks per dollar.[4] The difference can be explained in part by the fact that purchasing power parities reflect the prices of all goods and services, while exchange rates tend to reflect the value of goods and services traded internationally. For example, Kravis estimated that a dollar in the U.S. would buy 3.8 times as much telephone service as a mark would buy in Germany—but telephone calls are not an internationally traded service.

Also, deviations of exchange values from present purchasing power parities may reflect future expectations as much as current realities. For example, if participants in foreign exchange markets come to expect U.S. inflation in the future consistently to average higher in relation to German inflation than they thought in the past, they may shift out of dollar denominated assets into mark denominated assets. These capital account transactions can depress the value of the dollar even before enough actual inflation takes place to justify the new exchange rate in terms of purchasing power parities. Similarly, if participants in foreign exchange markets judge that future real economic growth will cause the demand for a country's exports to increase more rapidly than its demand for imports, the present exchange rate for its currency may be bid up in anticipation of the expected future improvement in its current account balance.

Short-Run Exchange Rate Fluctuations

With the necessary reservations, as noted, the purchasing power parity theory can be thought of as determining exchange rates in the long run. In the short run, exchange rates vary from day to day and month to month for reasons that are related only indirectly, if at all, to long-run changes in relative purchasing power and inflation rates. Among the important short-run factors influencing exchange rates are changes in aggregate economic activity, in interest rates, and in inflationary expectations.

Aggregate Economic Activity The national economies of the United States and other countries do not grow at the same steady rate year after year.

[4]Based on unpublished research by Kravis, reported by Alfred Malabre, Jr., "Despite the Dollar's Decline, U.S. Retains Top Living Standards," *Wall Street Journal*, May 1, 1979, p. 48.

Instead, there tend to be periods in which real output expands more rapidly than the long-run growth rate of potential real output alternating with periods in which real output grows more slowly or actually contracts. Furthermore, expansionary and contractionary episodes in various countries are not perfectly synchronized. This lack of synchronization creates short-run variations in the pattern of international trade and hence in exchange rates.

In a country where real aggregate demand is expanding relatively rapidly, part of the growth is met by an increase in imports of goods from abroad, which tends to move the country's balance of payments on current account from surplus toward deficit. Similarly, a country experiencing slowly growing real aggregate demand, or actual recession, tends to move from current account deficit toward surplus. Other things being equal, then, a nation's currency can be expected to depreciate as its real growth rate accelerates relative to that of its trading partners and to appreciate as its real growth rate lags behind that of its trading partners.

Interest Rates As shown in the previous section, exchange rates are sensitive not only to transactions taking place on current account but also to transactions taking place on capital account. In today's world economy, investment funds tend to be highly mobile among countries. Individuals, international corporations, and even national governments face the problem of balancing their portfolios among assets of numerous countries, all having various risks, liquidities, and expected rates of return. Other things being equal, an increase in the interest rate in any country will tend to attract internationally mobile funds, which will tend to move that country's capital account balance toward surplus and to cause its currency to appreciate. Similarly, a country in which the interest rate falls, other things being equal, will tend to experience a capital outflow and a depreciation of its currency.

Inflationary Expectations In saying that high interest rates attract internationally mobile funds, other things being equal, one of the things held equal is the relative riskiness of assets. In a given country, high nominal interest rates that simply reflect a high rate of domestic inflation are thus not necessarily attractive to international investors. As shown earlier, in the long run, the purchasing power parity theory suggests that such a country's currency will depreciate. It follows that for a given nominal interest rate, a country is likely to experience a capital outflow as the result of any development that makes international investors expect its inflation rate to accelerate relative to the rates of its trading partners.

EXCHANGE RATE POLICY

Two Possible International Monetary Systems

The long-run and short-run fluctuations in exchange rates discussed in the previous section are the result of current and capital account transactions. This section turns again to the official reserve account and the use of sales and purchases of foreign currency reserves as an instrument of policy. It begins by distinguishing two idealized international monetary systems, each characterized by a set of rules for governments to follow in the conduct of official reserve transactions.

Fixed Rates The first system is one of fixed exchange rates. Under this system, a group of countries (in the idealized form of this system, all countries) meet and agree on a set of "par" values for their currencies. The West German mark may be set at a par value of $.50, the British pound at a par value of $2, and so on. The countries then agree to hold substantial foreign currency reserves and to buy and sell from these reserves when necessary to offset potential deviations of exchange rates from their par values. Suppose, for example, that developments in the current or capital accounts led to an excess demand for marks, putting upward pressure on the international value of that currency relative to the U.S. dollar. Under the terms of the agreement, the German central bank would be obligated to sell marks and buy dollars in sufficient quantity to meet the excess demand at the par value of $.50. Or suppose that an excess supply of British pounds developed, putting downward pressure on that currency. The Bank of England would then step in and buy enough pounds to soak up the excess supply, paying for them with dollars from its foreign currency reserves. As long as all countries played by the rules, then, the actual exchange rates of all currencies would remain fixed at their par values.[5]

Floating Rates The alternative system is one of completely flexible or "floating" exchange rates. In terms of policy, this system is just the opposite of a fixed rate system. Under it, all governments agree to a hands-off policy on exchange rates. They conduct no official reserve transactions for intervention purposes. Exchange rates fluctuate up or down in accordance with supply and demand generated on the current and capital accounts alone.

The current world monetary system is a hybrid that fits neither of the idealized patterns perfectly. Before the current system and its evolution are described, however, some of the claimed advantages and disadvantages of the idealized fixed and floating exchange rate regimes will be discussed.

The Case for Fixed Rates

The case that can be made for a system of fixed exchange rates can be reduced to four principal arguments.

Real Effects of Currency Disturbances The first point made by proponents of fixed rates is that variations in exchange rates have significant real effects on the economy. When a country's currency appreciates, its export industries find it harder to compete in world markets. At the same time, industries that face import competition find it difficult to compete in domestic markets. When a country's currency depreciates, in contrast, export- and import-competing industries boom, but industries that rely on imported energy or raw materials suffer. If the appreciation or depreciation in question reflects fundamental long-term changes in patterns of world trade, these adjustments in import and export industries may be necessary and desirable. But it is argued that short-term random, cyclical, or speculative changes in exchange rates should not be allowed to disturb the domestic economy. After all, labor

[5]One extreme form of fixed exchange rate system, no longer in use, is a *gold standard.* Under such a system, different currencies—such as the dollar or the mark—are only local names for gold coins (or other gold backed currency) of different sizes.

and other factors of production cannot make costless moves from sector to sector at a moment's notice.

The "J-Curve" Effect A second reason frequently advanced for fixing exchange rates is that in the short run, the depreciation of a country's currency may worsen rather than improve its balance of payments on current account. To understand how this can happen, recall the earlier discussion of how the elasticity of demand for imports and exports affects the slope of the foreign exchange market supply and demand curves in a world where only current account transactions take place. The supply curve for dollars in Exhibit 23.2 was drawn with a positive slope on the assumption of elastic demand for imported goods. Exhibit 23.3 showed how the dollar supply curve would have a negative slope if domestic demand for imported goods were inelastic. Suppose now that both the domestic demand for imported goods and the foreign demand for U.S. exports are inelastic, creating the supply and demand curves shown in Exhibit 23.8. Here, the supply curve crosses the demand curve from right to left as the price rises. The market is in equilibrium at an exchange rate of 2 marks per dollar; however, the equilibrium is unstable. If the dollar depreciates to, say, 1.5 marks, an excess supply of dollars appears. This puts additional downward pressure on the exchange rate. Fluctuations in the exchange rate are thus not self-correcting in the short run, insofar as the current account is concerned.

J-curve effect The tendency for the depreciation of a country's currency to worsen its current account deficit in the short run and to improve it only after a lag.

A possible real-world result of the hypothetical situation shown in Exhibit 23.8 is the so-called **J-curve effect.** This effect, shown in Exhibit 23.9, occurs because import and export demands tend to be inelastic in the short run, although they are elastic in the longer run. When a country's currency first depreciates, few additional export sales are made immediately, and importers do not or cannot immediately reduce the quantity of goods they purchase. At the lower exchange rate, however, importers do have to offer

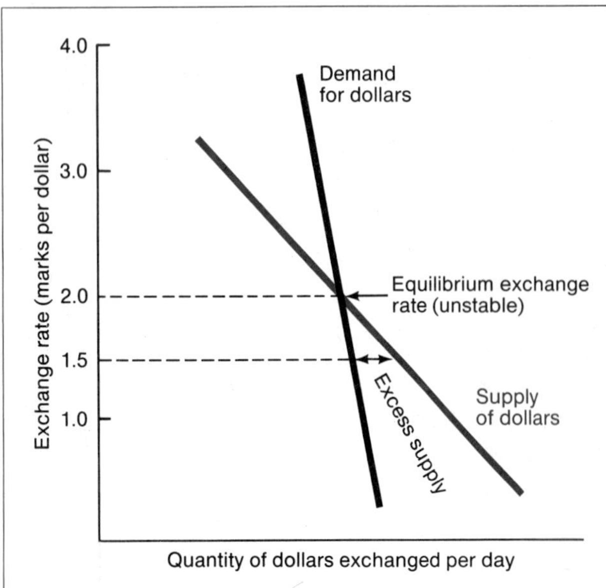

Exhibit 23.8
Foreign exchange market with extremely inelastic demand for imports and exports
This exhibit shows the dollar-mark foreign exchange market as it might look with extremely inelastic demand for U.S. goods in Germany and for German goods in the United States. The inelastic demand for U.S. goods in Germany makes the demand curve for dollars very steep. The inelastic U.S. demand for German goods gives the supply curve for dollars enough of a negative slope that it cuts the demand curve from the right as the exchange rate rises. The equilibrium exchange rate is 2 marks per dollar as the curves are drawn, but this equilibrium is unstable. For example, a depreciation of the dollar to 1.5 marks would create an excess supply (not an excess demand, as normally). This would put further downward pressure on the dollar rather than upward pressure toward equilibrium.

Exhibit 23.9
The J-curve effect
The so-called J-curve effect occurs when the demand for imports and exports is inelastic in the short run and elastic in the long run. As a result, a devaluation may initially worsen a country's balance of payments on its current account before eventually improving it. Here, the country has been experiencing a moderate current account deficit for some time. At the point shown, it devalues its currency. At first, the current account drops farther into deficit, but eventually it rises into surplus, following the J-shaped path shown.

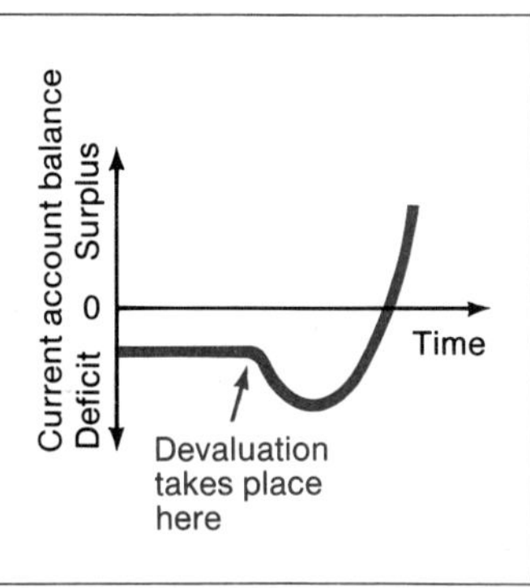

greater quantities of the domestic currency in order to buy the foreign currency they need to buy the unchanged physical quantity of imports. The current account balance thus moves toward deficit, putting further downward pressure on the exchange rate. Eventually, the lower exchange rate attracts new export buyers and encourages importers to find domestic substitutes. The current account balance then improves. The result is a pattern of events that, over a period of time, traces out a J-shaped curve—hence the name.

Proponents of fixed exchange rates argue that because of the J-curve effect, short-term fluctuations in exchange rates may not be self-correcting. If a disturbance in the exchange rate is expected to be only temporary, they say, why not short-circuit the J-curve by keeping the exchange rate fixed in the first place?

Inflationary Effects A third argument in favor of fixed exchange rates is based on the relationship between exchange rate variations and inflation. The previous section argued that countries experiencing relatively rapid inflation can expect their currencies to depreciate—in accordance with the purchasing power parity theory. However, the causation may also run the other way; a currency depreciation may cause domestic cost-push inflation. This occurs in part directly, because the prices of imported goods and raw materials rise, and in part indirectly, because domestic import-competing industries feel free to raise their prices when the prices of imports rise.

Under the proper conditions, a vicious cycle that runs something like this can be touched off: Inflation in, say, the United States causes the dollar to depreciate. Depreciation brings a round of cost-push inflation. International asset holders see the worsening inflation and react by pulling their funds out of U.S. banks and securities, thereby creating a capital account deficit. Especially if the J-curve effect of the depreciation is creating a current account deficit at the same time, the value of the dollar can plunge out of control in the absence of official intervention.

Meanwhile, a less inflationary country, say Switzerland, enters a "virtuous" cycle that is the mirror image of the vicious cycle described for the United States. Currency appreciation lowers import prices, further dampening inflation. International investors rush to put their funds in the ultra-safe Swiss franc, thereby creating a capital account surplus that causes further appreciation. But while the banks of Zurich grow fat, Swiss watchmakers find themselves increasingly priced out of the world market on which their livelihood depends.

The way to prevent such runaway vicious-virtuous cycles, it is said, is to prevent exchange rate fluctuations in the first place. Rather than letting differential rates of inflation disturb exchange markets, countries should use the time gained by exchange rate intervention to undertake domestic policies to control inflation.

Automatic Monetary Policy This leads to the fourth argument in favor of fixed exchange rates: The act of exchange market intervention itself automatically institutes the correct anti-inflationary monetary policy. Suppose, for example, that inflation begins to accelerate in the United States, putting downward pressure on the international value of the dollar. Under a fixed exchange rate system, the Fed would be obligated to go to the exchange markets to buy dollars, paying for them with foreign currency reserves. These dollars would go into the Fed's own accounts, thus disappearing from the money supply.

This contractionary monetary policy has several beneficial effects that help correct the original exchange market imbalance. First, interest rates tend to rise, encouraging a capital inflow. Second, international investors anticipate that the contractionary monetary policy will dampen inflation, which makes the dollar a less risky currency and further encourages capital inflow. Finally, aggregate demand in the United States is moderated, which moderates the demand for imports and improves the current account. All of this happens because the Fed's action in buying dollars through its "foreign desk" is a perfect substitute for buying dollars (that is, selling bonds) through its "open market desk."

Under floating rates, in contrast, central banks are not subject to the same kind of international discipline and may feel free to create more inflation. Fixed exchange rate advocates blame part of the increase in worldwide inflation over the last decade on the move toward floating rates.

The Case for Floating Rates

Advocates of floating rates remain unconvinced by the arguments in favor of fixed rates. They offer counterarguments to each of the four points just raised and provide some additional arguments of their own.

Counterarguments Floating rate advocates begin by pointing out that fixed rates do not truly protect the domestic economy from the real effects of international disturbances. For example, if inflation occurs under a fixed rate system, foreign competition may prevent prices from rising in industries facing strong international competition. As costs and prices rise in other sectors of the domestic economy, the industries facing foreign competition will be squeezed and resource allocation will consequently be disturbed.

Next, while acknowledging the J-curve effect as a short-run possibility for the current account, floating rate advocates believe it does not justify fixed rates. Why should it matter, they say, if devaluation temporarily causes a current account deficit if that deficit can be offset by a surplus on capital account? They dismiss the possibility that supply and demand curves for the foreign exchange market as a whole—including both current and capital accounts—can cross in the unstable configuration shown in Exhibit 23.8. It is nonsense, they say, to suggest that exchange rates shoot off to zero or infinity at the slightest disturbance; instability of that type simply does not exist.

Floating rate advocates are similarly unconvinced by the argument that currency depreciation creates a vicious cycle through cost-push inflation. The impact of exchange rate fluctuations on domestic inflation depends on whether the domestic money stock is held constant or increased. If the money stock is held constant—instead of being increased to accommodate the inflationary impact of currency depreciation—price increases in some markets will tend to be offset by price decreases elsewhere. Floating rate advocates concede that in a floating rate world, central banks would not always have the necessary discipline to avoid inflationary monetary policy, but they suggest that the blame should be placed on the banks, not on the monetary system.

Playing by the Rules In addition to disputing the arguments in favor of fixed rates, floating rate advocates advance a further argument of their own. The real trouble with a system of fixed exchange rates, they say, is that governments refuse to play by the rules. The rules call for exchange market intervention to be used only to iron out temporary fluctuations in exchange rates. Long-term variations, especially those arising from differential rates of inflation, are supposed to be handled by domestic macroeconomic policy.

In particular, governments tend to balk at subjecting themselves to the discipline of the automatic monetary policy that a fixed rate system implies. Suppose, for example, that a fixed rate system is in force, and, for some reason or other, downward pressure develops on the dollar. The Fed obediently buys dollars through its foreign desk, thereby propping up the exchange rate. But various domestic interest groups are immediately offended. The housing industry starts to squawk about high interest rates. Labor unions rebel at the threat of rising unemployment. The administration sees an election coming up and pressures the Fed to pursue expansionary domestic monetary policy. So at the same time the Fed buys dollars through its foreign market desk, it puts them right back into circulation through its open market desk. The continuing inflation pushes the current and capital accounts farther and farther into deficit. The U.S. government leans on its allies and trading partners to join it in defending the dollar through massive official reserve account purchases. But as long as the fundamental inflationary imbalance remains uncorrected, this effort only buys time and makes the crisis bigger when it comes.

But it is not necessary to deal in hypothetical cases to show the problems of a fixed rate system. It is time to turn from theory to a review of the postwar history of the international monetary system.

Bretton Woods

After World War II, the major trading nations of the world met under United Nations auspices at Bretton Woods, New Hampshire, to forge a new world monetary system of the fixed rate variety. The Bretton Woods conference also set up the International Monetary Fund (IMF), with headquarters in Washington, D.C., to administer the system. The rules of the international monetary game as it was played under the Bretton Woods system are presented here.

It was not quite an ideal fixed rate system. Instead, it featured what might best be called an "adjustable peg." Par values for each currency were established in terms of the U.S. dollar. Exchange rates were pegged at the par values; thus they were allowed to fluctuate under the influence of supply and demand within a narrow range of 2.25 percent above par to 2.25 percent below par. (The limits were only 1 percent until December 1971.) When the value of a currency rose to the upper limit or fell to the lower one, the government of the country in question was obligated under IMF rules to intervene and prevent further movement. A government faced with an excess demand for its currency at the limit rate had to sell enough of its own currency in exchange for dollars to soak up the excess demand. A government faced with an excess supply of its currency had to buy it in exchange for dollars if necessary to keep its price from slipping below the limit.

Although governments were supposed to intervene in exchange markets to counteract temporary disturbances, they had another option if they felt the disturbances reflected fundamental long-term changes. In the face of such changes, they could adjust the peg—change the par values of their currencies. This could be done in either of two slightly different ways. One way was to declare immediately a new par value above or below the initial value. The other was to float the currency temporarily, letting it find a new equilibrium value under the influence of supply and demand without government intervention. A new par value would later be fixed at the market determined rate when things seemed to have settled down. (A few countries, notably Canada, let their currencies float for years at a time in the postwar period. This, however, was considered to be a violation of at least the spirit, if not the letter, of IMF rules.)

Problems of the Bretton Woods System

Resisting Adjustment Under the Bretton Woods system, a country whose currency fell to the lower limit of the permissible range either was supposed to let automatic monetary policy do its job until the imbalance was corrected or was supposed to adjust the peg, make a new start at a new par value, and try to keep serious imbalances from arising again in the future. Unfortunately, governments often did neither when faced with downward pressure on their currencies. Fearing unemployment and high interest rates, they short-circuited the monetary adjustment mechanism. And concerned about possible sectoral effects, they resisted downward adjustment of their par value. In desperate attempts to prop up their currencies, they engaged in all sorts of trade restrictions. They imposed tariffs and quotas to try to improve current account balances, and they slapped on foreign exchange controls to prevent free international movements of capital, all in the hope of improving the capital account. But these mechanisms usually did little more than postpone the day of reckoning.

Crises Because adjustments were seldom fully automatic, the system was crisis-prone. Governments often resisted making small adjustments when the adjustments would have been only slightly painful. Instead, they waited for pressures to build up, and these pressures eventually tore the system apart.

Here is the scenario for the kind of international monetary crisis that repeatedly occurred under the Bretton Woods rules. Some country, say the United Kingdom, runs a persistent balance of payments deficit. A chronic excess supply of British pounds sterling appears on the world's exchange markets. The British government is forced to support the pound. It resists monetary restraint. Gradually, dollar reserves are run dangerously low, and the British government is forced to borrow from the IMF or the U.S. Treasury. It may try imposing exchange controls or other trade restrictions, but its efforts are met with threats of retaliation and domestic political resistence. It becomes harder and harder to keep the pound from breaking through the floor.

Speculation At this point, speculation enters the picture. Speculators are active all the time in international currency markets. Under the Bretton Woods rules, if I were a speculator, my game would work like this: Suppose the pound is floating between its upper limit of $2.45 and its lower limit of $2.35, changing a bit from day to day. If I buy 100,000 pounds today at $2.40, and tomorrow the vagaries of supply and demand carry the rate up to $2.41, I can change them back into dollars and pocket a clear profit of $1,000. The problem is that in normal times no one can be sure whether the pound is on its way up or on its way down. I might just as easily lose $1,000. Heads I win, tails I lose. Speculators are professional risk takers who perform a number of useful economic functions. In normal times, though, they do not play a very big role in the international payments picture.

But back to the scenario of the British government hanging desperately on the brink of a forced devaluation. At this point, I am faced with the kind of situation speculators are always looking for but are rarely lucky enough to find: the situation where heads I win, tails I break even. The question is: Will the pound hold at $2.35, or will it be devalued? Suppose I sell all the pounds I can get my hands on, borrowing them if necessary. If the pound is devalued to $2.10 tomorrow, I can buy pounds back to pay off the loans and make a huge profit. If the British government somehow muddles through, and the pound holds, I lose practically nothing. At the very worst, the pound will rise a cent or two off its floor and I will have to pay a few days' or weeks' interest on the loans.

The final scene in the sterling crisis is set when speculators start to pour hundreds of millions of pounds into the foreign exchange markets. The excess supply of sterling becomes overwhelming, and the last straw forcing an actual devaluation is the speculative pressure occurring in anticipation of the devaluation.

The End of the Bretton Woods System

In early 1973, an especially severe crisis occurred, involving the U.S. dollar, the German mark, and the Japanese yen. In response to this crisis, the major trading nations took the bold step of abandoning the adjustable peg and allowing their currencies to float relative to each other. The relative values of the yen, the dollar, and the mark were allowed to find their own levels under the influence of supply and demand.

The international monetary system that emerged from the crisis of 1973 is still a mixed system. It contains a number of features that do not conform exactly to a pure floating rate system. Although it is much more flexible than the adjustable peg, two important restrictions must be kept in mind.

First, not every currency floats against every other currency. Rather, the system is one in which major blocks of currencies float against one another. A number of Western European countries have attempted to peg their currencies against one another in an arrangement known as the European Monetary Union. Countries with strong trading ties to the United States have pegged their currencies to the dollar. Those with strong ties to Britain have pegged theirs to the pound. Movements between blocks have been substantial, though. Because increased flexibility has been introduced, several currencies have swung by as much as 20 to 30 percent. Occasionally there have been swings of 2 or 3 percent in a single day.

Second, governments have not taken a strictly hands-off attitude toward exchange rates. Instead, they have frequently intervened in foreign exchange markets to damp what they perceive to be temporary or unjustified fluctuations in exchange rates. This intervention is, however, not guided by any specific rules, as under the Bretton Woods agreements. The present mixture of floating rates and sporadic intervention is often referred to as a "dirty float."

The following case study illustrates the present international monetary system in action. The events it describes highlight a number of the features of the system that have just been discussed in theoretical terms.

Case 23.1
Carter's Dollar Rescue, 1978

As noted at the beginning of this chapter, international monetary events were very prominent in the news during 1977 and 1978. Exhibit 23.1 shows some of the important trends during that period—a swing in the current account balance from surplus to deficit, a decline in the trade-weighted value of the dollar on the foreign exchange markets, and a dramatic appreciation of certain "strong" currencies, notably the West German mark and the Japanese yen (the latter not shown).

Throughout the period, a substantial deficit on capital account added to downward pressure on the dollar. This deficit was most frequently attributed to the high rate of inflation in the United States compared with that of its major trading partners. In 1977, the United States experienced a 6.5 percent inflation rate while inflation in Germany was only 3.9 percent. Inflation in Japan was over 8 percent in 1977; but, importantly, it was on its way down from higher levels, while U.S. inflation was clearly on its way up. In Switzerland, not a major U.S. trading partner but a crucial international financial center, inflation had virtually been eliminated.

As long as the decline in the value of the dollar was gradual, the Carter administration did little to intervene in exchange markets. It was content to see heavy official reserve purchases of dollars by foreign central banks soak up the excess dollars created by the U.S. current and capital account deficits. Meanwhile, it hoped that the moderate depreciation would soon improve the current account balance. By the third quarter of 1978, however, the downward trend in the value of the dollar began to accelerate. The hoped-for improvement in the current account proved very slow in coming. It became increasingly difficult to convince international asset holders that anything serious was being done about inflation.

By October, the Carter administration saw it was time to act. On October 24, the president went on national television to announce a renewed anti-inflation policy featuring voluntary wage and price guidelines. He also pledged to reduce the budget deficit as a further anti-inflationary measure. International financial circles were disturbed, however, by the absence of any mention of monetary policy in the talk. They apparently decided that the anti-inflation package was just window dressing for domestic consumption. The run on the dollar continued.

Prompted by this further pressure on the dollar, the administration and the Federal Reserve finally took decisive monetary action on November 1. A dramatic new policy package to rescue the dollar was announced. Its main features were the tightening of monetary policy and the assembly of massive foreign currency reserves for exchange market intervention. The monetary policy was signaled by a full percentage point increase in the discount rate and a half percentage point increase in the federal funds rate. From November 1 through March 1979, the growth rate of the money supply slowed almost to a stop. The intervention package included drawing on the U.S. reserve position at the IMF, borrowing reserves from Germany and Japan through currency "swaps," and, for the first time ever, selling U.S. government securities denominated in German marks and Japanese yen directly to residents of those countries.

Effects of the November 1 initiative were felt immediately. Within a week, the dollar had climbed 7.7 percent from its low point at the close of trading on October 30. The gains held through the winter and into the spring of 1979. By the first quarter of 1979, the current account had swung back into surplus.

CONCLUSIONS

As the international economy enters the 1980s, the world of Bretton Woods fades more and more into history. The academic debates over fixed versus floating rates that characterized the fifties and sixties have been overtaken by events. At present, it is clear that the dirty float is here to stay for quite a while.

A floating rate world has not proved to be the promised land that some academic enthusiasts once thought it would be. It has not brought a halt to world inflation. It has not led to a dismantling of tariffs, quotas, and other barriers to free trade. It has not protected domestic economies from internationally generated disturbances. But, say floating rate advocates, it has not halted crime or illiteracy either; such expectations, in other words, were unrealistic to begin with. Something like the present system appears to be the only one possible in today's world. It is at least robust. It is hard to imagine, for example, that the Bretton Woods system could ever have accommodated the enormous international financial disturbances brought on by the rise of the OPEC oil cartel. And as long as the present system prevails, international monetary economics will continue to be a lively and exciting field of study.

SUMMARY

1. The many kinds of international transactions that take place in the world economy can conveniently be classified into three "accounts." The first is the current account, which comprises imports and exports of goods and services and unilateral transfers. The second is the capital account, which includes all international borrowing and lending and all international purchases and sales of assets for investment purposes. The third is the official reserve account, which is made up of central bank purchases and sales of foreign currency reserves. Because all international transactions are included in one account or another, the sum of the surpluses or deficits on these three accounts must always be zero (except for unavoidable statistical discrepancies).
2. The foreign exchange markets are made up of a whole complex of banks, specialized currency dealers, and government agencies through which currencies are exchanged for one another. Like other markets, they can be represented by supply and demand curves. A currency is said to depreciate when its value on the foreign exchange markets falls and to appreciate when its value rises. Fluctuations in exchange rates can result from shifts in supply

or demand arising in either the current or capital accounts. Often governments use official reserve account transactions to offset such currency fluctuations.

3. In the long run, international exchange rates tend to reflect, at least approximately, changes in the purchasing power parity of various national currencies. In the short run, changes in the growth of aggregate demand, in interest rates, and in inflationary expectations can cause substantial deviations from purchasing power parity exchange rates.
4. From 1944 to 1973, the international monetary system operated under a system of fixed exchange rates. Many observers of the international economy continue to favor such a system. They argue (a) that it shields the domestic economy from international financial disturbances, (b) that under flexible rates, depreciation of a currency does not necessarily improve the current account balance in the short run, (c) that a depreciating exchange rate can cause as well as be caused by inflation, thereby creating the danger of a vicious-virtuous cycle, and (d) that fixed rates impose automatic monetary discipline on inflationary countries.
5. Advocates of floating rates dispute each of these arguments and contend that fixed rate proponents exaggerate the inherent instability of the international economy. They see the unwillingness of governments to play by the rules of the game as a fatal flaw in all fixed rate systems. Experience under the Bretton Woods system appears to have justified this second criticism. At present, a floating rate system of some sort seems to be the only workable possibility.

DISCUSSION QUESTIONS

1. In your library, locate two copies of a good financial newspaper, such as the *New York Times* or *Wall Street Journal*—a current copy and one a year old (the latter probably on microfilm). In the daily table of international exchange rates, check the values of the West German mark, the Japanese yen, the British pound, and the Swiss franc. Are they currently moving up or down? How have they changed from a year previously? For a more ambitious research project, pick one of these currencies, and try to explain its movements in terms of the ideas presented in this chapter.
2. As another research project, try updating Case 23.1. A good place to start is with a general news index, such as the *New York Times Index*, beginning with March 1979.

SUGGESTIONS FOR FURTHER READING

Kindleberger, Charles, and Lindert, Peter. *International Economics.* 6th ed. Homewood, Ill.: Richard D. Irwin, 1978.

A comprehensive text on international economics; Chapters 13 to 22 deal with the issues of theory and policy raised in this chapter.

President's Council of Economic Advisers. *Economic Report of the President.* Washington, D.C.: Government Printing Office, annually.

Each year's report contains an up-to-date analysis of international economic developments and a discussion of policy alternatives facing the U.S. government in the year ahead.

Riehl, Heinz, and Rodriguez, Rita. *Foreign Exchange Markets: A Guide to Foreign Currency Operations.* New York: McGraw-Hill, 1977.

A nuts-and-bolts guide to how foreign exchange markets work.

Schmidt, Wilson E. *The U.S. Balance of Payments and the Sinking Dollar.* New York: New York University Press, 1979.
Discusses the balance of payments accounts and explains why, in the author's view, the balance of payments should not be a major policy concern under a floating exchange rate regime.

Yeager, Leland. *International Monetary Relationships.* New York: Harper & Row, 1976.
The historical chapters of this book provide a good discussion of exchange rate experience under various institutional arrangements in the past.

GLOSSARY

Absolute advantage In international trade theory, the ability of a country to produce a good at lower cost, measured in terms of factor inputs, than its trading partners'.

Accommodating monetary policy A policy under which the Federal Reserve System expands the money supply in an attempt to keep interest rates from rising when the Treasury sells bonds to cover a budget deficit.

Accounting profit Total revenue minus explicit costs.

Acreage controls Policies designed to raise agricultural prices by limiting the acreage on which certain crops can be grown.

Adaptive expectations Expectations about the rate of inflation or other future economic events formed primarily on the basis of experience in the recent past.

Aggregate A term used in economics to describe any quantity that is a grand total for the whole economy.

Aggregate demand The total value of all planned expenditures of all buyers in the economy.

Aggregate nominal demand schedule A graph showing the relationship between aggregate nominal demand (the nominal value of total planned expenditure) and nominal national income.

Aggregate supply The total value of all goods and services supplied in the economy; identical to national product.

Aggregate nominal supply schedule A graph showing the relationship between aggregate nominal supply (nominal national product) and nominal national income. The schedule has the form of a 45 degree line passing through the origin.

Agricultural marketing orders Agreements authorized by the Agricultural Marketing Agreement Act of 1937 that allow farmers collectively to control the quantities of particular farm products flowing to particular markets.

Anarcho-capitalism (radical libertarianism) A capitalist system under which no state exists and all goods and services—including defense, police, and court services—are supplied by private firms.

Antitrust laws A set of laws, including the Sherman Act of 1890 and the Clayton Act of 1914, that seek to control market structure and the competitive behavior of firms.

Appreciation A rise in the price (exchange rate) of the currency of one country in terms of the currency of another country.

Arbitrage The activity of earning a profit by buying a good for a low price in one market and reselling it for a higher price in another market.

Assets All the things to which a bank, other firm, or household holds legal claim.

Automatic stabilizers Changes in taxes, transfers, and government purchases that occur automatically as nominal GNP rises or falls.

Autonomous consumption The level of consumption shown by a consumption schedule for a zero disposable income level.

Balanced budget multiplier A multiplier showing how much equilibrium nominal national income will change in response to a change in government purchases matched dollar for dollar by an offsetting change in net taxes. The value of the balanced budget multiplier is always 1.

Benefit reduction rate The amount by which transfer benefits are reduced per dollar of earned income.

Bilateral monopoly A market in which both buyer and seller exercise monopoly power and neither passively accepts the demands of the other.

Birthrate *See* Crude birthrate.

Budget line A line showing the various combinations of goods that can be purchased at given prices within a given budget.

Capital As a factor of production, all means of production that are created by people, including such things as tools, industrial equipment, structures, and improvements to land.

Capital account The account whose transactions include all international borrowing and lending and all international purchases and sales of assets for investment purposes.

Capital inflow Purchases of domestic assets by foreigners and borrowing by domestic residents from foreigners.

Capitalism Any economic system based on private ownership of all factors of production in which owners of capital act as entrepreneurs and coordinate their activity through use of the market.

Capitalized value (of a rent) The amount equal to the value of the sum of money that would earn a periodic interest return equal to the rent if invested at the current market rate of interest.

Capital outflow Purchases of foreign assets by domestic residents and borrowing by foreigners from domestic sources.

Cartel An agreement among a number of independent suppliers of a product to coordinate their supply decisions so all of them will earn monopoly profits.

Centralized socialism A socialist system under which all capital and natural resources are owned by the government, which plans all production as if the economy were one big firm.

Circular flow of income and product The flow of goods from firms to households and factor services from households to firms, counterbalanced by the flow of expenditures from households to firms and factor payments from firms to households.

Civilian labor force All members of the noninstitutionalized adult civilian population who are either officially employed or officially unemployed.

Classical liberal capitalism A capitalist economic system in which government performs only the limited role of protecting property rights and settling private disputes.

Commodity inflation A variety of cost-push inflation in which a spontaneous increase in commodity prices is the initial source of general price increases.

Comparative advantage In international trade theory, the ability of a country to produce a good at a lower opportunity cost, in terms of other goods, than its trading partners'.

Complements A pair of goods for which an increase in the price of one causes a decrease in the demand for the other, other things being equal.

Concentration ratio The percentage of all sales contributed by the four or eight largest firms in a market.

Conglomerate mergers Mergers between firms that operate in unrelated markets.

Constant returns to scale A phenomenon said to occur when there are neither economies nor diseconomies of scale.

Consumer equilibrium A state of affairs in which consumers cannot increase the total utility they obtain from a given budget by shifting expenditure from one good to another. (In consumer equilibrium, the marginal utility of a dollar's worth of one good must be equal to the marginal utility of a dollar's worth of any other good.)

Consumer price index (CPI) A measure of the price level based on a weighted average of the prices of goods purchased by a typical urban consumer.

Consumption schedule A graphical or numerical representation of how nominal consumption expenditure varies as nominal income varies, other things being equal.

Contractionary gap The gap between planned expenditures and national product at the target level of national income when aggregate supply exceeds aggregate demand at that level.

Corporation A firm in which the ownership is divided into equal parts called shares, with each shareholder's liability limited to the amount of his or her investment in the firm.

Cost-push illusion The phenomenon that demand-pull inflation often looks like cost-push inflation to those caught up in it, because inventories cushion the immediate impact of demand on prices at each link in the chain of distribution from producers to retailers.

Cost-push inflation Inflation that is touched off by a spontaneous rise in wages, profit margins, commodity prices, or other elements of cost during a period of slack aggregate demand.

Craft union A union of skilled workers all practicing the same trade.

Crowding out effect The tendency of expansionary fiscal policy to cause a drop in private planned investment expenditure as a result of a rise in the interest rate.

Crude birthrate The number of people born into a population per thousand per year.

Crude death rate The number of people in a population who die per thousand per year.

Currency Coins and paper money.

Current account The account whose transactions include imports and exports of goods and services plus international unilateral transfer payments.

Death rate *See* Crude death rate.

Deficit In referring to government budgets, an excess of government purchases over net taxes.

Demand curve A graphical representation of the relationship between the price of a good and the quantity of it demanded.

Demand deposits Commercial bank deposits that depositors can withdraw by writing checks; commonly known as checking accounts.

Demand, law of *See* Law of demand.

Demand-pull inflation Inflation that is initially touched off by an increase in aggregate demand.

Demand schedule A table showing the quantity of a good demanded at various prices.

Demographic transition A population cycle that accompanies economic development, beginning with a fall in the death rate, continuing with a phase of rapid population growth, and concluding with a decline in the birthrate.

Depauperization Economic development of a kind that benefits the poorest of the poor, providing them not only with the material necessities of life but also with access to education, status, security, self-expression, and power.

Depreciation A fall in the price (exchange rate) of the currency of one country in terms of the currency of another country.

Diminishing marginal utility, principle of *See* Principle of diminishing marginal utility.

Diminishing returns, law of *See* Law of diminishing returns.

Discount rate The rate of interest charged by the Federal Reserve to member banks for reserves borrowed from the Fed.

Discretionary fiscal policy Changes in the levels of taxes, transfers, or government purchases made for the specific purpose of economic stabilization.

Diseconomies of scale A phenomenon said to occur whenever long-run average cost increases as output increases.

Disintermediation The large-scale withdrawal of funds from financial intermediaries by depositors in search of higher interest rates obtainable elsewhere.

Disposable personal income (disposable income) Personal income minus personal taxes.

Dissaving Negative saving—the difference between disposable income and consumption expenditure when consumption exceeds disposable income.

Distributive justice The principle of distribution according to innate merit. Roughly, the principle of "from each according to abilities, to each according to needs."

Dual economy An economy that is sharply divided into a modern, westernized industrial sector capable of rapid growth and a traditional rural sector that remains stagnant.

Dual labor market The division of the labor market into a primary sector, containing good jobs with established firms, and a secondary sector, containing low-paid, unstable jobs with marginal firms.

Dynamic efficiency The ability of an economy to increase consumer satisfaction through growth and innovation.

Econometrician A specialist in the statistical analysis of economic data.

Economic ideology A set of judgments and beliefs concerning efficiency, market justice, and distributive justice as goals of economic policy, together with a set of prejudices or beliefs concerning matters of positive economics.

Economies of scale A phenomenon said to occur whenever long-run average cost decreases as output increases.

Effective demand The quantity of a good that purchasers are willing and able to buy at a particular price.

Effective marginal tax rate The percentage of each dollar of additional earned income that a household loses through all explicit taxes and benefit reductions combined.

Efficiency The property of producing or acting with a minimum of expense, waste, and effort.

Elastic demand The situation where quantity changes by a larger percentage than price along the demand curve, so that total revenue increases as price decreases.

Empirical Term referring to data or methods based on observation of actual past experience or on controlled experiments.

Employed Officially, any person who works at least one hour per week for pay or at least fifteen hours per week as an unpaid worker in a family business.

Employment rate The ratio of the number of people employed to the number of people in the noninstitutional adult civilian population.

Entrepreneurship The aspect of economic decision making that consists of exploring for new alternatives, inventing new ways of doing things, being alert to new opportunities, taking risks, overcoming constraints, and experimenting with new objectives.

Event conditioned transfers Social insurance programs under which transfer payments are available to all citizens, regardless of income level, upon the occurrence of a specified event such as retirement, unemployment, or disability.

Excess quantity demanded The amount by which the quantity of a good demanded exceeds the quantity supplied when the price of the good is below the equilibrium level.

Excess quantity supplied The amount by which the quantity of a good supplied exceeds the quantity demanded when the price of the good is above the equilibrium level.

Excess reserves Reserves held by commercial banks in excess of required reserves.

Expansionary gap The gap between planned expenditures and national product at the target level of national income when aggregate demand exceeds aggregate supply at that level.

Expected real rate of interest The nominal rate of interest minus the expected rate of inflation.

Expected real rate of return The annual real net improvement in a firm's cost or revenue that it expects to obtain by making an investment; it is expressed as a percentage of the sum invested.

Expenditure approach A method of estimating aggregate economic activity by adding together the nominal expenditure of all economic units on newly produced final goods and services.

Explicit costs Costs taking the form of explicit payments to nonowners of a firm.

Extensive growth Growth based predominantly on the mobilization of increasing quantities of factor inputs.

Factor markets The markets in which the factors of production—labor, natural resources, and capital—are bought and sold.

Factors of production The basic inputs of natural resources, labor, and capital used in producing all goods and services.

Featherbedding The practice of negotiating purposefully inefficient work rules so that more workers will be needed to do a job.

Federal funds market A credit market in which banks can borrow reserves from one another for periods as short as twenty-four hours.

Final goods and services Goods and services sold directly for household consumption, business investment, or government purchase. Excludes intermediate goods sold for use as inputs in the production of other goods.

Financial intermediary Any financial institution that performs the function of channeling funds from savers to investors.

Fiscal policy The aggregate of policies that determine the levels of government purchases and net taxes.

Fixed inputs Inputs to the production process that cannot easily be increased or decreased in a short period of time (the quantity of fixed inputs employed by a firm defines the size of the firm's plant).

Fixed investment Purchases by firms of newly produced capital goods, such as production machinery, newly built structures, and office equipment.

Flows Processes occurring continuously through time, measured in units per time period.

Foreign exchange market The whole complex of institutions—including banks, specialized foreign exchange dealers, and official government agencies—through which the currency of one country can be exchanged for that of another.

Franchised monopoly A monopoly protected from competition by a government grant of monopoly privilege, such as an exclusive license, permit, or patent.

Frictional unemployment That portion of unemployment accounted for by people spending relatively short periods between jobs.

Full employment balanced budget rule A rule under which taxes and spending policy would be adjusted so that the federal budget would be in balance if the economy were at full employment.

Functional distribution of income The distribution of income according to factor ownership—that is, the distribution among workers, natural resource owners, and owners of capital.

General equilibrium analysis An approach to the study of markets along the lines of: If Event X occurs, the effect on Market Y will be Z, provided that other markets also adjust fully to the event in question.

GNP deflator A measure of the price level equal to the ratio of current year nominal GNP to current year real GNP times 100.

Government purchases of goods and services (government purchases) Expenditures made by federal, state, and local governments to purchase goods from private firms and to hire the services of government employees.

Gross national product (GNP) The dollar value at current market prices of all final goods and services produced annually by the nation's economy.

Homogeneous Having the property that every unit is just like every other unit.

Horizontal mergers Mergers between firms that are direct competitors in the same market.

Humphrey-Hawkins Act An act amending the Employment Act of 1946 by adding specific numerical policy targets for unemployment and inflation and by attempting to improve coordination of stabilization policies pursued by various branches of the federal government. Formally known as the Full Employment and Balanced Growth Act of 1978.

Hyperinflation Very rapid and sustained inflation.

Implicit costs The opportunity costs to a firm of using resources owned by the firm itself or contributed by owners of the firm.

Import quota A limitation on the quantity of a good that can be imported in a given time period.

Income approach A method of estimating aggregate economic activity by adding together the incomes earned by all households.

Income conditioned transfers Welfare or public charity programs under which transfer payments are available to citizens who meet some specified low income criterion.

Income effect The part of the change in quantity demanded of a good whose price has fallen that is attributable to the change in real income resulting from the price change.

Income elasticity of demand The ratio of the percentage change in the demand for a good to the percentage change in the income of buyers.

Incomes policy A policy that attempts to control wages, salaries, earnings, and prices directly in order to fight inflation.

Income velocity of money (velocity) The ratio of nominal income to the quantity of money.

Indexing The practice of automatically adjusting wages, salaries, or other payments to compensate for changes in the price level.

Indifference curve A graphical representation of an indifference set.

Indifference map A representative selection of indifference curves for a single consumer and pair of goods.

Indifference set A set of consumption alternatives each of which yields the same utility, so that no member of the set is preferred to any other.

Industrial union A union of all workers in an industry, including both skilled and unskilled workers and workers practicing various trades.

Inelastic demand The situation where quantity changes by a smaller percentage than price along the demand curve, so that total revenue decreases as price decreases.

Inferior good A good for which an increase in the income of buyers causes a leftward shift in the demand curve.

Inflationary recession A period of rising unemployment during which the rate of inflation remains high or even continues to rise.

Injections The part of total expenditures on domestically produced goods and services that does not originate from domestic households—that is, investment, government purchases, and exports.

Inside lag The delay between the time a policy action is needed and the time it is taken.

Intensive growth Growth based predominantly on improvements in the quality of factor inputs and in the efficiency with which they are utilized.

Inventory investment Changes in the stocks of finished products and raw materials that firms keep on hand. If stocks are increasing, inventory investment is positive; if they are decreasing, it is negative.

Investment The sum of fixed investment and inventory investment.

J-curve effect The tendency for the depreciation of a country's currency to worsen its current account deficit in the short run and to improve it only after a lag.

Keynesian cross A figure formed by the intersection of the aggregate nominal demand and aggregate nominal supply schedules.

Kolkhoz A Soviet collective farm.

Labor As a factor of production, the contributions to production made by people working with their minds and muscles.

Labor force *See* Civilian labor force.

Laffer curve A curve showing the relationship between a tax rate and the total revenue raised by the tax. At a zero or 100 percent tax rate, no revenue is raised; at some intermediate rate, tax revenue reaches a maximum.

Law of demand The law that the quantity of a good demanded by buyers tends to increase as the price of the good decreases and tends to decrease as the price increases, other things being equal.

Law of diminishing returns The law stating that as the quantity of one variable input used in a production process is increased (with the quantities of all other inputs remaining fixed), a point will eventually be reached beyond which the quantity of output added per unit of added variable input (that is, the marginal physical product of the variable input) begins to decrease.

Leakages The part of national income not devoted to consumption (saving plus net taxes) plus domestic expenditures on foreign-made goods (imports).

Liabilities Financial claims against a bank, other firm, or household by outsiders.

Liquid Description of an asset that can be used as a means of payment or easily converted to a means of payment without risk of gain or loss in nominal value.

Long run A time perspective long enough to permit changes in the quantities of all inputs, both fixed and variable.

Lump sum taxes Taxes that do not vary as income varies.

M_1 The measure of the money supply, defined as currency plus demand deposits.

M_2 M_1 plus savings and time deposits at commercial banks.

Macroeconomics The branch of economics devoted to the study of unemployment, inflation, economic growth, and stabilization policy.

Managerial coordination Coordination of economic activity through directives from managers to subordinates.

Margin, marginal Terms referring to the effects of making a small increase in any economic activity.

Marginal average rule The rule that marginal cost must be equal to average cost when average cost is at its minimum.

Marginal cost The increase in cost required to increase output of some good or service by one unit.

Marginal cost of pollution abatement The added cost of reducing a given kind of pollution by one unit.

Marginal factor cost The amount by which a firm's total factor cost must increase in order for it to obtain an additional unit of that factor.

Marginal physical product (of an input) The quantity of output, expressed in physical units, produced by each added unit of the input.

Marginal productivity theory of distribution A theory of the functional distribution of income according to which each factor receives a payment equal to its marginal revenue product.

Marginal propensity to consume The fraction of each added dollar of disposable income that goes to added consumption.

Marginal propensity to save The fraction of each added dollar of disposable income that is not consumed.

Marginal rate of substitution The rate at which one good can be substituted for another without gain or loss in satisfaction (equal to the slope of an indifference curve at any point).

Marginal revenue The amount by which total revenue increases as the result of a one-unit increase in quantity.

Marginal revenue product (of a factor) The change in revenue resulting from the sale of the product produced by one additional unit of factor input.

Marginal social cost of pollution The total additional cost to all members of society of an additional unit of pollution.

Marginal tax rate The percentage of each added dollar of income paid in taxes.

Marginal utility The amount of added utility obtained from a one-unit increase in consumption of a good.

Market coordination Coordination of economic activity using the price system to transmit information and provide incentives.

Market equilibrium A condition in which the separately formulated plans of buyers and sellers of some good exactly mesh when tested in the marketplace, so that the quantity supplied is exactly equal to the quantity demanded at the prevailing price.

Market justice The principle of distribution according to acquired merit. The observance of property rights and the honoring of contracts. Roughly, the principle of "value for value."

Markets All the various arrangements people have for trading with one another.

Market socialism A socialist system in which details of resource allocation are made through market mechanisms rather than through central planning.

Market structure Important characteristics of a market, including the number of firms that operate in it, the extent to which the products of different firms are diverse or homogeneous, and the ease of entry into and exit from the market.

Microeconomics The branch of economics devoted to the study of the behavior of individual households and firms and to the determination of the relative prices of individual goods and services.

Minimum efficient scale The level of output at which economies of scale are exhausted.

Monetarists Economists who believe that movements in the money supply are the primary causes of ups and downs in business activity.

Money Anything that serves as a unit of account, a medium of exchange, and a store of purchasing power.

Money demand schedule A schedule showing the quantity of money that people desire to hold in their portfolios given various values for the interest rate and the level of nominal income.

Money multiplier The ratio of the quantity of money to the total reserves in a banking system. Various money multipliers can be defined, depending on the definition of money used. For the U.S. banking system, the money multiplier is the M_1-to-total-reserves multiplier.

Monopolistic competition A market structure in which a large number of firms offer products that are relatively close substitutes for one another.

Monopoly power A seller's power to raise the price of a product without losing all, or nearly all, customers.

Monopsony A market in which there is only one buyer; from the Greek words *mono* ("single") and *opsonia* ("buying").

Multiplier effect The ability of a one dollar shift in the aggregate nominal demand schedule to induce a change of more than one dollar in the equilibrium level of nominal national income.

National income The total of all incomes, including wages, rents, interest payments, and profits received by households.

National product The total value of all goods and services supplied in the economy.

Natural monopoly A monopoly protected from competition by technological barriers to entry or by ownership of unique national resources.

Natural rate of unemployment The rate of unemployment that would prevail if the expected rate of inflation were equal to the actual rate of inflation.

Natural resources As a factor of production, everything useful as a productive input in its natural state, including agricultural land, building sites, forests, and mineral deposits.

Near monies Assets that are less than perfectly liquid but still liquid enough to be reasonably good substitutions for money.

Negative income tax A general name for transfer systems that emphasize cash benefits, beginning with a basic benefit available to households with zero earned income that is then subject to a benefit reduction rate of substantially less than 100 percent.

Net exports Total exports minus total imports.

Net national product (NNP) A measure of national product adjusted to exclude the value of investment expenditures that merely replace worn-out or obsolete capital goods. Officially, NNP equals GNP minus the capital consumption allowance.

Net reproduction rate The inherent long-term growth rate of a population, measured as the average number of daughters born to each female child over her lifetime.

Net taxes Total tax revenues collected by government at all levels minus total transfer payments disbursed.

Net tax multiplier A multiplier showing how much equilibrium nominal national income will change in response to a change in net taxes. The formula for the net tax multiplier is –MPC/MPS.

Net worth The assets of a bank, other firm, or household minus its liabilities.

Nominal rate of interest The rate of interest measured in the ordinary way, without adjustment for inflation.

Nominal values Measurements of economic values made in terms of actual market prices at which goods are sold.

Normal good A good for which an increase in the income of buyers causes a rightward shift in the demand curve.

Normal rate of return to capital The opportunity cost of capital to a firm—that is, the rate of return necessary to attract funds for investment from their best alternative uses.

Normative economics The part of economics devoted to making value judgments about what economic policies or conditions are good or bad.

Official reserve account The account whose transactions include purchases and sales of reserves of foreign currency by central banks.

Okun's law A rule of thumb according to which for each three percentage points by which real economic growth exceeds (or falls short of) the growth rate of potential real GNP in any year, the unemployment rate will tend to fall (or rise) by one percentage point.

Oligopolistic interdependence The necessity, in an oligopolistic market, for each firm to pay close attention to the behavior and likely reactions of its rivals when planning its own market strategy.

Oligopoly A market structure in which there are two or more firms, at least one of which has a large share of total sales.

Open market operation A purchase of securities from the public or a sale of securities to the public made by the Federal

Reserve for the purpose of altering the quantity of reserves available to member banks.

Opportunity cost The cost of doing something measured in terms of the loss of the opportunity to pursue the best alternative activity with the same time or resources.

Outside lag The delay between the time a policy action is taken and the time its effects on the economy are felt.

Parity price ratio The ratio of an index of prices that farmers receive to an index that farmers pay, using the years 1910–1914 as a base period.

Partial equilibrium analysis An approach to the study of markets along the lines of: If Event X occurs, the effect on Market Y will be Z, provided that the equilibrium of other markets is not disturbed.

Participatory socialism A socialist system under which the means of production are owned collectively by the workers of individual firms, who participate democratically in the process of management and share the profits of their firms.

Partnership A firm formed by two or more persons to carry on a business as co-owners. Each partner bears full legal liability for the debts of the firm.

Perfect competition A market structure characterized by a large number of relatively small firms, a homogeneous product, good distribution of information among all market participants, and freedom of entry and exit.

Perfectly elastic demand The situation where the demand curve is a horizontal line.

Perfectly inelastic demand The situation where the demand curve is a vertical line.

Personal distribution of income The distribution of income among individuals, taking into account both the functional distribution of income and the distribution of factor ownership among persons.

Personal income The total of all income, including transfer payments, actually received by households before payment of personal income taxes.

Phillips curve A curve showing the relationship between the rate of inflation and the level of unemployment. Inflation, usually placed on the vertical axis of such a figure, can be measured in terms of either the rate of change in wages or the rate of change in a price index.

Planned investment schedule A graphical representation of how the rate of planned investment for the economy as a whole varies as the expected real rate of interest varies, other things being equal.

Population trap A situation in which the rate of population growth rises above the rate of economic growth, halting the growth of per capita income and aborting the demographic transition.

Portfolio balance The idea that people try to maintain a balance among the various kinds of assets they own—including money, consumer durables, stocks, and bonds—shifting from one kind of asset to another as economic conditions change.

Positive economics The part of economics limited to making scientific predictions and purely descriptive statements.

Potential real GNP (potential real output) The level of real GNP that the economy could, in principle, produce if resources were fully employed.

Precautionary motive A motive for holding money arising from its usefulness as a reserve of liquid funds for use in emergencies or in taking advantage of unexpected opportunities.

Price discrimination The practice of charging more than one price for different units of a single product, when the price differences are not justified by differences in the cost of serving different customers.

Price elasticity of demand (elasticity of demand) The ratio of the percentage change in the quantity of a good demanded to the percentage change in the price of the good.

Price elasticity of supply (elasticity of supply) The ratio of the percentage change in the quantity of a good supplied to the percentage change in its price.

Price leadership A situation in an oligopolistic market where increases or decreases in price by one dominant firm, known as the price leader, are matched by all or most other firms in the market.

Price support A program under which the government guarantees a certain minimum price to farmers by undertaking to buy any surplus that cannot be sold to private buyers at the support price.

Price taker A firm that sells its outputs at fixed prices that are determined entirely by forces outside its own control.

Principle of diminishing marginal utility The principle that the greater the rate of consumption of some good, the smaller the increase in utility from a unit increase in the rate of consumption.

Producer price index A measure of the price level based on a weighted average of prices of crude, semi-finished, and finished producer goods bought and sold by private firms.

Production possibility frontier A curve showing the possible combinations of goods that can be produced by an economy, given the quantity and quality of factors of production available.

Profit-push inflation A variety of cost-push inflation in which a spontaneous increase in profit margins is the initial source of price increases.

Progressive tax A tax that takes a larger percentage of income from people whose incomes are high.

Protectionism Policies of shielding domestic industry from foreign competition.

Public goods Goods or services having the properties that (1) they cannot be provided to one citizen without being supplied also to that person's neighbors, and (2) once they are provided for one citizen, the cost of providing them to others is zero.

Purchasing power parity theory (of exchange rates) The theory holding that the price of a unit of Currency A in terms of Currency B will, in the long run, tend to be equal to the ratio of the price level in Country B to the price level in Country A.

Pure economic profit The sum remaining after both explicit and implicit costs are subtracted from total revenue.

Pure economic rent The income earned by any factor of production that is in perfectly inelastic supply.

Pure economizing The aspect of economic decision making that consists of choosing a pattern of activities from among a given set of alternative activities that will best serve a well-defined objective, subject to known constraints.

Pure monopoly A market structure in which one firm accounts for 100 percent of industry sales.

Rate of natural increase The current growth rate of a population calculated as the crude birthrate minus the crude death rate.

Rational expectations Expectations about the rate of inflation or other future economic events based on a rational weighing of all available evidence, including evidence on the probable effects of present and future economic policy.

Realized real rate of interest The nominal rate of interest minus the actual rate of inflation.

Real values Measurements of economic values that include adjustments for changes in prices between one year and another.

Reflation An expansion of aggregate demand after a period of high unemployment and decelerating inflation, bringing substantial short-term gains in employment with little or no inflationary penalty.

Regressive tax A tax that takes a larger percentage of income from people whose incomes are low.

Repurchase agreements Arrangements under which financial and nonfinancial firms sell securities subject to agreement to buy them back, often as soon as the next day.

Required reserve ratio The fraction of each type of deposit that the Federal Reserve System requires member banks to hold in the form of non-interest-bearing assets.

Reservation wage The wage (adjusted for nonmonetary advantages and disadvantages of a job) below which a person will not accept a job offer.

Residual charges Charges of a fixed amount per unit of waste imposed on all sources that discharge a given kind of waste into the environment.

Saving schedule A graphical or numerical representation of how nominal saving varies as nominal disposable income varies, other things being equal.

Savings deposits Deposits at commercial banks or thrift institutions subject to withdrawal at any time upon presentation of a passbook.

Scientific prediction A conditional prediction having the form "if A, then B, other things being equal."

Shortage As used in economics, an excess quantity demanded.

Short run A time perspective within which output can be adjusted only by changing the quantities of variable inputs within a plant of fixed size. *See also* Very short run.

Simple multiplier The ratio of an induced change in the equilibrium level of nominal national income to an initial shift in the aggregate nominal demand schedule. Using MPC to stand for the marginal propensity to consume, the value of the simple multiplier is given by the formula $1/(1-\text{MPC})$.

Socialism Any of a number of doctrines that include the following tenets: (1) that some major share of nonlabor factors of production ought to be owned in common or by the state, and (2) that justice requires incomes to be distributed at least somewhat more equally than under classical liberal capitalism.

Sole proprietorship A firm owned and usually managed by a single person, who receives all profits of the firm and who personally bears all of the firm's liabilities.

Speculative motive A motive for holding money arising from its fixed nominal value, when the nominal value of alternative assets is expected to decline.

State capitalism A capitalist system under which government intervenes widely in the market and provides an alternative to the market as a means by which individuals and firms can win control over resources.

Static efficiency The ability of an economy to get the greatest consumer satisfaction from given resources and technology.

Stocks Accumulated quantities existing at a particular time, measured in terms of simple units.

Stop-go policy A cycle of acceleration, inflationary recession, deceleration, and reflation brought about by alternating political pressures to do something first about inflation and then about unemployment.

Substitutes A pair of goods for which an increase in the price of one causes an increase in the demand for the other, other things being equal.

Substitution effect The part of the increase in quantity demanded of a good whose price has fallen that is attributable to the tendency of consumers to substitute relatively cheap goods for relatively expensive ones.

Supply curve A graphical representation of the relationship between the price of a good and the quantity of it supplied.

Supply schedule A table showing the quantity of a good supplied at various prices.

Surplus As used in economics, an excess quantity supplied. In referring to government budgets, an excess of net taxes over government purchases.

Target level of nominal national income (income target) The level of nominal national income judged by policy makers to be most nearly compatible with the goals of full employment, price stability, and real economic growth.

Target price A price guaranteed to farmers by the government; if the market price falls below the target price, the government pays the farmers the difference.

Tariff A tax levied on imported goods.

Tax-based incomes policy (TIP) An incomes policy employing tax incentives (penalties or rebates) to secure compliance with otherwise voluntary wage and price guidelines.

Theory of the mine The branch of economics concerned with the allocation over time of nonrenewable natural resources.

Thrift institutions Nonbank financial intermediaries primarily serving the interests of small savers and nonbusiness borrowers; thrift institutions include savings and loan associations, mutual savings banks, and credit unions.

Time deposits Deposits at commercial banks or thrift institutions subject to withdrawal without penalty only at the end of a specified period.

Total rate of return to capital The opportunity cost of capital plus pure economic profit, expressed as a percentage of the capital invested in a firm.

Transactions costs All costs of finding buyers or sellers to transact business with and of negotiating terms of exchanges, drawing up contracts, guarding against involuntary default or foul play, and so on.

Transactions motive A motive for holding money arising from the convenience of using it as a means of payment for day-to-day transactions.

Transfer payments All payments made by government to individuals that are not made in return for goods or services currently supplied. Social security benefits, welfare payments, and unemployment compensation are major forms of transfer payments.

Transitivity The situation where if A is preferred to B and B is preferred to C, then A must be preferred to C.

Unemployed Officially, any person without a job but actively looking for one.

Unemployment rate The percentage of the civilian labor force not employed.

Unit elastic demand The situation where price and quantity change by the same percentage along the demand curve, so that total revenue remains unchanged.

Utility The economist's term for the pleasure, satisfaction, and need fulfillment that people get from the consumption of material goods and services.

Variable inputs Inputs to the production process that can quickly and easily be varied to increase or decrease output within a plant of a given size.

Vertical mergers Mergers between firms that stand in a supplier-purchaser relationship to one another.

Very short run A time horizon so short that producers are unable to make any changes in input or output quantities in response to changing prices.

Wage-push inflation A variety of cost-push inflation in which a spontaneous increase in nominal wage rates is the initial source of price increases.

I N D E X